D1530557

REMOVED FROM
E.S. FARLEY LIBRARY
WILKES UNIVERSITY
COLLECTION

THE ART OF INTERACTIVE TEACHING

with Cases, Simulations, Games and other Interactive Methods

E.S. FARLEY LIBRARY
WILKES UNIVERSITY
WILKES-BARRE, PA

Edited by Hans E. Klein

H62
A3A78
1995

Copyright © 1995 by

Hans E. Klein
All rights reserved

Except as permitted under the Copyright Act of 1976, no part of this publication may be reproduced, stored in a retrieval system, or transmitted in any form or by any means without the prior permission of the publisher.

Produced and distributed by
WACRA - World Association for
Case Method Research & Application
23 Mackintosh Ave
NEEDHAM (BOSTON) MASSACHUSETTS 02192-1218 U.S.A.
Tel. +617-444-8982 FAX: +617-444-1548 Internet: hklein@bentley.edu

Library of Congress Cataloging in Publication Data

Klein, Hans Emil, 1939

Case Method Research and Application:
The Art of Interactive Teaching
With Cases, Simulations Games and Other Interactive Methods
Selected Papers of the Eleventh International Conference
on Case Method Research and Application at HEC, the
Ecole des Hautes Etudes Commerciales
MONTREAL, QUEBEC, CANADA

Bibliography: p.

1. Case Method Research and Research Theory
2. Interactive Teaching
3. Innovations in Teaching Accounting
4. Case Method Applications
5. The Case Method in Education
6. Cases in Various International Settings
7. International Cases for Various Teaching Objectives
8. How the Case Method is Viewed and Applied in: Africa, Mexico, Canada, Poland, France and Australia
9. Simulations: Creation, Production and Applications
10. Special Topics

ISBN 1-877868-06-X

Printed and bound by OMNI PRESS, MADISON, Wisconsin United States of America

CONTENTS

- CHAPTER ONE -
CASE METHOD RESEARCH AND RESEARCH THEORY

JI-201530

- CHAPTER TWO -
INTERACTIVE TEACHING

- CHAPTER THREE -
INNOVATIONS IN TEACHING ACCOUNTING

- CHAPTER FOUR -
CASE METHOD APPLICATIONS

- CHAPTER FIVE -
THE CASE METHOD IN EDUCATION

- CHAPTER SIX -
CASES IN VARIOUS INTERNATIONAL SETTINGS

- CHAPTER SEVEN -
INTERNATIONAL CASES FOR VARIOUS TEACHING OBJECTIVES

- CHAPTER EIGHT -
HOW THE CASE METHOD IS VIEWED AND APPLIED IN:
AFRICA, MEXICO, CANADA, POLAND, FRANCE AND AUSTRALIA

- CHAPTER NINE -
SIMULATIONS: CREATION, PRODUCTION AND APPLICATIONS

- CHAPTER TEN -
SPECIAL TOPICS

APPENDICES

AUTHOR INDEX

- A -

- B -

- C -

- D -

- K -

- L -

- M -

- N -

- O -

- P -

- Q -

- R -

- S -

- T -

- V -

- W -

- Z -

ACKNOWLEDGEMENTS

The editor wishes to express his appreciation to the individuals who have participated in the double blind peer review process. Their assistance in reviewing manuscripts and making suggestions represented an important contribution to the success of WACRA'94 in Montreal and facilitated the production of this volume. Special thanks go to Jane Stoneback, Amelia Klein, Murali Nair and Joëlle Piffault for coordinating and administering the peer review process for 150 submissions and to Tim Edlund for the peer review process for the Case Writers Colloquium. WACRA also gratefully acknowledges the support by Bentley College, HEC and the University of Massachusetts/Boston, faculty colleagues and staff and others.

Keith Absher, Abdel Agami, Doug Allen, James Allen, A.J. Almaney, Guy Archambault, Hanna Ashar, Michael Avramovich, Chi Anyansi-Archibong, Yezdi Bhada, Philip Baron, Julien Bilodeau, Clifford Brown, Don Brown, Michael Budden, John Burns, Floyd Byars, David Callaghan, Jim Camarius, Jim Carroll, Karen Cascini, Philippe Chapuis, Lal Chugh, Jay Conger, Mary Cooper, Phil Cooper, Marcel Coté, Gerald Crawford, Robert Crowner, Willem de Beer, Christiane Demers, Robert L. DeMichiell, Danielle Desbiens, Zdenek Drabeš, Yvon Dufour, Jim Gallagher, Tom Griffin, Donald Grunewald, Taïeb Hafsi, Francine Harel-Giasson, Harvard University Publishing Division, Sherman L. Hayes, Elizabeth Hawthorne, Jacques Hermant, Florence Jones, Veronika Kisfalvi, Lawrence Klein, Janko Kralj, Robert C. Lake, Bernard Lachance, Laurent Lapierre, Pierre Laurin, Phil Leblanc, Jens Lindemann, Stephen Lucas, Vince Luchsinger, Lynette Lahay, Erik Maaløe, Shirley Malone-Fenner, Brian MacIver, Jean Mathurin, Keith Martin, Joseph McHugh, Joseph Miller, Larry Minks, Robert Mockler, Denise Nitterhouse, Barra O Cinneide, Sean O Connor, Ronald Patten, Boris Popoff, John F. Quinn, George Radford, Catherine Rich-Duval, Alexander Romiszowsky, William Rotch, John Ruhe, Joan Sander, Wayne Sander, Don Shannon, H. Lee Schlorff, Hal Schroeder, Louis Seagull, John Seeger, Ronald Schill, Larry Smiley, Christopher Spivey, William Thomas Stevens, William Stewart, Ron Stiff, Nancy Strong, Mary Sudzina, Marilyn Thurston, Rocco Vanasco, Jill Lynn Vihtelic, Steve Tomczyck, Lourdes Vanasco, Rocco Vanasco, Steve Wernet, Joseph Wolfe, Willem van Woerden, Murray Young, Gerhard Zapke-Schauer, James Zeitler.

OTHER WACRA PUBLICATIONS

CASE METHOD RESEARCH AND APPLICATION:

<u>NEW VISTAS</u>, 1989, ISBN 1-877868-01-9, 544 pages, $35 plus $6 (overseas $8) for postage & handling.

<u>PROBLEM SOLVING</u>, 1990, ISBN 1-877868-02-7, 576 pages, $35 plus $6 ($8 overseas) for postage & handling.

<u>MANAGING CHANGE</u>, 1991, ISBN 1-877868-03-5, 573 pages (hardcover), $47 plus $6 ($8 overseas) for postage & handling.

<u>FORGING NEW PARTNERSHIPS</u>, 1992, ISBN 1-877868-04-3, 584 pages (hardcover), $49 plus $6 ($8 overseas) for postage & handling.

<u>INNOVATION THROUGH COOPERATION</u>, 1993, ISBN 1-877868-05-1, 735 pages (hardcover), $53 plus $6 ($8 overseas) for postage & handling.

Distributed by:

WACRA - World Association for
Case Method Research & Application
23 Mackintosh Ave
NEEDHAM (BOSTON) MA 02192-1218 U.S.A.
Tel.+ 617-444-8982 Fax:+ 617-444-1548
Internet: hklein@bentley.edu

PREFACE

This volume continues the annual presentation of selected papers resulting from international, interdisciplinary WACRA conferences devoted to the consideration of the case method, simulations, games, videos and other interactive methods, as research, teaching, training and learning techniques. Included are also a selection of international cases.

During the last 30 years the case method has enjoyed a steady and continuing increase in popularity and use. For example, applications in the field of education have increased in the past three years and continue to increase dramatically. The American Accounting Association and many leaders in university-level business education encourage the use of the case method and other interactive techniques to more effectively reach students, especially undergraduate accounting students who, in recent years, have turned to more "exciting" studies.

Presentations and discussions of scholarly work are primary means of communicating knowledge. Today, scholarship and research is increasingly international in scope. To facilitate research and promote cooperation internationally and across disciplines, the World Association for Case Method Research & Application (WACRA) organizes international conferences and publishes this volume of selected papers with the purpose of

- creating an International Forum for the discussion of contemplated, on-going or completed case method research,
- facilitating the exchange of experiences with existing case method applications and
- providing encouragement and an interdisciplinary, international structure for the discussion, development and dissemination of new avenues and approaches to teaching and training.

Months before the infamous "Wall" came down in 1989, WACRA had decided to hold its 1991 conference in East Berlin - then the capital of the German Democratic Republic (East Germany) - in order to build new bridges to colleagues in Central and Eastern Europe. WACRA '92 at the University of Limerick in Limerick, Ireland built on the 1992 conference with the theme "Forging New Partnerships with Cases, Simulations, Games, Videos and Other Interactive Methods." WACRA '93, in Bratislava, Slovakia, expanded the previous efforts to explain, research and advance the use of interactive methods with the theme "Innovation Through Cooperation." WACRA '1993 took on special significance for the Slovak conference hosts. They are charged by their society (as are Universities in other East and Central European countries) with preparing qualified economists, managers, teachers and leaders who will be able to facilitate the transition to a free market economic system. Indeed, managerial skills are important preconditions for the successful economic restructuring and further democratization of Central and Eastern European countries. There is no doubt in the view of many, that case study methodology can and should play a crucial role in the development of new curricula and the entire process of transformation. WACRA '94 was a record breaking conference in a number of ways (without taking away from previous years' conferences): First official bi-lingual WACRA conference, largest enrollment, most presentations, most interactive workshops, first video-recorded sessions. Delegates from around the globe reported on case method research, case writing, simulations, and new, innovative uses of media and interactive teaching methods and applications. "Learning by Doing," the conference theme, occurred in the lecture halls, workshops and inter-cultural pre-conference sessions and could be observed during social events.

Since 1989, WACRA has undertaken a series of important initiatives to assist developing democracies in Central and Eastern Europe to move toward a free market system. In 1990 and 1991, on the invitation of the Government of Czecho-Slovakia, WACRA conducted symposia in Prague to develop, together with government policy makers, educators and businessmen, strategic plans for various segments of society. Since then, the initial contacts have evolved into full partnerships between WACRA and Central and Eastern European institutions and also among WACRA members from all over the world. Members have collaborated on case writing, case teaching and training, management consulting, and curricula planning, to name just a few projects.

Delegates from thirty five nations attended the conference in Montreal. The papers and contributions presented in this volume were selected through a double blind peer review. The contributions are arranged in the following broad areas: Case Method Research and Research Theory (1), Interactive Teaching (2), Innovations in Teaching Accounting (3), Case Method Applications (4), The Case Method in Education (5), Cases in Various International Settings (6), International Cases for Various Teaching Objectives (7), How the Case Method is Viewed and Applied in: Africa, Mexico, Canada, Poland, France and Australia (8), Simulations: Creation, Production and Applications (9), Special Topics (10).

While editing the papers included in this volume, I have tried to maintain the character and thrust intended by their authors, despite the need to make, in some instances, alterations and amendments, in other cases, assisting the author in rewriting the paper. I have retained, to allow for flavor, alternate accepted (British) spelling, and have permitted slightly 'unorthodox' sentence structures to prevail, as long as the meaning was not distorted. In all, I have tried to maintain the author's opinions, views, suggestions and thoughts.

Hans E. Klein, Editor

CHAPTER ONE

A RESEARCH STUDY TO INVESTIGATE THE DEVELOPMENT OF REFLECTIVE THOUGHT PROCESSES OF PRESERVICE TEACHERS THROUGH THE USE OF CASE STUDIES IN EDUCATIONAL PSYCHOLOGY COURSES

James D. Allen
The College of Saint Rose
ALBANY, NEW YORK, U.S.A.

Abstract

The use of case studies in teacher preparation courses has expanded greatly during the last few years. This research investigates two major questions: (1) Do students in an educational psychology course where cases are used become more reflective about their actions than students in a traditionally taught educational psychology course? (2) Do these "case" students learn as much educational psychology content as students in a traditionally taught course?

INTRODUCTION

If one looks at the introductory chapters of most current educational psychology texts, one finds the authors describing to students the importance of developing into teachers who are reflective practitioners [e.g., Biehler & Snowman, 1993; Woolfolk, 1993]. Woolfolk [1993] describes reflective teaching as teaching that is "thoughtful and inventive" with an emphasis on "how teachers plan, solve problems, create instruction, and make decisions" (p. 8). She relates it to a teacher who has integrated the "art" of teaching (i.e., vision, intuition, talent, commitment, creativity) with the "science" of teaching (i.e., repertoire of techniques, procedures, and skills based on knowledge, theory and research). In other words, reflective teachers operate from an extensive knowledge base of content and pedagogy that is well organized around an integrated set of principles, and develop solutions to common classroom problems by knowing how to frame a problem, frame relevant questions regarding the problem, and consider alternative solutions to the problem.

Similarly, in reviewing the literature on reflection, Ross [1989] found the following used to define the reflective process:

- Recognizing an educational dilemma
- Responding to a dilemma by recognizing both similarities to other situations and the unique qualities of the particular situation
- Framing and reframing the dilemma
- Experimenting with the dilemma to discover the consequences and implications of various solutions
- Examining the intended and unintended consequences of an implemented solution and evaluating the solution by determining whether the consequences are desirable or not. (p. 22)

Ross continues her review by referring to Schon's [1983] perspective of reflective practice being grounded in a repertoire of values, knowledge, theories, and practices that teachers use to frame dilemmas and make judgements and decisions regarding solutions. She relates this to Liston and Zeichner's [1987] views that teachers use moral as well as educational criteria in examining the consequences of implemented solutions. Finally, Ross points out in her review that reflection by teachers "requires development of several attitudes and abilities, such as introspection, open-mindedness, and willingness to accept responsibility for their decisions and actions" as noted by Dewey [1933], and "the ability to view situations from multiple perspectives, the ability to search for alternative explanations of classroom events, and the ability to use evidence in supporting or evaluating a decision or position" as indicated by Kitchner and King [1981].

However, in many teacher preparation programs, students take educational psychology courses before they have personal teaching opportunities on which they can reflect. Wasserman [1993] describes how traditional teacher preparation courses often fail to prepare preservice teachers adequately for the transition from theoretical knowledge to classroom application due to the failure to help education students learn how to "make meaning" of classroom situations. She suggests that students must be given the opportunity to apply critical analysis to making meaning of classroom dilemmas by developing the skills of observation, comparison, extraction of main ideas, intuition, and application of facts and principles as applied to case studies. Since the primary focus of most educational psychology courses is to provide a theoretical and research foundation (i.e., the science of teaching) for students to use as a base to develop their personal teaching practices (i.e., the art of teaching), case studies provide a vehicle for students to reflect on realistic classroom dilemmas and apply the psychological theories and research findings they are learning in the course [Silverman, Welty, & Lyon, 1992]. Case studies allow students to develop and use analytic problem solving skills for making informed decisions about classroom events while considering multiple perspectives.

THE PEDAGOGY OF CASE STUDIES IN EDUCATIONAL PSYCHOLOGY CLASSES

In the teacher preparation program at The College of Saint Rose, all undergraduate education majors take EPY 350 - Educational Psychology (3 credits = 45 hours of instruction) during their junior year after completing a separate child or adolescent development course and before student teaching. This educational psychology course has a cross-section of students from all the education disciplines (Elementary Ed., Secondary Ed., Special Ed., Art Ed., Music Ed., etc.). Each semester there are approximately six course sections of EPY 350 with 25 students in each section. Usually two sections are taught by the author using a case study pedagogy, while the other sections are taught in a more traditional lecture and discussion style.

The "case" sections are structured so that coverage of content is interwoven with applying it to a case study. First, approximately four to five hours of class time are devoted to discussion and lecture related to content from an educational psychology text or other readings to provide a common knowledge base for all students. This is followed by a one to two hour session of analyzing and discussing a case which describes a teacher reflecting on a classroom or educational problem or dilemma in which the teacher is involved. This cycle repeats throughout the semester eventually covering six or seven case studies.

To promote active, but thoughtful, discussion of the cases, students are required to read and reflect on the case and to prepare an outline to bring to class. Students are given guidelines for constructing an outline which includes major topic categories for organizing their thoughts regarding the case (see Appendix A). The outline is to contain a list of the major problems and issues of the case both from the perspective of the teacher telling the story, as well as the reader's own perspective of the situation. These perspectives are to be supported by the particulars in the case (data/evidence) and related to the educational and psychological principles that have been discussed in class or students have learned elsewhere. Students are to list some possible solutions to the problems they identify and support their solutions based on sound theory and research. They are also asked to indicate what possible consequences might arise if these solutions are implemented.

Then, during the class discussion of the case, students are exposed to the multiple and different perspectives of the other students in class regarding the nature of the problems, possible solutions to the problems and corresponding consequences, and the educational principles used to support their analysis along with the underlying values associated with their decisions. Students are asked to consider these various interpretations, challenge those views which they see differently, and defend their own viewpoints when challenged, by citing relevant evidence from the case and relevant theory and research as it applies to the case situation being discussed.

After the class discussion of the case, students are asked to write a five to six page analysis of the case following evaluation guidelines given to them (see Appendix B). The emphasis is on the level of reflective analysis and the ability to synthesize theory into practical and realistic applications for the particulars of the case. The purpose is to help students see that classrooms are complex environments and realize that problems existing in classrooms seldom have simple solutions, but that though reflection, deliberation, and analysis, the actions they take in the classroom are more likely to create effective learning environments and make a difference in the lives of the students they will teach, as well as empower them as responsible and professional educators.

THE PROBLEM STATEMENT AND RESEARCH QUESTIONS

From a cognitive theoretical perspective on learning we know that students are more likely to find educational psychology principles and concepts more meaningful and retain these principles and concepts longer if they are actively generating their own understanding of them [e.g., see Wittrock, 1986]. In addition, the application of this information in "making meaning" of classroom situations by analyzing case studies of teaching dilemmas should enable preservice educators to become more "intelligent" professional decision makers when they enter real classrooms as teachers [Wasserman, 1993]. Lohman [1993], for example, points out that fluid abilities (intelligence) can probably be best promoted by first imposing "some organizational scheme on declarative knowledge," especially knowledge over ill-structured domains, by encouraging "students to identify main points, but from several different perspectives" via stories or case studies. Lohman cites Spiro et al. [1987] to argue that

> The best way to... instruct in order to attain the goal of cognitive flexibility... is by a method of case-based presentations which treats a content domain as a landscape that is explored by "criss-crossing" it in many directions, by reexamining each case "site" in the varying contexts of different neighboring cases, and by using a variety of abstract dimensions for comparing cases. (p. 178)

So, as described above, we can expect that students engaged in case study analyses should develop a more well defined "teaching" schema, with more connections to educational psychology principles and concepts and more ways to apply these concepts than students who are not exposed to cases.

However, the research base on case studies in teacher education is minimal. For me, as an instructor who uses cases in educational psychology courses that are part of a teacher preparation program, several questions need to be researched.

1. How effective are case studies as a pedagogical method in helping students become more reflective and improve their decision-making abilities to make sense of complex situations such as classrooms? After going through a course which uses a case-based approach, do students really think differently than students who go through a more traditionally taught educational psychology course? This question regarding students cognitive processes can be subdivided into the following three questions each considering a different aspect of reflection:

1a) Do students exposed to cases exhibit more cognitive flexibility and a greater degree of fluid abilities in solving problems?

1b) Do students exposed to cases base their decisions on values that could be said to be on a higher level of moral development?

1c) Do students exposed to cases become more "expert" in their thinking and think about classroom situations in more complex ways by considering multiple perspectives, applying theory to practical solutions, and considering the consequences of their suggested actions?

Or do some students come into the course "naturally" more reflective than other students and respond well to the case methodology, while other students continue to look for simplistic solutions to classroom situations even after exposure to cases? There is some research on reflective writing by education students to suggest that this last concern might be the case [Axelrod & McLane, 1993; Ross, 1989]. There is also research to suggest that the attitude of students toward education classes are more positive if they are taught by a case study approach than by a more traditional approach [James. 1992]. But do education students *reflectively think* any differently about classroom dilemmas as a result of a case-based course?

2. Do students in case study classes learn the same amount of content than students in traditionally taught educational psychology classes? Due to the approximately 25% of class time that students engage in discussions of cases, students are exposed to less direct coverage of some topics during lecture periods. Although an argument can be made that even if students are exposed to less content, what content is covered is learned more thoroughly due to the need to work with the information at higher cognitive levels (i.e., application, analysis, synthesis, and evaluation). Or as Lohman [1993] puts it:

> ...the motto might well be "less is more." A clear understanding of the key events, controversies, or concepts in a domain, along with the ability to connect these ideas both to each other and to a larger scheme is more important than a much larger base of fact and skill knowledge that is disconnected, is not tied with other learning, and can be applied only locally.(p. 21)

However, in New York, as in many other states, education students must pass a standardized test before gaining certification to teach, and a major portion of these tests focuses on topics covered in an educational psychology course (e.g., the "Professional Knowledge" section of the NTE). As states in the U.S. move more toward using performance assessments for granting certification to teach, it seems even more important that students be exposed to reflective case studies that investigate performances by teachers in the classroom. Nevertheless, is seems valuable to determine if students in an educational psychology class using cases achieve the same level of content knowledge than students in more traditionally taught courses.

3. Do students who have analyzed case studies perform any differently (i.e., become more reflective practitioners) than students who have not analyzed case studies? This, for me, is the BIG question. If students exposed to cases, or other reflective teacher education practices, don't perform any differently in the classroom than students who attend more traditionally taught education classes, does it really matter if cases are used? (Although the fact that the course instructor and students may find it more interesting than lectures may in itself be enough justification to teach with cases.) This is a research area that is particularly sparse due to the longitudinal and complex design that is necessary to answer this question. Although this third question is only tangentially addressed with the present research study, a follow-up study is planned to investigate this question in more depth by following the subjects of the present study into their student teaching in subsequent semesters.

METHOD

What follows is a description of the research conducted to answer questions 1 and 2 above.

SUBJECTS

The participants in this study were 106 undergraduate students taking EPY 350, an educational psychology survey course. The majority of the students were female (90%). These students were enrolled in five sections of the course taught by three different professors. For analysis purposes, sections 3 and 4, taught by Prof. A, were collapsed into one treatment group, and sections 2 and 5, taught by Prof. M, were similarly grouped together. Section 1, taught by Prof. L, became the third research group. Students self-selected which section they enrolled based on class schedules and which sections were still open when they went to register. Since students are not randomly assigned to treatment groups pre- and post-treatment data were collected to determine if significant differences in initial cognitive and reflective abilities existed between groups. Data collected on students are identified by social security numbers to assure confidentiality and to avoid researcher bias.

INSTRUMENTS

To measure levels of cognitive flexibility and moral decision making (questions 1a & 1b), data was collected within and across course sections using two different instruments. First, all students were given as a pre- and post-measure the Raven's Standard Progressive Matrices test which measures "the nonverbal component of Spearman's "g". This component assesses educative ability or the ability to make sense of complex situations, derive meaning from events, and to perceive and think clearly" [The Psychological Corporation, 1994, p. 86]. The use of this standardized cognitive abilities test to measure "fluid abilities" (viewing intelligence as a developing attribute rather than a stable one), characterizes student's ability "to solve...unfamiliar problems" or dilemmas "in a domain and" the ability "to impose multiple organizational schemes on their learning" [Lohman, 1993, p.21]. Second, all five sections of students were given as a pre- and post-measure the Defining Issues Test (DIT) to measure levels of moral reasoning and decision making ability [Rest, 1979]. According to Rest [1990] "the DIT is based on the fact that people judge different considerations as important in arriving at a moral decision about what to do" (p. 2). This corresponds to Schon's [1983] and Liston & Zeichner's [1987] perspectives of reflective teachers who use value and moral criteria in examining classroom dilemmas and making judgements when initiating actions to solve these problems. These pre- and post-test measures were used to record changes along these two factors of cognitive reflective ability.

To measure students reflective ability to consider multiple perspectives, apply appropriate educational psychology theory to analyze cases, and to note possible consequences of their solutions (question 1c), six written case outlines and four case analyses were collected from each of the students in the Case Study Group throughout the semester. To measure levels of reflectivity, the analyses of written cases are being evaluated by using the Framework for Reflective Pedagogical Thinking, a coding scheme developed by Sparks-Langer, et al. [1990] for use in analyzing reflection of students regarding educational situations. The framework consists of seven levels of language use and thinking that range from "no use of descriptive language" (level 1) to "explanations with consideration of ethical, moral, political issues" (level 7) (see Appendix C). Due to the enormous quantity of written material to analyze (approximately 1,100 typed pages), this analysis is incomplete and will not be discussed in the Results section of this paper.

To measure the amount of content that students learned (question 2), all sections of EPY 350 were given an educational psychology pretest and final exam constructed from a test item bank supplementing the required text. Test items reflected the content that all instructors listed on their syllabi and covered in class.

DESIGN & PROCEDURES

Treatment Groups

Three groups of students are compared as follows:

(1) Case Study Groups (CSG)

These two EPY 350 sections (n = 38) were taught during the 15 week semester using case studies as described on pages 2 & 3. In summary, students received traditional instruction in a combined lecture/discussion format over educational psychology content based on a standard educational psychology text [Biehler & Snowman, 1993] for approximately 3 days. This was followed by a day of discussion of a case of a teacher experiencing a classroom problem related to the educational psychology topics most recently discussed [Silverman, et al., 1993]. Students were required to prepare an outline before the case was discussed and a written analysis of four of the cases was required after the discussion. Six cases were discussed and used approximately 25% of the instructional time allotted for the class.

(2) Integrative Log Groups (ILG)

These two EPY 350 sections (n = 45) were taught primarily through traditional lecture/discussion format over the same content as the CSG and using the same text. However, the 25% instructional time spent on cases in the CSG was used for direct instruction on topics either not covered with the CSG or to provide greater depth on covered topics. However, students in this group were required to develop Integrative Log entries that attempted to develop "reflective" thought in a non-case manner (for examples see Appendix D). These entries were completed outside of classroom instructional time.

(3) Traditional Lecture Group (TLG)

This EPY 350 section (n = 23) was taught entirely through a traditional lecture/discussion format without any specific "reflective" treatments.

Phases of Research

Phase I of the research entailed collecting during the first week of classes pre-treatment data including baseline data on the two factors of reflectivity: fluid ability/problem solving (Raven's SPM) and moral decision making (DIT). Baseline data was also collected on content knowledge in educational psychology (EPY 350 Pretest), as well as appropriate demographics (survey).

Phase II of the study consisted of teaching each group as described above during the fifteen week semester. During this time all groups took 10-12 quizzes over the content. In addition, Students in the ILG were given five log entry assignments to complete during outside of class time, and students in the CSG were required to write and submit six case outlines and four case analyses for evaluation.

Phase III, during the last week of the semester, involved re-administering the Raven's SPM and the DIT to obtain comparison scores on the reflect thinking factors of problem solving abilities and moral decision making. Also a final exam was administered to measure amount of course content learned EPY 350 Post-test).

Phase IV consisted of data analysis to determine differences within and between treatment groups regarding levels of reflective decision making (question 1) and the levels of content knowledge achieved (question 2).

RESULTS

REFLECTIVE THINKING ABILITIES

Problem Solving & Decision Making

To determine if the case study method helped educational psychology students become more reflective in their problem-solving and decision-making abilities (questions 1a & 1b), a series of paired samples t-tests on pre- and post-tests data were conducted to analyze if any changed occurred on either the Raven's SPM or the DIT within each group. As can be noted from table 1, no significant differences were found on the DIT measure, although the Case Study Group had the largest positive change. For the Raven's SPM, all three groups did less well on the post-test than the pretest, and the Traditional Learning Group did significantly worse. (One possible reason for this may be due to the differences in administration of the pre and post Raven's. For the pre-test students were tested individually in a "testing room," while for the post-test they took the test as a group immediately after their final EPY 350 exam. Therefore, fatigue might have effected the post-test score on the Raven's SPM.)

TABLE 1
MEANS, STANDARD DEVIATIONS, AND T-TESTS ON PAIRED GROUP SAMPLES
FOR MORAL DECISION MAKING (DIT) AND PROBLEM-SOLVING ABILITY (RAVEN'S SPM)

Group		DIT Pre		Post	Raven's SPM Pre		Post
CSG	M	36.988		39.966	51.105		49.947
	SD	10.488		14.452	3.697		5.240
	n		26			38	
	t		1.175			-1.921	
	p		.251			.063	
ILG	M	37.309		37.188	49.718		49.231
	SD	13.409		13.214	7.041		6.834
	n		32			39	
	t		-.059			-.794	
	p		.953			.432	
TLG	M	35.282		37.329	50.174		48.000
	SD	15.130		13.240	4.638		5.665
	n		17			23	
	t		.585			-2.524	
	p		.567			.019	

To measure if there was any differences between groups on the post-DIT or post-Raven's measures after the different instructional treatments, an Analysis of Variance was conducted for each measure across the three groups. No significant differences were found in either the manner in which students in each group solved moral dilemmas on the DIT, $F(2,72) < 1$, nor in their fluid abilities to solve problems on the Raven's SPM, $F[2,97] < 1$.

CONTENT KNOWLEDGE

No significant differences were found on the EPY 350 pretest between groups, $F(2,103) = 2.012$, $p = 0.139$. Therefore to determine if the Case Study Group (CSG) learned the same amount of content as the more traditionally taught groups (question 2), an ANOVA was conducted. This analysis showed extremely strong levels of significance, $F(2,103) = 20.694$, $p < .0005$, so a series of post-hoc analyses (Scheffe tests) were conducted between the three pairs of groups. As shown in Table 2, significant differences were found between the CSG and each of the other two treatment groups (ILG & TLG), but there was no significant difference between ILG and TLG.

TABLE 2
MEANS, STANDARD DEVIATIONS, AND POST HOC COMPARISONS
OF EPY 350 POST-TEST FOR THREE TREATMENT GROUPS

Group	M	SD	Post Hoc Comparisons
CSG (n=38)	84.211	8.470	CSG > ILG, p < .001
ILG (n=45)	71.733	10.597	CSG > TLG, p < .001
TLG (n=23)	70.957	10.178	ILG > TLG, not significant

DISCUSSION

It appears that at least in the short term (15 weeks) case study methods of instruction, or more traditional methods of instruction, do not significantly change the way in which students think about moral or ethical dilemmas (question 1a). However, the positive direction of movement from pretest to post-test DIT scores of the Case Study Group suggests that if given more cases to analyze or by devoting more than 25% of the class time to cases, a larger increase in moral reasoning might occur. However, the dilemmas of the DIT are not classroom specific, so an additional analysis is under way of the case analyses and outlines that the Case Study Group students wrote. As mentioned earlier, analyses of four written cases by students in the Case Study Groups will be evaluated for levels of reflectivity by using the Framework for Reflective Pedagogical Thinking. It is hypothesized that although students may not progress to level 7 over the semester, they will show an increase in levels from the first case written early in the semester to the fourth case that is written later in the semester.

Regarding the Raven's SPM data, it appears the manner in which the post test data was collected may have been a major factor in the consistent decrease of pre- to post-test scores for all three groups. Giving the Raven's Post-test separate from the EPY 350 Final may have given more meaningful scores. Both fatigue and "end of the semester" anxiety and disinterest may have effected the manner in which students took the Raven's Post-test.

A major finding, however, is that instruction through the case method seems to significantly increase the level of educational psychology content knowledge that a student obtains when compared to more traditional instructional methods. Although all three instructional methods showed significant gains in the level of content knowledge that students obtained, the level of the students receiving case study instruction was significantly greater than the students receiving either of the other two methods of instruction. This would lend support to the cognitive theories of generative learning [Wittrock, 1986], since analyzing cases and writing case analyses require that students generate their own syntheses of how educational psychology theory applies to solving the case problems. This active generation and synthesis should help to more deeply process the educational and psychological concepts taught in the course. It should also help students to retain this information longer, and therefore be available the next year when these students do their student teaching.

This brings us back to what I consider the BIG question (question 3): Do students who have analyzed case studies *perform* any differently (i.e., become more reflective practitioners) than students who have not analyzed case studies? Or restated to address the movement of these students into their student teaching experiences next year: Do students who are exposed to cases during their preservice education behave more reflectively in their student teaching experience? This question will be addressed in a subsequent study. The author's intention is to continually collect data over the next 2-3 year period to develop an analysis which can be used to inform teacher educators, particularly educational psychology instructors, as to the advantages and disadvantages of the use of case studies as a reflective pedagogical practice. Hopefully, this information can also contribute to creating better curricular programming in teacher education institutions.

APPENDIX A
CASE STUDY OUTLINES

Name of Case: Maggie Lindberg

Problems   Evidence/Data
* Teacher's Perspective (Maggie's)

-

-

* My Perspective

-

-

Ed. Psych. Principles

-

-

Solutions   Consequences

-

-

Ed. Psych. Principles

-

-

APPENDIX B
CASE STUDY ANALYSIS GUIDELINES

A written analysis will be required for most of the case studies discussed. The analysis is to be typed, double-spaced, and follow APA writing style guidelines. The paper should be approximately 5-6 pages long. It should minimally contain the following information:

1. A clear statement of the problems in the case that the teacher must resolve. Both the teacher's perspective of the problems and your perspective should be identified. Often these two perspectives will not be the same. You need to state why these problems are important and cite specific data in the case that provides evidence that these, in fact, are problems. You must support your perspective based on the theory and principles of educational psychology presented in the assigned readings and discussed in class. Your thinking regarding the problem should reflect what you are learning from the educational theory and research. (This section should be approximately 1/3 to 1/2 of the total analysis.)

2. Some possible solutions to the problems. Try to be as specific as possible, citing a specific "plan of action" for the teacher to use to solve the problems. Your solution should be written clear enough so that the teacher in the case study could read your solution and begin trying it in her or his classroom tomorrow to solve the problems. Be sure to relate your solution directly to the readings assigned in class, both those under current consideration and any appropriate readings done earlier in this course or another course. (This section should be approximately 1/2 to 2/3 of the total analysis.)

APPENDIX C
FRAMEWORK FOR REFLECTIVE PEDAGOGICAL THINKING*

Level	Description
1	No descriptive language
2	Simple, lay person description
3	Events labeled with appropriate terms
4	Explanation with tradition or personal preference as the rationale
5	Explanation with principle or theory given as the rationale
6	Explanation with principle/theory and consideration of context factors
7	Explanation with consideration of ethical, moral, political issues

*Taken from page 27 of Sparks-Langer, G. M., Simmons, J. M., Pasch, M., Colton, A., & Starko, A. (1990). Reflective pedagogical thinking: How can we promote it and measure it? *Journal of Teacher Education, 41* (4), 23-32.

APPENDIX D
INTEGRATIVE LOG ENTRIES**

Integrative log Entry #1

It has been said that we teach the way we were taught. For this writing assignment be a reflective teacher-as-a-theorist/scientist, and consider the two teachers you have had whose teaching styles you would wish to emulate. Give thought to the experiences you had being a student in their classes, and briefly describe their teaching, especially their specific characteristics or teaching styles which you would incorporate into your own teaching. Remember, this is to be typed, and about two pages in length.

Integrative Log Entry #2

The American public schools have been called "the great arena of behavioral psychology." Reflect on your own education and discuss, in one or two type-written pages, how behaviorism was used in classrooms in which you were a student. Your discussion can include how behavioral practices were used to enhance your learning, motivate you, and/or mange the classrooms you attended.

Integrative Log Entry #3

In the current educational environment which stresses "Back to basics," it is unlikely that you will be asked to teach in a "Humanistic" classroom. It is likely, however, that you will be able to incorporate Humanistic concepts into your teaching. Give thought to yourself as a classroom teacher in the near future, and describe how you would incorporate Humanistic principles in a back-to-basics classroom.

Integrative Log Entry #4

For the area in which you expect to teach, select a topic of your choosing which you might realistically present to students. Discuss how your instruction might reflect the precepts of cognitive psychology. Focus on the nature of your students' schemas, and how you could present the material in a meaningful way in order to facilitate your students' construction of proper useful schemas.

** Note: I wish to acknowledge Dr. Robert Malloch at the College of Saint Rose as the author of these examples.

REFERENCES

Axelrod, P. & McLane, M. (1993 April). *Instructional strategies that support reflective teaching practices in special education courses*. Paper presented at the Council for Exceptional Children Annual Convention, San Antonio,Texas.

Biehler, R.F. & Snowman, J. (1993). *Psychology Applied To Teaching (7th ed.)*. Boston: Houghton Mifflin.

Dewey, J.(1933). *How We Think*. Chicago: Henry Regnery.

James, F. R. (1992). *Case-based or traditional didactic instruction: Which tells the story for preservice teachers?* Paper presented at the annual meeting of the American Educational Research Association, San Francisco, CA., April.

Kitchner, K.S., & King, P. (1981). Reflective judgement concepts of justification and their relationship to age and education. *Journal of Applied Developmental Psychology, 2*, 89-116.

Liston, D. P. & Zeichner, K. M. (1987). *Reflective teacher education and moral deliberation*. *Journal of Teacher Education, 38* (6), 2-9.

Lohman, D. F. (1993). Teaching and testing to develop fluid abilities. *Educational Researcher, 22* (7), 12-23.

Rest, J. R. (1990). *Information Bulletin*, the Center for the Study of Ethical Development, University of Minnesota (9/7/90)

Rest, J. R. (1979). *Development in judging moral issues*. Minneapolis: University of Minnesota Press.

Ross, D. D. (1989). First steps in developing a reflective approach. *Journal of Teacher Education, 40* (2), 22-30.

Schon, D. A. (1983). *The Reflective Practitioner*. San Francisco: Jossey-Bass.

Silverman, R., Welty, W., & Lyon, S. (1993). *Case Studies in Teacher Problem Solving*. New York: McGraw-Hill Primis.

Sparks-Langer, G. M., Simmons, J. M., Pasch, M., Colton, A., & Starko, A.(1990). Reflective pedagogical thinking: How can we promote it and measure it? *Journal of Teacher Education, 41* (4), 23-32.

Spiro, R. J., Vispoel, W. P., Schmitz, J. G., Samarapungavan, A., & Boerger, A. E. (1987). Knowledge acquisition: Cognitive flexibility and transfer in complex content domains. In B. K. Britton & S. W. Glynn (Eds.), *Executive control processes in reading* (pp. 177-199). Hillsdale, NJ: Erlbaum.

The Psychological Corporation (1994). *Resources for Measuring Educational Performance*. San Antonio: Harcourt Brace & Co.

Wasserman, S. (1993). *Getting Down to Cases: Learning to Teach with Case Studies*. New York: Teachers College Press.

Wittrock, M. C. (1986). Students' thought processes. In M.C. Wittrock (Ed.), *Handbook of Research on Teaching* (pp. 297-314). New York: Macmillian.

Woolfolk, A. E. (1993). *Educational Psychology (5th ed.)*. Needham Heights, MA: Allyn & Bacon.

CASE-BASED RESEARCH
PRACTICAL REFLECTIONS ON THE CRAFT

Brian Leavy
Dublin City University Business School
DUBLIN, IRELAND

Abstract

This paper presents the practical reflections of a 'working student' in the strategy field on the craft of case-based research, and is aimed in particular at researchers from any discipline who are setting out to use the case method for the first time. It begins with a brief review of the growing contribution that the case method is making to the strategy field and the potential that the method offers for further studies in this area. It then goes on to examine such basic questions as how and why researchers choose the case-based approach and how such an approach typically makes a value-added contribution to the field of interest. It concludes with a discussion of some of the skills, challenges and practical difficulties typically involved in the selection of case sites, the gaining and maintaining of access, and the collection and analysis of data, in this type of research.

INTRODUCTION

The 1990s may well turn out to be the decade when case-based research finally comes into its own in the social sciences. It is not so long ago that most case-based researchers found themselves on the defensive about the 'scientific' rigor of their methodology and about the capacity of this type of research to make generic value-added contributions to their fields of interest. As late as 1979 Van Maanen [1979] and his co-contributors to a special issue of the Administrative Science Quarterly still felt the need to "reclaim" qualitative methods for the social sciences generally, and early into the following decade Yin [1981: 58] was seeking anxiously "to reaffirm the role of the case study as a systematic research tool" and to "show that an acceptable craft had already emerged." Since then, however, the attractiveness and credibility of case-based research has been steadily rising (a process which has been affected by, and reflected in, the growing influence and stature of WACRA itself over this time). Over the last ten years or more some of the most influential research in the business studies field in general, and in the strategy field in particular, has been primarily case-based in approach. Porter's [1980, 1985, 1990] work on competition, the Montreal research on strategy formation [Mintzberg, 1978: Miller and Friesen, 1978, 1980: Mintzberg and Waters, 1982], the Burgleman [1983] study of internal corporate venturing, the research of Kanter [1983] and Pettigrew [1985a] on the management of strategic change, the Bradford studies [Hickson et al, 1986] on strategic decision processes, and Hamel's [1991] work on strategic alliances are among the more prominent examples.

Right across the board case-based research now has a strongly established pedigree in the business studies field. Even in areas like accounting and marketing, where large-scale statistical sampling methodologies have been particularly dominant, the credibility and contribution of case-based research is growing [Kaplan, 1986: Scapens, 1990]. In spite of this growing interest and stature many researchers, who are contemplating the choice of a case-based approach for the first time, are often daunted by what seems like the free-style, somewhat "messy," nature of the research process involved. The main purpose of this paper is to share with those who might be setting out on their first major project using a case-based approach the practical reflections of a "working student," which as Mills [1970: 215] has suggested can often be more valuable and interesting to other practitioners than "a dozen codifications of procedures" by methodological specialists. The remainder of the paper begins by examining the distinguishing characteristics of case-based qualitative research and the variety of approaches covered by the category. It then goes on to consider the factors that influence researchers to choose a case-based research design and how such an approach can be used to make a generic value-added contribution to the field of interest. The paper ends with a discussion of some of the practical challenges and difficulties involved and how they might be met and overcome. The author draws on his own experience with case-based research [Leavy, 1991: Leavy and Wilson, 1994] and on his exposure to the reflections of other researchers, directly and through the literature. He also draws freely on his earlier work on the same topic [Leavy, 1994].

CASE-BASED RESEARCH - CHARACTERISTICS AND APPROACHES

It is difficult to present either a precise definition for case-based research or any single code of procedure. This is at one and the same time part of its charm and its challenge. Case-based research is normally considered under the more general classification of qualitative research, though the two are far from mutually synonymous. The label qualitative research itself has "no precise meaning" and is "at best an umbrella term covering an array of interpretative techniques" [Van Maanen, 1979: 520], and the case-based approach, as we shall see, can cover a wide spectrum of possibilities. This can be seen most readily in the wide variation in the number cases that different researchers choose to study, and in whether it is primary or secondary case data that form the main basis for thematic analysis. In the strategy field, for example, some of the most prominent case-based research has ranged from classic studies of single cases using primary case data [Allison, 1971] to equally inventive studies involving 20 or more previously published cases [Porter, 1980, 1985: Miller and Friesen, 1978, 1980]. While recognising the potential of research based on already published cases this paper is mainly concerned with primary case-based studies and the skills and challenges involved.

The full range and variety in approaches is not adequately captured in terms of just numbers of cases and sources of data alone. By way of illustration let us compare and contrast the Bradford study [Hickson et al, 1986] on strategic decision making with Pettigrew's [1985a] research on strategic change. The Hickson et al [1986] research studied 150 strategic decision episodes across thirty different organizations, six of them in some detail, whereas Pettigrew's [1985a] project focused in depth on four cases of strategic change across the major divisions of the same company. These two studies represent quite a contrast not only in research design but also in underlying 'world view'. The first is largely functional-positivist in its philosophical underpinnings while the second is much more relativist and ideographic in its perspective and approach [Burrell and Morgan, 1979: Morgan & Smircich, 1980]. What they do have in common is the primary role played by descriptive data. According the Van Maanen [1979: 520] "doing description" is the "fundamental act of data collection in a qualitative study." The intensive Pettigrew research was primarily historical and ethnographic. The more extensive Hickson et al study was not as richly descriptive at the individual case level. However its large sample of 150 discrete decision episodes allowed the researchers to use descriptive statistics to augment their overall qualitative analysis with an added and insightful quantitative dimension. Both studies were primarily inductive. Neither used the techniques of statistical inference to test hypotheses or to try to establish causality. Both were more concerned with theory generation than with trying to prove or falsify established theories.

THE CHOICE OF A CASE-BASED APPROACH

What kind of criteria influence researchers to choose the qualitative case-based approach. "For the classic social scientist" according to Mills [1970: 135] "neither method nor theory is an autonomous domain; methods are methods for some range of problems and theories are theories for some range of phenomena." Many researchers find that the nature of the research question, and the current state of the field, drive them in the direction of case-based research. This, for example, is how Michael Porter [1991: 99], with a strong quantitative background in industrial economics, found himself drawn towards case-based research in his now seminal work on competition:

"In my own research, I pursued cross-sectional econometric studies in the 1970s but ultimately gave up as the complexity of the frameworks I was developing ran ahead of the available cross-sectional data. I was forced to turn to large numbers of in-depth case studies to identify significant variables, explore the relationships among them, and cope with industry and firm specificity in strategy choices."

However, while for many methodological purists the choice of problem should dictate the choice of method, as illustrated in the Porter example, there are many prominent practitioners, like Mintzberg [1979] and Pettigrew

[1985a] for whom the reverse is true. These researchers prefer to work with case-based approaches because they find this style of research more interesting. They like to use exploratory inductive approaches that bring them into close personal contact with organizations and their personnel, in preference to working with deductive approaches involving data collection methods that rely on surrogate measures collected at a distance, however interesting and elegant the techniques for doing so. As Mintzberg [1979: 584] described it "it is discovery that attracts me to this business, not the checking out of what we already know," and researchers like he and Pettigrew unashamedly choose their personal research agendas to suit their preferred style of empirical enquiry.

HOW CASE-BASED RESEARCH MAKES ITS CONTRIBUTION

As experienced editors like David Whetten [1989: 492] of the Academy of Management Journal will readily testify, the question of "what is a legitimate, value-added contribution to theory development" is often one that is neither easy to explicate nor to evaluate. Such contributions are usually easier to discern and evaluate in quantitative research that follows fairly precise and well-trodden methodological procedures, though many researchers with a pre-disposition for more qualitative approaches feel that relevance and impact are often sacrificed for rigor in such deductive, hypothesis- testing studies.

Throughout the social sciences, case-based qualitative researchers often differ from those with a preference for large scale quantitative techniques not only in method but also in the focus of interest. In the strategy field for example the quantitative researchers tend to focus on issues of content and structure in conditions of equilibrium. The emphasis tends to be on trying to determine through large-scale, point-in-time, cross-sectional studies what types of strategy and structure will represent the 'best fit' with the particular environmental and technological contingencies of the firm and industry in question. The process by which organizations go about achieving this 'best fit' is implicitly viewed as a black box by such researchers and tends to be of little theoretical interest to them. In contrast, case-based qualitative researchers like Mintzberg [1978, 1979] and Pettigrew [1979, 1985a, 1990] tend to be most interested in process issues. They are most curious about such questions as how strategic and structural change happen in real organizational settings in conditions of disequilibrium and transition. They tend not to accept the determinism of the equilibrium or contingency theorists and to believe that strategic and structural changes in organizations are not simply the result of some sharply defined and timeless imperatives (whether environmental or technological) but the rich, messy and often inconclusive products of the interaction of economic, political and cultural forces linking context, process and outcome in a dynamic, iterative and interactive way [Mintzberg et al, 1976: Pettigrew, 1985a: Leavy, 1991]. In short, case-based researchers tend to be interested in analysing and theorising about such dynamic, disequilibrium processes as strategy formation (as distinct from formulation), strategic change, innovation and industry evolution.

Case-based qualitative research, with its emphasis on dynamic processes and close-in methodologies, makes it contribution primary through induction. In its purest form the induced theory should emerge from the data. The classic 'manual' on the generation of such empirically "grounded theory" is the Glaser and Strauss [1967] book (see also Strauss [1987]), though ideas and approaches to the building of theoretical contributions from case-based research are developing all the time in quite inventive ways, as reviewed recently by Eisenhardt [1989] and Leavy [1992]. In the inductive mode of theory generation the researcher is ideally supposed to go into the field with little or no theoretical pre-conceptions. In practice, however, the researcher cannot be totally open-minded and some conceptual framework must be developed in advance to at least guide the efficient and systematic collection of data. However it is very important in this type of research to avoid premature categorization as much as possible in order to allow the key themes and factors on which subsequent theory will be built to emerge from the data.

There is no precise procedure for generating theory by such an inductive process and this is one of the method's most formidable challenges. However experience has shown that there are a number of broad strategies for theory generation which case-based researchers have used to great effect (see also Eisenhardt [1989]).

(i) **Pure induction:** To use a favorite aphorism of Pettigrew and other inductive researchers the central thrust of this approach is as far as possible to "let the data speak for themselves." Burgleman's [1983] study of internal corporate venturing and Hamel's [1991] research on inter-partner learning in strategic alliances are excellent examples of theory generation in the strategy field by almost pure induction.

(ii) **Synthesis from disparate literatures:** Bringing two or more disparate paradigms or literatures together to generate a new synthesis is probably one of the most powerful ways to make a valued-added contribution in any field and to give it new life and direction. The Caves [1980] and Porter [1980, 1981] cross-fertilization of the Industry Organization and Business Policy paradigms in the strategy field is a classic example.

(iii) Generating replacement theory: This approach involves using existing theory as a 'strawman'. The empirical analysis is directed at highlighting the inadequacies of the existing theory and at generating more empirically sound theory to replace it. The Bower [1970] study of resource allocation and the Mintzberg [1973] study of the nature of managerial work are two classic examples of this approach.

(iv) **Combination:** Some researchers have used approaches which involved some combination of the above three strategies to good effect. Allison's [1971] study of the decision process in the case of the Cuban Missile Crisis and the Bradford [Hickson et al, 1986] research on strategic decision making processes are excellent examples of the use of multiple perspectives and approaches in the analysis of qualitative data and the generation of new insights.

THE CRAFT SKILLS INVOLVED

At first sight case-based qualitative research can often be deceptively appealing, especially to those who might be uncomfortable with the concepts, techniques and technologies of more quantitative methods. Can anyone who is reasonably literate "do description" and analyse qualitative data at a level capable of making a substantial contribution? To examine this question it is interesting to look at how the better known exponents of this type of research actually characterise their approach in everyday language.

Many of these great exponents, when they reflect on what they do and how they do it, tend to converge on the notion of a craft process [Mills, 1970: Yin, 1981: Van Maanen, 1982: Pettigrew 1985b: Porter 1991]. Yin's [1981: 58] use of the phrase an "acceptable craft," quoted earlier, and Porter's [1991: 116] reference to the "crafting of empirical research" are typical of the way that case-based researchers characterise their approach. For example Mills [1970: 134] has described the classical social analyst as one "who has not been inhibited by method or technique" but has more typically "sought to develop and use in his work the sociological imagination" in the "way of the intellectual craftsman." Likewise Pettigrew [1985b: 223] has described his own case-based qualitative approach as a "craft process and not merely the application of a formal set of techniques and rules." He goes on to point out that, "contrary to the way the practice of research is often taught and written up, the activity is clearly a social and not merely a rationally contrived act," and that it has its "artistic and subjective sides." Van Maanen [1982: 15-19] in a very similar vein points out that "technique-dependent definitions of qualitative research" are "unlikely to encompass the diversity of uses" or adequately reflect "the artistry, the craft, (and) the workmanship involved."

The case-based method may involve "simple - in a sense inelegant - methodologies" [Mintzberg 1979: 583], when compared to more quantitative approaches. However, like the artist with a brush or the brain-surgeon with a scalpel, the use of such inelegant instruments can be quite elegant and sublime in the hands of those most skilled in their craft. So what kind of craft skills and artistry are involved? Mintzberg [1979: 584-5] sees two essential skills in the case-based inductive approach, the first is "detective work" or the "tracking down of patterns" in the data, and the second is "the creative leap" that generates fresh insight from these patterns. The creative leap seems to come from "subconscious mental processes" or "intuition." In Mintzberg's experience this intuition "apparently requires the 'sense' of things" that can only come from being close enough to the source of the data to really "understand what is going on" in real organizational terms. In a similar vein Pettigrew (in conversation with the author in 1985) crystallized the critical skills in this type of research as "real conceptual ability in order to be able to abstract from very rich descriptive data" and "kaleidoscopic reading in order to broaden the base from which concepts and insights might spring, which could be brought to bear on this data." Pettigrew's inclusion of 'kaleidoscopic reading' as a means for stimulating creativity and insight finds echoes in Mill's [1970: 221] reflection that "imagination" is often "invited" or "loosen(ed) up" by the "putting together of hitherto isolated items" and the finding of "unexpected connections." This approach has a sound basis in the modern literature on innovation, where it is now commonly held that the probability of generating frame-breaking ideas is enhanced by variety in approach, the cross-fertilization of ideas and by thinking that is deliberately prevented from converging too prematurely [Quinn, 1986: Peters, 1992].

DIFFICULTIES AND CHALLENGES

Up to this point we have dealt with the characteristics of case-based research, the factors influencing the choice of this approach, the broad ways in which it can be used to make a value-added contribution and the craft skills involved. We now turn finally to consider some of the difficulties and challenges that it typically presents in operation and how they might be overcome.

CHOOSING THE NUMBER OF CASES

One major issue that arises early on in most case-based research designs is the question of how many cases to study and how to select them. The debate about the relative merits of using single or multiple cases is still alive and unresolved, as the recent exchanges between Dyer and Wilkins [1991] and Eisenhart [1991] in the Academy of Management Review so readily attest. The key considerations are both epistemological and practical. The epistemological issue revolves around the question of how generalizable the findings are of any single case, a question that many quantitative researchers consider to be the major weakness of the case-based approach. The community of case-based researchers in general is less defensive about this than it used to be. As Mintzberg [1979: 583] has boldly demanded "what is wrong with a sample of one?" and "why should researchers have to apologize for them?." In biology, for example, few researchers involved in the intensive study of a single digestive system would feel in any way defensive about the scientific nature of their inquiry or the generic value of the insights to be gained from it. As long as the case is clearly an example of a generic class of process or phenomenon then the question of generalizability becomes less of an issue [Leavy, 1991]. Pettigrew [1985b: 242] supports the view that "even single case studies are capable of developing and refining generalisable concepts and frames of reference" while Mohr [1992: 79], in a stimulating paper at WACRA 1992, has shown how the single case can be used with confidence to establish causality by making a distinction between "physical causal reasoning" (through case analysis) and "logical causal reasoning" (through statistical analysis).

Most case-based researchers recognise that theory generation from cases is difficult without a research design that provides for some form of comparative analysis. This is one of the main considerations favouring a multi-case approach. The multi-case design trades off depth for breadth and may lose some of the most distinctive advantages of the case method in doing so (see the recent interchange between Dyer and Wilkins [1991] and Eisenhardt [1991] referred to earlier). In making this trade-off researchers should consider the opportunities presented for within-case comparative analysis as well as for the cross-case variety. For example, my own recent study of strategy formation was based on a research design involving four case studies of different organizations but the same research design also presented me with thirteen discrete leadership tenures or episodes within and across these organizations and a rich single case study of the deeply embedded linkages between industry evolution and firm level strategic change [Leavy, 1991: Leavy and Wilson 1994]. Such hybrid opportunities can emerge from the research process after the basic design has been chosen, as in my own case, or can be a deliberate element of the original design. The Hickson et al [1986] study on strategic decision processes, discussed in some detail earlier, and the study of Hamel [1991] into inter-partner learning in strategic alliances are examples of the more deliberate kind. The latter involved a two-stage design in which breadth (eleven cases) was used to reveal key conceptual categories and depth (two cases) was used to generate richer process insight.

GETTING AND MAINTAINING ACCESS

Case-based research usually requires a high degree of direct access to organizational personnel and archival material. Getting it can be difficult and maintaining it can be challenging. Case-based researchers therefore need to have good social skills. They also need to be well versed in the basics of organizational behaviour in order to accomplish their task of primary data collection with due sensitivity. The very presence of a researcher in an organization, asking certain types of questions and probing certain issues and episodes, can have unintended consequences, and leave a residue of concerns about why the study was undertaken and how the findings will be used, that management may have to spend considerable time and effort to address.

One practical approach to gaining access that I have used is for the researcher to make informal contact with a middle ranking executive through his or her own social and professional network and to have some exploratory and confidential discussions before any formal approach is made. Through this process the researcher can assess whether the case site is likely to be as appropriate or relevant to the project as had been hoped, whether the level of access to company personnel and archives that will be needed is likely to be forthcoming, and how best to make the formal approach. The formal approach is usually best made through the chief executive but it can often help if by that stage the request for cooperation is already expected. An important by-product of this approach is that it also allows the organization to say no without loss of face or damage to a relationship which may well be fruitful at some later stage. Soon after a formal approach has been accepted the senior officers of the organization will typically want an up-front meeting to establish the ground rules and mutual expectations. They will want to be comfortable with the aims of the research, the amount of executive time and effort required, the confidentially of the process and the plans for dissemination of the results.

It is difficult to be precise in advance, in this type of research, about exactly how much cooperation you will need, how many people you will want to interview and how much archival data you will need to collect. The organization's quite normal desire to have these requirements explicitly laid out may seem to overly constrain and circumscribe the potential of the inquiry. However in my own experience many of these restraints will usually be relaxed as the data collection proceeds, when a relationship of trust and credibility has been developed and the organization has had time to become more comfortable with the process. However there is always some risk that the organization may withdraw your access before you are happy that your data collection is complete. Such withdrawl is not uncommon and most case-based researchers will probably experience it at some stage during their careers. It can also be difficult to anticipate. For example Wilson [1980: 122] tells how at one of his case sites his continued presence had become "politically embarrassing" for the organization's leaders because of the issues that his research was probing and how he was prematurely asked to leave. In another case my own access was unexpectedly withdrawn when an incoming leader felt no longer bound by the commitments to the project given by his predecessor [Leavy 1993]. Mitigating this risk of access withdrawl may be one of the strongest pragmatic considerations favouring a multi-case design.

COLLECTING DATA - ARCHIVES AND INTERVIEWS

Company documents and personal interviews are the case-based researcher's main data sources and the collection of this data is usually a long, serial and labour-intensive process. My own comparative study of strategy formation [Leavy, 1991: Leavy and Wilson, 1994] involved a total of 70 personal interviews with nearly 40 respondents each lasting on average around two hours. The archival data used in the same study included over 105 annual reports, 200 press cuttings, and numerous in-house company documents and contemporary historical books and articles. The collection of the interview and archival data tended to be interleaved and the whole process to resemble detective work [Mintzberg 1979] with both data types complimenting each other in valuable ways. I found that interview data often led to the unearthing of more archival data, which in turn gave rise to further lines of inquiry to be pursued in future interviews. The archival data often helped to sort out the proper chronology of historical events where personal recollections were doubtful or inconsistent and interviews provided valuable interpretations of key events, and what they meant to those involved, that could not have been gleaned from any other sources.

Personal interviewing is the most intrusive on organizational time and resources and the schedule of interviews needs to be carefully worked out and managed. The most a researcher can reasonably expect is two interviews with any individual respondent. The second interview, where it can be secured, can often be the most valuable because much of the first session may be taken up with establishing rapport and credibility. The main challenge to the interviewer, particularly with an open-ended unstructured approach, is to keep the data channel as open as possible by going all out to make the respondent comfortable with the process. For example I tend early on in some interviews to point out that, since I am interested in getting the deepest possible insights into the process under study, I may raise some issues that the interviewees may not wish to discuss or elaborate on, and they should feel free to decline to do so without explanation. The onus is always on the researcher to use the interview time effectively, particularly with the most senior executives whose busy schedules will usually not accommodate a second opportunity. My own approach in this regard has been to try to become as fully informed as possible about the particular episodes or processes of interest from the most accessible data sources first, and to reserve the rarer data collection opportunities with the most senior executives for data which is likely to be unique because of the particular position or perspective of the respondent.

Data collection in this type of research does not lend itself easily to the use of either research assistants or to team-based approaches because of the long, serial and intensive nature of the process and the need for "continuous interaction between the theoretical issues being studied and the data being collected" [Yin, 1984: 56]. Parallel data collection is not impossible but it is difficult. Even where much time and effort are spent in carefully developing "common research protocols" [Leonard-Barton, 1992: 125], the high degree of consistency of approach required to make it work can still pose the most formidable of challenges. Finally, the practical guideline for when the data collection process should stop in case-based research, whether carried out by individuals or teams, is when the process has reached point of diminishing returns, where "additional data no longer add to the refinement of the concepts" [Burgleman, 1983: 225) or where "saturation of the core categories" is achieved (Hamel, 1991: 86).

ANALYZING THE DATA

The qualitative data involved in case-based research is, as Miles [1979: 590] has characterised it, an "attractive nuisance" which is typically rich in quantity and texture but can be difficult to organize, retrieve and analyse. Data retrieval is the first problem. Where are your most apposite illustrations and anecdotes when you need them? In most cases they are buried deep in your files. Many manuals on qualitative methods give practical guidance on cross-indexing and data organization. I have tried some of these with some success but in my own experience there is simply no substitute for knowing your data intimately and constantly interacting with it, whatever technique you decide to adopt. This is one of the benefits of collecting the data yourself and one of the main reasons why a team-based approach can be so difficult with this type of research. Furthermore the ability to draw on direct quotations will help to breath life into the description and analysis of the cases and it is important to record the data in the first place with this requirement in mind.

Case writing and analysis is an art in itself, as many WACRA members can attest from first hand experience, and whereas the quantitative researcher can lean mainly on sophisticated statistical techniques and procedures to reveal the relationships and patterns of interest the case-based researcher must rely more on literary skill and good prose. The case-based researcher is under more pressure than most not only to make interesting findings but to make the findings interesting. Like the "house of history" our house must "not only be secure" in the sense of scientific rigor but should be "handsome as well" [Gay 1988: 189]. The analysis begins with each case narrative itself. No matter how descriptive you try to keep it in the first instance the selectivity and structuring involved in the transformation of interview and archival data into a coherent narrative represents the first stage in the conversion of information into knowledge. The narratives form the more 'refined' database for comparative analysis and synthesis from which the real conceptual contribution is expected to emerge. The creativity and contribution in this type of research is often made through the writing process itself because "your themes often emerge quite late in the (research) process" as David Wilson, an experienced case-based researcher [Wilson 1980, Hickson et al 1986, Leavy and Wilson 1994] has pointed out (in conversation with the author). It is often through trying to find the most interesting way or ways to present, compare and analyze the data that the key relationships and categories emerge and the real contribution is made.

Like all research the case-based approach is 95% perspiration and 5% inspiration. However that 5% is particularly critical and challenging in qualitative research, where there is little scope for elegant methodology to distract from, or compensate for, thin data, unimaginative analysis or weak insight. This inspirational component, or 'creative leap,' is a mysterious process of the imagination which can often be coaxed, but be rarely commanded, through procedure or technique. While the final written form of any project tends to portray a deliberate, linear and logical sequence the process itself is usually more untidy, iterative and emergent in character, with literature and data typically interleaved and the researcher continually interacting with both in ongoing inner dialogue throughout the duration of the project [Glaser and Strauss 1967; Eisenhardt 1989; Pettigrew 1990]. "The research may begin with only a broad definition of the research problem, which is sharpened by a complex and evolving mixture of literature analysis; data collection; internal discussion; the uncovering of themes, patterns and propositions" which is then usually "followed by more data collection, and more polished and structured thematic writing" as the research proceeds [Pettigrew 1990: 279]. One indispensable technique for the case-based researcher is the keeping of a journal [Mills 1970] for continually recording 'research memoranda' [Glaser and Strauss 1967; Strauss 1987] to capture the inner dialogue in chronological sequence as the research progresses. As in other crafts where the creative leap is vital "even the slightest hint of an idea should be written down" in this journal [Chisholm 1992: 10], which will act as a vital repository for all kinds of elusive ideas that may enter this dialogue at any time of the day or night as the relentless search for insight continues. Over time what emerges from these ideas are recurring themes or central obsessions around which the researcher's intellectual curiosity begins to converge in an attempt to make some holistic sense out of the inner dialogue and draw fresh insight from it. It is from this process, and the ongoing production of working papers that makes it explicit, that the elusive but vital 5% inspiration is likely spring, and through which it can be most systematically encouraged.

CONCLUSION

Cased-based research is, as we have seen, a craft process. It is not the easiest of research approaches in spite of the relatively simple and inelegant technology involved. As Yin [1984: 56] points out the demands of this type of research "on a person's intellect, ego and emotions are far greater than for any other research strategy." It can often be the case that "the happiness of the result bears no relation to the difficulties overcome or the pains taken" to borrow William Hazlitt's [1826] somewhat poignant reflection on the mysteries of the creative process in the literature field. Most case-based researchers live with a high level of uncertainty about the potential quality of their contribution right through to almost the end of the process as the Bradford group's [Hickson et al, 1986: xii] references to "exhausting days closeted in discussion" and "wet and windy moorland walks searching for inspiration" so colourfully attests. However like most crafts it can be accessible and rewarding at some level to almost everybody, and the means of the most sublime and highest forms of human achievement for those who have the ability and obsession to perfect it. There is no substitute for learning by doing but it is my hope that this learning may be enhanced and accelerated, particularly for those being drawn to the approach for the first time, by the kind of 'working student' reflections on the craft that have been presented in this paper.

REFERENCES

Allison, G.T., Essence of Decision (Little Brown, 1971).

Bower, J.L., Managing the Resource Allocation Process (Irwin, 1970).

Burgleman, R.A. "A process model of internal corporate venturing in the diversified major firm," Administrative Science Quarterly (Volume 28 1983), pp. 223-244.

Burrell,G. & Morgan, G. Sociological Paradigms and Organizational Analysis (Gower, 1979).

Caves, R.E. "Industrial organization, corporate strategy and structure," Journal of Economic Literature (Volume 18 1980), pp. 64-92.

Chisholm, A. The Craft of Writing Poetry (Allison & Busby, 1992).

Dyer, W.G. & Wilkins, A.L., "Better stories, not better constructs, to generate better theory: a rejoinder to Eisenhardt," Academy of Management Review (Volume 16 1991), pp.613-619.

Eisenhardt, K.M. "Building theories from case study research," Academy of Management Review (Volume 14 1989), pp. 532-550.

Eisenhardt, K.M. "Better stories and better constructs: the case for rigor and comparative logic," Academy of Management Review (Volume 16 1991), pp.620-627.

Gay, P. Style in History (Norton, 1988).

Glaser, B.G. & Strauss, A.L. The Discovery of Grounded Theory: Strategies for Qualitative Research (Aline, 1967).

Hamel, G. "Competition for competence and inter-partner learning within international strategic alliances," Strategic Management Journal (Volume 12 1991), pp.83-103.

Hazlett,W. "Whether genius is conscious of its powers," reproduced in Frank Carr (Ed.) Essays of William Hazlett (The Scott Library - undated edition).

Hickson, D.J., Butler, R.J., Cray, D., Mallory, G.R. & Wilson, D.C. Top Decisions (Blackwell, 1986).

Kanter, R.M. The Change Masters (Simon & Schuster, 1983).

Kaplan, R.S. "The role for empirical research in management accounting," Accounting, Organizations and Society (Volume 11 1986), pp429-452.

Leavy, B. "A process study of strategic change and industry evolution: the case of the Irish dairy industry," British Journal of Management (Volume 2 1991), pp187-204.

Leavy, B. "The power and flexibility of case research in the study of strategy," in H.E. Kelin (Ed.) Forging New Partnerships (World Association for Case Research and Application, 1992).

Leavy, B. "Resource allocation and strategy in the IIRS 1960-88," Administration (Volume 41 1993),   pp. 16-39.

Leavy, B. "The craft of case-based qualitative research," Irish Business and Administrative Research (forthcoming 1994).

Leavy, B. and Wilson, D. Strategy and Leadership (Routledge 1994).

Leonard-Barton, D. "Core capabilities and core rigidities: a paradox in managing new product development," Strategic Management Journal (Volume 13 1992), pp.111-125.

Miles, M.B. "Qualitative data as an attractive nuisance: the problem of analysis," Administrative Science Quarterly (Volume 24 1979), pp.590-601.

Miller, D. & Friesen, P.H. "Archetypes of strategy formulation," Management Science (Volume 24 1978), pp921-933.

Miller, D. & Friesen, P.H. "Momentum and revolution in organizational adaptation," Academy of Management Journal (Volume 23 1980), pp.591-614.

Mills, C.W. The Sociological Imagination (Penguin, 1970 - First published by Oxford University Press, 1959).

Mintzberg, H. The Nature of Managerial Work (Harper and Row, 1973)

Mintzberg, H., Raisinghani, D., and Theoret, A. "The structure of 'unstructured' decision processes," Administrative Science Quarterly (Volume 21 1976), pp.246-275.

Mintzberg, H. "Patterns in strategy formation" Management Science (Volume 24 1978), pp.934-948.

Mintzberg, H. "An emerging strategy of 'direct' research," Administrative Science Quarterly (volume 24 1979), pp.582-589.

Mintzberg, H. & Waters, J.A. "Tracking strategy in an entrepreneurial firm," Academy of Management Journal (Volume 25 1982), pp.465-499.

Mohr, L.B. "Causation and the case study," in H.E. Klein (Ed.) Forging New Partnerships (World Association for Case Research and Application, 1992).

Morgan, G. & Smircich, L. "The case for qualitative research," <u>Academy of Management Review</u> (Volume 5 1980), pp. 491-500.

Peters, T. <u>Liberation Management</u> (A.A. Knopf Inc., 1992).

Pettigrew, A.M. "On studying organizational cultures," <u>Administrative Science Quarterly</u> (Volume 24 1979), pp.570-581.

Pettigrew, A.M. <u>The Awakening Giant:Continuity and Change in ICI</u> (Blackwell, 1985a).

Pettigrew, A.M. "Contextualist research and the study of organizational change processes" in E.E. Lawler, A.A. Morhman, S.A. Morhman, G.E. Ledford, T.G. Cumings & Associates, <u>Doing Research that is Useful for Theory and Practice</u> (Jossey-Bass, 1985b)

Pettigrew, A.M. "Longitudinal field research on change: theory and practice," <u>Organizational Science</u> (Volume 1 1990), pp.267-271.

Porter, M.E. <u>Competitive Strategy</u> (Free Press, 1980).

Porter, M.E. "The contribution of industrial organization to strategic management," <u>Academy of Management Review</u> (Volume 6 1981), pp.609-620.

Porter, M.E. <u>Competitive Advantage</u> (Free Press, 1985).

Porter, M.E. <u>The Competitive Advantage of Nations</u> (Free Press, 1990).

Porter, M.E. "Towards a dynamic theory of strategy," <u>Strategic Management Journal</u> (Volume 12 1991), pp.95-117.

Quinn, J.B. "Managing innovation: controlled chaos," <u>Harvard Business Review</u> (May-June 1986), pp.73-84.

Scapens, R.W. "Researching management accounting practice:the role of case study methods," British <u>Accounting Review</u> (Volume 22 1990), pp.259-281.

Strauss, A. <u>Qualitative Analysis for Social Scientists</u> (Cambridge University Press, 1987).

Van Maanen, J. "Reclaiming qualitative methods for organizational research," <u>Administrative Science Quarterly</u> (Volume 24 1979 - Guest editor's introduction to a special issue on qualitative methods), pp.520-526.

Van Maanen, J. "Introduction" in J. Van Maanen, J.M. Dabbs & R.R. Faulkner (Eds.) <u>Varieties in Qualitative Research</u> (Sage, 1982)

Whetten, D.A. "What constitutes a theoretical contribution?," <u>Academy of Management Review</u> (Volume 14 1989), pp.490-495.

Wilson, D.C. "Electricity and resistance: a case study of innovation and politics," <u>Organization Studies</u> (Volume 3 1982), pp.119-140.

Yin, R.K. "The case study crisis: some answers," <u>Administrative Science Quarterly</u> (Volume 26 1981), pp.58-65.

Yin, R.K. <u>Case Study Research:Design and Methods</u> (Sage, 1984).

THE CASE STUDY RESEARCH METHOD:
A MEANS OF UNRAVELLING THE TRANSFORMATION
PROCESS IN THE CZECH REPUBLIC

Anne Mills
Siobhan Bygate
BUCKINGHAMSHIRE COLLEGE BUSINESS SCHOOL,
A COLLEGE OF BRUNEL UNIVERSITY
UNITED KINGDOM

Abstract

The objective of this paper is to provide academic justification for the use of the case study method in the field of qualitative research. It aims to assess the organisational and managerial implications of the economic transformation process in the Czech Republic. The paper will divide into two parts. Part one will deal with the macro environment of privatisation and part two will evaluate the effect of the macro process at a micro level by means of a case study.

RATIONALE FOR CASE STUDY RESEARCH METHODOLOGY

The study of the transition process in the former Eastern Europe presents unprecedented challenges and opportunities for the researcher in the field of organisational behaviour. The events unfolding in the former communist states present unique opportunities to research into a completely new phenomenon in the history of political and organisational change - the transition from a command to a market economy and the transformation of industry from state to private ownership.

A primary challenge for the observer,however, is that accepted methods of developing theory described by Eisenhardt [1989] as:

`...combining observation from previous literature, common sense and experience', cannot be employed fully in relation to the study of the transition process within organisations in the former Eastern Europe. The researcher in the New Europe is faced with documenting and analyzing phenomena for which there is no existing body of theoretical knowledge. There have been no similar events in the past from which a body of literature could have been developed, or from which experience of similar situations could have been assimilated as a basis for future study. Additionally, even though a variety of former East European countries are simultaneously undertaking the transition process, their cultural and political composition and agendas for change are so diverse that they do not lend themselves very well to international comparative study. Concerning the issue of common sense, the gulf in culture and value systems between Eastern and Western Europe is so great that generally accepted assumptions concerning patterns of behaviour and beliefs are not necessarily transferable to this new context. That is not to say, however, that it is not possible to apply the constructs of academic rigour to research activity. It does, however, limit the sources of data and information available for the researcher from which to begin to develop a body of informed knowledge on the subject.

Since the situation is such that implementation of paradigm change is being undertaken simultaneously with its formulation, the study of organisational practice though the medium of case study analysis presents a possible route for the research to follow. The primary aim of the case study is to begin the process of theory generation. [Gersick, 1988]

Eisenhardt [1988] recommends that case study theory should begin with the initial definition of a research question which was in this context:

`To what extent have changing patterns of ownership resulting from the privatisation process influenced management decision-making within organisations?'

The shaping of the research by the use of relevant a priori constructs in relation to the functioning of organisations was also identified i.e. ownership, control and management decision making. This approach proved beneficial in the development of the emerging theory. In relation to the within-case versus cross case study technique, the latter was employed. A single company was selected to demonstrate the trends which were identified in the other companies interviewed.

The primary framework for analysis was through the application of grounded theory. Glaser and Strauss [1967] as summarised by Professor Barry Turner at a Research Seminar held at BCHE [1994].

TRANSITION WITHIN THE MACRO ENVIRONMENT

The transition process within the former Eastern Europe is being undertaken with the objective of meeting a simultaneous set of economic and political goals, which should lead to the emergence of a market type economy.

This study will focus upon the objective of privatisation i.e. the process by which private ownership of property is being re-established. The Czech Republic has been chosen as the country focus for the study. Located in the heart of middle Europe, the Czech Republic has a tradition of democracy and industrial development which predated the Communist takeover of 1949. In terms of its industrial structure, by the velvet revolution of 1989, 95% of all enterprises were state owned [Myant 1988]. Thus successful privatization, which is critical to the achievement of transformation, is a major priority for the Czechs. Additionally, the voucher method chosen by the Czechs and the Slovaks to transfer ownership of state property to private individuals is a unique and untried process which is worthy of analysis also.

Thus, the process of privatisation in the Czech Republic is concerned with both the transformation of organisations from state to private ownership and the process of dissemination of ownership to the population through the voucher privatisation scheme.

The legal framework for the implementation of the privatisation process is now in place. The application of the new laws is still in its early stages. For the Czechs, this presents the dual problem of undertaking a major economic and political change process and adapting to a new set of values and beliefs embodied in the rule of law.

From the organisational perspective, upon which the case study research focused, the issues relate both to the transformation of the organisation and its functioning under the newly developed system of private ownership.

The privatised ownership form addressed by this study is the Joint Stock company (akciová, společnost) defined in the Commercial Code in Trade Links (1992) as:

`a company whose capital stock is divided into a certain number of shares of a certain nominal value....The company is liable to the extent of all its assets if it fails to fulfil its obligations but its shareholders do not bear any such liability'.

This is the legal form which has been or is being adopted by state owned enterprises both in preparation for privatisation, and the accommodation of the diverse pattern of share ownership created by the voucher privatisation scheme. It is a complex legal entity which is suitable for large companies who are likely to trade their shares on the Czech and Slovak stock exchanges.

The legislation requires that joint stock companies must have a supervisory board comprising at least three members. Supervisory boards are elected by the General Meeting but, in organisations with more than 50 employees at least one third but not more than half the Supervisory Board must be elected by company employees. The overall management of the company however is the responsibility of the Board of Directors at least 3 members of which must be elected by the General Meeting of the shareholders or the Supervisory board [Trade Links 1992]

The macro process prescribes both the process and the expected resultant behaviour through the legal framework. It is difficult to evaluate the effectiveness of these processes in practice especially at a behavioral level. The case study method provides unique insights and situational analysis of the operation of the system of privatisation in an organisation.

Additionally, it is not possible to make generalised assumptions about behaviour change in this situation, from the study of the macro process alone. The case study method lends itself well to examining actual situations and emerging themes.

THE PRIVATISATION EXPERIENCE AT CASE STUDY LEVEL

This case study was chosen out of a total of three (diverse industries) in the Czech Republic, four similar interviews having been conducted in Slovakia in the same industry (i.e. furniture-making). It was felt that this company was a prime example of a joint stock company moving toward privatisation. Additionally, the case study interview displayed the themes recurring in most of the interviews with state enterprises undergoing transition, as well as some of the themes thrown up by interviews with newly established private enterprises in the Czech and Slovak Republics.

The interview was held in the managing director's office with both the managing director, finance department manager present as well as the external advisor. The interview lasted over three hours and consisted of an initial phase of unstructured questions allowing the managers to identify their own areas of importance and priorities in the transition process. Further questions were then asked in order to elicit deeper information on the central themes as identified by the interviewer. The interview was conducted in Czech with the external advisor translating. This member of the management team had had working experience abroad and possessed a high skill in English. Communication was therefore not impeded. The final results were analyzed by means of codifying contributions and identifying recurrent themes. Finally, the links between these recurring themes were extracted. The main examples illustrating the impact of ownership on management decision-making are discussed below.

The Company

Company F is a typical example of a medium-sized joint-stock company in the Czech Republic formed out of the remnents of the old regional Kombinat and employing 156 people. It is located in a small village in a rural, wooded area in northern Bohemia near to both the German and Polish borders, about 3 hours from Prague. This area has a long tradition of furniture-making and has old contacts with Germany, being part of the former Sudetenland. The other ex-branches and units of the regional furniture-making Kombinat had either stopped production due to unpaid debt or were very small and fragmented. Company F had continued to exist as a state enterprise, after separation from the Kombinat until the 1st of May 1992 when it became a joint stock enterprise prior to the first privatisation wave. The buying of shares began in January 1993 and the last shares in the company were bought by June of that year. The first general meeting with the new shareholders was held on the 30th of June 1993.

Privatisation and Ownership in Company F

The wide dissemination of actual share ownership and the limited knowledge and experience of shareholders lead to over concentration of power and influence amongst shareholders in the hands of the privatisation funds. The total 1500 shareholders in this company are represented by 36 people. These 36 investors represent 52% of all shares and therefore form the basic invested capital. The break-down of investors can be seen in Appendix 1. Managers reported that the individual shareholder had little influence and in fact the regional privatisation fund, which was also the regional bank was the single biggest shareholder.

In this company the shareholders and elected board of directors appeared to be acting according to a very different behaviourial pattern than managers. The managing director and finance department manager continually highlighted the lack of knowledge and the old style thinking of the shareholders. The external advisor experienced the dealings with the shareholders with great disillusionment and believed that they had lost interest after the initial euphoria of belonging to a propertied class. As an example of this he cited the first joint stock company meeting with the new shareholders when two halls had to be prepared. For the second meeting room for 500 shareholders was prepared but few turned up.

The three interviewees cited similar more widely known examples of this in bigger companies such as Škoda Plzeň and Česka Spožitelna savings bank as evidence of a general lack of interest amongst shareholders. It also appeared that the board of directors were blocking many decisions proposed by the management which were considered necessary to ensure the survival of the firm.

Sale of Basic Capital and Investment

Management had made a Spring proposal to sell off part of the basic capital of the company in form of number of buildings in a local village. This was also seen as a means of rationalising operations and generating desperately needed cash for reinvestment. Management had also located a potential buyer. Since the Commercial code states that any increase or reduction of capital stock has to be authorised by the general meeting of shareholders this proposal was made part of the Business Plan.[1] It was prepared by the Managing Director, the Finance Department Manager and the external Advisor, for the constituent meeting in June. The Business Plan was submitted in March 1993 and opinions of shareholders solicited. However, no reply was received until the June meeting when it was subsequently rejected outright with no substantiation of that decision. This illustrates the differing concept of ownership between the shareholders and elected board of directors on the one hand and the managers on the other. In this example the decision against the sale of property meant that the potential buyer was lost as well as the opportunity to raise essential revenue.

Conflict of Ownership and Control

The Managing Director felt that owners, as opposed to managers were only just beginning to realise what they had bought. The next stage was for the owners to realise the need to consider proposals put forward by management or suggest their own.

There appears to be an awareness on part of management of the required changes in company strategy. These changes are needed to accommodate new production requirements and new organisational arrangements, as a result of and appropriate to the emerging market relations. This awareness has been built up within and in relation to the company since the 1989 transformation.

The shareholders and board of directors, however, had only recently adopted the ownership role in relation to this company. Unlike management it had not experienced at first hand the changing market demand and demand structure. However the privatisation process envisages the right of the shareholders through their shares to "participate in the company's management, profits and liquidation balance, should the company be wound up".[2]. The scope of this participation in management is limited to the business of the general meeting convened annually.[3]

Concerning the role of the Board of Directors the Commercial Code does not contain any definition or limitation to the powers belonging to this body. According to the senior management in this company, i.e. the general manager, the finance department manager and the external advisor, the Board of Directors has the legal right to accept or reject sale of basic capital. It must also be involved in decisions on capital shares, investment and the commitment to contribute to the management of the firm. They also stressed that the Board of Directors were only interested in profit and could play no role concerning the production process.

When asked if the degree of involvement of the Board of Director affected the day to day running of the firm, management insisted that this was not the case. However, from the description of the issues where management decision-making was affected by the Board of Directors it would appear that there was a direct effect on the long term strategic planning. This inevitably influences the effective day to day running of the firm.

In practice the Board of Directors had been involved only negatively in strategic decision-making, e.g. their rejection of the Business Plan. Their only positive contribution was limited to a few individual operational issues, e.g. possible labour force reductions and regular monthly trips to the firm. No recommendations were made on these visits, much to the disappointment of the senior on-site management.

The limited knowledge and experience of owners in general is due to the nature of the former command economy. This has meant that the Board of Directors have been less than active in their role. On site mangers explained this in terms of the owners' outdated 19th Century attitude to property. The ideological interpretations of the capitalist system fostered by the old regimes had produced a peculiar attitude to property; a 19th century concept of laissez-faire capitalism with highly authoritarian ownership.

RESTRUCTURING ISSUES

Management decided to informally implement key changes in the organisation structure despite the fact that certain restructuring proposals contained in the Business Plan had been rejected by the Board. Some changes had already taken place and management were continuing to press ahead with other changes. They achieved this by circumventing the Board of Directors and taking on more responsibility.

Changes in production and managerial activity were felt to be necessary in order to survive in a transitional and market-type economy. The managing director pointed out that now no official reorganisation could occur due to Board opposition. However after closer questioning it transpired that the managing director and finance department manager had already made some significant changes before full privatisation had occurred. In 1992 they had created a commercial department and had since been trying to acquire the requisite skills themselves due to the shortage of skills in this area. While expressing frustration at the impediment caused by the Board of Directors' imperviousness to the proposed restructuring ideas, all the managers were confident that a reduction in the number of managers at head quarters from 23 to 15 could be achieved by June 1994. The board of directors had in fact nominally agreed that only 10% of the original work force could eventually be retained. When Company F separated off from the Liberec regional Kombinat it took with it 4 workshops plus 4 additional small workshops. The work force at this time had stood at over 360, and had now been reduced to 156. Managers expressed regret at the decision to reduce the work force, especially as they felt there were few alternative employment opportunities in the immediate locality.

They also expressed concern over how this reduction was to be achieved and were proposing two methods at the time of the interview. The first method relied on natural wastage primarily through retirement. For the remaining employees they accepted that an increased workload and greater flexibility were inevitable. They were uncertain as to the employee response to the change in job roles. The second method therefore cited increased use of technology, in particular computers.

RENUMERATION AND MOTIVATION

RENUMERATION

In the interviews the issue of low renumeration in newly privatised state-owned companies versus high renumeration in newly established private companies was commonly quoted as a major problem. Management in this company cited 1990/91 as a particularly difficult year because they were unable to increase wages due to the government policy of wage capping. Consequently, many well-qualified people left to join the newly established private sector. The top wage in a state-owned enterprise was 5000-6000 Czech crowns, that is wage band 8, applicable to managers of workshops of employing 50 staff. Meanwhile in newly established enterprises this restriction did not exist. The managing director claimed that this imbalance in renumeration arrangements was an on-going phenomenon and that Company F were now having to consider "over-payment" in order to attract high calibre employees.

The wage capping policy of the Czech republic was an attempt to control inflation, necessary for the arranged IMF loan. Wage capping restrictions in 1992 did not apply to enterprises with more than 30% foreign ownership, enterprises with less than 50% state ownership and any enterprise established since January the 1st, 1992. Since January the 1st, 1993 wage capping restrictions have been abolished but an amendment to the social and employment insurance legislation effectively continues to limit increases, in this case, to below 5%. Companies who fail to comply will be required to pay substantially increased social insurance contributions.[4]

"Street-wise" comments of a secretary in a foreign company earning more than a surgeon appeared to be founded in fact.

MOTIVATION

Despite the limitations of wage constraints there was still an awareness of the need for better quality of employees which, in spite of the very large labour pool available to the company, were in short supply. Management had identified the profile of a higher quality work force as being one which could work with less supervision than currently necessary. They cited lack of motivation as the major inheritance from the past which was braking present progress. They knew that employee behaviour in this respect had to be changed. The reference to "overpaying" any new appointees perhaps reflects traditional management values which are now being challenged.

There also appeared to be a growing awareness of the changing nature of management practice in terms of a move away from a bureaucratic and closely supervisory role to one of creative and independent thinking; decision-making unencumbered by inefficient levels of supervision. An example of the increasing commitment to the new rationale was the search for a new Deputy Director of technology and production. Jan, the managing director had assumed responsibility for both posts 3 months ago, despite the extra workload, because no appropriate person could be found. He was committed to employing only a person with the best skills and was thus prepared to wait. The same situation had occurred in the Commercial Department. The managing director was aware of the primary importance of this function and its central role in the future development of Company F. There were plans to extend this department by two more people bringing the total number employed in this area to four.

All managers reported increased overlapping of departmental activities which previously did not occur due to central control. In the past commands were passed down to companies and carried out by departments rather than developed in departments according to priorities identified by the companies.

MANAGEMENT LEARNING CURVE

Using the case study method to analyze the ownership issue allowed automatic progression to the study of the management decision-making process, as they responded to the privatisation scenario.

Management understanding of the interface between the policy of privatisation at a macro level and its operation in a fledgling market economy at micro-level had been developing since 1989. Through this experience management became aware for the first time both of the scope for management's own activities and of the power of their day to day knowledge. Consequently traditional assumptions about motivation and equitable renumeration levels were being challenged by real situations.

Regarding the relationship between ownership and management, the latter realised that a prerequisite for acceptance of the Business Plan by the Board of Directors was a greater awareness of the issues involved in the running of the company. The possibility of re-educating the Board of Directors was discussed, but strategies for this were not developed. However they believed that it was necessary to foster a cooperative spirit rather than allowing the situation to grow into an "us against them" scenario thereby achieving a change in attitude.

They were aware that the Board of Directors and the General Meeting would eventually have to accept the Business Plan as no other workable alternative had been proposed. Meanwhile management recognized the value of implementing aspects of the Business Plan piecemeal with or without seeking Board approval.

SUMMARY OF PRIVATISATION AND THE CONTROL/OWNERSHIP ISSUE

The issue of ownership, as might be expected, greatly influences management behaviour, although not always in the form expected, i.e. contributing to greater managerial effectiveness. It appears that the new market and customer demands have influenced operational activities and management practice to a greater extent than ownership. Markets and customers were and are the driving force to restructuring. Nevertheless the issue of ownership is an integral part of the macro transition to a market economy, although it has not as yet affected management practice directly in a positive form in this company. The effect of the owners, or shareholders, on management activity was felt by the three interviewees in September 1993 to be a negative one. They felt that both the shareholders at the first constituent general meeting and the chosen board of directors were unsympathetic. They lacked practical knowledge of the company and a market economy and were attached to old ideas. Consequently they refused to endorse management's proposals. The legal constraints to management decision-making vis-a-vis the Board of Directors and the annual shareholders meeting as laid down in the Commercial Code[5] ensured legal private ownership control but did little to effect a behaviourial change in the ownership-management relationship.

There was a growing belief amongst the managers interviewed, that as a company, they had progressed further along the learning curve than those to whom they were legally responsible. They identified the initial relationship of shareholders to their newly acquired property as one of "wild west capitalism," but acknowledged the slowly growing awareness on the part of the shareholders of the implications of owning property. Ultimately management had perhaps expected too much from the owners and the experience, which had initially made them feel isolated, had subsequently encouraged them to become increasingly self-sufficient. As a result of relying to a greater extent on their own knowledge and decision-making powers, they had also developed a higher estimation of their own managerial know-how.

The case study illustrates the fact that a change in the legal framework does not automatically elicit the intended behaviourial responses at management and ownership level. It is a learning process for all concerned. The case study in question provides a snap shot of this process, otherwise unattainable, by concentrating on the influence of new ownership patterns on management decision-making.

CONCLUSION

THE CASE STUDY METHOD IN RESEARCH AND TEACHING

Research

The application of the case study method to the organisational implications of privatisation reveals recurrent themes and allows their identification by the researcher. These findings provide the beginnings of a tentative theoretical model of organisational paradigm change in the Czech republic which could now subsequently be developed by future researchers.[6]

This issue is already being addressed by one of the authors who has constructed a questionnaire around the central themes identified in the course of[7]. This will be circulated to all the firms interviewed in all countries in order to attempt a longitudinal study with some quantitative back-up.

Teaching

At the time of writing it is planned to use this case study model in a seminar week in Osnabrück Fachhochschule, Germany in May 1994. The case study will be used to highlight the issues raised in lectures on East/Central Europe and as a format for students to develop their own case studies from the bare bones of other interviews given to them. It is planned that formal feedback will be solicited from students in written form.

ENDNOTES

1. p. 26 of the translation of the Commercial Code by Trade Links, 1992, "Czech Republic, Slovak Republic. A Businessman's guide to Czech and Slovak Legislation".

2. bid.

3. ibid.

4. Price Waterhouse, "Information Guide. Doing Business in the Czech and Slovak Republics." 1991, 1993, p72, "Working Conditions."

5. See Endnote 1.

6. Gersick 1988

7. The questionnaire was constructed upon the results of 15 various interviews with companies and agencies throughout Slovakia, the Czech Republic and Eastern Germany.

REFERENCES

Eisenhardt K.M. (1989), "Building Theories from Case Study Research," Academy of Management Review, Vol. 14, No. 4.

Gersick, C. (1988), "Time and Transition in Work Teams: Toward A New Model of Group Development," Academy of Management Journal, 31.

Myant, M. (1989), The Czechoslovak Economy 1948-1988.The Battle for Economic Reform, Cambridge University Press, London.

Hefortva, A (1992), Starting A Business in Czechoslovakia., Trade Links, Prague.

On small-scale privatisation: the "Act on the Transfer of Certain State-owned Property to Other Legal and Natural Persons," (No. 427/1990 Coll.), passed October 1990 and in effect since the 1st of December 1990.

32

On large-scale privatisation: the "Act on the Conditions for Transfer of State-owned Property to Other Persons" (No.92/1991 Coll. as subsequently amended), enacted in 1992 in the "first wave," the "second wave" starting in Autumn 1993.

On legal arrangements and delineations of responsibilities for the differing commercial entities, i.e. joint stock company, (akciová společnost) or limited liability company (společnost s ručením omezeným), etc., see "The Commercial Code," late 1991, which came into force in both the Czech and Slovak republic in 1992.

APPENDIX 1
OWNERSHIP IN COMPANY F

Shareholders	Shares
Regional Privatisation Fund	20%
2 Groups of Shareholders -informal groupings -individuals' investment money	20%
Various Newspapers	45%
National Property Fund (Shares awaiting sale)	7%
Small Privatisation Funds	5%
Restitution Fund	3%

The largest number of shares held by any one investor are those controlled by the regional privatization fund in this area. The shares held by newspapers do not represent a single cohesive grouping.

PASSIONATE PRACTICE MEETS COLD THEORY: ARE SCIENTIFIC RESEARCH RESULTS USEFUL IN THE ARTFUL DEVELOPMENT AND USE OF LARGE SCALE BEHAVIORAL SIMULATIONS?

Maureen Harris[1]
National-Louis University
McLEAN, VIRGINIA, U.S.A.
Joan Sander
The Bureau of Labor Statistics of the U.S. Department of Labor
WASHINGTON, D.C., U.S.A.
Wayne Sander
National-Louis University
WASHINGTON, D.C., U.S.A.

Abstract

Although the use of large-scale behavioral simulations continues to grow, there is inconclusive evidence that participants actually learn during or after simulations. An overview of literature reviews indicates that social science researchers investigated primarily simulation input and output factors, with several attempting to link output factors (performance not learning), with later managerial success [Keys & Wolfe, 1990]. Yet educators and trainers of adults do not seem to be influenced by the limited research results. On the contrary, they offer passionate and glowing anecdotes about conducting simulations and many point to adult education theory as all the evidence they need that simulations "work." With these disparate perspectives in mind, questions are offered to direct future inquiry.

INTRODUCTION

Thornton and Cleveland [1990] indicate that management simulations were an outgrowth of several major fields: military war games, operations research, role play and performance testing. Keys and wolfe [1988] noted that 95.1% of aascb schools use simulations in their coursework and in corporate training 29.5% of training time is devoted to simulation exercises. These statistics inform us that simulations are being widely used as a teaching methodology. Can educators then assume that a learning methodology that is widely used has a research base to support its effectiveness?

In this article the authors will explore three questions about simulations. The first question asks what has research provided in the way of understanding the effectiveness of simulations on learning and more specifically the question focuses on large scale behavioral simulations. The second question asks what are the practical problems which exists when evaluating the learning which occurs from simulations. The third question asks do the large number of learning variables within large scale behavioral simulations make generalizing the results too difficult.

A REVIEW OF THE REVIEWS

Since the purpose of this paper is to frame issues for discussion, we review five recent major literature reviews by Wolfe [1985], Hsu [1989], Thornton and Cleveland [1990], Keys and Wolfe [1990], and Tannenbaum and Yukle [1992]. We take the studies cited in them and their descriptions of the literature at face value. Any citations of individual studies are based on their initial review and analysis of those studies.

The literature can be broken down into three broad categories of studies. Firstly, there are studies that look at the learning output effects of simulations. Secondly, there are studies that examine the effect of input factors on either learning or group performance. Finally, there are studies that look at process factors that might affect performance or learning.

DO SIMULATIONS FOSTER LEARNING?

Large scale games or simulations are used often by educational institutions, especially business schools [Thorton & Cleveland, 1990; Tannenbaum & Yukl, 1992]. One might assume that the learning fostered by the simulations would be well documented by scientific studies. Yet, there is surprisingly little scientific research linking learning to these simulations, especially the behavioral and affective learning touted by many champions of simulations. Two types of studies have explored the relationship between simulations and learning.

The first type of studies sought to compare the learning from simulations with the learning from more traditional methods of instruction such as lectures and case studies. Hsu [1989] reported that the results of these studies were inconclusive, finding that 15 studies showed a positive effect as compared with other instructional methods or in promoting the learning objectives of college courses, 12 were inconclusive and 7 showed negative effects. At best, Hsu found simulations to be inefficient methods of learning theoretical abstractions and principles.

Beyond the ambiguous results of these studies, Hsu correctly points out that traditional measures of cognitive classroom performance may be inappropriate in judging the effectiveness of simulations on learning. By their very experiential nature, large scale behavioral simulations allow students to experience an abstraction of complex reality and learn how to work with the pressure, ambiguity, conflict, interpersonal relations, communication breakdowns and other messy but realistic aspects of organizational life.

Are cognitive learning goals, as expressed through course objectives, relevant to the real problems faced by people in real organizations? Firstly, it should not be surprising that few course designers have scientific studies on hand to test each of their learning objectives for utility in the real world. Even if they did, the temporal nature of courses means that these objectives must be based on an imperfect prediction of what problems students will later face in real life. Students take a course, complete it, and generally have limited long term contact with their professors. Further, many courses seem to be based on the implicit assumption that cognitive knowledge is either sufficient for success or that the other types of skills can be picked up elsewhere.

The second type of studies actually try to measure the effect of simulation learning on success in later life. A few studies actually tried to measure success five years after the simulation. Keys and Wolfe [1990] report on three interesting, but somewhat inconclusive studies. The first, by Wolfe, found that students with previous career success performed better in simulations. The second, by Wolfe and Roberts, in a 5 year follow up study, found that game performance was related to career mobility and career satisfaction. Yet, another five year follow up study by Norris and Snyder reported no clear associations between game performance and proximity to chief executive officers of companies.

While these studies appear to be a promising beginning for longitudinal research, two factors affect their utility for assessing student learning. Firstly, the use of game performance is not necessarily a good measure of the learning from simulations. High scores in a game or simulation do not necessary mean that students learned more than students in failing simulated companies. Learning might come from failure as well as success. In fact, the study by Wolfe that reports students with prior career success performed better in games than other students attests more to the skills and knowledge brought into the simulation than the learning during the simulation.

The second factor affecting the usefulness of these studies is the use of measures such as career mobility or proximity to the chief executive officer position. If real world organizations were all meritocracies, basing promotions on pure managerial skill, such a measure might be accurate. Yet we know that they are not.

In a study on the nature of managerial work, Luthans, Hodgetts, and Rosenkrantz [1988] found that there were differences between the way that successful and effective managers used their time. They defined successful managers as those managers who move up the organizational hierarchy quickly, while effective managers are those with subordinate satisfaction and commitment. They found that successful managers spent far greater time networking and less time on routine communication and managing human resources than did effective managers. If hierarchial positioning is the measure of learning from simulations and games, the studies might not be measuring managerial skills but rather posturing skills.

The other problem with career mobility measures is the possible effects of gender, race, national origin or religion on job level. In the United States, as well as other countries, there have been considerable problems with discrimination, especially at higher organizational levels. In light of legal experience, we should be at lease skeptical that upper level positions are filled exclusively, or even primarily, on the basis of managerial competence.

DO INPUT FACTORS AFFECT LEARNING FROM SIMULATIONS?

A second large group of studies attempted to measure the effects of a variety of input factors on the performance or learning that occurs in the simulation. These factors are perhaps, the most easily changed by the average facilitator of large scale simulations.

Keys and Wolfe [1990] reviewed a number of studies on these factors. They first found that the complexity level of the simulation affected the learning of cognitive knowledge. Simulations with medium to high complexity tended to create more learning than low complexity simulations. Although some of the effect might depend on student readiness for complex simulations [Thorton & Cleveland, 1990]. Secondly, they found that larger groups tended to have better performance and cognitive learning than smaller groups, although these effects changed over time. Thirdly, they found that factors such as being an "NT" on the Myers Briggs Type Indicator or having a higher grade point average correlated with simulation performance. Finally, they found that factors such as prior management success and prior group training correlated with simulation performance.

While these studies provide some help to the practitioner in selecting simulations and determining student readiness, their value is limited. In determining what effect these factors have on learning, the two problems discussed in the last section apply here. First, cognitive learning may not be the best measure of the effectiveness of simulations. Behavioral and affective learning may be as, if not more, important. Secondly, game performance is not necessarily a good measure of learning. Students may learn as much from failures as they learn from successes.

DO PROCESS FACTORS AFFECT PERFORMANCE OR LEARNING?

A third group of studies attempted to measure process factors which may affect performance or learning in simulations. The process factors identified were instructor reinforcement, feedback, and the use of supplemental materials.

Four studies reviewed by Keys and Wolfe [1990] investigated how instructors
influence players learning and performance. One study by Wolfe indicated that instructors guidance must be applied during critical stages in the development of the teams and at the debriefing stage of the simulation to ensure closure and summary insights are obtained from the experience. A second study by Dill, Hoffman, Leavitt, & O'Mara, also found that players could be influenced by the instructor. A third study by Starbuck and Kobrow found that an instructor influenced a team when suggestions reinforced the team's economic self-interest. A fourth study by DeBattista found that learning was greatest when weekly structured feedback was employed over the course of a simulation.

Wolfe's [1985] review of studies about the effects of debriefing on participants learning found that no research had been done on whether knowledge gains accompany debriefing or the type of debriefing exercises instructors can use for effective learning to take place. There is a recognition that feedback is important but there are no intervention models which explain the kind and type of feedback which is most appropriate to use in simulations.

Educators recognize the important role an instructor plays in the learning process and educational studies have been conducted to understand instructors influences. From the few simulation studies reviewed the applicability of the results was limiting. It is helpful for instructors to know there are critical stages during simulations when their guidance is important, yet the research begs the question what type of guidance is appropriate during simulations, especially during large scale behavioral simulations. Some studies support the importance of feedback but for large scale behavioral simulations, in which numerous learning activities take place, there is no information about the form the instructor's feedback should take in order to make an effective contribution to the experiential learning process. Supplemental materials, in the form of player's manuals or decision support systems [DSSs], provide feedback and guidance during simulations. From the studies reviewed by Keys and Wolfe [1990] noted that, even though many writers have recommended the use of decision support devices with simulations, research has provided mixed results, which is similar to the real world results. In one study by Affisco and Chanin no significant difference was found between the economic performances of teams using the DSS versus those that did not use it. Both groups did consider the same number of decision alternatives and the same amount of data during their decision making process which disagrees with Keys, Burns, Case, & Wells behavioral study which found significant attitudinal differences between a group that used computer-based work sheets versus those who used hand-scored work sheets.

The reliability research problem arises when investigating the effectiveness of supplemental materials in simulations. When one research investigation compares the use of DSS versus no DSS in one particular simulation it is difficult to use the results to determine the use of DSS in a different simulation. In studies which looked at attitudinal differences related to the use of supplemental materials the question can be asked, was the supplemental material the cause of the attitude differences. During a simulation, which is an experiential learning process, numerous interactive learning variables take place. Is it even possible to begin to control for all the different variables which take place during a simulation?

CAN ADULT EDUCATION THEORY INFORM SIMULATION RESEARCH AND PRACTICE?

Paradoxically, while empirical social science research has not validated that adult learning occurs during or after simulations, there has been a significant increase in the use of simulations in a variety of organizations in the last decade [Tannenbaum & Yukl, 1992; Thornton & Cleveland, 1990]. Keys and Wolfe [1990] suggest that this "gaming" movement is due in large part to the general acceptance among practitioners of a critical learning theory based in the adult education literature: the experiential learning cycle. The theory is based on the premise that adult learners with a developed mental model of management practice (or any discipline) learn optimally when allowed to practice and reflect upon behaviors that spring from those mental models. Learning is evident in this continuous cycle when adult learners change their behavior based on insights gained from experience [Kolb, 1971].

The experiential learning theory is clearly rooted in adult education research. Malcolm Knowles [1964] was among the first of adult education scholars to affirm that adults bring a wealth of information with them to a learning event, and it is often detrimental to their learning to offer them repetitive and thus meaningless declarative knowledge through lecturing. Other scholars concluded that adult learning was enhanced through active rather than passive participation in the learning activity [Kidd, 1973], that "meaningful" material was longer remembered and more apt to be put to use than principles that were not somehow related to the adult's personal experience [Darkenwald & Merriam, 1982], that a simulated practice of behavior provided a safer environment for the learner to test out actions and therefore learn from the consequences of the actions [Cross, 1981], that adults' learning events should be tailored to their needs rather than delivered in a standardized fashion [Knox, 1977], and that adults should be involved actively in the contracting and assessment of their learning experiences [Tough, 1971].

Given this core list of adult education theory, many adult educators and trainers have understandably deduced that simulations are a likely vehicle to enhance adult learning. However, to the authors' knowledge, there have been no adult education studies, qualitative or quantitative in nature, that have investigated whether simulations enhance adult learning. Additionally, the authors have not found adult education studies that attempt to measure the transfer of learning from simulations to the workplace. Perhaps no one has chosen this avenue of investigation in adult education because of a strong argument that has surfaced from the related disciplines of psychology and management: given that learning in simulations is individually tailored and so entangled with other variables, it is impossible to measure their unique contribution to adult learning [Thornton & Cleveland, 1990]. However, it may also be worth examining why researchers have generally attempted to measure the factors that facilitate learning and the external effects of learning from simulations, without having a conceptual understanding of the learning that they are trying to facilitate and transfer.

This examination is at the heart of how adult education theory and research methodologies can inform simulation research and practice. To conduct an inquiry into the very nature of learning in simulations, the researcher could conduct an inductive, exploratory study--the type of qualitative study that would not be found in *The Psychological Bulletin*, but would certainly be included in any adult education journal. For example, a grounded research method might involve a combination of observation and in-depth interviews with simulation participants using open-ended, think-aloud techniques. Studies of this nature would help to resolve the debate that continues among practitioners regarding the analysis of learning in simulations.

DOES SCIENTIFIC RESEARCH HELP EDUCATORS FOSTER LEARNING WITH SIMULATIONS?

The authors offer the following questions to help direct future inquiry: 1) How have scientific studies contributed to educators use and understanding of simulations? 2) Is it possible to define, measure, and evaluate learning and its benefits during or after simulations? If so, how? 3) What type of learning do simulations foster? 4)Does learning from simulations transfer to the workplace? Butler, Markulus, and Strang [1988] used Bloom's taxonomy of educational objectives as a guiding framework from which to view work undertaken by simulation researchers and to begin to answer the above questions. Bloom's Taxonomy classifies learning outcomes into three domains: (1) cognitive, (2) affective, and (3) psychomotor. The analysis of simulation research studies and articles found that most efforts have been focused on cognitive learning with little examination of the affective and psychomotor areas of learning. Even within the cognitive learning outcomes, researchers tended to focus on only two of the six cognitive levels, application and analysis. The other four levels; knowledge, intellectual ability/skill, synthesis, and evaluation were not investigated. Butler, Markulus, and Strang implored the simulation research community to move toward more rigorous research designs and to increase attention to learning outcomes. Many practical suggestions were presented about ways to develop stronger research designs. In the area of learning outcomes the suggestion was for researchers interested in experiential learning to examine affective and psychomotor learning as well as cognitive learning outcomes. Suggestions were not presented about how to examine learning. Finally, the authors would like to add a fundamental question to the ones stated above concerning learning with simulations: *Is simulation practice an art or science? or a combination of both?*

CONCLUSIONS

Many questions remain unanswered about the capability of simulations to foster learning. Different research studies focused on the pragmatic tests of the efficacy of simulation gaming vis-a-vis other teaching methods [Hsu, 1989]. A few studies did incorporate cognitive learning as a paradigm that could be used to guide research on learning outcomes. Wolfe [1985] stated that simulation success criteria have ranged from hard quantitative economic results to subjective written reports. Researchers have found that instructors have more or less counseled participants, team sizes have varied, and game complexity can span from four to fifty decisions per round. Many factors influence the effectiveness of a simulation. Is it even feasible to alter them one at a time to determine their individual impact on learning results?

The challenge facing the simulation research community is to debate the above question in order to focus more clearly on what researchers should be investigating. There exists a need to explore what type of learning outcomes occur with simulations since presently no answers exist. More studies need to be designed to investigate the experiential belief that effective learning is an active experience that challenges the skills, knowledge, and beliefs of participants. What effect does a large scale behavioral simulation have on participants as they experience a contrived, yet realistically challenging and psychologically safe learning environment in which they can investigate and employ new concepts, skills and behaviors?

Another question can be raised which asks if scientific research methods are appropriate for understanding the learning which occurs during a simulation. Educators who use simulations do not challenge the idea that learning occurs for participants, but participants each have their own learning brush and paints which they use as they experience their own learning outcomes. Should or can each painting be replicated? What is the purpose of studying how the different paintings emerge? Perhaps each painting should be accepted and valued for its unique contribution.

ENDNOTES

1. The authors Names appear in alphabetical order.

REFERENCES

Butler, R., Markulis, P. and Strang, D., "Where Are We? An Analysis of the Methods and Focus of the Research on Simulation Gaming," Simulation & Games (19, 1988), pp. 3-26.

Cross, P., Adults As Learners (Jossey-Bass, 1981).

Darkenwald, G. and S. Merriam, Adult Education: Foundations of Practice (Harper & Row, 1982).

Hsu, E., "Role-Event Gaming and Simulation in Management Education: A Conceptual Framework," Simulations & Games (20, 1989), pp. 409-438.

Keys, B., "Total Enterprise Business Games," Simulation & Games (18, 1987), pp. 225-241.

Keys, B. and J. Wolfe, "Management Education and Development: Current Issues and Emerging Trends," Journal of Management (14, 1988), pp. 205-229.

Keys, B. and J. Wolfe, "The Role of Management Games and Simulations in Education and Research," Journal of Management (16, 1990), pp. 307-336.

Kidd, R., How Adults Learn (Follett, 1973).

Knowles, M., "What We Know About the Field of Adult Ed," Adult Education (October 1964), pp. 67-73.

Knox, A., Adult Development and Learning (Jossey-Bass, 1977).

Kolb, D., "Individual Learning Styles and the Learning Process," working paper, Massachusetts Institute of Technology, Sloan School, 1971, pp. 535-571.

Luthans, F., R.M. Hodgetts and S.A. Rosenkrantz, Real Managers (Ballinger, 1988).

Tannenbaum, S. and G. Yukl, "Training and Development in Work Organizations," Annual Review of Psychology (43, 1992), pp. 399-441.

Thornton, G.C. and J.N. Cleveland, "Developing Managerial Talent Through Simulation," American Psychologist (45, 1990), pp. 190-199.

Tough, A., The Adult's Learning Projects (Ontario Institute for Studies in Education, 1971).

Wolfe, J., "The Teaching Effectiveness of Games in Collegiate Business Courses," Simulations and Games (16, 1985), pp. 251-288.

USE OF INTERVIEW RECORDINGS
TO TEACH/LEARN/DO SINGLE-CASE EVALUATION
RESEARCH ON PRACTICE INTERVENTIONS

Faye Y. Abram
Saint Louis University
ST. LOUIS, MISSOURI, U.S.A.

Abstract

The case method approach is used to evaluate practice interventions, specifically interviewing efforts, skills and competence. Students in social work practice and research courses viewed, rated, and compared two interview recordings. This learning exercise demonstrated not only a way to measure the quality of an interviewer's communications but also how to assess inter-rater reliability, as well as differences, changes or improvements in interviewing competence. The teaching of research and practice methods are experientially linked. Alternative ways to do this exercise, using audio or written process recordings and making comparisons across time and cultural groups, are discussed.

INTRODUCTION

Over the past decade, the use of the case study method as a tool for doing evaluation research has grown within such fields as education, business/organizational management, and social work [Merriam, 1988; Yin 1984/1989/1993; Feagin, et al., 1991]. Workshops, colloquiums, conferences, and several publications have appeared that are devoted to proselytizing and demonstrating the usefulness and applicability of the case method and related instructional approaches in a variety of settings. Moreover, advocates of the case study method have explored its application across international and cultural boundaries [Klein, 1993; Sue & Sue, 1990].

Within the social work profession, interest in the case study method is perhaps greatest when the case being studied is an individual, group or family that has engaged the services of a social worker. It is important to remember, however, that many different types of units of analysis can comprise the "case" in case study research. The case might be an individual, a program, a decision, an organization, a neighborhood, a single contact, an interview, or a critical incident to name some examples.

While much of the social work profession's "practice wisdom" was generated by the clinical case studies of clients, Rubin and Babbie [1993:392] have noted that the case study method "fell out of favor in the 1960s and 1970s, as skepticism grew about the objectivity and validity of qualitative case studies...[This was] accompanied by a demand for evidence generated from studies with experimental controls for internal validity. Today, however, a new wave of enthusiasm has emerged among social work researchers, educators, and practitioners for qualitative methods in general..." Becoming especially popular is the case study approach that combines qualitative and quantitative methods while using single-subject designs to evaluate the quality and/or effectiveness of one's own practice.

Several textbooks that are now commonly used in social work research courses include content on the case study method and/or a whole chapter on single-subject designs or qualitative research methods [e.g., Grinnell, 1993; Marlow, 1993; Rubin & Babbie, 1993; Royse, 1991]. Such books as Evaluating Your Practice: A Guide to Self-Assessment [Alter & Evens, 1990] and Evaluating Practice: Guidelines for the Accountable Professional [Bloom & Fischer, 1982] are devoted entirely to these modes of inquiry. Similarly, a number of social work practice texts include descriptions of the case study method, single-case evaluation, case studies, and self-assessment tools for evaluating practice competence [e.g., Compton & Galaway, 1989; Sheafor, et al., 1991; LeCroy, 1992; McClam & Woodside, 1994]. Meanwhile, the attraction of social workers to the case study method has been strengthened by the Curriculum Policy Statements of the profession's educational accrediting body [CSWE, 1988; 1992], which prescribe that the research content in programs of social work education must include qualitative and quantitative research methodologies for the systematic evaluation of practice.

Social work researchers using the case study method commonly analyze qualitative and quantitative data from recorded interviews, client logs, and time-series records. Somewhat less often, they have also used process recordings, narrative reports, audiotape transcripts, ethnographic interviews, and computerized records.

For instance, William R. Nugent [1992] studied the immediate affective impact that a clinical social worker's interviewing style (verbal behavior only) has on observers and clients, by examining a combination of qualitative and quantitative data from four simulated interviews and three "single-case experimental interviews." Not at all unexpectedly, Nugent reported that the results of his research illustrate that obstructive interviewing styles tend to elicit negative feelings and thoughts, while facilitative interviewing styles tend to elicit positive feelings and thoughts.

Given these developments, I have struggled with how to extract that which could promote increased linkage between research teaching and practice method teaching in the classroom, and boost students' practice and research competence as well.

BACKGROUND AND DEVELOPMENT OF THE EXERCISE

During my 20 years of teaching social work, I have taught a number of practice and research courses and experimented with several teaching approaches with students of varying backgrounds. Challenged by a new mandate to infuse content on research (as well as human diversity) into all areas of the curriculum so that social workers can both **use** and **do** research, my colleagues and I in the social work programs at Marygrove College and Saint Louis University began to assign more in-class, experiential learning exercises to heighten students' practice and research competence. After three years of sharing our teaching trials, errors and innovations, we have come to view one of the exercises (an application of the case study method) as a particularly useful and dynamic way for students to (a) evaluate practice interventions and (b) get a good handle on single-case research.

Traditional methods of teaching research and social work practice do not seem to work as well as experiential learning approaches. Like other educators, I have assigned the obvious textbook chapters and lectured on single-case research designs or interviewing skills. I have learned from students, however, that most spend their efforts memorizing lists of concepts, research terms, and interviewing techniques. They, therefore, rarely achieve the problem-solving and thinking skills desired and students seldom have the sense that they can actually **do** research because they have not done it. Similarly, students regularly report their impressions of an interview as good or bad, without being able to distinguish how facilitative or obstructive worker communications contribute to these impressions.

Students in my class have also been required to read journal articles that investigate the impact of social workers' interviewing styles. In addition, I have expected students to review research studies that illustrate the application of single-system technology to different-sized systems, from communities to individuals. Meanwhile, I have impressed upon students that clients are never to be used as "guinea pigs" for research or practice courses.

In addition to the above approaches, my colleagues and I have all used classroom simulations of interviewing. But students have reported that simulations often are artificial and difficult to take seriously. We have also video-taped students in the classroom. The "fishbowl" aspect of this exercise tends to make students self-conscious and to inhibit their performance, according to their evaluations of this exercise. We have frequently had students audio tape interviews in laboratory-like media centers as well as in field settings and real situations. This produces less anxiety but non-verbal communications are lost. With more student workbooks available, some faculty have assigned workbook problems and exercises in practice and research courses. Yet all of the above teaching/learning methods have yielded less than hoped for results.

Given the difficulties I have described, it was clear that a curricular innovation was needed, or that I would have to borrow, build upon, and use an existing approach in a new way. While searching for a better way to help students learn how to apply the essential practice principles and research skills in class, I came upon the idea of combining into one exercise two separate assignments that I had developed earlier and used for years: (1)

the process-recording and critique of a filmed interview in a social work practice course, and (2) the calculation of inter-rater agreement and correlation scores, as well as change and difference scores, in a research course.

DESCRIPTION OF THE EXERCISE: EVALUATION OF INTERVIEWER COMPETENCE

The combined exercise, using interview recording to do single-case evaluation research on practice interventions, was designed to more actively involve students and more effectively integrate research and practice learning. It was also designed so that students could quite easily transfer learning from this experiential exercise to systematically evaluate the quality and/or effectiveness of their own practice. Further, it was hoped that this approach might help to improve overall performance on exams, and enhance student demonstration of practice and research competencies in their work with clients in field placements.

I collaborated with Dorothy Seebaldt and Michelle Ventour, faculty who also teach social work practice courses, to produce a tool for assessing interviewer competence. The tool resulting from our efforts (See Appendix) was informed and guided by the works of several authors who have either developed or facilitated the utilization of helping checklists, self-assessment exercises, rating criteria, and other instruments for assessing interview(er) or social work(er) competence [e.g., Stiles, 1984; Kadushin, 1990; Sheafor, et al., 1991]. I first used what I have since decided to call the Interviewer Competence Questionnaire (ICQ) in a social work practice course in 1989.

The ICQ aims to assess how competently an interviewer conducted a single interview session, focusing on operationalized values, skills, and behaviors that distinguish the more competent interviewer from the less competent interviewer. This tool is best used to assess an initial interview, an interview for gathering information, rather than for changing behavior. The ICQ consisted of 12 clusters of interviewing skills. The listed clusters, each with five descriptive statements ranging from less to more competent, follow the interview process generally from beginning to end. The clustered skill areas are:

A. Initiating the interview
B. Nonverbal communications, attending behavior
C. Confidentiality
D. Questioning skills
E. Active listening and responding
F. Control/direction of the interview

G. Transitions
H. Barriers to effective communication
I. Ease of the interviewee
J. Accomplishment of interview purpose
K. Note-taking/recording
L. Termination

Before using the ICQ to rate an interview session, students are instructed to read the questionnaire very carefully and to review the sections of the textbook on interviewing skills [Hepworth and Larsen, 1990, pp. 28-192]. These sections have content on operationalizing the cardinal social work values, attending and active listening skills, communicating with empathy and authenticity, verbal following, exploring and focusing skills, as well as eliminating counterproductive communications patterns. Students are invited to ask questions and to identify any statements in the ICQ that seem unclear or confusing. There was discussion time to provide needed clarification before the interview was presented.

INTERVIEW I

Step 1: Viewing and Rating Interview I

Initially, students viewed the film "Studies in Interviewing I", with a running time of 17 minutes. The interview takes place in a department of social services office. The film is a recording of the initial contact between a social worker (the interviewer) and a woman who is seeking information about county aid (the interviewee). Students are instructed to independently, without any discussion, complete the ICQ when the film ends. When the ICQs are completed, ratings are recorded onto a ICQ Summary Rating Sheet and these sheets are collected. Then, during an open discussion period, we solicited students' reactions to and impressions of the interview. Most students agreed that the social work interviewer in Interview I seemed distracted, unfriendly, and not helpful. Interview I is generally seen as a session in which the interviewer did not demonstrate good interviewing skills.

Step 2: Calculating the Percent of Agreement and Correlation Between Two Sets of Ratings

Students are randomly paired and each student pair received two sets of ICQ Summary Rating Sheets completed by students in the class. When there was an odd number of students, the instructor (using a blind draw procedure) picked one ICQ Summary Rating Sheet from those collected and copied it so that each student would have two sets of ratings to work with. On the ICQ Summary Rating Sheet the 12 clusters of skills are listed A through L, with the number of the rating given for each letter cluster. Students then obtained two different measures of interrater reliability, the extent of consistency among different observers/raters in their judgements, by calculating the percentage of agreement and the degree of correlation in their independent ratings. Figure 1, which follows, is an illustration of how to calculate the percent of agreement and the degree of correlation in two sets of ratings.

TABLE 1
AN EXAMPLE ILLUSTRATING HOW TO CALCULATE PERCENTAGE OF AGREEMENT AND THE DEGREE OF CORRELATION IN STUDENTS' RATINGS OF INTERVIEWER COMPETENCE IN INTERVIEW I

Skill Cluster	Student X Ratings	Student Y Ratings	Agree=1 Disagree=0	X^2	Y^2	XY
A	2	2	1	4	4	4
B	2	2	1	4	4	4
C	0	0	1	0	0	0
D	1	2	0	1	4	2
E	1	2	0	1	4	2
F	3	3	1	9	9	9
G	1	1	1	1	1	1
H	1	2	0	1	4	2
I	1	1	1	1	1	1
J	1	1	1	1	1	1
K	0	0	1	0	0	0
L	0	0	1	0	0	0
Sum of:			Sum of:			
X = 13	Y = 16	A = 9	X^2 = 23	Y^2 = 32	XY = 26	

N = 12 pairs of ratings for skill clusters

Sum of Agrees	9	% Agreement is:
Total # Pairs	12	9/12 = 75%

Raw Score Computing Formula for Pearson's Correlation Coefficient:

$$r_{XY} = \frac{N \Sigma XY - \Sigma X \Sigma Y}{\sqrt{[N \Sigma X^2 - (\Sigma X)^2][N \Sigma Y^2 - (\Sigma Y)^2]}}$$

In the above formula, N = total number of pairs.
Σ = notation for "sum of"

$$r_{XY} = \frac{12(26) - (13)(16)}{\sqrt{[12(23) - (13)^2][12(32) - (16)^2]}}$$

$$r_{XY} = +.89$$

Table 1 shows the ratings on 12 interviewing skill clusters for two students in the class. The two raters agreed 75 percent of the time, which was about average for the class. If there was agreement 80 percent of the time or more in their ratings, most would assume that the amount of random error in measurement is not excessive. Some would argue that even 70 percent agreement would be acceptable.

The correlation between the two ratings is another measure of interrater reliability, presented in Table 1. This is a useful measure to calculate because although the two raters sometimes disagree on the exact rating, they both tend to give low (or high) ratings in a consistent fashion. That is, with ratings on a scale from 0 to 4, the difference between the two raters was rarely more than a single point. Sometimes the percentage of agreement was low but, because the ratings tended to move up and down together, the correlation would be high (sometimes over .80). This exercise demonstrates two relatively easy and practical ways to assess interrater reliability.

INTERVIEW II

Step 1: Viewing and Rating Interview II

The same process described above for preparing students to view and rate Interview I was followed for Interview II. This interview is a reenactment of Interview I, with the same worker/interviewer, the same client/interviewee, and the same presenting concern. Interview II, however, progresses very differently. Students independently rated the interviewer's skills in this session higher than they rated her skills in Interview I. The discussion which followed the completion of the ICQ clearly revealed that Interview II was seen as better than Interview I, the worker's communications as more appropriate and helpful.

Step 2: Computing Difference Scores, Improvements Between Interviews

To get a measure of the difference between Interview I and Interview II on the ICQ, each student's Summary Rating Sheets were returned. Students obtained a change/difference score by matching and then subtracting each skill cluster rating on Interview I from the corresponding skill cluster rating on Interview II. The ratings for Interview I were subtracted from the ratings for Interview II in order that any positive sign obtained for the remainder or difference would be indicative of improvement between the two interview sessions (See Table 2 below).

TABLE 2
HOW TO CALCULATE DIFFERENCE/CHANGE SCORES
BETWEEN ICQ RATINGS FOR INTERVIEW I AND II

Interview Cluster	Interview II Ratings	Change/ I Ratings	Difference
A	3	2	+1
B	3	2	+1
C	3	0	+3
D	4	2	+2
E	3	1	+2
F	3	3	0
G	3	2	+1
H	3	2	+1
I	2	1	+1
J	3	1	+2
K	2	0	+2
L	2	0	+2
Total	34	16	+18

Note: Positive change/difference scores can be taken as signs of improvement. The filmed reenactment of the interview session exaggerates the amount of improvement (more than 200%) that might be expected in reality.

Table 2 provides information about changes/improvements in specific areas of interviewing skills as well as overall change/improvement in the interviewer's total score. Again, students found the calculation of change/difference scores to be an easy straight-forward way to distinguish levels of interviewer competence.

ALTERNATIVE WAYS OF USING INTERVIEW RECORDINGS IN EVALUATING INTERVIEWER COMPETENCE

The ICQ can also be used to compare two interviews by the same interviewer at two points in time--if care is taken to keep constant (or to permit very limited variability in) the purpose and length of the interview as well as the critical attributes of the interviewee.

One year, we experimented with students audio-taping, then rating and comparing two of their own interviews. For each of these interviews students were asked to locate volunteers who were relatively unknown to them. Students were to obtain their consent to conduct a 30 minute social history interview for practice. The first of the two interviews had to be done before the third week of the practice class in order for us to have a baseline measure of each student's basic interviewing style and skills.

When student interviews were done, their audio tapes were collected, well before the content on interviewing was covered. Six weeks later the second set of audio-recordings were complete. Then, each student rated and compared their two interviews: Interview A (baseline interview before content/coursework on interviewing) and Interview B (after content/coursework on interviewing). Basically, the same steps outlined above for Interview I and II were followed for Interview A and B.

Most students observed a marked improvement between Interview A and B. As expected, better students (i.e., those with higher ratings on Interview A) showed less improvement, while those with lower initial ratings showed the most improvement. Interestingly, there was less inter-rater agreement for those receiving the top and the bottom ratings. It is believed that the discrepancy may have been greater at the top and the bottom of the scale because students who are excellent interviewers tend to be very introspective and to under-rate their performance, while students who are poorer interviewers often over-rate their performance because they have little self-awareness and limited ability to be introspective or provide self-criticism.

The students who rated and compared Interview A and B were able to see this exercise as a micro-simulation of the AB Single-Subject Research Design, with the interviewer (not the client) as the subject and the recorded interview session(s) as the unit of analysis. Moreover, I was able to reinforce the point that the BA designs have the weakest control for history and students were able to offer concrete and personal reasons why multiple-baseline and multiple-component designs would offer better control of extraneous factors, such as the history threat to internal validity. This exercise also enabled students to appreciate the simplicity and feasibility of doing single-subject research and its utility for the systematic evaluation of one's own practice.

The next planned variation on this exercise is to have a group of predominately African-American students and a group of mostly European-American students each view, rate, and compare ICQ ratings of a cross-cultural interview session in order to explore differences and/or similarities in ratings between these two groups of students. The interesting question is whether ratings of interviewer competence are general across cultures? Will there be greater agreement or disagreement when students rate cross-cultural interviews? Will the ratings for cross-cultural interviews not look markedly different from ratings of interviews involving intracultural communication?

DISCUSSION

The most important benefit of using interview recordings to teach, learn, and do single-case evaluation research on practice interventions is that **with this method students make the link between research and practice**. Abstract concepts become real for them and statistics meaningful.

It can be argued that the experiential learning exercise described herein is more than a bit too simplistic. After all, the twelve skill clusters for the ICQ were not constructed on the basis of factor analyses. There has not been any research on the ICQ to establish its degree of internal consistency, test-retest reliability and no real validity data are reported. Nevertheless, as a learning tool this exercise provides an excellent opportunity to see social work research in action on a topic relevant to social work education and practice. Initial student response to the exercise has been enthusiastic and most positive. Also, acknowledging the bugs in the works, students and faculty are working together to refine both the instrument and the process. Several future research projects are waiting in the wings.

REFERENCES

Alter, C. and W. Evens, <u>Evaluating Your Practice: A Guide in Self-Assessment</u> (Springer, 1990).

Bloom, M. and J. Fischer, <u>Evaluating Practice: Guidelines for the Accountable Professional</u> (Prentice-Hall, 1982).

Compton, B. and B. Galaway, <u>Social Work Processes</u> (Wadsworth, 1989).

Council on Social Work Education, <u>Curriculum Policy Statement</u> (Author, 1988).

Council on Social Work Education, <u>Curriculum Policy Statement</u> (Author, 1992).

Feagin, J., A. Orum and G. Sjoberg, <u>A Case for the Case Study</u> (University of North Carolina, 1991).

Grinnell, R. <u>Social Work Research and Evaluation</u> (F.E. Peacock, 1993).

Hepworth, D. and J. Larson, <u>Direct Social Work Practice: Theory and Skills</u> (Wadsworth, 1990).

Kadushin, A., <u>The Social Work Interview: A Guide for Human Service Professionals</u> (Columbia University, 1990).

Klein, H., <u>Innovation Through Cooperation</u> (WACRA, 1993).

LeCroy, C., <u>Case Studies in Social Work Practice</u> (Wadsworth, 1992).

Maple, F., <u>Dynamic Interviewing: An Introduction to Counseling</u> (Sage, 1985).

Marlow, C., <u>Research Methods for Generalist Social Work</u> (Brooks/Cole, 1993).

McClam, T. and M. Woodside, <u>Problem Solving in the Helping Professions</u> (Brooks/Cole, 1994).

Merriam, S., <u>Case Study Research in Education: A Qualitative Approach</u> (Jossey-Bass, 1988).

Neuman, W., <u>Social Research Methods: Qualitative and Qualitative Approaches</u> (Allyn and Bacon, 1994).

Nugent, W., "The Affective Impact of a Clinical Social Worker's Interviewing Style: A Series of Single-Case Experiments," <u>Research on Social Work Practice</u> (January 1992), pp. 6-27.

Royse, D., <u>Research Methods in Social Work</u> (Nelson-Hall, 1991).

Rubin, A. and E. Babbie, <u>Research Methods for Social Work</u> (Brooks/Cole, 1993).

Schulman, L., <u>The Skills of Helping Individuals, Families, and Groups</u> (F.E. Peacock, 1992).

Seabury, B. and F. Maple, "Using Computers to Teach Practice Skills," <u>Social Work</u> (July 1993), pp. 430-439.

Sheafor, B., C. Horejsi and G. Horejsi, <u>Techniques and Guidelines for Social Work Practice</u> (Allyn and Bacon, 1991).

Stiles, W. and W. Snow, "Counseling session impact as seen by novice counselors and their clients, <u>Journal of Counseling Psychology</u> (1984), pp.3-12.

Sue, D. and D. Sue, <u>Counseling the Culturally Different: Theory and Practice</u> (John Wiley & Sons, 1990).

Task Force on Social Work Research, <u>Building Social Work Knowledge for Effective Services and Policies: A Plan for Research Development</u> (Author, 1991).

Thyer, B. and K. Thyer, "Single-System Research Designs in Social Work Practice: A Bibliography from 1965-1990," <u>Research on Social Work Practice</u> (January 1992), pp. 99-116.

Yin, R., <u>Case Study Research: Design and Methods</u> (Sage, 1989).

Yin, R., <u>Applications of Case Study Research</u> (Sage, 1993).

APPENDIX
INTERVIEWER COMPETENCE QUESTIONNAIRE

A good test of what you have learned about interviewing is to have you personally conduct video/audio tape and analyze an actual interview. Ideally, this is to be done at the beginning of the course and again near the end of the course - in order for you to have pretest/post-test measures of your interviewing skills and to permit you to calculate change/improvement scores. The following is a structured interview assessment guide to facilitate your evaluation of your interviewing skills.

A. <u>Initiating the Interview</u>
   0. No attempt was made to set up the interview or prepare the interviewee for what would follow.
   1. Brief introductions, without attempt to put interviewee at ease.
   2. Greeting and introductions--tone and expression were acceptable.
   3. Warm greeting and descriptive introductions. Procedure <u>or</u> purpose was explained, but not both.
   4. Warm greeting and descriptive introductions. Procedure <u>and</u> purpose were both explained.

B. <u>Nonverbal Communications</u>
   0. Voice quality, gestures, facial expressions, <u>and</u> body orientation were inappropriate.
   1. Any three (3) of the following: looked bored; jerky, fidgety, or squirming movements; spoke to fast/slow or pitch too high/low or spoke in a monotone; posture rigid or slouched; speech is hesitant, interviewer stammered or shuddered.
   2. Any two (2) of the above. Sometimes voice quality, gestures, facial expressions, and/or body orientation were not appropriate.
   3. Any one (1) of the above. Most of the time, voice quality, gestures, facial expressions, and body orientation were appropriate.
   4. Throughout interview, pace/pitch was appropriate and speech fluent with good use of inflection; eye contact was maintained and facial expressions conveyed interest; posture was relaxed and movements fluid.

C. <u>Confidentiality</u>
   0. Confidentiality was not mentioned.
   1. Confidentiality was mentioned but not explained.
   2. Confidentiality was explained but not adequately.
   3. Confidentiality was adequately explained.
   4. Confidentiality was fully explained and the interviewee's consent or expression of comfort with proceeding was obtained.

D. <u>Questioning Skills</u>
   0. Often asked more than one question at a time, loaded questions, and/or ambiguous questions.
   1. Sometimes asked more than one question at a time, loaded questions, and/or ambiguous questions.
   2. Tended to ask mostly closed questions or mostly open-ended questions.
   3. Asked a good mixture of open-ended as well as closed questions <u>and</u> used questioning to obtain clarification, probe for specific details, and/or explore interviewee's feelings about a topic. (NOTE: Do <u>not</u> circle this rating without providing at least 3 examples of the latter in your descriptive analysis of the

interview.)

E. **Active Listening & Responding Skills**
   0. Rarely responded to interviewee's communication. Generally, followed interviewee's communications with a question and/or head nodding.
   1. Only minimally responded to interviewee's communications and only minimally demonstrated active listening. Generally and repeatedly used short encouraging responses such as "I see", "Mm-mmm", "Yes", "And?", "But?", or "Okay".
   2. Occasionally used short encouraging responses as well as restatement, paraphrasing, or empathic responses.
   3. Frequently used encouraging responses, restatement, paraphrasing <u>and</u> empathic responses. (NOTE: Provide at least 3 examples of the above.)
   4. Throughout the interview, used encouraging, restatement, paraphrasing, and empathic responses as well as summarizing responses. (NOTE: Provide example of <u>each</u> responding skill.)

F. **.Control of Interview**
   0. Lack of control to point of ineffectiveness or rigid over-control. Rarely directed the interview or talked too much.
   1. Often lost control or over-controlled throughout interview.
   2. Sometimes lost control or over-controlled at points in the interview.
   3. Maintained control and effectiveness, but with some obvious intrusions.
   4. Maintained control and directed the interview effectively without being intrusive.

G. **Transitions**
   0. Hopped from topic to topic or from one question to another without offering any transitions.
   1. Transition(s) provided but transition(s) was/were confusing, haphazard, or mechanical.
   2. Little evidence of logical orderly progression from one topic to another, but not haphazard or "slap-dash". Didn't go off on tangents.
   3. Logical, orderly progression with appropriate transitions provided in most instances.
   4. Communications flowed logically and orderly. Transitions are provided that link interviewee's last communication to your next question or comment. (NOTE: Give examples).

H. **Possible Mistakes and/or Barriers to Effective Communication**
   0. Made more than three (3) of the following mistakes: interrupted, advised prematurely, confronted prematurely, suggested what interviewee "should" or "ought" to do, lectured, blamed, criticized, threatened, labeled or stereotyped, used sarcasm, offered glib interpretation, and/or parroted or overused certain phrases/clichés. (NOTE: Identify <u>all</u> mistakes made).
   1. Made 3 different mistakes or repeated mistakes listed above. (Identify <u>all</u> mistakes made).
   2. Made 2 different mistakes or repeated mistakes listed above. (Identify <u>all</u> mistakes made).
   3. Only made one of the above mistakes throughout the entire interview. (Identify mistake made).
   4. Did not make any of the above mistakes throughout the entire interview.

I. **Ease of Interviewee**
   0. Much discomfort, ill at ease. No effort made to reduce discomfort.
   1. Some discomfort, lack of confidence, anxious, hesitant, hostile. Little or no effort made to reduce discomfort.
   2. No obvious discomfort. Little or no effort made to ascertain or increase ease of interviewee.
   3. Easy forthright manner. Little or no effort made to reinforce ease of interviewee.
   4. Quite at ease, comfortable, and confident. Praise used to reinforce ease of interviewee.

J. **Accomplishment of Interview Purpose/Objective(s)**
   0. Purpose was unclear and not accomplished.
   1. Only minimally accomplished purpose (e.g. social history is incomplete, assessment is confusing).
   2. Part of the purpose/objectives was/were accomplished. Some part(s) were not accomplished.

48

3. Purpose and objectives were accomplished satisfactorily.
4. Purpose and objectives were fully accomplished. Interview was comprehensive and information collected seems valid and reliable.

K. **Note-taking/Recording**
   0. There was no note-taking or recording of the interview.
   1. Note-taking or recording of the interview was distracting.
   2. Note-taking or recording of the interview was not distracting, but it was not explained.
   3. Note-taking or recording was explained but it still was somewhat distracting.
   4. Note-taking or recording was explained and it was not in any way distracting.

L. **Termination**
   0. Interview ended abruptly without closing salutation.
   1. Interviewee was thanked and "good-byes" were said.
   2. Some sort of wrap-up was provided. Interviewee was thanked and "good-byes" were said.
   3. Closing summary was provided. Interviewee was thanked and "good-byes" said.
   4. Interviewee's readiness to terminate was ascertained as well as interviewee's response to "anything else?" that needs to be covered at the time. Closing summary was provided with a discussion of what happens next.

CHAPTER TWO

AN ENHANCED SIMULATION APPROACH: INTEGRATING MULTIPLE TEACHING METHODS

Philippe Chapuis
Université du Québec à Hull
HULL, QUEBEC, CANADA
Benoît Bazoge
Université du Québec à Montréal
MONTREAL, QUEBEC, CANADA
Jérôme Morel
Groupe EIA
MARSEILLE, FRANCE

Abstract

Although management subject matters are now better taught, we still fall short when teaching decision-making. In the past few years, we have used a pedagogical formula that relies simultaneously on lectures, case studies, and business simulation. This combined approach has been tested on various student populations. It appears that business simulations used in a different pedagogical context, along with tailored seminars and constant consultation support, help attain higher learning objectives, preparing "managers-to-be" to take larger steps.

INTRODUCTION

The teaching of management in general and in particular of decision-making is often quite unsuccessful. Dissatisfaction is great and criticism can be scathing:

"[…] Students have a tendency to apply, in a fairly mechanical and scholastic fashion, standard analytical grids. And this in the "*best*" of circumstances. In the worst cases, these grids become virtually empty and serious interpretation mistakes occur (when) dealing with basic management concepts. […] We need to ask whether students understand that strategic analytical tools are heuristic, useful in construction/problem-solving and not pseudo-algorithms." [Martinet & Reiter, 1991]

In light of this, we have set out to reconsider how decision-making is taught. First, we question the methods employed and their appropriateness to the development of knowledge. Thus, we have developed and tested a pedagogical formula that relies on the simultaneous exploitation of a simulation along with lectures and personalized follow-up consultation. This formula consists of enriching lectures with specific exercises which fit the reality of the simulation, treating the members of competing teams as executives of enterprises that have external consultants (professors) at their disposal at any time. The simulation also serves to bridge the gap between the general theory taught and the more restrictive framework of simulations. This combined approach, novel in its content and especially in its implementation, has been tested with several very different student populations in Canada and in France.

THE LEARNING PROCESS

How should we teach? Instead of stating this question, why not ask: how do we learn? The underlying hypothesis suggests that educators, conscious of the learning process, could more suitably adapt their style to the discipline taught. While taking into account the specificities of individuals, the educator might anticipate potential difficulties and then, without eliminating all the psychological blocks, at least grasp them.

The media have echoed research related to the difference between the functioning mechanisms of the right and left hemisphere of the brain. Aside from invert proprioceptive pathways,[1] there exists also a functional difference, now well documented,[2] regarding perception and information treatment.

Neurophysiologists have introduced the term *hemisphericity* to designate, under certain conditions, predominance of one hemisphere over the other.[3] As Plato's postulates,[4] hemisphericity is more specialized in controlling verbal activities such as reading, rhythm and speech recognition. "Linear " hemisphericity is considered an analytical and precision tool; it is the logical and rational organ so dear to Descartes. The other, more syncretic, non-verbal and global [Myers, 1982 : 210] is specialized in form, melody and spatial pattern recognition. This is integration and synthesis hemisphericity. From the representation of images and models, from symbol and analogy manipulation, it supports intuition.

Naturally, it is the complementarity of the two hemispheres that gives perception and thought all its originality. "Global" hemisphericity, also referred to as the predominance of the right hemisphere, is not necessarily less complex or more simplistic than the other. " Linear " hemisphericity, or the predominance of the left hemisphere, is really superimposed on its counterpart. There exists a " global " dominance in a great number of perceptive and non-verbal tasks. Consequently, each individual perceives and treats everyday events in his own way. Objectivity is a myth because the observation of facts is altered by personal filters produced by values and emotions in each of us. Therefore, a great number of our behavioural patterns and courses of actions do not arise from the conscious thought process [Gazzanica, 1985]. Intuition is crucial and it often leads to original decisions made by business executives in successful enterprises (Iacocca, Steinberg, etc.).[5]

It is possible to imagine that the " logical-rational " side acts as a gateway to data and the " holistic-intuitive " side acts as an analysis and treatment centre [Chapuis: 1991, 1993]. While each person is different, no one apprehends reality with the same " left/right " configuration. Considering our personal characteristics, each and every one of us needs information to be more or less rich in one or the other treatment modes in order to understand. Likewise, in our interventions, we unconsciously favour a particular type of communication that represents our favourite channels. We tend to impose it implicitly on our audience. This results in professors with a " global " dominant using sketches, schemes, simulations without always deeming it necessary to back up these holistic methods with a written demonstration. On the other hand, the " linear " will use written documents to communicate information, without considering the use of exercises, schemes or drawings since they will be considered superfluous.

It is not surprising that most educators turn to teaching methods that are derived from Cartesian thinking since they themselves come from an academic environment that traditionally supports this approach. It is impossible to expect students to assimilate a global vision from sequential and linear means, forgetting in the process two important elements of creativity: incubation and illumination. Although we know that the decision-making process necessitates a dialogue between the two hemispheres, classical teaching continues to address one part of the brain almost exclusively: "linear-intellectual." The prevalence placed upon the analytical mental process in classical teaching ignores a part of the brain's potential.

THE LEARNING CONTENT

Questioning ourselves on management teaching in general and decision-making in particular, also sends us back to the nature of knowledge that we want to convey to students. Executive work integrates multiple learning: it is impossible to establish boundaries for it and its application is in perpetual motion. Learning management skills requires, at the same time, the assimilation of concepts, techniques and tools, and also an awareness of reality which will entail being faced with the management of personnel, materials, information and cash flows while confronted with time, resource and other pressure constraints.

Unfortunately, the pedagogical tools currently in use incite students to retrench in the relative comfort of an analyst's role. They avoid any involvement in the implementation of the selected outcomes and shun any responsibility for the consequences of their decisions. This criticism has been directed at MBA graduates [Bazoge & Zussman: 1988, Hall: 1988] as well as at students from Business Schools in France (ESC), whose analytical skills are hypertrophied while at the same time, they seem paralyzed when confronted with decision-making, particularly at the implementation stage [Martinet & Reiter, *Op. Cit.* ; Chapuis, 1991, 1993].

Thus it appears important that the future management graduate be introduced to the difficulties of decision-making in a systemic context and that they may recognize the multiplicity of the logic in action. The fear of the unknown causes serious cognitive blocks that need to be treated by practicing decision-making and action. The student, therefore, must be sensitive to the complexity of the decision-making process in order for this knowledge to shift from conceptualized to internalized.

The teaching of decision-making presents serious pedagogical challenges. First, the educator must not theorize to the point of leading others to believe that he teaches an exact science and must not confine himself to teaching exclusively techniques, grids and analytical methods, at the risk of producing what Stanley Shapiro calls: "The 'third generation idiot' is the student of a 28 year old assistant professor working, in turn, for a 35 year old associate professor, all three of them having virtually no business experience" [Meyer, 1991:30]. Unable to draw the relation between the theory learned and what he will be confronted with in his daily life as an executive, with this mechanist approach, the student is guided to reproduce the models learned without "comprehending" or seeing the limits of their application.

The other extreme is to opt for teaching methods based solely on practical experience. This consists in putting the students in situations where they make decisions without having assimilated the theory previously. This inductive method is based on the hypothesis that the student will be able to reconstruct the general from the particular and that knowledge is gained from the "doing" phase. So, without the enlightenment of a theoretical framework, that will centre on observed elements, is it reasonable to believe that the student will be able to step back when confronted with problems and that he will be able to identify or recognize his errors, even during a training period in business?

Between these two extremes, the educator must select his pedagogical methods. From this, the policy course exemplifies well the difficulty of teaching delta-type knowledge [Gilbert & Paquet: 1991]. In most management education, a large portion of the pedagogy is based on the lecture-reading dyad. Lectures and theoretical presentations by the professor are supplemented by discussion, course notes and a synthesis. Articles written by renowned authors establish the concepts and show the process, techniques and the tools appropriate for decision-making. These readings (if done) can be commented on and discussed in class. Well-known individuals may present their experiences to which could be added "question and answer sessions," synthesis and discussion periods.

In this style of teaching, knowledge acquisition can be gauged by exams. Essentially, exams measure the student's ability to regurgitate, as is, what has been learned. Due to the nature of the academic process that students go through, any student who has read the course material and attended class should succeed in these "bookish" knowledge tests. This type of teaching and the exam that is its corollary, stimulate the logico-rational hemisphere. They fulfill their role fairly well and this teaching style may train good analysts. It is probable, however, that we may lose a certain number of good students whose learning process is more global, thereby robbing businesses of creative candidates with strong potential.

In the category of more global approaches, there is the case method. Inspired by Platonist pedagogy, this method was initially developed at Harvard; it has since been revised and adapted to the point that in some cases it has moved completely away from its original holistic vocation. When properly used, policy cases describe business situations from which students extract a set of problems to then derive and prioritize these problems. Case studies stimulate group and class discussion as well as the writing of a summary document; sometimes, they encourage individual reading interest. The complexity and the integration of the problems presented, the absence of a single solution, compromises, and the discussion all offer the possibility for the right brain to blossom.

Unfortunately, case method teaching is not without its own problems. Paradoxically, this method is at once simple, complex and truncated. Simple, because one "only needs" to know the case well, the concepts that should be uncovered and how to conduct a group discussion. This apparent simplicity leads certain professors not to control the case discussion; we then witness discussion anarchy in the classroom which prevents the important points of the case from emerging. At other times, the discussion is too carefully planned; the professors sell and impose their own solution to the case as "the" solution (there is a virtual break of instructional notes which often are disguised answer sheets exchanged by students from year to year!). Complex, because when it is mastered, this method goes against students' basic expectation of a solution at the end of the case discussion. It also runs counter to teachers' expectations of showing themselves as the "ones who know." Finally, truncated, because it does not allow the students' involvement in the implementation of their own recommendations, nor does it allow them to take responsibility for the consequences of those decisions.

Business simulations constitute a different class of interactive pedagogical methods that have been available to management schools for the past twenty years. They help students manage a " virtual business " and recreate a dynamic competitive environment. The students are called upon to utilize their knowledge for a practical exercise within the limitations of the resources at their disposal at the time. Here are the most common pedagogical objectives sought by simulation users [Chapuis, 1991]:

- becoming familiar with the managerial process
- putting oneself in a virtually real situation
- practicing decision making
- solving problems other than functional
- mastering techniques and acquire knowledge
- differentiating between strategic choices and short-term decisions
- making a synthesis of the functional courses
- working in groups and experience group dynamics
- communicating one's own ideas (in writing and orally)

Perceived as a panacea when they were first introduced, business simulations have progressively lost their initial appeal. Still, they are pedagogical tools that seek to fill the gaps in traditional education. Well conducted, they are probably the single most realistic tool that approximates an internship in enterprise or the " real " professional life that students will encounter at the end of their training.

In fact, when operated under optimal conditions, a business simulation gives life to interdepartmental interactions within an organization which would otherwise remain obscure in the mind of the students until they worked in an organization. The business simulation also fosters the expression of creativity and the need for responsibility so that students may find their own solutions, contingent upon the competitive dynamics of all the participants, and then assume the consequences of their choices. Its playful nature renders it attractive, stimulating the student's appetite for knowledge. Beyond the business simulation's undeniable appeal in integrating knowledge, its more essential elements are: confrontation with the other teams, learning teamwork, leadership challenge, learning about political and social issues at stakes and above all its global approach, which promotes learning through discovery.

Furthermore, simulations help establish a real sense of collaboration not only between educators and students, but also between the student teams and within the teams themselves. This takes into account the social context and at the same time, it reenacts the dynamics of organizational life. It provides students with an ideal way to better perceive the dynamic relationships that exist between the elements of a complex system. This, in turn, encourages the participants' total involvement by letting them experience intensely an interpersonal situation while under stress. In order to grasp the implications of problems under uncertain conditions and of multiple information needing to be assessed in limited time frames, in simulation, the students are "forced" collectively to integrate their acquired knowledge.

A business simulation is not, however, a panacea. Its operation imposes constraints and presents potentially perverse effects if we are not careful. For example, certain students could be tempted to " try out " decisions without having done prior analysis, which would eliminate all possible induction and generalization. Others ingeniously try to decode the algorithms used by the computer, thereby wasting any opportunity to understand, from common sense, the environment in which they must develop. Still others try to win at all costs and will not shrink from any means to reach their end. We then witness such curious events as the "disappearance" of documents and diskettes, and nocturnal search of the trash baskets in the different meeting rooms !

THE CONCEPT OF ENHANCED SIMULATION

Executed under optimal conditions, a business simulation offers an important complement to traditional teaching methods. It lets students experience a competitive situation in a complex and progressive environment. They [students] can make decisions, test the validity of their decisions, analyze their results and then start all over again. Both right and left hemispheres are called upon to make a full contribution.

In our view, however, it is possible to push further the reconciliation between the two hemispheres and teaching methods. The spirit of competition that emerges during simulations explains the appeal simulations have for students, who develop an urge to fill any information gap simply to have the pleasure of testing their performance against their colleagues/competitors. Through this experience students eagerly search for knowledge that can be used in the short term. Our observation of their [students'] state of mind persuaded us to combine teaching methods and to integrate additional pedagogical tools during the course of the simulation. We then noticed that it was possible to "enhance" the simulation environment with the help of two accompanying methods:

CUSTOM SEMINARS

These seminars aim to present remodelled and simplified theoretical concepts that can easily be used in the simulation. They can be applied immediately to help student manage their enterprise. These seminars are short, practical and concrete in that they present the essence of a concept without giving too much detail. They are no substitute for full rigorous traditional lectures; they aim to retain the students' attention with their simplicity and their practicality. We have developed, for example, seminars on the evaluation of return on shareholder's equity, strategic-plan writing, establishing a value chain, commercial forecasting, management of cash-flow movements, oral presentation techniques, etc.

FIGURE 1
SAMPLE SCHEDULE FOR OF AN ENHANCED SIMULATION PROGRAM

	Friday	Saturday	Sunday	Monday	Tuesday	Wednesday
8h30	Student Briefing		Spreadsheets preparation	Decision no.1	Decision no.5	Decision no.9
9h00		Trial no.2		Results no.1	Results no.5	Results no.9
9h30	• General presentation	Seminars		Consultations with teams	Consultations with teams	Consultations with teams
10h00						
10h30	• Questions/ Answers	Trial results no.2				Decision no.10
11h00		Trial decision preparation no.3				Results no.10
11h30				Decision no.2	Decision no. 6	
12h00	Trial decision preparation no.1					Consultations with teams
12h30						
13h00		Consultations with teams		Results no.2	Results no.6	
13h30						
14h00	Consultations with teams			Consultations with teams	Consultations with teams	Decision no.11
14h30		Trial nº3	Decision no.1 preparation			Results no.11
15h00		Seminars				Consultations with teams
15h30	Trial no.1				Decision no.7	
16h00	Seminars	Trial results no.3		Decision no.3	Results no.7	Decision no.12
16h30				Results no.3		Seminars
17h00	Trial results no.1				Consultations with teams	
17h30		Decision tools preparation		Consultations with teams		Results no.12
18h00	Trial decision preparation no.2				Decision no.8	Student evaluations
18h30					Results no.8	
19h00		Consultations with teams		Decision no.4		
19h30				Results no.4	Consultations with teams	
20h00	Consultations with teams					
20h30				Consultation with teams		
21h00						
21h30						

In general, these seminars are offered during trial decision periods that precede the actual simulation. It is at this time that students realize their operational shortcomings. Students are free to attend but conscious of the difficulties they have already encountered, most want factual information. They therefore attend the seminars with interest rather than out of sense of obligation, knowing that the concepts presented will help them improve their performance. Even those who "know," or think they know, attend just in case something useful might come out. Sometimes, in order to stimulate their interest, several seminars are held at the same time, forcing team members to deploy, share this new information and then train each other. Some students become frustrated when they cannot attend a seminar because of lack of space. This "forces" us to surrender under pressure and offer the seminar again in order to maintain the equilibrium among the teams - even the chances for everyone! Students cannot stand to be surpassed by their colleague/competitors. After the seminar, they then have some time left during the trial decision periods and before the simulation competition to fine-tune and operationalize these concepts for their own benefit. They are learning while doing.

CUSTOM CONSULTATIONS

This type of consultation is a continuous monitoring of teams, similar to a typical group discussion of a case study. Here, however, it is related to their case and their decisions; the discussion is centred on their corporate results. We take great care not to lead the discussion, but rather to ask questions that help the students discover their mistakes on their own and also possible alternative solutions. We want to avoid taking a position and being too much in control. The word consultation here is intended more as therapeutic reassurance than expert advice. In most cases the consultation is arranged in response to a voluntary request from the teams. They must justify their decisions, dare to ask questions and push their reasoning to the limit. Our aim is definitely not to advise students as to what course of action they should take. Rather, it is to "coach" them in their thinking process. The intervention style is designed to force students to identify gaps in their understanding and to fill those gaps themselves and, by directed questions on the instructors' part, to learn how to deal with the situations they face.

This ongoing follow-up serves to personalize the relationship with the students and to establish trust between the professor and the students which in turn is conducive to inquiry. Since there are no witnesses during our meetings with individual teams, students feel more inclined to ask questions openly without fear of disapproving looks from the whole class. Students search for and recognize their shortcomings: they become more eager to learn. The teaching relationship becomes inverted: it is no longer the teacher who "pours out" his knowledge, but rather the student who questions. From our experience, these consultations are certainly what students remember as the most positive aspect of the enhanced simulation exercise.

KEY SUCCESS FACTORS

We have been conducting the same business simulation with identical seminar content and the same team of professors in different settings. We worked with a group of second-year and third-year bachelor-level students in France (ESC) and with another group of French students returning from a year of internship outside France (CESEM-4th-year) and also with a group of graduates starting a "mastère." Finally, we tested our approach in Canada at the MBA level and with Polish business economics professors and Romanian engineers in training.

Student's evaluations of this learning method are convincing. Regardless of the student group trained, the satisfaction index is greater than 80% with regard to the seminars' criteria of usefulness and over 85% in terms of the usefulness of consultations. The qualitative comments collected testify eloquently to the advantages of the method. The only negative comments concerned the logistics and the attitude of certain professors towards the students. For this reason it would seem helpful to also present here the difficulties encountered in the implementation of enhanced simulations.

First, this type of event requires using facilities in a different manner than for traditional lectures. Student teams of the same industry must work in rooms separate from each other to protect them from divulging competitive information and to allow professor-consultants to circulate in the different meeting rooms and answer questions without risking eavesdropping from competing teams. In addition, seminar rooms must be available on short notice and for short periods of time during the entire week to be able to offer seminars on [student] request. This [approach] may be incompatible with existing [institutional] course schedules. Most institutions are not prepared for this type of upheaval and often the most stimulating challenge for us has been to convince the university's administration to modify their class schedules to accommodate our needs.

We then need to develop seminars relevant to the simulation and to involve theory. Each simulation has its own peculiarities. Not all the themes taught in traditional courses are necessarily applied in any given simulation (for example: marginal analysis, learning curves, etc.). It is necessary to present only notions[themes] that will be directly used in the simulation. It is important to avoid short-cuts by drawing information from other courses offered in the curriculum for the sake of simplicity. Our own experience leads us to state that the task of developing a seminar forces the professor to reflect on the essence of his specialty, and this usually results in a more focused presentation. It is not always easy to identify all the difficulties that students may encounter and to propose appropriate [custom] seminars. Furthermore, there are time constraints that make it difficult to offer a large number of seminars. We must, therefore, be selective with our choice of interventions.

These simulations also require an imposing supervisory structure. The time investment expected of each professor is considerable, especially since the emphasis is on the quality of the intervention "customized" for each student team. This requires the participation of numerous teachers - who should be as versatile as possible - during several consecutive days. Not all teachers are prepared to make this kind of commitment for reasons of physical fatigue, scheduling constraints and, more prosaically, because of the heavy workload. The foremost difficulty for the hea [coordinator] of this type of intervention is to be successful in recruiting compatible teachers who are willing and able to "play" the game to the end.

The second success factor is the teachers' intimate knowledge of the simulation. Students appreciate being guided by educators who know the intricacies of the simulation's mechanisms, the rules of the game, the particularities, the order of importance of variables, etc. Even when the professor answers indirectly to questions, students are given to understand that the lack of rigour in the answer is voluntary and pedagogical and not due to the fact that the professor is experimenting with the variables at the same time as they are. We are trying to avoid creating the impression that if the professor is unsure himself, then the students do not have to know either. The second difficulty then lies in the challenge of finding teachers who regularly work with the simulation and thus remain familiar with the details from one year to the next.

The coordinator is yet faced with another major difficulty: that of ensuring that the teachers do not portray themselves as the holders of universal truth, placing more emphasis on their way of analysis. This perverse effect of the simulation is one of the major risks that confront the coordinator. In the course of action, it is difficult to intervene without offending the susceptibilities of young teachers unfamiliar with the constraints of co-teaching. Many [inexperienced teachers] merely recite the last popular book. Even worse, some only repeat what they have understood from their master's teachings (ref. "The third generation idiots")! It may be interesting to note, although opportunities for personal contributions are limited, for the most part they are unsuited for the type of teaching where students are expected to discover and invent. Professors must, in fact, respect the students' decisions and use them to help them uncover other avenues. Most of the time, it's an excellent, if not the best, learning opportunity. This presupposes putting together a pedagogical team that keeps from "playing" with or against the students. It is understandably tempting for the experienced teacher to impose his advice in order to counteract the "less successful" decision made by some team. Of course, when acting in this way, teachers show that they are knowledgeable, flatter their ego. . . but at the same time, frustrate the students even more.

On the other hand, one of the difficulties lies in promoting the proper amount of learning by trial and error without reducing the level of motivation because of experienced failure. As long as the consequence of the less successful decision is marginal, then the student is willing to accept the trial and error process. But the moment the stakes are higher, the risk of failure takes over in thr mind of the students and they then reject any suggestion of the need to participate in a learning process. It is possible, if we are not careful, to see student teams give up and drop out of the exercise. The effect on their ego can be so strong that, unlike their colleagues in other teams, they are not able to control the key variables of the simulation. In these cases, and only in these cases, should a professor intervene as an expert-adviser to help the team regain the courage to continue with the exercise.

Because of these different elements, we must stress the fact that the choice of professors is a delicate process. What is needed is a strong team of versatile, credible, supportive and even tempered individuals who are not going to regurgitate material from courses that are already developed in order to simplify their task. Teachers must be willing and able to take risks, since there will be times when direct intervention is call for, without preparation, during tense conflict situations. In fact, teachers must be vigilant since, under stressful conditions, students will naturally revert to their role of petitioners for certainties and reassurances. They demand precise answers from the consultant-professors who could inadvertently end up "playing" along with them, if they are not careful.

CONCLUSION

The training of decision-makers is far from clearly defined. Current results [achieved] are not convincing or satisfactory regardless of the pedagogical method used. It is apparent that in a great number of cases, the failure to get results through a lecture can be explained. The method is simply inadequate to reach the aim. Therefore, it is "normal" — and somewhat reassuring — to realize that such a format "just does not work." The teaching of decision-making entails particular difficulties since management is fraught with hazy, blurred, and ambiguous situations where certainties are rare and linearity is excluded. We believe that attempting to reduce the pedagogical relationships to a flood of notions [themes], typical of more or less passive methods, without considering the specifics, is to risk to further fragment an already complex reality and to hinder the learning process.

To teach decisiveness is to practice the subtle art of seeking a near-perfect equilibrium where cognition and perception for professors and students are in synchronization with opportunities in the environment and the vague elements of the management field. These are the conditions for pedagogical success that could free not only the learner, but also the professor from method-sclerosis, intellectual stagnation, stereotypes, unfounded certainties and the absence of learning strategies that are coherent with the brain's function and the subject being taught.

The costs associated with conducting such a business simulation may seem prohibitive *a priori,* but the real costs need to be assessed in light of the quality of the results that can be achieved when [the simulation is] carried out properly. Many institutions cannot afford to offer this kind of alternative to traditional teaching methods. Many are satisfied with half measures: simulations that last only a few days, without further concrete contribution. If we add up the time needed to learn the rules and mechanisms of the simulation, there is little time left for anything else. . . except maybe a self-satisfying fair.

Under certain conditions, integrating business simulations with other classical teaching methods to yield an enhanced pedagogical process, could result in reversing the direction and flow of traditional education. This composite approach would allow students to organize their knowledge from elements and thinking frameworks offered by the professor. It reamins the student's responsibility to construct his own knowledge base to higher learning objectives.

ENDNOTES

1.   The left hemisphere of the cortex controls our body right motor activities and the right side of the brain controls the left side of our body.

2.   For an expanded and general perspective read: Chalvin, 1986; Springer & Deutsch, 1988; Ornstein, 1986. For a more specialized view on the relationship between hemisphericities and cognition read: Arnt & Berger, 1978; Bever, 1983. To know more about the relationship between hemisphericities and decision-making read: Gevins, 1987, Chapuis, 1991, 1993.

3.   The left hemisphere is often referred to as the predominant hemisphere. But it is an oversimplification. In fact, one must know that:
   •   The left hemisphere is only predominant in 80% of right-handed men and 65% to 70% of right-handed women.
   •   Distribution on left-handed people is not symmetrical.
   •   There is a bilateral predominance in less than 5% of men, but almost 20% of women.

4.   In *Cratylus*, Plato clearly defines the complementary dichotomy: linear thinking <-> global thinking. He compares Hermogenes, whose hemisphericity is predominantly holistic to Cratylus, who, unlike the latter, is mainly stimulated by words and sentences. Plato also proves that both approaches coexist.

5.   The task and responsibilities of true leaders is best reflected by their creativity, according to Chester Barnard [1938].

REFERENCES

Arnt, S. , & Berger, D. , " Cognitive Mode and Asymmetry [...] ," Cortex, (1978), pp. 78-86.

Barnard, C. The functions of the executive, (Harvard University Press, 1938).

Bazoge, B. & Zussman, D. , " Le MBA en crise " in Education Canada, Canadian Higher Education Research Network Publication, (1988).

Beauvais, R. , L'hexagonal tel qu'on le parle, (Hachette, 1970).

Behrman, J. N. , & Levin, R. I. , " Les grandes écoles remplissent-elles bien leur mission?" Harvard l'Expansion, (summer 1984), pp. 65-73.

Bever, T. G. , "Cerebral Lateralization, Cognitive Asymmetry and Human Consciousness," in Cognitive Processing in the Right Hemisphere, (Academic Press, 1983), pp. 19-39.

Chalvin, D. , Utiliser tout son cerveau, (Librairies techniques, 1986).

Chapuis, Ph. , L'enseignement de PGE et l'utilisation des simulations, Rapport de recherche, E. S. C. (Tours, 1991).

Chapuis, Ph. , La formation des décideurs, Proceeding, Colloque International, Pédagogie de la prise de décision. ICN Nancy, (may 1992).

Chapuis, Ph. , Le mythe de Procuste au royaume de Janus, Proceeding, Congrès européen de systémique, (Prague, 1993).

Gazzanica, M. S. , " The Social Brain ," Psychology Today, (november 1985), pp. 29-38.

Gevins, A. , & Al, "Human Neuroelectric Patterns [...], " Science, (30/01/1987), pp. 580-585.

Gilles, W. , & Paquet, G. , " La connaissance de type Delta ," Le management en crise, (Economica, 1991).

Hall, L. , Report Card on Canadien MBA Programmes, Queen's University, 1986; McKibbin, Current Criticisms of Business School Curriculum, Management Education and Development, (McGraw Hill, 1988).

Martinet, A. Ch. , & Reitter, R. , " Remarques de synthèse," Rapport de correction sur les examens de sortie des ESC, (Paris: A. C. F. C. I. , 1991).

Meyer, E. , L'Expansion, (june, 19, 1991), p. 30.

Myers, J. T. , " Hemisphericity Research [...]," (Journal of Creative Behavior, 1982), p. 210

Ornstein, R. , The Psychology of Consciousness, (Penguin Books, 1986).

Platon, Œuvres Complètes, Tome V, Le Cratyle, (Les Belles Lettres, 1931), p. 54.

Springer, S. P. , & Deutsch, G. , Left Brain, Right Brain, (W. H. Freeman, 1985).

60

PERFORMANCE MEASUREMENT OF STUDENT ACCOUNTABILITY IN CASE STUDY IMPLEMENTATION

Robert DeMichiell
Fairfield University
FAIRFIELD, CONNECTICUT, U.S.A.
Ernest Pavlock
Virginia Polytechnic Institute and State University
FALLS CHURCH, VIRGINIA, U.S.A.

Abstract

The global world of business requires fast response, accurate reporting, and creative problem-solving. The manager of tomorrow will be immersed in business environments which will require effective leadership and responsive decision making. A student-driven learning model for business scenarios where the student is active in not only conducting the project work, but also in the planning and development of the approach, can provide more realistic results. Students must learn accountability standards by defining them for their project team and for each individual participant. Accountability requires definite performance measures. This presentation provides accountability measures derived from several undergraduate and graduate case study implementations over the past five years.

ACCOUNTABILITY IN STUDENT-DRIVEN LEARNING MODELS

Students perceive accountability as meeting the standards (established course requirements) imposed by the instructor. If these criteria are achieved in quality and quantity beyond some minimum expectation, the student will receive a high grade. When the instructor communicates these expectations clearly, quality and quantity become defined and there is a minimal 'expectation gap" between instructor and student. Students then decide on their degree of conformity and exert an effort to obtain a grade commensurate with this expectation. In traditional courses where lecture and examination are the primary teaching modes, the instructor-student expectation gap should be small since the course requirements can be stated in uncomplicated fashion.

However, in case study approaches involving student teams individual performance measures are more difficult to define because of several factors as follows:

a. Interdependence of student work (dependence on each other to provide and share information to meet team and individual objectives);
b. Interpersonal differences among students (personality impact on productivity);
c. Oral and written reporting (team reports indicating individual contributions);
d. More elusive criteria (such as creative analytical approaches, team project management, progress, and leadership);
e. Communication (within and outside the student team, including perhaps business clients involved in the case study); and,
f. Increased personal accountability to others (case study is examined by team but may very well include roles and responsibilities for each student).

Figure 1. Student-Driven Learning Model (SDLM)

Stage I: Preparation for Change
(Analysis) . Project Start-up Kit: General Scenario of Case-Study
 . Team Projects
 . The Process of SDLM
  . Creativity Lecture
  . Systems Thinking & Project Management
  . Student Roles, Responsibilities
  . Deliverables and Accountability
 . Planning for the Inevitable: Change
  . Examining the Possibilities, Best Solutions
  . Reasonable Project Terms and Conditions

Stage II: **Project Definition: Synthesis of Design Variables**
(Design)   . The SDLM Process: Revisited
  . Creative Departures by Students
   . Alternatives and Convergence to Reality
   . Student Personal Interest Profile
  . Capturing Major Activities of the Project
   . Videotaping Events, Audiotaping Interviews
 . The Student-Defined Project
  . Assumptions, Constraints, Scope
  . Team Organization
   . Contract for Deliverables, Approval
   . Presentations, Reports, Data Collection
    . Contract Deliverables
    . Milestones, Scope, Objectives

Stage III: Project Implementation
(Implementation)
   . Coordinating and Communicating Project Activities
  . Classwork and Independent Project Work
   . Teams and Individuals
  . Final Oral and Written Presentations, Evaluation

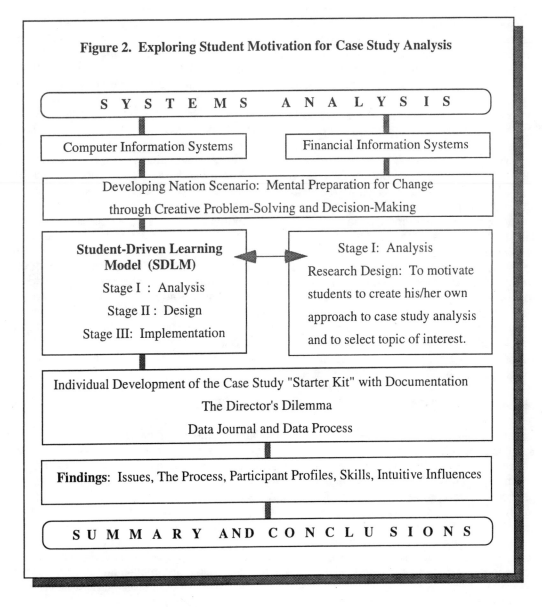

Figure 2. Exploring Student Motivation for Case Study Analysis

SYSTEMS ANALYSIS

Computer Information Systems | Financial Information Systems

Developing Nation Scenario: Mental Preparation for Change through Creative Problem-Solving and Decision-Making

Student-Driven Learning Model (SDLM)

Stage I : Analysis
Stage II : Design
Stage III: Implementation

Stage I: Analysis
Research Design: To motivate students to create his/her own approach to case study analysis and to select topic of interest.

Individual Development of the Case Study "Starter Kit" with Documentation
The Director's Dilemma
Data Journal and Data Process

Findings: Issues, The Process, Participant Profiles, Skills, Intuitive Influences

SUMMARY AND CONCLUSIONS

In order to minimize the expectation gap between instructor and student for case study methods, these factors must be addressed at the outset. In this way, students are given enough notice to determine one's level of conformity to course requirements with criteria different from a traditional course presentation. In addition, the performance criteria should state how they will be measured. Will students be assessed unilaterally by the instructor or will peer group evaluations be included in the measurement scheme?

If the case study methodology includes extensive student team activity, role-playing, and student-driven course requirements, performance measurement problems are exacerbated further. In order to preserve program academic quality [Schaffer, 1992], student participation in determining course requirements has to be supervised carefully. The key concept is to allow full student participation while maintaining high academic standards. High standards implies the need for specific criteria upon which the new performance measures can be based. New performance measures require that the process follows a student-driven learning model, such as the concept depicted in Figure 1.

At a previous WACRA Conference [DeMichiell and Wysocki, 1991], this model was presented as a concept focused on active student participation in the process of case study development and execution. Using the Student-Driven Learning Model (SDLM), students are provided a 'case starter" representing an actual business scenario involving information technology. Subsequently, students collect facts for the case, explore scope, assumptions, and constraints, and conduct the case study analysis for findings, results, and conclusions. The instructor acts more as a facilitator rather than a lecturer and provider of case study information.

The three stage approach of the SDLM suggests that students prepare for change, define and delineate the case study, and finally, implement a team action plan to conduct the project work needed to complete the self-assigned tasks. The major thrust of that presentation was on the overall process and on the creative aspects of student involvement in case study analysis.

In the following year, the creative approach was explored further [Pavlock and DeMichiell, 1992] with emphasis on student motivation (Figure 2). How can students be motivated to be active and reactive, to be both case designers and implementers, and to be team members as well as individualists? The SDLM provided the process which was used by several students in a graduate business administration class to uncover relevant issues in case study analysis of graduate program requirements. Students liked the opportunity to reflect and digress from initial considerations. They appreciated the complexity of dealing with problems with no right or wrong solution. They were concerned about performance measurement, since it appeared to them that the criteria would have to be different for such an approach.

IMPLEMENTING ACCOUNTABILITY PERFORMANCE MEASURES

This presentation addresses phase three of the SDLM, namely implementation. From a student point-of-view this phase has features important for academic survival; typically, most of one's grade is based on output, not only observed throughout the process, but also noted in the format and content of final oral and written reports. Performance measures of accountability should be made known to students at the outset so that the previously noted problematic factors (items a-f) are addressed.

The authors have used this approach with other undergraduate and graduate students at two different institutions of higher education in a variety of business case study settings. The courses have been in the areas of financial management, management of information technology, decision support systems, and computer systems analysis and design. Topics range from general management practice to specific database design. Case study scenarios depict situations which incorporate interdisciplinary, multi-cultural, and collaborative efforts. Although some attention is given initially to economic feasibility concerns, students are required to examine other technical, operational, and socio-humanistic factors in their pursuit of practical solutions.

Such focus is consistent with the need for students to take a more total systems approach to problem-solving and to take managerial control of case study progress from fact-finding to solution. This approach mimics the real world of business and will become even more important in the next decade. Business and industry strategies for the next century [Carlyle, 1991] indicate that lower level managers will be making more and faster decisions for the organization. They have the technology and the expertise needed to assemble and manipulate data for effective and responsive decision-making.

The proposed approach nurtures these attributes by requiring students to collect the right facts for the right reasons and in the right way. If one is to believe predicted mega trends for the next century [Naisbitt, 1990], the individual will be more of an influence on reality by taking a more active role in leading the effort for a better life; thus, students must be allowed to take a more active role in their learning process. In justifying their solutions, results must be presented effectively [Covey 1989]. It is not good enough just to present ideas or to discuss the reasoning behind the results. Students must be convincing (credible) and have pathos (empathy) as well. Although wide latitude is given to students in requirements definition, they are not allowed to escape careful scrutiny of presentation skills in oral and written format. It is suggested that students rate other students as one of the performance measures.

The underlying concept is to allow students to actively engage in planning and executing their work thereby making themselves, collectively and individually, accountable for their actions [Pavlock, 1990]. In essence, the students themselves become the criteria and set the standards of accountability. In implementing this procedure, it was clear that students were somewhat confused by the lack of detailed instructions and factual data on the case study. This approach is in keeping with the concept of investing in small starts [Peters, 1987] and building the case study as the course proceeds.

However, as project work proceeded and it became more clear that *they* would be responsible and accountable for planning, organizing, and conducting *all phases* of the case study, they went to work and conducted the work. Students practice the art of a learning organization, one in which the fifth dimension of total systems thinking [Senge, 1990] paves the way for realizing human potential to create the results they truly desire. A chaotic beginning, which sometimes is professed to be necessary in order to effect change [Peters, 1987], turned into more organized work flow sprinkled with some diversion to areas of particular interest to the team and/or individuals. However, the student-imposed schedule together with its information-sharing nature, quickly moved these digressions back to the mainstream activity of scenario-building [Hickman, 1984]. Visions were defined, opportunities and dangers were identified, key success factors emerged, and major events were planned.

Near the end of the case study, at which time the project work incorporated a heavy commitment of time for all students (completing the work and preparing the final oral and written reports), the accountability performance measures helped to focus them on the right issues. Students were placed on the path to developing a twenty-first century mind [Sinetar, 1991]. Certainly, they could not complain that the measures were too stringent, or unfair. They defined the very criteria on which they would be measured-the accountability standards. They knew them from their inception at the beginning of the case study and kept them in mind throughout the exercise.

RESULTS AND CONCLUSIONS: SOME PERFORMANCE MEASURES

Performance measures for assessing accountability have been derived from several scenarios over the past five years. Previous research efforts have been expanded to focus on student reporting of results during the implementation phase of the student-driven learning model. These outcomes were reported in previous WACRA presentations denoted in the list of references. New results in the form of accountability performance measures during the implementation phase of the process are reported at this time, as follows:
   a. Higher order thinking skills (critical analysis of assumptions, facts, and solutions);
   b. Differentiation of symptoms from causes of case study problems;
   c. Originality of problem-solving approach (team and individual efforts);
   d. Uniqueness and innovative thinking in approach to problem-finding, problem-solving
   e. Application and integration of subject matter expertise to case study methodology;
   f. Organization and planning by student team in conducting all case study activity;
   g. Development of realistic implementation plan with detailed task definition and schedule;
   h. Adherence to instructor-imposed guidelines and standards for quality and quantity;
   i. Justification of proposed solution with assumptions and constraints;
   j. Identification of major issues in total systems view of case study scenario;
   k. Completeness of analysis, findings, conclusions, and recommendations;
   l. Participation in process with emphasis on active as well as reactive student input;
   m. Use of computer-based tools (word processing, financial and presentation graphics);
   n. Presentation of results in oral and written form with consideration given to audience;
   o. Group decision-making effectiveness and efficiency;
   p. Visionary and flexible solution with awareness to change and responsiveness to change;

q. Incorporation of impact of solution on other internal and external elements; and,

r. Individual contributions (time, effort, completeness, accuracy, and responsiveness.

These suggested criteria may not be applicable for all case study scenarios. It is envisioned that the instructor would examine this list in light of the case study environment and objectives. Once the selection is made, perhaps with or by the students depending on the amount of control relinquished to them, the items on the list would be weighted (prioritized). A defined percentage of the student's grade would be governed by the nature of the case study, instructor objectives in presenting the case, student interest and personal schedule, degree of actual business involvement in case study analysis and execution, and any programmatic constraints.

In addition, if the course is team-taught, other scheduling and instructor preferences may introduce conflicts in conducting the case study. The authors have concluded that all of these factors must be considered in the design stages of teaching the course with specific case study methods. Once the audience is known (student academic background and business experience, perhaps through internships or other project courses), one can proceed to examine these performance measures to ensure student accountability. We have discovered that students move from confusion and complexity to organization and synthesis. In the final analysis, their evaluations of the process of determining their own academic fate indicate that it is time-consuming and inefficient, but that it is rewarding. Following graduation, students exposed to this student driven learning experience have taken the time to write of their on-the-job experiences and how the approach better prepared them for work and life.

REFERENCES

Alter, A. E., 'Putting Genius to Work," CIO Magazine (August 1990), Vol 3, No.11, pp.21-27.

Carlyle, R. 'The Tomorrow Organization," Datamation, (February 1, 1991), Vol. 36, No. 3, pp 21-27.

Covey, S. R. The 7 Habits of Highly Effective People (Simon and Schuster, 1989), pp236-260.

DeMichiell, R. and Wysocki, R. 'Facilitating Change with Cases Emphasizing Creativity," in Managing Change with Cases, Simulations and other Interactive Methods, Hans E. Klein, Ed., WACRA, 1991.

Hickman, C. R. and Silva, M. A. Creating Excellence (Signet, 1984), pp168-173.

Naisbitt, J. and Aburdene, P. Mega trends 2000 (Avon, 1990), pp322-335.

Pavlock, E. and DeMichiell, R. 'Uncovering Issues in Case Study Analysis: An Individualized Approach," in Forging New partnerships with Cases, Simulations, and Other Interactive Methods, Hans E. Klein, Ed., WACRA, 1992.

Pavlock, E., Sato, F. and Yardley, J. 'Accountability Standards for Corporate Reporting," Journal of Accountancy, May 1990.

Peters, T. Thriving on Chaos (Harper and Rowe, 1987), pp240-266.

Schaffer, R. 'The Quality Quagmire," CIO, Vol. 6, No. 3, pp28-31.

Senge, P. M. The Fifth Discipline (Doubleday, 1990), pp1-26.

Sinetar, M. Developing a 21st Century Mind (Villard, 1991).

THE APPLICATION OF CASE STUDY METHODOLOGY
TO GRADUATE BUSINESS EDUCATION

Peter W. Olson
Hartford Graduate Center
HARTFORD, CONNECTICUT, U.S.A.

Abstract

In universities, Total Quality Management (TQM) is learned through management case studies, however many of the cases, companies and situations are outdated. Therefore, it would seem appropriate to introduce a new methodology, *live case studies*. *A live case* study allows students to examine real companies with real problems in real time. The ability to apply learned skills during their educational experience is essential in a competitive world. When students learn how to define issues, they begin to determine what is critical. The live case studies and their ensuing discussions allows them to further examine the ever changing management process.

INTRODUCTION

One of the greatest challenges in education is to discover what it is that keeps alive in some students the natural spark of curiosity, eagerness, hunger for life and experience, and how we may rekindle that spark when it flickers out. If we ever solve that problem, we will be at the threshold of a *new* era, not only in education but also in human experience [Gardner, 1968].

Traditionally, there have been three ingredients that constitute the elements of the case method: the case report, the case analysis, and the case discussion. Every form of case method necessarily uses all three ingredients.

The outstanding applications of case method have been the Harvard Method, the Wharton School "Live" Case Method: Then and Now, and the Centre Europeen D'Education Permanente. The Harvard Method of reporting actual situations and analyzing case reports is the oldest and most generally respected form. To many people, it is the case method. Originated in the 1880s by Christopher Langdell at the Harvard Law School, this nondirective way of helping students to think for themselves slowly won acceptance in law, medicine, business administration, and social work.

A major aim of the Harvard method has always been showing students how to learn by independent thinking - discerning in the "ever-tangled skein of human affairs" principles and ideas which have lasting validity and general applicability [Redlick, 1914].

In the Harvard method, professors function as a catalyst: they assign cases for study and provide a permissive environment for group discussion. They do not attempt to cover a topic by "telling them" (the lecture method). Instead, they help the students to discover for themselves the facts and ideas - displayed in case reports - which are most meaningful to them.

The role of the Harvard professor, in such a course, has been described operationally by Glover and Hower: "Let me summarize what I think I heard you say, to see if I caught what you were driving at"... "Would you mind elaborating on that? I'm not sure it is clear to most of us."..."Is this what you mean?"..."I think I see your point, but I am having difficulty relating it to your previous interpretations (or to what Mr.--- has just said, or to the situation as developed in the discussion so far)" [Glover and Hower, 1953].

Another hallmark of the Harvard method is the completeness of their published case reports. For case writing, few institutions can equal the research division of the Harvard Business School. Members of its staff spend years in the field before writing case reports which faithfully describe actual situations. However, to some

68

students the Harvard reports have seemed overly detailed and time-consuming to read as preparation for case discussion.

The Wharton School "Live" case method was originated by Walter B. Murphy and instituted, in the early 1950s, at the Wharton School of Finance and Commerce. In its original form, each case was presented to students by an executive from an organization where the case situation had developed and where the difficulty recently had been, or currently was being, tackled. The immediacy of that approach was a convincing way to give what is nowadays referred to as "credibility" to the facts reported and immediacy to the issues, which students were invited to analyze and discuss.

The procedure for study was as follows: (1) a brief written statement of an actual difficulty was given to students the day before the first classroom session at which (2) an executive presented the case orally, allowing most of the hour for questions. (3) Next, students met informally, in small groups, and each student wrote a brief analysis of the problem, adding his or her own solution and summarizing the report in a one-page letter to the executive. (4) At the second meeting of the whole class a student led the discussion. The professor would then select ten reports which he considered as the best and forwarded them to the executive. (5) The executive studied those reports, added comments, and returned the material to the professor before meeting again with the whole class. (6) At this final meeting, the executive told the students about the historical solution to the problem, and commented on discussion of solutions by management and by students.

Over the years that approach has been considerably modified. In fact, the Wharton School has dropped the "live" part of the case method, however the authenticity of cases studied has been retained and the vitality of the approach has, in at least one course, been enhanced. These statements about current procedure were documented in a letter from Leonard Rico, Wharton School of the University of Pennsylvania. Here are the salient points:

"We emphasized exposure to the real world problems, doing this in several ways. Guest lecturers from area firms, provide students with up to date information from their own companies. And students do research in organizations. Numerous variations of what was formerly called the 'live' case method are applied by instructors in various Wharton disciplines.

In my own courses I use the Incident Process and the Harvard case method to bring reality into the classroom. I also use project teams to evaluate problems of human resources in area firms. Teams act as consultants on problems defined by executives. They then make oral reports to the class and to company representative, who evaluate these oral reports. Some firms also have teams report to representatives of upper management. Comments and suggestions on oral reports are incorporated into final, written reports which students submit at the end of the semester."

The Centre European D'Education Permanente (CEDEP), founded in 1971, is located in Fontainebleau, France, adjacent to the European Institute of Business Administration (INSTEAD). It constitutes a major development in the training of European executives. The principal teaching methods are participative, the Harvard case method, various forms of group dynamics and micro-computer assisted teaming.

The most innovative feature of this international Center is its associative and cooperative character. Originally founded by six major European industrial concerns, it now has a membership of 20 different companies from industry and service who actually manage the Center in collaboration with a staff of professional teachers, mostly from INSTEAD.

The major educational program of CEDEP is the General Management course: a 12 week program divided into six training periods of two weeks each with an interval of three months during which participating managers return to work in their respective companies. During the three month recesses, managers keep in touch with one another and with CEDEP staff members, INSTEAD provides backup services, such as library and duplicating facilities.

The major objective of CEDEP is rapidly to create a "critical mass" of executives who have followed the same type of management development program. Within each member company, this will stimulate the development of a coherent "business culture" which will permeate the organization with managerial values, principles, and styles that have been approved by member companies.

This working with, and in, current situations is well designed to foster continuing self-education by executives. The problem still remains, how to motivate students to learn and apply what they have learned in the real world of business management? Though, these three outstanding examples of differing applications show a few ways in which case material can be presented, analyzed, and discussed, where do we go from here? The next logical step would be to have students work with executives in real companies, with real problems and do it in real time. This application of the live case study methodology will be discussed in the next section.

INTRODUCTION OF THE "LIVE" CASE STUDY METHODOLOGY

Creating quality has become an essential factor of many successful global businesses, however business schools have not yet adopted the concept totally. We can no longer ignore the continuous improvement process, the American Assembly of Collegiate Schools of Business (AACSB) has required all business schools seeking accreditation during 1993-94 to demonstrate that they have implemented continuous improvement concepts to improve critical processes related to curricula, faculty and administration. AACSB has taken a bold step towards the new paradigm, quality education. This paradigm shift will continue through the 1990s into the new century, those universities that do not make the shift to the quality movement will be left behind.

In 1950, Dr. W. Edwards Deming introduced the *Total Quality Management* (TQM) process to the Japanese manufacturers, who embraced the process and refined it. The Japanese presently lead the world in several industries and have achieved their dream of financial stability. The Japanese learned a valuable lesson from Dr. Deming, that you need to apply what you have learned to current situations in a timely manner. In 1989, Deming said, "Transformation is required in government, industry, and education... Transformation requires [us] to move out of the present state. The transformation required will be a change state, metamorphosis, not mere patchwork on the present system ... We must of course solve problems and stamp out fires as they occur, but these activities do not change the system" [Deming, 1988].

Deming is correct and the proof is the outstanding performance of the Japanese companies in the global marketplace. In applying, his TQM process to education, we have an opportunity to create a quality atmosphere, and an environment that allows our students to experiment, develop and learn.

The Japanese word, *Kaizen*, continuous improvement, has application both in and outside the classroom. Educators, who have become aware of the TQM process, may have a tendency to expect immediate results after application, however we have learned that the TQM process in industry and education is a slow, methodical process, that requires the participants to change both their habits and their mind sets. It is with this in mind that the live case study was started. The students needed to apply what they had learned in the classroom in the real world. The concept of a live case study done by students for real business was immediately accepted by the local area executives. The AACSB requirement of instituting quality processes was being met.

The next section will discuss the case study methodology utilized by the students and the professor.

STEPS IN THE CASE METHODOLOGY

STEP 1: PREPARATION

Students began by reading all the literature that the company produced for customers, internal use and for information by other interested parties. Once all the literature was digested by the students, the professor began to discuss the case study in the classroom. If there was interest by a majority of the students the professor would have the students begin to examine the company in greater detail through the library resources, other industry experts, competitor analysis, periodicals, and any other pertinent information sources.

STEP 2: ORGANIZING THE EFFORT

Once the students have exhausted all the available sources of information concerning the company, it was time to organize the effort. However, before the students break into groups and begin their discussions, it is important to verify the information that they have collected. At this time, an executive from the case company should visit the class and fill in any gaps in their research.

The students now break into groups to discuss the issues that the company is facing, to identify the key problem/issue that needs to be addressed. During this step, students discuss what needs to be addressed and what tactics and strategies they will employ. Lively discussion of short-term and long-term strategies are initiated by the professor to alert the students of all the options that are available to them.

During this step, many students have the desire to solve all the company's problems and/or issues. There is a danger that should be noted here, students and the professor need to focus their efforts, or the case study will not be manageable. A good tactic at this point is to have each team of students prepare a summary of the facts and the strategies they would like to employ. Each summary should be distributed to all the teams for review and discussion.

STEP 3: FORMULATE THE KEY STRATEGIES

After a discussion of the facts and strategies, the students now can sort out the pertinent facts and focus their attentions on the key issues. It is recommended that the students break the issues into short term and long term categories. It is important that the students and the professor agree on what are the key issues, as well as what are short and long terms.

Once strategies have been summarized and written, it is appropriate to invite an executive of the case company to listen to the summarized reports. After the oral reports have been given the executive may choose to engage in open discussions with the students, further clarifying issues and strategies that are appropriate for the company. The executive should receive all summarized reports for review and to return with appropriate comments.

STEP 4: WORKING WITH THE CASE COMPANY AT THE SITE

All the above is not valid until the students can bridge this academic exercise to the real world. Small groups of students (no larger than four) begin to visit the company on a regular basis. If the students are to benefit from this exercise they must take an active role in the implementation of the strategy they designed. It is imperative that we develop critical thinking in our students, however we must be wary of motivating our students to think critically to the point where we are encouraging expectations that can not possibly be met. MacKenzie [1978] views one of the central tasks of educators as that of inculcating an awareness of the risks accompanying the activity of criticizing and challenging established values and practices. In other words, the students will learn that many of their strategies and recommendations will be met with resistance and hostility.

Deming states that, one-third of the people will become apathetic and disinterested, another third will be on the fence undecided, and the remaining third will actively engage in the process [Walton, 1986]. It is this one-third of interested participants in the company that will convince the other two-thirds to engage in the new opportunities.

This step may require additional time depending on the resistance of the company employees to working with students and/or outsiders. In every relationship a certain amount of time must pass to establish trust and credibility. At this point, the professor can become an important liaison between the student teams and the company.

Each student team needs to coordinate through the professor and a company representative, so all the efforts are directed and focused on meeting the strategies and addressing the key issues. It is important to note that coordination of all the teams is essential to a successful learning experience for the students.

STEP 5: MAKING THE FINAL PRESENTATION

After the students have completed their work at the company, the students, the professor and interested executives need to schedule a meeting where the students will summarize their findings and the results of their efforts. A written summary should be submitted to the company for their review and comments.

The written report format should include a brief historical background of the company and the industry, discussion of the key facts and the problem/issue, discussion of strategies and tactics, the selection and implementation of the strategy and tactics, monitoring and measurement of the implementation process, and a conclusion of actions taken, recommendations (short and long term) and future action plans for the company.

THE ACTUAL CASE STUDY

The study examines the TQM process in a real company, Praxair Surface Technologies, Inc. (PSTI) located in North Haven, Connecticut. PSTI applies hard, wear resistant thermal spray coatings to various industrial components in order to extend their useful life. Applications include components of gas turbine aircraft engines and airframes, steel rolls, textile equipment, petroleum and food industry equipment. PSTI has twenty-two international facilities located strategically throughout the world. The North Haven facility, built in 1961, primarily serves the original equipment manufacturer (OEM) aviation businesses in North America. The facility has 98 employees in production, engineering and sales.

PSTI was previously known as Union Carbide Coatings Service Corporation, a wholly owned subsidiary of the Union Carbide Corporation. In July, 1992, Union Carbide Corporation spun off the company to form the present PSTI. The company's annual sales worldwide in 1991 were $2.5 billion, of which $1 billion in sales was coating services.

In the late 1980s, the OEM aviation business became increasingly competitive, causing profit margins to shrink and customers to place more and more emphasis on cost, quality and delivery. A significant change needed to occur in the North Haven facility despite all of the current quality efforts, i.e. quality circles, quality improvement teams.

In 1987, a group of students became involved in the PSTI facility on a consulting basis. They found a receptive company who was in the middle of implementing the concepts of World Class Manufacturing (WCM). The PSTI strategy was based on five components: Just-In-Time (JIT), Total Quality Control, Total Preventive Maintenance, Simplicity, and Employee Involvement.

The student teams decided to examine the five strategies of World Class Manufacturing (WCM). In 1988 the management of PSTI implemented the five strategies and in early 1989, the JIT experiments were launched throughout the facility. The early successes led to better quality, cost and delivery. The students began working with production workers on the floor with great success. The idea of JIT lines gained popularity quickly and became a part of the manufacturing process. Teams of workers and students concentrated on particular job types, self-scheduling, daily and weekly meetings addressing quality problems and the continuous improvement process.

In the quality area, the "Jobs Done Right the First Time" indicator went from 96.8 percent in 1988 to 99 percent in 1992 [Adams, 1992]. The monthly "Non-conformance Costs" averaged $25,000 in 1988 and was reduced to $5,000 in 1992 [Adams, 1992]. The "Cost of Unquality" indicator, which is the ratio of monthly Non-conformance Costs divided by the Total Costs, fell from 4.8 percent in 1988 to 2.1 percent in 1992. On time delivery performance which had a dismal record of 68 percent in 1988 averaged 95 percent in 1992. Accepted expedited deliveries, those orders delivered earlier than the quoted turn time, went from 85 percent in 1990 to 100 percent in 1992.

Customers noticed the difference and praised the North Haven plant through thank you notes, telephone calls, better supplier ratings, preferred supplier status and various awards. The feedback was gratifying for both the students and the employees. In some cases, customers have formed long term partnerships with PSTI because of the dramatic improvements in quality, cost reductions and better deliveries.

The key problem that the students teams focused on was how does PSTI differentiate themselves in a highly competitive and saturated marketplace. Student teams examined the current market situation and found that PSTI had a current business mix of 88 percent OEM aircraft, 10 percent general engineering management (GEM), and 2 percent overhaul (O/H) aircraft components. The students recommended from their research that the current marketing mix would change due to the downturn in the aerospace industry until 1995. Travel growth rates for airlines would grow at a modest 5.2 percent for non-US airlines and 4.5 percent for US airlines through 2010. Long-term market predictions project the need for more than 6,000 new jets for 1992-2000 and for more than 32,000 jet engines during the next 20 years.

PSTI would need to redirect their mix to 69 percent OEM, 28 percent GEM and 3 percent O/H. The students also recommended that PSTI should ask customers to predict purchase orders for a minimum of a year. The lag in business slow down is typically 12 to 18 months behind. Likewise, business growth in the economy often lags the same period for PSTI. One explanation follows the logic that thermal spray coatings are the last operation a part undergoes and that time period can be 12 to 18 months.

Another student team examined the competition and determined that PSTI does not have the competitors on a global scale, rather the competition focuses on particular market segments. For example, OEM applications usually have one set of competitors totally different from the GEM applications.

For the OEM applications the competition is limited to qualified suppliers of the customers. Qualification often requires extensive engineering, testing and experience in the area. The competition mainly comes from the following companies: General Plasma, Inc., Sermatch, Klock, Plasma Tech Inc., and Cincinnati Thermal Spray. Unfortunately, neither the students nor the marketing executives could gather detailed information on these competitors, so students relied on other industrial experts for secondary information. This was the first time that PSTI had any current information on their competition. This proved to be a major differentiation for PSTI.

Additionally, many customers have internal thermal spray coating operations and are considered part of the competition. Due to cost reduction programs that have been enacted by customers, many have found it more efficient to have their own operation, however their costs have increased. Some of the competition is *buying* market share by cutting prices, so cost reductions are essential for PSTI to remain competitive in the industry. Companies like Sermatech and General Plasma are aggressively capturing market share with this tactic. The students agreed that this is not a healthy tactic and has long term disadvantages.

Another student team examined the perceptions customers have of PSTI and their competitors, especially in the OEM market. The measures of price, quality and delivery are continuously compared and contracts are awarded based on the customer's perceptions. Through a student survey of the customers, we learned that PSTI had a high price, but quality was better than most of the competition. However, PSTI did lose contracts strictly due to the higher price.

In July, 1992, a marketing study was completed identifying the strengths, weaknesses, opportunities and threats (SWOT) facing PSTI. From this study, a new market strategy was recommended to develop the maximum market differentiation. Differentiation is defined as the act of designing a set of meaningful differences to distinguish the company's offer from that of the competition's. In many cases, PSTI has differentiated themselves from their competitors but has failed to effectively promote this in the marketplace.

The students focused on "delivered value," and why customers will purchase from the firm that offers the highest delivered value. Delivered value is the difference between total customer value and total customer price. When two suppliers are seen as equal, one supplier can improve its offer in three ways. First, the supplier can augment total customer value by improving the product, services, personnel and/or image benefits. Second, a supplier can reduce the buyer's non-monetary costs by simplifying the buyer's time, energy and psychic costs. Third, the supplier can reduce its monetary price to the buyer.

Delivered value can be seen as the difference or ratio between total customer value and total customer price or the profit to the customer. A difference worth establishing to the extent that it satisfies the following criteria [Kolter, 1991]:

Important: The difference delivers a highly valued benefit to a sufficient number of buyers.

Distinction: The difference either is not offered by others or is offered in a more distinctive way by the company.

Superior: The difference is superior to other ways to obtain the same benefit.

Communicable: The difference is communicable and visible to buyers.

Preemptive.- The difference can not be easily copied by customers.

Affordable.- The buyer can afford to pay for the difference.

Profitable: The company will find it profitable to introduce the difference.

After several classes had completed the information search, collection of data, the analysis, the field work and the summarization, the students prepared the written report for PSTI executives. The students selected the *right* differences to pursue, since PSTI needs to establish their position in the marketplace. PSTI's image has been one of the most expensive suppliers in the market, however they are also one of the top performers in quality standards and on-time delivery performance. The students strongly recommended that PSTI concentrate on customer delivered value, the extra costs associated with purchases of equipment, training staff and employees, the time to get to the point of equivalent expertise, the perception of total customer price rises substantially thereby reducing total customer delivered value!

Dynamic positioning is the act of designing a company's offer so that it occupies a distinct and valued place in the target of the customer's mind. PSTI's typical positions to promote are: best quality, best service, lowest price, and most advanced technology.

For the appropriate competitive advantage selection, it is necessary to compare with the major competitor's standings on each identified competitive advantage position. The chart above suggests that since service is important to the customers, the company can afford to improve its service and do it fast; and the competitor probably can not catch up.

METHOD FOR COMPETITIVE ADVANTAGE SELECTION

Competitive Advantage	Company Standing	Competitor Standing	Importance of Improving Standing	Affordability and Speed	Competitor's Ability to Improve Standing	Recommended Action
Technology	8	8	L	L	M	Hold
Cost	6	8	H	M	M	Monitor
Quality	8	6	L	L	H	Monitor
Service	4	5	H	H	L	Invest

1=lowest, 8=highest L=Low, H=High

The future considerations that the students had for PSTI were to change the top-down management style to a bottom-up style using more tactics-driven strategies rather than trying to enter markets or implement poor strategies. To identify a tactic that will work, it is necessary to identify the company's strengths and quantify customer's wants. Students had completed a SWOT analysis and determined PSTI's strengths. Diversification will not be cost effective for PSTI, they need to focus their activities in key areas, i.e. OEM.

CONCLUSION

The application of the *live* case study methodology allowed the students to examine tasks rather than just reviewing the results of the task completed, it became apparent that this would be advantageous. Since most companies are *results oriented* and not process oriented, we would have to continuously monitor the results to give the company case feedback. The students literally became process consultants working with the company, assisting in the planning process, developing a marketing strategy for product introduction, analyzing the manufacturing flow through the facility, and critiquing the paperwork flow through the office. With the help of computer software packages, i.e. Lotus spreadsheet, the students were able to apply what they had recently learned in the classroom in the real world. Furthermore, students began to apply these new techniques at their own workplaces.

During the classroom discussions of the case study, students related issues to problems they experienced at work, and then return to then explore and develop the root causes for each issue. This application to an actual situation has assisted students in becoming critical thinkers, as well as critical decision makers. Many professors believe that the learning objectives of the students have been met after some discussion of a textbook case. The TQM process requires further examination by both professor and student. Critical thinking can only be accomplished with critical comparisons, which increases the student's critical awareness [Brookfield, 1989]. The comparison of the theory and the practical has proven most beneficial to the student's learning experience.

"A global marketplace, increased competition, and a continuing reorganization of work are the new realities facing today's organizations and their employees. To compete, nothing short of world-class performance will do. The limited demands on workers to know only one narrow repetitive job no longer apply. Now workers from the factory floor to the customer service companies, the choice is growing increasingly stark; go for world-class performance or be left behind" [Meister, 1994]. A major paradigm shift is occurring in education, that will change how we educate our executives in the future. The old paradigm was to train employees in the standard operating procedures of the organization and they will be productive. The new paradigm is that an organization's work force is its primary resource for creating value. Work force-based competitive advantage is proving more enduring than technology-based competitiveness, which quickly slips away as new technologies become equally accessible to companies on a global basis [Porter, 1985]. Therefore, if an organization is to survive all efforts have to be focused on work force excellence, from hiring to training/education practices. It is only through these efforts that excellence can be achieved and maintained.

This case methodology has presented another opportunity to academia, that of strategic alliances between universities and the private sector. This new strategic alliance has produced some interesting results that has added to the classroom experience. (1) Company executives are taking an active role in the development of the student (employees) learning objectives. We have company representatives regularly visiting the classrooms discussing their experiences and working with our students. The linkage of the university and the business community can become a strategic alliance, if each communicates their goals and objectives to the other in a clear and concise manner [Olson, 1993]. (2) Students are applying what they have learned in the classroom in the workplace. Deming's Reaction Model shows a significant correlation between newly acquired skills and job satisfaction. As skills are utilized by the learner at the workplace, the learners job satisfaction increases proportionally. Quality will be improved only when our attitudes are improved, which is a function of our self esteem and worth coupled with our utilization of our skills. (3) Informal surveys of student's expectations and productivity levels at their workplaces have risen sharply since the conception of this case study methodology. Though these surveys are not conclusive, there is a positive relationship between what a student learns in the classroom and what the student learns in the field.

Many university quality systems advocate the improvement of education, but fail to provide a methodology that insures that the student has a quality experience, that will translate into higher productivity levels in the workplace. Quality is an attitude, a philosophy, a process that never ends. Just as some products have a shelf-life, knowledge also has a shelf-life. In order for education to be an effective learning experience students must engage in activities that they will face in the real world, they must be faced with deadlines, problems, and crises. Knowledge actually should be referred to as, "JIT Knowledge," following the TQM process terminology. The more real world activities education can engage in, the better the student's learning experience and ultimately, the better the business executive's performance. Education needs to foster a continuous improvement attitude in the curricula, so total quality education becomes the rule, not the exception.

REFERENCES

Adams, David, Interview at Praxair Surface Technologies, Inc. (1992).

Brookfield, Stephen D. Developing Critical Thinkers: Challenging Adults to Explore Alternative Ways of Thinking and Acting. (Jossey Bass, 1989).

Deming, W. Edwards. Deming at Work in Management (Doubleday and Company, 1988).

Dolter, Philip, Marketing Management: Analysis, Planning, Implementation and Control. (Prentice Hall, 1991).

Gardner, John W. No Easy Victories (Harper & Row, 1968).

Glover, John D. and Ralph M. Hower, "Some Comments on Teaching by the Case Method," The Case Method of Teaching Human Relations and Administration: An Interim Statement (Harvard University Press, 1953).

Meister, Jeanne C. Corporate Quality Universities: Lessons in Building a World-Class Work Force. (Irwin, 1994).

Porter, Michael E. Competitive Advantage: Creating and Sustaining Superior Performance. (Free Press, 1985).

Olson, Peter, "Another Way to Make your Mark," The Hartford Business Journal. (1993).

Redlich, Josef, "the Common Law and the Case Method in American University Law Schools," Carnegie Foundation for the Advancement of Teaching, Bulletin No. 8 ((1914), p.12.

Walton, M. The Deming Management Method. (Putnam, 1986).

THE EXPORT FEASIBILITY ANALYSIS FOR SMALL BUSINESSES: A LIVE-CASE FORMAT THAT ADDRESSES THE EMERGING BREED OF INTERNATIONAL COMPETITOR

Nicholas C. Williamson, Stephen R. Lucas & Benton E. Miles
The University of North Carolina at Greensboro
GREENSBORO, NORTH CAROLINA, U.S.A.

Abstract

The live-case, export feasibility analysis format has application in a variety of settings in university classrooms as well as in company settings not having access to universities; it is easily transportable and applicable in any country. The export feasibility analysis focuses on small businesses and international settings. Students are engaged in practical study of international consequences for a real-life firm. The firm benefits by having an exhaustive study conducted that addresses the firm's export potential in a target foreign country. Each project team conducts a feasibility analysis and plans how the company can become one of the emerging breed of international competitors in the targeted country.

INTRODUCTION

This paper presents a concept referred to as an export feasibility analysis for small businesses. Historically, U.S. small business owners were reluctant to view themselves as active players in international markets. For many of these owners, crossing state lines for commerce purposes seemed like a formidable task. To consider international business opportunities was beyond their consideration. This paper serves as a way that universities can assist small businesses in overcoming their reluctance to participate in international opportunities.

The semester-long export feasibility analysis discussed in this paper is a means by which the course in international marketing can come "alive" for the students in the class. The obvious benefit of the analysis is two-fold: (1) the students in the class are engaged in a practical study of international consequences for a real-life firm that takes them beyond the classroom and into the companies in their geographical region and, thus, the students are confronted with real managers, CEOs, etc., their products/services, and their problems, and (2) the firm is benefitted by having an exhaustive study conducted for them that addresses the export potential for their firm in a targeted country and allows them to engage in dialogue with university students. The process enriches both parties.

The complexity of operating in foreign markets, whether it be international sourcing, selling products or services, or manufacturing, is formidable. However, the opportunities to discover and function in new market settings is reason enough for companies to explore selected foreign countries and their potential for enhancing the company's profit picture.

The challenge for the professor of record is to find a way to make the course come alive so that students will be involved and, yet, will assure that course objectives will be met. Thus, an export feasibility analysis was created to bring real-life situations into the classroom and cause students to be exposed to marketers with export potential in a very personal way by advising them based on an information search using the vast wealth of indexes and statistical compilations available to the public today.

The export feasibility analysis for small businesses is transportable; that is, it can be used in classrooms (or indeed in company settings not having access to universities) throughout the world. The learning situation presented by this "live-case" medium is extremely beneficial to the student and the firm. University goodwill is enhanced within the business community, student self-confidence is heightened, and student resumes are enriched.

RATIONALE AND OBJECTIVES FOR THE PROJECT

The course project is positioned on these two foundations: (1) Global marketing expanded rapidly in the 1980s, and that growth can be expected to extend into the next century, and (2) Marketers in all industrialized countries will have to re-think how they will act toward the new, emerging breed of export competitor.

The use of the export feasibility analysis is applicable to any country in the world. It is not just a matter of the U.S. marketer looking at foreign markets; it is also a matter of foreign marketers looking at the U.S. market and other markets that can be identified through an export feasibility analysis as a viable market.

Objectives of the export feasibility analysis for small businesses are several:

1. to understand the movement toward a global economy and the interdependency of the various countries,
2. to delineate the dimensions of the various international markets,
3. to identify those companies within the immediate regional, geographical area that can participate in an export feasibility analysis, and
4. to determine the degree of operation within foreign markets by firms in the region.

AN ANNOTATION OUTLINE OF THE EXPORT FEASIBILITY PROJECT

An annotated outline with moderate detail of the export feasibility analysis project is provided below. Of vital importance in the successful completion of this ambitious project is the access to secondary sources of information most commonly located in the university library. Exhibit 1 provides a listing of the information sources that are considered appropriate for use in this project.

EXHIBIT I
SOURCES OF INFORMATION

DICTIONARIES
> The International Business Dictionary and Reference
> Encyclopedia of International Commerce
> Dictionary of Business and Management

COMPANY AND INDUSTRY INFORMATION
> American Export Register. New York: Thomas International Publications. Annual. Information on firms, buying agents, and governments throughout the world for selecting American materials, products, or services.
> Hoover's Handbook of World Business. Austin, TX: The Reference Press, 1991. One page profiles of countries and international corporations.
> Bergano's Register of International Importers. Fairfield, CT: Bergano Book Co., 1992. Contacts for direct exporting arranged by country with a product categories index.
> Directory of Leading U.S. Export Management Companies. 3rd ed. Fairfield, CT: Bergano Book Co., 1991. An export management company provides a full range of export services.

TRADE INFORMATION
> National Trade Database (NTDB).

FOREIGN COUNTRY INFORMATION
> Directory of European Business. London: Bowker-Saur Ltd., 1992. Includes information relating to the operating environment in the 35 countries covered. Details of the top 4,000 leading business and government organizations.
> Europa Year Book. London: Europa Publications. 2 volumes. Annual. Data provided on each country includes: recent history, economic affairs, basic economic statistics, constitution, government, political parties, diplomatic representation, religion, public holidays. Also lists leading newspapers, periodicals, publishers, radio and TV, banks, insurance companies, trade and industrial organizations, railroads,

shipping firms, tour organizations.

Foreign Economic Trends. U.S. International Trade Administration, Dept. of Commerce. Washington D. C.: U.S. Govt. Printing Office. Brief reports for over 100 countries, covering the current economic situation, trends, 1 and their implications for U.S. businesses operating overseas.

Overseas Business Reports. U.S. International Trade Administration, Dept. of Commerce. Washington D.C.: U.S. Govt. Printing Office. Reports on over 100 countries containing brief information on industry trends in the country, foreign trade outlook, transportation, and utilities, distribution, and sales channels, advertising and research, banks and credit, trade regulations, guidance for business travelers, sources of economic and commercial information, market profiles.

Background Notes. U.S. Department of State. Bureau of Public Affairs. Office of Public Communication. Washington D.C.: U.S. Govt. Printing Office. 2 volumes. Pamphlets featuring information about a country's people, land, history, government, political conditions, economy, and foreign affairs.

Demographic Yearbook. New York: United Nations. Statistics covering population, births, deaths, life expectancy, marriages, divorces for about 250 countries.

Statistical Yearbook. New York: United Nations. Annual. Sections cover: Population, manpower, agriculture, forestry, fishing, industrial production.

Exporter's Encyclopedia. Dun's Marketing Services. Annual with updates. Importing, exporting, travel, communications, and research information for approximately 170 world markets.

Importers Manual USA. San Rafael, CA: World Trade Press, 1993. The single-source reference encyclopedia for importing to the United States.

Direction of Trade Statistics Yearbook. Washington, D.C.: International Monetary Fund, Annual totals for value of exports and imports in U.S. dollars and arranged by country.

International Trade Statistics Yearbook. New York: United Nations. v. 1: Trade by country. v. 2: Trade by commodity.

Africa South of the Sahara. London: Europa Publications Limited. Annual. Essays on regional issues followed by surveys of individual countries. Includes statistical summaries.

Encyclopedia of the Third World. New York: Facts on File, 1992. Country summaries, including statistical tables and a bibliography for each nation.

Far East and Australia. London: Europa Publications Limited. Annual. Essays on significant regional issues followed by country surveys. Includes statistical summaries.

U.S. - East European Trade Directory. Chicago: Probus Publishing Company, 1991. Reference for conducting business in Poland, Hungary, Czechoslovakia, Bulgaria, Yugoslavia, Romania, Albania. Also includes relevant American addresses.

U.S. - Soviet Trade Directory. Chicago: Probus Publishing Company, 1991. Lists of addresses, both Soviet and American, arranged in broad topical categories.

ECONOMIC INFORMATION

Survey of Current Business. U.S. Dept. of Commerce. Washington, D.C.: Govt. Printing Office Monthly.

World Economic and Business Review. Cambridge, MA: Basil Blackwell. Annual. Country business summaries emphasizing important economic and political events of the year. Extensive statistical information.

World Economic Outlook. Washington, D.C.: International Monetary Fund. Annual.

INDEXES

Public Affairs Information Service Bulletin.

Area Handbook Series. This is a series of books targeting different countries.

The skeletal outline for export feasibility analysis for small businesses is as follows:

I. Situation Analysis
A. Description of the Company
　　1. History
　　　　The student team is to provide a brief description of the company and it is discussed in the first meeting with company representatives and the students. The company information is obtained through the prime candidate. The prime candidate is the head of exporting; if none exists then the head of marketing will be the contact. The students will then familiarize the class in a one- to two-minute

presentation.

2. Size

The team provides a brief description of the company in regard to revenue.

3. Product Lines

A general description is required providing information as to what the client firm produces and sells.

4. Current Domestic Market Area

This is the geographic area where the company presently sells its products.

B. Management's Propensity to Devote Resources to International Markets

1. The term, production resources, refers to the manufacturing capacity of the company. The ideal company for an export feasibility analysis is one who has at least 20 percent unused production capacity. This type of company is relatively more hungry for new ideas and more receptive to new ideas in regard to how to use the capacity profitability.

2. Marketing Resources

This portion of the project deals with the propensity of the company to devote salespeople to the marketing opportunity which the student group identifies.

C. Production Capacity, Unused

One looks at how much production would be created if the company worked full time without adding fixed costs under the current scenario. (For example, determine hours/days mandatory vacations and people working less than full time; then subtract from the ideal, the current production level being realized; next, divide the difference by the ideal that was formerly computed and that will equal the unused production capacity percentage.) The best scenario is usually a 20 to 40 percent unused production capacity. If the company's average profit is one percent of average sales, that is $100,000 in profits before taxes on five million dollars in sales. If gross margin is 50%, a ten percent increase in sales will generate two hundred and fifty thousand dollars in extra gross margin dollars, thus, greatly increasing profits before taxes. A fairly small increase in sales will increase the profit line significantly.

Those companies in the 5 to 15 million dollar sales bracket are likely candidates for this kind of study. Whereas companies that have below five million sales are too stretched resource-wise to offer the students any help (personnel to advise them). Usually a minimum of 15 hours of key staff time are required. If one is over 15 million dollars in sales, the likelihood is that the company is already exporting; this is generally true because the company in this category will have the specialists that are necessary to do the detail work needed for an export feasibility analysis. Thus, in those situations, no student teams are needed.

II. Foreign Market Analysis and Selection

A. Choice of and Rationale for Target Market

The choice of a target market usually comes from a foreign market considered by the company. If no foreign market is selected by the company, the students will use the National Trade Data Bank (NTDB). The NTDB shows where the largest markets are for similar products exported by U.S. manufacturers. The theory underlying the NTDB search is for one to target a market(s) that is already developed for the company by existing exporters. Further, the client company is advised to go in with their product(s) as a "me-too" product. This approach is not pioneering. The pioneer very seldom makes money. The "me-tooers" enter without market development costs and, as a consequence, can charge a lower price than the early companies.

B. Market Potential

The potential market is chosen by looking at the magnitude of revenues generated by U.S. exporters who export products similar to that market. Alternatively, one secures information on market size from the consulate for the country (consulates to the U.S. are located in Washington, DC). The university or city library serves as the source for locating exporters; the document's title is, "Exporters Encyclopedia of Overseas Business Reports," filed in the U.S. Government Document Section.

C. Restrictions on Product Entering the Chosen Market

Information pertaining to the question of possible restrictions obtained from the "Exporters Encyclopedia of Overseas Business Reports" and from interview with freight forwarders listed in the yellow pages of one's local telephone directory (freight forwarders are companies which consolidate the shipments of many small-scale exporters so as to achieve a low cost in transportation).

D. Identification of Factors that will "drive" Demand in the Chosen Foreign Market

One tries to link demand to the product with variables expressed in a country's demographic profile; for instance, the demand for disposable diapers in a country is likely driven by the number of live births in a country.

E. Analysis of the Competition

Typically, knowledge of foreign competitors is the most difficult information to come by in the export feasibility project. Even in the U.S., it is troublesome. Again, the consulate and the embassy will be helpful.

III. Marketing Strategy

The student team is challenged to condense the strategy into a 100-word statement. If a student team cannot summarize the marketing strategy in 100 words or less, it is viewed that the team has obviously not become involved in the core of the project to a sufficient degree. The team must have an in-depth knowledge in order to render an explanation of a complex assignment in a simplistic manner.

IV. Marketing Mix

A. Product

1. Product Specification Changes

The greatest incident of product specification changes occurs in the marketing of consumer package goods to lesser-developed countries. Such changes are enacted in 90% of the export transactions. The marketing of other types of products to other types of markets typically requires fewer product specification changes. For example, when consumer electrical appliances are manufactured in Europe, the appliances need to be reworked to meet the electrical requirements used in the various countries.

2. Description of Changes in Profits

The profits referred to are projected manufacturing profits and they will be dictated by what is determined in the product changes to be specified.

B. Price

1. Description of Price Levels

For many types of products the prevailing price levels for competitive products can be calculated by using data taken from the NTDB. In this procedure, one divides the total sales revenues generated from exporting a given product (where revenues are established on a "free along-side" containership basis) to a particular market by the total number of units of the product sold to that market. This yields a competitive price per unit of an item.

2. Description of the Source of Price Escalation

One can get these sources of price escalation by soliciting an international freight transportation price quote from a freight forwarder. The forwarder has access to software which calculates these items automatically enroute to the specification for the international freight price quote (includes tariffs, levies, port charges, and other pertinent items).

3. Determination of Price Reduction

The next step is for the student team to determine by how much the ex-works (this term refers to the price for a product quoted by a manufacturer whereby the buyer must take possession of the product at the loading dock of the manufacturer at the place of production) price must be reduced in order for the product to be competitive in the target foreign market.

The student records the ex-works price and adds on to this price the cost of inland freight. One then compares that price with the free, along-side price calculated in above. If this price exceeds the price, then the manufacturer will likely have to reduce the price for the export market.

4. Possible Problems with Foreign Exchange

Problems with foreign exchange are most frequent in exporting products to various South American countries and any country that was formerly a member of the Soviet Bloc. If a country is short of foreign exchange (hard currency in the country's central bank), then counter trade (this term refers to a type of transaction where goods are traded for goods rather than for money) will likely need to be used by the exporter.

C. Promotion

1. Promotion Strategies

The great majority of promotional activities will be centered on the use of "push" strategies (a push strategy by the manufacturer requires the effective use of the manufacturer's salesforce and representatives as well as heavy trade promotion to push to product down through the channels to the ultimate company) where salespeople are key instruments in promotion. "Pull" strategies (a pull strategy by the manufacturer requires heavy spending on consumer promotion in order to build consume demand so that consumers will, in turn, request the product be carried by their retailer and this request for the product will be repeated back up through the channel of distribution to the manufacturer) which require intensive use of the mass media in foreign countries are likely to be uneconomical for a company that is just starting to penetrate a new market. This is true because pull strategies are efficient only if mass distribution has already been accomplished.

2.   Cultural Issues

Cultural issues are primarily an obstacle in the promotion of consumer goods particularly foods and personal items such as cosmetics. Other items are relatively, little effected by cultural issues.

3.   Conduct of Business

It is a practice for a producer to pay a foreign distributor for promoting a product by permitting the distributor a discount off the producer's regularly published, domestic wholesale price.

D.   Channel of Distribution
1.   The optimal channel of distribution is primarily a function of the nature of the product and the intensity of after-sales service that is required. For example, the greater the level of after-sales service that is required, the more direct is the channel of distribution.
2.   Typically, small companies which have no prior experience in exporting are going to be the most receptive to using a pure international marketing company such as an export management company (EMC) or an export trading company (ETC). The appeal lies primarily in the notion that an export management company or an export trading company turns all fixed export costs into viable export costs for a producer. This is true because an EMC or ETC performs all of the export marketing functions and only gets paid if the EMC/ETC makes a sale in the target foreign market; under this arrangement, there are no out-of-pocket costs to the producer.

V.   Improvements in the Company Likely to be Created

Any financial benefits that are forthcoming to the producer as a consequence of making sales in the target foreign market can be used to support domestic competition (U.S.). Everything else being equal, the company which has successful international business activities, will tend to competitively dominate a purely domestic company as a consequence.

VI.   Description of Risks and Financial Impact

A financial analysis of the impact of the company's profit and loss statement using three scenarios is the final portion of the project. Students are encouraged, through this final step, to view their work in three dimensions from the "soaring star" to the "crash of great hopes."

If the faculty member is hesitant to begin to undertake the assignment of this ambitious project as a class requirement and needs further advice and assistance, oftentimes there are personnel available in one's geographical area whose job entails the promotion of international trade. In North Carolina, for instance, the North Carolina Small Business and Technology Development Center has designated personnel whose specialty is to assist small businesses in exploring the export trade possibility. These personnel are extremely knowledgeable about the exporting process and can serve as vital support personnel for the faculty member.

GUIDELINES FOR STUDENT CONSULTING TEAMS

After structuring the export project, the faculty member must be attentive to the student team and its contacts with the client firm. Below are suggested guidelines developed through experience and recommended by the authors for student conduct when students are in a consulting role and dealing with the business community.

1.   Crisis Control. As we all know, a little bad publicity is worse than a lot of good publicity. It is important for the faculty member responsible for the student involvement in the live-case format to maintain a close relationship with the business client in order to intervene if the relationship between the client and the student team members is not a positive one. One must remember that we are working with students, many with limited business experience, and this is a learning experience for them as well as a learning experience for the business client.
2.   The First Meeting. Arrange the first meeting of the student teams and the clients in a controlled environment such as a classroom at the university with the faculty member present. This will help ensure there will be fewer misunderstandings as to the responsibilities of the student teams and the business clients.
3.   Client Commitment. Obtain a commitment from the business client to allocate an appropriate amount of time to the student team and for at least some of the meetings to take place at the client's place of business.
4.   Confidentiality. The faculty member and student team must guarantee that all information obtained

pertaining to the client and the client's business will remain confidential. This agreement to confidentiality is permanent. This means that, if any report or publicity release containing reference to the client is anticipated, one must first obtain the client's consent. Last, the students will not engage in any direct competition with the client firm. (Beguin, 1992, p. C-1)

5. Maintaining a Business-Like Climate. At all times, the student team should not discuss the project's information with outsiders (this means anyone not in the class). At no time should the student team ridicule the client firm. Above all, the student team should show respect for the client. (Beguin, 1992, p. C-1)

6. Business Ethics and Legalities. If a student team discovers that certain acts have the appearance of being unethical or illegal, the student team should report the matter to the faculty member. The rule to follow first is to use discretion. After the faculty member has investigated the concern reported by the student team, the faculty member will make the decision whether or not to continue; it is possible that a case may have to be discontinued. (Beguin, 1992, p. C-1)

7. Access to Records. The client must be willing to share confidential records needed by the students to be able to make a recommendation pertaining to the particular issue. The students must also be willing to sign a confidential statement and understand the seriousness of what they have been asked to sign.

8. Periodic Reviews. The faculty member must conduct periodic reviews of the progress of each student team during the semester.

9. Access to Expertise. The faculty member must be able to assist the students in obtaining any outside needed expertise (for example, other faculty members, members of SCORE, and counselors from the Small Business Development Center).

10. Treatment of Recommendations. Both the client and the students should understand that the client is under no obligation to implement the team's recommendations. However, it is exciting to the students, the faculty member, and the client when the recommendations are implemented and are found to be useful.

CONCLUDING STATEMENT

The complex topics of export trade, the global economy, and the characteristics of international markets can be integrated in the export feasibility analysis project. The methodology provides students with opportunities to work with key personnel in a company while building their resume with a significant entry. The challenge to the professor and student is formidable but certainly worthwhile.

REFERENCES

Anonymous, "Comparison Shopping Service Offers Custom Export Market Research," Business America, March 1990, Volume 111, No. 6, pp. 14-15.

Beguin, Verona (ed.) Small Business Institute Student Consultant's Manual: A Practical Guide for Student Consultants. Washington, DC: U.S. Small Business Administration and the Small Business Institute Directors' Association, 1992.

Chait, A. L., "In Complexity Lies Opportunity," Across the Board, January 1994, pp. 16-21.

Chernoff, J. & Price, M., "Eastern Europe Markets Bubble With Hope," Pensions & Investments, January 1994, Volume 22, pp. 3, 84.

Delphos, W. A., "TDP Funds Overseas Projects," Global Trade, January 1992, Volume 112, Issue 1, pp. 28.

Hill, H. & Phillips, P., "Trade is a Two-Way Exchange: Rising Import Penetration in East Asia's Export Economies," World Economy, November 1993, Volume 16, Issue 6, pp. 687-697.

Hitchcock, E. & Tiberio, D., "Show Me the Way," Journal of European Business, January/February 1993, Volume 4, Issue 3, pp. 31-32.

Jayne, E. R., "Business Prospects in a Competitive World," Business Economics, January 1994, Volume 29,

84

Issue 1, pp. 24-26.

Manwell, E. R., "Forming a Foreign Sales Corporation Can Shield Rental Income From Tax," <u>Journal of Taxation of Investments</u>, Winter 1993, Volume 10, Issue 2, pp. 158-161.

Montias, J. M., "The Sequencing of Reforms," <u>Challenge</u>, September/October 1990, Volume 33, Issue 5, pp. 12-14.

THE UTILIZATION OF SIMULATIONS AND CASE STUDIES IN A WORLD ORDER STUDIES SEMINAR

Raymond McCandless
The University of Findlay
FINDLAY, OHIO, U.S.A.

Abstract

Simulations and case studies have been used in world politics courses for many years. In this paper, the author reports on the use of these teaching vehicles in his Seminar on World Order Studies. Students enrolled in the class developed simulations and case studies for use in a local high school. Discussion in the paper focuses on: 1) why case studies and simulations are extremely relevant in the teaching of a world order course; 2) the student experience in developing and implementing case studies/simulations; 3) an assessment of this teaching experience and future application.

INTRODUCTION

The Seminar on World Order Studies was first taught at The University of Findlay (formerly Findlay College) in the spring semester of 1983. The course is listed as an upper-level (400) political science course and has been offered on an every third year cycle since its inception. Our political science curriculum at The University of Findlay is fairly standard, presenting students with traditional course selections such as comparative politics, American politics, Western political thought, etc. I do not believe that there are a great number of small colleges/universities that offer a course on world order studies, although I do not have the survey data to support my claim. Many academics may consider the world order perspective on international relations to be too far removed from mainstream thought within the discipline to be added as a permanent component to their curriculum.

Similar to peace studies courses, the purpose of world order studies is to encourage individuals and groups to identify threats to human survival and to consider various strategies and tactics which will assure a future based in peace and justice. Richard A. Falk, a major contributor to the field of world order studies, offers the following definitional comment:

> Such an approach is concerned with understanding the extent to which past, present, and future arrangements of power and authority are able to realize a set of human values - including peace, economic well-being, social justice, and ecological balance - for people throughout the globe. At the same time, its primary intention is to sharpen understanding of what is really happening rather than to specify solutions prematurely. [Falk, Kim, Mendlovitz, 1982, 1]

International scholars who have adopted this perspective believe that thinking, writing and dialogue within the discipline have for too long ignored normative or value considerations. Even those scholars not directly identified with world order studies have noted this unfortunate lack of attention. For example, J. David Singer states, "Specialists in world affairs have a special responsibility to not only teach and conduct high-quality research, but to address the major problems confronting the global village....The human condition is, on balance, morally unacceptable" [qtd. in Viotti and Kauppi, 1987, 580]. Many professionals within the field have ultimately reached the conclusion that there is a place for both empirical international relations theory and normative theory.

COURSE DEVELOPMENT

It was my belief that the unique nature and orientation of world order studies demanded an equally original teaching approach. I recognized from the onset that both the instructor and the students were being asked to step out of safe, predictable parameters of behavior and procedure for this specific seminar. Many students expressed an initial uneasiness with the course's subject matter. This may be partially explained by the fact that contemporary students of the social sciences are not always comfortable when asked to think about their chosen field of study in a prescriptive, value-oriented manner. One of the criticisms of the scientific or behavioralist approach which has come to dominate the social sciences is that it does not allow us to ask fundamentally relevant, normative questions, such as "Can we make a difference?" John T. Rourke, in a popular, current international relations text, reflects on this shortcoming. He states:

Behavioralists, from their "value-free" or "scientific" perspective , are more disinterested in the good or ill of world politics. They tend to operate from a value-free posture, neither condoning nor condemning what is. They only describe what is and why and try to predict what will be. This value-free approach has been the source of some criticism of behavioralism by those who contend that the problems and stakes of the world are too great to be studied dispassionately. [1991, 29]

Rourke's criticisms of behavioralism may be somewhat overstated. However, I do not believe that it is entirely inappropriate to suggest that the behavioralist methodology has had an impact on the way students approach the study of social phenomena and what they perceive to be the prescribed role of the social scientist in our society.

It is certainly beyond the purview of this paper to investigate all of the possible reasons why students approached this course with a certain amount of trepidation. It could simply be that all students have an aversion to courses with a syllabus longer than two pages! Since I dislike simplistic answers and want to believe that students retain knowledge from other courses, I found myself partial to the former explanation. Also, my discussions with students, all either juniors or seniors, did seem to validate this. The majority of the students realized early into the course that world order studies was just not quite the same as taking more traditional courses in political science. I am still waiting for at least one student to directly speak to the behavioralist-normative dichotomy expounded upon at the beginning of this section.

As stated earlier, I thought that to effectively teach this seminar, I had to be open to nontraditional teaching methodologies. Specifically, these had to be methods which complemented the pro-active, creative orientation of the world order approach. Beyond gaining an understanding of reading assignments, students needed to connect with the "doing" or personal and social commitment side of politics. My emphasis was not on having students accept one view of future world order, for example, the formation of a world government. Student adoption of some ideological construct was not the objective. The primary goal was to assist in developing or enhancing within students a sense of passion, or at the very least, a deep concern for the four issues which form the centerpiece of world order studies: peace, economic well-being, social justice and ecological balance. Activism and devoting personal time to solution-oriented thinking can come only after this well of passion has been tapped in some way.

The world order seminar was designed as a four-credit course. Each student had to enroll in the three-hour segment of the course titled "Understanding and Promoting Just World Order." Students were also required to sign up for a one-hour lab section. In the three-hour portion of the course, students became familiar with world order studies through instructor presentations and the discussion of assigned readings. The lab section was reserved for the creation of workshops which would include case studies and simulations which related to world order values. This is the course activity which certainly demands further explanation.

Students were divided up into four different groups or committees. Each group was to formulate a "world order workshop." The four workshops were labeled as follows: Peace Studies, Social Justice, Ecology and Economic Well-being. The workshop titles/topics were drawn from the world order literature which designated these to be primary world order values. The plan was to implement these workshops in a local high school. Each workshop would consist of two class day presentations. The group would spend the first class period introducing their issue or presenting a case study. The second day was to be devoted to the implementation of a simulation or another activity pertinent to the workshop topic.

It is necessary to explain why I thought it important for students to engage in this type of teaching activity. As discussed throughout this paper, world order studies emphasizes preparation for activism. One of the assigned texts for the course, Towards a Just World Peace: Perspectives from Social Movements, by Saul H.

Mendlovitz and R.B.J. Walker [1987], contains essays which articulate the need for the development of a globalist perspective, and most importantly, the formulation of actions and initiatives at the local level. The authors' primary message in the text is the importance of linking the global with the local if we are to be serious about the achievement of a sustainable world peace. I wanted to offer my students a course experience which would present them with this type of opportunity within the community of Findlay. Thus, this was the basis for the creation of high school workshops.

It was obvious to all of the students who were sitting in a classroom listening to lectures from a teacher with a monotone delivery that this was not the best way to stimulate interest in a subject, and certainly not an approach that would inspire activism. I strongly suggested to the students that they incorporate some type of experiential element into their workshop presentation. There was certainly precedent established for the use of this type of educational technique in the workshops. Gaming, the case study method and simulations have all been used for years in political science and international relations to instigate the type of response that I had in mind. For example, in 1963 Harold Guetzkow and his associates developed a simulation for teaching high school students the major principles of international relations [Guetzkow et al., 1963]. As reported by Joyce and Weil, this simulation consisted of:

Five "nation" units; in each of these nations, a group of participants acts as decision-makers and "aspiring decision-makers." The simulated relations among the nations are derived from the characteristics of nations and from principles that have been observed to operate among nations in the past....Together, the nations play an international relations game that involves trading and the development of various agreements....The nations can even make war on one another, the outcome being determined by the force capability of one group of allies relative to that of another group. [1986, 375]

Probably the best known simulation activity employed in international relations is the model United Nations. William A. Hazleton and James E. Jacob begin their article on the model UN experience with the comment that "their (simulations) major attraction is that simulations and games make politics come alive as they capture the interest and excitement of students....the overall experience may serve as a stimulus for related course enrollment and even future involvement in public service or politics" [1982-83, 89]. This notion of involvement or activity is what drew me towards the idea of utilizing simulation procedures in my class.

Foster, Lachman and Mason [1980] present an argument which very clearly demonstrates how well student participation in simulations dovetails with the goals of a world order course. They state:

Perhaps the most important and certainly the most neglected type of learning related to simulations is verstehen. "Verstehen," as the Germans termed it, is a process of subjective understanding or interpretation. Human action has meaning not only to the observer of the action, but also to the actor....Since students cannot directly experience much that ought to be known, it is possible to reconstruct the environment of particular social events and have students "relive" them. This is essentially what role-playing simulations attempt to do. [1980, 228-29]

Course objectives such as student involvement in confronting value questions and ethical dilemmas significant in international affairs; the exploration of the consequences of nation-state policy decisions; and the creation of the type of excitement that may eventually translate into activism seems to stand a better chance of being created if this approach to learning is operationalized. A critical assumption underlying this whole teaching enterprise is that the college students' work in creating the workshops, specifically the simulations or case studies plus their on-site involvement in administering the workshops, produces the same results as stated above.

THE WORKSHOPS

There were certain hurdles which had to be overcome in the creation of these workshops, the most basic one being that some of the students had little or no experience with the case study/simulation method. Besides teaching the content matter of the course, it became my responsibility to also instruct students in these unique approaches to learning. Two books which I found to be helpful in accomplishing this endeavor were Simulation and Gaming in Social Science [1972] by Michael Inbar and Clarice S. Stoll and Learning through Simulation Games [1973] by Philip H. Gillespie. In the latter work, the author provides useful information in Appendix I titled "How To Design Your Own Simulation Game" [226-229]. Gillespie states:

When I am asked the question "How do you design the simulation game?" I respond, "Let's write a game." When I do this, I follow a very simple four-point outline: 1. choose an objective; 2. identify the major systems that relate directly to the issue that is stated in the objective; 3. specify one problem to solve that typifies the issue identified in the objective; 4. impose a structure on the game. [1973, 226]

Even though I knew my students would not be developing simulations as complex or involved as the ones discussed in either the Gillespie or Inbar and Stoll book, I did hope that guidelines such as those stated above would help give focus and direction to their efforts.

Source material on the case study method was also provided to the students. I did not want to overwhelm the students with a voluminous amount of educational theory and information on this topic. I found it best to provide them with case studies which they could use as models in building their own works. For example, Frederick H. Hartmann, in his text The Relations of Nations [1983], has a chapter titled "Studies in Collective Security: Ethiopia and Korea" [368-388]. These case studies on the attempt to apply the collective security principle in two different situations provided the students with concrete examples of what we were attempting to create for our workshops. Over the course of the semester, the lab sessions became informal meetings, where through trial and error, we constructed exercises appropriate to each workshop.

There were a number of very positive outcomes associated with these lab sessions (beyond the obvious one, which was to create workshop simulations and/or case studies). Students were being asked to work with the course material in a creative manner. The point of learning about world order studies was not to become well-versed enough in the subject matter to merely pass a test or answer classroom questions, but to be successful in the implementation of a high school workshop. As the semester progressed, I detected an increased student confidence and willingness to discuss global issues in a manner much more characteristic of the activist and less like the "ivory-tower" academic. "How can we get high school students interested in these issues?" "What will help these students to remember the points we want to make in this short two-day presentation?" These were fundamental concerns expressed by the college students in the lab sessions.

The construction of the case studies or simulations also assisted the college students in organizing their thoughts about a particular global issue. For example, when I taught the course in 1983, students on the Social Justice Committee decided to focus upon the issue of human rights abuses. The students on the committee had recently completed a course on Latin American politics. The first day of the workshop, students utilized their allocated 50 minutes to present a case study on the human rights abuses occurring in El Salvador. There was a great amount of media attention being focused on this issue in the mid-1980s. After a first day filled with substantive information, it was important to have the opportunity to discuss in more generalized terms the problem of human rights abuses. The college students had a clear objective for the second day--to demonstrate that it is difficult to reach a consensus on the definition of social justice and to further illustrate how ethics and morality may be compromised in the name of national interests. The high school class was divided into three groups representing the USSR, USA and El Salvador. The first task of each group was to put together a declaration of human rights which reflected the values and ideology of the country they were representing. At least five principles had to be generated for each declaration. After each declaration was displayed on an overhead, a representative was chosen from each group and a meeting was held to work out a compromise document. This led to a very productive discussion involving the entire class.

Over the years, students would create other case studies based upon historical events/situations (e.g., Cuban Missile Crisis, Persian Gulf War, Pinochet's Chile) which would act as vehicles to provoke discussion and a consideration of the current principles, structures and practices which define contemporary world politics. Admittedly, none of these would represent very sophisticated utilizations of the case study/simulation method of teaching, but they served their purpose quite well. Besides engaging in an activity which had hopefully raised the political awareness of their audience, the college students had been forced to integrate information, which initially may have seemed disconnected, into an organized, imaginative forum.

All of the workshops administered over the years had much in common in terms of organization and objective. For example, a group of college students who organized an Economic Well-being workshop were able to demonstrate the significance of political and economic theory in their high school presentation. On the first day of their workshop, the students presented two divergent theoretical perspectives on the causes and cures for the disparity of wealth among nation-states. Their instruction on the major principles of dependency and conventional theories of economic development prepared the high school students for the following day's activities. A fictional country named "Turbulence" was described on a one-page handout. The economic, social and political characteristics of the country resembled those of a less developed country in the throes of modernization. The country profile also included information on the material and strategic resources possessed by Turbulence which made it of interest to other powerful nation-states. The high school class was then divided into the following groups: USA, USSR, the incumbent government of Turbulence and the revolutionary force in Turbulence. Each student group was to construct a statement which suggested a solution to the present political and economic difficulties of Turbulence. Since there was limited time, the workshop facilitators were only able to provoke a discussion regarding various perspectives on economic development. They had planned a number of other intervention activities which would have led to further discussion and interaction of the groups. This problem with time has been a consistent problem regarding the implementation of student developed case studies and simulations.

ASSESSMENT AND FUTURE APPLICATION

It is important to stress that the major purpose of this exercise was not to create historical case studies and simulations of publishable quality, but to have the college students become involved in the process of case study and simulation creation and implementation because of certain assumptions regarding learning benefits that could be gained from this process. To summarize, it was my belief that college student engagement in this endeavor would: 1) assist in the development of an "activist" orientation which is critical in a world order/peace studies course; 2) motivate student involvement and study of course material; 3) allow students (both college and high school level) to connect political principles with reality, a benefit directly linked to the case study/simulation approach to learning; and finally, 4) involve students and instructor in an exciting, creative educational venture.

I have taught this seminar on four different occasions. I have determined there is a need to develop some type of testing instrument which would assist in determining whether or not the stated objectives are actually being met. It is a requirement of the University that faculty members administer a course evaluation form at the end of each semester in several classes. I have always had this course evaluated. Student response has been overwhelmingly positive, but it has been difficult to discern from this opinion survey if the specific goals have been achieved. An end of workshop survey is also administered in the high schools, but this instrument is also in need of some fine tuning. I am somewhat reticent to commit myself to this project because of the difficulty researchers have had in evaluating the impact of nontraditional types of teaching such as simulations.

Students were required to complete end of the semester "reflection papers" in which they were asked to evaluate course activities and responsibilities. Naturally, students focused on the workshop experience in these papers. Even the students who had certain ideological problems with the world order approach registered satisfaction with the course activities. Some students expressed satisfaction simply because the course was "different" while others noted that it was "fun and exciting to actually try to teach the information we are learning." Several students revealed that the "possibility of embarrassment in the high schools" made them work harder in putting together their workshop. I was surprised that a number of students wrote that they enjoyed the course but found it to be the "most difficult course I have taken during my college career." There was no consensus on the reasons for the difficulty which included a number of diverse sources: the creation of the case studies/simulations, going into the high schools, or the course material itself. What I found to be most encouraging is that a large number of students wanted to take other courses designed in this manner. In fact, one student bluntly asked, "Where can I sign up for World Order Studies II?"

I am committed to the workshop feature of this seminar, even though I do not have irrefutable evidence to support my assessment that course goals were being met through current course design. From a personal perspective, there were a number of benefits which I gained from teaching this course. First, the course afforded me the opportunity to discuss teaching and learning strategies with undergraduates. Since a great amount of my time is devoted to teaching, it has been extremely fulfilling to share with students some of the teaching strategies I have found to be successful and not so successful over the years. Second, as someone who did not have a great deal of experience with simulations, this course led to the investigation of what I have found to be an excellent teaching tool. I have experimented with simulation designs in other political science courses. It is my hope to eventually have my students become involved with a Model United Nations program. Third, the workshop approach helped me solidify a stronger link between local high schools and The University of Findlay. Besides opening up the possibility for the implementation of similar programs in the high schools, I found it beneficial to become more well acquainted with the views and social science background of future college students. Finally, a college student noted in his reflection paper that the workshop experience had made him more empathetic to the instructor's task in the classroom. This result alone justifies the continued application of the workshop approach.

REFERENCES

Falk, Richard, Samuel S. Kim, and Saul H. Mendlovitz, eds., <u>Studies On A Just World Order, Volume 1 - Toward A Just World Order</u> (Westview Press, 1982).

Foster, John L., Allan C. Lachman, and Ronald M. Mason, "Verstehen, Cognition, and the Impact of Political Simulations," <u>Simulation and Games</u> (June 1980), pp. 223-241.

Gillespie, Philip H., <u>Learning Through Simulation Games</u> (Paulist Press, 1973).

Guetzkow, H., et al., <u>Simulation In International Relations</u> (Prentice Hall, 1963).

Hartmann, Frederick H., <u>The Relations of Nations</u>, 6th ed. (Macmillan, 1983).

Hazleton, William A. and James E. Jacob, "Simulating International Diplomacy: The National Model United Nations Experience," <u>Teaching Political Science</u> (Winter 1982-83), pp. 89-98.

Inbar, Michael and Clarice S. Stoll, <u>Simulation and Gaming in Social Science</u> (The Free Press, 1972).

Joyce, Bruce and Marsha Weil, <u>Models of Teaching</u>, 3rd ed. (Allyn and Bacon, 1986).

Mendlovitz, Saul H. and R.B.J. Walker, eds., <u>Towards a Just World Peace: Perspectives from Social Movements</u> (Butterworths, 1987).

Rourke, John T., <u>International Politics on the World Stage</u>, 3rd edition (The Dushkin Publishing Group, 1991).

Viotti, Paul R. and Mark V. Kauppi, <u>International Relations Theory: Realism, Pluralism, Globalism</u> (Macmillan, 1987).

CONTINGENCY AND CASE DESIGN:
EACH DISCIPLINE NEEDS ITS OWN CASE APPROACH THE EXAMPLE OF MANAGEMENT AND ENTREPRENEURSHIP EDUCATION

Louis Jacques Filion
École des Hautes Études Comerciales de Montréal
MONTRÉAL, QUÉBEC, CANADA

Abstract

This paper highlights the differences between managers and entrepreneurs. It shows that the self-awareness attributes of managers and entrepreneurs differ considerably. Know-how is also different, with managers' know-how being focused on resource organization and entrepreneurs' know-how on defining contexts. The paper discusses the consequences of these differences on education. For entrepreneurship education, it is suggested that the design of cases in the form of edited interviews with real-life entrepreneurs will have many advantages. By studying their progression, student entrepreneurs learn how to define contexts from real-life patterns. It concludes that each discipline will be better served by cases designed to satisfy its own specific attributes.

INTRODUCTION

It seems to be an unstated rule that the case method should be applied in a fairly standard way in different management disciplines, with cases written so as to allow readers to diagnose a business situation, identify problems and develop solutions [Ronstadt, 1980; Erskine et al., 1981; Christensen, 1992]. However, it may be useful to consider the possibility of designing cases using the contingency approach [Lawrence and Lorsch, 1967], where adjustments are made to the case design and use to reflect teaching objectives that are coherent with the specific aspects of each discipline. This paper examines some of the differences between the activity systems of managers and entrepreneurs and highlights the educational consequences for each group. It also suggests how the nature of entrepreneurship as a discipline could be taken into account to design cases that would satisfy its own specific requirements.

MANAGEMENT AND ENTREPRENEURSHIP: SOME DIFFERENCES

Mintzberg [1975], Boyatzis [1982], Kotter [1982] and Hill [1992] all examined the work of managers. Filion [1988] reviewed the literature on entrepreneurs and studied the activity systems of 100 entrepreneurs in 15 countries [1990, 1991]. Wortman and Birkenholz [1991] made an overview of the field of entrepreneurship. Their work, and that of other authors [Timmons, 1978; Hornaday, 1982; Brockhaus and Horwitz, 1986; Hisrich, 1986], reveals considerable differences in the operating methods of managers and entrepreneurs, as Table 1 shows.

Managers pursue objectives by making effective and efficient use of resources. They normally operate within frameworks previously defined by someone else.

The organizations created by entrepreneurs, however, are really an extrapolation of their subjective worlds. What entrepreneurs do is closely linked to how they interpret what is happening in a particular sector of the environment. Their own knowledge of a specific market or the development of a new product or manufacturing process will lead them to envision and market something different. They define ways of doing things that reflect what they themselves are, and their success depends on how appropriate and different what has been defined is and how it meets changing needs. Not only do entrepreneurs define situations, but they imagine visions of what they want to achieve. Their main task seems to be to imagine and define what they want to do and, often, how they are going to do it.

TABLE 1
DIFFERENCES IN THE ACTIVITY SYSTEMS OF MANAGERS AND ENTREPRENEURS

Managers	Entrepreneurs
Work on efficient and effective use of resources to reach goals and objectives	Set a vision and objectives and identify resources to help realize them
Key is adapting to change	Key is initiating change
Work pattern implies rational analysis	Work pattern implies imagination and creativity
Operate within an existing framework	Define tasks and roles that create an organization framework
Work centred on processes that take the environment into account	Work centred on the design of processes resulting from a differentiated view of the environment

Generally speaking, management is associated with rationality and entrepreneurship with intuition, although in both cases these should be considered to be predominant rather than exclusive attributes. Entrepreneurial activities require a systemic framework that includes concepts [Peterson, 1981; Drucker, 1985], although on a different level to management, and managerial activities demand elements of intuition and imagination. However, the conceptual activities and skills of the two groups being different, their educational requirements should also be different.

TABLE 2
KEY DIFFERENCES BETWEEN MANAGERIAL AND ENTREPRENEURIAL EDUCATION

Managerial Education	Entrepreneurial Education
Affiliation culture supported	Leadership culture supported
Centred on group work and group communication	Centred on individual progression
Works on the development of both sides of the brain with emphasis on the left side	Works on the development of both sides of the brain with a strong emphasis on the right side
Develops patterns that seek abstract, general rules	Develops patterns that seek concrete, specific applications
Based on the development of self-awareness with emphasis on adaptability.	Based on the development of self-awareness with emphasis on perseverance.
Focused on acquisition of know-how in management of resources and own area of specialization	Focused on acquisition of know-how directed towards the definition of contexts that lead to the occupation of a market space

ENTREPRENEURIAL AND MANAGERIAL EDUCATION

These basic differences between managers and entrepreneurs demand fundamentally different educational and training methods. In education generally, emphasis is placed on knowledge acquisition, whereas in management education it is placed on acquisition of know-how, and in entrepreneurship education, on self-awareness [Gasse, 1992]. Table 2 examines the consequences of the differences listed in Table 1 on educational approaches.

This limited comparison brings out two complementary concepts: know-how and self-awareness. Both are manifested differently in managers and entrepreneurs. In terms of self-awareness, many authors insist on the adaptability of managers [Archambault, 1992; Hill, 1992], whereas for entrepreneurs one of the key words is perseverance [Hornaday, 1982; Filion, 1991]. In terms of know-how, managers must use rational approaches, but within a pre-defined working framework. Entrepreneurs, on the other hand, must take an imaginative approach and define their own working framework. They must identify a niche and then imagine a vision, or a space to be occupied on the market and a type of organization needed to do so. Research on entrepreneurial activity systems shows that an entrepreneur's work consists mainly of defining contexts and working frameworks [Filion, 1990].

The following sections examine some specific aspects of entrepreneurial education and suggest how the case method could be used to provide better support for the particularities of the discipline.

SPECIFIC ASPECTS OF ENTREPRENEURIAL EDUCATION

In any educational program, what is important is not just what is learnt, but how it is learnt; in other words, the learning pattern established. Participants in an educational program should feel comfortable and ready to play the new role for which they are being prepared. An entrepreneurship program should therefore concentrate on the development of self-awareness and the acquisition of know-how rather than simply on the transmission of knowledge. The self-awareness to be learnt should focus on autonomy, self-confidence, perseverance, determination, creativity, leadership and flexibility [Timmons, 1978; Hornaday, 1982; Brockhaus and Horwitz, 1986; Hisrich, 1986]. The know-how developed should focus mainly on how to define situations; this, as we saw earlier, is the main activity of entrepreneurs: knowing and understanding markets, identifying business opportunities, selecting targets, imagining visions, designing and structuring organizations and animating those organizations. Basic management know-how is also useful: in addition to the PODC subjects (planning, organizing, directing and controlling), it could include accounting, finance, marketing, information systems, etc. Care is needed, however, because all too often entrepreneurship and small business programs take on a management perspective, because this is what the program designers are used to. They are familiar with it. In some cases, existing management courses will be included in an entrepreneurship or small business program with no attempt to adapt them to reflect the entrepreneurial or small business context.

TABLE 3
GUIDELINES FOR ENTREPRENEURSHIP EDUCATION ACTIVITIES

- Each course should be designed to allow participants to identify what they want to learn and to define the framework within which it is to be learnt [Filion, 1989].
- Include multi-instruction strategies.
- Be concrete and practical.
- Introduce material that will be useful in practice once the course is over.
- Each course should be seen by participants as a learning activity and not just as the transmission of knowledge by the teacher.
- Each course should include interaction with real entrepreneurs through case studies, videos, meetings with entrepreneurs in the classroom and field work in which at least one entrepreneur is studied in depth.
- Each course should include personal follow-up of each participant's learning objectives. Entrepreneurship education resembles leadership education in that it requires at least a minimum of individual follow-up.
- Case studies should be properly adapted to the characteristics of the field. They should help participants learn to understand contexts and define situations.

Here, contingency is vital if participants are to leave the program properly prepared to succeed in their new entrepreneurial roles. Specialists in the field have already shown that entrepreneurship programs should be different from administration programs [Gibb, 1987; Brown and Burnett, 1989; Kirby, 1989; Thorpe, 1990; Johannisson, 1991; Filion, 1992; Ulrich and Cole, 1992]. Béchard and Toulouse [1993] even developed a sophisticated grid to classify entrepreneurship education approaches as such. Table 3 sets out some guidelines for the development of entrepreneurship education activities and programs.

Program details will depend on institution level: elementary, secondary, college, undergraduate or graduate university level, entrepreneurship centers and adult education services with no prerequisites and offering non-credited tuition. At the elementary and secondary levels, programs should focus mainly on self-awareness. The aim here is to develop "entrepreneuriability" [Fortin, 1992]; that is, preparing students to create their own jobs by launching their own enterprises. At the college and university levels, the focus should be on both self-awareness and know-how.

Given the learning needs involved - understanding contexts and defining situations - experience tends to show that entrepreneurial self-awareness and know-how are best taught using written and personal testimonies and descriptive cases based on edited interviews with entrepreneurs. Table 4 shows the subjects covered by this type of case.

TABLE 4
EDITED INTERVIEWS WITH ENTREPRENEURS
AS CASES IN ENTREPRENEURSHIP EDUCATION:
THE SUBJECTS COVERED

- Family origins
- Key elements in the entrepreneur's personal history
- The circumstances that led the entrepreneur to develop an interest in the field
- The entrepreneur's personality and personal attributes
- Identification of opportunities
- Vision of the niche to be occupied
- Vision of the type of organization needed to occupy the niche
- Difficulties encountered and means used to overcome them
- Present situation Vision of the future

More than a decade of research into entrepreneurial activity systems and experience in entrepreneurship education has taught the author the importance of adapting entrepreneurship education to reflect what entrepreneurs are and what they do. This means considerable differences in, for example, the use of cases in entrepreneurship education as compared with management education. The teaching objectives in the two fields are quite separate. In both, if the use of cases is to be valid, it must reflect the context of the discipline itself and the types of self-awareness and know-how required by the people doing what the students are being trained for. Entrepreneurs are often "deviants," playing very different business roles from managers. For them, self-awareness means identifying with models and understanding how to develop and express their differences, whereas for managers it means learning to adapt to existing organization methods and cultures. Managers need to learn how to understand organizational contexts and adjust to them; entrepreneurs must identify opportunities and conceive a way to exploit them. For managers, know-how means mastering their specialty areas; for entrepreneurs it means defining contexts from latent elements. Potential entrepreneurs - or students - clearly have much to learn from listening to experienced entrepreneurs describing how they succeeded by imagining something new. Table 5 shows some of the advantages of using edited interview cases as an entrepreneurial education approach.

Here, both case design and the use made of the cases are important. For example, a case may be used to teach students to assess the strengths, weaknesses and coherence of the entrepreneurs studied. However, it would be far more interesting to use it to teach them how to define contexts by having them draw up a questionnaire or exercise that would help them develop their own approach and framework for understanding and defining contexts. They could then go on to make a comparative study of how entrepreneurs did it and how they themselves would have done it. For instance, looking for elements of similarity in the detection of opportunities is always stimulating. Defining the characteristics of their environment, imagining a vision and the type of enterprise they need to realize their vision, and comparing all this with how a real entrepreneur did it, provides a fascinating learning experience for students.

TABLE 5
EDITED INTERVIEWS WITH ENTREPRENEURS AS CASES
IN ENTREPRENEURIAL EDUCATION: SOME ADVANTAGES

- The process is structured by the entrepreneur's own progression rather than by the precepts of case designers
- The entrepreneur's enthusiasm is reflected in the case and arouses student interest in entrepreneurship as a career
- Students see how each entrepreneur's own self-awareness develops and are better able to situate themselves in terms of their own entrepreneurial characteristics
- Students are often fascinated by how entrepreneurs have used their deviances to develop something different. They learn that they can be themselves and still succeed
- Students see how the entrepreneurs understand their environment and define their own business context
- Entrepreneurs and potential entrepreneurs often need concrete examples in order to learn. They know that the cases contain real-life situations, and this seems to stimulate their learning
- The imaginative dimension expressed by entrepreneurs seems to provide a powerful reference point for potential entrepreneurs in terms of how to direct their thought and perception processes.

A further advantage of edited interview cases is that they provide a great variety of elements. Class discussion can be extremely rich. People identify different elements and develop different interpretive scenarios. In this way, student entrepreneurs are introduced to many enjoyable aspects of entrepreneurship. And what an opportunity that is in the sometimes all-too-grey world of organization.

CONCLUSION

Experience shows that as we become more specialized in an area of education, we like to develop better-adapted teaching material. The classical management case pattern, concentrating on diagnosis and problem-solving, does not seem appropriate in the early stages of basic entrepreneurial education, although it might be useful later. Education that is properly adapted to the activity systems of entrepreneurs will benefit from the description and explanation by the entrepreneurs themselves of how those systems were designed. Contact with real entrepreneurs, in person or on video, is fine. But contact through edited interviews will lead to a deeper understanding of what people need to be and to do to become successful entrepreneurs. Thus, the design and use of edited interviews as cases seems to support the challenge of entrepreneurship education. The contingency approach is useful in ensuring that what we do is better adapted to the context in which we do it.

REFERENCES

Archambault, G., "Le perfectionnement des managers: au-delà des modes et des engouements." Gestion (May 1992), 6-15.

Béchard, J.P. and Toulouse, J.M., "Entrepreneurship Training: A Look from Educational Sciences." Maclean Hunter Entrepreneurship Chair Working Paper No. 93-03-01 (March 1993).

Boyatzis, R.E., The Competent Manager: A Model for Effective Performance. (Wiley, 1982).

Brockhaus, R.H. Sr. and Horwitz, P.S., "The Psychology of the Entrepreneur" (1986). In: Sexton, D.L. and Smilor, R.W. (Eds.), The Art and Science of Entrepreneurship (Ballinger, 1986).

Brown, R. and Burnett, A., "Enterprising Graduates and the English Graduate Enterprise Program 1985-1989." Paper presented at the 12th National United Kingdom Small Firms Policy and Research Conference, London (1989).

Christensen, C.R., Teaching and the Case Method. (Harvard Business School, 1992).

Drucker, P.F., Innovation and Entrepreneurship (Heinemann, 1985).

Erskine, J.A., Leenders, M.R. and Mauffette-Leenders, L.A., Teaching with Cases. (University of Western Ontario, 1981).

Filion, L.J., The Strategy of Successful Entrepreneurs in Small Business: Vision, Relationships and Anticipatory Learning. (1988). Ph.D. Thesis, University of Lancaster, Great Britain (UMI 8919064).

Filion, L.J., "The Design of Your Entrepreneurial Learning System: Identify a Vision and Assess Your Relations System." Third Canadian Conference on Entrepreneurial Studies (September 1989). Published in: McKirdy, J.G.M. (Ed.), Proceedings of the Third Canadian Conference on Entrepreneurial Studies (1989), 77 - 90.

Filion, L.J., "Vision and Relations: Elements for an Entrepreneurial Metamodel." Tenth Annual Babson Entrepreneurship Research Conference, Babson College, MA (April 1990). Published in: Churchill, N.C. et al. (Eds.), Frontiers of Entrepreneurship Research 1990. Proceedings of the Tenth Annual Babson College Entrepreneurship Research Conference, Babson (1990), 57-71.

Filion, L.J. Vision et relations: Clefs du succès de l'entrepreneur (Montreal, 1991).

Filion, L.J., "Ten Steps to Entrepreneurial Teaching." Paper presented at the 2nd NEDI (National Entrepreneurship Development Institute) National Conference on Entrepreneurship Education, Moncton (Canada) (June 1992).

Fortin, P.A., Devenez Entrepreneur (Québec, 1992).

Gasse, Y. "Prospectives d'une éducation entrepreneuriale: vers un nouveau partenariat éducation-organisation." 9th Annual Conference, Canadian Council for Small Business and Entrepreneurship, Victoria (Canada) (October 1992).

Gibb, A.A., "Enterprise Culture - its meaning and implications for education and training." Journal of European Industrial Training (1987). 11, 2: 3-38.

Hill, L.A., Becoming a Manager: Mastery of a New Identity. (Harvard Business School, 1992).

Hisrich, R.D., "The Woman Entrepreneur: Characteristics, Skills, Problems and Prescriptions for Success" (1986). In: Sexton, D.L. and Smilor, R.W. (Eds.), The Art and Science of Entrepreneurship (Ballinger, 1986), 61-81.

Hornaday, J.A., "Research about living entrepreneurs" (1982). In: Kent et al. (Eds.), Encyclopedia of Entrepreneurship (Prentice-Hall, 1982), 20-34.

Johannisson, J.A., "University training for entrepreneurship: Swedish approaches." Entrepreneurship and Regional Development (1991), 3, 1: 67-82.

Kirby, D.A., "Encouraging the Enterprising Undergraduate." Education and Training (1989), 31, 4: 9-10.

Kotter, J.P., The General Managers. (Harvard Business School, 1982).

Lawrence, P.R. and Lorsch, J.W., Organization and Environment: Managing Differentiation and Integration. (Harvard University Press, 1967).

Mintzberg, H., "The Manager's Job: Folklore and Facts." <u>Harvard Business Review</u>, (July-August, 1975), 49-61.

Peterson, R.A., "Entrepreneurship and organization" (1981). In: Nystrom, P.C. and W.H. Starbuck (Eds.), <u>Handbook of Organizational Design</u>, Vol. 1 (Oxford University Press, 1981).

Ronstadt, R., <u>The Art of Case Analysis</u>. (Lord Publishing, 1977).

Thorpe, R., "Alternative Theory of Management Education." <u>Journal of European Industrial Training</u> (1990), 14, 2: 3-15.

Timmons, J.A. (1978). "Characteristics and role demands of entrepreneurshipˆ." <u>American Journal of Small Business</u> (1978), 3, 1: 5-17.

Ulrich, T.A. and cole, G.S., "Instructional strategies for entrepreneurial education." In: <u>Proceedings, ICSB 37th World Conference</u> (June 1992), 586-605.

Wortman, M.S. and Birkenholz, W., "Entrepreneurship research on a global basis: an empirical based model" (1991). Proceedings, <u>ICSB 36th World Conference</u>, Vienna (June 1991), Vol. 1: 67-77.

ROLE PLAYING: AN INTERCULTURAL EXAMPLE

Timothy Wilson
Clarion University
CLARION, PENNSYLVANIA, U.S.A.
Gunnar Bålfors
University of Umeå
UMEÅ, SWEDEN

Abstract

Although role playing may be thought of as being primarily a form of a game, this pedagogical approach is boundary spanning with regard to this conference -- it also involves contributions from cases, simulations and is truly a form of interactive method. An example of a multicultural role playing exercise is given and the effectiveness of this exercise is discussed.

INTRODUCTION

The call for papers for this conference requests research and applications in the use of cases, simulations, games, videos and other interactive methods. The topic of games certainly is important as a pedagogical tool and is not to be overlooked as an opportunity to bring creativity to the classroom. Role playing as a form of play is general and pervasive. Across cultures, one of the first games children learn is one of imitation. Over time, this imitation evolves from one of mimicking sounds and movements to one of taking on the perceived actions and activities of others, the playing of roles. Dessler [1991] has indicated that role playing, as a management development activity in industry, has found wide usage as a means for improving sales, leadership, and interviewing skills. It has been characterized as an enjoyable and inexpensive way to develop new skills. Other authors have suggested that it is the form of action training that offers the quickest and surest approach to achieve behavior change among participants [Odiorne and Rummler, 1988]. It also has been suggested that games, as a form of play, provide a motivational mainstay in organizations and have a long history of a method for stimulating sales efforts for instance. In this regard, Anderson [1993] has indicated that managers would be better served by making the job itself more playlike instead of simply adding a layer of play on top of the job. Whereas work tends to wear individuals out, play [games] brings with it energy, stamina and excitement. It therefore was suggested that a sense of freedom, competition and stimulation be brought into the workplace.

The purpose of this paper is to describe how the general aspects of role playing were adapted to the specific, important example of teaching differences in negotiation style across cultures and to indicate some results from initial classroom use. This situation arose within the context of a masters level international marketing/business course development [Wilson, 1994]. It is thought to have enough importance in content and conduct to attract general interest among users of participant pedagogy in educational situations and so is reported in this conference.

BACKGROUND

INTERCULTURAL NEGOTIATIONS

The role of understanding culture in international business has been firmly established. Hall, who has written what is considered to be the seminal US text on understanding culture, has said, "Though the United States has spent billions of dollars on foreign aid programs, it has captured neither the affection nor esteem of

100

the rest of the world. In many countries today Americans are cordially disliked; in others, merely tolerated. The reasons for this sad state of affairs are many and varied, ... I am convinced that much of our difficulty with people in other countries stems from the fact so little is known about cross-cultural communication" [Hall, 1959, pp. 1-2]. Consequently, textbook authors invariably include culture as one element in the international environment that must be understood and frequently refer to the "primacy of the host country" as a determining constraint for conducting business [Jain, 1990, pp. 228-232]. It follows that negotiations are impacted by culture. In surveying the literature on negotiating style Graham et al [1992] have noted, "In order for American firms and Soviet enterprises to achieve potential commercial successes, managers from both cultures must understand the negotiation styles [i.e., the behaviors, attitudes, and expectations] of their exchange partners. Such an understanding is critical, if not imperative, because it enables each side to better predict the negotiation partner's behavior and/or tactics."

ROLE PLAYING

Role playing has been identified as one example of a broader class of educational devices called action training that include management games and incident processes. Although role playing may be thought of as being primarily a form of a game as suggested above, this pedagogical approach is boundary spanning with regard to this conference. In this regard Odiorne and Rummler [1988, 223] have suggested the unifying thread in action training approaches is that they require some simulated behavior on the part of the individuals involved. Further, case studies are one source of potential material for action training. This relationship is shown in Figure 1. Within this context, role playing exercises are ones in which participants are asked to play a part, or "role," in a session. The professor/instructor/trainer becomes a director, and the case, problem, or facts are presented by the "director" to develop a situation in which roles are to be acted out. In its simplest form, participants are only asked to describe the role they might take; in its more common form, however, dialogue and actions are developed by participants. Although entertainment is an essential element in the success of this approach, full benefit comes from attainment of the pre-established objectives and the feedback to participants, both from peers and their director [Odiorne and Rummler, 1988].

Nevertheless, role playing exercises have their peculiarities. To be useful, it is essential that exercises be associated with the ongoing activity for the individuals who are being trained and that objectives be developed for the exercises in advance. Additionally, it is generally felt that they afford feedback on the effects of that behavior from both the trainer and peers.

FIGURE 1
BOUNDARY SPANNING NATURE OF ROLE PLAYING

METHODOLOGY

In preparation for a "personal selling/negotiation" session in a masters level international marketing/business course, the Graham, Evenko, Rajan (GER) paper was assigned as one of several papers that was to be read over the month between which class meetings were held. This practice was common. In the five months over which the course was conducted, students were responsible for 24 readings that included 500 pages [Wilson, 1994]. In this instance, they were told in advance that a role playing assignment would be conducted so that it was important for them to be in class and prepared for the particular day in which the exercise was conducted.

The GER [1992] paper was used to construct an exercise for our Swedish students. In this paper, it was noted that US businessmen tended to utilize a problem-solving style. That is, they tended to utilize a set of negotiation behaviors that were cooperative, integrative, and information-exchange-oriented. Soviet businessmen, on the other hand, favored a competitive style. That is, they tended to be competitive, inflexible, confrontational, and secretive.

The situation that was developed for role playing was one with which the Swedish students could identify. It had a Swedish intermediary who had the opportunity to negotiate a deal between a potential Russian buyer and an American supplier for a piece of manufacturing equipment. One complication that was added was that the Soviet buyers had no hard currency and would thus have to bargain to pay for the equipment with output from its operation. The characteristics for the supplier and buyer were drawn from the GER article. The Americans were to be problem solvers and the Soviets were to be competitive. The Swedes, on the other hand, were to be flexible and adapt to the styles of their counterparts. A constraint that was placed on the negotiation was that the three parties were not permitted to meet as a group, and the responsibility for imposing this discipline was left up to the Swedish intermediaries. If the three parties met, the Soviets and Americans were permitted to deal directly, effectively freezing out the Swedish intermediaries from the transaction.

On the morning in which the exercise was conducted, the class was divided into four groups of three individuals each. Each group had a "US" supplier, a "Swedish" intermediary, and a "Soviet" buyer. Essentially, the suppliers and buyers were to supply boundary conditions under which the intermediaries worked. The objectives of the exercise were to:

1. illustrate that different negotiating styles exist,
2. demonstrate that these styles require flexibility in response, which might make negotiations more or less pleasant, and
3. show that a degree of patience must be developed in negotiating situations.

Feedback was to be provided through intergroup comparisons of performance as well as informal discussions of the common roles played by individuals in each of the groups.

Before the break that separated the first and second hour of the class, students were given individual sheets that described the exercise and their role in it. They were asked to read the sheet over the break and not to discuss it with other members of the class. (It is felt that they complied with this request.) These sheets for the American supplier, the Swedish intermediary, and the Soviet buyer are shown in Figure 2. In the second hour, the groups were briefed individually concerning their role in the exercise -- American suppliers were briefed as a group; Soviet buyers likewise, and then the Swedish intermediaries. Overheads that summarized the descriptive write-ups were used and suggested behavior was extended. It was explained that the purpose of the exercise was not competitive. That is, it was not the purpose of any one group to get a better deal than others, but rather to understand what is involved in negotiating trade agreements. Students were asked to carry out their negotiations during breaks (students were given 15 minutes break each hour), over lunch and throughout the evening before the next day's class. Additionally, individuals were asked to take notes on meetings both with regard to content and time taken in meetings. Forms were supplied to them for this purpose, as well as for preparing strategy and tactics for their meetings.

FIGURE 2A
GENERAL INSTRUCTIONS

This exercise has been developed to present students with some experience in cross-cultural negotiations. Its purpose is not to develop any judgement on a "right" or "wrong" approach to negotiation, but rather to develop some appreciation for types of negotiation styles that may develop in the international marketplace. Neither will any judgement be made on winners or losers, although the "deals" that are made among various teams will be compared -- as will the negotiation experiences.

You will be asked to play a particular role, as designated above. The reason for this role assignment will be made more clear at the end of the exercise, but it remains sufficient now to say that role playing is a very effective means of learning. You are therefore asked to play your role as seriously as possible for the duration of this exercise.

FIGURE 2B
INSTRUCTIONS FOR SOVIET ENTREPRENEUR

You are a Russian entrepreneur who needs a particular piece of equipment to open a business. Possession of this equipment will place you in a "can't miss" position. At the stage the market presently is in, you can sell everything that you make and thus there is virtually no risk in purchasing this equipment. If you can get this piece of equipment, you can develop an income stream that is two to ten times the average Russian income -- you will not be rich, but you will live very comfortably. Further, the income stream will present enough money to pay for the machine within a year or two after it is put into operation.

You do not know exactly what one of these machines costs, but you suspect that a fair price may be $1 million (about 7.5 million SEKr). You therefore would like to buy the machine for about $0.75 million if you could, but you might consider paying as much as $1.25 million.

Your one problem is that you have no money, nor do you have much hope of getting any. You thus would like to pay for your equipment with proceeds from your sales. You could conceivably pay for the equipment in one year, but would prefer to take two years and three would even be better.

You have the opportunity to get this equipment from a Swedish distributor. You will have to negotiate the price and terms that are satisfactory to both of you.

Basically, you will approach negotiating as a distributive bargainer. That is, you feel compelled to get your adversary to see things your way. You get personal satisfaction in outbargaining your competitors, and you think that to give in on a point is a particular sign of weakness. In fact, the word "deal" has strong negative connotations in Russian. "Competitive," "inflexible," "confrontational," "uncompromising," "tough," "hard," "stubborn," and "rigid" are terms that describe your style.

You do not mind being confrontational in your style, nor are you particularly inclined to hurry the negotiations. The longer you wait to get the equipment, however, the longer you wait to get its benefits.

As a Russian, you are almost obligated to interrupt or disrupt negotiations at some point during their conduct for your potential benefit.

FIGURE 2C
INSTRUCTIONS FOR AMERICAN SUPPLIER

You are a major American equipment manufacturer who would like to "crack" the Russian market. Initial presence there could benefit you in the long run. You have the opportunity to get into this market through a Swedish intermediary who will contact you with a possible deal for you. The opportunity to deal through an intermediary suits you just fine. Although you have your own sales force in the US, the opportunity to get into an international market without extra expense on your part fits well with your strategy.

You would like to sell 10 extra pieces of equipment this year if you could. Your starting price for bargaining in the US is $1.5 million and would like to sell at that price if possible. Your full cost, breakeven price (0 profit) is $1.0 million, but you could sell for less on a contribution to margin basis. Under no circumstance, however, should you sell below $0.8 million.

Your normal deal is cash, net 90 days, but it is not unusual for customers to wait 180 days before paying without penalty. Beyond 180 days unpaid accounts are accessed a 10% penalty.

Your general arrangement with distributors is to have them take any mark-up they receive as payment for services rendered. You are not in the practice of paying distributors a commission on their sales. Your position is if you sell direct, the price you charge, about $1.1 million is enough to guarantee them a profit if they sell at the same price.

You are to use a problem solving approach in your negotiations. That means that you should 1) attempt to obtain a suitable profit from your negotiation, while 2) establishing a sense of satisfaction for your negotiating partner, also.

You would like to build this business and an effective international distribution network would be an attractive way for you to proceed. You should try to the extent possible to find out what your negotiator's needs are and attempt to establish a settlement within his/her needs.

FIGURE 2D
INSTRUCTIONS FOR SWEDISH INTERMEDIARY

You have an unique opportunity. You know a Russian entrepreneur who wants to buy a machine for his/her business, and you also know a representative of a US company who sells machines.

The profit margin between buyer and seller is large enough to attract you. Although you do not know exactly what it will be until you get information from the potential buyer and seller, you might expect it to be about $100,000 dollars (750.000 SEKr).

Your responsibility is to act as an intermediary to set up a deal between the Russian and the US person. As befits a Swedish person, you have complete freedom in how this deal is to be structured.

You have the opportunity to either talk to the potential seller, or the potential buyer first. You are under no time constraints to complete this deal, but naturally the sooner it is completed, the sooner you may get your money.

You may have to borrow money to support this purchase. If you do, the amount of interest you will have to pay is a straight 15% per year. That is, if you must borrow $1 million for one year, you will pay $1.15 million after a year, or $1.075 million after 6 months, etc.

You are to be flexible in your style. You should adapt to the style presented by your negotiating partner. You may expect that the two may be different. Your only responsibility is to structure a deal that is beneficial to you.

You should be aware of one thing, however. You have no contractual relationship with either party. If either one becomes aware of the other by you naming them, they could deal directly. You should thus be careful about maintaining source and customer secrecy.

English, the accepted language of commerce, was to be used as a conversational medium in all discussions. Students were left to develop their own scripts and strategies within the framework outlined in the role descriptions of Figure 2. Periodic checks were made during the day to see if contacts had been made and that progress was occurring. Debriefing was made in the first hour of class the next morning.

RESULTS

Each of the four groups reached a settlement -- three without apparent difficulty and one under the crisis conditions of settlement outside the classroom, but during the review of results from the other three groups. In the "crisis" situation the "American" supplier balked at selling a piece of equipment for what he considered less than a reasonable profit margin. The settlement in that situation captured the settlements in each of the other groups. There was a compromise; less now, but a promise of better returns in the future. The best any Swedish intermediary was able to do was a 10 percent mark-up over the price agreed to with the American supplier.

It was evident that some aspects of reality were captured in the exercise. Haas [1992] has indicated that a successful new industrial sale requires 4.3 sales calls on average, with a usual range of 3 to 6 calls. Three of the groups obtained agreement in five meeting couples and the other in three, where a "meeting couple" is defined as a meeting with both a buyer and a seller. Further, intermediaries indicated that it was much more agreeable working with the problem-solving participants than their more competitive counterparts as would seem consistent with Sheth's observations on dyadic interactions [1976]. They also tended to spend more time with the Soviet buyers.

The major difference from reality was time spent -- not only the overall time but the per meeting time. The whole process was covered in less than twenty four hours, a time period imposed by the exercise. In a real situation this process would be expected to take anywhere from three months to several years. Further, the

104

groups that took five meeting couples tended to spend an average of fifteen minutes per meeting; the group that took three meeting couples took 25 to 30 minutes per individual meeting. In "real life" these individual meetings would undoubtedly take an hour or two. The reduction that was observed could be rationalized by the simplifications imposed by the simulation and the fact that a lot of the socialization necessary in first time business situations was accomplished by having student participants who knew each other.

Nonetheless, the exercise appeared to have a positive impact on the students. In the exit survey of the course, each element of the course was evaluated by students on 1 to 5 "very important in my education" to "worthless" Likert scale [Wilson, 1994]. This exercise received the highest average grade awarded by the class, 1.3 where 1.0 would be a perfect score. Thus, it was perceived as being very important in students' development. On the other hand, the Graham, Evenko, Rajan reading on which the exercise was based received a score of 2.27, nearly identical to the average reading score of 2.28, which suggested the students appreciated the contribution the action portion of the exercise made. That is, they apparently thought they gained "by doing" as compared to just reading about these differences in an article.

DISCUSSION

Although role playing is recognized as an effective means of training working managers, it tends not to be utilized very heavily in academic programs. This may be an oversight. Certainly, case studies and computer based simulations tend to get greater usage. Arguments have been extended suggesting that the student is but one client being served in the academic process, the business organization hiring students being the other [Lichtenthal and Butaney, 1991; Meyers and Worthing, 1984]. In this regard, there has been criticism of MBA programs by executives who suggest that students lack "people" skills upon graduation [Business Week, 1992]. One possible way of overcoming this weakness would be to utilize more role playing exercises in individual courses across the curriculum.

A basic difficulty that exists at this time in the use of more role playing exercises in class is a lack of established exercises across a range of the business functions. One contribution of this paper, thus, is the reinforcement of the suggestion that such exercises readily come from case studies. It is foreseen that in that portion of the discussion where implementation is covered that some attention be given by case facilitators to having some portion of the implementation step acted out by students. The wide application of role playing in management training [Dessler, 1991] would suggest that its greater use in an academic environment also would make a positive contribution to student development.

The example presented here, although coming from a reading and not a case, illustrates that role playing can be effective -- as judged by students as relating to their futures. Two factors undoubtedly may have contributed to this judgement. First, the situation was one with which the Swedish students could identify. The Soviet market was opening up at the time, and it was one in which some form of barter would probably be necessary. Sweden was geographically situated to act as an intermediary to this market, and the US likely would be a supplier to this market. Thus, a realistic, meaningful situation was captured and likely appreciated by students. Secondly, the role sheets illustrated in Figure 2 guided the students' conduct. The utility of such instructions in getting potentially competing groups to cooperate is appreciated in role playing management [Ordiorne and Rummler, 1988].

CONCLUSIONS

It has been suggested that role playing exercises may be useful in classroom situations in which a premium is placed not only on getting students to learn to think, but also to learn to do. Indeed, role playing exercises may be a natural addition to cases in the implementation stage of discussions. A specific situation has been described in which students have been relatively satisfied in its effectiveness in adding to their education in an intercultural exercise.

REFERENCES

Anderson, Joseph V., "Put Work and Play into Marketing," Industrial Marketing Management 22, (1993), pp. 1-6.

Business Week, "The Best B Schools," (October 26, 1992), pp. 60-70.

Dessler, Gary, Personnel/Human Resource Management 5th ed. (Englewood Cliffs, NJ: Prentice Hall, 1991), pp. 293-294.

Graham, John L., Leonid I. Evenko, Mahesh N. Rajan, "An Empirical Comparison of Soviet and American Business Negotiations," Journal of International Business Studies 23-3, (1992), pp. 387-418.

Haas, Robert W., Business Marketing Management: An Organizational Approach (Boston, MA: PWS-Kent, 1992), pp. 517-520.

Hall, Edward T., The Silent Language (Garden City, NY: Doubleday & Co., 1959), pp. 1-2 et seq.

Jain, Subhash C., International Marketing Management 3rd ed. (Boston, MA: PWS-Kent, 1990).

Lichtenthal, J. David and Gul Butany, "Undergraduate Industrial Marketing: Content and Methods," Industrial Marketing Management 20 (1991), pp. 231-239.

Meyers, Patricia W. and Parker M. Worthing, "Marketing Educators as Artists: Lessons from History and Beyond," Marketing Comes of Age - 1984: Proceedings of the Southern Marketing Association, David M. Klein and Allen E. Smith, eds. (1984), pp. 243-246.

Ordiorne, George S. and Geary A. Rummler, Training and Development: A Guide for Professionals (Chicago, IL: Conference Clearing House, Inc., 1988), pp. 218-235.

Sheth, Jadish, N., "Buyer-Seller Interactions: A Conceptual Framework," in B.B. Anderson, ed. Advances in Consumer Research III (Cincinnati, OH: Association for Consumer Research, 1976), pp. 382-386.

Wilson, Timothy, "International Marketing in Sweden: Course Content and Conduct," Proceedings of Midwest Marketing Conference, in press.

CHAPTER THREE

PROBLEM-BASED LEARNING IN ACCOUNTING:
FROM HIPPOCRATES TO PACIOLI

Julien Bilodeau & Réal Labelle
ÉSG - Université du Québec à Montréal
MONTREAL, QUEBEC, CANADA
Pascal Dumontier
ÉSA - Grenoble II
GRENOBLE, FRANCE

Abstract[1]

Problem-based learning is a method that follows a structured approach focusing on the student. The emphasis is less on the teaching of the concepts that relate to specific disciplines than on the use of such concepts to adequately solve meaningful problems. This article has three objectives. In the first part, we suggest a reflection on the professional education process and on how traditional accounting programs have tried to meet the cognitive objectives implied by this process. We then explore how the PBL method could be adapted to the teaching of accounting. In the third part, we describe an experiment conducted with students enrolled in a graduate program. In conclusion, we present several research questions that need to be answered on this subject.

INTRODUCTION

Problem-based learning (PBL) is a learning method that follows a structured approach focusing on the student. It is different from the more traditional teaching approaches which are often centred on the professor. The emphasis is less on the teaching of the concepts that relate to specific functional areas of accounting (financial, managerial, systems, tax & auditing) than on the use of such concepts to adequately solve meaningful problems. In Canada, several Schools of medicine have adopted PBL. In these Schools, learning is mainly based on the solution of practical or theoretical problems. Students approach these problems by working in groups. Under the supervision of a professor (tutor), they identify and analyse each problem and then try to figure out means to solve them. Their work mostly involves readings, group discussions, practical assignments, laboratory experiments or other relevant activities.

PBL attempts to optimize the learning conditions by facilitating the use of relevant prior knowledge and by simulating real world settings. It stimulates motivation by involving students in their professional training. It develops their autonomy by improving their analysis and problem solving skills. It also uses the student's abilities and skills for team work.

This article has three objectives. In the first part, we suggest a reflection on the professional training process and on how traditional accounting programs have tried to meet the cognitive objectives implied by this process. We then analyse how the PBL method could be adapted to accounting education. In the third part, we present the results of an experiment conducted by one of the authors with students enrolled in a master program. In conclusion, we present several research questions that need to be answered on this subject.

ACCOUNTING PROFESSIONAL EDUCATION

Those involved in accounting education have several challenges to meet. Namely, they are related to the following problems:
- the body of knowledge that students must master is ever increasing while the programs cannot expand

at the same pace,
- the lack of integration among the disciplines which make up any accounting program,
- the need for continuing education after graduation in the face a rapidly evolving environment,
- the difficulty that students have in applying their theoretical knowledge to real life situations.

These challenges are not particular to accounting education. Similar challenges must be met in other fields as well. For instance, Abrahamson 1979 and Guilbert 1981 made a list of several "diseases" affecting programs in the field of medicine.

Before presenting PBL as a means to take up those challenges, it might be useful to first consider the professional education process and the ways in which traditional accounting programs have tried to meet the cognitive objectives that this process implies. As mentioned by Williams & al. [1988, p. 164]: "We need to know more about what and how our students learn and what role we play in the process, in order to know what to teach and how to teach it."

In order to educate professional accountants, Business Schools have at least two missions:
- to teach the discipline's specific knowledge, and
- to allow the students to develop their natural skills and abilities.

These missions can be analysed using Bloom's 1969 taxonomy[2] which proposes six learning levels corresponding to as many cognitive objectives:

1. *Acquiring knowledge* implies recalling definitions, concepts, facts, methods, rules, models...

Most of the accounting programs attempt to reach this first level objective by breaking up the business world in different functional areas such as auditing, taxation... and by calling upon specialists to teach them. This method affects (or is the consequence of) the way the university is structured; that is, by departments, services or sectors regrouping professors by disciplines. In such a structure, the probability of forgetting that acquisition of knowledge constitutes only part of the learning process and of equating the evolution of a program with the addition of more courses is high. If even the way programs are structured does not induce professors to go beyond their specialization, one must not be surprised that the students have problems integrating and applying what they have learned to solve real life problems.

2. *Understanding* means to be able to repeat what we have learned in our own words, to explain, translate, interpret, summarize and extrapolate without necessarily relating it to other material or seeing its fullest implications.

In a final examination at the end of a lecture, a student may show a good knowledge and understanding of the subject. However, these often do not take the test of time due to poor integration of the subject.

3. *Application* is the use of theoretical concepts in concrete situations. Principles, general rules and theories are recalled and the suitable ones are applied to actual and specific situations.

Lectures do not easily allow to go beyond this third learning level. In fact, they usually offer students few opportunities to activate and elaborate on prior knowledge in order to apply it in a context similar to the one in which they will practice. Based on Anderson's 1977 work, Schmidt [1983, p. 12] mentions that these three conditions are nevertheless essential in order to optimize learning:

"In conclusion, education should help students in activating relevant prior knowledge, provide a context that resembles the future professional context as closely as possible, and stimulate students to elaborate on their knowledge. If one or more of these conditions are not met, the quality of instruction will suffer."

4. *Analysis* implies distinguishing, detecting, discriminating, comparing or ranking.

For instance, we analyse financial statements. It is a search for components, for the cause and effect relationship, for the organization principles, for models. The analysis of complex cases to understand a situation by identifying the strategic problems, the causes, would allow to meet this objective [Thakur & Vosikis 1990, p. 34].

5. *Synthesis* is the amalgamation of parts and elements to make up a whole, a plan, a structure that we could not perceive before.

The actions of drafting a report, producing, creating, initiating, deducing, documenting, modifying, proposing, planning, developing, combining and organizing are part of this level. According to Thakur & Vosikis 1990, a case study where one needs to develop a set of strategic alternatives and a recommended plan of action would be a good way to exercise synthesis. Most accounting programmes do not include much courses using the case study approach. According to Bernard et Prégent 1989, this method would better be suited to attain and go beyond the application level.

6. *Evaluation* implies the ability to give an opinion, to assess, to argue, to validate, to recommend, to decide, to consider, to standardize.

The closer we get to this upper level of the learning process, the less important the memory's role becomes while the thinking and judgement abilities become of the utmost importance. At the end of his university learning process, the future professional accountant should therefore demonstrate that, besides his technical knowledge certifying his competence, he possesses the following aptitudes and skills:
a) to point out and define the client's or company's financial or related problems based on the information he gathered, the symptoms he noted or the mandate he obtained;
b) to show judgement in distinguishing important from secondary problems, in analysing them from a qualitative and quantitative point of view and in choosing practical solutions among possible alternatives;
c) to communicate either verbally or in writing in a clear and logical manner and to meet the user's needs;
d) to show autonomy in efficiently completing the task notwithstanding the pressure in an unstructured environment.

In the medical education literature, PBL is described as a useful alternative to conventional teaching methods [Schmidt 1983]. It is suggested that PBL could be an efficient remedy to the "diseases" previously mentioned. In Canada, many medicine Faculties have adopted the PBL method[3]. Can this model fit accounting education? The next section attempts to answer this question.

PBL: FROM HIPPOCRATES TO PACIOLI

This section's objective is to explore how the PBL method could be adapted to accounting education. In order to achieve this, we rely on the work of Schmidt [1983], Dumais [1993] and Labelle, Crôteau & Chaîné [1992]. We mainly refer to the way PBL is actually used at the "Centre hospitalier universitaire de l'Université de Sherbrooke."

The PBL process usually requires the formation of small groups of 8 to 12 students. Members may regularly switch from one group to another to allow them to develop their adaptability toward different work teams. The process starts with a problem presented in a text that can be a few lines or a few pages long including appendixes such as the following:

The President of a family business meets with his accountant and formulates the following comment:
"My brother and I do not agree any longer on the way our trucking family business should be managed. I would like to buy him out." or, The firm's partner gives you a pension plan draft agreement while mentioning: "Mrs. Smith, Vice-president, human resources, wants our opinion on this document before taking any decision. Prepare a report on this subject for me."

When the problems given to the students require the acquisition of skills relating to an activity or a project, in engineering for example, this method is referred to as "Project-based learning." These group projects often result in objects or documents such as an intervention plan, a model, a report. When multi-disciplinary case studies are not used only to review subjects previously seen in class but to acquire additional information or knowledge (theory, models, concepts...), they relate more the PBL method than to the case method.

The task of the group of students is to work toward the solution of the problem or the completion of the mandate using a systematic approach to analyse it, formulate learning objectives and gather additional information. The method is composed of three phases, each divided in several steps (table 1). The PBL's first seven steps as used by the University of Sherbrooke are identical to the ones described in Schmidt [1983]. They are borrowed from the scientific approach while the last three, added by the University of Sherbrooke, make the group raise a research question and assess its performance and the one of its members. A professor acts as a tutor[4]. A three hours tutorial takes place twice a week. During the first 60 to 90 minutes, the group completes the third phase of the previous problem; then, after a break, it analyses a new problem following the steps of the first phase. Each step is explained below by presenting its objectives and a description of the students' approach.

TABLE 1
ACTIVITIES RELATED TO THE PROBLEM-BASED LEARNING METHOD

First phase : Define the problem & formulate learning objectives

1. Read the problem & clarify terms, concepts & data
2. a) Precisely define the problem or mandate
   b) Draw up a list of questions, transactions requiring an explanation
3. Analyse the problem, suggest explanations
4. Draw a systematic inventory of the explanations inferred from step 3
5. Formulate learning objectives

Second phase: Individual study

6. Collect additional information outside the group

Third phase: Synthesis

7. Synthesize and validate the newly acquired information by applying it to the problem
8. Raise a research question
9. Assess the group performance
10. Assess the performance of individual students

PHASE 1: DEFINE THE PROBLEM & FORMULATE LEARNING OBJECTIVES

1. Read the problem and clarify terms, concepts and data
Objectives:
- Quickly identify the significant clues tied to the problem or the elements of the mandate,
- Identify the appendixes or portions of the text containing information about the questions to deal with,
- Use accounting or management terminology rigorously,
- Determine the environment of the problem (type of transactions or events, diagram of the relations between the various participants or companies, concerns, objectives or client's interests).

Each student reads the problem with maximum concentration, establishing his objectives, raising questions, showing critical mind as if he/she would be reading a contract. Throughout this reading, problems, information or key words, reactions, ideas or points of view are either underlined or noted in the margin to be presented to the members of the group in the subsequent steps. These notes are formulated in such a way so as to direct the analysis. For example, instead of simply writing "audit" in the margin besides a paragraph that deals with that issue, the student tries to be more precise in order to remember within which context he will have to demonstrate his current knowledge or acquire new one; does-it deal with the "implications of an initial audit mandate," "the drafting of an audit programme," the consideration of "the underlying audit risks."..?

The group agrees on the definition of the significant terms based on each member's knowledge and, if needed, with the help of a dictionary. While avoiding that this phase be completed superficially, it should not last long but allow a proper segregation between the terms that can be clarified immediately and the notions that will acquire their precise significance only after their analysis and study.

2. a) Precisely define the problem or mandate
Objective:
- Get used to come up with an accurate definition of the problem by keeping key elements and discarding secondary ones.

After a moment of reflection, students agree on a text summarizing the situation and its foremost characteristics. When the situation is complex, this summary will identify the secondary issues. They emphasize the relationships, the logical links among the questions addressed. Most of the time, there is a major problem (scenario) to which questions or ideas noted at the time of reading get linked. This scenario is summarized in a single line. This is not the diagnosis but rather the identification of the consultation's reason including its main circumstances, the role to play. Most of the scenarios will propel the student closed to the top of the organizational structure. He must determine accurately why his services are required? What is his task or mandate in the circumstances? Is-he acting as an auditor, a management consultant, an expert-witness, a controller...? The answer to these questions will influence the way the issue will be addressed.

2. b) Draw up a list of questions, transactions requiring an explanation
Objectives:
- Identify and associate the significant clues to precisely define and put in its context the problem, the questions to be addressed or the mandate,
- continuously raise questions about the situation, the sequence of events, their relationship, the usefulness of the financial statements or other tables that may be comprised in the problem,
- get used to plan ahead any discussion or work.

Students review the clues and the problems they have identified and point out those requiring explanations. They note on a board the most relevant questions without trying to answer them. These questions may be part of an explicit mandate where, for instance, you have to determine how to account for a specific transaction or they may constitute implicit problems that must be identified from clues or symptoms as in medicine. For example, the tax implications of a decision, erroneous analysis already performed by the executives involved in the problem, financial statements that need to be restated, conflicts of interest and other code of ethics related issues, the necessity to establish financing requirements as a result of a recommended project, a critical financial position that prevents management from completing its expansion project or consider a share issue... could constitute implicit problems.

The problem may include one or several tables or sets of financial statements. The latter often include data which will require analysis in order to recommend relevant solutions to the problems addressed. Before starting the analysis, it is imperative to establish their usefulness within the context. What is their role? Are-they under litigation? Is their presentation in line with the reader's needs or in accordance with GAAP? Are-they audited? By whom? Are-there the financial statements of a company to be acquired, a company that requires financing to expand or to correct its financial situation? Will-they be used to establish or justify the pricing policy? Such a list could be lengthened indefinitely. The members of the group must realize that each and every question raised requires a different analysis from both a qualitative and quantitative point of view to solve it.

This list represents the group's consensus on elements, transactions, phenomenon, symptoms, tables, relationships that require an interpretation or an explanation. Without being exhaustive, this list will help the group to sort the questions and reach agreement on a plan of the work or analysis to complete within the next hour.

3. Analyse the problem, suggest explanations or formulate hypotheses
Objectives:
- Optimize learning by facilitating the activation of prior knowledge and the creation of links between the latter and the knowledge to be acquired during the personal study period (phase II),
- Promote an efficient encoding of knowledge by linking it to a real life situation.

The problem's analysis is done using the list completed during the previous steps. It requires a careful perusal of the text stating the problem to gain a clear impression of the situation described, which translates into ideas and assumptions about the structure of the problem [Schmidt 1983]. It is a case of finding the causes of the symptoms and problems, of explaining them, of organizing them in a logical manner. To formulate hypotheses, students rely on two sources: prior knowledge that they recall and rational explanations which, although logical, are not necessarily true, that they share with the group. Dumais 1993 points out that this is where the participation of everyone is the strongest. Everyone suggests ideas and then clarifies, develops, modifies or goes thoroughly into them. This brainstorming does not only aim at putting forward hypotheses, but at testing and enhancing them. This analysis effort could result in the following reflections: "Could-it be that the company's problems be explained by...?," "Does the company have the financial resources to have a pension plan (PP)?" After discussions, each relevant assumption is retained by the group and noted on a board. While discussing, the need for new knowledge (ex: fiscal implications of a PP) is identified and noted on another board meant for all questions which need to be studied or for the learning objectives.

114

4. Draw a systematic inventory of the explanations inferred from step 3 and organize them

Objectives:
- Develop the intellectual skills needed by the professional candidate to be able to organize, make up links and draw up priorities,
- get used to complete an assignment or a discussion by summing up,
- link the present knowledge of various disciplines to the one to be acquired in the next study period.

At this stage, the group draws up a systematic list of the hypothesized explanations written down on the board and produces a synthesis. The group excludes all irrelevant elements and organizes, groups the others in a logical sequence or according to their importance. This global view takes shape in a plan or a diagram showing the links between the problems and all the standpoints (accounting, fiscal, administrative) from which they should be examined.

In the case of problems requiring a quantitative analysis (ex: a price, a cost, a net present value, restated financial statements...), the group determines precisely all data required to solve them. As a doctor chooses a diagnosis instrument according to the circumstances, the group selects a relevant analysis or calculation model. In the pension plan example, the group could have drawn the diagram below:

5. Formulate learning objectives

Objectives:
- Involve students in the identification of their learning needs,[5]
- get students to draw up a study plan corresponding to the specific needs identified above, to establish priorities, to foresee the sources of information, to determine how they will spend the time available.

This step has almost been completed while performing the previous ones, i. e., when students deficient knowledge, smatterings, uncertainties were written down as questions to be researched on the board reserved for this use. Students complete this list by precisely defining the study matters or required information they need to solve previously identified problems. A study plan is then prepared for which the group agrees on priorities and on the breakdown of available time. It also attempts to identify the most relevant sources of information. In the pension plan example, the following questions could have been raised:
- What is a PP? Detailed examination of the project clauses submitted by an expert.
- How does this project fit in the actual remuneration policy of the company?
- What are the costs (discounting)? Where will the funds come from? Links with other projects needing important outlays (budget)?
- What would be the effect on financial statements? On the audit mandate?
- What are the tax implications for the company? For its employees?

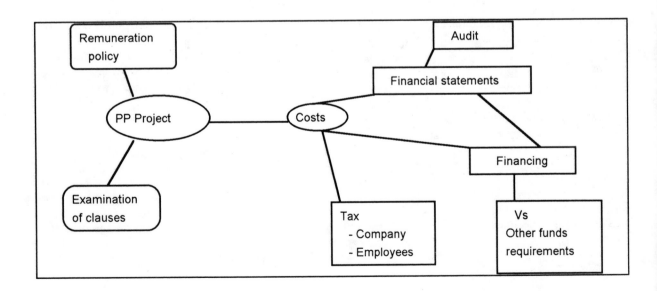

PHASE 2: PERSONAL STUDY

<u>6.   Collect additional information outside the group</u>
Objectives:
- Collect and master the information necessary to explain and solve the problem,
- gain the required skills and abilities for an autonomous apprenticeship.

Members of the group generally have two or three days to personally gather the information relating to the explanation of the problem and to the learning objectives. They consult various sources such as the library resources, their personal documentation, financial data bases, video cassettes or computer assisted learning software. This could also be an opportunity to question expert professors or practitioners during sessions organized by the tutor (why not ask the real actors of the practical problems submitted to the students to intervene?) .

To fully take advantage of this phase, the University of Sherbrooke students are encouraged to compel themselves to the following discipline [Dumais 1993]:
- Review the list of study questions prepared by the group and adapt it to personal needs by precisely formulating each learning objective;
- plan the period by conveniently breaking down the time available between hours devoted to concentrated work and to other personal activities;
- identify the most relevant sources of information;
- quickly distinguish and reject the irrelevant information;
- derive what is important by underlining, reformulating or summarizing it;
- note the ambiguities to be discussed by the group;
- end the study period by a synthesis of newly acquired knowledge;
- note the quality of references used to share them with colleagues
- complete this step by doing an evaluation of the process followed and of its efficiency.

PHASE 3 : SYNTHESIS

<u>7.   Synthesize and validate the newly acquired information by applying it to the problem</u>
Objectives:
- Elaborate knowledge from problems or practical situations,
- apply, formulate, verify or criticize newly acquired knowledge,
- test its understanding with the help of peers assessment and criticism,
- integrate knowledge, organize its structure in memory, increase its retention and facilitate its access in the future.

Students rejoin in small groups and, after having briefly commented and criticized the sources used for their personal study, agree on a formal discussion plan. Most of the time, the group redo the problem analysis by drawing up a new diagram. It is the discussion, and not the recitation of the newly acquired knowledge, and its application to complex practical situations that constitutes the focus point of this step. Newly acquired knowledge is shared, applied, criticized, corrected and completed. Members of the group use this discussion with peers to test their understanding and to reach an agreement on the problem's explanations or the formulation of recommendations as they would do, for instance, if they were sitting a an executive committee.

<u>8. Raise a research question</u>
Objectives:
- Arouse scientific curiosity,
- share the pleasure of discovering and understanding the limits of current knowledge.

In a round-table discussion, the group tries to put in perspective research questions that are still left open or that they would like to study in more depth.

<u>9. Assess the group performance</u>
Objectives:
- Analyse what is happening within the group, how it progresses, why each of its members enjoys or not being part of it,

- identify the strengths and weaknesses and agree on improvement objectives.

To assess the group's performance, two aspects are considered: a) the quality of the analysis process and the progress realized by the group in its learning path; b) the group's dynamic, the relationships and the working climate. Dumais [1993] strongly suggest not to elude this step even if it is difficult for a group to stop and assess its functioning. The group is a powerful instrument to maintain individual motivation, to acquire communication skills and to show human concerns.

10. Assess the performance of individual students
Objective:

- Acquire the intellectual discipline needed to complete an activity by writing down a summary of what has been done and what is left to be done, discipline that will prove valuable for continuing education purpose during the professional life.

On an individual basis, students list the learning objectives they master and the subjects they have completed, noting the best sources of information for review or consultation.

EXPLORATORY STUDY

In this section, we describe a practical experience conducted in the spirit of PBL with the second year students of the masters degree in management of the University of Grenoble II Business School. This experience, without scientific pretention, took place during a seminar on financial diagnosis. The 36 hours of the seminar were shared between lectures (30 %), case studies (55 %) and periods where problem-based learning was used (15 %). For the PBL portion of the seminar, in accordance with what this method involves, the task mainly consisted in organizing the environment in which the students were responsible of their learning process.

In a first experience, students used "Syface[6]," an educational software meant to allow them to complete their learning of financial analysis concepts and put their knowledge into practice. This method has been well greeted. These computer assisted learning devices may be useful during the second phase of PBL, i. e., during the personal study.

In a second experience, as per step 5 of PBL, students agreed on the key characteristics of an enterprise which should be examined for diagnosis purpose (see appendix 1). Then, working in small groups of 4 or 5, they had recourse to the data base called "DIANE" (for "Disque pour l'ANalyse Economique") and to other sources of information (PBL-step 6) to complete a report presenting the financial and economic diagnosis of a company of their choice. In addition to containing thousands of French companies annual reports, this data base comes with a software permitting the analysis of the data it contains. Finally, as per step 7 of the method, reports were presented to the members of the group and a discussion took place to share the information gathered.

SUMMARY AND RESEARCH PATHS

In this article, we have first proposed a reflection on the professional education process and on how traditional accounting curricula have tried to meet the cognitive objectives implied by this process. We have then explored how the PBL method, currently used to teach medicine at the University of Sherbrooke, could be adapted to accounting education. Finally, we have described an experiment conducted by one of the authors with students enrolled in a graduate program.

The theory seems to indicate that PBL could prove to be a useful add-on or could even replace traditional accounting teaching methods. However, the adoption of this method poses many problems that this article does not obviously pretend to resolve. To conclude, we are proposing a certain number of empirical or logistical research questions which remain to be addressed. Other disciplines such as medicine and engineering have already raised those questions and have started to address them. It also constitutes an interesting accounting research issue.

1. What would be the effect of PBL on the quality of professional accounting education? Does-it improve the learning and retention abilities and does it improve the way knowledge is applied in solving problems. The PBL hypothesis could be tested through an experiment similar to the one used in medicine by Schmidt 1982. A practical accounting problem could be submitted to several small groups of students (experimental groups). They would then study a text containing new relevant information. Problems would then be

submitted to these experimental groups as well as to other control groups that would only have studied the text. The effect of the PBL approach would be tested by comparing the ability of each of the two groups in solving the problems by using the information contained in the text.

2. How can such a programme, based on the use of problems that provide for a "cumulative, integrated, progressive and coherent learning" [Engel 1991], be elaborated?

3. Is there a danger for students to become too dependent upon this small working groups environment? How will they react in the workplace facing a complex problem by themselves?

4. What is the cost associated with the PBL method compared to the one of traditional methods? and some related questions: Assuming the total time spent on study remains the same for students, how to translate the current lectures of traditional programs into PBL programs? How to convert the current workload of professors into tutorial activities? How to resolve the problem associated with the increased number of rooms necessary for small groups' meetings?

5. The problems associated with accounting education programmes are well known, but what are the chances, in the short run, for a real change in the way the accounting is taught to happen? How to face the resistance to change?

APPENDIX 1
ELEMENTS OF A COMPANY'S DIAGNOSIS

1. Context
   - Brief history
   - Portfolio of activities - Major and secondary
   - Point of view: Who does the diagnosis? From which point of view (actual or potential shareholder, lender...)? What for? In what conditions or economical context?

2. Economic diagnosis
   - Products portfolio: What is the products portfolio in each main activity? What is their stage of development, maturity? Their strengths? Their weaknesses? Their position towards competition...?
   - Market research
   - Distribution, pricing, advertising policies etc.

3. Social diagnosis
   - Age pyramid of employees
   - Socio professional category
   - Hiring policy
   - Formation policy
   - Indicators of the social balance sheet, etc.

4. Financial diagnosis
   - Activity, productivity, profitability evolution
   - Liquidity and financial equilibrium analysis (working capital, treasury and working capital requirements)
   - Analysis of the changes in the use and sources of funds
   - Treasury analysis etc.

5. Conclusions
   - Strengths and weaknesses
   - Possible improvements (how?)
   - Future outlook
   - Recommendations (from the point of view of the diagnostician).

ENDNOTES

1. This article is part of a research project sponsored by the "Ordre des comptables agréés du Québec" (C. D. Mellor scholarship) and the University of Québec" (Fonds de développement académique du réseau) to whom the authors are grateful.

2.   Miller & al. 1978 refined Bloom's taxonomy and contributed many of the descriptive verbs and terms used thereafter to describe the levels.

3.   Namely, McMaster University, University of Sherbrooke and University of Montréal (September 1994).

4.   For a description of the possible type of tutor's interventions as a guide to the problem analysis process and to the group's functioning, see Dumais 1993

5.   It is the students' responsibility to find the learning objectives but they can be guided by their tutor during the tutorial. If needed, the tutor could be more directive during this step in order to get the students to find the objectives listed in the tutor's guide [Dumais 1993].

6.   "Syface" is a financial analysis educational software which was developed by one the author, Pascal Dumontier, and Bertrand Brisson of University of St-Étienne.

REFERENCES

Abrahamson, S, "Diseases of the Curriculum," *Journal of Medical Education* (53, 1979), pp. 951-957.

Albanese, M. A., Mitchell, S., "Problem-based Learning: A review of Literature on its Outcomes and Implementation Issues," *Academic Medicine* (vol. 68, number 1, January 1993), pp. 52 - 81.

AA A, "Teaching and Curriculum Section," *Report of the 1992-1993 Outcomes Assessment Committee*, 59 p.

Amesse, F., Comtois, J., Livick, V., Pelletier, M., Savoie, R., Rapport du Gr. de travail sur la formation en sc. compt. soumis au Comité des affaires académiques de la CREPUQ, (December 1992), 17 p.

Barrows H S, "A taxonomy of problem-based learning methods," *Medical Education* 1986, pp. 481-486

Bernard, H., Prégent, R., *Atelier de formation pédagogique, la préparation systématique d'un cours*, Manuel du participant (August 1989), 73 p.

Big Eight Accounting Firms Sponsoring Partners, *Perspectives on Education: Capabilities for success in the Accounting Profession* (1989), 15 pages.

Bloom, B.-S., *Taxonomie des objectifs pédagogiques*, Montréal, tome I, Domaine cognitif, Education nouvelle (1969), 232 p.

Dumais, B., "L'apprentissage par problème, description des étapes de l'APP," pp. 11-30. In: *L'apprentissage par problème: un programme centré sur l'étudiant*. Sous la direction des professeurs Des Marchais J. E. et Dumais, B., Faculté de médecine, Un. de Sherbrooke, Sherb., Qué. (1993), 395 p.

Engel, C. E., "Not Just a Method But a Way of Learning." In Boud, D., Feletti, G., *The Challenge of Problem-Based Learning*, (St-Martin Press 1991), pp. 23-33.

Guilbert, J. J., "Les maladies du Currilum," *Revue française d'Éducation Médicale* (6, 1981), pp.13-16.

ICACB, *The board of examiners' report on the 1991 uniform final examination*, 39 p.

Labelle, R., Crôteau, O., Chaîné, J., *Cas de comptabilité: méthode et outils d'analyse*, (Science et culture 1992), 355 p.

Managing Change with cases, simulations, games and other interactive methods, ed. by Hans E. Klein, (WACRA 1991).

Miller, H. G., Williams R. G., Haladyna T. M., "Beyond Facts: Objective Ways to Measure Thinking" (Educational Technology Publications 1978), in AAA Teaching and Curriculum Section, *Report of the 1992-1993 Outcomes Assessment Committee.*

Norman, G., "Research in the Psychology of Clinical Reasoning : Implications for Assessment" (Cambridge Conference IV, 1989).

Norman, G., Schmidt, H. G., "The Psychological Basis of Problem-based learning: A Review of the Evidence," *Academic Medicine* (vol. 67, number 9, September 1992), p. 557 - 565.

Norman, G., "Problem-solving skills versus problem-based learning," pp. 297 - 299. In: *L'apprentissage par problème: un programme centré sur l'étudiant.* sous la direction des professeurs Des Marchais J. E. et Dumais, B., Faculté de médecine, Université de Sherbrooke, Sherbrooke, Québec, 1993, 395 p

Schmidt, H. G., "Problem-based learning: rationale and description" *Medical Education* 1983, pp.11-16.

Schmidt, H. G., "Activation and Restructuring of Prior Knowledge and their Effects on Text Processing," in Flammer, A., Kintsch, W. (eds), *Discourse Processing* (North-Holland Publishing 1982).

Sequencing accounting curriculum content: a basis for restructuring, (Proceedings of the CAAA Education Congress May 1991).

Thakur, M., Vozikis, G., "Pedagogy and the case method: a comparative analysis," *Canadian journal of administrative sciences* (Vol. 7, no. 1, Mars 1990), pp. 29-36.

The bachelor of accounting program, Brock University, Ontario, (Proceedings of the CAAA Education Congress May 1991).

Walton, H. J., Matthews, M. B., "Essentials of problem-based learning," *Medical Education* (23, 1989), pp. 542-558.

Williams J., Tiller M., Herring III H., and J. Scheiner, "A Framework for the Development of Accounting Education Research" (AAA 1988).

LEARNING BY DISCOVERING: USING A CASE IN AN INTRODUCTION TO ACCOUNTING COURSE

Michel Blanchette and François Brouard
Université du Québec à Hull
HULL, QUÉBEC, CANADA

Abstract[1]

This paper[2] explains the main characteristics of a learning tool designed to encourage students to use their common sense and to actively participate in class. The case "Le Banquier" is a role-playing game developed specifically for the very first class of an Introduction to Accounting course. A special feature of this case is that it allows students to develop professional skills in addition to acquiring technical knowledge.

INTRODUCTION

Historically, the primary role of a public accountant has been the preparation of financial statements [Côté and Tremblay, 1991]. As the 21st century approaches, that role is exploding, becoming proactive and future-oriented. The public accountant is a change agent who can influence many types of decisions in many fields, including finance, fiscal law and human resource management[3]. Many studies have shown that accounting information has significant explaining power in terms of behaviour [Watts and Zimmerman, 1986; Boland and Gordon, 1992].

In a university-level Introduction to Accounting course, one usually deals with financial statements, ledgers, and a few theoretical principles, all of which are treated in a somewhat isolated manner. Our observations are that this way of doing things has undesirable consequences. First, it invites students to memorize the various topics, which gives them temporary knowledge that rapidly fades away. Second, it encourages them to neglect the concepts and focus on technical details. In short, the way training is done does not encourage them to demonstrate their professional abilities.[4]

To remedy this we have created a learning tool that requires the skills and the participation of the students in the classroom. This tool, the case "Le Banquier", requires their interactive participation and allows them to discover the main concepts on their own.

The main objective of this paper is to present the characteristics of the case "Le Banquier" as a learning tool that can allow students to learn by discovering. The second objective is to discuss the advantages and disadvantages encountered while using the case during an Introduction to Accounting course at the Université du Québec à Hull.

The rest of this paper is divided into four sections. In the next one, we explain the objectives and the learning techniques we are aiming for. We then present the main characteristics of the case "Le Banquier" and how it is used in class. We then discuss the results that we observed after using the case. Finally, we present our conclusion.

LEARNING BY DOING

In an Introduction to Accounting course, there are usually a number of "technical" training objectives. These deal with the acquisition of knowledge, understanding and application, i.e., the three first levels in Bloom's taxonomy. Because of this, the lecture method has been favoured up to now in such courses because it fits well with the objectives [Prégent, 1990].

Starting from the hypothesis that the lecture method is the one most frequently used in Introduction to Accounting courses, we believed that an innovative teaching technique would stand a good chance of being interesting for the students. The method would focus on them, which could motivate them, and would certainly bring a certain variety to the courses.

LEARNING OBJECTIVES

More and more, Canadian professional accounting bodies are requiring that students demonstrate professional abilities in such areas as judgment and communication [CGA, 1994; CMA, 1994; CICA, 1993]. Although an Introduction to Accounting course includes a significant amount of technical knowledge, it would be desirable that teachers use pedagogical techniques that allow students to develop their professional abilities. This does not mean reducing the amount of technical knowledge, but rather adding the development of abilities that the lecture method imparts only with great difficulty. This would be possible by making better use of the time available. The objectives are therefore of two types: technical knowledge and professional abilities.

Technical knowledge

The technical knowledge to be acquired falls into the following areas: the needs of the users of accounting information; the role of accounting information; certain accounting principles such as conservatism, reliability, historical cost and matching; the accounting equation and the balance sheet; the notions of "fixed date" and "financial period". This knowledge is basic and provides the students with a conceptual framework that will allow them to integrate the subject matter that flows from it. Examples of this are: knowledge about the users of accounting information and their needs in order to understand the rationale behind and the specific rules governing the presentation of financial statements (the short- and long-term classification of a balance sheet); the accounting principle of conservatism that is useful for understanding measurement rules such as the lower of cost and market (short-term investments and inventory), etc.

Professional abilities

Many professional abilities can be developed through interactive teaching techniques. They are in fact quite general and apply to most disciplines. The professional abilities we are most interested in are the following: judgment, which is closely related to the ability to structure and synthesize both qualitative and quantitative information; communication, through the efficient and favourable presentation of relevant information; and certain aspects of human behaviour such as ethics, emotion and negotiation.

LEARNING BY DISCOVERING

The idea of integrating objectives related to both technical knowledge and professional abilities in a single pedagogical tool is particulary innovative when applied to an Introduction to Accounting course. The teaching techniques that are most relevant to the acquisition of such abilities are those that focus on discussion, working in groups and individual work [Prégent, 1990; Bhada, 1993]. It is in this context that we are proposing the use of role-playing as a teaching technique.

Role-playing

In role-playing, students are not force-fed knowledge through lectures or lengthy normative deductions; instead, it is arrived at inductively. During role-playing, students use a decision-making process that relies on realistic information like that encountered in practice [Prégent, 1990]. It is therefore desirable that participants make certain errors and pull off some "good shots", such as poorly presenting information and seeing undesirable decisions as a result; omitting information, with unfortunate consequences; revealing disadvantageous facts, but having a positive effect on credibility; etc. We hope that students will come to realize that certain accounting policies designed to structure financial information logically can help in decision-making. In financial accounting, such policies correspond to generally accepted accounting principles.[5]

This way of doing things motivates students because they are directly involved and because role-playing is based on situations that are encountered in practice. It is also likely to be effective in the long run because students find it easier to remember concepts that they have discovered as opposed to those described by a teacher. In other words, we don't teach students that accountants invented debits and put them on the left, invented credits and put them on the right, that entries always have the same number of debits and credits, and that the sum of these entries constitute financial statements that can allow users to make decisions. Instead, we make them play the role of users who, as a result of discussions at their level, deduce the main concepts that underlie accounting.

Preparation

For students to learn by discovering, it is essential that they not have been previously exposed to the subject matter. Of course this implies that it has not been touched upon in class beforehand, but also that the students not have done any preparatory work. The latter condition is often difficult to achieve during a semester since students often do preparatory reading before coming to class (and this is most desirable!). On the other hand, this is not the case at the very first class of the semester. It is for this reason that the case "Le Banquier" has been designed to be used during this first class.

Even in an Introduction to Accounting course it is possible that some students have received some training in accounting even before the course starts.[6] The teacher will have to take that into consideration. One way to reduce the negative impact in such cases is to make these students play the role of critical observers. We will come back to this in the section on suggested procedure.

"CASE" OR "ROLE-PLAYING?"

A case is usually a written description of a practical problem. The situation to be analyzed can include all kinds of real information. A case often gives students a situation that is quite close to what they are experiencing or will experience and lead to decisions similar to the ones they will actually have to make.

In role-playing, some students are called upon to act in a brief scenario, in front of their peers, which is very similar to real-life situations. Often, they are not given a text; they receive only general instructions which differ from individual to individual. Each student improvises and tries to act out the feelings, behaviours and attitudes of the person whose role he or she is playing. [Prégent, 1990]

In methodological terms, "Le Banquier" is basically a role-playing exercise, but its content is similar to that of a case. The instructions given to the students are detailed enough to allow an analysis similar to what one would expect in a case study but the main element is a brief role-play by three actors.

THE CASE "LE BANQUIER"

The case "Le Banquier" is a learning tool designed to combine both technical knowledge and professional abilities objectives. It emphasizes student participation and discussion. In this section we will present the main characteristics of the case and a procedure for using it that, in our opinion, maximizes the odds that the activity will meet the stated objectives.

CASE CONTENT

"Le Banquier" is a role-playing exercise in which students are chosen to simulate the decision-making process of a banker who must decide how much to lend to two borrowers. The exercise is built around the interviews during which the borrowers must make their case to the banker. He must then make a decision solely on the basis of the arguments used during the interviews and some additional information that has been given to him. The case is presented as a statement of role-playing rules, to which participants' instructions are attached. The teacher also receives a pedagogical briefing note.

Statement of role-playing rules

The statement of role-playing rules is presented clearly and concisely. After reading it, the students and the teacher should understand exactly what they are trying to accomplish and how they are going to do it. It is critical that there be no misunderstanding at this point in order that the activity not stray from the objectives or require more time than has been allowed.

The main role-playing rules are as follows. The participants must follow the instructions given and stick to the facts given in the description of their role. The banker is the one who decides when the interview is over. The teacher and the students who are observing are not allowed to intervene during playing even if there are factual or procedural errors. Such errors should be identified during the plenary discussions at the end since that is part of the main objective of the activity, learning by discovering.

<u>Participants' instructions</u>

The instructions are presented as appendices. A description of each of the players, i.e., the banker and the two borrowers, as well as their role and objectives, are given in the first series of appendices. The second series contains additional information about events that happen after the role-play.

The information in the appendices is relatively simple but it is presented in random order. It includes quantitative elements that are more or less precise, such as the annual salary of the borrowers and the municipal assessment of the properties they own, and qualitative elements such as the risk aversion demonstrated by the banker and the fact that the borrowers are attached to some of their physical assets. There is some extraneous information. This diversity of information is essential if the activity is to cover both technical knowledge and professional abilities.

The literary style in the appendices is relatively humorous, which tends to create a more relaxed atmosphere and make the activity less formal [Barsoux, 1993]. In fact, one must remember that this case is designed to be used in the first class of an Introduction to Accounting course. It is therefore possible that the students will not be used to or prepared to speak in front of an entire class.

<u>Pedagogical briefing note</u>

The pedagogical briefing note provides some additional information designed to help the teacher manage the activity and guide the discussions. It suggests ways of adapting the activity to groups of different sizes and lists some related subjects that could be discussed. Finally, it presents a list of proposed solution factors.

It goes without saying that there is no single answer to this case since the outcome depends on the role-play and the interpretations given to it. From the viewpoint of the learning objectives, however, it is not the solution that counts, it's the way one gets to it. The list of proposed solution factors is designed only to help the teacher orient the discussions so that the most important elements are brought to light.

PROCEDURE

The procedure is essential if the activity is to succeed. If the suggested procedure is not followed, the creative process of learning by discovering may become a rather passive one for the students. That is why we suggest that the teacher refrain from explaining the main components of a balance sheet before doing the role-playing exercise. In fact, we expect the students who play the role of the banker to ask the borrowers for a list of their assets that could be used as collateral for the loan, as well as a list of their debts, in order to evaluate the credit risk they represent. However, please note that although this information is equivalent to a balance sheet, the borrowers in the role-play have no idea, or perhaps only a vague idea, of what a balance sheet is. Therefore all they know is that they need money and all they have is a list of random information that they must structure, synthesize and present in a manner that will convince the banker to give them the loan they are asking for. It is this absence of previous training that allows learning by discovering. Here is a fairly specific description of the suggested steps to be followed in using the case. To visualize the classification of students, see FIGURE 1.

1. The teacher distributes the statement of role-playing rules to the students and ensures that it is well understood.
2. Initially, three teams of five participants are put together using students who have no previous academic or practical training in accounting. The descriptions of the roles are then distributed: appendix A is given to the banker's team, appendix B to the first borrower's team and appendix C to the second borrower's team. At this stage, it is imperative that each team have only the appendix that describes its role. Hence the banker does not know the situation and objectives of the borrowers and vice-versa. The remaining students are grouped in teams of three to five people who will act as critical observers.[7] The teacher gives them one or more appendices and ask them to concentrate on specific points such as: the ability of the borrowers to present their case; tools and techniques they used (or could have used) to win (or improve their position) in their negotiation; to whom they would lend if they were the banker, etc.
3. Preparation time of 20 to 30 minutes is allowed for each team to put together its arguments. During this time, the three initial teams select a representative who will participate in the role-play.

4. The role-play is acted out. The banker interviews the first borrower, then the second. It must be noted that during the role-play, the 12 remaining members of the initial three teams, the teacher and the critical observers do not have the right to speak.

5. Appendix D, which contains additional information that could be useful, is given to the banker; he is given 5 to 10 minutes to reach a decision and communicate it to everyone.

6. During the plenary discussions that follow, the teacher helps the group do a self-evaluation and to discover what can be learned from the case. At this stage, all students are invited to present their point of view.

7. Appendix E, which includes subsequent humorous information, is given out and the activity is brought to a close.

It takes about two to three hours to complete the activity. That includes the explanations, time to read the material, preparation, the actual role-play and the plenary discussions. Everything is done with minimum intervention by the teacher, except in leading and guiding the plenary discussions. No preparation is required, nor is it even desirable, on the part of the students before the activity.

FIGURE 1
CLASSIFICATION OF STUDENTS

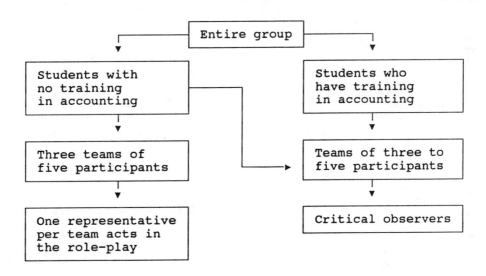

RESULTS OBSERVED AFTER USING THE CASE

In this section we will discuss the advantages and disadvantages we have observed after having used the case in class and we will then present some statistical results to verify that the learning objectives have been met.

ADVANTAGES AND DISADVANTAGES

Up to now, the case "Le Banquier" has been tested with three groups during the fall semester in 1993 and the winter semester in 1994 at the Université du Québec à Hull. Our overall observations, which follow, are very positive.

The main advantage of this case is that it allows students to develop professional abilities. However, an activity designed to develop such abilities might give the students the impression that technical knowledge is less important. The activity takes time and does not cover as much technical knowledge as a three-hour lecture. On the other hand, the knowledge acquired is better understood and better integrated. For example, a teacher in a lecture could list a number of users of accounting information and explain their needs; while just two are seen with the case "Le Banquier", but they are studied in more depth.

The fact that the students themselves play the roles gives the course an interactive dimension. Students are very creative when given a chance to express themselves. And we have seen to what extent that can be a driving force. In fact, what impressed us the most during the activity was the enthusiasm and the motivation demonstrated by the students. They were actively and emotionally involved. The role-playing created a relaxed atmosphere that lasted well beyond the first course. In addition, the opinions of those who expressed themselves were listened to and respected, which created a climate of confidence between the students and the teacher. It is reassuring for students when the discussion deals with a "real-life" situation that is at their level. Things could hardly be otherwise since they control the activity. The psychological gap between teacher and students seemed less great than when the lecture method is used.

As for the technical knowledge, it seemed to us that the students really learned by discovering. Given that the activity took place during the very first class, no student had done any prior reading before the class, which gave a maximum of value added for a minimum of preparatory work. This way, students who had never done any accounting had no choice but to discover!

The critical observers, who are only spectators during the actual role-play, participated fully during the plenary discussions. Those who had already been exposed to accounting seemed to realize that certain concepts they thought they had mastered had subtle aspects that they had not fully grasped. A good example would be that they were aware of the reliability principle but had never made the link with the historical cost principle. The discussions during the role-playing exercise and in subsequent classes seemed richer to us than when the first class was given using the lecture method.

Finally, it is difficult for a teacher to facilitate a role-play since he is not the one who controls it (except for the plenary discussions). There is always the risk that students' participation will not rise to the teacher's expectations. Delegating to the students a significant part of the responsibility for their learning can have undesirable consequences. One example would be a conflict between two students. Some uncontrollable factors might also put the activity at risk, such as having a group in which all the students had previous training in accounting. We have not had such problems up to now but we are aware that they could occur.

STATISTICAL TESTS

Hypotheses

The idea of adding professional abilities as an objective in an Introduction to Accounting course is interesting but risky. One danger is that focusing on professional abilities may cause us to neglect the basic technical knowledge that is so important in such a course. Starting from the premise that technical knowledge is more important than professional ability, we believe that technical knowledge is an important stake (We are aware that this is a debatable premise.). In fact, it is desirable that students in an Introduction to Accounting course develop professional abilities, but not at the expense of technical knowledge. What good is it if students have good judgement but haven't acquired technical knowledge that is essential to an accountant, such as accounting principles and the accounting equation?

We decided to compare the results of a test group with those of a control group on a question regarding the enumeration and understanding of some technical knowledge dealt with in the case "Le Banquier". The same question was asked to all students during an exam; it dealt with the users of financial statements and their needs. Here is the question: "Choose three groups of users of accounting information and discuss, for each one, the extent to which financial statements drawn up according to generally accepted accounting principles meet one of their needs or specific objectives". If the performance of the test group is not significantly inferior to that of the control group, we can then conclude that the students in the test group reached the stated objectives. That assumes that the control group met those objectives. Here is the hypothesis we tested:

The results of the test group, on a question involving technical knowledge dealt with in the case "Le Banquier", are not inferior to those of the control group.

On the other hand, it is recognized that the lecture method helps reach lower level learning objectives (acquiring information, understanding and application) while methods that focus on the students, such as role-playing and the case method, are designed to help reach higher level objectives [Prégent, 1990]. The case "Le Banquier" therefore has a stronger chance of contributing to the development of professional abilities than the lecture method. We have not tested this hypothesis in the current exploratory phase but it would be interesting to do so in future research.

Sample

The sample included a test group and a control group. These groups were made up of students who had taken the Comptabilité I or Comptabilité administrative I courses (Accounting I and Administrative Accounting I) in the fall of 1993 or the winter of 1994 at the Université du Québec à Hull. The course contents are the same in terms of the subjects dealt with in the case "Le Banquier". However, the professors who gave the courses to the two groups are different. In addition, the students registered for these courses have different characteristics. The Comptabilité I course is for students in the accounting program whereas the Comptabilité administrative I course is designed for students in the general administration program. TABLE 1 presents details about the sample.

TABLE 1
SAMPLE DETAILS (NUMBER OF STUDENTS)

	Fall 1993	Winter 1994	Total
Test group	61[1]	27[2]	88
Control group	68[1]	46[1]	114
Total	129	73	202

[1] Students registered for Comptabilité I.
[2] Students registered for Comptabilité administrative I.

It should be noted that all the students who took the Comptabilité I course in the fall of 1993 and the winter of 1994 were tested. For the Comptabilité administrative I course, only one group out of a possible 10 was tested.[8]

Methodology and results

First, we used an analysis of variance to measure whether there was a significant difference between the results of the test group and those of the control group.[9] We used this statistical procedure for each semester separately and for the sample as a whole. In all cases, there was no significant difference between the results of the two groups at the level where $\alpha = .05$.[10]

Certain characteristics of the students are likely to bias the results. For example, the results of one of the groups could have been caused by a greater number of hours of study rather than the pedagogical method used by the teacher. Some students are part-time, others full-time; they are sometimes registered for day courses, other times registered for evening courses; some are between 20 and 22 years of age and have little practical experience, others may have years of experience; some may have acquired knowledge of accounting prior to the course and others are being exposed to it for the first time; some are motivated, others less so; the abilities, aptitudes and learning styles can vary considerably from one person to another, etc. The list could be longer. All of these factors can bias the results. To take their effect into account, we have introduced covariates and classification variables in the statistical procedure.[11]

Second, we have done an analysis of covariance to identify the influence of one or more variables on the results of the students. The covariates and classification variables that we used are as follows: age, sex, grade point average, number of credits obtained, grades for certain courses, and the fact that the students were registered full- or part-time. The only significant covariate was the grade for the Informatique de gestion course (Introduction to Management Information Systems; t=3.39; p=.001; n=79). In all cases, there was no significant difference between the results of the two groups at the level of $\alpha = .05$[10].

Limits of the statistical tests

The limits of the statistical tests are certainly important. First, it is difficult to test for the professional abilities dealt with in the case "Le Banquier" by using written examinations. We have not tested this aspect.

We have limited our statistical test to the evaluation of some technical knowledge, dealt with in the case "Le

Banquier" and easily measured by a written exam. It is difficult to state that the question chosen measures perfectly and only the knowledge acquired through the case. In this regard, we consulted several other teachers. Our tests are based on the premise that the questions selected do a good job of measuring the areas of technical knowledge aimed at. We are also well aware of the fact that a number of other variables other than the case "Le Banquier" may have influenced the acquisition of knowledge. We have used covariates to control such effects. One of the limits is the possible omission of important covariates.

CONCLUSION

The case "Le Banquier" was developed to allow participants to discover some concepts in an Introduction to Accounting course and to act out certain behaviours that were likely to help them develop professional abilities. It seeks to be an alternative to the traditional lecture method that is teacher-centered. Just the opposite: the ball is in the students' court and they must take on a greater share of the responsibility for their learning. The case is a role-playing exercise in which students simulate a realistic decision-making process. It has the advantage of bringing an interactive dimension to a course that often uses the lecture method. One of our observations has been that the students participated enthusiastically, not only during the activity, but also in subsequent courses. On the other hand, there is a danger, that of neglecting important technical knowledge in such a course, in favour of professional abilities that can, after all, be developed in other courses.

To evaluate the results obtained after using the case "Le Banquier", we compared the results of a test group and a control group to the same technical knowledge question. The results showed that the performance of students who participated in the case "Le Banquier" was not significantly different from that of the students who took the same course from a teacher who used the lecture method. These results suggest to us that learning tools, such as the case "Le Banquier", in addition to helping develop professional abilities, can be just as relevant to the acquisition of technical knowledge; the main characteristic of learning is discovery.

One avenue for further research would be to measure whether the knowledge and abilities acquired have a lasting effect (six months, a year or more). In order to do so, this approach would have to be used for a significant part of a course by a test group; later on, the test group's results would be compared to those of a control group.

ENDNOTES

1. This paper was originally written in French. Cet article est disponible en français.
   Sommaire Cet article présente les principales caractéristiques d'un outil pédagogique motivateur faisant appel au jugement et à la participation en classe des étudiants. Cet outil, le cas «Le Banquier», est un jeu de rôles conçu pour être utilisé lors de la toute première séance d'un cours d'introduction à la comptabilité. Une de ses caractéristiques est qu'il vise autant le développement de compétences professionnelles que l'acquisition de connaissances techniques.

2. The authors would like to thank their colleagues Diane Bigras and Sylvain Durocher who agreed to allow their students to participate in this project; Madeleine Lussier, Louise Briand, Gilles Poirier, Thérèse Roy and Tomasz Skapski for their comments; the Université du Québec à Hull for its support, especially Élyse Amyot for her collaboration in the processing of the data as well as Martin Tousignant and Francine Dion. The opinions expressed in this paper are those of the authors.

3. For example: the decision to invest in a project is often made with the help of a discounting model in which much of the information is taken from the financial statements; the capitalization of certain disbursements in the balance sheet entails an increase in taxable income and in the tax burden; the negotiation of an agreement between the union and the employer usually takes into account the past and projected performance of earnings.

4. Many authors agree with this [AECC, 1990; Sundem, 1993].

5. This is consistent with the purpose of accounting, which is to supply decision-makers with information [Watts et Zimmerman, 1986].

6.   At the Université du Québec à Hull, about half the students who register for an Introduction to Accounting course already have a certain amount of practical or academic training in accounting.

7.   Kejzar [1992] presents an application of role-playing and, in particular, the possibility in large groups for individuals to play the role of observers.

8.   The case "Le Banquier" was developed in the fall of 1993 for use in an Introduction to Accounting course. At the Université du Québec à Hull, two courses were targeted: Comptabilité I and Comptabilité administrative I. We did not test any Comptabilité administrative I group in the fall of 1993 because we had not obtained the required administrative authorizations at that time and had not made contact with the teachers who give the courses. In the winter of 1994, one of them used the case and we were therefore able to test it.

9.   Stuhler [1989] did some statistical tests to measure the performance of students who participated in cases. Smith [1990] presents some criticisms of the evaluation of the case method, especially about the comparison of the results of a test group with those of a control group.

10.   We did some parameter and non-parameter testing (on the rank ordering). The results were similar in both cases.

11.   Smith [1990] discusses evaluation methodology of the case method. He mentions, among other things, the possibility of testing students before and after use of the case. We have not done such pretesting.

REFERENCES

AECC (Accounting Education Change Commission), Position Statement No 1, Objectives of Education for Accountants, Bainbridge, WA: 1990.

Barsoux, J.C., "The Laugh that Dare not Speak its Name", Journal of General Management, 1993, pp.43-47.

Bhada, Y.K., "Interactive Instructional Methodology in the Educational Framework", Innovation through Cooperation with Cases, Simulations, Games and other Interactive Methods, H.E. Klein (WACRA 1993), pp.65-72.

Boland, L.A. and I.M. Gordon, "Criticizing Positive Accounting Theory", Contemporary Accounting Research, vol. 9, no 1, Fall 1992, pp.142-170.

CICA (Canadian Institute of Chartered Accountants), Programme en vue de l'admission au sein de la profesison de comptable agréé, Les ordres de comptables agréés du Canada et des Bermudes, 1993.

CGA (The Certified General Accountants Association of Canada), Annuaire CGA, Vancouver, 1994.

CMA (Corporation professionnelle des comptables en management accrédités du Québec), Guide de la profession, Montréal, 1994.

Côté, Y.A., Tremblay, D., Le cadre théorique de la comptabilité générale, Éditions du renouveau pédagogique, Montréal, 1991.

Kejzar, I., "Using Interactive Training Methods Group Work and Roleplaying", Forging New Partnerships with Cases, Simulations, Games and other Interactive Methods, H.E. Klein (WACRA 1992), pp.387-391.

Prégent, R., La préparation d'un cours, Éditions de l'école polytechnique de Montréal, 1990.

130

Smith, G., "Evaluating Case Study Effectiveness", <u>Problem Solving with Cases and Simulations</u>, H.E. Klein (WACRA 1990), pp.223-233.

Stuhler, E.A., "Research into the Case Method in a Non-Case Environment, Cognitive Learning", <u>Case Method Research and Aplication: New Vistas</u>, H.E. Klein (WACRA 1989), pp.157-168.

Sundem, G.L., <u>La formation comptable en vue du XXIe siècle</u>, Conférence dans le cadre du symposium à l'intention des professeurs en sciences comptables organisé par l'Ordre des comptables agréés du Québec, Montréal, 1er octobre 1993.

Watts, R.L. and J.L. Zimmerman, <u>Positive Accounting Theory</u>, Prentice Hall, 1986.

USING NON-TRADITIONAL TEACHING METHODOLOGIES IN THE INTRODUCTORY ACCOUNTING SEQUENCE

Cheryl McConnell and Marlene Donahue
Rockhurst College
KANSAS CITY, MISSOURI, U.S.A.

Abstract

In 1992, the Accounting Education Change Commission (AECC) issued a position statement calling for changes in the content and pedagogy of the first college course in accounting. The position statement encouraged the use of cases, simulations, group projects and other participatory teaching techniques. This paper describes one college's implementation of the AECC position statement in its introductory accounting course sequence.

INTRODUCTION

Since the Accounting Education Change Commission was organized in 1989, there have been extensive discussions about the need to use active and participatory learning techniques in accounting courses. Historically, accounting faculty have been hesitant to use such techniques because of the lack of curricular resources, time constraints to cover necessary technical material and the faculty's own lack of experience using case, group and discussion methods.

The objective of this paper is to discuss how cases, group problems and oral and written reports were integrated into the introductory accounting sequence at a small, private comprehensive college. The paper discusses specific curricular resources developed to achieve course objectives. The paper also gives examples of student reactions to the changes in course approach and pedagogy.

The authors believe this paper is of interest to an interdisciplinary, international forum because of the following factors:
1. Although related to the accounting discipline, the techniques and experiences discussed in the paper are relevant to all disciplines which have technical content or a high level of time constraints because of the quantity of material that must be covered.
2. The paper discusses the objective of integrating an international element into traditional accounting courses. It is noted in the paper that of all the elements which were integrated (oral and written reports, ethical and international perspectives), student responses indicated that they wanted the international perspective integrated to a higher level.

ACCOUNTING EDUCATION CHANGE COMMISSION (AECC)

The AECC, created by the American Accounting Association in 1989, was organized to serve as a catalyst for improvements in the education of accountants. It was formed with the support of all major professional accounting firms and accounting organizations. In the four years since its inception, the AECC has issued the following position and issues statements:

Position Statements
1. Objectives of Education for Accountants
2. The First Course in Accounting

Issues Statements

1. AECC Urges Priority for Teaching in Higher Education.
2. AECC Urges De-coupling of Academic Studies and Professional Accounting Examination Preparation
3. The Importance of Two-Year Colleges for Accounting Education
4. Improving the Early Employment Experience of Accountants
5. Evaluating and Rewarding Effective Teaching

In addition to issuing the above statements, a major role of the AECC has been to award $2.5 million in grant money to implement changes in accounting programs. The AECC has completed its grant process and has awarded ten grants to four-year and graduate programs and two grants to two-year institutions. The grants to the two-year institutions were awarded to work toward improving the introductory accounting sequence.

AECC POSITION STATEMENT #2 - THE FIRST COURSE IN ACCOUNTING

The AECC emphasizes the importance of the first course in accounting to both business and accounting majors. For business students not majoring in accounting, the first accounting course helps students understand the role and process of providing accounting information for decision-making purposes. For accounting majors, the first accounting course shapes students' perceptions of the accounting profession, the aptitudes and skills needed for successful careers in accounting, and the nature of career opportunities in accounting [AECC, 1992].

According to AECC Position Statement #2, "...the primary objective of the first course in accounting is for students to learn about accounting as an information development and communication function that supports economic decision-making.... For example, the course should help students perform financial analysis, derive information for personal or organizational decisions and understand business, governmental and other organizational entities" [AECC, 1992]. To achieve these objectives, the AECC states that the first course should be a rigorous course which focuses on the use of accounting information as well as the preparation of accounting information.

The AECC recognizes the importance of attention to pedagogy in the effort to achieve the objectives stated above. AECC Position Statement #2 states, "Teachers of the first course in accounting should put a priority on their interaction with students and on interaction among students." Faculty is urged to promote student involvement by using methods such as cases, simulations and group projects. They also urge universities to utilize their most effective instructors in the first course in accounting.

IMPLEMENTATION OF AECC POSITION STATEMENT #2

The purpose of this section of the paper is to describe the implementation of AECC Position Statement #2 at a small, private comprehensive college. The description will include a brief summary of the old curriculum, a review of the new curriculum, examples of actual projects, cases and curricular resources used in the classes and a summary of student responses to the course changes.

OLD CURRICULUM

The old courses, Accounting 001 and 002, were traditional introductory accounting courses which were primarily financial in nature. The courses emphasized the recording of transactions and the preparation of financial statements. Teaching methods consisted of lecture and the review of assigned problems. All undergraduate business majors were required to take the AC001 and AC002 sequence.

NEW CURRICULUM

The new courses, Accounting 10 and 11, were changed to provide a balance between financial and managerial accounting issues. The objectives of the new courses are as follows:

1. To present accounting as an information development and communication process.
2. To focus on decision making and problem solving skills as well as technical competence.
3. To substantially increase the use of active and cooperative learning techniques.
4. To substantially increase the use of oral and written reports.

5. To integrate ethical, international and timely business issues into each course.

AC10 - Financial Accounting
    AC10 is an introduction to financial accounting which includes such topics as the accounting cycle, accounting for major business transactions, reporting and evaluating financial results, accounting for merchandising operations, inventory, long-term assets, liabilities, internal controls and investments. Integrating the objectives into this highly procedural course proved to be challenging because of its high information content and time constraints. The integration of objectives was achieved by reducing the technical details on certain financial accounting topics. For example, instead of presenting and preparing problems on both the income statement and balance sheet methods of computing the allowance for bad debts, the classroom discussion now concentrates on the conceptual need for accounting estimates and how they impact the financial statements. One method of estimating the allowance for bad debts is then demonstrated and the students are assigned homework problems to reinforce the calculations. All financial topics were analyzed to assess whether there was unnecessary duplication or complexity which could be eliminated to allow the students to concentrate on more thoroughly understanding accounting concepts.
    The introductory financial accounting course was changed from a preparer orientation to a user orientation. Transactions are introduced by analyzing their impact on the financial statements and cash flows. Journal entries are given as examples of how a transaction flows from the economic event to its appearance on the financial statement.
    Because of the time constraints mentioned above, it was difficult to integrate active and participatory learning techniques to the extent originally desired. It was decided to begin such techniques on a small scale in AC10, Financial Accounting, and to expand their use and scope in AC11, Managerial Accounting. The following table illustrates how oral and written reports and ethical and international perspectives were integrated into the AC10 curriculum:

TABLE 1

ELEMENT TO BE INTEGRATED	CURRICULAR EXAMPLE OF INTEGRATION
Oral Reports	Students, as members of in-class groups, present the results of classroom assigned problems. For example, students may be assigned to discuss the strengths and weaknesses of the internal controls described in a short chapter case. Each group will then give oral reports on their conclusions.
Written Reports	After discussing the solution to a problem in class, students are asked to write a memo to a fictional supervisor which defines the problem and explains the correct solution.
Ethical Perspectives	Cases and vignettes are discussed utilizing the cases provided by the Arthur Andersen Ethics Program and the AAA Project on Professionalism and Ethics.
International Perspectives	When studying GAAP and the FASB, students also study the proposed globalization of accounting standards. Students discuss the advantages and disadvantages of uniform standards as well as the potential impact on traditional financial statement presentation.

AC11 - Managerial Accounting
    AC11 is an introduction to managerial accounting which includes such topics as cost identification and behavior, cost-volume-profit analysis, relevant costs for decision-making, capital budgeting, financial statement analysis and the statement of cash flows. Integrating the new course objectives was again achieved by analyzing topics to eliminate unnecessary duplication and complexity. A decision-making orientation is now

134

achieved by focusing the classroom discussions on understanding the needs of the internal management information user and by providing the appropriate accounting information necessary to aid in the decision-making process.

Since time constraints were not as severe in the AC11 course, active and participatory learning techniques were fully integrated to the extent originally desired. The techniques and assignments were sequenced to be more complex and challenging than the techniques and assignments in AC10. The following table illustrates how oral and written reports and ethical and international perspectives were integrated into the AC11 curriculum:

TABLE 2

ELEMENT TO BE INTEGRATED	CURRICULAR EXAMPLE OF INTEGRATION
Oral Reports	Students, as members of a group, give a short 5-10 minute presentation on an element of financial statement analysis and a long 45-60 minute presentation on an emerging issue in management accounting. See Appendix A for details on the oral report assignments.
Written Reports	Students prepare a project paper analyzing the annual report of a company of their choice. The assignment is structured to require students to find outside resources about their company and the industry in which it operates. See Appendix A for full details on the written report project.
Ethical Perspectives	Cases and vignettes are discussed utilizing the cases provided by the Arthur Andersen Ethics Program and the AAA Project on Professionalism and Ethics.
International Perspectives	One of the long oral report topics is the proposed globalization of accounting standards. In addition, several short Harvard Business School cases and exercises involving international companies and elements are discussed.

STUDENT RESPONSE TO CURRICULUM CHANGES

Comprehensive statistical analysis of student performance before and after the curriculum changes cannot be calculated due to marked differences in exam formats and objectives. On similar individual test problems in the financial accounting course before and after the curriculum changes, mean scores were within 5 percentage points. Caution is urged in making any further generalizations or interpretations regarding exam assessment because of the differences in testing instruments.

Written student responses on anonymous student evaluations have been positive. The instructor asked the students to write their reactions to the use of the oral and written reports and case studies described in Tables 1 and 2 of this paper. All responses were positive to very positive, with selected comments summarized below:

"The cases gave me a feel as to what input a managerial accountant adds to the decision-making process of a business. The accountants must provide past and future information relevant to the issues by using their communication skills. The management accountant must also have skills in marketing and finance so that he or she understands the dynamics of the decision-making process."

"I now realize that there will be more to my job than simply accounting. Marketing, sales, management and other financial and international topics may relate or be relevant to decisions I make or participate in."

"I better understand everything that is involved in an accounting decision. Most of the work and problems given to us in classes are in a refined form that is easy to understand. The cases gave mostly raw data that, at first, didn't look like it fit together. So I now realize that we will be the ones who have to relate all the data and present it in an understandable way."

"Over the years working my way up in the small CPA firm environment, I have come to realize how important it is to be able to explain, verbally and written, what you know. This is a very hard thing to master and I personally need to work very hard to improve my skills in these areas."

"I now realize how important it is for me to understand marketing and finance so that I can use my accounting skills to explain things which can be very important to the decision process. Accountants can play an important part in decision-making. I also realize how important my oral skills will be."

"As a salesman and a marketing major, I am not particularly fond of accounting. However, I must admit the material covered in this class has been the most helpful in understanding the inner workings of business of any class I have ever taken."

On college administered student evaluations, many students commented that the international perspective portion of the course needed to be increased and integrated more fully into each appropriate topic.

SUMMARY AND CONCLUSIONS

Integrating the new objectives in the introductory accounting sequence is a step forward in achieving the overall goals promulgated by the AECC. As with any curricular change, the results must be evaluated over a period of time. Comprehensive assessment tools must be developed to measure whether the new objectives are being achieved. Assessment tools must also be developed to assure that the curricular changes are having a positive impact on students majoring in accounting.

APPENDIX A
CURRICULAR RESOURCES FOR MANAGEMENT ACCOUNTING

ORAL REPORT ASSIGNMENTS

Financial Statement Analysis

Students are divided into groups and are asked to give 5-10 minute presentations on one of the following elements of financial statement analysis:
- Objectives of financial statement analysis and the importance and limitations of accounting data
- Time series analysis (percentage and trend)
- Common-size financial statements
- Profitability ratios
- Solvency ratios
- Structure ratios
- Operating cycle ratios
- Market ratios

Groups are evaluated on the following factors:
- Accuracy of information
- Depth of topic analysis
- Use of outside resources and examples
- Presentation style
- Completeness of the presentation handout
- Presentation delivery within the requested time frame
- Responses to student and instructor questions
- Effective group interaction

Groups are encouraged to present the information in a clear and engaging manner. Examples and outside resources are vital. Each group should develop a one-page summary of the presentation to hand out to the class and the instructor. Students are given the following procedural steps to help them get started:
- Read the appropriate segments in the accounting textbook
- Review the topic in other resources (texts, journals, current events)
- Meet with your group to brainstorm on how to present the information

-Prepare the presentation and summary
-Practice the presentation

Emerging Issues in Management Accounting
    Using the same evaluation criterion described above, student groups give 45-60 minute presentations on emerging or current issues in management accounting. The topics vary each semester, but examples of recent presentations include the following:
        -Just-in-time production and inventory
        -Globalization of markets and accounting standards
        -Activity based costing
        -Total quality management-How to measure its success or failure
        -Corporate cash management
        -Impact of computerization and robotics in manufacturing
        -CMA exam - past, present and future
        -Employment opportunities in management accounting

WRITTEN PROJECT PAPER

The purpose of the written project paper is threefold:
1. To familiarize the students with all aspects of a company's annual report, including but not limited to the president's letter, the financial statements, the footnotes and the audit opinion.
2. To help students discover information resources available to help analyze a company's strengths and weaknesses. Among available resources are the Wall Street Journal, published industry ratios, current newspaper articles and current journal articles.
3. To help students analyze the information gathered and to have them demonstrate their understanding of the company and its industry by preparing a company analysis as described below.
The student papers should include the four following sections. The questions asked in sections 1 and 2 are examples of the issues that should be considered in describing the company and its industry. In these sections, students are encouraged to not limit their analysis to the questions asked. They are encouraged to be creative in learning about and describing their company and its environment.

Section 1 - Company description
    What type of company is it?
    What do they produce and sell?
    How long has it been in business?
    What areas of the business are they emphasizing in the future?
    What areas of the business are they phasing out?

Section 2 - Industry description
    Who are the company's major competitors?
    Where does the company fit in the industry?
    What are the threats to the industry in the current business climate?
    What are the opportunities for the industry in the current business climate?

Section 3 - Financial Statement Analysis
    Students should specifically answer each of the following questions. They are asked to give supporting evidence for their conclusions.
        a. How well did your company do in the most recent year?
        b. Was the company "better off" at the end of the year as compared to the previous year? How?
        c. How do you explain the difference between the company's income (loss) and its change in cash for the current year?
        d. Is it becoming easier for the company to meet its current debts on a timely basis?
        e. Is the company collecting its accounts receivable more rapidly?
        f. Is the company's investment in accounts receivable decreasing?

g. Are dollars invested in inventory increasing?
h. Is the company's investment in plant assets increasing?
i. Is the stockholders' investment becoming more profitable?
j. Is the company using its assets efficiently?
k. Did the amount of research and development increase during the last three years?
l. Is the current market price of the company going up or down?
m. Is the earnings per share increasing or decreasing? Why?
n. Compare the company's book value and market value per share. Why are the values different?
o. Compare the company's accounts receivable and inventory turnovers to the industry averages.
p. What current events have happened at your company since the annual report was issued?
q. What accounting methods were used for inventory? depreciation?
r. What segments or products would you advise your company to emphasize? Why?
s. In what part of the world is your company most profitable?
t. What kind of contingencies does your company have?
u. Was the report audited and by whom? So what?
v. Prepare a graph showing a five year trend analysis for sales, net income and earnings per share.
w. Would you sell merchandise on account to your company?
x. Would you lend money to your company on a 10 year note?
y. Would you buy stock in your company at the current market price?

Section 4 - Company Summary
Based on you research and analysis in sections 1 through 3, prepare a comprehensive summary of your company's strengths, weaknesses, opportunities and threats.

REFERENCES

Accounting Education Change Commission, "AECC Urges De-coupling of Academic Studies and Professional Accounting Examination Preparation: Issues Statement No. Two", Issues in Accounting Education (Fall 1991), pp. 313-314.

Accounting Education Change Commission, "AECC Urges Priority for Teaching in Higher Education: Issues Statement No. One", Issues in Accounting Education (Fall 1990), pp. 330-331.

Accounting Education Change Commission, "Evaluating and Rewarding Effective Teaching: Issues Statement No. Five", Issues in Accounting Education (Fall 1993), pp. 436-439.

Accounting Education Change Commission, "The Importance of Two-Year Colleges for Accounting Education: Issues Statement No. Three", Issues in Accounting Education (Spring 1993), pg. 191.

Accounting Education Change Commission, "Improving the Early Employment Experience of Accountants: Issues Statement No. Four", Issues in Accounting Education (Fall 1993), pp. 431-435.

Accounting Education Change Commission, "Objectives of Education for Accountants: Position Statement No. One", Issues in Accounting Education (Fall 1990), pp. 307-312.

Accounting Education Change Commission, "The First Course in Accounting: Position Statement No. Two", Issues in Accounting Education (Fall 1992), pp. 249-251.

American Accounting Association, Committee on the Future Structure, Content, and Scope of Accounting Education (The Bedford Committee), "Future Accounting Education: Preparing for the Expanding Profession," Issues in Accounting Education (Spring 1986), pp. 168-195.

Campbell, Jane E. and William F. Lewis, "Using Cases in Accounting Classes", Issues in Accounting Education (Fall 1991), pp. 276-283.

138

Christensen, C.R., D.A. Garvin, and A. Sweet, editors, <u>Education for Judgment: The Artistry of Discussion Leadership</u> (Boston: Harvard Business School Publishing Division, 1991).

Cottell, Philip G. and Barbara J. Millis, "Cooperative Learning Structures in the Instruction of Accounting", <u>Issues in Accounting Education</u> (Spring 1993), pp. 40-59.

Knechel, W. Robert, "Using the Case Method in Accounting Instruction", <u>Issues in Accounting Education</u> (Fall 1992), pp. 205-217.

Libby, Patricia A., "Barriers to Using Cases in Accounting Education", <u>Issues in Accounting Education</u> (Fall 1991), pp. 193-213.

May, Claire Arevalo, <u>Effective Writing: A Handbook for Accountants</u>, Third Edition (Englewood Cliffs, New Jersey: Prentice Hall, 1992).

Porter, Lyman W., and Lawrence E McKibbin, <u>Management Education and Development: Drift or Thrust into the 21st Century?</u> (New York: McGraw-Hill, 1988).

Scofield, Barbara W. and Linda Combes, "Designing and Managing Meaningful Writing Assignments", <u>Issues in Accounting Education</u> (Spring 1993), pp. 71-85.

Stanga, Keith G. and Robert R. Ladd, "Oral Communication Apprehension in Beginning Accounting Majors: An Exploratory Study", <u>Issues in Accounting Education</u> (Fall 1990), pp.180-194.

Stocks, Kevin D, Ted D. Stoddard, and Max L. Waters, "Writing in the Accounting Curriculum: Guidelines for Professors", <u>Issues in Accounting Education</u> (Fall 1992), pp. 193-204.

ENVIRONMENT AND ACCOUNTING: DEVELOPMENT AND USE OF THE ULTRA/BRAER CASE

François Brouard and Michel Blanchette
Université du Québec à Hull
HULL, QUÉBEC, CANADA

Abstract[1]

This paper[2] explains how problem-based learning (PBL) served as the conceptual framework for writing and using a fictitious case about environmental problems and their impacts. A major oil spill in the Saint Lawrence Seaway, close to Quebec City, is the central problem described in the ULTRA/BRAER case. By providing accounting students with a realistic scenario, the case should enable them to identify environmental problems, thereby preparing them to adopt a leading-edge attitude towards the environmental challenges of tomorrow.

INTRODUCTION

In the accounting profession both practitioners and academics recognize that major changes are needed in the development of new approaches to traditional teaching methods and to different aspects of training. The work undertaken by the American Accounting Association [Bedford, 1986], the Accounting Education Change Commission [AECC, 1990], major accounting firms [Arthur Andersen & Co. et al., 1989] and certain committees of Québec universities [CRÉPUQ, 1991] shows this quite clearly. One of the roles of today's and tomorrow's public accountants is to adapt the information system to changes that affect organizations. It is therefore essential that they receive initial and ongoing training that is at the leading edge of current topics related to public accounting.

The rapid evolution of the legal, political, socio-cultural and economic frameworks of which accounting is a part requires pedagogical material that deals with real and current problems so that students will be moved to tackle tomorrow's challenges. Among the phenomena that make up a growing part of this evolving context, we have identified environmental problems and their impacts. Indeed, they are an international phenomenon that public accountants in all countries will have to deal with if organizations are to be held accountable for their social responsibilities to various users [CICA, 1992; 1993a; 1993b].

The objective of this paper is to explain how a case dealing with environmental accounting was developed and to suggest various pedagogical strategies for its use. The remainder of this paper is divided into four sections. The first one describes the conceptual framework. The second section explains the development of the ULTRA/BRAER case. In the third section, various strategies for using the case are discussed. Finally, we present our conclusion.

CONCEPTUAL FRAMEWORK

LEARNING AND TEACHING METHODS

The first objective of teaching is learning. A definition of learning may allow us to remember more clearly what it is about. "Learning is an individual and voluntary act that happens when a person becomes able to know, to do or to feel something new, whether or not others have learned the same thing." [Tousignant and Morissette, 1990, p.5]

To achieve a certain degree of learning (if not a degree of certain learning!), the choice of teaching methods must be done carefully. Teaching methods can be grouped in two broad categories. The first includes teacher-centred approaches while the second includes interactive approaches that are student-centred.

Various factors must be analyzed before choosing a method. These include the subject (nature of the subject matter, objectives, expectations), the students (nature of the student population, preferences, abilities, background, interests, autonomy, maturity), the professors (style, patience, personality, need to evaluate) and physical and material conditions (size and makeup of the group, time, space) [Bhada, 1993; Chhokar, 1990; Prégent, 1990].

There is a consensus that there is no "best" recognized teaching method per se [Bhada, 1993]. According to Prégent [1990], approaches to teaching that are more student-centred seem to generate more significant learning and stand a better chance of increasing memorisation and the transfer of learning than teacher-centred approaches.

PROBLEM-BASED LEARNING (PBL) V. CASE STUDIES

Bhéreur et al. [1993] identify five pedagogical systems in the development of a curriculum: 1) an interactive lecture given to groups of 30 to 40 students; 2) a lecture given to large groups; 3) individual learning; 4) tutoring (Oxford style); and 5) problem-based learning (PBL).

There is a great deal of confusion in the terminology used, whether one is talking about PBL or case studies [Barrows, 1986; Dooley and Skinner, 1977]. Our aim is not to sort out this confusion by establishing a taxonomy. According to Prégent [1990], PBL, like case studies, is part of the category that includes discussion or working in teams. In our opinion, and that of Barrows [1986], case studies are a part of PBL. Given their numerous similarities, case studies and PBL will be treated as one and the same for the purposes of this paper.

In PBL, the subject matter to be covered is divided into modules. The contents of a module are examined through one or more problems to be solved that are similar to what the students will encounter in their professional work. They have not received any special training before solving a problem. They first work as a team for some time; then there are meetings between the students and the professor. The problems serve as catalysts in the organization of other academic activities. Students do their individual work from the point of view of trying to understand and solve the problem they are given. [Bhéreur et al. 1993; Walton and Matthews, 1989]

The role of the professor is to guide the students in the identification of the problem, its analysis and solution. The students are the ones who make the decisions. Special attention must therefore be taken to ensure that the learning objectives are adequate and are met. The professor may also suggest certain documentary resources and challenge the process and the proposed solutions.

As Bhéreur et al. [1993] rightly point out, a PBL approach is centered on students rather than on the subject matter. Issues about learning strategies at the undergraduate level are an international problem found both in North America and in Europe [De Ketele, 1993]. As we have already indicated, the accounting profession shares this concern about better learning, as stated by professors [Bedford, 1986], certain employers [Arthur Andersen & Co. et al., 1989] and a joint group [AECC, 1990].

Certain universities use PBL in the fields of medical science, engineering and biology [Bhéreur, 1993; Woods, 1993]. We must stress, however, that the interactive lecture method with groups of 30 to 40 students is the one most used in our institution. Even if this is not a PBL system, partial adoption is possible in certain courses. PBL was the conceptual framework for the development of the ULTRA/BRAER case.

DEVELOPMENT OF THE ULTRA/BRAER CASE

There are certainly pressing needs for the development of cases. Certain authors stress that a case has a shelf life of two to three years; new cases should therefore be continually under development [Desbiens and Berneman, 1991; Leenders and Erskine, 1989].

There are a number of sources for the information required to develop new pedagogical material. Almaney [1993] provides a list that includes annual reports, financial statements, government reports, historical background on organizations, videos, newspapers, interviews with leaders, industry information (CD-ROM, index), etc. Hafsi and Piffault [1993] indicate that the École des hautes études commerciales de Montréal favours library research for the development of cases. This approach is different from the one suggested by Leenders and Erskine [1989], who favour interviews with organizations or their leaders. We favoured library research.

There are a number of phases in the development of a case, i.e. feasibility study, planning, writing, and evaluation [Bédard et al., 1991; Dekker-Groen, 1990]. We will deal with some aspects of the development.

FEASIBILITY STUDY

The feasibility study phase includes, among others, definition of the objectives and questioning the usefulness of a case study. The undergraduate policy of the Université du Québec identifies the end purposes and the characteristics of training at that level. Undergraduate training therefore aims at developing students' ability to analyze and to synthesize, to learn on their own in a continuing manner, to adapt easily to change, to relate their field of expertise to others, to determine the objective value of statements they make or that are made to them, to understand, interpret and communicate information well, to intervene effectively, to measure the social and ethical impact of their activities, to communicate and to develop their initiative and their creativity [UQ, 1992].

With a case study we hope that students registered in an accounting course will understand better the stakes and the complex nature of environmental problems and the role of the public accountant in the identification of solutions, and discuss the consequences of environmental issues in terms of financial accounting. We want to ask students specifically to identify the financial accounting problems and their consequences for the presentation of the financial information of an entity.

After identifying the accounting problems, our expectations are that the students will classify them according to certain priorities, identify measurement, recognition and presentation alternatives for the information in financial statements, and discuss the relevance of each option. Finally, the student who plays the role of a public accountant seeks a solution for each problem.

PLANNING

The planning phase includes the identification of the subject areas and the general orientation of the case. The ULTRA/BRAER[3] case is part of environmental accounting. One definition of the environment could be: "all of the natural conditions in which we live, i.e., the air, the water, the earth, the flora, the fauna, as well as the non-renewable resources such as combustible fossils and minerals" [CICA, 1993a, p.v]

Environmental accounting is part of the greater field of social accounting. Social accounting can be defined as: "Accounting whose purpose is to identify, measure and present information on the costs of an economic activity for the community, and on the advantages that it derives from that activity. The objective of social accounting is to evaluate the positive effects (the advantages or social benefits) or the negative ones (social costs) of the activities of an organization on the financial situation and the physical and moral well-being of both the people directly associated with the organization in question (personnel, members, clients, suppliers, investors, etc.) and third parties who benefit or are harmed by the activities of the organization because of its location or for any other reason." [Sylvain, 1982, p.468]

The interesting aspects of social information about the environment deal with air (acid rain, selling the right to pollute, ozone layer, greenhouse effect), water, toxic substances (chemical products, pesticides), solid waste and dangerous waste (radioactive products), public health and the destruction of sites. Many recent examples illustrate the impact of such problems for organizations and individuals: Bhopal in India, Exxon-Valdez and the Love Canal in the United States, Chernobyl in the USSR, the Amazon forest in Brazil, etc.

Environmental accounting problems are multi-level, which raises a number of questions about accounting research [CICA, 1993a]. Should organizations capitalize or expense environmental costs? Should such costs be charged off to a previous period, to the current period or to subsequent ones? When should a subsequent expense be recognized as a liability? How should subsequent costs be estimated and measured?[4] What information should be given about the environment?

Here are the problems given in the case: an oil spill in the Saint Lawrence Seaway by an oil tanker chartered by an organization, the time of the expense recognition as a result of the disaster and the presentation in the financial statements, various contingencies, the accounting treatment of the prevention cost of damages, the accounting for an investment in an organization set up to act in emergencies, the recognition of site restoration expenses and other minor problems. In developing the case we varied the types of situations and the level of abstraction related to the different problems, including the presentation of a decision for discussion purposes, the confrontation of various options and the role playing of an event where the problem is not explicit.

WRITING THE CASE

The writing phase includes collecting the information, selecting the problems and the actual writing of the statement, the solution elements and the pedagogical notes. As we have stated, the oil spill is the heart of the case. We told the story from that basis, adding various other problems in order to make it an interesting case that touches on other aspects of environmental accounting, including prevention and site restoration. We also wrote solution elements and pedagogical notes for the professor.

We took special care during the writing to ensure the quality of the case. For example, we tried to be precise about the facts selected, to write about them objectively and to present the story logically (chronology of events) and realistically [Bédard et al., 1991].

Real event
Our case is based on a real event that made international headlines. The oil tanker Braer foundered north of Scotland in January 1993 and caused significant ecological damage [The Economist, 1993]. We tracked down various stories in daily newspapers that dealt with this catastrophe [La Presse, 1993; Le Devoir, 1993; The Ottawa Citizen, 1993]. Since the sources were primarily the international press agencies (Agence France Presse, Associate Press, Presse Canadienne, Reuters, United Press International,), the same information is available internationally.

When such a catastrophe occurs, one of the interesting elements is that many newspapers publish stories about it. This allows us to increase the quantity of information about a particular event. In our case, there were reports suggesting the adoption of a standard that would require that ships on the Saint Lawrence Seaway have double hulls. Even though a report had been published a few years beforehand, the newspapers talked about it and we included it in our case as additional information. This problem creates a lot of interest because everyone feels moved by this type of catastrophe.

Transposition to Canada
The event was transposed to the Canadian waters of the Saint Lawrence Seaway to increase the involvement and motivation of the students with regard to a problem that has such important economic and accounting consequences. To remain as realistic as possible and to enrich the event, other problems related to circumstances described in the case and having accounting repercussions were selected from newspaper articles. The city of Québec was chosen as the site for many reasons. First, the event could well have happened there since the tanker that foundered north of Scotland was en route to St-Romuald in the suburbs of Québec, where there is an important oil company. Second, the city of Québec and the Île d'Orléans are important tourist sites and are part of the international heritage sites of UNESCO. A map illustrating the exact location of the catastrophe was prepared.

STRATEGIES FOR USING THE ULTRA/BRAER CASE

Given the time and effort needed to develop a case, it is essential to maximize its use through various means [Damle, 1989]. As Bhada [1993] and Prégent [1990] indicate, certain conditions must be met in order to make optimum use of teaching methods in general and interactive methods in particular.

The level of objectives targeted by the case study are at the high end of Bloom's taxonomy (analysis, synthesis and evaluation). The ability to favour autonomous and continuous learning is moderately high. The degree of control exercised by the student is high. It is preferable to limit the number of students in each group. The number of hours required for preparation, meetings and correction is moderately high. This type of method is favoured when one is seeking identification of the elements of the problem and of possible alternatives rather than searching for a solution. In the context of an environmental problem, searching for a solution would in any case be premature and idealistic.

USE IN ACCOUNTING THEORY

The Accounting Theory course at the Université du Québec à Hull (UQAH) is part of an undergraduate university program[5]. The course is divided into more than 20 modules. Social accounting is one of them. The modules that precede the one on the environment provide the students with some tools. In one of them, the different points of view (economic, moral, legal, psychological, etc.) that must be considered during the problem solving and the debate on possible solutions are discussed. Another module deals with basic accounting concepts (going concern, stable monetary unit, etc.), the objectives of financial information and financial statements, the characteristics of information (usefulness, comparability, verifiability, etc.), the definition of elements (asset, liability, charge, etc.) and the recognition and measurement principles.

Since the ULTRA/BRAER case fits in the framework of problem-based learning, environmental problems served as a catalyst for the organization of certain academic activities. For the two-week period during which the ULTRA/BRAER case was discussed in class, there were: an industrial visit to a pulp and paper company, a conference on the environmental balance sheet of that company, the writing of comments by the students, a debate that followed the comments on that balance sheet, the presentation of a video on the financial empire of which the company is a part and a discussion of the advanced accounting themes related to the video.

Many of the characteristics of undergraduate training identified during the feasibility study can be addressed through PBL. In fact, that is why the ULTRA/BRAER case was developed. We used the following problem-solving steps in the Accounting Theory course at the UQAH:

1. Identify the problems (for example, after reading the case)
2. Analyze the information (and research information as required)
3. Define the problems and identify their relative importance
4. Identify possible solutions
5. Compare the options identified in terms of Canadian accounting standards
6. Evaluate the advantages and disadvantages of each option (consequences)
7. Draw a conclusion after evaluating the options in relation to the objectives of the users
8. Propose means for putting the proposed solutions into effect

Exam

The ULTRA/BRAER case was first used as a question on the final exam in the Accounting Theory course during the winter semester of 1993 at the UQAH. At that point, the case was a first draft that was obviously not as complete as it is now since writing a case is an evolutionary process! This 60-minute question was worth 35% of an exam that counted for 30% of the final grade for the course. This type of question is typical of the type encountered by Canadian candidates facing entrance exams as chartered accountants (CA) or certified management accountants (CMA).

Discussion in class

Among the stages of the problem-solving process, this case focusses on identifying problems and evaluating their relative importance. As shown by the comments of the examiners of some professional Canadian accounting bodies, these are particularly important [CICA, 1993c; SCMA, 1993][6].

In the Accounting Theory course, we used discussions in small groups followed by plenary discussions. Beforehand, the students had written up the elements of the solution. As opposed to lectures, the role of the professor in PBL and in case studies is to manage the logistics and the group dynamics in order to maximize learning. Active participation by the students is essential to effective learning.

A number of variations could be used if time permitted. Instead of asking the students to prepare in advance, they could be placed in small groups and asked to draw up a draft solution after identifying the problems. By splitting up the case and providing the information piecemeal, students could be forced to seek additional information (Pigors' technique); by presenting the events in chronological order, students would have to react instantly to each new piece of information.

Term paper

Students could be required to write an official paper or to present their conclusions to the class, or both, in order to evaluate their written and oral communications abilities. Such a paper could also be in the form of a grid for correcting the case.

Other

In other circumstances, we could use a role play in which various individuals or groups (owner, corporate comptroller, auditor, ecologists, media) would debate their points of view on the problems identified. Dramatic effects could be introduced by using a film or a video on the topic since they allow the transmission of ideas that are often difficult to verbalize. Specific questions could be asked after showing the video. To complete the case, various information supplied by the media could be used to make the case even more life-like; that would also allow us to link the problem being studied to daily life.

OTHER USES

The ULTRA/BRAER case could also be used in other financial accounting courses or in other disciplines by changing the work assignments or by adding information. Using different participants eliminates the need to reinvent the wheel. In accounting, we could, for example: use a team from another country assigned to clean up the site in order to discuss the problems related to foreign currencies; incorporate it in an auditing course to identify audit implications related to environmental problems (ethics, auditors' opinion on the financial statements of the organization); the taxation aspects could also be examined from the point of view of the deductibility of the amounts in question.

In fields such as management, this theme could also generate discussions about the ethics of managers and the accountability for certain events. The case could also be used as the basis for a problem in biology by adding information on the affected flora and fauna. By incorporating appendices on the oil products spilled, chemists could try to solve the problems encountered by the participants in the case. Public relations professors could use the scenario to discuss crisis management.

CONCLUSION

In the last few years the environment has been a constant preoccupation for accountants in all countries. Using a case that deals with contemporary environmental problems should allow accounting students to think about the appropriate accounting treatment and the presentation of environmental financial information.

In problem-based learning (PBL), various aspects of a given problem are dealt with. PBL is an interesting way to approach the development of new pedagogical practices in accounting. According to the accounting profession, searching for new ways of learning is essential in order to maintain the professional qualities that tomorrow's challenges will require. This kind of interactive approach favours learning and changes the role of the professor by increasing the focus of training on the problems that students will have to face in their professional careers.

The ULTRA/BRAER case describes a fictitious situation, i.e. an important oil spill in a Canadian seaway. After identifying the related problems (accounting treatment of the cost of preventing damages and of restoring the site), students must classify them according to certain priorities. They must identify alternatives to the measurement, accounting and presentation of information in the financial statements and discuss the relevance of each solution. Finally, for each problem the student playing the role of the public accountant must seek a solution.

This type of case could also be used to discuss themes other than financial accounting. We are thinking especially of ethical questions related to environmental problems, to community relations issues (employees, government) and to issues of responsibility (social responsibility for the businesses and individual responsibility for the managers). A PBL case allows for a number of pedagogical use strategies, including discussion in class and report writing. A professor can modify the strategies from one semester to the next in order to explore their effectiveness.

As Bisters and Ernsteins [1993] rightly point out, training in environmental problems depends on increased awareness on the part of the students, on a change in the relationship between the students and the professors, on an interdisciplinary point of view, given the complexity of the problems, on the simulation of real problems and, finally, on learning by doing.

ENDNOTES

1. This paper was originally written in French. Cet article est disponible en français.
    Sommaire L'apprentissage par problèmes (APP) sert de cadre conceptuel à ce texte qui décrit l'élaboration et l'utilisation d'un cas fictif portant sur des problèmes environnementaux et leurs impacts. Le problème principal du cas ULTRA/BRAER consiste en un important déversement de pétrole qui survient dans le fleuve Saint-Laurent près de la ville de Québec. L'objectif visé est d'aider des étudiants en sciences comptables à identifier les problèmes et ainsi mieux les préparer à affronter les défis de l'avenir en matière environnementale.

2. The authors would like to thank their colleagues Madeleine Lussier, Diane Bigras and Louise Briand for their comments and the Université du Québec à Hull for its financial assistance in the development of the case.

3. The case is available in English and in French. Interested parties can reach François Brouard at the Département des sciences comptables of the Université du Québec à Hull, P.O. Box 1250, Station B, Hull, Québec, Canada, J8X 3X7.

4. "The world environmental debt today could well reach the billion dollar mark." [Rubinstein, 1991, p. 36]. By itself, this observation gives one pause since the information distributed by organizations does not reflect this reality. Since organizations have a social role to play, it is, therefore, important that public accountants help them play this role actively and effectively.

5. The Accounting Theory course is currently in the sixth and last semester of an undergraduate program leading to a bachelor of accounting degree. It is a program that leads to the practice of public accounting since it is an important step before admission to professional accounting bodies in Quebec.

6. In fact, the most important of the five deficiencies noted during a number of years by the CICA Board of Examiners, the first one analyzed was "important problems that were neither seen nor analyzed". One of the important services that chartered accountants can provide for their clients is the diagnosis and resolution of problems but that, in practice, the problems in a given situation are not always obvious. Candidates often have difficulty spotting and analyzing problems to which their attention has not been drawn. This inability to spot problems or elements that are not obvious raises serious questions about their ability to function as public accountants [CICA, 1993c].

REFERENCES

AECC, Position Statement No 1 - Objectives of Education for Accountants (Accounting Education Change Commission, 1990).

Almaney, A.J., "Using «Live» Organizations as Cases Studies in Strategic Management Courses" in Innovation Through Cooperation with Cases, Simulations, Games and other Interactive Methods, H.E. Klein (ed.) (WACRA, 1993), pp.151-159.

Arthur Andersen & Co and al., Perspectives on Educational Capabilities for Success in the Public Accounting Profession (Arthur Andersen & Co., Arthur Young, Coopers & Lybrand, Deloitte Haskins & Sells, Ernst & Whinney, Peat Marwick Main & Co., Price Waterhouse, Touche Ross, 1989).

Barrows, H.S., "A taxonomy of problem-based learning methods", Medical Education (1986), pp.481-486.

Bédard, M.G., P. Dell'Aniello and D. Desbiens, La méthode des cas (Gaëtan Morin, 1991).

Bedford, N. (chairman) - American Accounting Association (AAA) Committee on the Future Structure,

Content, and Scope of Accounting Education, "Future Accounting Education: Preparing for the Expanding Profession", Issues in Accounting Education (Spring 1986), pp.168-195.

Bhada, Y.K., "Interactive Instructional Methodology in the Educational Framework" in Innovation Through Cooperation with Cases, Simulations, Games and other Interactive Methods, H.E. Klein (ed.) (WACRA, 1993), pp.65-72.

Bhéreur, P., P. Richard and M. Chaput, «L'apprentissage par problèmes (APP), une approche pédagogique novatrice (Le cas du baccalauréat en biologie de l'UQAM)», Actes du Colloque international Enseignement supérieur: stratégies d'apprentissage appropriées (Université du Québec à Hull, août 1993), pp.59-83.

Bisters, V. and R. Ernsteins, "Interdisciplinary Training in Environmental Education through Simulation and gaming" in Innovation Through Cooperation with Cases, Simulations, Games and other Interactive Methods, H.E. Klein (ed.) (WACRA, 1993), pp.145-150.

Chhokar, J.S., "Learning how to Learn the Use of Unstructured Case Discussion and Seminar" in Problems Solving with Cases and Simulations, H.E. Klein (ed.) (WACRA, 1990), pp.125-130.

CICA, Annales de l'examen final uniforme 1992 (Canadian Institute of Chartered Accountants, 1993c).

CICA, Coûts et passifs environnementaux : comptabilisation et communication de l'information financière, étude de recherche, (Canadian Institute of Chartered Accountants, 1993a).

CICA, Environmental Stewardship: Management, Accountability and the Role of Chartered Accountants, Report of the Task Force on Sustainable Development, (Canadian Institute of Chartered Accountants, September 1993b).

CICA, La vérification environnementale et la profession comptable, étude de recherche, (Canadian Institute of Chartered Accountants, 1992).

CRÉPUQ, Rapport du Groupe de travail sur la formation en sciences comptables (Conférence des recteurs et des principaux des universités du Québec, octobre 1991).

Damle, C.S., "The Case Method of Instruction in Management Education A Critical Review" in Case Method Research and Application: New Vistas, H.E. Klein (ed.) (WACRA, 1989), pp.3-15.

De Ketele, J., «La situation en Europe», Actes du Colloque international : Enseignement supérieur: stratégies d'apprentissage appropriées (Université du Québec à Hull, août 1993), pp.11-26.

Dekker-Groen, A.M., "Problem Solving with Cases in Higher Engineering Education" in Problems Solving with Cases and Simulations, H.E. Klein (ed.) (WACRA, 1990), pp.211-221.

Desbiens, D. and C. Berneman, "To Write or not to Write Cases: That is the Question" in Managing Change with Cases, Simulations, Games and other Interactive Methods, H.E. Klein (ed.) (WACRA, 1991), pp.181-185.

Dooley, A.R. and W. Skinner, "Casing Casemethod Methods", Academy of Management Review (April 1977), pp.277-289.

Hafsi, T. and J. Piffault, "Developing Cases and Case Method Teaching in a Context of Scarce Resources" in Innovation Through Cooperation with Cases, Simulations, Games and other Interactive Methods, H.E. Klein (ed.) (WACRA, 1993), pp.271-279.

La Presse (6, 12, 13 janvier 1993).

Le Devoir (6 janvier 1993).

Leenders, M.R. and J.A. Erskine, Case Research: The Case Writing Process (School of Business Administration The University of Western Ontario, 1989) (third edition).

Prégent, R., La préparation d'un cours (Éditions de l'École Polytechnique de Montréal, 1990).

Rubinstein, D.B., «Une comptabilité verte», CA Magazine (mars 1991), pp.35-42.

SCMA, Examen d'admission et solutions de 1993 (Société des comptables en management du Canada, 1993).

Sylvain, F., Dictionnaire de la comptabilité et des disciplines connexes (Institut canadien des comptables agréés / Ordre des experts comptables et des comptables agréés - Paris / Institut des reviseurs d'entreprises - Bruxelles , 1982) (deuxième édition).

The Economist (January 9th, 1993).

The Ottawa Citizen (January 6th, 9th, 10th, 11th, 1993).

Tousignant, R. and D. Morissette, Les principes de la mesure et de l'évaluation des apprentissages (Gaëtan Morin, 1990).

UQ., Les études de 1er cycle (Université du Québec (UQ), 1992).

Walton, H.J. and Matthews, M., "Essentials of problem-based learning", Medical Education (1989), pp.542-558.

Woods, D., Improving Teaching and Learning (Canadian Academic Accounting Association Education Committee, Teaching Workshop, Carleton University, June 10, 1993).

CHAPTER FOUR

SHOW, DON'T TELL:
TEACHING BEHAVIORAL KNOW-HOW
THROUGH THE CASE METHOD

André Cyr and Maria Dame
École Nationale d'Administration Publique
MONTRÉAL, QUÉBEC, CANADA

Abstract

This paper presents the results of a development project of six case-studies aimed at teaching behavioral know-how, that is, the interpersonal and political skills needed to operate effectively in a consultation environment. These case studies were developed in response to the training needs of graduate students who were about to begin a practical training session as public sector consultants. The paper is divided into two major sections. The first part describes the context in which these case studies were developed and the methodology which was used. The second part presents one of the case studies and briefly describes its classroom use.

INTRODUCTION

This paper presents the results of a development project of six case-studies aimed at teaching behavioral know-how in the specific context of consultation assignments in public or parapublic organizations. These case studies were developed in response to the training needs of ÉNAP[1] graduate students who were about to begin a practical training session as public sector consultants. In the Fall of 1991, ÉNAP initiated a new Masters in Public Administration (MPA - Option B) in which students could complete a practical training session (PTS) as part of their degree requirements. These PTS's provided the students with an opportunity to complete a consulting assignment in a real-life situation. The case studies described in this paper are based on the experience of the first group of trainees.

The paper is divided into two major sections. First, we shall describe the context in which these case studies were developed and the methodology which was used. In the second section, we shall present one of the case studies and briefly describe its classroom use.

THE MPA PROGRAM - OPTION B

Option B of the MPA program is designed for students who intend to become consultants, analysts or researchers in public or parapublic organizations. In addition to the provincial, federal or municipal public service, these also include institutions such as hospitals, school boards, junior colleges, universities, cultural organizations, etc. The program offers four areas of specialization: organizational design and analysis, accounting and financial management, program evaluation and human resource management.

STUDENT POPULATION

Option B students are generally under 30 years old. Depending on their area of specialization, they have completed an undergraduate degree in disciplines such as psychology, sociology, management, political sciences, accounting, etc. As a rule, these students have had very little working experience before entering the program. Typically, they have held summer or part-time jobs that where totally unrelated to their field of study.

152

At best, they may have held a temporary job in their field.

PRACTICAL TRAINING SESSIONS

At the end of their course work, Option B students must choose between a thesis and a practical training session in a client organization. Most students select the PTS option which in effect become an entry level job, thus allowing them to put that crucial "first line" on their curriculum vitae.

PTS's are carried out under the joint supervision of an ÉNAP faculty advisor and a local advisor from the client organization. These sessions include two major dimensions. First, they are designed to help students integrate the knowledge they have acquired in the course of their program. In this respect, PTS's provide them with an opportunity to apply these theoretical constructs, models and methodologies to concrete problems and situations. Secondly, and perhaps more importantly, PTS's allow student to learn the interpersonal skills that are an essential element of the consultant's trade.

PTS ISSUES

THE STUDENTS' POINT OF VIEW

The first PTS's began in January 1993 and went on for 15 weeks. They were monitored very carefully in order to obtain an accurate assessment of the main problems experienced by the first group of 30 trainees and their client organization. All trainees were interviewed individually in the middle and at the end of their practical training session. At that time, moreover, a sample of 15 trainees were invited to a collective debriefing interview. This interview was videotaped and analyzed in detail in order to highlight the most common issues and problems brought up by trainees.

None of the participants mentioned any serious technical problems with respect to the day-to-day accomplishment of their PTS assignments. By and large, trainees had the necessary know-how or knew where to find the answers to the technical problems they encountered along the way.

Virtually all students, however, mentioned problems related to what could best be described as the general area of "behavioral know-how", such as discovering the dynamics of the interpersonal relationships involved, identifying the key actors and the major issues at stake, learning to keep expectations within realistic limits, dealing with the anxiety caused by the arrival of a consultant in the organization, etc. In this respect, the most frequent problems mentioned by students included:
- How to enter the organization: the importance of first impressions
- How to define a mandate clearly so as to avoid generating unrealistic expectations,
- Becoming aware of the anxiety caused by the arrival of a consultant in the organization,
- How to demonstrate empathy without becoming involved in the personal problems of one's contacts within the organization,
- How to avoid becoming involved in the inevitable power struggles and political battles within the organization,
- How to present the conclusions of an analysis in a matter which is acceptable to the primary client, and finally,
- How to leave the organization once the assignment has been completed.

Further to the collective interview, the trainees who had the most interesting experience were asked to participate in an in-depth personal interview. These interviews were recorded on audio tapes and transcribed in full so as to allow for a very detailed analysis.

THE CLIENT ORGANIZATIONS' POINT OF VIEW

The most frequent complaint on the part of client organizations was that PTS trainees had a tendency to be arrogant, to apply textbook solutions indiscriminately, and that they were often insensitive to the interpersonal and political aspects of their assignments. In fact, discussing these issues with PTS students and primary clients in the host organizations highlighted two diametrically opposed views of the students' role and status in the organization.

Typically, the students saw themselves as trainees in a learning situation. Many among them felt somewhat insecure as to whether they would be able to live up to their client's expectations. They often turned to their local advisors for guidance on specific issues. Local advisors, on the other hand, usually regarded their PTS trainee as full-fledged consultants who would be able to "solve the problem". As one of the student indicated during the interviews, he was introduced at the first staff meeting which he attended with his client as, "Here is the guy who has the answers to our current problems". In addition, other members of the client organization tended to see PTS trainees as powerful consultants with a mandate to "get things done". In a context of generalized budget cutbacks and rationalization programs, this view often led to extremely defensive attitudes on the part of staff members. As a result, PTS students often found it difficult to obtain the necessary information. This in turn exacerbated their own sense of insecurity. Hence, they tended to fall back on the technical aspects of their mandate, which was often perceived as arrogance by members of the host organizations.

SHOW, DON'T TELL...

While the dynamics of this situation became readily apparent to the interviewers who looked at it from a more distant perspective, it remained largely elusive to the students themselves. Furthermore, it also quickly became obvious that there was indeed very little point in *telling* the students about these aspects of their task because of the indifference or the hostility with which such statements would be met. There is no point, for instance, in telling students not to be arrogant; because in their own mind, they are certainly not. Similarly, telling them that certain forms of behavior may be misconstrued as arrogance is not very helpful either, because it is an intellectual observation which is interpreted as a value judgment on the part of the instructor. However, *showing* a situation in which a given character's behavior is perceived as arrogance is another matter.

What was needed, in sum, was a way of bringing the students to *see* these problems for themselves, so that they would realize the necessity of allowing for such factors in the course of their PTS. Ideally, moreover, students should develop an awareness of these factors *prior* to the beginning of their practical training sessions. While these elements had been explicitly presented in various courses and seminars, the message simply did not seem to register. Students who had not actually *been* in an organization could not relate these factors to any tangible personal experience, and therefore tended to dismiss them as being irrelevant to the execution of their assignment. More experienced students usually felt threatened and, as a result, became very defensive.

In order to address these problems, we decided to write a series of case studies based on the actual experience of the first group of PTS students. These case studies were written as short stories, that is, without interpretative positions or value judgements. In literary writings, for instance, the text does not usually *explain* the motivations underlying a given character's behavior; instead, it shows the character in action, leaving the reader free to draw his/her own conclusions.

The case writer's task, in this instance, is twofold. First he/she must "read" the situation correctly. Interviews with different members of the client organization and with students will indicate how these participants saw the situation from their respective perspectives. Once this has been done, the case writer must then reconstruct the story in order to tell it from the perspective of an unseen narrator. This process also allows the writer to highlight the most significant aspects of the situation at hand. The purpose of this reconstruction exercise is to produce a text that will evoke in the reader the same emotions as those felt by the original actors, although in a more condensed and less personal manner. An image, as the saying goes, is worth a thousand words. The same can be said about mental images.

CASE STUDIES

It would be impossible due to space constraints to present the six case studies that were developed in the course of this project. We shall therefore restrict ourselves to one case study in order to illustrate the approach.

ALBERT BASTARACHE AND THE NEW WORLD CONSERVATORY

Albert Bastarache and the New World Conservatory is a four-part case study illustrating some of the pitfalls faced by inexperienced consultants. Albert Bastarache's PTS assignment consisted in recommending an appropriate administrative structure for the reorganization of the New World Conservatory, a professional music school in the Montreal area. At the time, the conservatory was considering several alternatives and wanted an assessment of the legal, financial, operational and structural implications of each of them. In its initial form, the mandate was therefore much to broad for a single individual, even more so in the case of an inexperienced consultant. At the insistence of his faculty advisor, Bastarache succeeded in restricting the assignment to the structural implications of the different alternatives under consideration. Even in its scaled-down version, however, his assignment was still a "tall order" in view of his very limited professional experience.

When Bastarache arrived at the Conservatory on a cold, snowy January morning, he discovered, much to his dismay, that nobody was aware of his mandate and that his arrival was totally unexpected. He had negotiated his assignment directly with the dean of the conservatory with whom he had had one meeting only, and he had made no preliminary contacts before entering the organization. The dean was absent when Bastarache arrived, and he had not told Odette Roy, his secretary, about Bastarache's assignment. Ms. Roy had been working at the Conservatory for forty years, and she was, in several respect, the most powerful person in the institution. Bastarache eventually discovered that the dean was usually absent because he was heavily involved in the promotion of the conservatory's activities within the arts industry.

After Ms. Roy had recuperated from the shock of Bastarache's arrival, she directed him to a comfortable office in a remote corner of the building and presented him with an impressive stack of administrative documents on the conservatory's recent history. Bastarache was literally "snowed-in". He then secluded himself in the quietness of his office and started reading, leaving the door ajar so that he could hear the students who were rehearsing all day long. Bastarache read for three weeks during which he made no contacts whatsoever within the organization. When his reading phase was over, he decided to go on a tour of similar institutions in Montreal and Quebec City.

This phase lasted for another three weeks, after which Bastarache decided that he was ready to write his report. The Conservatory did not insist on his presence, so Bastarache decided to work at home where he could use his personal computer. Bastarache spent close to a month on his report, and gradually came to the realization that he was not going anywhere. The whole exercise was turning into another academic term-paper. He could not write anything worthwhile about the conservatory because he had in fact hardly ever been there. At that point, he went back to the conservatory and started doing what he should have done in the first place; he started meeting people. The image of the conservatory which he obtained further to these meetings was markedly different from his earlier "documentary" image. Once again, however, Bastarache was not very persistent. He had written a note to all student representatives in which he briefly explained his assignment and asked to meet them. When he did not receive any answers, he did not pursued the matter any further.

During the second part of his assignment, Bastarache developed a close working relationship with Marcel Boucher, the dean's administrative assistant. Boucher was an astute political operator who had several points of contention with his boss. He was quick to see how he could use Bastarache's report against the dean. Without realizing it, Bastarache was gradually drawn into Boucher ongoing battle against the dean. The first version of his report was heavily critical of the dean and was written in a language that did not befit his position as a consultant. At the insistence of his faculty advisor, it was substantially amended and edited before being presented at the Conservatory.

According to the standards of consultation, Bastarache's performance was therefore far from successful: his mandate was poorly defined; his entry into the organization was a fiasco; his interpersonal and political skills were next to nonexistent. Had he been working for a consulting firm, his performance would in all probability have led to his dismissal. That being said, *Albert Bastarache and the New World Conservatory* is nevertheless a very rich case study. Bastarache was a bright young man who had had good grades throughout his studies. His shortcomings were behavioral rather than technical. He was simply not able to translate his technical knowledge into usable practical tools. The case study is divided into four parts, each corresponding to a phase of his assignment (i.e. entry, documentation, etc.) The text contains no opinion statements or value judgments on Bastarache's performance. It simply describes what happened with occasional direct quotations from the key actors. Yet, when it is used in the classroom, students are quick to see the problems and to discover the actor's motivations. For instance, they point out that Bastarache's own insecurity makes him literally run away from his assignment whenever he has a chance, or that Boucher was able to capitalize on that insecurity in an attempt to use Bastarache's report to his own advantage.

CONCLUSION

In addition to *Albert Bastarache and the New World Conservatory*, three other case studies on PTS students and two case studies involving senior consultants were also written. These served to illustrate certain consulting issues that had not surfaced during the interviews with the PTS students. These six case studies were use in the preparatory workshops for PTS students in December of 1993. The second series of PTS's began in January 1994. The case study considerably improved the preparatory workshops, as was reflected in the mid and end of session questionnaires completed by students and their advisors. Students arrived in the organization with much clearer picture of their role, of the limitation of their assignments and of the potential pitfalls.

ENDNOTES

1.   ÉNAP: *École nationale d'administration publique,* or National School of Public Administration.

156

IMPROVING CASE DISCUSSION
THROUGH COOPERATIVE LEARNING

William Cooper
North Carolina A&T State University
GREENSBORO, NORTH CAROLINA, U.S.A.
Charles Malone
North Carolina A&T State University
GREENSBORO, NORTH CAROLINA, U.S.A.
James Harris
North Carolina A&T State University
GREENSBORO, NORTH CAROLINA, U.S.A.

Abstract

Cooperative learning is a group structure that can be used to stimulate case discussion. This paper discusses some approaches for implementing cooperative learning techniques as well as pitfalls that an instructor should seek to avoid in the process of introducing cooperative learning techniques in the classroom.

INTRODUCTION

As instructors attempt to stimulate classroom discussion through greater use of cases, they are experimenting with new and unique group structures. One technique that is gaining in popularity is entitled "Cooperative Learning" [Astin, 1993; Marzano, 1992]. Cooperative learning attempts to give structure to students in developing case discussion and gives the instructor guidance for more effective monitoring of student responses. This presentation contains a description of cooperative learning, recommendations regarding the implementation of cooperative learning, and possible pitfalls that should be avoided.

As described by Cooper et al [1990, p. 10], cooperative learning is "an instructional technique which requires students to work together in small fixed groups on a structured learning task." Activities utilizing cooperative learning techniques can address several dimensions of learning [Solomon and Davidson, 1993; Marzano, 1992]. While the structured learning task can take a variety of forms, the case method is particularly benefited by cooperative learning since it fosters interrelationships among students in goal formation, task development, and the assignment of rewards. Cooperative learning structures promote active learning [Millis, 1991; King, 1992] and collaboration and interdependence are important aspects of cooperative learning [Mauro and Cohen, 1993].

IMPLEMENTING COOPERATIVE LEARNING

Group formation is a critical task that the instructor should consider because each method has certain potential social and educational benefits. For example, if the instructor seeks to stimulate discussion from all groups, then heterogeneity may be desired within groups and students should be assigned to groups based upon ability as measured by grade point averages. Students with highest averages would be grouped with weaker students. One might expect this attempt for equalization across groups to lead to more stimulating discussion within the group and better participation outside the group. However, while noting that most cooperative learning models advocate the above described distribution, Astin [1993] suggests that research should address the group composition issue. In addition to ability, a variety of factors such as academic major, courses completed, gender, race, ethnicity, and work experience could be considered in assigning students to groups [Cottell and Millis, 1994]. Student-completed data sheets may be useful in this process [Cottell and Millis, 1994].

Randomization could be used by the instructor to assign students to groups in situations in which the students are fairly homogeneous or if the instructor lacks information regarding the abilities of the students. The randomization method could be humorous and generate initial support for the case groups.

An alternative to instructor-formed groups would be to allow the students to form their own groups. Given that student-formed groups are more voluntary than instructor formed groups, the expectation is that this may help to establish a harmonious work environment within the group. Feichtner and Davis [1985] contend that students prefer instructor-formed groups because within student-formed groups there may be subgroups which are dysfunctional to group performance. Furthermore, students may benefit from learning to work with group members with whom they were previously unfamiliar and may develop new friendships [Feichtner and Davis, 1985].

What is the optimal group size? Group size may depend in large part on the class enrollment. For some relatively simple tasks, groups of two may be adequate. Cottell and Millis [1994] advocate groups of four students. Based upon a study of a variety of group activities, Feichtner and Davis [1985] recommend that groups of four to seven students tend to have greater resources than smaller groups while possessing greater cohesiveness than larger groups. At many universities a large percentage of students have part-time jobs to finance their education [Cottell and Millis, 1994]. Instructors need to recognize that differing class schedules and the demands of work make it difficult for groups to meet outside of class time. Smaller groups facilitate arranging meetings [Feichtner and Davis, 1985]. Additionally, some class time should be set aside to permit groups to make meeting arrangements.

The number of groups will be a function of the class enrollment and group size. Case discussion may be more lively in classes of moderate size. With respect to the stability of groups, Feichtner and Davis [1985] claim that permanent groups offer advantages with regard to cohesiveness and the development of task effectiveness.

Regardless of the method, once the groups are formed, the instructor is then free to approach the case in any manner desired. Long cases that would be difficult for a two or three person group to address can be handled by combining two or more groups. Other situations could involve particularly difficult cases in which experts could be designated within each group. Each expert would then interact with experts from other groups within the class to develop a common solution for a portion of the case and then bring that solution back to the original group. In summary, cooperative learning provides a structure within the classroom as the students move from case to case.

POSSIBLE PITFALLS

Cottell and Millis [1994] and Ekroth [1990] have noted that faculty encounter several barriers to changing their teaching approaches. Included among the barriers to change are anxiety by faculty and students relating to change as well as the desire by faculty to entertain and be the center of attention [Ekroth, 1990]. One of the most difficult aspects of cooperative learning is that it can require considerable time. It is very easy for an instructor to become impatient and try to speed the process along. Often, particularly in an undergraduate environment, the solutions given by the students are crude and fail to include key components the instructor feels should be highlighted. The instructor needs to be willing to wait and allow the case to unfold. Also, through careful planning and the use of some cooperative learning techniques, one can reduce concern regarding the time factor [Cottell and Millis, 1994].

A second problem that is ingrained in the formation of groups is the "free rider" [Feichtner and Davis, 1985] or "hitchhiker" [Cottell and Millis, 1993]. Students who fail to participate are often hidden by the actions of other group members. Frequently, better students resent this problem and will rebel if it is allowed to persist. One solution to this problem is to rotate roles within the group [Cottell and Millis, 1994]. For example, members may take turns as the presenter and the recorder of the case solution. Ideally, the group itself will monitor individuals but situations may develop in which the instructor may need to intervene [Cottell and Millis, 1994]. Peer assessment of individual contributions may also encourage group members to contribute [Cottell and Millis, 1994].

A third problem, and one that has no easy solutions, is grading. Assigning an identical grade to all members of a group masks individual contributions while, on the other hand, trying to identify each student's input is difficult. There are only partial solutions to the grading problem. One alternative would be to limit the number of points given to each case thus minimizing the effect of grading error. However, if too few points are allocated to the group activities, then students, as rational decision makers, may fail to seriously address the cases. Another grading alternative would require students to evaluate each other member of their group. Feichtner and Davis [1985] recommend that with any group work there at least be some use of peer evaluation in the grading process. Michaelsen [1992] and Cottell and Millis [1994] provide some good suggestions for peer evaluation of group work. A third approach would be to sit with each group and formulate a grading scheme. Each of these grading alternatives has its own set of problems, but if used in combination with other methods, the final grade should be viewed as reasonably fair to all students.

Cooperative learning will not work unless both the instructor and students buy into it. It is important to communicate to your students through the syllabus and class discussion the nature of cooperative learning, group case assignments, and the class expectations [Cottell and Millis, 1994]. Students must be motivated to become involved. Explanations as to why methods are adopted may facilitate adaptation to new methods [Ekroth, 1990]. Students need to understand that individual accountability continues to exist despite the assistance provided via cooperative learning from the instructor, the group, and the class.

REFERENCES

Astin, A., "What Matters In College? Implications For Cooperative Learning of a New National Study," Cooperative Learning & College Teaching (Spring 1993), pp. 2-8.

Cooper, J., S. Prescott, L. Cook, L. Smith, R. Mueck, and J. Cuseo, Cooperative Learning and College Instruction: Effective Use of Student Learning Teams (Long Beach, CA: Institute of Teaching and Learning, 1990).

Cottell, P. and B. Millis, "Cooperative Learning Structures in the Instruction of Accounting" Issues in Accounting Education (Spring 1993), pp. 40-59.

Cottell, P. and B. Millis, Cooperative Learning and Accounting (South-Western Publishing Co., 1994).

Ekroth, L., "Why Professors Don't Change," Teaching Excellence (Winter-Spring 1990).

Feichtner, S. and E. Davis, "Why Some Groups Fail: A Survey of Students' Experiences With Learning Groups," The Organizational Behavior Teaching Review (Volume IX, Issue 4, 1985), pp. 58-73.

King, A., "Promoting Active Learning and Collaborative Learning in Business Administration Classes, in T. Frecka (Ed.), Critical Thinking, Interactive Learning and Technology: Reaching for Excellence in Business Education (Arthur Andersen Foundation, 1992), pp. 158-173.

Marzano, R., "The Many Faces of Cooperation Across the Dimensions of Learning," in N. Davidson and T. Worsham (Eds.), Enhancing Thinking Through Cooperative Learning (Teachers College Press, 1992).

Mauro, L. and L. Cohen, "The Concept Attainment Model of Teaching: Connections With Cooperative Learning," Cooperative Learning (Winter 1993), pp. 7-11.

Michaelsen, L., "Team Learning: A Comprehensive Approach for Harnessing the Power of Small Groups in Higher Education," To Improve the Academy (Volume 11, 1992), pp. 107-122.

Millis, B., "Fulfilling the Promise of the "Seven Principles" Through Cooperative Learning: An Action Agenda for the University Classroom," Journal on Excellence in College Teaching (Volume 2, 1991), pp. 139-144.

Solomon, R. and N. Davidson, "Cooperative Dimensions of Learning," Cooperative Learning (Winter 1993), pp. 37-43.

CRITERIA FOR THE SELECTION
OF CASE STUDIES OF LEADERSHIP

Roger Smitter
North Central College
NAPERVILLE, ILLINOIS, U.S.A.

Abstract

Higher education has witnessed a proliferation of programs for the study of leadership. Case studies are often integral to the instructional practices in such programs. The paper lays out a set of criteria for the selection of case studies of leadership, focusing on the works of leadership theorists such as Gardner, Rost, Burns and Roesner. A case study of leadership is examined using these criteria.

INTRODUCTION

Leadership studies have emerged as a significant interdisciplinary force in higher education. Speaking to a 1993 conference on liberal arts and leadership, [Marietta College, 1993] Howard Prince, Director of the U of Richmond Jepson School of Leadership, noted that "leadership studies" is a growth industry in American colleges and universities. He cited figures which put the number of leadership programs well over 700. Since 1991, two national organizations for the study of leadership, the Association of Leadership Educators and the National Clearinghouse for Leadership Programs, have been established. Numerous conferences have been sponsored. A new publication, The Journal of Leadership Studies, appeared in late 1993.

Leadership continues to be a popular topic in traditional academic disciplines. Business schools as well as schools of public administration, health, and education offer courses and whole programs in leadership.

By its very nature, the teaching of leadership should (and does) make extensive use of interactive teaching methods, relying heavily on case studies. For example, the index for a recent Harvard Business School catalog of case studies includes a separate section entitled "leadership" [1993]. Textbooks in the disciplines include many more "leadership" cases.

Drawing on the work of major theorists such as Burns [1978], Gardner [1990] and Rost [1991], this paper seeks to establish **criteria** for the selection of case studies in the teaching of leadership. A case study of leadership will then be analyzed. "leadership" case.

CRITERIA

DOES THE CASE PORTRAY LEADERSHIP AS A POSITION WITHIN A HIERARCHY OR A RELATIONSHIP AMONG PARTICIPANTS?

Gardner [1990] and Rost [1991] both make this a fundamental distinction in their conceptualization of leadership. They note that traditional wisdom equates position within an organization with leader. After all, most persons in business and politics aspire to a **position** which will give them some form of power or prestige.

Gardner [1990] argues strongly for a distinction between leadership and related concepts such as status, power, authority and elites (pp. 2-3). He readily recognizes the overlap among these but he consistently reminds readers that without a relationship of some kind with followers, leaders have nothing:

Confusion between leadership and official authority has a deadly effect on large organizations. Corporations and government agencies everywhere have executives who imagine that their place on the organizational chart has given them a body of followers. And of course it has not. They have been

162

given subordinates. Whether the subordinates become followers depends on whether the executives act like leaders (p. 3).

Gardner goes so far as to reject the word follower, preferring the word **constituents** to label the other half of the leadership relationship.

Rost [1991] suggests that leadership is "an influence" relationship among leaders and followers" (p. 102). He focuses on the active, not passive, nature of followers. He recognizes that the relationship is inherently unequal because the influence patterns are not equal (pp. 102-103).

The application of this criteria for case selection is straightforward. One effective case scenario would show one character, well established in the organizational hierarchy, being surpassed in leadership skills by another character who understands relationships with followers. Another scenario would be to have students select for promotion to a leadership position from several characters in a case, with the issue revolving around the characters' abilities to form relationships with followers.

DOES THE CASE CAST LEADERSHIP AS A TRANSACTION OR AS A TRANSFORMATION?

This distinction comes from Burns [1978] who saw transactional leadership as an "exchange ... to realize independent objectives." However, in transformational leadership, "Leaders ... shape and alter and elevate the motives and values and goals of followers," performing a teaching role. The transformation occurs in the "pursuit of higher goals...that represent the collective...interests of leaders and followers" [Burns, 1978, p. 425]. He adds:
> The premise of this leadership is that, whatever the separate interests persons might hold, they are presently or potentially united in the pursuit of "higher" goals, the realization of which is tested by the achievement of significant change that represents the collective or pooled interests of leaders and followers (p. 425).

This distinction represents a major shift in thinking about leadership. Burns said older models saw the leader engaging in a kind of exchange with followers, getting them to do something for the leader's interest if the leader did something to advance the followers' interests.   In similar fashion, Rost [1991] talks about mutual purposes becoming common purposes (p. 103).

This criteria would best be put to work in selecting cases which show the differences between the two forms of leadership. As with test number one, two characters with different concepts of leadership would serve well in such cases. Students could also be put in the role of a leader who needs to define the transforming goal in the case. Cases about conflict are often useful in this regard.

DOES THE CASE CAST LEADERSHIP AS A PROCESS OR A SINGLE EVENT?

Gardner [1990] sees leadership as a series of actions, not a "single act" (p. 1).   Burns [1978] casts leadership as a "reciprocal process" (p. 425).   The theorists are saying that no one event can capture what a leader is or does. Even great speeches (such as the Gettysburg Address) are the product of many events and are followed by other events. The point is that each action derives its meaning from the context of preceding and following actions by the leader and others. Obviously, no one case can provide all the information leading up to a decision. However, students need to have enough information to put an action into a context which provides some of the meaning of an act of leadership.

In applying this test, the instructor obviously needs to find cases of sufficient length so as to supply the context for a leadership decision.   It would be useful for students to sort through the facts of the case to find those which define the leadership activities of the characters.

DOES THE CASE RAISE ISSUES OF ETHICS AND VALUES?

Leadership cannot be separated from fundamental questions of values. Gardner's [1990] list of the task of leadership includes several which imply an understanding of the ethics of an organization: **envisioning goals** and **affirming values** (including the regeneration of values), and **representing the group, serving as symbol** (pp. 11-23).   He also lists several attributes of leaders which imply the issue of ethics: **judgement-in-action; willingness to accept responsibilities; courage, resolution, steadiness;** and **capacity to win and hold trust** (pp. 48-54).   Gardner devotes a full chapter to the "moral dimension" of leadership (pp. 67-80).

Returning to the concept of **relationship**, we can see that all acts of leadership involve other persons. Questions of ethics are inherent in any kind of relationship. Leaders make decisions which affect many people either directly or indirectly (as in the case of a decision which affects the future for an organization). Interestingly, in the Foreword to Rost's book where he criticized Rost for underestimating the crucial importance of concepts such as values, ethics and morality [Rost, 1991, xii].

Obviously many cases on ethics in business and medical education already exist. It would be useful to reconceptualize these as leadership cases.

DOES THE CASE SUGGEST THAT LEADERSHIP LEADS TO CHANGE OR THE INTENTION OF CHANGE?

Rost [1991] argues for a position which is at odds with many leadership theorists, especially Burns [1978]. Rost argues that leadership is not something we define after the fact. Rost says leadership emerges in the here and now out of a relationship which purposefully sets about to create change. Furthermore, according to Rost, "Intention must be demonstrated by action" (p. 114) and the change must be "substantive and transforming" (p. 115). Rost takes issue with Burns for conceptualizing leadership as a product, not a process (pp. 115-116). Rost also argues that leaders and followers intend changes over time. The efforts of leadership seldom result in a single, isolated change (p. 117).

Effective cases need to supply readers with considerable description of characters actions and words. From these actions and words, students should deduce the intent to the leaders.

WHAT FORMS OF POWER ARE AVAILABLE FOR LEADERSHIP FUNCTIONS IN THE CASE?

Teaching about the leaders and power is one of the more difficult tasks in teaching leadership. Power is not the same as leadership. However, power is something that is inherent in the leadership process. Gardner [1990] devotes a full chapter to a discussion of power. "By definition," he says, "leaders always have a measure of power. But many power holders have no trace of leadership" (p. 56).

Rost [1991], Gardner [1990] and Burns [1978] all distinguish between various forms of power, arguing that leaders should not use coercion. Coercion implies a "uni-directional" rather than the preferred "multi-directional" relationship with followers [Rost, pp. 105-106]. Rost embellishes his point by saying:

Deciding what is coercive or not coercive is a bit more tricky than deciding whether the relationship is multidirectional. The key word is influence, so concentrate on a clear understanding of influence as the basis for a relationship. If influence is what makes the relationship tick, then it is leadership. If not, some other relationship is happening (pp. 106-107).

It should be noted here, as an aside, that students will encounter this "other" kind of relationship in the world beyond the classroom. They need to be exposed to cases which help them appreciate power the importance of power in leadership relationships.

Applying this question to the case selection, the obvious contrast would be between the use of coercive and noncoercive power in a case study. Students could also be asked to play the role of a character in the case and speak or write about the sources of power they could draw upon. The well worn but still relevant analysis of Raven and French [1959] provides a useful way to assess the sources of power in a case.

DOES THE CASE RAISE ISSUES OF DIVERSITY IN LEADERSHIP?

Two key forms of diversity entail gender and ethnic differences. Certainly case studies should provide a diverse set of characters for students to analyze. Care must be given however in analyzing the behavior of any character from a single frame of reference.

Roesner [1990] suggests that "women's ways of leading" are more likely to be characterized as transformational in nature, while male styles are transactional. Drawing on the work of Gilligan [1982], Helgesen [1990] observed that women are more likely to use relationships rather than power as the basis of leadership.

In a concise summary of the work on ethnic diversity and leadership, Conrad [1994] suggests that Latin cultures define leadership along three dimensions: honoring one's family through hard work; doing one's duty for others, not necessarily for an organization; and avoiding public confrontations, especially showing deference for superiors. He concludes: "These values lead to a high level of concern for interpersonal relationships and the feelings of other people, a more participatory, open-door leadership style and a preference for face-to-face

164

communication" (p. 416). Conrad sees similarities between Latin and African-American concepts of leadership, especially in the development of cooperative work teams (p. 417).

HOW DOES THE CASE PORTRAY FOLLOWERS?

Leadership implies the presence of followers. It may well be the case that the concept of "follower" will be more difficult to define and analyze than that of "leader." Rost [1991] notes that many theorists have trouble with the connotations for the word follower. He prefers to see followers as active, not passive, participants in the leadership process (p. 107). Gardner [1990] prefers the word constituents to followers, suggesting the collaborative relationship they have with leaders (p. 2).

The work of Kelly on "followership" [1988] casts the follower role as integral to any understanding of leadership. His principle is that followers help create a particular type of leader. He assesses followers along two dimensions, active-passive and critical-non critical, creating four types of followers, "active", "sheep", "cynics" and "yes people".

Too many cases supply a significant amount of detail about the person cast as "the leader" in the case. Instructors need to select cases which also supply detail on the nature of the followers and subordinates in the case. Once students know an equal amount of information about both roles in the case, they can begin to see the importance of understanding the nature of followers.

DOES THE CASE RAISE THE ISSUE OF LEADERSHIP AND VISION?

Former US President Bush's problems with "the vision thing" may pale in comparison to the attempts of theorists to define its role in leadership. Burns's [1978] implies that a transformational leader has a something in mind which is bigger than the immediate concerns of followers. Gardner thoughts on vision emerge in his definition of leadership: "the process of persuasion or example by which an individual (or leadership team) induces a group to pursue objectives held by the leader or shared by the leader and his or her followers" [1990, p.1].

The best analysis of vision comes from the work of Nanus [1992] who defined vision as a "realistic, credible, attractive future for an organization" (p. 20). The vision provides direction and focus to all of the energies of the organization. While he states it is seldom a result of methodical, linear planning, it can be assessed using a variety of tools. This concept is one of the most elusive in the theory and may well be taught better by use of concrete events in cases.

Several questions spring to mind for the instructor selecting cases. Does the case show a character developing a vision of any kind? Are there characters with competing visions? Can the case be used to force students to develop and articular their own vision for an organization?

CASE REVIEW

The case selected for analysis, "Leading a Corporate Task Force," is the case used in the chapter on leadership in a popular textbook on small group communication [Cragan and Wright, 1991, pp. 142-143]. It is copied as an appendix to this paper. While offered in a textbook on group communication, the case has application to organizational behavior and management courses as well.

In brief, the case tells the story of a rising executive in a corporation, Mary Schilling, who makes bad choices about the membership of a task force. Mary allows her former supervisor to dominate the group and fails to quell a brewing conflict between two factions within the group. The task force fails to achieve its goals and Mary is removed from the assignment.

Prior to writing this paper, the author has used this case several times, with mixed results as measured by the quality and quantity of case discussion. Given the criteria outlined above, what is the potential of the case for teaching leadership?

The case is especially useful to illustrate the distinction between leadership as *position* and as *relationship*. Mary too readily assumes that because she has a position in the corporate hierarchy, she is the leader. The members of the task force clearly see the complex web of relationships within the group, especially noting the presence of her former supervisor. The case supplies enough detail to show the *process* nature of leadership. The meeting-by-meeting summary of what happened nicely illustrates how Mary's former supervisor, Tom, presence of her former supervisor. The case supplies enough detail to show the *process* nature of leadership. The meeting-by-meeting summary of what happened nicely illustrates how Mary's former supervisor, Tom, unintentionally compounds the problems for Mary by bailing her out when the group had reached an impasse. While a cursory reading of the case would suggest Mary was at fault for not exerting the authority of her position, a closer reading of the process shows now the Tom-Mary relationship is at the heart of the failure of leadership.

The case also illustrates nicely that Mary had several *power* resources to draw upon in exerting her leadership. She apparently was on a "fast track" with the corporation, having demonstrated proficiency in previous tasks. She had the right traits and potentially other power resources, but failed to translate these into leadership.

Finally, the case presents a useful reversal of typical male and female ways of leading. Mary believes that her position alone is enough to lead the group while Tom has some savvy about the importance of relationships within the group. Unfortunately, Tom does not have (or at least express) enough savvy to know from the start that his presence on the task force would create problems for his protege, Mary. Mary ignores relationship issues as well, failing to deal with the conflict of the marketing and sales people until too late. Her one attempt at creating a relationship with Sally is perceived as too heavy handed to be effective.

A number of problems exist with the case, however. The lessons about *change, vision, transformation,* and *followers* are all taught by bad example. It is clear that Mary intends change. But she seems to have little in the way of a vision for the direction of that change. If we had more facts about the product mentioned in the case, it would be possible to have students develop a vision for Mary.

Also, Mary cannot find the overarching principle or goal which will enable her to engage in transformational leadership. In fact, she hardly engages in transactional leadership until the one inept act with the other female on the task force.

The Kelly model of followership could be applied to the subordinates in the case. However, because we know so little about them, they remain one-dimensional characters.

The case does not raise significant questions of *ethics* for analysis. While Tom may have had an obligation to refuse Mary's offer to be part of the task force, his decision to participate hardly raises an issue of intentionally foiling her efforts. The other characters had an obligation not to carry personal conflicts into the task force. But, because we know so little about them, it is difficult to raise ethical questions about their behavior.

All in all, the case is adequate for teaching leadership in organizations. Given this analysis, a number of teaching strategies spring to mind for focusing on the strengths of the case. Because it so nicely illustrates the distinction between leader as position and leader*ship* as relationship, it would be especially useful as a case for undergraduates who are about to begin their careers in the business world. The case can teach as a example of what not to do in a leadership position. However, when measured against the questions presented in this paper, its has limited potential.

The analysis of this particular case reveals that the nine questions posed above provide a useful framework for case selection. These questions also provide guidance in teaching the case in the classroom.

REFERENCES

Burns, J. Leadership. NY: Harper, 1978.

Cragan, J. & D. Wright. Communication in Small Group Discussions, 3/e. St. Paul: West, 1991.

Conrad, C. Strategic Organizational Communication, 3/e. Fort Worth: Harcourt, Brace, 1994

French, J. & B. Raven. "The Bases of Social Power," in Group Dynamics: Research and Theory, D. Cartwright & A. Zander (eds.), 3/e. NY: Harper, 1968 pp. 259-269.

Gardner, J. On Leadership. NY: Free Press, 1990.

Gilligan, C. In a Different Voice. Cambridge: Harvard, 1982.

Harvard Business School 1993-94 Catalog of New Teaching Materials. Cambridge, MA: HBS, 1993.

166

Kelly, R. The Power of Followership. NY: Doubleday, 1989.

Marietta College "Leadership and Liberal Arts Conference, April, 1993.

Nanus, B. Visionary Leadership. San Francisco: Jossey-Bass, 1992.

Rost, J. Leadership for the Twenty-First Century. NY: Praeger, 1991.

A NEW KIND OF CASE-STUDY: USING BUSINESS BEST SELLERS IN THE BUSINESS POLICY COURSE

Donald Grunewald and Philip Baron
Iona College
NEW ROCHELLE, NEW YORK, U.S.A.

Abstract

Using a best selling business book provides a method for students in the Business Policy course to study business strategy and learn about a large corporation in depth. This assignment gives the student the opportunity to read at least one good book about business. One benefit to students is increased business literacy. Students also have something current about business to talk about during job interviews. Examples of assignments and books that have been used are discussed in this paper.

The undergraduate Business Policy (Strategic Management) course is often taught by using the case method of instruction. Cases are generally regarded as especially good vehicles for giving students an understanding of the general management view of an organization. CEO's are often faced with broad issues and problems which are complex, unstructured, ill defined, sometimes difficult to assess and often unique. [Cote and Piffault, 1992]. The board of directors also faces such issues in its functions. These decisions must be made under uncertainty in a dynamic environment.

The reasoning process involved in this kind of decision making requires the ability to think abstractly. That ability, called cognition, includes perception, memory, language, concept formation, problem solving and information processing. Case analysis requires precisely those skills. In turn, it reinforces and refines such abilities.

Cases are further useful for analyzing past actions of organizations, identifying major problems facing the institution, developing alternative courses of action, deciding one or more actions to be taken and finding the strategic issues involved. They are often better than lectures for these purposes. Learning involves recreating experience in new terms and applying it to new situations. That is precisely what is involved in business decision making. In other words, wisdom often can't be told, it must be experienced. Cases, especially case histories, enable students to see patterns in development and similarities in situations. The case method enables students to identify and solve problems in real world situations. Further, they sharpen integrative capabilities.

In most undergraduate business policy courses, cases are used from a variety of organizations, familiarizing students with varied organizations. This is useful to them in a number of ways. Large multinational corporations, new enterprises, public and other non profit organizations, organizations of all kinds in crisis (such as potential bankruptcy or dissolution) are illustrative of the types of organizations represented in the business policy course. They face common problems and experience similar evolutionary processes.

Sometimes a case is used for one class session. Long, complex cases may carry over several class sessions. Series cases may be used to enable students to study organizations in depth longitudinally over time as they face multiple decisions.

Most business policy courses at the undergraduate level supplement cases by lectures from the professor and other experiences such as readings, discussions of text books, debates, videos and computer simulations.

The authors of this paper have found all of these devices useful in the undergraduate business policy course. Cases are often presented in class by student groups and then discussed in detail by the entire class.

Sometimes written reports on a case are used to help improve student writing skills and enable the instructor to better measure the capability of student analysis.

Moreover, the authors have been experimenting with a variant on the traditional case method of instruction. They have been motivated by the knowledge that it is crucial in Business Policy for the students to learn much about at least one large corporation in depth. The experience of these faculty members is that there is much support for the premise that intensive learning provides a superior basis for generalization. Using a best seller business book provides an opportunity for such in depth study of some organization. This kind of experience also means that students have the opportunity to read at least one well written book about business. One benefit to students is increased business literacy. Students have something current about business to talk about during job interviews.

Each year for the past six years, the instructors of the business policy course at Iona College have chosen a different business best seller for a two part written assignment. All undergraduate students in the business policy course have the same assignments regardless of who their instructor is.

Books used in recent years are the following: <u>Barbarians at the Gate</u>, by Bryan Burroughs and John Helyar; <u>The Deal of the Century</u>, by Steve Coll; <u>The Taking of Getty Oil</u>, by Steve Coll; <u>The House of Nomura</u>, by Albert J. Alletzhauser; <u>The Third Century</u>, by Kotkin and Kishimoto; <u>Greed and Glory in Wall Street</u>; <u>The Fall of the House of Lehman</u>, by Ken Auletta.

Students are required to prepare two written assignments based on the book that is being read and supplemented by additional specified sources. In one of the assignments, students are requested to apply the book's ideas (such as a hostile leveraged buy out) to a company of their choice from among several assigned industries.

For example, relevant to the year we required students to read <u>Barbarians at the Gate</u>, students were assigned to address the below listed issues in their first written report (all reports written in memorandum form and style of 3 to 5 single spaced typed pages):

1. A brief summary of the book which specifically focuses on:
   a. Ross Johnson's career moves
   b. the significant individuals and groups involved in the LBO
   c. the major events during the LBO
2. An assessment of the external environment of RJR Nabisco, prior to the LBO, in terms of some of its perceived opportunities and threats. By opportunities and threats we mean environmental conditions and developments with a potential effect on RJR Nabisco's future. These effects can be positive or adverse. Significant factors can be observed by analyzing the following:
   a. markets/economy
   b. competition
   c. technology
   d. government/society
3. Describe and discuss some of the cultural and political factors characterizing the management of RJR Nabiso prior to the LBO. Point out how these factors could have influenced RJR Nabisco's managers in making their strategic choice of the LBO.

These assignments can only be handled adequately by students who have read the entire book and assigned supplementary supporting readings and who have regularly attended lectures offered by the instructors on the business policy principles involved.

In this particular assignment, a sequel report was required. It had to be a again written in memorandum format and style:

1. The various stakeholders of RJR Nabisco, who have a stake in the outcome of the LBO, and how they are going to be affected by it.
2. An alternative strategy that RJR Nabisco could have pursued to solve some of its problems as perceived by Ross Johnson.
3. Some of the strategic decisions by Kolberg, Kravis and Roberts after the LBO through December 31 of this year.
4. Performance of both RJR Nabisco and Kolberg, Kravis and Roberts since the LBO through December 31 of this year.

To prepare for the second assignment, students were required to track KKR and RJR Nabisco in the <u>New York Times</u> and <u>The Wall Street Journal</u> daily.

The authors expect that work done on such assignments will result in the following goals being attained: Students will learn the details of the operation of a large multinational business. Students will have read an important book and experienced the relating of knowledge to the matter at issue. Students will have learned something about the impact of major issues such as the threat of a hostile takeover on a corporation, the role of a chief executive officer in a company, how business environments change and influence outcomes and correlative matters.

Because the business policy course attempts to simulate the circumstances of a professional environment, criteria used in evaluating the papers by the instructors are professional business standards. Accordingly, writing is of overriding importance- proper English and proper form and style. Reports not written at a minimally acceptable level of proper English (all words spelled correctly, all rules of grammar obeyed, structured well, coherent, clearly articulated and focused and devoid of slang, jargon, clichés and street language are given lower grades.

Beyond writing, integration of information and knowledge from the textbook and other sources, evidence of having understood the assignment, research and independent work, clear and logical thinking supported by evidence and completeness are the basis upon which the instructors grade the written assignments.

Experience over the past six years with using best seller current business literature in the business policy course has been very positive. Students have enjoyed an assignment that focuses in depth on a major firm or issue that they can comprehend and the evolution of which they can follow. Alumni indicate that they continue to track the company or major issues involved in the assignment years after graduation.

Pedagogically, it is helpful to illustrate a number of strategic management concepts, such as SWOT analysis, by using a company that all students have studied in depth. This also helps illustrate the importance of environmental scanning, the nature of general systems theory and the open system concept.

Grading these student reports on the best seller in business takes much time. On the other hand, it is relatively easy for the instructor to separate the original thinkers and other outstanding students from average and weaker students who have written the assignments. It is apparent that grading
can be done more fairly than with other written assignments.

This type of assignment goes to the essence of developing cognitive thinking and analytical skills. It heightens awareness of the importance of reading in conceptual intelligence.

The authors of this paper intend to continue assigning current business books that are best sellers to students in the Business Policy course. They are convinced that it is an especially effective way to prepare students for the real world. Further application of this technique is urged by colleagues. Replication is needed to confirm the results obtained by the authors. Information from such use will be welcomed.

REFERENCES

Alletzhauser, Albert J., The House of Nomura, Harper Perennial, New York, 1990.

Anderson, John R., Cognitive Psychology and Its Implication, W. H. Freeman and Co., 1990.

Auletta, Ken, Greed and Glory in Wall Street, Random House, New York, 1986.

Burrough, Bryan and John Helyar, Barbarians at the Gate, Harper and Row, New York, 1990.

Coll, Steve, The Deal of the Century, Atheneum, New York, 1986.

Coll, Steve, The Taking of Getty Oil, Atheneum, New York, 1987.

David, Fred, Strategic Management, Second Edition, Merrill Publishing Co., Columbus, Ohio, 1989.

Eysenck, Michel W., A Handbook of Cognitive Psychology, Lawrence Erlbaum Associates, London, 1984.

French, Wendell L., Kast, Fremont E., and Rosenzweig, James E., Understanding Human Behavior in Organizations, Harper and Row, New York, 1985.

170

House, R.V. and Singh, J.V., "Organizational Behavior: Some New Directions for Industrial/Organizational Psychology", <u>Annual Review of Psychology</u>, 38, pp. 669-718.

Klein, S.B., <u>Learning</u>, McGraw Hill, New York, 1984.

Kotkin, Joel and Kishimoto, Yoriko, <u>The Third Century</u>, Crown, New York, 1988.

Latham, G.P., "Human Resources Training and Development", <u>Annual Review of Psychology</u>, 39, pp. 545-582.

Luthans, Fred, <u>Organizational Behavior</u>, Third Edition, McGraw Hill, New York, 1985.

Martin, G. and J. Pear, <u>Behavior Modification: What It Is and Hot To Do It</u>, Third Edition, Prentice Hall, Englewood Cliffs, N.J., 1988.

Schultz and Schultz, S., <u>Psychology and Industry Today, An Introduction to Industrial and Organizational Psychology</u>, Macmillan, New York, 1990.

INDUSTRY PROFILES:
COMBINING QUALITY MANAGEMENT
AND THE CASE METHOD

Bonnie Farber
San Jose State University
SAN JOSE, CALIFORNIA, U.S.A.

Abstract

This paper describes how the *case method* is combined with (1) *the industry profile* and (2) *homeworks using quality management tools* to improve business students' competencies in the synthesis of information and the evaluation of service quality in comparative industries and firms. Student leadership, teamwork, and training skills are also exhibited during the semester as each student group of five persons becomes the quality analyst for a specific industry and leads the rest of the class in discussion, using the combined industry profile and case method information.

BACKGROUND ON SERVICES MANAGEMENT AND QUALITY

From a theoretical standpoint, service quality may be defined as translating the future needs of customers into measurable characteristics, so that products and services can be designed and delivered to give satisfaction or value at a price that the customer will pay [Deming, 1986]. Management of service quality is the application of quantitative methods and human resources to control and improve: (1) materials and services supplied to a service firm; (2) work processes or technology used to create services; and (3) organizational focus on meeting customer needs.

Quality management uses a preventive approach philosophy that requires suppliers, company managers and employees, and customers to jointly analyze inputs (e.g., machines, methods, materials, and people), work processes and outcome products and services in order to continuously improve the service system. Process management tools have been developed in the manufacturing sector that are now adapted to service firms; these include process flow charts; cause and effect diagrams, histograms, pareto charts, scatter diagrams, trend charts and control charts.

As future managers, students must learn to be observant of the levels of service in their business operations; it follows they must learn research tools that will help them focus clearly on work processes and customer value, as well as on financial projections and marketplace results. With this in mind, the approach to teaching service operations management outlined in this paper is highly integrative across operations, human resources and marketing disciplines. The students' general area of study is service quality; they accomplish this by engaging in a series of class activities that combine to generate a holistic picture of what managers must accomplish to successfully manage service firms today.

RATIONALE OF PROPOSED TEACHING SYSTEM

The strongest rationale for using an industry profile teaching technique is that it familiarizes students with a cross-section of service industries using a common theoretical thread of service quality. Students learn about service quality and firms' goals, characteristics, and tasks from a comparative perspective across industries which better prepares them to apply traditional operations, human resources, and marketing theory in multiple settings. They also learn where the service sector is headed in the U.S., where they individually fit in as future managers, and what they might expect as future customers of service firms.

The learning platform is highly deductive, deriving from peer discussions about industry articles and cases; identified learning goals of the course range from quality management tool application to problem resolution and solution evaluation during case analysis to traditional strengths, weaknesses, opportunities, threats (SWOT) analyses using media information on industries. The use of this technique is in response to the call for better prepared business graduates who are able to provide the firms that hire them with value-added strategies for responding to customers' needs and the service firms' goals of quality and productivity.

COURSE CONTEXTUAL BACKGROUND

The host course for this combination technique is a service operations management course designed for business undergraduate seniors. Students focus on how to provide quality products and services to their customers by integrating the operations, human resources, and marketing functions of service businesses. The case method is combined with an industry profile technique as the primary mode of instruction; students are asked to relate text readings and skill-based homeworks with industry and case analysis and current news articles on a regular basis. Students achieve understanding of quality goals such as building customer loyalty, achieving total customer satisfaction, and mobilizing both employees and customers for maximum quality service.

FIGURE 1
GRADING SCHEME

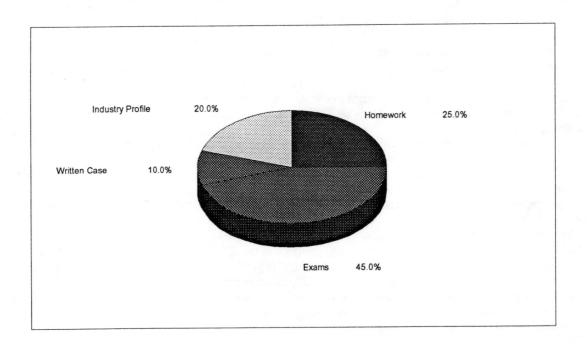

CONFIGURATION OF ASSIGNMENTS

Each student is involved in a series of activities during the semester; these comprise: (a) group participation in the analysis of quality in a designated service industry with resultant oral presentations; (b) written analysis of a case study to be integrated into the oral presentation about the industry studied; (c) homeworks requiring the practice of quality management tools; and (d) written examinations. Figure 1 shows the grading scheme for the course based on the above work list.

INDUSTRY PROFILE

Each student team signs up for a class date during the semester when it will present an oral report on service quality issues in a designated service industry. Oral reports include any related case studies indicated in the syllabus. Groups are responsible for coordinating additional source material, e.g., outside videos, extra readings or articles, related to their topic, which provide a conceptual background for their oral report. Groups are graded on their professionalism, their creativity, and most importantly, their ability to stimulate audience interest and discussion among their classmates. Peer evaluation is used also to measure the impact on the class of the group's performance on their oral report day>

Selection of the industries in any semester may be attributed to (a) current news worthiness of the industry, (b) availability of appropriate cases, and (c) instructors' levels of interest and expertise in specific industries. Industries that have been used include auto services repair, airlines, banking, express delivery, restaurant, hotel, retail/department store, legal, financial, and health services. Highly motivated students may request a specific industry when there exists sufficient reason to believe it will enhance their oral presentations to the benefit of all students.

Industry Profile Guidelines

Student groups are created in the first week of class in a non-structured fashion. A limit of five students per group is the norm. Written guidelines for performance on the industry profile group project are handed to students at the outset of the course. The following questions are written to the students' point of view and aid them in preparing for oral presentations (* indicates concepts specifically reinforced in the homework assignments).

(a) What are the core and supplemental services in your industry?
(b) What is the growth picture for supply and demand/markets?
(c) How would you define your industry's key work processes?*
(d))Flowchart critical inputs, processes, and outputs.*
(e) Are there aspects of your industry which are likely to become obsolete? How soon might this occur?
(f) What external environments provide threats to your industry? How?
(g) What do quality and productivity mean to managers in your industry?* To customers in your industry?*
(h) Which companies are the quality leaders? What are they doing?
(i) What does your case analysis offer to us in terms of learning about quality management applications in your industry?

Students are expected to plan 45 minutes for their presentations, including any (short!) videos or other information they may pass out to classmates. The quality of their support materials is critical to the presentation. They need to share their information with their classmates, not just with the instructor. Students prepare professional overheads or handouts that their classmates can focus on during class. All classmates are asked to fill out a presentation evaluation form for each oral presentation during the semester. This peer evaluation contributes to students' overall presentation grade.

CASE STUDY ANALYSIS

Due to the fact that services management is still in an infant stage of recognition among would be business textbook writers, the selection of cases is limited. However, three separate texts on service management concepts have been used successfully in this course and the author is confident that more will appear as this field of study matures:

(a) Fitzsimmons, J. and Fitzsimmons, M. <u>Service Management for Competitive Advantage.</u> c. 1994. McGraw-Hill, Inc.;

(b) Lovelock, C. editor. <u>Managing Services: Marketing, operations and human resources.</u> 2nd edit. c.1992. Prentice-Hall.; and

(c) Sasser, E., Hart, C. and Heskett, J. <u>The Service Management Course: Cases and Readings,</u> c. 1991 with companion text <u>Service Breakthroughs,</u> c. 1991. Free Press.

The critical factor in selecting a case for this particular class is the case's potential for a discussion of quality management and strategies leading to total customer satisfaction. Cases that focus heavily on financial or accounting information analysis would not be as useful in this context. It is necessary to review the cases and to prepare questions in accord with service operations management and quality management objectives.

Guidelines for Writing Case Analyses

Students are reminded that case decision makers need to avoid (a) looking for one right answer, (b) letting personal opinions cloud their viewpoints, and (c) looking for the answer only in the textbook. Also, students who do not present on an industry profile day are expected to prepare a one-page written summary sheet on the assigned case. The following guidelines are provided to aid their case analysis.

(1) Follow the basic decision making sequence of:
   (a) identify services management issues or problems and key players;
   (b) gather points of data or facts from the case material or other sources (e.g., newspapers);
   (c) come up with alternative action strategies;
   (d) defend the choice of selected service management strategies;
   (e) evaluate potential consequences of implementing the chosen action strategy on quality, productivity, and customer satisfaction.

(2) Identify theoretical frameworks from which to analyze data from the case:
   (a) use services management text vocabulary and theories when applicable to the analysis of the case;
   (b) describe any philosophies or values held by key players in the case, or write down your assumptions of their beliefs, values, goals, and management styles, especially with respect to quality;
   (c) consider the specific questions provided about each case;
   (d) brainstorm among students to determine your own values and philosophies about management and quality in this scenario.

(3) The following questions are to guide you in analyzing all business cases in this course:
   (a) What is your company's mission and philosophy at this time in the company's history?
   (b) What are the firm's key objectives?
   (c) How would you define your company's key market area?
   (d) What are the long and short term objectives of the company?
   (e) What five factors would you like to know about your competitor's future plans?
   (f) What conflicting goals are present among the players in the organization that keep the firm from successfully implementing their strategy?
   (g) Functional strategies should be designed to support overall mission statements, to improve likelihood of success, and to give guidance within business units. What functional strategies has your company employed in marketing, finance, and accounting, research and development, personnel policies, and operations to insure meeting their stated goals? To insure service quality?

(4) Write-ups should be limited to 10 pages, and presented professionally on white 8.5 x 11 paper; title page should include case title, student names and id numbers, and date. Do not put cases in folders or plastic/paper covers. Cases are due on the day of your oral presentations.

HOMEWORK ASSIGNMENTS RELATED TO QUALITY MANAGEMENT TOOLS

When studying service quality, one can do service process or task blueprints, one can gather physical data such as finished products (food items, repaired automobiles), observe employees in action to assess both their performance and motivation, or collect customer satisfaction cards to determine customer satisfaction levels. One can also analyze critical service incidents to assess root causes of service problems. Since a combination of these methods is preferred, students perform several service homeworks that enhance their observation and evaluation skills in the context of multiple industries.

These homeworks include: (a) service process flowcharts; (b) performance chart analyses; (c) root cause analyses of service problems; (d) importance/performance maps; and (e) manager quality interviews. Students can do these projects in pairs, or if they prefer due to logistics constraints, they can do them individually. The homeworks are done in the context of the industry profile the students are involved with; however, in most cases students within the groups are asked to base their homeworks on different or competing units or firms in order to get a broader perspective about quality in that industry. Figure 2 portrays a sample flowchart.

FIGURE 2
FLOWCHART OF HOTEL SERVICE

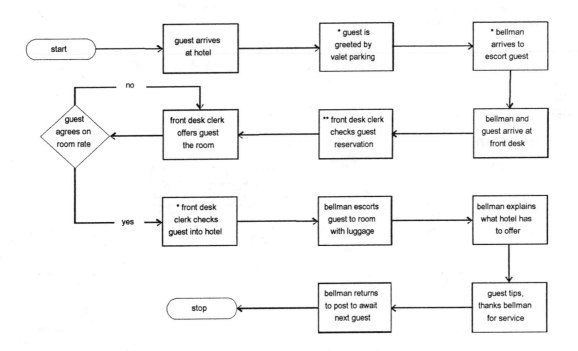

* critical point
** high failure

Service Process Flowcharts

Students are asked in their first homework assignment to individually create a service flowchart that diagrams the flow of a selected service their group assigned industry might provide to customers. They list inputs and outputs, and use appropriate flow chart symbols to diagram the service from customer contact points to service delivery points. Students are also asked to designate those process steps that they believe might be critical to the entire operation and also those steps that might have high rate of failure and why.

Service process flowcharting or service blueprinting derives from the job analysis domain. Students benefit from analyzing service processes because they learn to:

1. identify processes underlying service operation goals;
2. identify the jobs that service personnel currently perform;
3. identify performance dimensions of each job;
4. evaluate processes from a layout or logistics standpoint;
5. determine points where customer/employee interaction occurs;
6. pinpoint built-in performance delays and rework probabilities; and
7. continuously improve service processes.

FIGURE 3
CAUSE EFFECT DIAGRAM OF SLOW TELEPHONE SERVICE

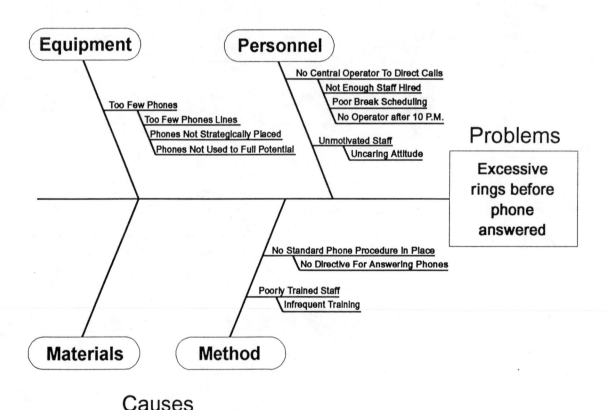

Performance Chart Analyses

This homework requires students to design a one or two variable employee task performance measurement system for a local service firm, and to actually measure employee service productivity over several time periods. They submit performance control or rating charts together with a one-page memo for service operations improvement based on their limited observations of service successes and problems. The managerial skills that are emphasized in this homework include: (1) designing a performance measurement system; (2) setting realistic criteria for service performance; (3) gathering employee performance data through observation or use of products or services; and (4) making recommendations for operational improvements. The students are also asked to select a specific service problem that they have observed to be used in the subsequent homework on root cause analysis.

Cause and Effect Analyses of Service Problems

Students are asked to submit a cause and effect diagram (Figure 3) that organizes potential root causes of an observed problem into four categories: people, machines, materials, and method type. Students also must submit a one-page prioritization sheet that specifies which root causes indicate system deficiencies which might be acted upon by altering the service flowchart or making some other operational change. Factors to be considered in this prioritization list include:

(a) What would be the cost of not correcting service errors? (*Hard costs* = dollars that must be expensed at the time the error occurs, e.g., amenities, rebates, transportation, letters, phone charges and replacement costs; *soft costs* = costs related to events occurring as a result of an error, e.g., productivity is decreased by 20 percent; *opportunity costs* = future sales that lost as a direct result of the error.)
(b) How common is the root cause and where in the system does it show up (or how close to thecustomer?);
(c) How immediate is the need for operational change to impact on the customer?
(d) What kind of investment would it take to make the changes? How realistic it this?

TABLE 1
SERVQUAL: A BENCHMARKING INSTRUMENT

Reliability	involves consistency of performance and dependability. It means the firm performs the service right the first time, and honors its promise, e.g., *accuracy in billing, keeping records correctly, performing the service on time*.
Responsivemess	concerns the willingness or readiness of employees to provide service. It involves timeliness of service, e.g., mailing a transaction slip immediately, calling the customer back quickly, giving prompt service.
Tangibles	include the physical evidence of the service, e.g., *physical facilities, appearance of personnel, tools or equipment used to provide the service*.
Assurance	involves security, credibility, courtesy, and competence. It means that the firm will make it a point to guarantee its service, e.g., *knowledge and skill of the contact personnel, physical safety and confidentiality for customer, company name and reputation*.
Empathy	is the communication, understanding/knowing the customer, and access the organization and customer have to each other, e.g., *providing individualized attention, explaining the service itself, accessible service*.

Importance/Performance Analysis

In this homework students are asked to consider the role of the customer in setting performance standards and in providing feedback to service firms. The technique of importance/performance analysis is a marketing based tool that is used by service firm managers to analyze product or service attributes on two dimensions: (1) how important is each attribute to the customer? and (2) how well is the service operation doing in providing the service to the customer? Attributes should vary as much as possible across five categories of service quality attributes [Parasuraman, A., Zeithaml, V.A. & Berry, L.L., 1985]. These 5 categories are presented in Table 1.

TABLE 2
HOTEL IMPORTANCE PERFORMANCE DATA ON 4 POINT SCALES

#	ATTRIBUTE NAME	IMP.	PERF.
1	Courtesy Staff	3.83	2.63
2	Promptness of Service	3.63	2.73
3	Did you feel welcome	3.60	3.15
4	Was the staff helpful	3.56	3.00
5	Design of Hotel	3.41	3.05
6	Informative Staff	3.41	3.29
7	Quality of Food	3.38	3.03
8	Quality of Beverage	3.37	.311
9	Hotel Security	3.29	2.00
10	Accurate Billing	3.27	3.02
11	Cleanliness of Bedroom	2.52	2.25
12	Cleanliness of Bathroom	2.43	2.49
13	Clenliness of Public Areas	2.37	2.35
14	Staff Grooming	2.05	3.33

FIGURE 4
IMPORTANCE-PERFORMANCE GRAPH

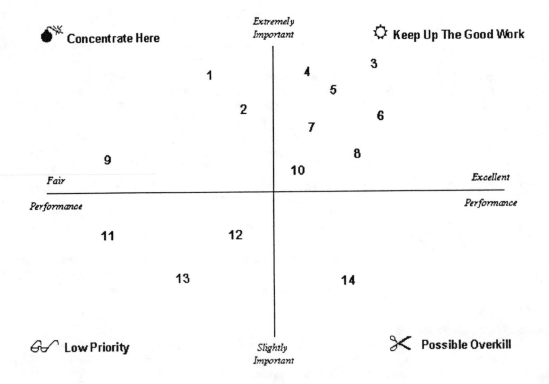

Students must contact a service firm in their industry and request permission to gather data on both customers' views of how important selected attributes are and how well that operation is doing. Students may use either a questionnaire format with live customers or available data from the service operation. Once the data are collected they may be recorded as in Table 2 and plotted as in Figure 4.

Lastly, students prepare a one-page analysis of which of four management strategies are appropriate for handling each attribute of the service operation. Generally four basic strategies are possible when analyzing graph results: (1) concentrate your attention here; (2) keep up the good work on these; (3) low priority--look at them when you can; and (4) possible overkill--could they be cut out?

Service Firm Quality Values Assessment

This final homework exercise requires students to conduct personal interviews with managers and employees of local service firms in their industry. Students prepare a written set of interview questions that elicit statements from managers and employees about quality and service management in their units. A written transcript of the answers to these interview questions are submitted, and shared orally with classmates during a designated class session. The principal objectives emphasized in this assignment are (a) the identification of company/employee philosophies and values regarding quality and the customer and (b) the assessment of how aware managers are in local service firms about theoretical principles of quality in service operations.

CONCLUSION

The teaching system developed for service operations management is highly integrative using multiple teaching methods, i.e., case study, industry scanning, and management tool application, as well as comparative across industries. This combination of tools and foci provides business students with a vast amount of information and application in a variety of industry settings where the students could be future employees, and certainly future customers.

The course begins with the essential philosophy of quality and value for the customer and leads the student into strategic thinking through industry profiles and case analysis all the way to implementation of quality management tools in local operations. Students remain highly involved due to the back and forth nature of practice and evaluation activities, and continuous exposure to both classroom and service unit sites. Students learn practical research techniques including measurement systems and survey analysis as well as multiple reporting methods, e.g., executive memos, charts, handouts, displays, and formal written/oral reports.

Students are able to analyze the service that they themselves receive from a more sophisticated vantage point, and at times have indicated that they are better able to demand levels of service clearly and without embarrassment after completing this course. Some students exhibit increased frustration due to the fact that they have passed their immediate supervisors in terms of knowledge about quality and service management. Overall, the student feedback is positive towards both the content and the workload, due to its highly relevant nature.

A general concern for the continuation of this type of course is that of finding more cases written towards integrating operations, human resources, and marketing with a overriding philosophy of service quality and customer value. This is a case writing arena that is wide open. Cases that can be used to integrate across disciplines provide the foundation materials for improving student learning levels in upper level business classes. Overall, it would appear that the future holds much promise for creative teaching in the services management field.

REFERENCES

Deming, W. E. Out of the Crisis, 2nd. edit. (Cambridge, Mass: MIT Center for Advanced Engineering Study, 1986)

Parasuraman, A., Zeithaml, V.A. & Berry, L.L. (1985), "A Conceptual Model of Service Quality and its Implications for Future Research", Journal of Marketing, 49 (Fall 1985), pp. 41-50.

LEARNING THE DOING, DOING THE LEARNING: HEALING FOR DAMAGED EMOTIONS

Jaclyn L. Eterovich
Cleveland State University
CLEVELAND, OHIO, U.S.A.

Abstract

Healing for Damaged Emotions is a localized community program for intervention/pre-vention regarding an outreach approach for those individual adults who are suffering pain from multiple causes, such as: divorce, job loss, personal injury, disease, and any other human need which can be administered to by a holistic approach. This program gives hope, encouragement, and strength to allow an individual to take control and responsibility for going forward with one's own life situation. It is an individual empowerment program in which participants gain support from both professional and nonprofessional participants.

Written handouts are supplied to provide numerous choices to invite ongoing interaction with the larger community to meet the needs within the individual's family, social, and occupational environment. Extending beyond the six teaching/support sessions are workshops designed to facilitate the change process and enhance self-motivation. This enables the individual to strengthen his/her objectives and goals for personal change, wholeness, and integrity.

INTRODUCTION

The foundation of this program is contained within the educational concept of a new organization entitled Noah's Ark Revisited, Inc. It's inspiration began with the Christian biblical scripture as follows, "Two can accomplish more than twice as much as one, for the results can be much better. If one falls, the other pulls him up; but if a man falls when he is alone, he's in trouble" [Ecclesiastes 4: 9, 10].

The original focus for this inspiration is the human element of emotional pain. The causes are multitudinous and originate from past hurtful experiences in the context of the individual's biological framework, environment, and personal history. Painful memories and feelings not yet unlearned continue to negatively impact the choices/behaviors of individuals in the current events of their lives. Figuratively, they become a pain to themselves and to others.

An individual's emotional pain creates isolation from within and among others. When paid becomes intolerable, conflicting, and personally dysfunctional, individuals seek to enter private counseling or join one of the many recovery programs for dealing with pain. Twelve-Step Programs having a strong spiritual component, continue to thrive and become more specialized. Alcoholics Anonymous, Over-eater Anonymous, and Emotions Anonymous are among many existing examples. Alternate types of support groups dealing with issues of incest, co-dependency, and abuse are also gaining popularity both locally and nationally.

These social groups foster self-determination through the collective struggle of people seeking to improve conditions affecting their lives. Through these many recovery programs, persons enter a process to transcend dependence and move toward interdependency. This process allows individuals to be more independent and less enmeshed within their intimate world of relationships. Theoretically, Noah's Ark Revisited Inc., exists to teach and promote healthy, interdependent lifestyles, while connecting individuals/families with local community services.

Most participants have already experienced some of the above programs and continue to search for more individual, affordable self-help. Recovery from emotionally painful environments is often a lifelong process because life's hurts occur daily and these participants are among the most vulnerable high-risk populations for dysfunctional lifestyles.

REPORT ON THE FIRST COMMUNITY PROGRAM FOR
HEALING OF DAMAGED EMOTIONS

Fifteen adults responded to the community advertisement to meet in the local library. Each person had cooperated with an interview and personal assessment with the teacher prior to the community gathering. Confidentiality was explained and a pledge was later signed. Each person understood the format for each session. A study book was given for optional reading throughout the three month period. Participants were encouraged to submit questions for large group discussion. The teacher invoked an attitude of respect for the opinions of each individual and encouraged freedom to express opinions openly in a non-judgmental manner.

The format for each session was simple. A short social period prefaced the hour of teaching, followed by interspersed periods of quiet reflection, journal writing, skill building exercises, and small group discussions using the teacher's guided questions. The teacher concluded by inviting comments from the larger group of fifteen persons. Those who desired could remain for another hour to continue informal questions and conversations.

TEACHER'S GENERAL OBSERVATIONS

At the first gathering, participants arrived too early and sat silently in a circle, showing little effort to communicate with each other. Everyone refused the refreshments and chance to socialize. With a sense of desperation, they diligently scanned all the reading material in their folders. The teacher was uncomfortable with the group's obstinate lack of communication, yet obvious dedication to apply themselves to the program.

Beyond the initial discomfort, most thrived. A few raced ahead by reading the optional book before the second session. Throughout the sessions, alterations became evident. In general, there was less anxiety, depression, anger, and hostility and more peace, tolerance, hopefulness, and an eagerness for improving the quality of their lives. An atmosphere of self-respect prevailed. Group serenity was evident as an attitude to accept the unchangeable and put energy into the possibilities for future changes.

A few left the program because they had reached their capacity for self-awareness, or because they were not yet ready to let go of damaging addictions. These however, did absorb some benefits even though their capacity for change was reached prematurely. For the majority, many benefits could be listed. However, only a few are highlighted in the three following case study excerpts. Concluding is a sketch of the content of the program and optional workshops.

PERSONAL PROGRAM EVALUATION
THREE BRIEF CASE STUDIES

CASE A: ANN

Ann, age 68, was referred to the program by a drug counselor. She had taken various prescription drugs habitually for thirty years, resulting in drug abuse. With medical supervision, she was receiving care for many physical ailments. She was chronically depressed throughout most of her life. Her manner was soft-spoken, polite, and passive. Married and divorced twice from the same man, she suffered from unresolved complicated grief issues. Her daughter and two younger sisters provided the most support for her.

Reading and retaining information was difficult for Ann. Both short-term and long-term memory were affected by age and drugs. Group acceptance allowed her to enjoy the community aspect of caring. The loneliness of her married life and current living situation caused her to be more dependent on others than necessary.

In the process of the program, Ann talked honestly about herself. At first, she was unable to identify her feelings. Once she began to use more expressive words, past painful memories surfaced. Moments of childhood and marital abuse shared with the supportive group provided much emotional relief. Her tears suppressed for thirty years began to flow.

When asked what she was most grateful for during the three month period, Ann quickly said that the ability to cry gave her a feeling of being really alive and alert to life. She also gained much self-confidence. Her relatives felt less burdened and more hopeful since Ann showed willingness to make more independent decisions for herself. Her previous habit of attracting attention through self-pity and excessive complaining was greatly diminished.

CASE B: BOB AND BETH

As a middle-aged couple having teenagers and dual careers, life was very stressful. They tried renewal weekends, marriage counseling, church fellowship groups and sports activities to relieve the stress they each felt. Beth eagerly attended the first session. Through strong coercion, Bob came the following week. Her controlling behavior and jealous attitude were easily observed. A private call to the teacher the following day indicated that she was very upset by the fact that she felt like a four year old child pouting because she had to share her toys with other children. The toys represented her husband.

Beth discovered that her over possessiveness toward Bob was a very destructive force in their marriage. She stopped blaming Bob and saw the need to change herself. Within those two months, she read material concerning manipulative behaviors and relationships. Beth also learned skills to reclaim boundaries that were lost in other such relationships affecting her nursing career. Eventually, Beth became aware for the first time that she had repressed most of her childhood memories after age seven. She decided to seek individual counseling.

Bob enjoyed a happier, more peaceful marriage. For him, the program helped focus on his caffeine addiction. He reduced his coffee intake from 12 to 3 cups of coffee daily. His wife and co-workers noticed some positive benefits. As a direct result of learning and practicing assertive skills, Bob noticed many rewards with his boss and co-workers. As his stress on the job decreased, his level of job satisfaction increased very significantly. Bob and Beth continued with the optional workshops. Their improved attitude, self-esteem, and respect for each other was most rewarding for the teacher. Both felt less marital stress as they established new boundaries within the family. Their teenage daughters were very pleased with the results.

CASE C: CAROL

Carol was the most emotionally damaged individual in the group. Privately, she told the instructor about her efforts to resolve the anger from her dysfunctional childhood. She was a victim of incest and endured years of verbal abuse from both parents. Her alcoholic, incestuous father created fear and chaos in the family. Carol's mother developed severe mental problems and remains institutionalized. Her marriage was unrewarding. Drug addictions were ruining her children's opportunity for independence and happiness. The teacher assessed that Carol could try attending the sessions conditionally. This decision was influenced by the knowledge that she had participated in many Twelve-Step programs and support groups. Her level of pain seemed manageable in a group setting. She was also receiving occasional counseling, but could no longer afford it.

Carol thrived on affirmation and kindness from the group. Embarrassment surfaced because she couldn't follow verbal or written instructions. With the guidance of the teacher and encouragement from the group, she learned that her abusive childhood caused her to fail in school. As a child, she believed she was dumb. She felt panic and fear in school.

Through self-awareness and determination, she practiced decision making skills in the form of statements both for and against issues. Carol acquired the skill to make simple step-by-step analyses for basic problem solving situations. Carol began to believe she was a capable and intelligent person, resulting in diminished feelings of helplessness. However, her anger increased when she compared herself with others. No one else had to work as hard to survive. Others were enjoying achievements in many areas which seemed unreachable to her.

Although Carol's sadness still prevailed, she became empowered to implement some positive changes in her life. She discovered how much she was really loved by her husband and acknowledged that she withdrew from the relationship because of her difficulty with the issue of trust. She began using a method of journal writing with the help of a social worker and Christian minister. Carol is improving one day at a time.

HEALING FOR DAMAGED EMOTIONS

TEACHING/SUPPORT SESSIONS

I.   Emotions (defined)
   A. Self-protection mechanisms
   B. Verbal expressions and their impact
   C. "Feeling" words listed

II. Self-Esteem (defined)
   A. Memories
   B. Behaviors - response or reaction
   C. Relationships

III. Boundaries (defined)
   A. Healthy vs. unhealthy
   B. Competing ethics
   C. Individual needs for respect

IV. Addictions (defined)
   A. Truths/myths
   B. Workaholism/perfectionism
   C. Personal choices - recognizing destructive forces

V.   The Cycle of Abuse (defined)
   A. Stressors
   B. Cognitive restructuring
   C. Affirmation techniques

VI. "Creating Your Future"
   A. Applications from previous sessions
   B. Use of community resources
   C. Evaluation

FACILITATED WORKSHOPS

VII. Attitudes/Humor

VIII. Affirmations/Imagery

IX.   Motivation

CONCLUSION
READER'S REFLECTION

THE ANALOGY OF NOAH'S ARK

Noah and his wife left the Ark with their three sons and their wives, from which the whole earth was populated. Noah was chosen by God to be in a covenant relationship. It was not his choice to be chosen, but it was his choice to say yes, participating in a mutual relationship with God. He was a good man, though not perfect: once in a drunken, naked stupor, he cursed his youngest son. Yet Noah strived to respect God, family, and creation.

Accordingly, he agreed to an unknown covenant. Daily, God specified the structure. Noah applied himself diligently to the work of building an Ark. His energy, determination, and steadfast effort defied the resistance of the evildoers of that age. God was saddened by the despoiling of His creation. Although it seemed that destructive forces were stronger than His beautiful world, in time a flood changed the course of history.

Today, evil, chaos, and pain are still powerful forces. Noah's example of an individual's faithfulness to co-create a better world for successive generations, brings hope. Is it possible the world could perish if individuals don't choose wholesome values and systems? Is there an urgent need? How important is it toward world peace that individuals become empowered and energized with positive values and forces?

REFERENCES

Augsburger, D. (1981). Caring enough to confront. Ventura, CA: Regal.

Alberti, R., & Emmons, M. (1990). Your perfect right. SanLuis Obispo, CA: Impact.

Baldwin, C., & Orange, C. (1993). New life, new friends. New York: Bantam.

Block, D. (1990). Words that heal. New York: Bantam.

Bramson, R. (1988). Coping with difficult people. New York: Dell.

Branden, N. (1985). Honoring the self. New York: Bantam.

Branden, N. (1987). How to raise your self-esteem. New York: Bantam.

Branden, N. (1992). The power of self-esteem. Deerfield Beach, FL: Health Communications.

Cloud, H., & Townsend, J. (1992). Boundaries. Grand Rapids, MI: Zondervan.

Colgrove, M., Bloomfield, H., & McWilliams, P. (1991). How to survive the loss of love. Los Angeles: Prelude.

Covey, S. (1990). The seven habits of highly effective people. New York: Simon & Schuster.

Hart, A. (1990). Healing life's hidden addictions: Self-hatred, worry, entertainment, food, sex, shopping, codependency, control, exercise, work, & other addictions. Ann Arbor, MI: Servant.

Jampolsky, G. (1979). Love is letting go of fear. Berkley, CA: Celestial Arts.

Koch, K., & Haug, K. (1992). Speaking the truth in love. St. Louis, MO: Stephen Ministries.

Lasater, L. (1988). Recovery from compulsive behavior. Deerfield Beach, FL: Health Communications.

Leehan, J. (1993). Defiant hope: Spirituality for survivors of family abuse. Louisville, KY: Westminster/John Knox.

Martin, S. (1988). Healing for adult children of alcoholics. Nashville, TN: Broadman.

McKay, M., & Faning, P. (1992). Self-esteem. Oakland, CA: Harbinger.

McKay, M., Rogers, P., & McKay, J. (1989). When anger hurts. Oakland, CA: New Harbinger.

Miller, J. (1989). Addictive relationships: Reclaiming your boundaries. Deerfield Beach, FL: Health Communications.

Moustakas, C. (1961). <u>Loneliness</u>. Englewood Cliffs, NJ: Prentice-Hall

Moustakas, C. (1974). <u>Portraits of loneliness and love</u>. Englewood Cliffs, NJ: Prentice-Hall.

Muller, W. (1993). <u>Legacy of the heart: The spiritual advantages of a painful childhood</u>. New York: Simon & Schuster.

Neal, C. (1993). <u>Fifty-two ways to reduce stress in your life</u>. Nashville, TN: Thomas Nelson.

NiCarthy, G. (1986). <u>Getting free: You can end abuse and take back your life</u>. Seattle, WA: Seal.

Null, G. (1993). <u>Change your life now: Get out of your head, into your life</u>. Deerfield Beach, FL: Health Communications.

Paul, M. (1992). <u>Inner bonding: Becoming a loving adult to your inner child</u>. New York: Harper Collins.

Seamands, D. (1981). <u>Healing for damaged emotions</u>. Wheaton, IL: Scripture.

Shostrom, E., & Montgomery, D. (1990). <u>The manipulators</u>. Nashville, TN: Abingdon.

Tannen, D. (1986). <u>That's not what I meant</u>. New York: Ballantine.

Tannen, D. (1990). <u>You just don't understand</u>. New York: Ballantine.

Viscott, D. (1992). <u>Emotionally free</u>. Chicago, IL: Contempory.

Viscott, D. (1976). <u>The language of feelings</u>. New York: Pocket.

Waitley, D. (1984). <u>The psychology of winning</u>. New York: Berkeley.

Whitfield, C. (1993). <u>Boundaries and relationships</u>. Deerfield Beach, FL: Health Communications.

Wild, G. (1992). <u>Free from the past</u>. Nashville, TN: Thomas Nelson.

Wilson, S. (1990). <u>Released from shame</u>. Downers Grove, IL: Intervarsity.

USE OF CASE STUDIES FOR STIMULATING THINKING AND LEARNING

Samuel J. Zeakes
Radford University
RADFORD, VIRGINIA, U.S.A.

Abstract

The use of the case study approach to stimulate thinking and learning in an upper-level biology class, Parasitology, proved to be a very powerful teaching-learning approach. An example of the exercise, some specific advantages for using the approach in teaching, along with ways for incorporating the technique/s into other disciplines will be presented.

KEY CONCEPTS

Writing Intensive
Collaborative Learning
Cognitive Development
Creativity

Critical Thinking
Problem Solving
Discipline Specific Vocabulary Development

INTRODUCTION

Biology 361, Parasitology, was taught using a writing intensive approach. The class consisted of 19 students (sophomores, juniors and seniors) majoring in biology, medical technology, pre-medicine, or other areas of allied health.

Students were assigned (as an out of class reading), the chapter on parasitic flukes (trematodes) from the course text. The chapter material was presented and discussed in class using a lecture-discussion format. Students were exposed to the subject material for the case study via lecture, laboratory and reading assignments.

The case-study consisted of a five-minute in class writing exercise. Students were asked to produce a case study dealing with a parasite (a fluke) that had already been studied. They were to present the writing as a medical case study, emphasizing symptoms, pathology, epidemiology and diagnostic features, in such a way that enough information would be provided for other members of the class to make a correct diagnosis. They were not to name the parasite described in their case study.

The case studies were collected, names removed, photocopied, and a booklet of all the case studies prepared for each student. The booklets were distributed to each student and they were asked to evaluate the other case studies (18 total) using a scale from 1-10 (10 being the highest). The criteria for evaluation were **symptoms**, **pathology**, **epidemiology** and **diagnosis**, along with the question of "Was enough information provided so that a correct diagnosis could be made?" They were also asked to name the parasite described in each of the case studies.

188

DISCIPLINE:	Biological Sciences
CLASS:	Parasitology
STUDENTS:	Sophomores, juniors, seniors (allied-health majors)

SETTING: Write a case-study dealing with one of the trematodes (flukes) we had studied. Present the writing as a medical case with emphasis on **SYMPTOMS**, **PATHOLOGY**, **EPIDEMIOLOGY** AND **DIAGNOSIS** in such a way that enough information would be provided for other members of the class to make a correct diagnosis. Do not name the parasite.

CRITIQUE: Collected the case-studies from the 19 students, cut off the names on each paper, photocopied them and prepared a booklet for each student of all case-studies. Handed out the booklets to each student during the next class and asked them to evaluate the other students' writing based on a scale of from 1-10 (ten being the highest).

***Was enough information provided for you to make a correct diagnosis?

ORIGINAL TYPEWRITTEN, <u>UNCODED</u> VERSION OF ONE STUDENT'S CASE STUDY

Location: Vietnam

A young Vietnamese boy, who after suffering from fever and diarrhea was taken to the local health clinic. With no real laboratory equipments at the clinic to do a proper examination, you decided to keep the boy there for observation. After a week, the boy began having epigastric pain and that he had not been eating well. Now as the symptoms get worse, you decided to sent out some of the boy's fecal materials to a hospital for examination. One and a half weeks later, the result of the fecal examination came back, indicating that there were numerous eggs of the trematode with an average size of 29 μ m x 160 μ m and some that were larger, around 35 μ m x 200 μ m. The eggs appeared to have an operculum and a small process at the abopercular end. However, the hospital was not able to identify the specific trematode that produced the eggs. But while you were waiting for the result, the boy began experiencing pain around the area of the liver and also appeared to be jaundiced. Now with the symptoms and eggs description in mind, you think you have an idea of a causative trematode. But you want to be sure, so you check on the boy's history before the onset of the symptoms and other members of his family. You discover that their diet consist of mainly vegetables and that almost every chore that the boy has done was with some other member of his family. But you do not hear any health complaints by his family. However, you were told that the boy had been eating a lot of fishes at a food stand. Now you know what the trematode that is causing the infections.

ORIGINAL TYPEWRITTEN, <u>CODED</u> VERSION OF ONE STUDENT'S CASE STUDY

Location: Vietnam

A young Vietnamese boy, who after suffering from [1]*fever* and [1]*diarrhea* was taken to the local health clinic. With no real laboratory equipments at the clinic to do a proper examination, you decided to keep the boy there for observation. After a week, the boy began having [1]*epigastric* pain and that he had not been [1]*eating well*. Now as the symptoms get worse, you decided to sent out some of the boy's [4]*fecal materials* to a hospital for examination. One and a half weeks later, the result of the fecal examination came back, indicating that there were numerous [4]*eggs* of the [4]*trematode* with an average [4]*size* of 29 μ m x 160 μ m and some that were larger, around 35 μ m x 200 μ m. The eggs appeared to have an [4]*operculum* and a small process at the [4]*abopercular* end. However, the hospital was not able to identify the specific trematode that produced the eggs. But while you were waiting for the result, the boy began experiencing [1]*pain* around the area of the [2]*liver* and also appeared to be [1,2]*jaundiced*. Now with the symptoms and eggs description in mind, you think you have an idea of a causative trematode. But you want to be sure, so you check on the boy's history before the onset of the symptoms and other members of his family. You discover that their diet consist of mainly [3]*vegetables* and that almost every chore that the boy has done was with some other member of his family. But you do not hear any health complaints by his family. However, you were told that the boy had been eating a lot of [3]*fishes* at a food stand. Now you know what the trematode is that is causing the infections.

TABLE 1
KEY TERMS USED IN IDENTIFICATION OF PARASITE
FROM CASE STUDY

Code # 1 SYMPTOMS	Code # 2 PATHOLOGY	Code # 3 EPIDEMIOLOGY	Code # 4 DIAGNOSIS
Fever	Epigastric	Young Boy	Fecal
Pain (liver)			Eggs: average size 29μ m x 160μ m
Epigastric pain	Jaundice	Fish	
Diarrhea	Liver	Vegetables	Trematode
Not eating well			Operculum
Jaundice			Abopercular

ADVANTAGES OF THE CASE STUDY WRITING EXERCISE

1. Students were writing in their discipline.
2. Students were involved in evaluation-they were participants and spectators.
3. Students were using scientific terminology.
4. The exercise helped indicate what students understood.
5. The exercise helped indicate areas that I as a professor needed to clarify.
6. The exercise allowed students an opportunity to practically apply what they were learning.
7. The exercise did not involve a significant amount of out-of-class grading time for the professor.
8. The exercise involved the whole class--time was well spent because it involved interaction among all students.
9. Much of the responsibility for learning was given back to the student.
10. A simple writing exercise, it provides a very powerful learning experience because of the components and does not require a lot of "grading time" by the professor because everyone is included in the evaluation. Everyone is both student and teacher.
11. Students had to read and write and think--then apply.
12. The exercise simulated activities that students might experience in their future careers.

REFERENCES

Zeakes, Samuel J. "Use of Case Studies for Stimulating Thinking and Learning in Biology," College Teaching (Winter, 1989), 37(1): pp. 33-35.
1.   ÉNAP: *École nationale d'administration publique,* or National School of Public Administration.

CHAPTER FIVE

THE ART OF INTERACTIVE TEACHING:
WHAT WE CAN LEARN FROM
ONE-ON-ONE INSTRUCTION IN MUSIC

Richard Kennell
Bowling Green State University
BOWLING GREEN, OHIO, U.S.A.

Abstract

The interactive nature of the case method is fundamental to transferring important problem solving strategies to our students. One-on-one instruction in music shares many aspects of this type of spontaneous and seemingly improvised instruction. Music teaching is an ideal context in which to study the underlying principles of interaction. This paper first reviews a social learning theory called scaffolding that was inspired by the writings of Russian cognitive psychologist Lev Vygotsky. Then, it extends our understanding of interactive teaching through a study of one-on-one music teaching.

PRACTICAL KNOWLEDGE

At the 1992 National Conference on Piano Pedagogy in Chicago, renowned pianist and pedagogue John Perry (University of Southern California) said, "Not only is it often difficult to verbalize what we do in teaching music, our subject matter - what we teach - is also often impossible to verbalize" [Perry, 1992]. This statement nicely differentiates between the two forms of professional knowledge that Professor Donald A. Schön calls "Reflection in Action" and "Knowing in Action" [Schön, 1983].

Writing from a background in Technology Management, Architecture Education, and Urban Planning at the Massachusetts Institute of Technology, Dr. Schön is interested in the exercise of professional knowledge in a wide range of human experience. In contrast to the formal body of knowledge that is created by a profession through technical rationality, Schön focuses on the day-to-day application of that knowledge by practitioners. He describes a kind of professional knowledge that can be exhibited but is difficult to verbalize. To Schön, some knowledge can only be revealed in the act of doing. Examples of this type of professional knowledge include throwing a curve ball, walking a tightrope, and playing a musical instrument.

Verbal descriptions alone are insufficient to describe such complicated activities. Either our words are inadequate or the practitioner's art is so automatic that the action's separate components are invisible, even to the performer! Schön calls this type of knowledge "Knowing in Action." When a professional is engaged in the act of professional performance - pitching a curve ball, walking a tightrope, or performing a musical instrument - s/he is demonstrating Knowing in Action.

Schön stresses two important assumptions concerning this special type of knowledge: "Competent practitioners usually know more than they can say", and "In the midst of practice, practitioners exhibit a capacity for reflection on their intuitive knowing...and use this to cope with the unique, uncertain and conflicted situations of practice" [Schön, 1983, p. viii].

In a professional practice, the practitioner is often responsible for applying Knowing in Action to bring about improved performance in another person. The novice presents a set of on-going problems which the expert must deal with on a moment to moment basis. The expert's problem solving actions in this context represent another form of professional knowledge. Schön calls this "Reflection in Action."

Reflection in Action is also highly automated. Its exercise by a professional practitioner is so automatic and transparent, that the expert practitioner does not have time to ponder what to do next. The expert performs almost an improvisation characterized by its spontaneity, energy, direction, and style. It is this spontaneous execution of professional knowledge that Schön feels is so important albeit so little understood.

It is critical to separate our understanding of the word "reflection" - which might suggest a looking back on our actions at some interval of time - from Schön's intention for the phrase "Reflection in Action." His meaning is clearly not retrospection but an active, immediate, and automatic application of problem solving skills for the moment.

If we apply these two notions of professional knowledge to the applied music lesson, we recognize the teacher's exercise of personal musicianship as "Knowing in Action" and the teacher's suggestions and interventions within the lesson as "Reflection in Action." Schön comments, "Insights (into Reflection in Action) can be found in certain deviant traditions of education for reflection in action: Athletics and coaching, apprenticeships in industry and the arts, especially education for the arts, in the studios and in the conservatories of music and dance" [Schön, 1987].

APPLIED MUSIC LESSONS AS REFLECTIVE PRACTICUM

Schön provides a label for the "deviant" teaching-learning contexts which he speculates might provide insight into his Reflection in Action. He calls such settings "Reflective Practica." There are several characteristics of a reflective practicum. In a Reflective Practicum...

FIGURE 1
CHARACTERISTICS OF REFLECTIVE PRACTICA

"People learn by doing."

"They do this together, with one another who are trying to do the same thing."

"They function in a virtual world which represents the world of practice but is not the world of practice."

"Students can run experiments cheaply without great danger, and where you can control the pace of doing."

"Students interact with someone in the role of coach, more like a coach than a teacher."

[Schön, 1987]

To Schön, a teacher is an expert who is an authoritative role model in our mainstream education institutions. A coach, however, is the traditional role for an expert in the deviant education practices. Students engage in a dialog with a coach. This dialog consists of more than words, it involves doing or performing. The coach's demonstrations are followed by the student's performance. The student's performances are in effect messages to the coach: "This is what I make of what you said" [Schön, 1987].

If researchers like Donald Schön are interested in studying the application of professional knowledge in day-to-day problem solving, they could hardly find a better laboratory than applied music lessons! Studio instruction in music exemplifies the qualities of Schön's "Reflective Practicum." Private music lessons are almost universally available around the country and the world. They are formal, repetitive events. They are somewhat predictable and engage the same individuals over a long period of study. While important conventions are followed, each lesson results in a unique interchange between the expert teacher and the novice student. Private music lessons may even be characterized as being unstable and unpredictable. At the start of each lesson, there is the potential for exhilaration or defeat, success or failure, order or chaos.

Private music lessons, therefore, provide an ideal context in which to study Reflection in Action. We should be able to observe the expert's professional knowledge as s/he makes choices in the reflective practicum which we call the lesson.

To Schön, reflective practica [Schön, 1987] start with an element of confusion, anger, and mystery. Whenever faced with a new problem, the student is vulnerable, out of control, and lacking in confidence. In fact, even the teacher's own statements may not be understood by the student at the start. But through engaging in a dialog of words and actions, students acquire the means to achieve competence. There is a gradual convergence of student capabilities and task requirements until mastery is achieved.

Along this convergence, there is a succession of interactions between the expert and the novice. To Schön, the exercise of the teacher's Reflection in Action follows a moment of surprise or an unanticipated problem. The puzzling, interesting, and problematic moments in the music lesson would initiate the teacher's professional problem solving action. Two events are now of interest: The student's specific problem and the teacher's corresponding intervention. Here is a sampling of teacher interventions from applied music lessons:

FIGURE 2
STUDENT PROBLEMS-TEACHER INTERVENTIONS

The Student's Problem	The Teacher's Intervention
Student plays f natural, instead of the written f sharp.	"That's an F sharp, not an F natural!"
Student fails to play a written crescendo.	"That's a crescendo!" or
	"What does that v-shaped marking mean to you?" or
	"Like this [teacher plays desired crescendo]" or
	[teacher makes crescendo gesture with hand while student plays...]
Student does not keep a steady pulse while executing steady 16th notes...	"Let's slow down the tempo here..." or
	"Let's rewrite the rhythm of the 16th notes. Play dotted-eighth sixteenth notes instead of even 16ths
Student starts playing in the wrong spot in the music.	"Start here [teacher points to starting place in the music]"

To Schön, these seemingly spontaneous solutions to student problems are examples of Reflection in Action. They are automatic, requiring little conscious attention. If the student's performance produced some unanticipated result, however, the teacher's problem-solving strategies might be elevated to a higher level of consciousness. This prompts the teacher to then consider the underlying assumptions for prescribing this particular intervention strategy, to restate the problem, and to craft a new strategy for this particular student. Schön believes "...it is the entire process of reflection in action which is central to the 'art' by which practitioners sometimes deal with situations of uncertainty, instability, uniqueness and value conflict" [Schön, 1983, p. 50].

SCAFFOLDING

Schön's description of the context of professional knowledge suggests that it is important to focus on the strategies that experts employ to solve moment-to-moment problems in a professional practice with novices. If, as Schön assumes, practitioners may not be able to verbalize all that they know, the teacher's special knowledge may be revealed through actions and choices rather than through words.

You will recall that Schön's professional practice consisted of one professional assisting another individual overcome some deficiency or problem. Some professional practices, however, have one additional important feature - the problem to be solved is actually introduced by the professional. Once the problem has been defined for the novice, the role of the expert is to act as a "scaffold" to support the student's attempts to solve the problem.

Several other writers have referred to this special teaching-learning context as "joint problem solving" [see Vygotsky, 1978, Wertsch, 1985 and Cole, 1985]. Still others have built on the metaphor of a scaffold to focus on expert interventions in joint problem solving contexts [see Bruner, 1985, Wood, Bruner, and Ross, 1976 and Wood, Wood and Middleton, 1978].

A joint problem solving context is created when a more experienced person [the expert] assigns a specific task to a less experienced person [the novice]. Furthermore, the expert has responsibility for bringing about improved performance of the assigned task by the novice over a period of time. During this succession of interactions, responsibility for task execution is gradually transferred from the expert to the novice [Wertsch, 1979].

In the early stages of the interaction, the expert serves as a scaffold to the novice until s/he is able to perform the task independently. A scaffold then is a metaphor for the supportive actions of the expert in a joint problem solving context. A scaffold is used to reach beyond one's current capabilities. It is temporary and is removed when no longer needed.

Wood, Bruner and Ross [1976] studied expert interventions in a familiar joint problem solving context. From systematic observations, they described six different categories of scaffolding strategies which experts employed in the joint problem solving context:

FIGURE 3
SCAFFOLDING STRATEGIES

1. Recruitment - The tutor's first and obvious task is to enlist the problem solver's interest in and adherence to the requirements of the task. ["Have you studied Hindemith yet in theory class? This next piece is by Paul Hindemith."]

2. Reduction of Degrees of Freedom - This involves simplifying the task by reducing the number of constituent acts required to reach solution. ("Play only the rhythm of this melody and use just one pitch...")

3. Direction Maintenance - Learners lag and regress to other aims, given limits in their interests and capacities. The tutor has the role of keeping them in pursuit of a particular objective. Partly it involves keeping the child "in the field" and partly a deployment of zest and sympathy to keep him motivated. ("I'd like you to prepare this new piece for our recital in four weeks...")

4. Marking Critical Features - A tutor by a variety of means marks or accentuates certain features of the task that are relevant. His marking provides information about the discrepancy between what the child has produced and what he would recognize as a correct production. ("That note is an F sharp, not an F natural...")

5. Frustration Control - There should be some such maxim as "Problem solving should be less dangerous or stressful with a tutor than without"... ("I know this is hard, but just do your best.")

6. Demonstration - Demonstrating or "modeling" solutions to a task, when closely observed,

involves considerably more than simply performing in the presence of the tutee. It often involves an "idealization" of the act to be performed... ("Listen to this..." [followed by a live or recorded performance]).

[Wood, Bruner and Ross, 1976 p. 98]

Wood, Bruner and Ross suggest that scaffolding strategies are discrete classes of expert-novice interactions. They are generative in the sense that they can be adapted to meet the particular needs of the moment. For example, there are several ways a teacher might employ Recruitment to focus the student's attention to a task. Likewise, there are an infinite number of ways to Mark a Critical Feature - either of the piece itself or of the student's performance of the piece. There are also many different ways that a teacher might offer a Demonstration - in the same medium or in an alternative medium.

If experts utilize scaffolding strategies to solve problems in joint problem solving contexts, what rules determine the selection of each scaffolding strategy? Three writers have offered different explanations for the selection of a specific scaffolding strategy.

Jerome Bruner [1985] proposed that it is best to present scaffolding strategies in a specific order, an order of presentation theory. Starting with Recruitment, a teacher would next Demonstrate the task, then Reduce Degrees of Freedom, and finally Mark Critical Features to achieve mastery. Again, a new task would be defined and the presentation order would be repeated.

Wood, Wood and Middleton [1978] proposed that a hierarchy exists among the different scaffolding strategies. This hierarchy ranged from greatest teacher involvement (Demonstration), to moderate teacher involvement [Reduce Degrees of Freedom), then to minimal teacher involvement (Marking Critical Features). To Wood, Wood and Middleton, the selection of a specific scaffolding strategy was governed by the rule:

"If the child succeeds, when next intervening offer less help. If the child fails, when next intervening take over more control. (p. 133).

The selection of an appropriate scaffolding intervention would thus be dictated by the teacher's assessment of the child's performance.

Kennell [1992] proposed that it is the teacher's attribution of the cause of the student's problem - not just the student's success or failure - that determines the selection of the appropriate scaffolding strategy. Kennell theorized that any performance failure could be caused by several different factors, such as an attention deficiency ("I have done this before, I just forgot to do it now..."), a conceptual deficiency ["I don't understand what you want me to do..."), or a skill deficiency ("I just can't do that...").

A musical task, in fact, combines both conceptual and skill dimensions. To present a satisfactory performance of a piece of music - to solve a musical problem, if you will - the performer must understand what the composer wants to be done (conceptual mastery) and the performer must be able to execute those ideas on an instrument (motor skill mastery). The failure to effectively execute a musical problem may therefore represent a deficiency in conceptual understanding, a deficiency in motor skill capability, or both. Furthermore, if the failure cannot be attributed to either of these deficiencies, it may represent a simple failure of attention or memory.

To Kennell, the teacher's selection of a specific scaffolding strategy was determined by his or her attribution of student failure to one or more of these possible explanations. Scaffolding strategies imply that the music teacher possesses a limited pallet of generic solutions to be matched with an infinite variety of musical problems. It is the artistry of the applied music teacher - once the appropriate strategy has been selected - to generate the contextually specific version of that strategy to fit the specific problem at hand.

In a music lesson, the teacher must possess both a detailed knowledge of the task, a detailed knowledge of the student, and a practical knowledge of these Reflection in Action principles. It is no accident that music students study with the same teacher for several years. The teacher must know which problems - embedded in the assigned task - the student has already mastered, which problems are solvable only with the teacher's assistance, and which problems are not solvable, even with the teacher's assistance.

FIGURE 4
TEACHER SCAFFOLDING MODEL

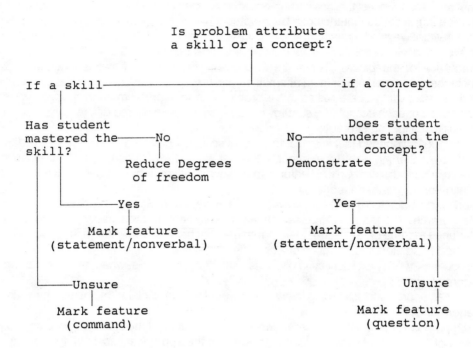

[Kennell, 1989 p. 47]

THE ART OF INTERACTIVE TEACHING

Donald Schön has described a special kind of practical knowledge which he has observed among various professionals. He refers to this special professional knowledge, Reflection in Action. He recognized that this knowledge was often difficult if not impossible to articulate - even by effective practitioners! He even has suggested that we should look for examples of Reflection in Action within the professional practice of conservatory music teachers.

I suggest that not only does our professional practice of studio instruction meet Schön's criteria for a Reflective Practicum, our experience and competence in expert-novice problem solving might be beneficial to other teaching professions. Schön's search for an understanding of Reflection in Action, for example, might benefit from scaffolding theory. Scaffolding theory offers a potentially useful vocabulary to study interactions between experts and novices across different disciplines.

The professional practice of applied music instruction represents an important human learning context. Schön may call it a "deviant" tradition in education. I prefer to call it a fundamentally human form of teaching and learning.

Do you recall earlier that I cited the work of Jerome Bruner and his colleagues who originally identified the six different scaffolding strategies? I stated that they studied a familiar joint problem solving context. Do you have any idea what special human relationship they studied?

They observed parents working with their children.

Scaffolding theory provides a direct link between teaching music today and the grand daddy of all instruction, Parenting. In a sense, it connects what we do in transmitting the culture of music with the timeless flow of human history. Our relationships with our students are personal, intimate, and caring because we may have borrowed the successful techniques that parents have used in teaching their children from the dawn of time. And we may have refined these techniques far beyond childhood instruction to the most advanced levels of performance.

Just think about the vocabulary we hear in and about the studio: "My kids...", "I just love the way you express that..." Even these familiar expressions may be vestiges of the first human educational institution, the family. And reflect for a moment on the esteemed lineage of applied instruction. We take great pride in the line of succession from our teacher's teacher to our teacher to us because we are a family!

Scaffolding Theory offers us a new way to conceptualize what we do in teaching music. It illuminates the moment to moment decisions that we make almost automatically. It raises new questions and suggests new possibilities.

Rather than viewing music, dance, and athletic coaching models as deviant educational traditions, I suggest that these teaching-learning systems are in fact cultural extensions and elaborations of the original and most powerful teaching tradition, the family. Perhaps it is the institution of schooling - corrupted by the inefficiencies of scale of the industrial revolution, dehumanized by bureaucracy and emphasizing a form of knowledge that elevates "knowing" above "doing" - that is truly the deviant tradition in human history.

But most important, scaffolding theory affirms our professional practice of teaching music. It reveals the highly complex problem solving activities that expert musicians must master to become successful teachers. Scaffolding Theory gives us a brief glimpse into the artistry involved in interactive teaching, involved in teaching music.

REFERENCES

Bruner, J.(1985). Vygotsky: a historical and conceptual perspective. In J. V. Wertsch (Ed.], *Culture, Communication, and Cognition: Vygotskian Perspectives* (pp. 21-35). Cambridge: Cambridge University Press.

Bruner, J. (1986). Actual minds, possible worlds, Cambridge, MA: Harvard University Press.

Cole, M. (1985). The zone of proximal development: Where culture and cognition create each other. In Wertsch, J. V. (Ed.), *Culture, Communication, and Cognition: Vygotskian Perspectives* (pp. 146-161). Cambridge: Cambridge University Press.

Kennell, R. (1989). Three teacher scaffolding strategies in college applied music instruction. *Dissertation Abstracts International*, 50, 2822-A. (University Microfilms No. 89-17656)

Kennell, R. (1992). Toward a theory of applied music instruction. *The Quarterly Journal of Music Teaching and Learning.* 3(1), 5-16.

Perry, J. (1992). *Qualities of successful teachers.* Paper presented at the meeting of the National Conference on Piano Pedagogy, Schaumburg, IL.

Schön, D. A. (1983). *The reflective practitioner: How professional think in action.* New York: Basic Books.

Schön, D.A. (1987). *Educating the reflective practitioner.* Paper presented at the meeting of the American Education Research Association conference, Washington, DC.

Vygotsky, L. S. (1978). *Mind in society: The development of higher psychological processes.* Cambridge: Harvard University Press.

Vygotsky, L. S. (1987) *Thought and language* (A. Kozulin, Trans.). Cambridge, MA: The MIT Press. (Original work published in 1962).

Wertsch, J. V. (1979). From social interaction to higher psychological processes: A clarification and application of Vygotsky's theory. *Human Development*, 22 (1979), 1-22.

Wertsch, J. V. (Ed.) (1985). *Culture, communication, and cognition: Vygotskian perspectives*. Cambridge: Cambridge University Press.

Wood, D.J., Bruner, J.S., and Ross, G. (1976). The role of tutoring in problem solving. *Journal of Child Psychology and Psychiatry*, 17, 89-100.

Wood, D., Wood, H. & Middleton D. (1978). An experimental evaluation of four face-to-face teaching strategies. *International Journal of Behavioral Development*, 1, 131-147.

TEACHING INTERRELATIONSHIPS AMONG DISCIPLINES THROUGH CROSS-INSTITUTIONAL PARTNER TEAMS

Sheila Anne Webb
Humboldt State University
ARCATA, CALIFORNIA, U.S.A.

Abstract

At the three year junction of a seven year project, case studies were introduced (a) to assist cross-institutional partners in solving partnership infrastructure problems, (b) to define parameters for the partnership in the context of a school setting, and (c) to prepare at risk high school students to work on inter-disciplinary curriculum projects with teams of teachers representing a variety of partners-- university, community college, a K-12 school district, county office of education, businesses, parents and other community members. The student population, considered at risk for dropping out, required a more relevant curriculum to retain students.

INTRODUCTION: PROJECT DESCRIPTION

Project PARITY (Promoting Academic Retention for Indian Tribal Youth) is a coalition of partners working in consonance to retain American Indians in formalized schooling K-12 and assist them in matriculating with a degree objective in higher education. The partnership model was adopted to provide broad-based support for the students and to serve as a curriculum and staff development source for a new educational delivery system that would include interdisciplinary curricula and cross-institutional team teaching. The partners included teachers in the areas of mathematics, science, language arts and social sciences from Humboldt State University, College of the Redwoods, the nearby community college, and the Klamath Trinity Joint Unified School District.

Other primary partners were representatives from the Humboldt County Office of Education, Hoopa Tribal Association, parents, local businesses and specialized school district support programs such as the Title V program. Among the PARITY members were counselors, teachers and administrators. These members held a common vision that an expanded educational community could provide an environment that offered students academic confidence and thus retain them in formalized schooling K-16.

PARITY's model develops four principles: (1) learn about and respect the student population; (2) incorporate the students' and community's values and interests into a relevant curriculum; (3) combine resources to enhance learning; (4) maintain high expectations. Through staff development and team approaches, faculties from the school districts and institutions of higher education work with community members to develop new course offerings that demonstrate the interrelationships among disciplines. PARITY employs the "next step" concept in the students' educational careers. Making the transition from one institution to the next (middle school to high school, high school to college) is de-mystified through faculty and student exchanges and sharing of resources at all sites. What results is a community support system for students through this partnership, through family participation and through business sponsorships.

PARITY serves the Native and non-Native American Indian student populations in a mountainous area of northern California in a 1,100 square mile reservation school district. PARITY's model, however, is not restricted to Native Americans; it may be applied to other under represented populations.

The curriculum is designed to retain students in formal education by providing materials relevant to students' interests and to enrich students' academic confidence and academic advancement. PARITY incorporates Native American social, cultural and historical contributions into the curriculum. By building on students' experiential knowledge, the curriculum encompasses elements in the natural environment and the importance of interrelationships among the disciplines. A "school without walls" occurs as students study outdoors at various locations and with a variety of teachers representing the cross-institutional partnership.

This enhanced curriculum meets the requirements of high school graduation and college entrance and has resulted in unanticipated outcomes such as dramatic increases in students' standardized test scores. PARITY's approach leads to a greater understanding of the students' surroundings and their relation to a larger, exciting world of learning, academic adventure and exploration.

Structurally, the partnership model of PARITY is designed to develop peer and collegial relationships across institutions and across grade levels. Preparation to work on cross-institutional collaboration that includes shared accountability for project outcomes requires all participants to attend workshops on partnership development. PARITY includes school district, community college, university personnel and community and business members working together. Since each institution forms its own type of educational "culture", PARITY participants examine the following areas to reach an understanding and appreciation of the diversity of educational perspectives within the group. These areas represent dimensions of culture in educational settings: (1) work tempo and the nature of professional time; (2) professional focus from theoretical to practical; (3) career reward systems; and (4) sense of personal power and efficacy. Additionally, all partners are required to participate in two annual orientation workshops that address Native American social, cultural and historical contributions.

PARITY began in 1989 with a one year planning phase followed by three additional years 1990-1993 of full funding from the California Academic Partnership Program. Funding from that source includes a 1994 dissemination phase. Throughout this funding, the project experienced many successes including increased (a) teacher job satisfaction, (b) student standardized test scores, (c) student retention, and (d) expanded partnership development. Partners were pleased with the outcomes and decided to seek additional funding through the Post-secondary Educational Commission Dwight D. Eisenhower Mathematics and Science Education Grant source. Funding was granted October 1993 to September 1996.

This second tier of funding added a layer of complication to the initial PARITY plan, which was now termed PARITY I. The new focus was PARITY II involving an expanded partnership that seemed somewhat unwieldy. There were ongoing challenges with PARITY I due mainly to the distance between project sites. The county office of education and institutions of higher education are located on the Pacific Ocean coast while the Klamath Trinity Joint Unified School District is sixty miles north and east inland through a mountainous region. Large amounts of personnel time and travel, plus organizational challenges to convene all partners to maintain effective communication and collaboration, were ongoing elements that threatened the partnership model. Additionally, the number of disciplines involved required special collaborative efforts among cross-institutional faculties in addition to requiring these individuals to attend whole group meetings. During the process of deciding to pursue Eisenhower funding, the partners refined the interdisciplinary approaches to mathematics and science only, but requested the partnership expand to an additional Indian reservation, which is a three hour drive south and east from the institutions of higher education. The second reservation school district, Round Valley Unified School District, gladly joined a partnership that had experienced three years of partnership and student success. PARITY II encompasses the two largest Native American communities in northern California including nine tribes and is geographically dispersed over two hundred and ten miles of rough, rural terrain.

USE OF CASE STUDIES

During the planning phase to develop PARITY II, it became apparent that geographical challenge plus an expanded number of partners would require a well thought out plan to keep the PARITY members cohesive and the project's focus attainable. The partners decided to use a case study model as a means of exploring solutions to problems that may occur. The case studies were developed through PARITY I experiences and expanded to encourage additional critical thinking to explore a variety of options as solutions for PARITY II. The sampling of case studies, which have been abbreviated, provided herein discuss the three different uses of the case study model.

PARTNERSHIP DEVELOPMENT CASE STUDIES

The need for partners to examine a variety of case studies pertaining to partnership development was important as PARITY I expanded to another distant site with the addition of new partners and became known as PARITY II. Prior to beginning PARITY II, the PARITY II partners had several meetings in which a variety of partnership situations were presented via a case study model. The purpose of the meetings was to have partners pre-think potential pitfalls to the partnership and experience solving problems as a group before actual problems occurred. Partners met on Saturday sessions. At the first meeting, they were introduced to the case study model and worked through a short sample. For the other sessions, they were mailed two studies to read prior to the Saturday sessions. They spent the mornings on one study and the afternoons on another. The Director for PARITY I remained the Director for PARITY II. She had attended a Management Development program at Harvard University and worked extensively with the case study model.

Since the case studies used in this phase and the others are long, four to ten pages each, space does not allow their inclusion here. However, a summarized version of the studies which removes a number of characters and sub-complications is presented to indicate the nature of the studies. The style of the summarized presentation incorporates the study situation and relevant questions relating to the situation into one narrative. The second person "you" is utilized as a summary of the actual character(s) named in the fuller study to encourage the reader to identify with the protagonist facing the situation.

The short, introductory study can be summarized as follows:

You were establishing rewarding success with partnership development during a planning grant and successfully applied for and was awarded an implementation grant. Your steering committee included two higher education partners--administrators and faculty from a university and a community college-- administrators and teachers from K-12, community members, parents of currently enrolled K-12 students, K-12 student representatives and representatives from two businesses. Planning went smoothly with everyone mutually agreeing on goals, objectives and activities. During the first semester of the implementation phase, the K-12 teachers suddenly felt vulnerable. They complained of being in a "Glass Bowl", taken from the privacy of their classrooms, placed in a larger public arena and expected to be solely responsible for project student outcomes. How can you develop a shared accountability concept and reality when the teachers are responsible for their students' learning as well as school and community perceptions of a school's educational delivery system that begins in each classroom? Other project partners are not on the school's payroll or subject to yearly internal school evaluations for continued employment. What can the project do to alleviate the "Glass Bowl" mentality experienced by the classroom teachers?

An example of a more involved case study is summarized below:

You have a complicated project in terms of number and types of partners plus a focus on two critical discipline areas such as mathematics and science. You wanted to create cross-institutional/agency peer relations, so you formed project goal-oriented subcommittees. You encouraged partners interested in topical areas to join the subcommittees of their choice. You also asked each subcommittee to participate in the democratic process and internally elect a chair. The outcome was more than you had anticipated. Each committee elected a representative from different partners. Your different subcommittees are chaired by a business person, a K-12 classroom teacher, a parent, a community member and a professor from higher education. You charged the chairs to develop agendas and maintain minutes of each meeting then took the responsibility of distributing these items to all partner participants as a means of information sharing. You used subcommittee reports at whole group meetings to develop what seemed to you like dynamic growth in meeting project goals. You dutifully did all your annual reports which included minutes of subcommittee meetings and had a wonderful sense that the project was proceeding beyond baseline expectations. However, during the second year of the project, you received more than one telephone call that indicated your project participants were not following partner infrastructure process. Only a handful of parents knew about the project. The business representative was an engineer who did not have a direct reporting line to the CEO. The project at the university was housed in one college and the dean had not communicated positive project outcomes to the Vice President of Academic Affairs or the President, who had been embarrassed because of lack of knowledge during a luncheon with the county superintendent of schools who praised the project. What can you do about these site-based infrastructure communication issues?

The purpose for using the case study model with partners planning to expand an existing partnership was to provide an avenue for partners to analyze potential problems, collaborate on options, plus make judgments and engage in strategic planning to avoid some of the pitfalls described in the studies. Although this technique was new to the partners, the situations were real enough to engage their interest and stimulate interaction. The studies provided opportunities for partner members to get to know each other and work together on strategic planning of issues that weren't an eminent threat in terms of being reality based on a set of individuals within the group. Most of the participants considered the studies fun, challenging and they looked forward to working on them as a group. The ultimate outcome was that working on the studies created greater group cohesion prior to the actual implementation of PARITY II.

PARTNERSHIP PARAMETER CASE STUDIES

The second level of case study usage focused on solving negative, unanticipated outcomes that the project's partnership may have unwittingly created. Since the participants had experience in strategy building from probable situations that a partnership may encounter as discussed in "Partnership Development Case Studies", this level focused on real problems. Utilizing the case study method at this level helped define the parameters of an energetic partnership. Although the project was intended to provide an enhancement to the existing educational system, at times the enthusiasm of the participants, especially as student academic successes increased, seemed boundless.

The example below demonstrates this level of case study usage and follows the summarized format discussed in the previous section. The format is utilized to provide only an overview of both the case study situation and some of the attendant questions asked relating to it.

The case study can be outlined as follows:

Case studies like the one above were used, as needed, to help solve emerging problems in the partnership model. These problems emerged due to the success of the project and the enthusiasm of more people to join as partner participants. The expanded number of people and additional partner site demanded that parameters be established for the project within the context of working cooperatively with school districts. The case studies provided an avenue to open discussion within the case study context and yet solve, as a group, problems that could threaten to cripple the project's ability to meet its goals and time lines.

Some of the other case studies used at this level were aimed at developing peer relationships across institutions, agencies and community groups. Although the partners had discussed how the dimensions of "culture" in educational settings may vary from institution to institution in any of the following four ways: (1) work tempo and the nature of professional time; (2) professional focus from theoretical to practical; (3) career reward systems; and (4) sense of personal power and efficacy, from time to time a situation would arise that emanated from one of these four areas. For instance, sometimes, a classroom teacher couldn't understand why a university professor with "all the time in the world" could travel to the school site at a particular time. Mini case studies were created to help cross these institutional "cultural" barriers. They helped open discussion and solve misunderstandings. Frequently, those who were experiencing a problem, were asked to try to write a case study of their own that described the situation and left an opportunity to examine options and a variety of solutions.

INTERDISCIPLINARY CURRICULUM CASE STUDIES

Each of the partners, which included teachers, administrators, community and business members from various institutions, had gained experience in working with the case study model through partnership development scenarios and unanticipated faction scenarios. Some had even attempted to write mini case studies as they developed cross-institutional, peer relationships. Although no one was an expert in writing case studies, the partners saw value in using the model for students to help them anticipate potential situations and to give them an opportunity to collaboratively build strategies to solve problems. Since developing new curriculum materials was part of the project's objectives, incorporating case studies for at least high school students seemed worth pilot testing. The cross-institutional content area teachers met regularly in subcommittees and took on the task of attempting to write case studies for high school students. They brought to the task their enthusiasm experienced in working on case studies and hoped to transmit that enthusiasm to the students. Because they wanted to be careful about encouraging open discussion and yet keeping all discussion focused, they felt that cross-institutional team teaching the case studies would be the most comfortable avenue for implementing the case studies in the classroom.

One of the focus areas for interdisciplinary work was the development of Supply Creek Trail, which is close to the high school in the Klamath Trinity Joint Unified School District. Several people within the partnership were interested in the trail because it provided an opportunity to experience a school "without walls" and to create a high school project for community service. The science cross-institutional partners were interested in the trail because the creek provides a good example of a lotic (flowing water) environment and an opportunity to study aquatic biology, fresh water insects and their ecological roles in freshwater environments. Within science, they envisioned the interrelationships of physical, earth and life sciences in terms of energy, systems, interactions and patterns of change in the creek and the surrounding environment. The mathematics cross-institutional partners were interested in the trail because the natural environment could provide hands-on experience in applying mathematics such as using triangulation to calculate board feet in trees and estimating volume and velocity in the creek water. The Forest Service offered to help survey the trail, to provide additional young trees in areas that would benefit from reforestation and to offer advice regarding flora and fauna protection. The Tribe thought the trail, once established, could be marked with signs in both the Native American and English languages that were constructed by the students with the help of the tribe. The trail would become an educational trail for the local schools, community and any other schools that would like to visit. The initial difficulty was that the trail had been strewn with litter and was unmarked.

The first step involved all the teachers visiting the Supply Creek site to become thoroughly familiar with the environment. They met as a combined science and mathematics group to discuss the characteristics of the student learners and the dynamics of student group interaction, especially since they would have the students in an open environment outside of the school. They decided they wanted to try using case studies to help students engage in critical analysis and reflection. They felt by using case studies prior to actual field experience, the students could "rehearse" or become familiar with the complexities of interdisciplinary approaches and cross-institutional team teaching in an outdoor setting. The case studies were kept necessarily short, typically two to four pages long and dealt with interpersonal communication skills as well as interdisciplinary scenarios. The teachers felt that the expanded educational community working cooperatively with the students and the combination of a science/mathematics approach would be in consonance with the Native American view of harmony and the interrelatedness of nature.

Since the project is only in the pilot testing phase of these case studies, the studies are not summarized here in the same manner as the other case study examples. Briefly, however, one case addresses student interactions in discovering various types of litter along the trail. Its focus is outcome-based on impact on the community. The situation includes a team of teachers from the institutions of higher education, tribe, Forest Service and high school who are assisting students in using survey equipment to lay out the trail, measuring devices to define animal tracks, and field guides to identify plant life. The students are separated into three groups, all working within hearing range of each other. Students discover condoms, soda pop and beer cans in the underbrush. Their immediate response is to joke about the discovery and signal their friends in other groups. The study draws on scenarios of hygiene in handling these items and scenarios of community impact by responding openly to friends in front of this community team of instructors. Students explore other options for dealing with their discovery.

The second level of case studies involved student scenarios of cooperative learning in discovering portions of an ecosystem. The studies described students in imaginary classes who were given information about flora and fauna and measurements taken to determine the age of trees and plants. In each of three cooperative learning groups, students arrived at different conclusions regarding the ecosystem. Each group justified its solutions and presented its findings to the whole class. The mathematics and science teachers who team taught the classes favored one group response over the other two. From an interdisciplinary viewpoint, students were asked why the instructors would choose that particular group's response. What other options could the instructors have viewed as a logical, "correct" solution. Naturally, the instructors in the scenario had traditional discipline specific "correct" solutions. Students were asked to analyze the instructors' response and reflect on their own solution to "convince" the instructors that other solutions were feasible from the data given.

The concept of using the case study method with high school students, although in its infancy in utilization on this project, is to provide the students with a new method of learning that requires critical thinking, analysis, and interaction among the teachers and students. Since the project utilizes team teaching on a cross-institutional model and interrelates subject matter that traditionally had been presented as discrete educational units, students have no experience in dealing with either the numbers of instructors or the content. The case study approach was used to assist students to gain familiarity with the complexities of interrelated content materials and multiple instructors while employing critical thinking skills and utilizing analysis.

SUMMARY

Project PARITY in converting from one funding source to another reduced its broad-based curriculum focus to the interrelationships among mathematics and science, but expanded its partnership model to include a larger geographic area and more partner institutions. In an attempt to provide creative, innovative, interactive thinking, the case study model was adopted at several different levels. The first level was to assist in partnership development and the second to assist in defining partnership parameters. Partnership members working on these two levels included adults from the school district, higher education, county office of education, community and businesses. The exploration for multiple solutions to problems examined through a case study mode seemed appealing enough to pilot test the case study model with high school students. The specific purpose was to help students learn methods of problem solving as well as particular content. That level of pilot testing is still being refined. Teachers writing case studies find the task somewhat tedious but enjoy implementing them and revising them. The biggest value in utilizing case studies was the exploration and application of knowledge within the context of a given set of information. Project partners and students could "rehearse" potential outcomes given a path of critical analysis that lead to a scenario of action. Interactive discussion would led to reflective thinking and perhaps the proposal of another solution. Interpersonal relationships among partners and students were strengthened by this discussion model.

Partners felt better equipped to deal collaboratively with an extended educational community concept to develop and deliver a new approach to curriculum. They could foresee potential pitfalls in a partnership model if communication and infrastructures were not sustained and develop parameters for the project's function within the school system. Overall, they felt more confident in working as a team and appeared to fully respect each other's perspectives.

Working with case studies at the partnership level provided the instructors with a new viewpoint regarding the potential for using case studies with high school students. The instructors had gained confidence in utilizing and even constructing case studies since they had used them extensively in the partnership development process. Although the interdisciplinary curriculum does not solely include case study techniques, the students have responded positively to the ones that are used. Students' standardized test scores in the project's content areas have risen as much as 34%. Although the case study techniques cannot be isolated from other project activities, the use of case studies can certainly be considered a contributing factor to the rise in the scores. Students also identify their greater enjoyment of the curriculum as part of the increases.

Project PARITY will continue until at least 1996. It is estimated that several case studies will be developed, pilot tested and revised for usage at the secondary level. Overall, the project has experienced incremental, ongoing success in utilizing case study methodology. An unanticipated outcome of first introducing the case study technique at the partnership level was that the teachers would embrace the method and develop it for secondary students.

ANDRAGOGY AND BASIC STATISTICS

Tom F. Griffin, III, Michael C. Budden & Robert C. Lake
Auburn University at Montgomery
MONTGOMERY, ALABAMA, U.S.A.

Abstract

This paper is an account of an exploratory attempt to use self-directed assignments based on principles of adult education in a college level, basic statistics course. Andragogy, as defined by Knowles, is the art and science of helping adults learn. In contrast, pedagogy is the art and science of teaching children. This paper reviews the differences in assumptions of andragogy and pedagogy and discusses the gap filled by experiential learning in adult education.

INTRODUCTION TO ANDRAGOGY

Malcolm S. Knowles is one of the nation's leading authorities on adult education and training. According to Knowles *andragogy* was first used by Alexander Kapp in 1833 to describe the educational theory of Plato. The term fell into obscurity for nearly a hundred years before being used in 1921 by Rosenstock. Rosenstock expressed the opinion that adult education required special teachers, special methods and a special philosophy. Andragogy is the method of teaching adults as distinguished from pedagogy, teaching children.

According to Knowles [1984], the pedagogical model emphasizes the role of the teacher in making decisions about how and what is learned. It is teacher centered education based on the following assumptions:

1. *The need to know.* Learners only need to know that they must learn what the teacher teaches if they want to pass and get promoted; they do not need to understand how what they learn will apply to their lives.
2. *The learner's self-concept.* The teacher's self-concept of the learner is that of a dependent personality; therefore, the learner's self-concept eventually becomes that of a dependent personality.
3. *The role of experience.* The learner's experience is of little worth as a resource for learning; the experience that counts is that of the teacher, the textbook writer, and the audio-visual aids producer. Therefore, transmittal techniques--lectures, assigned readings, etc., are the backbone of the pedagogical methodology.
4. *Readiness to learn.* Learners become ready to learn what the teacher tells them they must learn if they want to pass and get promoted.
5. *Orientation to learning.* Learners have a subject-centered orientation to learning; they see learning as acquiring subject matter-content. Therefore, learning experiences are organized according to the logic of the subject-matter content.
6. *Motivation.* Learners are motivated to learn by external motivators--grades, the teacher's approval, and parental pressures.

This is supported by Rogers' [1972, pp. 272-279] view of the assumptions implicit in an education based on Theory X assumptions about human nature.

1. The student cannot be trusted to pursue his own learning.
2. Presentation equals learning.
3. The aim of education is to accumulate brick upon brick of factual knowledge.
4. The truth is known.
5. Creative citizens develop from passive learners.
6. Evaluation is education and education is evaluation.

Experiential learning is based on Theory Y assumptions about human nature. As a result, the assumptions on which experiential learning are based, contrast sharply with traditional education. The assumptions of the experiential approach are as follows:

1. Human beings have a natural potentiality for learning.
2. Significant learning takes place when the subject matter is perceived by the student as relevant to his own purposes.
3. Much significant learning is acquired through doing.
4. Learning is facilitated by student's responsible participation in the learning process.
5. Self-initiated learning involving the whole person--feelings as well as intellect--is the most pervasive and lasting.
6. Creativity in learning is best facilitated when self-criticism and self-evaluation are primary and evaluation by others is of secondary importance.
7. The most socially useful element of learning in the modern world is the process of learning, a continuing openness to experience, an incorporation into oneself of the process of change.

Andragogy, the art of helping adults learn, is appropriate only for adult learners. It is a grave error to use principles of andragogy in the education of non-adults, those not equipped to benefit from this methodology. The distinguishing characteristic of the adult learner is the self-concept of being responsible for one's own learning. The adult learner is self-directed in learning that which is of significance to the learner's purposes. Knowles observes that American culture assumes much slower development of an individual's self-directedness than is possible. Therefore, our educational institutions practice pedagogy to an extent that is inappropriate. The individual's abilities to be self-directed lags behind the natural growth in the need to be self-directed. The increasing gap between the ability to be self-directed and the need to be self-directed produces tension, resistance, resentment and often rebellion in the individual.

Knowles andragogical model is based on several assumptions, below:

1. *The need to know.* Adults need to know why they need to learn something before undertaking to learn it. Tough [1979] found that when adults undertake to learn something on their own they will invest considerable energy in probing into the benefits they will gain from learning it and the negative consequences of not learning it. The first task of the facilitator is to make the learner aware of the need to know.
2. *The learner's self-concept.* Adults have a self-concept of being responsible for their own decisions, for their own lives. Once they have arrived at this concept, they will resent and resist situations in which they feel others are attempting to impose their will on them. This does not prevent them, however, from retreating back to previous school conditioning when they are in an activity called "education" and saying "teach me." If the teacher assumes that they really are children, and treats them accordingly, conflict with their need to be self-directed is inevitable.
3. *The role of learner's experience.* By virtue of having lived longer and accumulated more experiences, adult learners bring these experiences, a rich resource for learning, to the learning experience. Devaluing, or failing to value, the experiences of adults will cause them to feel rejected.
4. *Readiness to learn.* Adults become ready to learn those things they need to know and be able to do in order to cope effectively with their real-life situations. The subject matter to be learned must be introduced into the life of the learner.
5. *Orientation to learning.* Adults are motivated to devote energy to learn something to the extent that they perceive that it will help them perform tasks or deal with problems that they confront in their life situations. They learn new knowledge, understandings, skills, values and attitudes most effectively when they are presented in the context of applications to real-life problems.
6. *Motivation.* While some adults are responsive to external motivators (better jobs, promotions, higher salaries, and the like), the most potent motivators are internal pressures (the desire for increased job satisfaction, self-esteem, quality of life, and the like). Normal adults are motivated to keep growing and developing, but this motivation is frequently blocked by such barriers as negative self-concept as a student, inaccessibility of opportunities or resources, time constraints, and programs that violate the principles of adult learning.

ASSIGNMENTS IN STATISTICS BASED ON ANDRAGOGY

The traditional approach to the teaching of basic courses in statistics relies heavily on lecture presentations of material from a suitable textbook followed by solving applicable problems. Students may be assigned homework problems to work and/or may work problems in class.

The course in statistics that is the subject of this paper relied on a non-traditional assignment for students in a first course in statistics. The assignment involved requiring students to collect data on some phenomenon from an area of their own personal interest. The area of interest could be anything the student chose. Some students chose leisure activities: fishing, jogging, etc. Some students chose work-related subjects and some chose other topics of personal interest (auto safety, smoking/non-smoking, etc.). Such assignments are not new to college courses, but they are usually reserved for higher level courses that follow basic statistics (e.g., marketing research, production management, etc.).

The assignment required students to collect data that could be used to measure the probability of success in a Bernoulli process, and was therefore called the Self-Directed Bernoulli Application (SDBA). Students could then use the Binomial Distribution to make estimates about the likelihood of any number of successes in a given number of trials. The estimates could then be compared to the actual data collected in order to make judgements about the suitability of the Binomial for the process the student investigated. Where applicable, the analysis was extended to other distributions covered in basic statistics (e.g. Poisson, Hypergeometric, Normal and Exponential distributions). More important than the details of the analysis is the approach of allowing students to select the subject of the "problems" they were required to work.

The traditional statistics course and the assignment above can be evaluated with Knowles' andragogical model to determine if the SDBA fills a gap between the traditional course and the needs of adult learners.

1. *Need to know.* Good textbooks will attempt to select problems that demonstrate the applicability of statistics to the student's chosen career field. Likewise good teachers will try to make the benefits of learning the required material known to students. The SDBA enhances the *need to know* value of the course because it allows students to work on a problem from their own lives.

2. *The learner's self-concept.* The traditional statistics course allows the student almost no opportunity for self-direction. A given number of concepts and distributions must be learned by the student and the student must work the assigned problems from the book. The SDBA allows students to direct the learning to an area of their own choosing. Further, it allows them the freedom to conceptualize the problem (i.e., conceive of the Bernoulli process, determine what will be a "success," etc.).

3. *The role of the learner's experience.* The traditional statistics course does not make use of the rich experiences that adult learners bring to the classroom. Problems and examples from the textbook and the lectures are standardized for everyone in the class. No individualized work is undertaken. The SDBA individualizes the course and draws from the experience resource of every member of the class.

4. *Orientation to learning.* The traditional statistics course may or may not deal with problems that confront the learners in their life situations. Each person brings a different life situation to the class, and the book and lectures may or may not be relevant to them. By contrast, SDBA is individualized and has the opportunity to reach the life situation of each student.

5. *Motivation.* The traditional statistics course and the SDBA may rely on external motivators (grades, etc.). However, to the extent that the student does select topics that enhance job satisfaction, self-esteem or quality of life, then these internal motivators will enhance learning.

It would appear that the SDBA has the opportunity to fill a gap in the needs of adult learners. If this is true, then one would expect adult learners to achieve higher levels of performance and higher levels of enjoyment from the course. However, not all students in a basic statistics class are adult learners. Many will opt for selecting a topic for their SDBA that is nothing more than a convenient way of getting through the course. Twelve or thirteen years of pedagogy is no preparation for andragogy. As a result of previous conditioning it is easy for students to fall back to the "teach me" or "just tell me what to do" mentality of the child learner.

RESULTS

Although it is believed that the course produced higher levels of scholastic achievement than would have been the case without the SDBA, no scientific evidence of this is available due to the exploratory nature of this investigation. The use of the SDBA was not done within the context of a controlled experiment and no

210

achievement benchmarks were available for comparison. This remains an area ripe for further research.

Other indications of success relating to the affective domain are available from student course evaluations done at the end of the course. Again, this data is not part of a controlled experiment and no benchmarks were available for comparison. Only one student from a class of 32 students, 3.1%, dropped the course as compared to approximately 20% usually dropping this course. Sixteen students gave written comments about the course and thirteen were highly favorable. The favorable comments included comments indicating interest in and liking of statistics. The unfavorable comments were from students who desired more structure (i.e., "teach me"). A total of 31 students gave answers to a structured questionnaire. The evaluation of "overall instruction" was excellent by 13 students, good by 13 students, average by one student, fair by 3 students and poor by 1 student. Only one student disagreed with the statement "My interest in the subject was stimulated by the course." Only one student (the same student as the previous question) disagreed with the statement "This course was an excellent learning experience."

DISCUSSION

The use of self-directed assignment and other elements of course design consistent with andragogy would appear to offer promise for improving the quality of existing statistics courses. Again, it is not suggested that any conclusive evidence is presented in this paper. However, it does appear to be an area that should be investigated further.

REFERENCES

Knowles, Malcolm, The Adult Learner: The Neglected Species. 3rd Edition, (Gulf Publishing Company, Houston, 1984).

Rogers, C. R., Freedom to Learn. (Merrill, Columbus, Ohio, 1972).

NEW CONTEXTS FOR EDUCATIONAL CASE STUDY APPLICATIONS: FROM THE CLASSROOM TO COMPETITION AND BEYOND

Mary R. Sudzina
The University of Dayton
DAYTON, OHIO, U.S.A.
Clare Ryan Kilbane
St. James the Less Elementary School
COLUMBUS, OHIO, U.S.A.

Abstract

This paper presents an example of how case-based teaching was used to prepare a team of five undergraduate preservice teachers for a national case study competition. The use of cases in this "new context" extended the method's benefits beyond the university curriculum in unexpected ways. As these preservice teachers practiced their problem-solving skills, they also learned to research, network and collaborate to compete. These experiences resulted in a sense of personal and professional empowerment among team members and inspired them to establish a similar competition at their home institution, and to present their findings through presentations and symposia.

INTRODUCTION

The use of the case study method is gaining momentum in the United States in the preparation of preservice teachers [White & McNergney, 1991]. Teacher educators have discovered that the case study method provides a valuable link to the "real world" of teaching, and well as opportunities beyond field placement experiences for preservice teachers to carefully reflect and critically analyze teaching incidents and to develop schemas appropriate for future classroom practice [Henson, 1988]. During the last several years, the number of case study texts for education published in the United States has increased dramatically, reflecting a growing interest in applying cases to teacher preparation and in university case study text adoptions. One of the early texts was Greenwood and Parkay's Case Studies for Teacher Decision Making [1989],followed by others including Russo's Confronting Educational Issues: Decision Making with Case Studies [1990], Kowalski, Henson and Weaver's Case Studies on Teaching [1990], Silverman, Welty and Lyon's Case Studies for Teacher Problem Solving [1992]. Shulman's Case Methods in Teacher Education [1992], and Kauffman, Mosert, Nuttycomb, Trent and Hallahan's Managing Classroom Behavior: A Reflective Case-Based Approach, [1993]. The integration of case study texts into the teacher education curriculum offers multiple opportunities for preservice teachers to connect theory and practice while at the same time promoting the development of problem-solving, networking, and research skills [Sudzin & Kilbane, 1992]. Cases can also be used to focus on specific issues in teaching such as multicultural and diversity issues [Sudzina, 1993].

One result of the growing interest in case-based pedagogy, application, research and texts has been the establishment of a national team case competition sponsored, in part, by the Association of Teacher Educators, the American Association of Colleges for Teacher Education, the Commonwealth Center for the Education of Teachers at the University of Virginia, and the National Education Association. The competition, inaugurated in 1992 with the financial support of Allyn & Bacon Publishers, has attracted attention as the first event of its kind in the field of teacher education. This paper chronicles the transition and adjustments a teacher educator and a group of preservice teachers made from the application of the case study method in their university classrooms, to their preparation for participation in a national team case competition, to the impact of this experience on their subsequent personal and professional activities. Dr. Sudzina, the first author of this paper, was the competition team faculty advisor; Clare Ryan Kilbane, the second author and currently an elementary teacher, was the preservice teacher team captain.

THE COMPETITION

Teams of prospective teachers from across the United States and Canada were encouraged to submit a proposal to the Second Commonwealth Center Invitational Team Case Competition, held at the University of Virginia, early in 1993. The competition, scheduled for four days in May, was billed as "an event designed to test teachers' abilities to defend their ideas about teaching and learning before an eminent board of judges from various disciplines and a gallery of interested observers" [Ford, 1993]. Teams were encouraged to be diverse in the areas of age, gender, racial composition, ethnic make-up, subject-matter specialties and professionally relevant experiences. They were also asked to communicate the extent to which case based teaching was used at their institution.

During the first day of the competition, the four invited teams (The University of Calgary, The University of Dayton, The University of Hawaii, and The University of Vermont) and the defending champions (Hampton University) traveled to Thomas Jefferson's Monticello, visited with the other participants and met the competition organizers and student assistants. The second day, each team received instructions, was assigned a computer and work space, and given the written case. The case was selected from a text, then in press, whose co-authors included several teacher educators from the host institution [see, Kauffman et. al., 1993]. Teams were allowed six hours to research, diagnose, and prepare a written analysis of no more than five typed pages. The following day, each team received forty-five minutes to orally present their analysis to the judges. This presentation consisted of a ten minute overview from the team captain and the remainder of the time was to be spent responding to questions posed by three provocateurs. The winner was announced that evening at a banquet in the Dome room of the University of Virginia's landmark Rotunda building. On the next and final morning, a session was held for the purpose of sharing information about each school's teacher education program as well as reflecting and offering feedback regarding the competition experience.

PRELIMINARY PREPARATION: THE ROAD TO VIRGINIA

Both authors were interested in the case study method as a result of conducting research together examining case-based pedagogy from the points of view of a professor and preservice teacher [Sudzinand Kilbane, 1992]. When the announcement for the Second Invitational Team Case Competition arrived, the authors went about the task of selecting a team with the intention of attending the competition, and doing their best to win.

Comprising the Team: Selecting for Personal Qualities and Diversity

The procedure for team selection corresponded to the Commonwealth Center selection criteria in the call for proposals. Personal qualities of candidates were also considered in terms of writing, research and presentation skills, problem-solving, leadership, and collaboration abilities. Additionally, candidates were sought who were interested in competing, intrinsically motivated, compassionate, goal-oriented and diligent. The final team was composed of four females and one male, which included four Caucasians and one African-American. The "developmental design" resulted in selecting one senior who had completed student teaching, two juniors who were enrolled in methods courses and two sophomores who were currently completing their educational psychology requirements. Team members were currently enrolled or had completed Dr. Sudzina's case-based *Teaching and Learning* class.

Case-Use Survey

To meet the request for information concerning case-based teaching at their institution, the team wrote and administered a survey within the Department of Teacher Education. The data and responses received from the various professors in the department affirmed previous notions of the wide-spread use of cases at every stage in the program. What was surprising was the variety of case resources and implementation in these courses. For example, some professors were using novels and film as cases, and writing their own cases in addition to using case texts. Students were also writing cases about their field experiences dilemmas in an effort to communicate and problem-solve classroom observation issues.

Additional information about the use of cases across the university was acquired from the Associate Provost for Academic Affairs. This interview found that case implementation workshops were provided for university faculty each academic year. Cases were a large component of instruction in business, law, psychology, and engineering in addition to education. This information expanded team perspectives about the use of the case study method and reinforced the importance of their participation in the upcoming competition.

Writing the Proposal

This was a "first" professional writing experience for four out of five of the team members. The preparation of this document was the team's first cooperative effort, and one that set the stage for future collaboration. Each member of the team took responsibility for a certain part of the proposal's production. Team members who had a talent for writing compiled the team's biographies and did most of the writing in the document. Team photos were taken and included in the proposal. Those who were proficient at using the computer entered data and generated the graphics and flow charts which made the completed work look truly professional. Others organized and complied the required ten copies.

The final document surpassed everyone's expectations. It was ten pages, bound, and included two color team photographs. The result of this collaboration was a proposal in which everyone took pride and, subsequently, earned the team an invitation to the competition. This was a visible sign that five very diverse students who hadn't known each other previously could work together with a similar goal in mind.

DEVELOPING THE SKILLS TO COMPETE

The prospect of a *team* case competition was particularly intriguing as it offered an unusual opportunity for preservice teachers, who were used to competing exceptionally well individually, to preview an unknown situation together and collaboratively find the best solutions(s). Many skills needed to be developed for successful team collaboration, skills that are often not acquired in an undergraduate teacher preparation program. Collaboration was key because those who could pool their knowledge and resources to arrive at well-thought out and well-rounded solutions would be successful competitors, and, ultimately, teachers.

Team Building

Team building played an important, if not essential role in the preparation process. Before the team could work together however, there had to be a certain amount of familiarity, camaraderie, and trust developed. The construction of the initial proposal did a great deal to achieve this. But it was still apparent that the team was made up of five students who had achieved on their own but now needed to learn to work together for success. "Working dinners" were held weekly at the university that combined social and professional knowledge as each member shared their career aspirations, family background and areas of expertise. Team members presented at a symposium together at the university [see, Sudzina, Ahlgren, Belanich, Damon, Kilbane, Miller & Young, 1993] and continued to define and refine their roles within the team. They sat in on some classes together using case study analyses and kept each other up to date on what needed to be done. They audiotaped problem solving sessions to learn to listen and acknowledge others' contributions. They brunched together and analyzed videotapes of the previous year's competition. Although this was a difficult process, individuals struggled to put personal differences aside to attain synergy so that the team as a whole would be stronger than any single individual.

Case Analysis and Problem-Solving

While each of the team members had experienced the use of cases before, their experiences were different in many respects. Although several had shared required courses in which cases were used, they found that they each had specific schemas with which they thought about cases. Content knowledge as well as personal and professional experiences provided a wealth of information but the team needed to make this information collective. Before the team could develop a strategy for team preparation, it was important to assess the team's current facility with the method. To discover this, the team took a sample case study, sent by the Commonwealth Center with the call for proposals, and worked to analyze it. (This was the same case which was used in the first competition that took place a year earlier.) Each team member read the case and met together to analyze it as a group. The team leader facilitated the discussion and an audio recording was made of the entire session. From this experience, the team not only developed a knowledge for each other's problem-solving styles, they also acquired important information about where they were and where we had to go. With an audio cassette to review with an unbiased perspective, the team captain and faculty advisor were able to listen for "blind spots" in the team's analysis, identify each team member's problem-solving style and diagnose the team's ability to collaborate. During the next eight weeks, the team's preparation focused on developing teamwork, collaboration and presentation strategies. Additionally, team members meet once a week to discuss cases with an Honors/Scholars section of educational psychology whose focus was case analysis, application, and research.

Research and Content Area Knowledge

In addition to the team's efforts to promote collaboration, critical thinking and a multi-perspective analysis, the team also had to develop a facility for applying content specific knowledge to cases. They also had to learn to back up "gut feelings" with grounding in professional literature. The faculty advisor modeled these strategies and mentored the team as they practiced distinguishing between responses based on generalizations and those based on theoretical applications and research. Adding credibility to opinions and analyses was an important and powerful professional lesson. The team began to review the knowledge which they had obtained through various courses in teacher training and discern which theories would be the most useful in case analysis. This prioritizing and selection was, they realized, a higher order thinking skill. It was quite a discovery when team members realized that they each favored different psychological theories. They also realized that each had "favorite" educational trends and researchers.

Team members began to think about their own thinking as well. In addition to a review of previously learned information, they also practiced finding additional information to assist in their problem-solving efforts. Each team member practiced conducting ERIC searches on different educational issues including multi-culturalism, inclusion, journaling, education of the gifted, and urban teaching. This skill was a new acquisition for over half of the team members who had never before been challenged to use computer information indexes, and to apply that information to specific situations.

Strengthening Presentation and Writing Skills

Even the best ideas can be diminished unless they are clearly presented in verbal and/or written form. Through team discussion, it became apparent that the quality of the analysis would suffer if it could not be effectively communicated. Developing a strategy for writing a collaborative document and refining presentation skills became the team's next challenge. Together, the team began to formulate how the paper would be written. In addition, the faculty advisor modeled techniques of professional writing including the use of APA style for documentation, a form that had not been emphasized in the teacher education program. At this point, the team also began to determine a strategy for the oral defense. Through practice, the team began to develop a "feel" for each other's areas of expertise. Team members became comfortable with giving way and conceding to each others responses. They also began to support one another by adding additional information to responses on a case. It became understood that if one member was best at fielding questions regarding, for example, exceptional students, the others would allow them first crack at it. In essence, the team developed a non-verbal understanding with each other or a "sixth sense."

In addition to planning the strategy for the actual competition, the team also engaged in activities which would enable them to develop these skills. Collaboratively, the team produced a poster display for a university symposia which celebrated undergraduate research and special projects. Members of the teams took turns staffing the presentation and answering questions from observers. This provided additional practice in communicating about the competition in a professional setting [see, Sudzina, et. al., 1993].

Mock Simulation - Putting It All Together

In an attempt to prepare as much as possible for the actual competition and to further build team confidence, a mock simulation of the competition was set up. The team met in the library for six hours one Sunday. Using a case selected by the faculty advisor, they discussed, researched and prepared a five-paged typed analysis according to competition guidelines. On Tuesday, they presented their findings to the Honors/Scholars class, who had also read the same case.. To further replicate the competition format, the team leader gave a ten minute case overview and the remainder of the time was spent answering questions from the provocateurs (the

Honors/Scholars students). This simulation resulted in increased team confidence. It also revealed areas for further improvement.

THE COMPETITION EXPERIENCE

The team looked forward to the competition with certain expectations which were not only met, but surpassed. Team members expected to learn about different teacher education programs, meet other preservice teachers, practice problem-solving and analytical skills, and have fun. They didn't expect the unsolicited affirmation they received regarding their personal and professional abilities from judges and other teacher educators, an experience which broadened their perspectives and actions regarding future professional goals and opportunities.

DEVELOPING TEAM IDENTITY AND VISIBILITY

Upon arrival at the competition, the University of Dayton team became known as the "Green Team." This name, a result of the forest green UD tee-shirts donned by the team members, developed both team visibility and increased morale. It gave the individual team members a sense of unity and identity regarding their common goals and the university philosophy of "Learn, Lead, Serve.". As the team learned about the programs of other universities, they felt reaffirmed about their own preservice preparation and experiences.

SOLVING THE CASE

Analyzing the Problem
The case was set in an upper-middle class suburban setting and dealt with the behaviors and attitudes of gifted/high achieving students whose beloved teacher had left. In addition, it addressed the experiences of a novice teacher who needed to develop a relationship with this class of students. The team's mock simulation made it possible for them to get immediately to work on the case. The team read the case, discussed it on an audio recording, and then made a list of research to be gathered. They brainstormed on chart paper which was then hung on the walls of the work space. While three members of the team went to conduct research in the education library, the remaining team members began to write the paper. The remainder of the afternoon was spent refining and revising the document to meet the 5 p.m. deadline.

The Oral Defense
The team reconvened in their advisor's room early in the evening and worked through the early morning hours to practice their oral defense skills and the team leader's opening statement. They were cross-examined on their written statements, research, conclusions and consequences of the case. Additional research was discussed, areas of expertise affirmed, and team etiquette reviewed.

Teams drew lots for the order of their oral defense and Dayton was slated to go on second out of the five teams. The three provocateurs' questions were challenging and required higher-order thinking skills in addition to a working knowledge of theory and practice. Questions were specific to each team's written analysis. Advisors were permitted to attend each defense; team members were restricted to their own presentation. Each team's defense was videotaped.

OUTCOMES

The winning team, The University of Calgary, was announced after dinner that evening. Team advisors, who had seen all the presentations, concurred that the mature graduate Calgary team gave a masterful and creative presentation and defense. Although the young UD team was disappointed with the outcome, they received many complimentary and supportive comments by judges and observers after the banquet, an unexpected outcome..

On the flight home from the competition, the team had the chance to reflect on how much they had learned and how far they had come together in order to compete at Virginia. They agreed that this event was one of the highlights of their teacher preparation career. Individual team members expressed an interest in hosting a regional team case competition to offer other preservice teachers a taste of their overwhelmingly positive experiences. Their advisor then suggested submitting a panel proposal to national conference to report about these experiences. Departing from the plane for summer break, they all agreed to meet in early fall for further discussion.

BEYOND THE COMPETITION

While the immediate results of the case competition are known, the long-term effects of this experience on individual participants are still being realized. The use of cases in this new preservice context served as a catalyst for further case-based activities, preservice leadership skills, research and scholarship, and concrete applications to a novice teacher classroom.

FEEDBACK AND DEBRIEFING

Some of the best indicators of the effectiveness of this instance of case application happened *after* the competition. The judges' feedback received several weeks later served as a springboard for further reflections on the competition and motivated the team to continue to work together. Team members would probably not have thought about the competition, and communicated with each other over the summer, if not for the written comments from the judges, distributed by their faculty advisor. The time lapse enabled the team to view the judges' comments, as well as the video tape of their performance and that of the winning team, with the kind of objectivity they had learned to use in case analysis. Feedback in written and video form served as a important tool in the learning process as it reinforced individual and team strengths and suggested areas for personal and professional improvement. The team was continuing to learn from their competition experience as they shared with each other impressions, insights and recommendations for future case applications and activities.

PANEL PRESENTATION

Motivated by the positive written and verbal feedback they received, and their own sense of professional empowerment in "surviving and thriving" at the competition, the team collaborated with their faculty advisor to present a panel discussion at a national curriculum conference [see, Sudzina, Ahlgren, Damon, Miller and Young, 1993] in the fall. Team members discussed case preparation, the competition itself, and how that experience changed and expanded the way they viewed their roles as future teachers, professionals, researchers, and educational leaders. Turning their experiences into a case, they provided conference participants with a rationale and ideas for implementing case studies into the teacher education curriculum. Additionally, they showed a video clip from the competition, and prepared a case for the audience participation. For all of the participants, this was their first conference presentation and a natural extension of their competition preparation: organizing, collaborating, writing, presenting, and answering questions. The session went very well. For further individual feedback, the presentations were also audiotaped. This conference experience seemed to further whet the preservice teachers' appetites to host a case competition at their home institution.

MINI CASE COMPETITION

The team sought and gained the support of the Dean of the School of Education to sponsor a mini case competition second semester. Invitations were sent out to over 50 regional university and college teacher preparation institutions. Fourteen schools responded and four schools were invited to the one day competition. Team members took charge of all the details from selecting the case and formulating judging criteria, to planning the banquet and reserving meeting rooms. Faculty judges, invited by team members, represented six academic disciplines. Their former team captain, a first year teacher, was also invited back to judge.

The mini competition, a "condensed" version of the Commonwealth Center competition, took place on the last Friday in February. Competing teams were given the same case to solve from Managing Classroom Behavior: A Reflective Case-based Approach (Kauffman et. al., 1993), and asked to prepare a specific outline for the judges to follow. Participating faculty team advisors were offered a case study workshop in the morning hosted by the case competition team to share ideas about case-based teaching from faculty and student perspectives. In the afternoon, teams were individually questioned by two provocateurs, School of Education faculty, while the judges observed and ranked overall team responses. A reception and banquet were held that evening and prizes awarded. The event was videotaped and copies sent to participants along with judges' comments. Several of the competing teams expressed an interest in hosting the competition next year and it is expected that it will become an annual regional event.

RESEARCH AND SCHOLARSHIP AWARDS AND RECOGNITION

As a result of their involvement case-based teaching, (the national case competition, the mini competition, the Stander Symposium for Undergraduate Research, a national curriculum conference panel presentation, a case workshop for faculty, and written research associated with case-based teaching), four of the five team members have been recognized for their outstanding achievements in the 12 months since the competition. The national case competition team leader, a co-author of this paper, won the prestigious Dean's Research Award at graduation and was listed in Who's Who in American Colleges and Universities. The two junior team members also won this award upon their recent graduation. One of the sophomore team members, now a junior, was recently elected to Who's Who, and has won a summer fellowship to a national program at Phillips Exeter Academy in Andover, Massachusetts. The other sophomore team member, also a junior, has assumed leadership of a new team participating in a virtual team case competition, the first international e-mail preservice case competition, hosted by the Commonwealth Center at the University of Virginia. All attribute their case competition experience as a major influence in their continued scholarly and leadership activities.

IMPACT ON A NOVICE TEACHER

The skills developed to analyze cases, collaborate, motivate team members, and present findings to both judges and provocateurs have contributed to the success of the team captain in her first year of teaching, particularly in regard to classroom management and school socialization. As a fourth grade teacher, she used the objectivity gained through case analysis daily. In many instances, she was able to remove herself from "touchy" situations and make use of broader perspectives to view classroom occurrences as a third person observer. This objectivity removed her from highly emotional issues and allowed for more logical, reflective decisions. She also found herself identifying problem situations and applying educational theory and practice to them rather than just going with her gut instinct. Additionally, she used her research skills to search the literature about difficult problems and issues.

Collaboration with fellow teachers and auxiliary staff is often a challenge for first year teachers. The collaborative nature of the case competition fostered the development of this novice teacher's cooperative skills with the school psychologist, nurse, reading specialist, parents and fellow teachers. The ability to acknowledge each person's expertise and put personal differences aside to focus on the best interests of the child was learned through the team's case competition preparation. Equally, the motivational and facilitating skills used as team captain have helped to "get the ball rolling" on professional committees.

Finally, the professional skills necessary for presenting and defending the team's analysis before an audience of eminent educators has played an integral role in entry year teaching confidence and communication. The articulate and comfortable presentation style developed for the oral defense has been helpful during parent-teacher conferences, open house, school board meetings, and daily classroom instruction. The practice defending her professional judgement in front of the provocateurs has paid off every time she explained her judgements to her students' parents. The social networking skills used at the competition have assisted this first year teacher in setting up effective lines of home-school communication and fostering strong parent support for her innovative teaching practices. "In short," she says, "my first year teaching has been made easier in many ways by my participation in the competition."

SUMMARY AND CONCLUSIONS

Case-based teaching as a strategy to effectively weave theory, practice, and problem-solving in preservice teacher education has attracted the interest of teacher educators, researchers, professional education associations, and publishers alike. A result of this mutual interest has been the sponsorship of a national invitational team case competition for preservice teachers. Preparing and participating in the Commonwealth Center's Second Invitational Team Case Competition served as a catalyst for a team of undergraduate preservice teachers to reflect on their personal and professional roles and goals as future educators.

Team members collaboratively developed skills of: leadership, cooperation, problem-solving, networking, writing, researching, and oral presentation. The utilization of cases in this fashion inspired these future educators to extend this learning beyond the university classroom, to professional competitions and conferences, and into an elementary classroom. Team members felt enriched and empowered from these experiences. Several team members have assumed leadership roles within the university and community, and have expressed the desire to continue to write, research, and present collaboratively. It appears that the competitive aspect of case analysis served to encourage, rather than discourage, a sense of professionalism, camaraderie and desire for excellence from these preservice teachers. Even though this team came home from the competition "empty handed," they came home far from "empty headed." The case competition experience provided a springboard to new contexts for educational case study applications for these future educators, and their faculty advisor.

REFERENCES

Greenwood, G. and H. Parkay, Case Studies for Teacher Decision Making (McGraw Hill, 1989).

Harrington, H., "The Case as Method," Action in Teacher Education (Winter 1990-1991), pp. 235-241.

Henson, K., "Case Study in Teacher Education," The Educational Forum (Fall 1988), pp. 235-241.

Ford, R. E., "Champions Hail from North Country," Commonwealth Center News, Volume 6, (Fall/Winter 1993).

Kauffman, J.M., Mostert, M.P., Nuttycombe, D.G., Trent, S.C., and Hallahan, D.P., Managing Classroom Behavior: A Reflective Case-based Approach. (Allyn and Bacon,1993).

Kowalski, T., R. Weaver and K. Henson, Case Studies on Teaching (Longman, 1990).

Russo, F., Confronting Educational Issues: Decision Making with Case Studies. (Kendall/Hunt, 1990).

Schulman, J., ed., Case Methods in Teacher Education (Teacher College Press, 1992).

Silverman, R., W. Welty and S. Lyon, Case Studies for Teacher Problem Solving (McGraw-Hill, 1992).

Sudzina, M., "Dealing with Diversity Issues in the Classroom: A Case Study Approach." Paper presented at the annual meeting of the Association of Teacher Educators, Los Angeles (February, 1993).

Sudzina, M. and C. Kilbane, "Applications of a Case Study Text to Undergraduate Teacher Preparation." In Forging New Partnerships with Cases, Simulations, Games and Other Interactive Methods, ed. H. Klein (World Association for Case Method Application and Research, 1992).

Sudzina, M., K. Ahlgren, L. Belanich, K. Damon, C. Kilbane, B. Miller, and M. Young, "Applications of the Case Study Method in the Department of Teacher Education." Poster presentation at the Fourth Annual Stander Symposium to Celebrate Undergraduate Research, The University of Dayton, Dayton, OH (March 1993).

Sudzina, M., K. Ahlgren,K. Damon, B. Miller, and M. Young, "Competition, Collaboration, and Case-based Teaching: Reflections from an Invitational Team case Competition." Panel presentation at the annual JCT Conference on Curriculum Theory and Classroom Practice, Bergamo Center, Dayton, OH (October 1993).

White, B. and R. McNergney, "Case-based Teacher Education: The State of the Art." Paper presented at the Case Method in Teacher Education Conference, Harrisonburg, VA: James Madison University (June 1991).

SIMULATIONS AND THE ADULT LEARNER: THEORY AND APPLICATION

Elizabeth M. Hawthorne
The Pennsylvania State University
READING, PENNSYLVANIA, U.S.A.

Abstract

Many professional education faculty teach adult students whether in continuing professional education settings or in graduate programs. While the differences in the settings are not inconsequential, the similarities are compelling. Therefore, I am drawing from adult learning and adult education theory as well as simulation theory to (1) make the case for the benefits of simulation for adult students and (2) to outline a simulation that has proven effective with graduates students in a Program in Higher Education.

INTRODUCTION

This article is not unlike Midsummer's Night Dream in which there is a play within a play. In order to explain the factors that are involved in deciding how to select a particular pedagogy, I will necessarily discuss some of the factors that should be brought to bear in making these decisions. Similarly, the "problem" that students are challenged with in the simulation that I am discussing, concerns the development of a curriculum using the same principles I used to select the pedagogy.

According to McKeachie et al. [1986], teaching involves the learner, the content, the instructor, the context, and the pedagogy. The instructor's background, resources, skills, and interests are a crucial dimension of the instructional situation. I shall not elaborate on the instructor's role beyond simply cautioning instructors to consider their own circumstances and inclinations before embarking on a new instructional strategy, since the strategy itself is generally not the key to successful learning, but the Gestalt of the model is. Here I will focus on the learner and the pedagogy.

THE LEARNERS

One view of adults as learners is drawn from Sternberg's triarchic model of intelligence [1990]. This model specifies the following kinds of intelligence:
(1) analytic,
(2) experiential or applied, that is, the individual has the ability to automatize certain cognitive processes that are used often, and
(3 contextual, when the individual has street smarts--the ability to manipulate his/her environment.

Houle postulated a typology of the structural forms of learning by professionals that was later modified by Cervero and Dimmock [1987]. The modified typology included inquiry, the "spontaneity of the discovery process" [Houle in Cervero and Dimmock, p. 126]; the processes of group instruction and self-instruction, and the performance. This typology can be a helpful way to organize teaching and learning in concert with the triarchic model of intelligence the former being the process and the latter is the outcome.

Mezirow expanded these concepts. His theory of adult learning as a transformative experience describes how adults make meaning of their experience. Adults construct, confirm, and reformulate their experiences (p. xii). The construction of experience is drawn from within the individual; the meaning that one gives to experience is acquired and validated through social interaction. Mezirow posited a tripartite model of social learning based on Jurgen Habermas's work that includes instrumental learning, learning to control and manipulate the environment; communicative learning, learning to understand the meaning of what is being communicated, and reflective learning, that is, learning to understand oneself.

Habermas [in Mezirow, 1991] viewed modernity as the crumbling of traditional authority structures which mandates a new self-directedness in learning. While adult students are frequently self-directed learners, this concept compels the instructor to seek ways to ensure that their learning experiences in formal educational settings leads them to be self-directed learners throughout their lives. This implies the freeing of the adult student from dependency on the teacher and the necessity to guide students to control their own learning. In this sense, self-directed learning [Mezirow, 1985] is the capacity of critical self-reflection and for changing one's life. While they bring to formal learning experiences specific goals, and are unenthusiastic about investing their time and energy in activities and assignments whose pertinence is not clear [see Caffarella and O'Donnell, 1987], we are obliged to assist adult students in learning about their own learning, the meta-cognition approach discussed by McKeachie et al. [1986] or the meta-curriculum Weinstein addresses [1990]. Self-directed learning involves creative problem-solving and reinforcement of self-discipline [Knowles, 1980].

Characteristics of adult learners vary from the advanced professional to the undergraduate student returning after years of absence from schooling. Yet adult students do share some characteristics which are pertinent to our understanding of the learning environment. In contrast to traditional undergraduate students, adult students are older and, therefore, often work more slowly, but with greater accuracy [Cross, 1981]. They bring a breadth and depth of life experience to draw upon [see also Freire, 1970]. Similarly, they have experienced role differentiation, which suggests that they are simultaneously balancing multiple roles including the student role. Often adult students have clearer goals than younger students or actively seek assistance in obtaining clarification and direction. They take their learning seriously [Niemi, 1985]. The assignment, then, is to know who the adult learners are as we find them. Building upon the learners' own histories, instructors need to capitalize on the strengths these students bring to the learning situation by guiding their paths of self-understanding. This self-understanding is a self-conscious effort facilitated by the instructor through active problem solving and reinforcement of self-discipline. Thus will adult students be able and willing to continue to learn about themselves as well as their worlds.

SIMULATION

Simulation is an instructional method that allows students to experience real situations by creating a context in which there is a challenge for action requiring a definition of a problem that is likely to have multiple workable answers. Sternberg outlined some differences between problem solving in "real life" as compared with problem-solving in school [1990] that are depicted in Table 1. A major difference between the two is that school provides a structure and framework that real life does not. Simulations are an effort to bridge the gap between the two kinds of problem solving in order for learners to develop suitable skills to address problems confronted in real life. In simulations, too, students work in groups returning to the instructor for advice. Reinforcement is sporadic, but likely more than would be the case in real life! Simulations like the real world provide opportunities to apply knowledge. Students therefore have to make decisions about their sufficiency of knowledge, understand what they already know that is pertinent. Simulations should be an impetus for learners to acquire needed information so that they obtain the experience of identifying information needs and sources as well as problem solving skills. That is the heart of self-directed learning. Simulations have particular validity over real world experiences because in an educational setting the instructor creates a non-threatening environment in which students can experience both success and failure in their efforts. Adult students can draw up their reservoir of life experiences, but more importantly, they will seek out additional knowledge in service of the problem-solving task. This is responsive to the adult students need for relevance. The simulation is then a story created by the students that has the added value of acting as a memory aid that will help them retain information.[1]

Games and simulations have been found to be effective pedagogical strategies for teaching complex concepts. Simulations were found in one study to be more effective in teaching goal-setting skills by management students than the case study method [Wheatley, Hornaday and Hunt, 1988].

TABLE 1
REAL LIFE VS. SCHOOL

	REAL LIFE	SCHOOL
Problem	has to be defined	is given to student to find the right answer
Feedback	little	considerable
Problem-solving	in groups	solitary

[From Sternberg, 1990]

Further, a simulation is reality without the "responsibility" inherent in actual applications, e.g., performing surgery, flying airplanes. Because of the reduced risk involved, simulations are readily applicable to novices starting to learn about a particular field or skill. Simulations afford students the opportunity to work with actual materials that are the same or similar to those they would encounter in real life. Simulation gives students tools for continuing their own self-learning [see Cervero and Dimmock, 1987]. Simulations are transformative in the sense that the learners rehearse future roles by learning techniques and information that help them manipulate their environment. Diverse social communication experiences enable students to create meaning of what they experience, observe, and feel and the means to understand themselves. "This problem-solving process of attempting to understand requires an openness to different perspectives so that a learner becomes reflective or critically reflective in the course of interpreting the activity [Mezirow, 1991, p. 85]."

An additional benefit of simulations is cost savings. Simulations relieve instructors of the time consuming task of arranging and supervising internships. Transportation costs are eliminated, and costs of insurance, when appropriate are not incurred. In many cases, too, internships with experiences as specified as in some simulations may not be available. While there are costs of designing and evaluating simulations, these are likely to be substantially lower than providing real life learning experiences in many instances. Thus there are distinct advantages in the use of simulations under specified conditions.

SETTING FOR THE SIMULATION

The scene is a graduate preparation program for community college faculty and administrators. The students are adults with limited to extensive professional experience in two-year college settings. The elective course, Community College Curricula, is a simulation that also includes direct instruction (lectures, discussion, outside reading) to introduce students to the tools and resources they may require to complete the simulation. The activities are designed to develop desirable or necessary competencies for college administrators drawn in part from the limited research in this area that indicates that desired capabilities include knowledge of post secondary education, positive interpersonal skills, managerial and problem-solving abilities [Paris, 1985], and communication skills [Dowdeswell and Good, 1982]. Specific competencies, e.g., creating an evaluation design, were integrated into the simulation based on the instructor's knowledge of administrative roles in higher education (although more research in this area would provide helpful guidance for program planning).

The simulation activity is to design a curriculum for a two-year college in the United States. At the end of this problem solving activity, students are expected to be able to understand and have shown evidence of their ability to apply at least one curriculum design model and methods of evaluation appropriate for evaluating curriculum in two-year colleges (specific competencies). Students will have enhanced their knowledge of the range and potential of curricula in two-year colleges, faculty, students, and the institutional context for curriculum development in two-year colleges (knowledge of post secondary education), know the role of external organizations in curriculum development and evaluation, and have additional methods of communication to use in practice (communication skills). Further, students will have self-consciously experienced work in groups that they can use for critical self-reflection (positive interpersonal skills). The panel of experts, which critiques students' work, address student judgment regarding use of data and program planning (managerial ability).

ASSUMPTIONS UNDERLYING THE DEVELOPMENT AND DESIGN OF THIS COURSE:

- Students have some experience in or familiarity with two-year colleges. If not, they will actively seek information and ask questions in class to become familiar with these institutions.
- Students in the course will actively seek out readings that will build their background knowledge of community, junior, and technical colleges.
- In order to evaluate a program of any kind, it is most effective to develop the evaluation design (research design, methods, and instrumentation) before designing the program. When designing the program, the evaluation design can help form the program design and the program design will contribute to modification of the evaluation design.

INSTRUCTOR'S ROLE

The instructor first provides students with the tools/knowledge/information that are required to initiate the simulation, here, the concepts of curriculum design, the organization, design, and structure of curricula offered by two-year colleges; the relationship between assessment and planning, and evaluation design principles. Second, the instructor provides a reading list to all students for their reference. Required reading addresses curriculum design and evaluation issues. Directions on accessing Internet for additional resources could be provided if students have access to appropriate technology. Third, the instructor makes available resources that are not readily available in the institution's library, for example, the forms for program approval from a variety of state agencies. Fourth, the instructor assists students in forming their work groups. Fifth, the instructor provides instructions for the work groups. Finally, once the stage is set, the instructor's role is to serve as a facilitator and resource person for the groups.

THE ASSIGNMENT

Following is the set of directions provided to the students: Curriculum design goes beyond content and scheduling. There are many constituencies whose interests are pertinent and many considerations of the context in which the curriculum will be applied that must be factored in at the beginning. The assignment is for the group to develop a proposal for a new program to be submitted to the state agency for review. All materials requested by the state will be expected to be provided, so it is essential to contact the proper sources for data and other information AT ONCE in order to have this information in time for the final report.

At the end of the first class meeting, student groups will be formed (groups will be a maximum of four students; minimum of two) and each group will be expected to come to a consensus on a state to which they wish to turn their attention for this assignment. Once you select a state, identify a community, technical, or junior college in that state. The flow chart in Figure 1 can be used as a guide for curriculum development in the contemporary community college in the United States.

FIGURE 1
MODEL FOR CURRICULUM DESIGN

(1) Environmental Scan-----> (2) College-----> (3) Program Selection------> (4) Accrediting Standards------> (5) Curriculum Design and Evaluation Design Techniques -----> (6) Design Curriculum -----> (7) Prepare Review Materials -----> (8) Plan and present Curriculum

(1) After first defining the pertinent service area (e.g., county, state, region), gather data on the environment with consideration to the following conditions: social, cultural, environmental, political, economic, and demographic. Gather information on potential audience for college programs, e.g., community organizations, employers, social groups, and the like.
(2) Gather data on the college. These data should be pertinent to the development of curriculum including the background and number of faculty, current enrollment and student characteristic data, available equipment and faculties; administrative structure; and fiscal issues.

(3) Based on the gap between the service area's needs and the College's curriculum, identify a suitable area for program development keeping in mind the (4) requirements of accrediting bodies both regional and programmatic. Data from the environmental study will assist in defining the knowledge, skills, and attitudes desirable for the selected program area.

(5) Select desired curriculum design approach including theory and rationale and models. Develop a scheme to evaluate the proposed curriculum. (6) design the curriculum taking into account the environmental and college data. Construct a budget and assess its viability in the current fiscal environment; if necessary, identify realistic external sources for funds. Modify the curriculum design on the basis on the evaluation you conduct. Evaluation will include specifying a design and the evaluation criteria. (7) Prepare materials for review within the College, e.g., college curriculum committee or whatever structure is in place in the institution. Prepare materials for external review following the requirements of the agencies, e.g., state higher education agency (e.g., the community college board). Almost all state community college/higher education agencies require some form of program approval for new programs. States vary considerably in the scope of their oversight and in the kinds of information they require in order to review a proposed program.

(8) Present curriculum design to a team of administrators from local community colleges on (date), so a professional presentation is expected. The presentation should include a rationale for the selected curriculum, the complete curriculum, including costs, and the evaluation design. The review panel will be prepared to ask groups questions about the viability of the design and implementation of the curriculum.

Finally, each student will prepare a recommendation for a grade for themselves and for members of their work group with a rationale for all recommended grades.

CONCLUSIONS

This activity requires students to seek information, apply knowledge, work in a group, reflect on their own contributions to the work, and is compatible with theory on adult learning and adult students. The activity provides students with experiences that allow them to rehearse skills and behaviors that have been found desirable for college administration positions. Within a broad framework, students have considerable latitude in applying different curriculum design approaches and different evaluation designs, which encourages their creativity and their problem solving skills. They have to read about community colleges, the students, the faculty, and their resources in order to accomplish the assignment. They often have to contact practicing professionals for advice, information, and the like, thereby expanding their own knowledge of information sources in the field as well as their own ingenuity in ferreting out such sources. The use of information is functional, that is, it serves to accomplish the task, which satisfies the adult student's need for relevance and useful value; yet it extends beyond application to synthesis, analysis, and evaluation which fosters their critical thinking skills and their judgment. Finally, in this simulation, the learners develop communication skills--verbal, visual, and written through their work as part of a group and in making a formal presentation to a professional audience.

This simulation has some weaknesses in that the student only selects the premise of the assignment through enrollment in the particular course and has no choice but to design a curriculum. A serious flaw in this simulation is that it requires students to follow conservative approaches, because they are learning how things are done in the real world rather than how to reconstruct the world. While this prepares individuals to move into positions in the current world, it does not fully prepare them to create new tools, new realities. Therefore, simulations should be designed to include a strong component focusing on meta-cognition whereby students are encouraged to consider their own ways of knowing and doing and be ready to move beyond the way things are to the way things could be.

ENDNOTES

1.   I am indebted to W. L. Scheller, University of Toledo, College of Engineering, for focusing on these notions.

REFERENCES

Caffarella, and O'Donnell. "Self-Directed Adult Learning." Adult Education Quarterly. 37:4, Summer 1987,

224

199-211.

Cross, K. Patricia. Adults As Learners. San Francisco: Jossey-Bass, 1981

Dowdeswell, W. H. and Harold M. Good. "Academic Management--The Case for Challenge." Canadian Journal of Higher Education. 12:3, 1982, 11-24.

Freire, Paulo. Pedagogy of the Oppressed. New York: Herder and Herder, 1970.

Knowles, Malcolm. The Modern Practice of Adult Education. Chicago: Association Press, Follett Publishing, Co., 1980.

McKeachie, Wilbert J., Paul R. Pintrich, Yi-Guang Lin, David A. F. Smith and Rajeev Sharma. Teaching and Learning in the College Classroom. A Review of the Research Literature. 2nd edition. Ann Arbor, 1986.

Mezirow, Jack. A Critical Theory of Self-Directed Learning. New-Directions-for-Continuing-Education; n25 p. 17-30 Mar 1985

Mezirow, Jack. Transformative Dimensions of Adult Learning. San Francisco: Jossey-Bass, 1991.

Niemi, John A. "Fostering Participation in Learning." Involving Adults in the Educational Process. Sandra H. Rosenblum, editor. New Directions for Continuing Education. #26. San Francisco: Jossey-Bass, June 1985, 3-12.

Paris, Gyorgy. "The Responsibilities of Managers in Education." Higher Education in Europe. 10:3, July/September 1985, 15-18.

Sternberg, Robert J. "Real Life vs. Academic Problem-Solving." In Intelligence and Adult Learning. Robert A. Fellenz and Gary J. Conti, editors. Bozeman, MT: Center for Adult Learning, Montana State University, March 1990, 35-40.

Weinstein, Claire. "Strategies and Learning." In Intelligence and Adult Learning. Robert A. Fellenz and Gary J. Conti, editors. Bozeman, MT: Center for Adult Learning, Montana State University, March 1990, 17-34.

Wheatley, Walter J., Robert W. Hornaday, and Tammy G. Hunt. "Developing Strategic Management Goal-Setting Skills." Simulation and Games. 19:2, June 1988, 173-185.

INTERACTION-BASED SELF-ASSESSMENT OF COLLEGE TEACHING

Norman H. Hadley
Memorial University of Newfoundland
ST. JOHN'S, NEWFOUNDLAND, CANADA

Abstract

The author argues that anonymity-based evaluations of college teaching encourage students to operate outside of effective communication. The author proposes an interactive system of evaluating college teaching which is individualized and initiated by college teachers with the collaboration of their students. The author's interactive-based self-assessment of teaching provides a framework for college teachers to: (1) reflect on their self-assessments, (2) account for discrepancies between their self-assessments and student's impressions of their teaching, (3) modify their self-evaluations and (4) modify their teaching and/or manner of relating to their students.

INTRODUCTION

Communication cuts across all behavior settings including the evaluation of college teaching. Even in our sleep behavior we do not escape communication. Communication occurs in our dreams. We see ourselves talking to others and we see the actors in our dreams communicating with us.

According to Bandler, Grinder and Satir [1976] the essential components of communication include "the self," "other," and "context." See Figure 1. Bandler, Grinder and Satir [1976] identified blaming communication, placating communication, super-reasonable communication, irrelevant communication and a fifth positive pattern, congruent communication. **When we ask our students to evaluate our teaching without revealing their identities, we are encouraging our students to operate outside of effective communication. Indeed, anonymity-based evaluations do not qualify as interpersonal communication.** The article is based on the author's teaching while on leave at Brandon University.

PATTERNS OF COMMUNICATION

FIGURE 1
COMPONENTS OF COMMUNICATION AND CONGRUENT COMMUNICATION STANCE

According to Bandler, Grinder and Satir [1976] congruent communication takes the other person, self and the context of the message into account. Figure 1 illustrates that "self", "context" and "other" is recognized in communication. Blaming communication is characterized by statements of "disagreement" which ignore the "other person" and the context of the communication. See Figure 2. People who use super-reasonable communication seem to be very intelligent" but they are using their "intellect" to avoid their feelings [Bandler, Grinder and Satir, 1976]. See Figure 3. Because the human elements, "self", and "other", are subtracted from the communication the words are spoken in a monotone as if emitted by a computer.

FIGURE 2

BLAMING COMMUNICATION

FIGURE 3

SUPER-REASONABLE COMMUNICATION

Placating communication subtracts the "self" and the "context". (Figure 4). It can be summarized in one word "agreement." Placaters put themselves "down," assume an apologetic position and responsibility for everything. In irrelevant communication the person avoids important issues by ignoring the feelings of the listeners, ignoring his or her own affect, and ignoring the context. See Figure 5.

FIGURE 4

PLACATING COMMUNICATION

FIGURE 5

IRRELEVANT COMMUNICATION

ANONYMITY-BASED EVALUATION OF COLLEGE TEACHING

Anonymity-based systems of evaluation are based on distrust rather than trust and on a lack of interest in developing trust and effective communication between teachers and students. Anonymity-based evaluations approximate a monologue with the student holding the speaking floor. I argue that such methods encourage **blaming communication** because the college teacher is essentially subtracted from the communication process. (See Figure 2) Indeed, because anonymity-based evaluations **do not permit a reply**, it is difficult to see how they qualify as communication.

In anonymity-based systems college teachers do not have the opportunity to even temporarily seize the speaking floor. Often the feedback which they receive is limited to a profile of the results. If the students have made an error they have no way of alerting me to it, nor do I have any way of knowing whether or not they have made an error. Supposedly, the anonymity has advantages for the evaluators -- and I say this with tongue in cheek. The college teacher cannot ask the evaluator for clarification and he or she cannot explain the circumstances surrounding specific teaching methods. The teacher cannot apologize for an honest error. The anonymity does not even permit the evaluator to "take a second look".[1]

The major justification for anonymity-based evaluations is that the students will be more likely to provide an accurate appraisal if they can hide in the shadows. What is most feared, however, is that the college teacher will adjust the grades downward for those students who assigned unfavorable ratings. This stance can be challenged. A college teacher who is inclined to respond in such an unethical manner will undoubtedly find opportunities to behave unethically and hence signed or unsigned forms would have little or no bearing on how the college teacher treats his or her students.

INTRODUCING STUDENTS TO THE SYSTEM

I administered the forms similar to the one depicted in Figure 6 at the conclusion of a unit on confrontation. The students' evaluation of my teaching was a practical application of their confrontation skills. The students understood that they would be required to sign their forms and that I would reply in writing to their comments. They also were informed that I would return the evaluation forms to them after I had entered my comments. The students were also invited to respond to my comments and/or modify their comments or add additional comments.

MY REFLECTIONS

There is a uniqueness about my method: (1) It **invites students to reveal their identities by signing their names to the evaluation forms**. Having students acknowledge their presence encourages them to base their comments on observation and reflection. (2) **The method permitted me to communicate with my students and they with me**. The form was designed so that the students responded in the centre column and I responded to their statements on the right side of the page. See Figure 6. This characteristic gives the student an opportunity to give sensitive, constructive feedback, and it gives the college teacher an opportunity to respond to their feedback, to reinforce confrontation skills and to initiate changes in teaching.

STUDENTS' REACTIONS

The reaction of my students to communication-based self-assessment was threefold: (1) they expressed no hesitation about signing their names to the evaluation forms, (2) they expressed excitement about the fact that the forms would be returned for their perusal and (3) they expressed satisfaction with the system and commented favorably on the uniqueness of the evaluation system.

COMMUNICATION-BASED SELF-ASSESSMENT

Communication-based self-assessment presupposes a system of evaluation which is individualized and initiated by college teachers with the collaboration of their students. Presumably self-initiated self-evaluations are less threatening than externally imposed evaluations. Periodically college teachers write a one-page evaluation of their teaching. The students are invited to comment on the self-evaluations and the college teacher responds in writing to the students' comments. Figure 6 illustrates only one of many possible versions of communication-based self-evaluation of college teaching.[2]

Self-Evaluation of College Teacher	Invited Comments of Student	College Teacher's Reply to Student's Comments
Focus 1: Focus 2: Focus 3: _____ Teacher's Signature	_____Student's Signature	_____ Teacher's Signature

FIGURE 6. COMMUNICATION-BASED-SELF-EVALUATION OF COLLEGE TEACHING

When the self-assessments do not coincide with the external evaluations, college teachers have several options. These include: (1) reflecting on their self-assessment, their students' comments and their replies to the students' comments, (2) attempting to account for the discrepancies between their self-assessments and their students' impressions of their teaching, (3) modifying their self-evaluations and (4) modifying their teaching and/or manner of relating to their students.

Communication-based self-assessments also provide students with a format for expressing positive reinforcement for identified teaching responses. Because we know that our students will to respond to our self-evaluations, the evaluation system has a built-in accuracy check on the reporting of self-observations. **Self-observation and self-recording conforms to the scientist-practitioner guideline of employing "least restrictive" and least "intrusive interventions." Self-observation and self-recording is an established method of assessment and has the potential of generating behavior change in its own right because of the reactive effects of self-monitoring.** [3]

CONCLUDING STATEMENT

I have found the process and outcome of communication-based self-assessments to be positive. There were, of course, unpleasant moments, because I am not perfect and because I cannot expect every student to comment favorably all of the time. At the very least, communication-based self-assessment encourages dialogue and thereby improves and maintains positive interpersonal relations between students and college teachers. I welcome the sensitive confrontations and comments of my readers and I shall respond in writing.

ENDNOTES

1. For a detailed study of reexamining events and their interpretation in clinical practice and research, the reader is referred to Novey [1968].

2. Students could be asked to identify "critical incidents" which could be used as the foci in communication-based self-assessments. It is not difficult to identify critical incidents in educational settings. One only has to listen to students describing their teaching-learning experiences. A number of critical incidents come to mind - quizzes, scholarly papers, practical projects and individual or group presentations. I have used critical incidents to refer to events in teaching and learning which students have collaboratively identified as being "important." However, the established method of critical incidents originates with the work of Flanagan in the 1950s. The methodology has recently been rediscovered in the context of the scientist-practitioner model in applied psychology [Woosley, 1986].

3. Maletzky [1974] argues for self-recording produced treatment effects. Theory and research in self-monitoring provide a useful framework for examining communication-based self-assessment. The early article by

McFall [1976] and the recent work by Kanfer and Gaelick-Buys [1991] provides a useful overview of self-monitoring as a method of assessment and behavior change.

REFERENCES

Bandler, R., J. Grinder, and & V. Satir., Changing with Families, (Science and Behavior Books, 1976).

Flanagan, J., "The critical incident technique," Psychological Bulletin, (1954), 51, 327-358.

Kanfer, F.H. and L. Gaelick-Buys., "Self-management methods," In F.H. Kanfer & A.P. Goldstein (Eds.). Helping People Change: A Textbook of Methods (4th ed.) pp. 305-360). (Pergamon Press, 1991).

Maletzky, B.M., "Behavior recording as treatment: A brief note," Behavior Therapy, (1974), 5, 107-112.

McFall, R.M., "Parameters of self-monitoring," In R.B. Stuart (Ed.), Behavioral self-management: Strategies, Techniques, and Outcomes. (Brunner/Mazel, 1976).

Novey, S., The Second Look: Reconstruction of Personal History in Psychiatry and Psychoanalysis (John Hopkins Press, 1968).

Woosley, L.K. "The critical incident technique: An innovative qualitative method of research," Canadian Journal of Guidance and Counselling, (1986), 20, 242-254.

ACKNOWLEDGEMENTS

An earlier version of this paper was presented by the author on December 10, 1993 at a seminar sponsored by the Seminar Committee of the Faculty of Education at Memorial University of Newfoundland. I am indebted to Mrs. Carolyn Lono for preparing the many revisions, to Diane P. Janes, M. Ed., for the graphics and to Dr. Frank Riggs for administrative support.

STRATEGIC MANAGEMENT: EVALUATING THE CASE METHOD

David Jennings
Nottingham Trent University
NOTTINGHAM, ENGLAND

Abstract

The paper considers the use of case studies in the teaching of strategic management. The usefulness of the method is open to question due to issues relating to the realism of cases and a diversity of academic views concerning the nature of the strategy process. A questionnaire based survey of UK lecturers is used to answer a number of fundamental questions concerning lecturer's objectives in using case studies, the effectiveness of the case method, problems and difficulties and the comparative strengths and weaknesses of other methods in the teaching of strategic management.

STRATEGIC MANAGEMENT AND THE CASE METHOD

The origins of the use of the case method in business education can be traced back to the first decade of this century and the earliest attempts at education and training by the Graduate School of Business Administration of Harvard University. This tradition continues to flourish and has in turn been extended to new areas of management education, including strategic management.

Case studies are now extensively used in the teaching of strategic management. The majority of strategy texts include the familiar form of case study, lengthy descriptions of companies and their environments, with the intention that the material will form a basis for students to acquire insight and practice the skills of strategic management. The authors provide a common rationale for the use of cases in teaching strategic management. The popular text by Mintzberg and Quinn introduces case material as 'a rich soil for investigating strategic realities'. This is to be achieved both through description of strategic situations and through the students development of prescriptive analysis. While the authors warn that involvement in a real organisation is the ideal way to understand strategy each of the cases is seen as providing 'the data and background for making a major decision' as well as an opportunity to understand the realities of a particular organisation.[Quinn and Mintzberg, 1991]. Similar justifications are provided in other popular texts with cases included; 'to simulate the reality of the manager's job' [Jauch and Glueck, 1988] and to 'provide an opportunity to analyse the strategic issues of specific organisations in ... depth ... and often to provide solutions' [Johnson and Scholes, 1989].

STRATEGIC MANAGEMENT CASES: SOME QUESTIONS

The above assertions are based upon the belief that the case study captures enough of the strategic realities of a situation to provide a worth while exercise in analysis and decision making. But how realistic are strategic management case studies?

There are limits upon the ability of case writers to depict the realities of organisations. Strategic management case studies contain a variety and often a depth of information, but, as with any other act of reporting, the information is limited. With some notable exceptions - for example the research for the Swatch case study [Pinson, 1987] - the amount of time that senior executives will spend in interview constrains the case writers' understanding of the company. There are also issues of confidentiality and unintended bias that reflect a managers particular organisational and professional perspective. Faced with these limits on the information available the case writer's task becomes one of achieving sufficient information for the task at hand, in order to produce a training device that will prove worthwhile in developing the students skills and understanding. The case writer acts as an editor selecting and emphasising amongst the various issues and perspectives that have been encountered to provide an apparently comprehensive, ordered and coherent document.

There is a second and deeper question concerning the nature not of case studies but of the strategy process, the process which the case method is attempting to simulate. There is a lack of academic agreement concerning the nature of the strategy process. In a review of the strategic management literature Mintzberg [Mintzberg, 1990] recalls the fable of the blind men who are asked to describe an elephant. Like the elephant the literature of strategic management is vast and varied and each study is usually concerned with a part of the whole. From that literature Mintzberg identifies ten schools of thought concerning the nature of the strategy process. The schools identified vary profoundly in their assumptions. For the prescriptive schools (the design, planning and positioning schools), the strategic decision making process bears a strong resemblance to the typical case study session. Strategy is a conscious process, determined at a point in time, by a clearly identified set of actors, through an act of creativity or analysis. In contrast descriptive studies of the strategy process find the process to be based upon vision (the entrepreneurial school), a political process, organisational culture or organisational learning. For each of these schools strategic decision making is a less overt process, a process that typically extends over a considerable period of time [Mintzberg et al, 1976 and Quinn, 1980] and one that is not primarily based upon analysis.

Can the case method prepare students for involvement in the strategy process? Or, as Mintzberg claims [Mintzberg, 1990], does the use of cases lead to a misleading simplification of the realities of the strategy process which may in the extreme prove dangerous by leading managers to lose touch with the real sources of strategic understanding, encouraging them to remain in their offices 'waiting for pithy reports instead of getting outside where the real information for strategy making usually has to be dug out' [Mintzberg, 1990]. Mintzberg's conclusion is contentious [Goold, 1992], but there is clearly an established body of observation and theory concerning the nature of the strategy process that supports the conclusion that the case method is a questionable way of preparing students for participation in the strategy process.

Despite these issues concerning strategic management case studies the case method remains a central part of strategic management teaching. The continuing use of cases invites a number of fundamental questions:

Why do lecturers and instructors use case studies to teach strategic management. What are their objectives in using case studies?

How effective are cases in meeting those objectives and what are the problems and difficulties in using case studies?

How do other teaching methods compare with case studies in terms of their comparative strengths and weaknesses?

THE RESEARCH

In order to help answer these questions a questionnaire-based survey of lecturers involved in postgraduate and post experience management education was undertaken. The principal question included in the questionnaire was open, inviting the respondents to describe their main objectives in using case studies as part of the teaching method. Respondents were asked to rank those objectives in order of importance and also to use a five point scale (excellent to poor) to evaluate the degree to which, in view of the general performance of their students, each of the objectives was attained. The remaining questions sought to identify the other methods used in the teaching of strategic management and to evaluate their strengths and weaknesses compared to the use of case studies, to estimate the number of cases used and the main problems, obstacles and difficulties that the use of cases involved.

The questionnaire was administered by post to a sample of lecturers at UK higher education institutions. The sample was drawn from the membership list of BETA (The Business Education Teachers Association). Strategic Management (also known as Business Strategy or Business Policy) is a common subject in UK business schools, it is to be expected that all business schools on the BETA mailing list would be involved in teaching the subject. The questionnaire was sent to a named person at forty nine institutions, sixteen questionnaires were returned, a response rate of thirty two per cent. All of the responses were usable.

RESEARCH FINDINGS AND DISCUSSION

OBJECTIVES IN USING CASE STUDIES

The lecturers were asked to state their objectives in using case studies as part of the teaching method.

TABLE 1
CASE STUDY OBJECTIVES

OBJECTIVE.	EXPRESSED AS:	AS A PROPORTION OF ALL OBJECTIVES CITED
ILLUSTRATIVE		34%
	to illustrate - discussion points - the methodology of real world decisions - to add to experience of organisations	
INTEGRATIVE		12%
	to integrate - the activities of functional areas - theory and practice - knowledge about various subject areas	
INFORMATION SKILLS		4%
	to develop - research skills - information handling skills	
STRATEGIC ANALYSIS / STRATEGIC THINKING		18%
	to encourage - the development of analytical skills - strategic thinking	
COMMUNICATION AND INTERPERSONAL SKILLS		15%
	to develop - group working - report writing - presentation skills	
PEDAGOGIC EXPEDIENCE (using cases to maintain the		16%
teaching process, in contrast to a student based learning objective) to - provide interest and stimulate discussion - to prevent boredom		

Typically each lecturer was seeking a number of objectives in using cases, the sixteen respondents listed a total of sixty seven objectives. These could be categorised to identify six sets of objectives.

Table 1 shows case users to be seeking a variety of objectives through the case method. The most commonly cited objectives are illustrative, the use of cases to provide description of real world situations, this use accounted for one third of all responses and was cited by over eighty per cent of the respondents.

There are a further four major sets of objectives. Integration, using cases to develop the participants understanding of interactions and relationships whether that is between various business functions, or the interaction between theory and practice or the relationships between various academic subject areas. The objective of developing strategic analysis and strategic thinking. The development of communication and interpersonal skills and the use of cases to facilitate the teaching process for example through avoiding boredom, pedagogic expedience. Each of these four sets of objectives brought a similar number of responses (twelve to eighteen per cent of responses). The development of research and information handling skills was of minor significance accounting for under five per cent of the objectives cited.

The pattern of responses is surprising in its generality. Overall the case users are concerned with objectives that are either illustrative or concern a range of understandings and management skills most of which are required by, but not exclusive to, the strategic decision making process. In general these objectives do not suggest that a particular school of thought concerning the strategy process, nor a group of schools (for example based upon a prescriptive viewpoint), is implicit in use of the case method.

THE EFFECTIVENESS OF CASE STUDIES

The research assessed effectiveness in two ways, success in achieving the participation of students and achievement of objectives. The case method is a participative form of teaching typically involving three phases, preparation (as a group or individual exercise), presentation and discussion. In general the use of cases appears to be associated with high student participation. Considering all of the phases of a case exercise, seventy five per cent of the respondents rated student participation as one or two on a five point scale, excellent to poor.

To explore the success of the case method in achieving the particular objectives (outlined in Table 1) a five point rating scale was used for respondents to evaluate the performance of their students. The results are summarized in Table 2.

TABLE 2
PERFORMANCE IN ACHIEVING OBJECTIVES

OBJECTIVE.	RATING.
1. COMMUNICATION AND INTERPERSONAL SKILLS	91%
2. INTEGRATIVE	71%
3. PEDAGOGIC EXPEDIENCE	67%
4. ILLUSTRATIVE	62%
5. STRATEGIC ANALYSIS / STRATEGIC THINKING	57%

(rating is based upon proportion of an objectives ratings achieving the first two points of a five point scale 'Excellent' to 'Poor') (omitting 'Information Skills' due to low number of responses).

The case method appears to be a highly successful vehicle for the development of communication and interpersonal skills. This use requires the case study exercise to be structured to provide opportunity for reporting, group work and possible role playing. Any deficiencies in the case material may be compensated for by the process that the student is required to undertake.

The least successful use of cases is in the development of strategic analysis and strategic thinking. The objective received both the lowest overall rating (57%) and was also the only objective where performance was rated as poor by some respondents. At the same time case studies do not appear to be particularly successful in their most commonly cited purpose, their use as illustrative documents.

The respondents were asked to identify the main problems, obstacles and difficulties that they encountered in using cases. The replies are idiosyncratic with specific concerns not being widely shared, however the issues identified can be summarised to a number of headings that reflect various aspects of the operation of the case method (Table 3).

Overall the problems and difficulties indicate that cases often fall short of the particular requirements of the course on which they are used and may not provide the user with a convincing and realistic document. The limited success of cases in achieving their main objective, illustrative use, gains some explanation from the problems of 'relevance'. The reported lack of public sector, U.K. and European cases and cases including women managers, the age of the case material and its cultural context, all limit the illustrative potential of the case method. The problems that result in a case not providing sufficient scope for analysis, lack of information and the encouragement of a particular solution, obviously limit the achievement of objectives directed toward developing the skills of strategic analysis and strategic thinking.

These failings may not be intrinsic to the case method. Many of the problems, such as relevance, the demands on students time and the issue of providing sufficient scope for analysis, could in principle be resolved by case users producing their own case material. Even so there are dilemmas, for example between writing a case to suit the availability of student time and the inclusion of sufficient data to support analysis.

Many of the respondents identified a problem with resources, however the issue needs to be interpreted against the number of cases that are used by lecturers. From the survey, usage by individual lecturers ranges from three cases in a years teaching to over fifty, the most common quantity being between eleven and fifteen cases a year. The intensive use of cases makes it infeasible for most users of case material to write all of their own material, unless such case writing is based upon cooperative effort, for example by a faculty.

TABLE 3
PROBLEMS AND DIFFICULTIES

RESOURCES
Published cases are often expensive, as are texts including cases. There is a lack of time for writing case writing. Colleagues may be reluctant to share case material. The use of cases requires a high level of staff commitment.

RELEVANCE
There is a lack of public sector material, U.K. material, cases that provide a European perspective and of material that includes senior women managers in key roles. The company depicted in the case may be unknown to the tutor and students. It can be difficult for the tutor to understand the material. It can be difficult to judge whether a case will 'work', many cases may be discarded after one use. After considering the cases complexity and topic it may be questionable whether the case material is correct for the course. Cases can be used indiscriminately. Case material can become dated. Cultural differences can be difficult. It can be questioned whether the case is 'real' or a projection of the authors own views.

DEMANDS ON STUDENTS TIME
There may be too much or too little information for the time available. Students, especially part-time students, may not give the case a full reading. The resulting discussion can be too open for the time available.

SCOPE FOR ANALYSIS
The case may encourage a particular solution. Many cases lack information giving industry background and there may be a lack of material for conducting analysis.

OTHER LEARNING METHODS

All but one of the sixteen lecturers reported using other methods in the teaching of strategic management. The various methods were evaluated by the respondents to identify their strengths and weaknesses compared to the use of case studies. The responses are summarized in Table 4.

A range of alternative teaching methods are available and each method has significant strengths and weaknesses. Most lecturers employ multiple teaching methods and the various methods are most likely used to complement each other and to add variety to the overall teaching method.

The case method is not unique in providing real world insight. Other methods can be used to provide this dimension of the learning experience whether that is through use of video, the inclusion of guest speakers or the orientation of tutorials and seminars to a current or company issue. Company based and consultancy projects located in live organisations appear to be particularly promising in terms of their realism and the range of skills involved.

TABLE 4
OTHER LEARNING METHODS

METHOD

LECTURE WITH DISCUSSION
    Strength
        Good coverage of material
        Ability to focus on issues
        Clear communication of knowledge of the subject
        Efficient
    Weakness
        Low participation, low reflection
        No / low skill development
        Student boredom
        Low absorption of information

GUEST SPEAKERS
    Strength
        From 'the real world'
    Weakness
        May communicate realism poorly

VIDEOS
    Strength
        Depict real life
    Weakness
        Insufficient availability

TUTORIAL
  BASED ON CURRENT ISSUES
    Strength
        Current
        Student participation
        Provides a range of views
        General statements can be derived
    Weakness
        Difficulty in maintaining direction
        Possible dominance by strong individual
        Students may seek definite answers

  BASED ON AN ARTICLE
    Strength
        Directs toward specific issues
    Weakness
        Low student credibility
        Possible low participation

SEMINAR, SUBJECT OR COMPANY FOCUSED
    Strength
        Focused discussion
        Up to date
        Real companies
        Involves preparation and research
    Weakness
        Situation may allow non participation, lack of
        research and preparation

BUSINESS GAMES
    Strength
        Complex
        Helps develop scenarios
        Competitive situation
        Participants can see the effect of decisions
        Interest
        Hands on experience
    Weakness
        Lack of realism, static aspects
        Time consuming
        Costly and demanding on staff resources

COMPANY BASED PROJECTS
    Strength
        Discovery
        Understanding
        Develop research skills
        Model testing
        Relevance, through self selecting organisation
        Self direction and management
    Weakness
        Restrictions on information access
        Time consuming
        Difficulty in application of theory
        Difficulty in generalising findings

CONSULTANCY PROJECTS
    Strength
        Includes responsibility to client
    Weakness
        Little or no scope for experimentation
        May not be controllable

CONCLUSION, GETTING THE MOST OUT OF CASE STUDIES

The survey results indicate that case studies are a major method in the teaching of strategic management. All of the respondents used case studies and the most common rate of use, between eleven and fifteen cases per year, indicates that for strategic management case study forms an important part of the teaching method. Cases appear to be a successful way of teaching the subject. Student participation is reported as high as is general performance in achieving teaching objectives.

The research confirms the importance of cases in the teaching of strategic management but it also helps to define the role of case study teaching. Cases have their major use as illustrative material. In addition case teaching in strategic management is as much concerned with developing widely defined general management skills as it is concerned with developing strategic analysis and strategic thinking. The objectives that are being sought through the use of case study appear to be sufficiently general as to support the use of the case method by all strategic management lecturers and instructors, whether they adhere to a cultural, political or analytical understanding of the strategy process. Cases are a relevant teaching method regardless of school of thought concerning the strategy process.

The study supports a number of proposals that would improve the effectiveness of case studies in the teaching of strategic management.

Firstly, as case writers we need to ask: are the results surprising? The personal view of this author is 'yes'. If I have to locate myself within strategic management, my inclination is to follow a prescriptive approach, the positioning school [Mintzberg, 1990] as developed by Michael Porter [Porter, 1985]. The implicit objective behind cases that I write has been to 'tell that tale', to provide a teaching vehicle that will help students to develop their analytical skills. If cases are to achieve their full potential use their authors need to ask how well their material,

238

and the way that it is structured and presented, will serve the objectives of other lecturers, who may be more concerned with illustration, the demonstration of other themes and the development of other skills.

Secondly, there is a need to reconsider the way that case bibliographies and data bases describe cases. For strategic management cases the descriptors usually include, industry, topics(s), length of case and date. This is useful information in the search for material to fit the needs of a course, however the search process could be improved by including terms that directly reflect the common objectives of case users.

Finally, times change but there may always be work for case writers. In the UK there appears to be an unmet need for cases that provide a European perspective and also for material that includes senior women managers. As society and business continue to change the stock of case material will always need rebuilding. The case writer needs to be in touch with how those changes are being interpreted by the case user.

REFERENCES

Goold, M., "Learning and Planning: A Further Observation on the Design School Debate", Strategic Management Journal (Vol. 13, Issue 2, 1992), pp.169-170.

Jauch, L.R. and Glueck, W.F., Business Policy and Strategic Management (McGraw-Hill, 1988).

Johnson, G. and Scholes, K., Exploring Corporate Strategy-Text and Cases (Prentice Hall, 1989).

Mintzberg, H., Raisinghani, D. and Theoret, A., "The Structure of 'Unstructured' Decision Processes", Administrative Science Quarterly (June 1976), pp. 246-275.

Mintzberg, H., "Strategy Formation Schools of Thought", in Fredrickson, J.W., Perspectives on Strategic Management (Harper Business, 1990).

Mintzberg, H. and Quinn, J.B., The Strategy Process, Concepts, Contexts and Cases (Prentice-Hall 1991).

Pinson, C., Swatch (European Case Clearing House Ltd., Cranfield Institute of Technology, 1987).

Porter, M.E., Competitive Advantage: Creating and Sustaining Superior Performance (New York Free Press, 1985).

Quinn, J.B., Strategies for Change: Logical Incrementalism (Irwin, 1980).

CHAPTER SIX

A DIALOGUE OF THE DEAF?[1]

Emmanuel Kamdem
École Supérieure des Sciences Économiques et Commerciales (ESSEC)
DOUALA, CAMEROON

Abstract

At a meeting the progress of a project they are carrying out in partnership, Jimmy, and American businessman, and Mamadou, an African businessman, get into a discussion of management principles and practices. They end up realizing that their project depends on one essential element: cultural values. These values may, at one and the same time, contribute to and detract from the success of their project.

A DIALOGUE OF THE DEAF?

Jimmy, an American businessman, and Mamadou, an African businessman, meet to discuss an industrial project in which they are partners. A portion of their conversation follows.

Jimmy: So, Mamadou, how's our project coming along?

Mamadou: Not too badly, my friend, except that since the new production unit started up, I've been really swamped. We've run into all kinds of technical glitches, administrative hitches and personnel problems. I feel as if I have a thousand problems to solve every day. Otherwise, it looks good, provided I stay on top of everything.

Jimmy: Remember what I keep telling you: managing a company is like running an obstacle course. There are obstacles everywhere and you have to be constantly ready to surmount them, otherwise you'll give up right away. You have to be vigilant, plan carefully and, above all, avoid improvising. In business, it just doesn't pay.

Mamadou: You're right, Jimmy. Planning, evaluating, scheduling, and so on, it's what we all learned at university and continue to learn at the seminars we go to. In your country, things run smoothly because the rules of the game are clear for everyone, and everyone knows what they're supposed to do. Over here, we have to explain everything, remind everyone of everything, and always be looking over people's shoulders to be sure they're doing their work, even the ones who've lived in countries like yours.

Jimmy: That's why, in our previous conversations, I've always insisted that you have to properly train the people you work with, instead of simply considering them employees who draw a salary. That's participatory management: you get your employees to collaborate with you, rather than placing constraints on them or helping them.

Mamadou: You know, Jimmy, everything you've said makes sense. It works where you come from. Participatory management, making a company more human, and so on. Apparently the Japanese are big on it right now...

Jimmy:	Look, here's an example: we've been sitting here talking for about an hour, and your commercial representative, a university graduate who has more than three years of seniority, has called you twice simply to ask whether he can give preferential prices to certain customers.
Mamadou:	To you, it seems so simple! But it's more complicated than it looks. Once, just to see what would happen, during my annual vacation, I let him set the special prices we give to certain important customers. And what do you think I discovered when I got back? He was giving special prices to whomever he felt like, especially to certain customers who buy negligible amounts from us. He told me it was a way of holding on to these customers and attracting new ones. In point of fact, nothing was being done openly and formally, and the situation was frustrating for certain customers, who let me know indirectly.
Jimmy:	If you find that bringing authority back up to your level makes things easier, why are you complaining about being overloaded?
Mamadou:	Of course it doesn't make things easier. But, for the time being, it's hard to do things any other way.
Jimmy:	Let's take another example. When the new production unit started up three years ago, we set certain objectives together. Achieving the objectives was intended to strengthen the project (inspection and testing of the old machines, skill upgrading or gradual retraining of the machine operators, restructuring of the customer network, etc.). A budget was allocated, and the operations were to be completed in two years. We're in the third year and things are barely getting started.
Mamadou:	Don't be so pessimistic, Jimmy. It's true, I've barely begun putting in place the structures and the people we need to achieve the objectives. We'll get there, but it will just take longer. But better late than never.
Jimmy:	Listen, Mamadou, when you've got a scheduled project for which resources have been provided, you can't delay it indefinitely with no valid reason.
Mamadou:	Do you really think there's no valid reason?
Jimmy:	What is it then? I'd like to know.
Mamadou:	Often you have to be careful not to breathe down people's necks. You have to take each person's pace into account.
Jimmy:	Well, I find your pace pretty slow.
Mamadou:	It all depends on how you see each person's pace.
Jimmy:	Well, if you don't mind, let's go back to the problem of maintenance of the new facilities. They cost us a lot of money so it's in our interest to ensure they're maintained properly. As we agreed, the maintenance specialist will be spending some time here to evaluate the work of the local crew.
Mamadou:	Oh, yes. I had almost forgotten. Thanks for reminding me. When do you think he'll be available?
Jimmy:	In the fall or next spring.
Mamadou:	As long as it doesn't coincide with Ramadan. Most of our maintenance people are Muslim and

when they're fasting, absenteeism goes up and productivity goes down. When you say fall or spring, exactly which months are you talking about?

Jimmy: If you want, it could be either during the last quarter of the year, or before the next annual vacation. When is Ramadan?

Mamadou: There's no specific period; it changes every year. We'll know the exact dates in a few weeks.

Jimmy: In that case, let me know as soon as you find out so I can talk to the specialist and find out when he's available.

Mamadou: By the way, Jimmy, what finally happened to your friend Bob, the one who was looking for industrial partners in Africa?

Jimmy: Well, Bob's story is quite a funny one. After several less-than-successful attempts, he gave up. Right now, he's in Central Europe, where he hopes to do better. You know, the countries in that area have recently opened up to the market economy, and there's a lot of interest on the part of European, American and Japanese investors.

Mamadou: Are you saying those investors aren't particularly interested in Africa?

Jimmy: No, I wouldn't go that far. The proof is that we're working together. But it isn't easy to do business with you people, because you combine everything: business, politics, the family, the village, religion, etc. In the United States, we say: "Business is business." That's the basis on which we work.

Mamadou: Yes, but do you think we can do business without taking into account everything you just listed?

Jimmy: That's not quite it. I simply meant that being an entrepreneur or the manager of a business is a job, or an occupation, that has basic rules, requirements, ups and downs, and so on. If you take that into account, you should be able to find an efficient approach that will enable you to achieve your performance objectives.

Mamadou: I agree completely with your analysis. But, you know, everything depends on what you mean by objectives and performance.

Jimmy: Look, management isn't literature or philosophy. Those activities have their requirements, just as management has its. Above all, you have to keep things separate. Do you really think an individual or a group will agree to put money into a project, to recruit people, to train them and pay them to manage it, and not want to end up with positive, concrete results?

Mamadou: Do you think you can manage a project without taking into account all the unknowns that crop up? The politicians, the friends, the relatives and all the others who won't let you get your work done and who don't understand anything when you talk to them about objectives or performance.

Jimmy: So, what should we do to improve things?

Mamadou: That's The question I've been asking myself, day and night, ever since I decided to become an entrepreneur in my country.

INSTRUCTIONAL NOTES FOR A DISCUSSION OF THE CASE

CASE OBJECTIVES

The case has three main objectives:
- to show the importance of intercultural misunderstandings in communication and, generally, in behaviour;
- to identify and to analyze the source of these misunderstandings, as well as their impact on behaviour within an organization;
- to lead to possible research topics on interactions between culture and management.

ORGANIZATION OF THE DISCUSSION

The following suggestions can be used to lead a discussion of the case:
- identify and explain the main sources of misunderstandings that arise in the conversation between the two partners;
- discuss the impact that these misunderstandings may have on the behaviour of the two men and on the development of their partnership project;
- discuss how the misunderstandings can be reduced so that the two partners can understand each other better.

ENDNOTES

1. This case was inspired by a text written by G. Amado, C. Faucheux and A. Laurent (1990): "Changement organisationnel et réalités culturelles". It is intended to serve as the framework for an educational discussion. No judgment of the administrative situation referred to is implied.

REFERENCES

"AMADO, G.; FAUCHEUX, C.; LAURENT, A. "Changement organisationnel et réalités culturelles" in J.-F. CHANLAT (dir.), L'individu dans l'organisation : les dimensions oubliées, QuEbec, Les presses de l'Université Laval, Éditions ESKA, 1990, p. 629-662.

"DESAUNAY, G. "Les relations humaines dans les entreprises ivoiriennes", Revue Française de Gestion, No. 64, September-October 1987, p. 95-101.

"D'IRIBARNE, P. La logique de l'honneur. Gestion des entreprises et traditions nationales, Paris, Éditions du Seuil, 1989.

"ETOUNGA-MANGUELLE, D. L'Afrique a-t-elle besoin d'un programme d'ajustement culturel?, Yvry-Sur-Seine, Éditions Nouvelles du Sud, 1990.

"HALL, E.T.; HALL, M.R. Guide du comportement dans les affaires internationales, Paris, Éditions du Seuil, 1990.

"HENRY, A. "Peut-on redresser une entreprise africaine en respectant la parole des ancêtres?", Annales des mines, gérer et comprendre, September 1988, p. 86-94.

"HENRY, A. "Les possibilités d'une efficacité spécifique des entreprises africaines", PME Gestion, ESSEC Douala / HEC Montréal, Vol. 2, No. 4, April 1991.

"HOFSTEDE, G. "Relativité culturelle des pratiques et théories de l'organisation", Revue Française de Gestion, No. 64, September-October 1987, p. 10-21.

"KAMDEM, E. "Culture, temps et comportements au travail. Éléments pour une étude des facteurs culturels du management", <u>Gestion, revue internationale de gestion</u>, Vol. 11, No. 3, September 1986, p. 36-43.

"OLOMO, P.R. "Comment concilier tradition et modernité dans l'entreprise africaine", <u>Revue Française de Gestion</u>, No. 64, September-October 1987, p. 91-94.

GDYNIA PORT AUTHORITY

Christopher B. Spivey
The Citadel
CHARLESTON, SOUTH CAROLINA, U.S.A.
Tadeusz Koscielak
Ministry of Privatization
WARSAW, POLAND

Abstract

Gdynia Port Authority is an undergraduate level case study of a proposal for a capital improvement project for the grain handling facility at the port of Gdynia, Poland. The construction of new facilities and the installation of new machinery will reduce operating costs, increase grain storage capacity, and speed up loading and unloading. This case presents a capital budgeting problem in which the student must identify marginal costs and marginal returns, and decide whether or not the net marginal returns justify the investment. This case is based on field research.

GDYNIA PORT AUTHORITY

The Port of Gdynia is located on the Baltic coast just north of Gdansk, and was built after the First World War when the treaty of Versailles gave Poland an opening to the Baltic. The treaty also declared the port city of Gdansk (Danzig) a free city, but its Germanic composition at that time convinced Poland that they needed port facilities on Polish soil. The construction of the port at Gdynia during the interwar period included a grain handling facility built in 1937. In 1992 these facilities were basically unchanged: 55 years old and in serviceable condition, but obsolete and fully depreciated. Some minor improvements had been made by adding automatic controls to some functions, and by replacing some machinery. Basically, the grain facility continued to operate the same way it had since 1937, with the same physical plant.

In early 1992 the port's board of directors was considering a capital improvement project for the grain handling facility that would increase the grain storage capacity, decrease operating costs, and speed up loading and unloading.

At this time the grain facility could handle up to 250 metric tons per hour (for export) with the old pneumatic machinery. With this obsolete equipment, however, the 250 tons per hour pace can not be maintained. The maximum import rate is about 3,500 tons per day and the maximum export rate is about 2,500 tons per day. Import capacity exceeds export capacity because imported grain stored in the silos can be loaded onto trucks or railcars faster than grain coming the other way can be unloaded into the silos.

Although the grain facilities at Gdynia occasionally handle rapeseed or rye, almost all of the grain shipped through the port is wheat. The 21 silos at the port can store around 12,000 tons of various grains. These silos store grain that will be shipped to different destinations, so the 12,000 ton storage capacity is only rarely available to service a single shipment. If storage is not available in the silos, grain must be loaded onto the ship directly from trucks or railcars - presently a cumbersome process that ties up vehicles, ships, and facilities. The capital improvement plans call for a large increase in silo capacity, to 25,000 metric tons, allowing for better scheduling. Although this improved scheduling capability is important, the main source of the port's increased grain handling capacity will be the more efficient loading and unloading system; direct from truck or railcar to ship. The new facilities will include two truck turning stations and a railcar turner. With this system, the vehicles are unloaded by turning them over and dumping the grain into a loader. The new system will allow ships to be loaded simultaneously from truck, railcar, and silo. This faster loading will allow both ships and vehicles to spend less time in port.

Poland is an agricultural country that usually exports wheat, but trouble in agricultural production in a few recent years had seen net wheat imports, including imports through the Port of Gdynia. By 1991, however, the farm sector had recovered somewhat and Gdynia handled around 450,000 tons of wheat that year, almost all export. The board of directors expected future grain shipments to be mostly wheat exports. Considering Poland's wheat growing capacity compared to its projected need for wheat, the board expected grain exports through the facility at Gdynia to increase to around 900,000 to 1,000,000 metric tons annually. This could not happen, of course, unless the handling capacity increased.

Mean low water depth alongside the grain dock is 9½ meters, allowing only ships less than 15,000 tons of displacement to dock there. 10 meters from the dock the water depth is 12 meters, allowing ships up to 25,000 tons to be unloaded if they anchored out 10 meters from the dock and used an extended unloading boom. This is the deepest grain dock in Poland. Business from larger ships is usually lost to Hamburg. With Hamburg charging a handling fee of $4.50 per ton and Gdynia charging $7 (all charges paid in U.S. dollars) some shippers in western Poland find it cheaper to use Hamburg to reach the overseas market, in spite of high overland shipping costs. The capital improvements include a dock extension to deeper water, and will allow ships up to 70,000 tons to dock. Kaliningrad and Rostock are marginally competitive ports, but are no serious threat to Gdynia. Gdansk, however, could pose a serous threat to Gdynia's grain shipping operation by building a modern grain facility and taking away the business needed at Gdynia to make the new facilities profitable.

The renovation project is expected to cost about $12,000,000: $5,000,000 for machinery, $5,000,000 for construction costs, and $2,000,000 for freight, taxes, customs charges, and other costs. Although both the machinery and the construction are expected to last as well as the old equipment - over 50 years - they have an estimated useful economic life of 10 years and will be depreciated over 10 years. The machinery will be imported, and the price is quoted in U.S. dollars. The construction and other costs (total $7,000,000) are priced in Polish zloti at ZL11,500 to the U.S. dollar. In recent years the Polish zloti has shown a rapid and persistent decline in value relative to hard currencies. The board of directors expects this to continue. The Gdynia Port Authority has almost ZL60 billion available for these capital improvements, and up to $10 million is available through a 10 year 8½% fixed rate non-amortized dollar loan arrange by Cubic Marine Co. of Great Britain.

The old machinery operates on 930 kilowatts of power and loads 250 tons of grain per hour. The new machinery operates on 200 kilowatts and can load 400 tons per hour. A kilowatt of energy costs ZL500, but this is expected to increase sharply as the power plant adjusts to a market economy. It now takes 40 men to run the grain operation in 4 shifts, with 10 men per shift. The new machinery will cut this number drastically, to a total of 10 people. Labor costs would go from ZL4.75 billion to ZL1.75 billion, including payroll taxes. There are other costs involved in operating the grain facility. An annual ground rent is paid to the local government, there is a tax on asset value similar to a property tax, a tax on "surplus" similar to an income tax, a tonnage fee incurred by the shipper, and other minor costs. With the exception of the income tax, all of these costs are fixed costs or otherwise not attributable to the capital improvement project. The board considers the status of the corporate income in Poland to be very uncertain, and wants an analysis on a pre-tax basis.

Should the Gdynia Port Authority board of visitors upgrade the grain handling facility?

TEACHING NOTES

Although debt service will have to be paid in U.S. dollars, the handling fee received by the port authority is also in dollars, minimizing exchange rate risks. In fact, there is change to come out ahead on currency exposure since part of the costs faced by the grain elevator are in deteriorating zloti.

Can the interest be paid? If the tonnage of grain handled is increased to 550,000, the increase in cash flow can pay the interest.

Will earnings improve? Expenses will change: fixed operating costs (labor) will decrease by $261,000, energy will decrease by 14 cents per ton, interest will increase by $1,020,000 (8½% of $12 million), and depreciation will increase by $1,200,000 (straight line, $12 million/10 years). This is a net increase in expenses of almost $2 million annually. The cost of energy, the only variable cost listed here, will decrease from 16 cents per ton to 2 cents per ton if the new machinery is installed. With a revenue of $7 for each ton of grain handled, around 720,000 tons will have to be processed before earnings improve.

Should the improvements be made? Do the benefits exceed the costs? Exhibits A and B show the projection of cash flows that depend on the adoption of the capital improvement project. If the port can maintain the $7 per ton fee, an 8½% cost of capital would require the handling of between 650,000 to 700,000 tons to generate a positive net present value. If Gdynia were forced to lower its fees to $4.50 per ton to meet competition from other ports, they would need to handle a little less than 800,000 tons to generate a positive net present value. A 12% cost of capital would increase these figures to roughly 710,000 tons and 850,000 tons respectively. The 900,000 to 1,000,000 tons per year projected by the board of directors is higher than all of these figures. If the board's projection is credible, the improvements should be made.

EXHIBIT A
RENOVATION PROJECT NET PRESENT VALUE AT VARIOUS TONNAGE RATES ($7/TON)

	450,000 tons	500,000 tons	550,000 tons	600,000 tons	650,000 tons	700,000 tons	750,000 tons	800,000 tons
Additional Revenue[1]	None	$ 225	$ 450	$ 675	$ 900	$1125	$1350	$1575
Labor Costs Saved[2]	413	414	413	413	413	413	413	413
Labor Costs Incurred[3]	(152)	(152)	(152)	(152)	(152)	(152)	(152)	(152)
Energy Costs Saved[4]	72	72	72	72	72	72	72	72
Energy Costs Incurred[5]	(9)	(10)	(11)	(12)	(13)	(14)	(15)	(16)
Marginal Return	324	548	772	996	1220	1444	1668	1892
Annuity Factor 6.5613								
Present Value	2126	3596	5065	6535	8005	9475	10944	12414
Initial Investment	-12000	-12000	-12000	-12000	-12000	-12000	-12000	-12000
Net Present Value	($9874)	($8404)	($6935)	($5465)	($3995)	($2525)	($1056)	$ 414

1. $7 x tons over 450,000
2. ZL4.75/11,500 = $413,000
3. ZL1.75/11,500 = $152,000
4. 450,000 x 16c = $72,00
5. 2c x tonnage

EXHIBIT B
RENOVATION PROJECT NET PRESENT VALUE AT VARIOUS TONNAGE RATES ($4.50/TON)

	450,000 tons	500,000 tons	550,000 tons	600,000 tons	650,000 tons	700,000 tons	750,000 tons	800,000 tons
Additional Revenue[1]	None	$350	$700	$1050	$1400	$1750	$2100	$2450
Labor Costs Saved[2]	413	414	413	413	413	413	413	413
Labor Costs Incurred[3]	(152)	(152)	(152)	(152)	(152)	(152)	(152)	(152)
Energy Costs Saved[4]	72	72	72	72	72	72	72	72
Energy Costs Incurred[5]	(9)	(10)	(11)	(12)	(13)	(14)	(15)	(16)
Marginal Return	324	673	1022	1372	1722	2069	2418	2767
Annuity Factor 6.5613								
Present Value	2126	4416	6706	9002	11299	13575	15865	18155
Initial Investment	-12000	-12000	-12000	-12000	-12000	-12000	-12000	-12000
Net Present Value	($9874)	($7584)	($5294)	($2998)	($701)	$1575	$3865	$6155

1. $7 x tons over 450,000
2. ZL4.75/11,500 = $413,000
3. ZL1.75/11,500 = $152,000
4. 450,000 x 16c = $72,00
5. 2c x tonnage

AN IDENTITY STUDY OF FIRM MERGERS:
THE CASE OF A FRENCH SAVINGS BANK

Bertrand Moingeon
Bernard Ramanantsoa
HEC Graduate School of Management
PARIS, FRANCE

Abstract

During the implementation phase of firm mergers, many problems often arise. The human ones seem to be the most difficult to deal with. The merging of firms and the setting up of a new structure lead to existing identities being challenged. The case study of a French savings bank created by the merger of several organizations gives an empirical illustration of the theoretical framework we suggest to use in order to get a better understanding of those problems. A study of identity goes further than cultural approaches which remain at a descriptive level (describing problems more than explaining them). The analysis of the firm's identity brings to light root causes of the "cultural clashes."

As the business media periodically remind us, problems often appear during the launch of a merger between companies. It is usually the custom to set apart the human problems from the technical ones. Those last ones are usually considered as being easier to solve. In some cases, the implementation of the solutions does not succeed as planned. It is then, that the companies' managers discover that a problem identified as purely technical is really a problem of human dimension that they had overseen. Many well documented studies give an exact idea of the type of difficulties which can occur (e.g. [Buono, Bowditch, Lewis, 1988], [Buono, Bowditch, 1989]). Some researchers have especially analyzed the cultural collisions coming with those strategic movements (e.g. [Walter, 1985]). The empirical study that we have made meets that view point. Beyond the description of the feeling of the people involved in a merger, beyond the discovery of problems, it seems very important to us to find a way to identify the roots of those problems. The identity perspective which we suggest will allow for the understanding of the "why" of these problems.

A STUDY OF THE IDENTITY: THEORETICAL FOUNDATIONS

The notion of identity goes back to the existence of some characteristics which explain the specificity, the stability and the coherence of an organization [Larçon, Reitter, 1979]. More precisely, the identity goes back to the existence of a system of characteristics which has a pattern which gives the company its specificity, its stability and its coherence. The reader may wonder why one speaks of the identity of a company instead of its culture. Many studies of culture give a detailed description of how an organization runs. The authors are driven to bring into light some standards of behavior, some rituals, to describe the organization of the time and the space, and to emphasize the existence of some myths, etc. It is true that those symbolic products are specific to the organization which is being studied. But the description of those symbolic products, indispensable as they are for a diagnosis of an identity, is nevertheless insufficient. It is necessary to identify the elements generating those symbolic products, which we call the "why" of the culture of the company. The symbolic products constitute in fact the visible manifestation of a common organizational imagery ("imaginaire organisationnel") [Reitter, Ramanantsoa, 1985]. It is necessary to study together those symbolic products and this imagery if one wants to understand the running of an organization.

Several theoretical perspectives (psychological, sociological, psycho sociological, etc.) can be adopted to study the identity of a company. We shall strongly suggest here a sociological approach inspired by the theory of the habitus and of the field [Bourdieu, 1989, 1990].

This theoretical choice undoubtedly brings up several questions. In fact in the theory proposed by Pierre Bourdieu, each individual has a specific habitus which is the product of a particular history. "The conditionings associated with a particular class of conditions of existence produce habitus, systems of durable, transposable dispositions, structured structures predisposed to function as structuring structures, that is, as principles which generate and organize practices and representations" [Bourdieu, 1990, 53]. Early experiences play an important role in the formation of the habitus. Each one of us has embodied a certain number of values, a certain number of standards of behavior of which we are no longer aware. They are a part of us, they work without our awareness and they help us to define our vision of the world. Then how can we explain the existence of a common organizational imagery? How do we explain the existence of a common denominator at the level of the individual imagery?

A first answer consists in the emphasis of the presence in certain companies of a strong homogeneity of origin and of social trajectory (some consulting firms come to mind). The way to recruit in those companies is to choose employees with a similar habitus. It all happens as if there was a "selection of habitus at the entrance." But such an explanation can only deal with a restricted number of organizations.

One can reverse the study by saying that the individuals choose to work in those organizations which are compatible with their habitus. That proposal is similar to the one suggested by the psychoanalytical psychology in which the choice of a company by an individual is explained by his psychological economy. A "psychological contract" would then be established between the two parties. But for such a contract to be sealed, it is necessary for the individual to find the organization which suits him or her the best and for there to be a choice of companies (which is not always possible depending on the state of the economy). Even in good times when one can choose the company for which he or she wants to work, the newly-hired employee may find the image he or she now has of the company is not the same as the image he or she held before joining the company. Certain individuals feel chained (the economic situation keeping them from quitting) to an organization which does not appeal to them. Because they do not agree with the collective imagery they will not only invest the minimum amount of themselves in the organization, but also, they will have a very distant and even painful rapport with it.

A second possible response further emphasizes the existence of an acculturation mechanism. It appears that once individuals are in an organization for a long period of time they tend to internalize the values and norms of that organization. How can one realize that this is happening? The company, in being a field, exercises its influence on the habitus. As we have already mentioned, the structure of the habitus itself brings about a certain inertia. However, this structure is not rooted. If the first experiences of an individual have played such an important role in the formation of the habitus, they could, nevertheless, have evolved in function with later experiences. Therefore, one should not conclude that the habitus are structures which can be changed at will. The Directors in upholding the charters of the company and other creeds which have been imposed on the staff of the organization, in hoping to rapidly and durably change the culture of their organization have often experienced several disappointments. The habitus cannot be changed by decree as some recipes for the cultural management of an organization would like for you to believe. The formation and the reproduction of a collective imagery take a long time.

At the beginning of this paper we emphasized the existence of a causal relationship between the organizational imagery and the symbolic products. The definition of the notion of identity which we have held shows that, in time, the company has some relative stability. This stability is linked to the stability of the organizational imagery. Up to now, the question has been how has the imagery survived among the individual people. We believe that two complementary answers can be brought forward. First of all, the organization's staff plays a key role in the acculturation process of the new employees. They initiate them to the "home team spirit" and in that way then transmit the organizational imagery. The second response goes back to the symbolic products. Some of these such as certain myths, rituals, and organizational routines contribute to the collective imagery. There exists a circular causation process between the organizational imagery and the symbolic products. Therefore, the players and certain symbolic products assure the transmission of a heritage of imagery at the foundation of the company's identity.

It comes from this fact that in studying the identity, it is not enough to just describe the symbolic products (as many authors dealing with the culture of a company have done). To limit oneself to what can be observed prohibits the understanding of the roots of the culture, its essence, what proceeds it. On the other hand, an analysis of the imagery disconnected with the symbolic product would keep one from understanding how this imagery persists and survives in the individuals. In order to completely understand the identity of a company it is necessary to study the symbolic productions and the organizational imagery at the same time.

According to the definition which we have proposed, the identity reflects the existence of a system of characteristics which has a particular pattern that bestows to the company its specificity, its stability and its coherence. This definition does not mean to say that each characteristic is specific to that company. It is the particular pattern itself which defines the specificity.

We believe that the richness of this approach in terms of the identity can only be completely revealed once the identity is seized relationally, meaning in reference with other identities. In effect, by studying an organization's identity, one can realize what renders it different from the others - specifically. In other words, a study of a particular organization cannot take place autonomously but must be done with reference to the previous works or in parallel with other studies. In this way one can identify those characteristics within a company which are "firm specific" and those which are not. For example, if one compares two companies in the two different sectors, it could be that the observed differences are really differences reflected in the identities of two different sectors. This same reasoning can be true for different countries or regions. It is for this reason that the identity of a company reflects those elements of a national, regional and /or sectoral identity.

By recognizing the existence of different levels of identity, the question of how these different levels relate is brought up. How can one become aware of the articulation amount of these different levels? The theory of the field proposed by Bourdieu can answer this question. According to this theory, the social field is made up of a group of fields which are in turn made up of sub-fields functioning as fields, etc. It is possible to update at each level, the existence of common properties but also of a relative autonomy as compared to the larger field in which the field being studied is located. Therefore, a division within a company can be apprehended as a sub-field of a company's field which has a relative autonomy, meaning, from the point of view of the identity, having singular symbolic products and collective imagery. Only now, if one compares different divisions of a firm, and if one updates the existence of a common denominator on the level of the imageries, and if one identifies symbolic products on the level of the company as a whole, can one be justified in speaking of the company's identity. Otherwise, if the company is part of a national network then it could be that beyond the differences that exist between the entities within the network, there exist similarities which distinguish the companies in the network from those other companies in the sector. This is notably the case with the network of the French "Caisses d'Epargne." (Please see the case study.)

A STUDY OF THE IDENTITY: METHODOLOGICAL CHOICES

We are now going to describe how a diagnosis of an identity can be made. The study of symbolic products requires a competence in the matter of observation. One has to be able to recognize the rituals, to identify myths, the organizational routines, the work methods, etc. All of this information can be derived from internal documents, by interviews done with members of the organization or also by ethnographic research. However, if one wants to go beyond the description state, one has to proceed with inference in order to establish the link between the observed symbolic products and the organizational imagery. This is not an easy task as we have already proven, the imagery is not directly accessible. The habitus, in being the main generator for the applications and for the representation, functions without the knowledge of the agents.

The existence of a common imagery counts on a certain degree of "sameness" at the level of the staff of the same organization. This "sameness" is the product of the incorporation by an agent of certain specific properties of the organizational field. To arrive at the organizational imagery often requires a genuine work of socio-analysis [Moingeon, Ramanantsoa, 1993]. According to Schein, the staff of a company shares a set of basic assumptions of which they are not aware: "As the values begin to be taken for granted, they gradually become beliefs and assumptions and drop out of consciousness, just as habits become unconscious and automatic" [Schein, 1985, 16]. If we recognize along with Schein that the members of an organization have in their heads a set of basic assumptions of which they are not aware, we believe that these could exist only if the constituent schemas of perception of the habitus allow it.

The study of the organizational imagery can be facilitated by the evocation of three different internal images of the firm [Larçon, Reitter, 1979]: its image in the eyes of its members, their common views on what constitutes ideal qualities, and the way they picture the power distribution.

There are contexts which are more favorable than others in the study of identity. We feel that the period just after the launch of a merger is particularly interesting to study for two reasons. First of all, several companies are involved in a merger. This allows for a comparison which makes it possible to reveal more clearly the specificity of each organization. Secondly, it is often the case of a phase of change during which the existing identities are held back. The human problems, the conflicts which may appear, are made up of the particular symbolic products. This allows for a more direct-access to the imageries. The number of inferences which allow for the release of symbolic products to the imagery is reduced which minimizes the risk of erroneous interpretations.

One of the research hypothesis which we hope to validate by means of this study which we are now going to present is that the problems which appear during the launch of a merger are partially explained by the existence of a confrontation of different imageries.

THE CASE OF THE CAISSE D'EPARGNE OF FRANCHE-COMTE

Before approaching the particular case of the Caisse d'Epargne of Franche-Comté, a few historic points related to the history of the network of the French Caisses d'Epargne need to be made clear. These points are important in the understanding of the context in which this particular merger was located.

The first French Caisse d'Epargne was created in Paris in 1818 by a few philanthropists. Their objective was to teach to as many people as possible "the proper use of money" by demonstrating, notably, the benefits of savings. By refusing a charitable procedure which would lead to the recreation of an obedient link which previously united the rich and the poor, or a procedure which would have been a state-run management of poverty, they opted for a pedagogical procedure, which was, in their eyes, the only method capable of realistically consolidating the new social order with the liberal politics in place at that time. A basic network of Caisses d'Epargne was in place during the 19th century (more than 500 autonomous Caisses each having a statue of "private bodies of public utility" existed in 1880). "Primary schools of capitalism" [Duet, 1991], the Caisses d'Epargne invited their client to regularly deposit their savings in a "Livret," a kind of savings account. The money collected with the aid of this Livret was managed by the state via the "Caisse des Dépôts et Consignations." The effects this state tutelage had on the strategy of these institutions are still visible to this day. It was not until the end of World War II that a process of diversification was undertaken, albeit one that remained closely controlled by the state. For a very long time, the role of the Caisses d'Epargne was limited to that of a collector of funds, while the banking functions that determined how those funds were to be used were assured by the "Caisse des Dépôts et Consignations."

After the reform law of 1983 and the banking law of 1984 (to which the Caisses d'Epargne are attached), a "Centre National des Caisses d'Epargne" (CENCEP) was created to bring the French Caisses d'Epargne under one roof. Sociétés Régionales de Financement (SOREFI) were set up to serve as regional banks for the Caisses d'Epargne. The SOREFI were credit institutions (financial corporations), with the status of Private Limited Companies. They were responsible for managing "everyday resources": current accounts, vouchers, mortgage accounts, etc. They were set up to decentralize throughout the network the financial functions previously ensured by the Caisse des Dépôts et Consignations. The latter remained in charge of reemploying funds collected by the Caisses d'Epargne on the Livrets. The Caisses d'Epargne, under the law of 1983, changed their statute and became "non-profit-making credit institutions." Despite the fact that the CENCEP had been set up, the different Caisses d'Epargne continued to function in a highly autonomous fashion. Some people even went so far as to compare them to "little kingdoms" set apart from the rest of the "banking world." The Director of a Caisse was appointed by the "Orientation et Surveillance" Council (COS), which was likewise responsible for how the establishment was run. This Council itself was made up of staff from the Caisse, local politicians and representatives on behalf of individuals. This last group was the largest. In reality, the Director of a Caisse had considerable freedom. The Council generally functioned as a recording room "mastered" by the Director. The Caisses enjoyed close ties with the life of the locality in which they were "rooted." After the Minjoz law of 1950, the Caisses were authorized to use part of the funds collected to make loans to local communes. They also took part in cultural development by acting as patrons, as well as by sponsoring the town's sporting associations. Their leaders had always been considered as local dignitaries. They often entertained close relations with local politicians (Mayors, members of parliament, etc.). In 1990, the Caisses d'Epargne network numbered 186 autonomous entities. Each Caisse possessed agencies that in many cases resembled administrative bodies rather than local banks (with the exception of those whose internal architecture had evolved during the 1980s). The employees were situated behind a counter and, in some cases, were even separated from the clients by a hygiaphone.

For almost 150 years, the Livret was the only product offered to clients. Half of the aggregate amount in 1990 was derived from funds collected in this way. Nevertheless, the product was aging and was no longer as successful as it had been in the past. It was unable to stand up to competition from other, more profitable ways of placing one's savings. Confronted in this way with a powerful run on financial products at the expense of cash savings (Livrets), CENCEP leaders decided that the strategy and structure of the network would have to be thought through in depth. Above all, they felt that a marketing effort would have to be made and that restructuring the network was inevitable. To help them in their undertaking, they addressed themselves to the McKinsey Consulting firm.

The conclusions reached by the consultants were clear and reinforced the feelings of the CENCEP leaders. McKinsey showed in particular that sizable economies would have to be sought and that the Caisses d'Epargne would have to be given the opportunity of functioning like fully-fledged banking institutions. In 1991 and 1992, 31 new regional Caisses d'Epargne were created by the merger of 186 local Caisses with 22 SOREFI. The new entities are responsible for their own balance sheets, assure the totality of the banking inter-mediation functions and have full control over their commercial and financial policy.

The formation of the Caisse d'Epargne of Franche-Comté

Franche-Comté is a region in the eastern part of France. It includes 4 departments: Doubs, Haute-Saône, Jura and the Territory of Belfort. It has a population of about 1.1 million. In 1990, there were 11 autonomous Caisses d'Epargne in Franche-Comté: Belfort, Besançon, Lure, Luxeuil, Vesoul, Gray, Dole, Champagnole, Lons-Le-Saunier, Saint-Claude and Montbéliard. There was also a regional firm, set up in 1985, which served as a bank for the 11 Caisses: the SOREFI of Franche-Comté.

In November of 1991 the creation of the Caisse d'Epargne of Franche-Comté was the result of the merger of all 11 Caisses and the SOREFI. The new regional Caisse has a head-office and 7 commercial Groups. Unlike the old local Caisses, these entities are not autonomous but answer directly to a regional head-office. Their task is to coordinate the commercial activities of the 124 local branches, none of which were dismantled as a result of the merger.

Results of the identity diagnosis

While the merger was being launched we took on a series of semi-directed interviews with the staffs of the different organizations. We soon realized that there was a large gap between the answers given by the former SOREFI employees and those of the former employees of the Caisses d'Epargne, whatever their original Caisse was. We therefore, updated a communality of perception among the members of the eleven former Caisses d'Epargne. The interviews we were able to conduct with the staff of the former Caisses in other regions confirmed this fact. We have inferred from this the existence of a common imagery which in turn attests to the existence of an identity of the network of the Caisses d'Epargne itself. This does not mean that local Caisses did not have their own specific identity (a deeper study of three former Caisses lead us to emphasize the existence of "firm-specific" characteristics). But, once the responses of the staff of the former Caisses were compared with those of the former SOREFI employees, the differences among the various Caisses seemed secondary. As one former Caisse d'Epargne noted: "The head-office brings together people of all horizons: the former local Caisses, SOREFI, new recruits. But with Caisses d'Epargne colleagues, things are different, there is undeniably a common way of thinking, things are smoother, less complicated."

In the first attempt at diagnosing the identity, we looked to identify the problems experienced by those individuals who were involved in this merger. The main themes encountered in the interviews are: loss of autonomy ("When I was with the Caisse d'Epargne of Besançon, I had much more freedom than here. You can't take a piss without filling out a report"), too much red tape ("Things become inefficient when they get too heavy"), different working methods between the Caisses d'Epargne and the SOREFI ("we (former SOREFI staff) and the Caisses have different working methods"), problems in human relationships between the Caisses d'Epargne and the SOREFI ("Sometimes there are tensions," "problems are due to our different cultures, both professional and general"), nostalgia ("SOREFI was a small team of 50. At the new Caisse ... some of the friendliness, the warmth, has gone," "The Caisse d'Epargne spirit has disappeared. It may develop in due time"), imbalance of power ("The SOREFI people have seized power. I call that carrying out a hold-up on the Caisses d'Epargne"), etc.

An exhaustive analysis of the problems expressed lead us to ascertain that a good number of these problems were related to the uneasy relationships between the two clans: former Caisses d'Epargne staff and former SOREFI staff. This problem is fundamental in that most of the other problems are related to it. Our hypothesis is that these problems constitute the symbolic products which can be explained by the confrontation of two different organizational imageries.

Internal image of the company

It is important to realize, for example, that disharmony related to the work methods is a symptom of an even deeper disharmony on the company's and its profession's image. In fact, it is a symbolic struggle in which the stake is essential for the staff of the new entity. This stake is to be able to improve one's own vision of the world, one's organizational imagery. "In the Caisse d'Epargne of Besançon we used to have our own rhythm, a rapport with clients, which maybe other local Caisses did not enjoy in terms of volume or variety of clients. But the main difference is with SOREFI people. Sometimes there are tensions. We don't have the same way of handling business and customer relations. All is not wrong of course, but what to do ? (silence)." The conflict between two different organizational imageries reveals this disharmony while the work methods have a direct impact on the functioning of the company: "We have to learn to live together, and often find that problems are due to our different cultures both professional and general. So we have different ways of doing things, and, ultimately, it shows on the working relations, on the internal functioning of departments."

The violence of some of the arguments used with regard to the banks shows that a veritable "cult of difference" exists among former local Caisses staff. "The Caisse d'Epargne's view of things is not that of a banker. In my view our relationship with clients is a highly distinctive one. Our clients don't walk into a Caisse d'Epargne as they would walk into a bank" (17 years' seniority). "The Caisse d'Epargne should not end up just like any other bank. Never! I've been here for ten years and I can assure you that we don't have the same aims as a bank. We don't try and sell at all cost. That's why we have a good relationship with our clients." With the formation of a new organization, the former Caisses d'Epargne feared the disappearance of the specificity of the organization: "I fear that the restructuring will destroy whatever it was that made Caisse d'Epargne. One should not forget that at first we had a social mission. But now, I fear that by wanting to become a bank just like the other banks we will go further and further away from that mission. And that surely is a very unfortunate thing" (18 years' seniority). The members of the staff of the former Caisses denounce the creation of a new field which has a logic not in accordance with their collective imagery. For former SOREFI staff, on the other hand, the Caisse d'Epargne is a fully-fledged bank that should become even more so in the future: "The Caisse d'Epargne should affirm itself as a bank in the strong sense of the term," or again "At the moment, we are fighting to be a bank." "The main task of the Caisse d'Epargne was to collect funds for "Caisse des Dépôts et Consignations" (State). Now this won't do anymore. We simply have to be commercially as active as the other banks" (former SOREFI employee).

The fact to remember in this study of the internal image of the company is the clash of two opposing visions which attest to the existence of significant differences on the level of the organizational imageries.

Internal image of ideal qualities

Here again it is possible to bring out significant differences between former SOREFI staff and former local Caisse staff. For the employees of the old Caisses, the main qualities are devotion and loyalty to the firm. Importance is attached to starting "at the bottom" and having experience in the field. Seniority is an important criterion inasmuch as it is a way of evaluating loyalty to the Caisse d'Epargne. Over the years, people acquire the "Caisse d'Epargne spirit": "For us, you see, joining the Caisse d'Epargne was like joining a large family and we had to learn the ropes."

For former SOREFI staff, the main quality is competence, which is attested by having diplomas. "For me, the important thing is competence. To be competent, contrary to what people at the Caisse believe, is not to be old" (former SOREFI). They feel that a "managerial culture" is needed, and reproach members of the former Caisse staff for their lack of dynamism: "At the Caisse d'Epargne there is a drama where managerial culture is concerned." For them, work-methods and behavior should be geared towards a search for greater efficiency. They tend to associate seniority with inertia, routine, lack of self-questioning, etc. - in other words, with a whole bundle of attitudes that stand in the way of this search for efficiency.

Internal image of power distribution

Even if everyone agrees on the point that the former SOREFI globally took over the power (they now have a majority of the key positions), opinions are very different with each original company. The former Caisse staff resents the "hold-up" perpetrated by SOREFI staff : "The SOREFI people have seized power. I call that carrying out a hold-up on the Caisses d'Epargne (....) They fill all the management posts and that's it. No one stepped forward from the Caisses d'Epargne. Caisses d'Epargne people never used to step forward." The organizational routines which functioned in the old Caisses drove the employees to "wait in line" for promotion which were principally based on seniority. We have here an example of mutual reinforcement which existed between symbolic products and organizational imagery. The routines which were in place were explained by the organizational imagery (especially the importance given to company loyalty as an ideal quality) and in their own right, the routines contributed to the perpetuation of this imagery by becoming the standards for behavior for the new employees. The members of the former SOREFI staff see their accession to power as justified by their competence: "We, the members of the former SOREFI staff, have practically all ended up at the Caisse's head-office. Some people accuse us of having got the upper hand. For me, it's just a question of competence."

For those salaried employees who were interviewed, the power is in the hands of the former director of the SOREFI, now president of the new Caisse. However, the staff of the former Caisses does not have any animosity towards him: "I think that Mr. T controls the company, he is the company. Well, the company is made of its staff, but he is the leader. It seems that, even if not everyone agrees with this or that policy, this or that implementation, this or that thing, everyone has a great deal of respect for Mr. T, a certain admiration" (Former SOREFI). "People acknowledge Mr. T as the leader of the company because he was able to put his foot down at the right moment. He set things right in certain Groups" (former Caisse). There are two possible explanations as to why the former Caisses d'Epargne have a rather favorable opinion of the current president. The first is linked to his personality. It would seem that he has a certain charisma: "Everybody recognizes that he has a lot of charisma" (former SOREFI). Otherwise, in certain Caisses d'Epargne, the directors in place were all powerful and sometimes perceived as unjust. Several of those little kings were beheaded as a result of restructuring, a move that certain employees viewed as "justice being done": "some of the directors acted like dictators."

Symbolic Products

We will not go back to the study of the problems which arose during the launch of the merger, problems which could be considered as symbolic products representing the conflict among the different imageries. We have chosen to concentrate here on one particular example of a symbolic product: the myth. Discussions about the myths can be heard among former Caisses staff concerning the time when the Caisses d'Epargne played a major role in social development: "In the past, the Caisses d'Epargne were social. It was our predecessors who created the public baths and gardens," or again "One should not forget that at first we had a social mission." This myth of the "altruistic company" goes back to the origins of the Caisses d'Epargne and is explained by the internal image held by the staff of the former Caisses, an image which remains perpetual. The myth exists to remind the older employees and to teach the newly hired employees that the Caisse d'Epargne is not a banking institution like the others. An other persistent myth is that of the teller becoming the boss: "At the Caisses d'Epargne, you started behind the counter and, in time, ended up as boss." Here again, there exists a clear link between the myth and the emergence of ideal qualities (the most important quality being company loyalty proven by seniority). In the new company, this myth is now being questioned which then leads to an overhaul of the imagery: "At Caisses d'Epargne, you could start at the bottom of the ladder and end up at the top. With the restructuring, I'm not sure that things will still work out this way" (18 year's seniority).

CONCLUSION

In order to study the identity of an organization it is not enough to just produce a description of the rituals, myths, etc. One has to look to identify the logic behind the work, to question the "why" of certain symbolic products. This procedure will lead to an updating of the existence of the organizational imagery. In the first part of this paper, which was devoted to the presentation of a theoretical framework, we showed how this imagery is reproduced and we emphasized the role played by people and certain symbolic products (organizational routines, rituals, and myths). Then we put forward the methodological procedure for diagnosing the identity. This diagnosis is particularly interesting as it intervenes in the launch of a merger. In effect, it permits one (as the case study presented in the third section illustrates) to get to the root problems which can appear following a company merger. These problems are but often visible manifestations of a conflict among the different organizational imageries.

REFERENCES

Bourdieu, P., <u>Distinction. A Social Critique of the Judgement of Taste</u> (London, Routledge, 1989) (Originally appeared in 1979).

Bourdieu, P., <u>The Logic of Practice</u> (Stanford, Stanford University Press, 1990) (Originally appeared in 1980).

Buono, A.F. and J.L. Bowditch, <u>The Human Side of Mergers and Acquisitions. Managing Collisions Between People, Cultures, and Organizations</u> (San Francisco, Jossey-Bass, 1989).

Buono, A.F., Bowditch, J.L. and J.W. Lewis, "The Cultural Dynamics of Transformation: The Case of a Bank Merger" in Kilman, R.H., Covin, T.J. et al., <u>Corporate Transformation: Revitalizing Organizations for a Competitive World</u> (San Francisco, Jossey-Bass, 1988).

Duet, D., <u>Les Caisses d'Epargne</u> (Paris, PUF, 1991).

Larçon, J.P. et R. Reitter, <u>Structures de pouvoir et identité de l'entreprise</u> (Paris, Nathan, 1979).

Moingeon, B. and B. Ramanantsoa, "Socioanalysis: a Method for Diagnosing the Identity of an Organization," International Conference on Socio-Economics, Society for the Advancement of Socio-Economics (New School for Social Research, New-York City, March 1993).

Reitter R. et B. Ramanantsoa, <u>Pouvoir et politique. Au-delà de la culture d'entreprise</u> (Paris, McGraw-Hill, 1985).

Schein, E.H., <u>Organizational Culture and Leadership</u> (San Francisco, Jossey-Bass, 1985).

Walter, G.A., "Culture Collisions in Mergers and Acquisitions" In Frost P. et al. (eds), <u>Organizational Culture</u> (Beverly Hills, Sage 1985).

SAVING A UNIQUE ECOSYSTEM
WITH A DEBT-FOR-NATURE SWAP

Michael Tucker
Fairfield University
FAIRFIELD, CONNECTICUT, U.S.A.

Abstract

Conservation International proposed a debt-for-nature swap with the government of Madagascar. Financial modeling is needed to determine the total investment that would be required to sustain the fourteen year project under a most likely economic scenario. While finance is involved in the determination of an adequate level of funding, the case addresses considerably broader issues of global environmental degradation and what may be done to reverse it.

INTRODUCTION

Jane Ransom, a recent MBA graduate, was scheduled to begin work at a Fortune 500 corporation as a financial analyst in four months. With free time on her hands and a commitment to ecology, she decided to offer her expertise to Conservation International (CI). When she spoke with Mark Geist, CI's treasurer, he told her that her timing was perfect.

"We're putting the finishing touches on our deal with the government of Madagascar to do a debt swap," Geist said. "Most of the money will be coming from the Agency for International Development. Sometime soon, we've got to figure out just how much money we'll be asking for. That's where you come in. AID is a stickler for details. They'll want annual projected expenses in dollars and a full write-up of financials."

Jane quickly learned that while CI had plenty of talent in the sciences, particularly biology, people with business backgrounds were in short supply. The first budget Mark handed her was denominated in local currency and inflation had been omitted. The budget was also rife with inconsistencies making it difficult to figure out just who was spending what money when.

Just as she thought she was getting a handle on the budget figures, Bill Dickson, the Madagascar project director, called to tell her that the education part of project had been scrapped. "It was too expensive to run the education program and manage the conservation district," he explained. He faxed her a new set of numbers cautioning her that these, too, were in Malagasy francs (FMGs), subject to change and did not take inflation into account. "Coming up with some inflation assumptions and projections is up to you," he said.

Jane learned that a major investment bank working with CI could buy Madagascar's debt at a 50% discount from face value. Further talks with creditors and the Madagascar government altered the terms slightly. CI would have to make a 5% interest payment to creditors prior to swapping the funds into FMG. This effectively reduced the immediate gain on the swapped dollars from 100% to 90%, still a very attractive return compared to a direct exchange of dollars for local currency.

As proposed, the project would be operational for a fourteen year period. It was designed to set up conservation management in the Zahemena Natural Integral Reserve. The reserve, an area of over 283 square miles, was currently managed and maintained by just three full-time employees. The goal of the project was to bring in experts to train Malagasies in conservation management to expand the number of reserve employees. After an initial start-up period, management of the project would be turned over to local control.

The United States Agency for International Development found the project's goals and duration attractive, prompting it to offer to pay for up to 75% of the financing. Commitment to funding was dependent on a finalized project proposal and determination of the amount, in dollars, that would be required to sustain a fourteen year project in a country with a rocky economic past and an uncertain future.

It was up to Jane to come up with an appropriation request in dollars. Besides accounting for inflation and translating budget figures into dollars, she would also need to estimate how much could be earned on investments in Madagascar banks on the swapped debt proceeds in years prior to its expenditure. Estimating the impact of inflation on bank interest, the budget and currency translation was going to call on all her expertise.

BACKGROUND OF DFN SWAPS

The huge runup of LDC debt was economically tied to the rapid increases in oil prices of the 1970s and early 1980s. Awash with oil profits, petroleum producing countries deposited large amounts of money in Western banks. The banks in turn found themselves in need of major borrowers. With worldwide commodity prices rising in tandem with oil prices, LDCs with natural resources or viable cash crops capable of generating export dollars became major borrowers. The bank honeymoon did not last long. A combination of commodity price deflation, beginning in 1982, and poor or no returns on the investment of the borrowed capital transformed much of the over $1 trillion in LDC debt into non-performing assets on the balance sheets of many banks.

As borrowers stepped-up exploitation of natural resources in an attempt to service their outstanding loans, damage to ecosystems was ignored. With more countries rushing crops and raw materials to market, a commodity glut ensued. Prices quickly declined and LDC foreign exchange dropped. Continued debt service became nearly impossible for many countries. LDC's were viewed as bad debtors and new investment capital grew scarce.

Exacerbating LDC problems was the continued population growth which put further pressure on the environment. LDC governments, lacking funds for basic human services, did not set a high priority on conservation projects fearing such actions might discourage the limited foreign capital still available for resource development projects. Rational ecological management was next to impossible with expanding and impoverished populations demanding more land for subsistence agriculture.

Lenders holding non-performing loans began to write them down, selling what they could. Secondary debt markets blossomed with LDC debt selling at large discounts from face value. Some LDCs offered to swap discounted debt for local currency at face value stipulating that the proceeds be used for approved projects within the country. Chrysler, for example, purchased a discounted Mexican bond which it later swapped at face value using the pesos to build a Mexican assembly plant [Purcell and Canavan, 1989].

Some economists fault swaps, arguing that they are potentially inflationary because LDC governments are, in effect, merely printing money. In practice, most swaps, and DFN swaps in particular, involve small sums which are typically spent over time resulting in little or no inflationary impact. One study showed that a $50 million infusion of new money into the Costa Rican economy produced only .5% additional inflation [Dogse, 1991].

For banks holding discounted debt, selling the debt at market rates clears their books of non-performing assets. This creates a book loss if the debt had not previously been written down to market value. On the plus side, from a cash flow standpoint, selling non-performing assets at a discount means positive cash flow where none existed. Creditors, however, have expressed concerns about the possible "moral hazard" inherent in allowing debtors to retire loans at substantial discounts [Sundaram 1990]. "Free riders," banks that don't participate in the sale of discounted debt but stand to gain from the participation of their competitors were yet another potential obstacle to swaps. Nonparticipating banks could profit if enough debt is sold by other institutions so as to increase the possibility, and the market perception, that the remaining debt will be bought at a higher price.

DFN swaps were first proposed in a 1984 New York Times article by Thomas Lovejoy as a way to address the joint problems of environmental degradation and the unmanageable debt burdens of LDCs. Conservation International completed the first DFN swap with the Bolivian government three years later [Burand 1988]. By developing a conservation plan in conjunction with local Bolivian environmental groups and including those groups in the ongoing management of the project, CI set a precedent for local conservation group input and involvement.

MADAGASCAR

Madagascar, with per capita income of about $200 per year, has been described as one of the ten poorest countries in the world. Although it has had GDP growth averaging 2% annually, a population increasing at 2.9% per year has resulted in eleven million people sharing an economy expanding too slowly to maintain their meager living standards [Africa South of the Sahara 1993, Rajcoomar 1991]. In addition, because GDP calculus ignores environmental degradation, it is possible for a country to have measurable economic growth even as natural resources are depleted beyond the point of recovery. Satellite photographs of Madagascar show how destructive deforestation can be. The island is now surrounded by an orange tinted ocean awash with the country's soil confirming its status as the most eroded place on earth.

Having been 21% forested as late as 1980, Madagascar's forest cover has been reduced to only 10% of its land mass [Africa South of the Sahara 1992]. Primitive slash-and-burn agriculture has been largely blamed for the denuded landscape. Vast tracts of forest have been eliminated to bring ever more marginal land under cultivation and to provide 81% of the country's fuel requirements. Deforestation is an unsustainable economic strategy that destroys the potential wealth of unique ecosystems. Rather than seal off threatened areas under armed guard, it is the goal of conservation groups to properly manage ecosystems in such a way that income might accrue to the local populace. For example, in Madagascar, at least one medically and economically important plant, the rosy periwinkle, has been identified [Jenkins 1987]. This plant, found only on the island, provides the most effective treatment of childhood leukemia.

POLITICS

Following independence in 1960, Madagascar experienced a series of economic reforms under the guise of socialism including the nationalization of various private enterprises and the adherence to fixed exchange rates. In the late 1980s, support from a defunct Soviet Union abruptly ceased. The country turned to the West for economic aid and assistance in rebuilding its economy. Following the government's disavowal of communism, large amounts of external debt were forgiven, particularly by France. Still, $3.5 billion of loans remain outstanding; a sizeable sum considering the country's annual GNP of just over $2 billion.

In 1989, constitutional reforms established a multiparty system signaling at least a potential cessation of the parade of strongman rulers who have dominated the post-independence period. The International Monetary Fund (IMF) and the World Bank began consulting with government leaders seeking ways to move the country toward a free market economy that would eventually attract new investment.

Conservation groups recognizing the dire straits of the island's ecosystem have targeted the country for environmental investment. With its external debt selling at a discount, the use of DFN swaps was clearly an attractive financing vehicle. In 1990, the World Wildlife Fund (WWF) and CI concluded two DFN swaps retiring $8 million in debt. Recognizing that attitudes as well as economic policy needed to be changed, as part of its conservation program, WWF introduced an ecology curriculum into all the country's schools [UNESCO 1991].

Conservation is not new to Madagascar, the French colonial government saw the importance of preserving parts of the island in its pristine state as long ago as 1927. At that time several reserve areas were established. One of those areas was the Zahemena Natural Integral Reserve.

FINANCES

Recently the IMF and the World Bank, in talks with Madagascar, expressed concern that too many swaps could create a large infusion of new currency leading to inflation above the already high five year average of 12.5%. Bowing to their concerns, Madagascar has set a $1 million ceiling on the amount of swapped funds that CI can invest directly in the economy in any given year. Any funds swapped above the $1 million ceiling must be invested in one year government bonds which have paid a 9.75% fixed rate since 1983.

Taking into consideration the $1 million ceiling, CI has decided to fund the project with a series of four swaps. Initially it will use $1.4 million dollars to buy Madagascar debt. Three additional equal installments at the beginning of each of the next three years would complete the funding. Just how much each of the next three swaps would amount to was yet to be determined.

Debt purchased to be swapped in future years will be exchanged for FMG at prevailing exchange rates. With the government's expressed desire to move toward a free market economy, CI believes it is likely that its currency will be allowed to float freely on the world market. Under relative purchasing power parity (RPPP), FMG exchange rates relative to the U.S. dollar are likely to change in response to inflation differentials between Madagascar and the United States [Copeland and Weston 1983]. For example, assuming that U.S. inflation is 6% the following year (and over the fourteen year period), Madagascar inflation of 12.5% and the current exchange rate of 1885 FMG to the dollar, the number of FMGs projected to be exchanged per dollar at the end of the year would be calculated as follows:

$$Excge_1 = 1885 * \frac{1.125}{1.06}$$

In each subsequent year, the number of FMGs exchanged per dollar would increase proportionately to the ratio of Madagascar to U.S. inflation.

Madagascar has four major banks offering both time deposits and demand deposit accounts. Given the large sums of money CI will be keeping on deposit over the fourteen year period, a former finance minister has advised CI that interest rates with any of the banks are negotiable. One assumption being considered is the expectation of earning interest of at least 1.5% above inflation on deposited funds.

THE PROJECT

CI has established a local management board (ACTMB) consisting of eleven business and former political leaders to act as go-between with the government and to participate in overseeing the eventual allocation of swapped funds. The board has expressed an interest in using some of the funds to finance local business ventures. CI has thus far resisted any uses other than conservation. Together with local conservation groups and CI personnel in the country, all of whom are scientists, an initial budget has been proposed covering the first four years of operations. The budget shown in Table 1 does not take inflation into account.

It is expected that in the fifth year local management will be sufficiently well trained to assume complete control of the project. This is anticipated to result in a 5% reduction in operating costs in that year compared with year four. The project will be phased out beginning in year 12 at which time operations will be reduced to 75% of the prior year's level. The next two years will wind down to 50% and 25%, respectively, of the eleventh year's level of operations.

Typically, conservation groups have increased local employee compensation at the rate of inflation. As a general assumption, other budgeted costs will be expected to increase in tandem with inflation.

Given likely investment earnings, the planned $1.4 million initial debt purchase and expected operating costs increasing at the rate of inflation, Jane must determine how much funding will be required for the three subsequent equal debt purchases to sustain the fourteen year project. To calculate the funding required, she will need to construct a financial model incorporating all the assumptions. In addition, once funding levels have been established, CI staff would like to know how many years the project could be sustained under inflation projections above the expected 12.5% Jane has been asked to use in the initial model.

TABLE 1
REAL ESTIMATED OPERATING COSTS IN LOCAL CURRENCY

YEAR	ANNUAL EST FMG OPTG. COSTS
1	892,289,444
2	796,097,894
3	815,074,943
4	893,651,168

REFERENCES

Africa South of the Sahara 1993, Europa Publications, 22nd edition, 1992, 494-512.

Burand, Deborah, "Doing It Naturally: The Greening of International Finance," International Financial Law Review, September 1989, 37-39.

Copeland, Thomas E. and Fred J. Weston, Financial Theory and Corporate Practice, Second Edition, 1983, Addison-Wesley.

Dogse, Peter and Malcolm Hadley, "Debt for Nature," UNESCO Environmental Briefs, UNESCO, 1991.

_____, Peter and Bernd von Droste, Debt-for-Nature Exchanges and Biosphere Reserves: Experiences and Potential, UNESCO, Paris, 1990.

International Financial Statistics, February 1993, 336-337.

Hammond, Allen, ed., *The 1993 Information Please Environmental Almanac*, compiled by World Resources Institute, Houghton-Mifflin, 1993, New York, 394-395.

Jenkins, M. D., ed., *Madagascar: An Environmental Profile*, International Union for Conservation of Nature and Natural Resources, United Nations Environment Programme, 1987, Gland, Switzerland.

Lovejoy, Thomas, "Aid Debtor Nations' Ecology," The New York Times, Oct. 4, 1984, A-31.

Purcell, John F. H. and T. Chris Canavan, "The Developing Country Loan Market: How it Works and Why Its Future is Bright," in Steven M. Rubin, ed., Debt Equity Swaps in 1990s, Volume 1, November 1989, The Economist Publications.

Rajcoomar, S., "Madagascar: Crafting Comprehensive Reforms," *Finance & Development*, Sept. 1991, 46-48.

Sundaram, Anant K., "Swapping Debt for Debt in Less-Developed Countries: A Case of a Debt-for-Nature Swap in Ecuador," International Environmental Affairs, Winter 1990, 67-79.

UNESCO, *Environmental Brief*, UNESCO, 1991, 9.

PROTEC INSTALLATIONS LIMITED

Hal Schroeder
University of Lethbridge
LETHBRIDGE, ALBERTA, CANADA

Abstract

Started in 1986, Protec Installations Ltd., an electrical contractor, was among Canada's 100 fastest growing companies by 1992. Non-union contracts had been increasing, so well qualified electricians were available at hourly rates well below those of union contracts. However, in 1992 the new provincial government introduced a Fair Wages Policy which required that minimum rates well above non-union wages must be paid on all large projects which received government funding. Protec would need to make some major changes if its growth strategy was to be maintained.

INTRODUCTION

In October, 1993, Erin Strench, President and General Manager of Protec Installations Ltd. in Richmond, British Columbia (B.C.) faced a decision which might significantly change the direction of his electrical contracting firm. The company had experienced outstanding growth since it started in 1986 in an environment where non-union contracting had increased considerably and qualified electricians were available at hourly rates well below those of union contracts. The B. C. government's 1992 Fair Wages Policy required that non-union contractors on large government-funded projects pay higher wages which would increase Protec's labour costs on such contracts by about 15 percent. More labour legislation had since been introduced and Erin knew that drastic changes would be needed if Protec's growth strategy was to be maintained.

COMPANY HISTORY

Protec Installations Limited was incorporated on December 13, 1985 and opened for business on February 1, 1986. This was not his first business venture. Having graduated from the British Columbia Institute of Technology in 1969 with a diploma in electronics technology, he had an interest in research and development in solid state motor control. After jobs with several electrical contractors, he bought Harrington Electric Co. in 1975 and in 1977 he started another contracting company Westec Electrical Services Ltd. The recession of the early 1980s devastated both the economy and Westec and in 1983 he sold the business to Granby Electric Corp. of Richmond, B. C. He stayed with the company as a project manager but found that did not suit his character. In his words, "I'm not cut out to be an employee. I like the dynamics of being an employer" [Stueck, 1993].

In 1986 he was an employer again, but he and his wife Beverly were the only employees and they had no clients. But he was well prepared. Since his college days he had received a diploma in business management through night classes at the University of British Columbia and certification from the Canadian Institute of Quantity Surveyors. His years in contracting had also given him a wealth of experience and numerous contacts in the industry.

It was also the year of Expo 86 in Vancouver. A deserted stretch of shoreline was to be transformed into a world showpiece where virtually every square foot needed to be wired. With deadlines approaching, many understaffed and burnt-out contractors were working around the clock and new contractors provided fresh resources. It was a good "kick-start" for Protec; in six weeks their crew completed $300,000 worth of construction [Stueck, 1993] in the Brunei, Malaysian, Romanian, Saudi and Singapore pavilions.

A downturn was expected after Expo, but that did not materialize. With careful bidding on contracts to install electrical systems in commercial and light industrial projects Protec soon became a major competitor. By 1988 it employed over sixty electricians and apprentices and had six radio- dispatched vehicles to service clients' needs [Vancouver's Business Report, 1988]. By 1992 Protec had become the largest non-union electrical contractor in B. C. with nearly 150 employees [Richmond Review, 1992] and ranked 61st in Profit magazine's list of Canada's fastest growing companies [Spence, 1992]. Total revenue had multiplied over twenty times in six years from under half a million dollars in 1986 to over $11 million in 1991; net income before taxes had grown from under $79 thousand in 1986 to over $610 thousand in 1992. The Richmond Chamber of Commerce named Strench executive of the year.

COMPANY MISSION AND STRATEGY

COMPANY MISSION

Like other areas, electrical contracting had been changing significantly over the years. Basic services like running power lines to buildings, installing power outlets and light fixtures, ensuring adequate breaker boxes, providing the requirements for major appliances were still needed and were best provided by well trained electricians. However, technological developments had raised sophistication and complexity in the field far beyond these levels. From its start in 1986 Protec had kept pace with changes in the industry and by the early 1990's the primary focus of the company was on the concept, engineering, design/build, installation and project management of electrical systems, lighting and power, security and fire alarm systems mainly for commercial, multi-unit residential buildings, office and retail developments and light industrial projects [Stueck, 1993]. Maintenance and servicing of existing electrical systems were also offered. Although there were many contractors who offered some of these services, Protec prided itself in what was informally called "the full meal deal." A balanced team of professional employees was to provide a single-source, comprehensive range of expertise and services to satisfy the needs of even the most demanding clients in areas like preliminary designs for development permits, final engineering drawings, budgets, firm pricing and total electrical installation.

Several affiliated companies were formed to ensure that the range of services offered kept pace with technological change. Logical Solutions Ltd. was formed in 1988 to provide expertise in data, voice and fibre optic installations. Logic Installations Ltd., specializing in building automation and industrial controls was introduced in 1991. QS Electrical Design Inc. provided engineering and drafting (both manual and CAD) services while Western Logic Technologies Inc. added emergency electrical service and commercial and industrial automated control installations. If other capabilities were required, its joint venture entity, Protec Western Ltd. could engage other companies which had the necessary capabilities. Protec was anxious to maintain its reputation of being able to work with others to meet all clients' requirements.

POLICY AND STRATEGY

Strench said he was not philosophically opposed to unions but Protec was an open-shop or non-union company. This meant that electricians at Protec were paid $20 per hour as compared to about $25 or more at companies which employed members of the International Brotherhood of Electrical Workers (IBEW]. He suggested that he would like to see a healthy balance with about half the industry consisting of unionized companies because unions had a lot to offer. Protec's policy and procedures manual had been designed to resemble a union agreement to incorporate the strengths of that system. But there was no doubt in which half he would like his company. His previous companies were unionized prompting him to now suggest that "... in the old days ... the bank owned the company and the unions ran it. I now own the company and also run it" [Stueck, 1993]. In addition to ownership and control, the saving of about twenty percent on labour costs obviously provided a substantial competitive advantage in bidding for contracts.

While Protec had no union, Strench considered the company fortunate to have a group of loyal and dedicated employees who recognized the philosophy of the company and were prepared to work in that framework. According to Strench [1993] the lower wages made it possible for the company to employ more people, avoid short term layoffs with temporary "make-work" projects, provide an income that was still above average and leave employees with a greater sense of belonging to the organization. For middle management there was a heavy emphasis on training to develop management skills, computer literacy and estimating capability in its on-site training facility. A large room with audio-visual equipment and smaller rooms were available for meetings and presentations to help the flow of information for the company's team approach to project management. Effective supervision was considered the key to the success of major projects, all of which used a project manager, an estimator, a foreman and a purchasing manager.

ORGANIZATIONAL STRUCTURE, MARKETING AND FINANCE

The company was divided into four units - i) large projects and ii) medium projects which were managed by Vice President of Operations, Mike Roper and iii] a service/small job division and iv] administration which were Erin's responsibility. Recently the company introduced a human resources manager who was to develop a total quality management program for both the office and the field.

Although the company did not employ sales representatives, some marketing was conducted by estimators and project management teams. The firm was promoted as a proactive contractor whose main mission was to meet the requirements of its clients. A major selling point was that the synergy among well trained employees and complementary affiliated companies and the ability to work with others in joint ventures made it possible to meet a wide range of clients' needs. Keeping close relationships with existing clients and working with them on their new projects from the outset was also emphasised. In addition, an effort was made to keep in touch with the movement of investment capital and remain strategically aligned with general contractors who dealt with new developers.

Protec had a one million dollar line of credit with the Canadian Imperial Bank of Commerce (CIBC) and the relationship between Strench and the company's bonding agent Jardine Rolfe Ltd. dated from the time of Erin's previous companies, providing the company with the lowest rates in the industry. Careful financial management had allowed Protec to take the trade credit 2% - 10 day cash discount at all times since the company was started.

OPEN AND CLOSED SHOPS IN THE INDUSTRY

In electrical construction, as in general construction, there was a large number of relatively small competitors in the industry. In 1991 the number of general construction companies in B. C. was estimated at nearly eleven and a half thousand and an estimated 915 electrical companies operated in the province.

For some years the industry had been unionized to some extent. In unionized companies, sometimes called closed shops, agreements generally required that workers become union members before or shortly after they started on that job. However, a trend towards non-union arrangements, sometimes referred to as the open shop movement, was becoming recognizable by the mid-1970s During the economic recession of the early 1980s organized labour lost more ground while the non-union sector grew. This expansion was particularly notable in electrical contracting for multi-unit residential buildings, office buildings and retailing facilities. In 1988 the number of unionized electrical companies was down to 154 compared to 659 non-union companies. By 1991 the numbers were 132 and 783 respectively with non-union companies now at 85 percent. The percentage of the overall payroll of the two sectors, however, remained relatively constant during that time. In 1988 union companies held about 45 percent of the industry's total payroll; in 1991 this was still estimated at just over 45 percent.

According to Statistics Canada [1991], the average annual employment income of electricians working thirty or more hours per week for 49 or more weeks per year was $39,477 in 1990. The 45 percent or so who worked less during the year had an average employment income of $32,390 per annum. Similar figures for other construction occupations included carpenters: $31,202 and $22,966; brick and stone masons: $31,546 and $24,940; and plumbers: $38,511 and $31,753 respectively. Within each of these groups, however, there was considerable disparity between the wages of the union and non-union employees. Hourly rates among non-union contractors could also vary. According to estimates by the Quantity Surveyors Society of British Columbia [1993], non-union electricians' rates varied from about 65 to 80 percent of union rates. Benefits and benefit/wage ratios also varied to some extent for electricians and other construction workers. Examples are provided in Appendix 3.

THE RESPONSE OF ORGANIZED LABOUR

Having lost its dominant position in the market, the International Brotherhood of Electrical Workers [1992] undertook efforts to roll back non-union contracting. Local 213 in neighbouring Burnaby B. C. struck a Market

Recovery Committee and contracted with a B. C. Research and Communications firm in an attempt to recover the market share which had been lost to non-union competition. With unemployment levels high and the economy in recession, unionizing non-union shops was difficult in much of North America so other means to regain strength were sought. According to Cockshaw's [1993], the International Brotherhood of Electrical Workers (IBEW) had used job targeting programs in some parts of the U. S. to win jobs which would otherwise have gone to non-union shops. An extensive study of such programs by Cockshaw's found that the type of plans that were most acceptable to union members had all working members pay a given amount into a fund which was then used to reimburse workers if they were paid under scale or to contractors if they paid on scale.

In British Columbia another approach became possible. The pro-business Social Credit provincial government was becoming increasingly unpopular due to scandals and leadership problems early in the 1990s. The other major political party in the province at the time was the New Democratic Party (NDP] with a social democrat orientation that was generally supported by organized labour. Since British Columbia did not have legislation requiring disclosure of contributions to political parties, it was not clear whether this included financial support for the NDP in the 1991 election. It was however, very evident that the NDP was committed to creating a "level playing field" in the industry even though it did not intend to outlaw the non-union sector. Item 7 of their election platform said, [i]t's time to put one-sided and extreme labour laws behind us" [IBEW, 1992]. They promised to introduce a new Fair Wage and Skills Development Policy if elected.

In fall, 1991 the New Democratic Party swept into power and the Policy was interpreted as a popular measure. Colin Snell, secretary-treasurer of the B. C. Provincial Council of Carpenters, argued that an opinion poll suggested the policy was supported by 70 percent of British Columbians. Said Snell [1993], "[i]t is an NDP election promise that the new government intends to keep." In March, 1992 the policy was introduced by an order in council and announced in a press release by the Minister of Labour, Moe Sihota.

FAIR WAGE POLICIES BRITISH COLUMBIA

· In forty years leading up to the most recent revision, changes in government had brought several dramatic reversals in fair wage policies in B. C. In 1951 the B. C. government introduced a law requiring wages in the amount prevailing in the market. In 1973 the NDP government replaced it with one that required contractors on public works to be party to a collective agreement. In 1976 this was reversed again requiring fair wages as prevailing in the market. The goal of the 1992 policy was to revert once again to conditions similar to those of 1973, but instead of mandating union shops, it required the payment of minimum wages considerably greater than non-union rates on most major building construction receiving provincial funding. Selected excerpts of the policy are presented in Exhibit 1 on page 7.

EFFECTS OF THE B C FAIR WAGE POLICY

The Fair Wage Policy had the immediate effect of giving the construction industry a third category of wage rates. Union rates were unchanged; non-union rates remained as before in private sector projects but for most government-funded projects the policy minimums now applied. These rates for the classifications covered were estimated to average at about 87 percent of the union rates. Employment income of non-union construction workers on projects covered by the policy was increased, although that increase might not continue on projects in the private sector.

The cost of construction in the public sector was increased relative to the private sector. Non-union contracts had accounted for about two thirds of B. C. government-funded construction. According to the Quantity Surveyors Society's [1993] estimates these costs increased between six to seven percent, affecting government construction costs by approximately $30 to $35 million between the effective date March 30, 1992 and June 30, 1993.

Changes in unemployment costs may also have resulted. Union workers had generally worked less weeks per year thus collecting more unemployment insurance than non-union workers. With increased rates for non-union workers, they might now similarly be hired for less hours thus increasing unemployment insurance payments.

EXHIBIT 1
GOVERNMENT OF BRITISH COLUMBIA
FAIR WAGE AND SKILLS DEVELOPMENT POLICY
(Selected Excerpts]¹

A. Preamble

1. Cabinet has directed that a fair wage and apprenticeship policy will apply to all building construction undertaken by the Province, its Crown Corporations and agencies which received monies for building construction.

2. This policy will not apply to building construction of less than $1.5 million to Provincially subsidized social or student housing projects or where the Provincial Government contribution to the project is less than $500,000.

B. Policy Requirements

Where a contract for building construction worth $1.5 million or more is entered into by the Province, a Crown Corporation or an agency funded by the Province or a Crown Corporation, the Minister responsible shall ensure that:

1. Wages paid under the contract for building construction are not less than the rates (combined hourly rate and benefits] set out in the attached schedule for each classification of construction worker.

2. The contract requires that:
   a] tradespeople employed on a project covered by this policy hold either a B.C. Certificate of Apprenticeship or a B.C. Certificate of Qualification (T.Q. Certificate] or both.

For contractors, the effects were mixed. While Policy rates were still lower than union rates, the competitive advantage of non-union contractors in the market affected was reduced, thus reducing the competitive disadvantage of union shops. In electrical contracting the labour costs of some non-union firms on provincial government-related jobs would be affected substantially. Firms emphasizing the low end of the range of non-union rates would require a labour cost increase of nearly 33 percent of their previous rates ($16.50 to $21.93 per hour] on government jobs. For contractors at the high end of the range the increase was just over seven percent of previous labour costs ($20.43 to $21.93 per hour]. With changes in benefits, however, the total cost increase might constitute up to about fifteen percent of previous costs.

FURTHER GOVERNMENT ACTION AND THE RESPONSE OF BUSINESS

In October, 1992 the government introduced Bill 84, The British Columbia Labour Relations Code, resembling the laws of the 1973 NDP government on matters like union certification, picketing and replacement workers. In April, 1993 the government announced its intention to also change the Employment Standards Act. Several issues were placed on fast track review so they could be quickly expedited, including the elimination of contracting out, revision of the Employment Standards appeals process and the right to pay in lieu of extended notice of termination.

The Coalition of B. C. Businesses was generally opposed to the policy and much of the legislation. It was an affiliation of about thirty industry organizations representing over 50,000 small and medium-sized firms in B. C. This sector of the economy was estimated to create about ninety percent of new jobs. Achieving this performance required flexibility and the ability to adapt quickly to the frequent and significant changes happening in the workplace. In voicing their opposition to some of the changes, the Coalition emphasized that laws intended to provide justified protection for employees "must also be consistent with goal of maintaining the economic success of the businesses that created the jobs" of those employees to being with. The capacity of business to compete successfully in a demanding marketplace should not be undermined (Coalition of B. C.

---

¹Source: Government of B.C., FWSD Policy, 1992. Selected minimums specified in the schedule are shown in Appendix 3.

Businesses, 1993).

NOW WHAT?

For many non-union contractors, including Protec, the open shop movement had been a major determinant of strategy since the early to mid-1980s. The Policy eroded this central pillar of their strategy. In Erin's words, "you have control of your business one day; the next day that control is lost" (Strench, 1993]. As the largest non-union contractor in B. C., Protec was particularly affected. The strategic expertise it had acquired with regard to a specific feature of the external environment had been seriously weakened for a part of the market namely all government-related projects. He realized, of course, that private sector projects were not affected, but was reluctant to abandon the public sector entirely. Working in both markets, however, posed the thorny question of whether to use different rates on different projects or have a major competitive disadvantage in private sector projects.

In a way, he wished the government would simply reverse its policy but also knew that was unrealistic, wishful thinking. As the representative of electrical contractors in the Coalition, he was intimately familiar with the government's legislation and attitude and realized that the chances of reversals were, at best, extremely slim. From the perspective Protec's strategic management, it would be best to adopt a worst case scenario and assume that no reversals were forthcoming before the next election.

In deciding what direction to now take, Strench noted several features of the company and its environment. Obviously there were areas in North America which did not have such strong fair wage policies and in Eastern Europe there had been a monumental move away from government control of the economy. In the Vancouver area there had been a large increase in investment from other Pacific Rim countries. There were also exciting technological developments which were changing traditional electrical contracting.

Erin had confidence in Protec's human resources. The field crew included nearly fifty qualified electricians and over fifty apprentices, generally "happy campers who did not feel ripped off" with hourly wages of $20.00 for journeymen and percentages of that rate for apprentices varying with their level of training. The company avoided excessive debt, owned its premises, and its key employees were willing to make some personal sacrifices to help it succeed. The ability to diversify was present and the prevailing culture of the organization welcomed the challenge of trying something new rather than simply doing what others were already doing. The firm had been successful in achieving growth and profit objectives in most of seven years and Strench was determined to have that continue. He likened himself to an "elephant with a long memory who tucks away ideas when they come along" and gathers information on suppliers, competitors, clients, market trends, statistics and anything else that may be important from whatever source it might happen to come [Strench, 1993].

REFERENCES

Coalition of B. C. Businesses, "A Submission to Employment Standards Act Review Committee Position Paper Summary - Expedited Issues Review" (June, 1993).

British Columbia, Government of, Honourable Moe Sihota, Minister of Labour and Consumer Services and Minister Responsible for Constitutional Affairs, "Fair Wages and Skills Development Policy" (March, 1992).

Cockshaw's Construction Labor News and Opinion, "Job Targeting becomes Potent Union Weapon," Cockshaw's Construction Labor News and Opinion (July, 1993, vol. 23, #7) pp. 1-2,6,8.

International Brotherhood of Electrical Workers - Local 213, Letter to members (January 29, 1992)

Quantity Surveyors Society of British Columbia, "Analysis of the Impact on Construction Costs of British Columbia's Fair Wage and Skills Development Policy," (August 17, 1993).

"Richmond Business," Richmond Review, (Dec. 2, 1992) p. A15.

Snell, Colin, "A fair appraisal of fair wage policy" Vancouver Sun, (August 2, 1993) p. D1.

273

Spence, Rick, "Class of '92," Profit (June, 1992, vol. II, #2)
pp. 15-25.

Statistics Canada Census 1991, Catalogue 93-332, Employment Income by Occupation.

Strench, Erin, Information from company records and personal interviews, (October 14 and 15, 1993).

Stueck, Wendy, "Live Wire," Business in Vancouver (February 16-22, 1993, # 173) pp. 8-9.

Vancouver's Business Report, "Protec Specializes in Computer Related Support Systems," Vancouver's Business Report (April, 1988, vol. 2, #6) p. 37.

TEACHING NOTE
PROTEC INSTALLATIONS LIMITED

INTENDED COURSE

This case is intended for an integrative, capstone Policy-Strategy course for fourth year undergraduate or graduate level management/business students.

OVERVIEW

The case takes place in the Province of British Columbia, where historically politics has tended to be rather polarized. The generally pro-business Social Credit government prior to the 1991 election had become increasingly unpopular due to suspicious
activities and leadership problems. The election was won by the
New Democratic Party with a social democrat orientation generally supported by organized labour.
Prior to the election, the open shop movement had been growing for some time. An increasing number of contractors, including Protec, were using non-union workers who were paid lower wages than unionized workers. The new government, however, introduced a Fair Wage Policy which required payment of wages at or above specified minimums.

IMMEDIATE ISSUE

The immediate issue thus is to determine what strategic alternatives are available to Protec in the face of this change in the legal environment, to evaluate those alternatives and select the one considered most appropriate.

BASIC ISSUES

1. Strategic Management in a political environment prone to drastic changes.
2. The merits and demerits of Fair Wage Policies.

TEACHING OBJECTIVES

1. To have students simulate strategy formulation in a setting where a major component of the company's strategy has been weakened for part of its market.
2. To familiarize students with the arguments for and against fair wage policies.

SUGGESTED ASSIGNMENTS/QUESTIONS

1. Why is Erin Strench so involved with B. C. Coalition of Businesses in opposing the fair wage policy? Discuss.

2. Discuss the arguments for and against fair wage policies.

3. What strategic alternatives were available to Protec after the fair wage policy was introduced? Evaluate those alternatives, decide which one(s) you would choose and explain why.

SUMMARY ANALYSIS

Question 1
In getting involved in opposition to the policy, Strench was practising effective strategic management. He may have been opposed to the policy philosophically and in representing the non-union contractors in the Coalition to voice that opposition, he might be viewed as defending both them and free competition in general. However, by familiarizing himself with the policy and the attitude of the government, he was strengthening Protec's ability to formulate its strategy in response to the new legal environment. In so doing he was gaining a competitive advantage over the very contractors he represents.

Question 2
Fair Wage policies have long been the subject of disagreement. Following are some of the points of contention.
1. What is fair is very much a subjective matter. Like beauty, it is often "in the eye of the beholder."
2. It is argued that fair wage policies increase fairness by controlling the growth of non-union contracting and helpingto equalize wages. Opponents contend that this encourages and rewards inefficiency.
3. Proponents suggest that increased wages boost demand for goods and services and thus reduce unemployment. The response to this often is that fairness would then demand that such increases should go to all workers rather than a select few.
4. Advocates of the policy say it would be desirable to take wages out of competition and have contractors compete on management skills and material inputs. This is resisted on the grounds that an item which accounts for 25 to 40 percent of government construction costs should not be exempt from the forces of competition.
5. Supporters of fair wage policies allege that non-union contractors can unfairly capture economic rents by keepingthe difference in wages greater than the difference between union and non-union bids. Fair wage policies are to prevent this. Foes of the policies argue that there are no such rents available to begin with because the large number of small contractors in the industry ensures that none of them has the required market power.
6. Defenders say that such policies improve resource allocation where the government has monopsony power; this is disputed on the grounds that the government does not have monopsony power in the construction market.
7. Backers of such policies maintain that they reduce volatility and regional disparity of workers' incomes, but this too is said to promote inefficiency.

Question 3
There were various strategic options available to Protec. Relocating or expanding to neighbouring Washington State or Idaho or Alberta, if they preferred to stay in Canada, might be considered. Projects in other Pacific Rim countries, Eastern Europe or third world regions were other alternatives. Since the Fair Wage Policy's rates were still lower than union rates, competing with a reduced competitive advantage was another possibility. Students may note that, while revenue increased from 1991 to 1992, net income decreased by over fifty percent. More alert students, however, will see that the cost of sales remained relatively constant suggesting that this option may be viable if the cause of the increased overhead could be removed. There remained, however, the question of whether Protec's growth and profit objectives could be achieved with this strategy.
Avoiding the effects of the policy by focusing on projects in the private sector was another possibility. More discerning students may recognize two less obvious options. First, as suggested in question 1, Protec was developing a strategic strength and competitive advantage by becoming more familiar with a major feature of the legal environment and improving the ability to manoeuvre the company accordingly. Second, as shown in Appendix 5, unionized contractors still had a huge share of the industrial market. In reading the section on affiliated companies, it might be noted that Protec had already begun to diversify by beginning to move into this market niche.

APPENDIX 1
SUMMARIZED PROTEC INCOME STATEMENTS - 1986 TO 1992

	1986	1987	1988	1989	1990	1991	1992
Revenue	472,463	1,920,059	3,729,273	5,251,878	7,981,100	11,094,732	11,330,173
Cost/Sales	315,101	1,443,173	3,060,749	4,394,083	6,366,376	9,269,381	9,392,463
Gr. Prof.	157,362	476,886	668,524	857,795	1,614,724	1,825,351	1,937,710
Overhead	78,385	346,716	444,572	653,025	1,050,593	1,215,097	1,641,271
N. Income*	78,977	130,170	223,952	204,770	564,131	610,254	296,439
*Before Taxes					Source:	Protec	Records

APPENDIX 2
PROTEC REVENUE, COSTS AND INCOME TARGETS - 1993 TO 1997

	1993	1994	1995	1996	1997
Revenue	13,330,173	15,330,173	17,330,173	19,330,173	20,000,000
Cost of Sales	10,997,393	12,609,067	14,210,742	15,754,091	16,200,000
Gross Profit	2,332,780	2,721,106	3,119,431	3,576,082	3,800,000
Overhead	1,799,573	1,916,272	1,992,970	2,029,668	2,000,000
Net Income*	533,207	804,834	1,126,461	1,546,614	1,800,000
*Before Taxes				Source:	Protec Records

276

APPENDIX 3
SELECTED HOURLY RATES IN 1992 B. C. CONSTRUCTION
BY CLASSIFICATION AND TYPE

CLASSIF.	UNION	FAIR WAGE MINIMUM	NON-UNION LOW	NON-UNION HIGH
CARPENTERS	$22.72	$20.27	$16.22	$19.81
ELECTRIC.	25.41	21.93	16.50	20.43
LABOURERS	20.37	18.19	11.47	14.62
PLUMB/PIPE	24.17	20.83	16.96	19.94

SOURCES: QSSBC AND B.C. FWSD POLICY. NOTE: RATES SHOWN ARE UNWEIGHTED AVERAGES AND EXCLUDE MOST BENEFITS. BENEFIT/WAGE RATIOS VARIED AMONG CLASSIFICATIONS AND TYPES AND BENEFITS RANGED FROM $4.00 TO $7.09 PER HOUR.

APPENDIX 5
ESTIMATED MARKET SHARE OF ELECTRICAL CONSTRUCTION
(Percentages)

CONSTRUCTION CATEGORY	UNION	NON-UNION
NEW INDUSTRIAL	90	10
NEW COMMERCIAL	40	60
RENOVATION COMMERCIAL	15	85
INSTITUTIONAL	50	50
SERVICE	25	75
HIGH-RISE RESIDENTIAL	15	85

SOURCE: IBEW - LOCAL 21 3

APPENDIX 4
SELECTED B.C. CONSTRUCTION STATISTICS - 1988 & 1991
(Estimates)

ITEM	UNION		NON-UNION	
	1988	1991	1988	1991
NUMBER OF CONSTRUCTION COMPANIES	1,406	1,269	7,904	10,218
NUMBER OF ELECTRICAL COMPANIES	154	132	659	783
NUMBER OF EMPLOYEES - ELECTRICAL COMPANIES	1,345	2,483	2,726	4,838
PAYROLL OF ELECTRICAL COMPANIES P.A./MILLION	$75.9	$119.2	$94.1	$141.9
SALES OF ELECTRICAL COMPANIES P.A./MILLION	190	298	269	405
PURCHASES OF ELECTRIC. MATERIALS P.A./MILLION	95	149	148	223

SOURCES: PROTEC & W.C.B.

PRIVATIZATION ON A SCALE:
"THE CASE OF THE CZECH AND SLOVAK REPUBLICS"

Juraj Sipko
University of Economics
Ministry of Finance
BRATISLAVA. SLOVAKIA
Hans E. Klein
Bentley College
WALTHAM, MASSACHUSETTS, U.S.A.

Abstract

Economic reform in the former Czechoslovak Federal Republic - CSFR - presumes rapid and extensive privatization as a necessary precondition for real transition to a market economy. After the successful introduction of the two first steps of economic reform, macroeconomic stabilization and price liberalization, a favorable environment is in place for the last, but the most difficult, step of transition to a market economy, the process of privatization. As is well known, the economy in all former socialist countries was dominated by government owned firms. The Czechoslovak government controlled 97% of all production in the 1980's. The purpose of this paper is to analyze the large-scale privatization and to discuss the positive and negative features of the voucher method of privatization used in the former Czechoslovakia.

INTRODUCTION

Economic reform in the former Czechoslovak Federal Republic - CSFR - presumes rapid and extensive privatization as a necessary precondition for real transition to a market economy. After the successful introduction of the two first steps of economic reform, macroeconomic stabilization and price liberalization, a favorable environment is in place for the last, but the most difficult, step of transition to a market economy, the process of privatization. As is well known, the economy in all former socialist countries was dominated by government owned firms. The Czechoslovak government controlled 97% of all production in the 1980's.

Czechoslovakia chose a novel method of privatization, mass auctioning of large production units, the so-called "voucher method." The voucher method of privatization had two primary advantages: it enabled Czechoslovakia to privatize a large number of companies in a short space of time. It also overcame the obstacle of a poorly developed capital market. There was (and is) a lack of a private savings and expertise necessary for the functioning of a domestic capital market.

By using the voucher method it was possible to accelerate the whole process of economic reform, which is very important at this point in the development of the national economy. An additional benefit of the voucher method is that state assets are distributed in a relatively equitable way. This allows the perception that everyone benefits from privatization and avoids the large sell-off of assets to foreign companies common in other countries. The purpose of this paper is to analyze the large-scale privatization and to discuss the positive and negative features of the voucher method of privatization in the former Czechoslovakia.

GRADUALISTS VERSUS RADICALS

The transition process in the CSFR from a centrally planned economy to a market economy was the main topic of discussion after the "velvet" revolution of 1989. Macroeconomic stabilization and price and trade liberalization were introduced at the beginning of 1991.[1]

After the establishment of a successful macroeconomic stabilization policy and liberalization of prices and trade it was necessary to begin privatization. In comparison with macroeconomic and price policy and trade liberalization, privatization is more difficult. The government as well as economists were convinced that private ownership of the means of production was also necessary for a market economy. The heavy state involvement in the socialist economy was widely seen as having contributed to the weak performance of the socialist block in the post second world war period.

There were two views on large-scale privatization: "gradualist" and "radical." The latter group argued that the only way for successful economic reform should be mass privatization of state assets as soon as possible. For that purpose they suggested a non-standard method of privatization, the use of "vouchers" as the main instrument for the distribution of shares. The leader of the radical group, the former Federal Minister of Finance, Vaclav Klaus, argued that the privatization by vouchers would be both faster and more equitable.

The "gradualists" argued that privatization should be introduced slowly so as to avoid a large jump in unemployment that would be accompanied by quick adjustment to a market economy. This group was represented mostly by economists from the 1960's, which had wanted to introduce the so called "socialism with a human face."

TRANSITION FROM STATE OWNERSHIP TO PRIVATE

The transition from the state-owned enterprises (SOEs) to private was divided in two parts: small and large privatization.

THE SMALL PRIVATIZATION

In the former CSFR, small privatization started at the end of 1990 and was organized as a public auction. The volume of auctioned units was estimated to have been around 27,000 units of small and medium size shops, retail and wholesale stores.

Before the auction, the book value of each enterprise was estimated. The eventual selling prices were on average only 59% of estimated book value, though some attractive businesses in Prague and Bratislava sold at prices above book value. The small privatization was finished in 1991, with the great majority of small units successfully privatized.

The agricultural sector was a special case of privatization because approximately two-thirds of agricultural land was already private.[2] However, under the previous system, the government used the land and formed cooperatives without paying rent to the legal owners. Returning full control over land to the legal owners was complicated by the existence of these cooperatives. It was inefficient for the cooperatives to break up into separate farms (it was typical that various landowners owned many separated pieces of land). The details of agricultural land privatization are still to be decided, it will likely involve the formation of joint-stock companies in which both the owners of plots and workers are issued shares.

THE PRIVATIZATION OF LARGE ENTERPRISES

Companies entered the privatization process without attempts by government to reorganize enterprises to make them more attractive. It was felt that government would not have enough information to transform enterprises and that the private sector would do a better restructuring job. Moreover, such reorganizations would have delayed the entire privatization program.

The privatization of large units proceeded in two waves. The first wave took place in 1992 and 1993. The new shareholders will be receiving their stocks [certificates] this summer. The second wave began in the summer of 1993. The Czech Republic[3] will continue to use a voucher method, but Slovakia will be use public auctions and tenders.

Companies privatized in the first wave were those better prepared for the transition to market ownership. 6,000 state-owned enterprises were eligible for privatization in the first wave, 4,400 from the Czech Republic and 1,600 from Slovakia. However, only 988 from the Czech Republic (with a total book value of 212,5 billion Czechoslovak crowns) and 503 from Slovakia (with a book value of 86,9 billion Czechoslovak crowns) entered the first wave. The 1491 companies privatized in the first wave represented 55-65% of all state property and left another 35-45% of the state property to be privatized in the second wave.

The large-scale privatization will cover 55-60% of all property. Another 10% will be privatized through the transformation of cooperatives, 15% through transfer of ownership to municipalities, about 5% of state property will be restituted to previous owners and 10-15% will be privatized later.

From the beginning it was necessary to set up a book value (evaluation) for every company. The book value of companies was estimated according to the method of "competitive projects," i.e., estimating the value of a company by the value of its most sophisticated project. In many cases the estimates were very crude and very poor predictors of a firm's desirability in the auctions.

THE NEW PHENOMENON IN PRIVATIZATION - THE VOUCHER METHOD

The large-scale privatization has one distinctive feature: investment points for assets which were distributed for a nominal fee to all eligible citizens. Without the use of investment points it would have been impossible to implement the decisive change in property rights in the Czechoslovak economy within a short period of time [Klaus, 1992]. From the beginning, the proponents of the method argued that the gains resulting from the redistribution of state property would be much larger than the possible negative impacts of a voucher privatization. The problem with a voucher system was seen in the dispersion of ownership and the inability of individuals to effectively influence business's managers.

In the former CSFR every citizen older than 18 years was entitled to buy a voucher booklet. The price of a booklet was 1,000 Czechoslovak crowns (roughly 35 USD, or one third of the average monthly salary at the time) plus a 35 crowns registration fee. However, the total registration fee of 1,035 crowns fee was largely symbolic: the book value of a voucher booklet was estimated to be 30,000 crowns according to official data.[4]

The process of selling joint-stock companies for investment points proceeded in five auction "rounds" (see Table 1).

TABLE 1
THE SCHEDULE FOR THE FIRST WAVE OF PRIVATIZATION

Round	Start	Deadline for Points	End of Allocation Round
Zero	March 1, 1992	April 2	May 15
First	May 18	June 18	June 30
Second	July 8	July 28	August 18
Third	August 28	September 15	October 6
Fourth	October 14	October 27	November 17
Fifth	November 23	December 2	December 22

Source: Voucher Privatization 2, No. 7, 8, 9, 10, 11, 12, 13 and 14, 1992, Center of Voucher Privatization, Prague

ZERO ROUND

Before the auction began all companies were divided into shares according to their estimated book values. The voucher holders then had to decide whether to invest as an individual investor or to use an Investment Privatization Fund (IPF) as an intermediary. These are comparable to mutual funds in the countries with well-developed sectors for financial services. Booklet vouchers were bought by 8,560,000 (Czechoslovak) citizens. 72% invested their vouchers in IPFs.

FIRST ROUND

For the first round, the government set a price of 100 investment points = 3 shares for any company. Individuals and IPFs bid for the shares of the companies. The disposal of assets of a firm depended upon supply and demand. If demand for shares was greater than 125% of the outstanding shares, then no shares were sold and the company was moved to the next round. If demand was greater than supply but less than 125% of supply, then the entire company was sold to the bidders. Each bidder received a fraction of shares proportional to the number of shares he originally bid for. The shares in companies for which supply was greater than demand, were sold to the indindividuals who demanded them. The leftover shares moved for sale to the next round. During this round individual investors as well as IPFs focused on joint-stock companies which, in previous years, had reached relatively high levels of efficiency.

In the first round, individual investors and IPFs used 92% of all investment points. In the course of the first round 38% of all offered shares were sold. The remaining 62% of offered shares were invested in the 421 joint-stock companies in which demand was higher than supply (more than 125%). During the first round, 48 companies were fully sold.

For the second round, the price of shares was updated from first round according to first round relation between demand and supply. Thus, firms which were oversubscribed in the first round had their share prices increased and undersubscribed firms had their share price reduced. Shares of 1443 companies moved to the second round.

SECOND ROUND

The price of shares of some companies increased twelvefold on the second round. The highest price of shares was 400 investment points per share. The cheapest shares were 10 investment points per share. In this round, 24% of (unsold) shares were sold to individual investors who were focusing on the current profitability of companies and to IPFs which were focusing on companies with strong long-term prospects.

Thus, after the first two rounds, 53% of the original number of shares were sold and 74 companies were sold completely, while 441 firms were over-subscribed. One fourth of the original total of investment points were invested in the 120 companies that were fully sold in the first two rounds.

THIRD ROUND

This round was characterized by the largest differences in share prices. The price of shares of companies over-subscribed in the second round increased from 400 to 800 investment points per share. While for the companies with the lowest demand, the price decreased from 100 investment points for 10 shares to 100 investment points for 97 shares in the third round. Thus, the spread between the highest and the lowest price was 776:1.

Predictably, decreasing the prices increased the demand for shares of companies which were perceived to be attractive. The share prices dropped so low for some of these firms that they became over-subscribed in this round. Similarly, demand for the most attractive shares fell due to the rise in prices for those shares.

During the third round, 24.5% shares were sold, representing 10.7% of the original shares offered. 171 companies were fully sold. After three rounds 66.7% of all shares were sold.

FOURTH ROUND

At the beginning of this round, government officials asked the IPFs to follow the same investment strategy as in the previous round. In this round the prices of the most attractive shares increased to 1,000 investment points per 1 share. The lowest share price was 100 investment points for 60 shares. The spread between the highest and the lowest price was 600:1. In the fourth round, 369 companies were over-subscribed of which 224 were over-subscribed in the third round (see Table 4). This is a large number of repeated over-subscriptions relative to other rounds. During this round, 37% of the shares were sold (12.4% of the original shares). 80 companies were fully sold. In the first four rounds, 79% of all shares were sold. 93% of all disposable investment points were used and successful offers were 34,7%. Before the start of the last round, 79% of the companies had been sold and 93% of all disposable investment points had been used.

FIFTH ROUND

For the fifth round (as for they hand done for round four), the government officials appealed to IPfs to repeat their strategy from the previous round. Because the fifth round was to be the last one in the first wave of voucher privatization, investment points invested in over-subscribed companies would be lost forever. This round was more successful than all previous rounds. During the fifth round, 65,5% of the shares were sold. 40 more companies were fully privatized. In 40 cases IPFs reduced their demand. In the end, 117 companies were over-subscribed, 73 in the Czech Republic and 44 in Slovakia (see Table 2).

TABLE 2
DEMAND AND SUPPLY IN THE FIFTH ROUND

Demand/Supply	Number				
	Com-panies	Offered Shares (mill.)	Ordered Shares (mill.)	Sold Shares (mill.)	Sold Shares (%)
Oversubscription of Supply	1 079	54	37,21	37,21	68
Decreasing Demand by IPFs	40	3.74	3.90	3.74	100
Oversubscription of Demand	117	4.16	6.25	0.00	0
CSFR	1 236	62.50	47.36	40.95	66
Czech Republic	818	38.95	28.62	24.49	63
Slovakia	418	23.55	18.74	16.46	70

Source: Voucher Privatization, 2, Center for Voucher Privatization, No. 11, 1992, Prague.

The fifth round was best from the point of view of successful offers and repeated over-subscriptions (see Table 3). The shares of the companies over-subscribed in the last round will be sold after the creation of the secondary market for stocks.

OVERVIEW OF ALL ROUNDS

In the course of the first wave of privatization, Slovak investors as well as Slovak IPFs invested more in the Czech Republic than Czechs invested in Slovakia. Czech IPFs and citizens allocated only 1% of all investment points in Slovakia, while citizens and IPFs from Slovakia invested around 10% of all investment points in companies located in the Czech Republic. The flow of investment points between both republics was determined by the economic structure. The structure of Slovak economy is different than the structure of the Czech economy. One tenth of the production in Slovakia is related to military procurement. Additional production capabilities are concentrated in heavy industry (steel, aluminum, etc.). These sectors were not expected to flourish. In many instances, Slovak companies produce semi-finished products as well as component parts for Czech companies. Investment points allocated to over-subscribed companies became worthless after the fifth round. This represented 44 million investment points, around 7% of all investment points which were used in round five. During the five rounds, 92.8% of all shares were bought with 98.8% of all disposable investment points.

TABLE 3
SUCCESSFUL ORDER AND PERCENTAGE REPEATED OVERSUBSCRIPTIONS

%	Rounds				
	1	2	3	4	5
Successfully Order	38	37	11.8	34.7	86.5
Repeated Oversubscriptions	0	9.5	3.0	61.0	2.0

Source: Voucher Privatization, 3, Center for Voucher Privatization, No. 14, 1993, Prague.

During the first wave of voucher privatization, 291 of 1491 firms were fully privatized. The remaining 8% of the shares not allocated in the first wave are now the property of the National Property Fund and will be sold in the secondary markets.

The first wave of the large privatization ended January 31, 1993. Each participant in the "big lottery" received a statement listing shares owned from the Centre of Voucher Privatization in February. According to the schedule of large privatization everyone received shares during May and June. The shareholders meeting of all privatized firms took place in June 1993. Individual investors have now the right to control the privatized companies.

According to the average book value of companies in the course of the first wave, individuals invested vouchers better than IPFs. The best investment outcomes were obtained by those who bought shares in the second round and the worst by those who bought in the first round. Around 90% of all shares purchased in the first round were cheaper in further rounds (see Table 4).

TABLE 4
THE FIRMS AND PRICES OF SHARES IN THE FIRST WAVE
OF VOUCHER PRIVATIZATION

Firms and Price of Shares	Rounds				
	1	2	3	4	5
Firms Offering Shares	1 491	1 443	1 369	1 317	1 236
Firms Over-subscribed	421	439	507	369	117
Under-subscribed	1 022	930	811	868	*
Sold	48	72	51	80	40
Total Sold	48	120	171	251	291
Maximum price of share (shares:price)	3:100	10:100	97:100	60:100	60:100
Minimum price of share (shares:price)	3:100	1:400	1:800	1:1000	1:1000

*During the first wave of privatization, 278 million shares of all applicable firms(book value 278 billion CSK) were sold, i.e., 92.8%, and8,440 billion investment points were used .
Source: Voucher Privatization 2, 3, Center for Voucher Privatization No. 8, 9, 10, 11, 12, 13 and 14, 1992-93, Prague.

The shares purchased in the first round were disproportionately bought by individual investors. In the first wave individual investors obtained 101,800 000 shares and spent 2,4 billion investment points, in comparison with IPFs which obtained 176,000,000 shares for 6,135 billion investment points (see Table 5).

TABLE 5

Purchasers of Shares(%)	Rounds					
	1	2	3	4	5	Total
IPFs	39.7	28.8	11.1	9.7	10.7	100
Individual Investors	19.1	26.7	12.7	19.7	2621.8	100
Total	58.8	55.5	23.8	29.4	32.5	-

Source: Voucher Privatization 3, Center for Voucher Privatization No. 14, 1993, Prague.

INVESTMENT PRIVATIZATION FUNDS

During the first wave of large-scale of privatization, IPFs played a very important role. The IPFs were established as joint-stock companies. 436 IPFs participated in the first round (refer to Table 6). The main role of the IPFs was to collect vouchers from individuals before the auction and to invest them during the five rounds of privatization. The 14 largest IPFs, organized by banks, saving and insurance companies, controlled 36.1% of all investment points.[5]

TABLE 6
CONCENTRATION OF INVESTMENT POINTS IN IPFS

Allocation of Investment points

Investment points	Number of IPFs	Allocation of Investment Points (%)
200 - 1000	6	27.2
100 - 199	5	6.8
50 - 99	3	2.0
10 - 49	44	11.6
5 - 9	44	3.5
1 - 4	105	3.1
.5 - .9	53	0.4
.1 - .49	101	.3
.01 - .09	67	.04

Source: Federal Ministry of Finance, Center for Voucher Privatization, December 1992, Prague. the Table was constructed from available published data.

SECONDARY MARKETS

According to the schedule of mass privatization, stock exchanges were established in both republics at the beginning of April 1993. The delay of creating secondary markets hampered the success of the privatization effots. The lack of skills and expertise by some IPFs caused addtitional difficulties. It seemed that some IPFs desired to play an important role in the process of voucher distribution to acquire or outright buy voucher booklets, but did not want to participate in a secondary market.

Without some regulation of IPFs activities it is be expect that competition will force some of the poorly managed IPFs into bankruptcy. Another problem is the dispersion of ownership because of the large number of shareholders. IPFS are now restricted and cannot control more than 20% of the shares of a company. However, some funds have begun to influence the management of companies in partnership with other large investors. In many cases IPFs working together have begun to improve the management of companies.

Before the auction, the only condition for establishing an IPF was the requirement to have 100,000 crowns on deposit in a bank. The majority of funds used their initial capital during the advertisement campaign and now most of the funds suffer from liquidity problems. Before the auction, some IPFs promised their shareholders that in one year's time they would return to the investors 10, 12, 15, even 20 times the value of their original investment. However, after more than one year, none of these promises have been fulfilled. The main reason for the present situation is that government did not create, on time, the institutional framework for a secondary market.[6] It is clear that the ultimate success of the voucher privatization will depend on the successful functioning of secondary markets.

INSTITUTIONAL STOCK MARKET FAILURE

As described earlier, in order to achieve the main goal of the large privatization, it will be necessary to create functioning Stock Markets in both republics. The absence of well-functioning secondary markets will lead to problems for the privatization efforts. During the various stages, valuations of companies were based on book values. The secondary market create market values for all shares.

The introduction (and the ability to attract) of foreign capital is delayed by the lack of legislation. Foreign capital is important for the privatization efforts and can help alleviate the problem of capital shortages suffered in both republics. Facilitating capital mobility into the former Czechoslovakia will also help to accelerate the process of privatization, help to avoid liquidity problems and the potential collapse of the secondary markets; an event which could lead to the failure of the entire process of mass privatization.

CONCLUSION

The introduction of mass privatization is a very important part of the economic restructuring plan. The former Czechoslovakia was the first ex-socialist country to introduce large-scale privatization. The Czechoslovak experience will provide valuable insights for other countries that decide to privatize large segments of their state enterprises. The first wave of privatization now completed revealed some strengths and also some weaknesses.

The institutional framework has played an important role during the first wave. In some companies the National Property Fund still controls more than 50% of all shares. The commission for setting prices created a big spread between the second and third rounds. In many instances the of share-price was too high in one round and too low during the next round.

The distribution of vouchers was very organized as a process for creating a primary market. In order to continue in the first wave of the large-scale privatization, it was necessary to establish securities markets. The delay in introducing these market represented one of the greatest obstacles to the success of the first wave of privatization. The distribution of vouchers was unique from a technical point of view. It will, in the future, influence the process of corporate governance, because of the dispersion of ownership.

Another problem area is the lack of legislation concerning the operation of IPFs. The delay in legislation will cause difficulties in the future. Also, a large number of funds have encountered liquidity problems. It is expected that increased competition will eliminate poorly managed funds. At present, there is a shortage of information regarding the financial condition of some IPFs and as a result, it is difficult for individual investors to evaluate the value of their investments.

The lack of legislation concerning foreign investment continues to cause difficulties. The shortage of domestic capital and the barriers to foreign capital can lead to unfavorable conditions in the future.

In order to improve and accelerate the process of privatization in other post-socialist countries (on the basis of knowledge and experience gained from the former Czechoslovakia) it is necessary to accept and use some techniques and practices of Western countries and companies which were applied during privatization efforts in those countries, e.g., forms of leveraged buyouts or management-employment buyouts.

ENDNOTES

1. The former Czechoslovakia is the only country within the ex-socialist region which accomplished very impressive results from the point of macroeconomic stabilization. After price liberalization the consumer price index moved to around 12% per year, the purchasing power of the exchange rate of the Czechoslovak Crown stabilized, indebtedness was the lowest within all of Eastern and Central European countries.

2. Cooperatives are being transformed into several kinds of new entities in accordance with Federal Law on *Regulation of Property Relations in Cooperatives 42/1992.*

3. Czechoslovakia in 1992 decided to split into two separate countries: the Czech Republic (approximately 10 million people) and Slovakia (approximately 5 million people). The split occurred against the desires of the majority of the the population. Puplic opinion polls, just before and after the split, indicated and continue to so, that between 60 -70% of the population in both parts of Czechoslovakia favored "some" kind of union overtwo sovereign states.

4. Kyn estimated that the book value of one voucher book was 12.000 Czechoslovakian crowns.

5. The large IPFs were established by Komercni Banka (Commercial Bank), Investicna Banka (Investment Bank) in both republics, Ceska a Slovenska Poistovna (Czech and Slovak Insurance company), Slovenska Sporitelna (Slovak Ins. Co.), etc.

6. In accordance with a *Stock Exchange* law, two institutions, one in Prague, one in Bratislava were established. In Prague there are 23 seats for brokers (5 from private brokerage firms), while in Bratislava there are 18 seats, with no private brokerage firms. The largest IPFs from both countries will be on both stock exchanges.

288

DOCKSIDE REFINERY LTD

Ann Brown
City University Business School
LONDON, UK
Stavros Spanos
IT-Technomen Ltd
NICOSIA, CYPRUS

Abstract

This case covers 8 years in the life of a company. It outlines the strategy, objectives and business operations of the company. The way in which Information Technology has been developed and put to use is described from the first steps. It is clear that better value could be obtained from the existing investment. At the close of the case in 1993 the company is facing a severe threat. The case questions revolve around how to get the investment in IT to make maximum contribution to the survival of the company.

INTRODUCTION

Dockside Refinery Ltd (DRL) is the only petroleum refinery on the island country of Maumi. It is now, in late 1993, facing a major competitive threat to it's existence from imports. One of several initiatives proposed for countering the current threat is that of making more effective use of Information Technology.

There has been a steady stream of investments in Information Technology over the last 8 years. At the beginning of the period, the company owned no computers and few staff had any knowledge of how to handle this new resource. It takes time to learn how to exploit Information Technology successfully. The present case concerns the choices made over this period in developing and supporting the new computing facilities at the company and the use to which these have been put.

THE COMPANY

BACKGROUND

The company started operations in 1972, after a two year construction period. The largest shareholder is one of the major international oil companies, Moboil, with a 50% control of the shares. Next is the Maumi government with a 35% share in the company. The rest belongs to other local interests, including some of the marketing oil companies present in the country. One of the biggest industrial units in the country, the Dockside Refinery has always been considered a strategic investment for the country's economy. The Board of Directors has nine members, the Chairman traditionally appointed by the government of Maumi. The Managing Director of the Refinery, Peter White, is a non voting member of the Board of Directors.

Due to the relatively small size of the company and its remote geographical position, the parent company, has chosen to exert minimal control. It has preferred to influence direction mainly through its role as the Technical Advisor. At the board level decision making is by consensus and the members appointed by either of the main shareholders have never interfered with the day-to-day management of the company, or blocked any important decisions brought for approval by the top management of the refinery.

MISSION AND STATUS OF THE COMPANY WITHIN THE MARKET

The mission statement of DRL is " ... *to meet as closely and as economically as possible the requirements of the Maumi market in petroleum products*". The two major shareholders have agreed to operate the refinery on a "*cost-plus*" basis.

The eight oil marketing companies and a small number of other companies that trade propane gas, are the customers of the Refinery. These companies are responsible for buying the crude oil from abroad and transferring it to Maumi. The amount of crude oil supplied by each company is proportional to its share of the market. The relations between DRL and its customers are governed by a processing agreement signed between each one and the Refinery. The crude is processed at the Refinery and the resulting oil products are returned to the original owners. DRL ends up each year with zero reserves. At all stages of this cycle, the crude and products remain the property of the supplying companies. DRL only provide the service of processing it to produce the oil products. The "*cost-plus*" mode of operation means that for the services it provides, DRL charges a "*processing fee*" to cover its capital investments and operating costs. The Return On Capital Employed (ROCE), for the shareholders, is guaranteed in the form of a premium charge on these costs. After an agreement between the government and the parent oil company, it was set at 15%. This "profit" is collected from the customers and is returned to the shareholders as dividend.

Being the only refinery in Maumi, DRL does not face any direct competition from another refinery. However, a major threat is the fact that its customers (the oil marketing companies) can always import gasoline and other petroleum products, directly from abroad. DRL can justify its existence as a business, only with the foreign exchange savings it makes for the users and the Maumi economy in general, by putting on the market petroleum products that cost less than the CIF (Cost Insurance Freight) cost of imported finished products. *Consequently, the need for DRL to be a profit making enterprise becomes identical to minimising the cost of the finished products required by Maumi*. From the viewpoint of the government, this is the main strategic objective and as long as it continues to be met, it will always be willing to invest further in order to sustain the company's operating status.

PLANT & OPERATIONS

The refinery is an integrated continuous flow operation that works on a 24 hour basis. It uses three shifts of operating personnel working an average of $35^{1}/2$ hours each week. The design capacity is approximately 780,000 tons of crude oil annually, assuming 340 operating days per year. The main products of the refinery are liquefied petroleum gas (LPG), premium and regular gasoline, aviation turbine fuel, automotive gas oil (Diesel), light fuel oil, heavy fuel oil and bitumen. There is no storage of the above products in the refinery. DRL is connected to it's customers storage facilities by a pipe network, through which the products are transferred directly after production.

Oil refining today is not a labour intensive operation. DRL has mainly pneumatic control systems. This technology achieves partial automation, but overall control is exercised through human intervention from the control room. In order for the plant to be totally handled by a computer the pneumatic control systems currently in place would have to be replaced with electronic control systems, involving further large scale investment.

The Refinery is normally operated by a shift of nine people who are responsible for both the production and the delivery of products to the customers. The work of this team is backed up by craftsmen in the service departments, all qualified engineers and technologists. DRL employs a total of 140 people, including the top management. To be employed in any capacity, a candidate must be at least a graduate of secondary education, and will then spend one year under training. The first six months are covered by a formal training scheme and the next six months include a lot of on-the-job training.

COMPANY STRUCTURE - THE FOUR DEPARTMENTS

The company is organised into four Departments: Administration, Engineering, Operations, and Technological (see Figure 1). The biggest department, Operations is responsible on a 24-hour basis, for receiving, storing, processing the Crude oil and controlling the delivery of the products to the customers. The total personnel employed in the department is 52. Directly below the Department Head there is the Refinery Information Manager, Ian McGregor, and the Head of Refinery Operations who manages the smooth switching between and functioning of the five shifts. Each shift has seven operators, its own supervisor and deputy supervisor.

The Technological Department monitors both the quality of the products and the performance of the plant. It constantly inspects the installations and undertakes all trouble-shooting, determines optimal operating conditions, recommends modifications to improve efficiency and/or increase the processing capacity of the various units. It employs 19 people. The Inspection unit monitors the plant and performs various metallurgical tests, to identify possible problems caused by corrosion, metal fatigue etc. Finally, there is the Technological section which includes a fully equipped chemical laboratory where all tests for quality control of the finished products are performed on a 24 hour basis. This section also employs scientists who study the efficiency of the current production methods and make suggestions for further improvements.

The Administration Department handles all matters relating to Finance, Personnel, Safety, Training, and Information Technology and employs a total of 17 people. The Oil Scheduling section is also located in this department. This section co-ordinates the incoming quantities of crude and its return as finished product to the owners. It is in constant contact with the Operations Department, customers, and the Government's Customs Officers.

FIGURE 1
ORGANISATION CHART FOR DOCKLANDS REFINERY

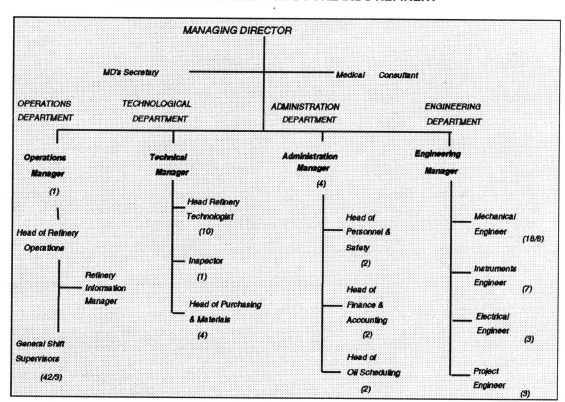

The Engineering Department carries out all predictive maintenance and repair work. It assists the Technologists in developing plant modifications and executes the resulting engineering projects. It employs a total of 44 people. The Mechanical workshop handles the work on the piping, cranes and other mechanical parts of the plant. The Electrical & Instruments workshop handles all the work on the electronic and pneumatic automation systems. The Office Engineering & design section prepares and keeps drawing records of every modification and handles project management.

THE MANAGING DIRECTOR AND STRATEGY MAKING

The Managing Director, Peter White, together with the heads of the four Departments form the top management team. All are engineers apart from the Administration Manager, John Connell, who is a Chartered Accountant with a first degree in Computer Science. John Connell is the only member of the top management team with any background or understanding of Information Technology.

Decision making at Dockside Refinery, always involves Peter White one way or another. He was chosen for this position after serving for years as an operations supervisor. He has a proven ability to manage people, and a deep knowledge of the Refinery operations. A qualified, experienced engineer, he feels quite comfortable moving around the plant area, being able to understand most problematic situations and contribute in the search for solutions. A true workaholic, he likes to be on top of everything and to give his personal contribution to every matter, even if doing so, leads him into the sphere of duty of the department Heads.

Strategy forming is an on-going process, where plans are regularly reviewed under all new external and/or internal developments. Peter White, in co-operation with the rest of the team, takes all strategic decisions and draws guidelines and policies for the operation of the company. There are regular strategy meetings. These are held in addition the daily morning meetings where the team deals with the everyday management of the company.

RELATIONSHIP WITH THE TECHNICAL ADVISOR

The parent company, Moboil, is also the official technical advisor of the company on all matters related to refining. It currently manages 20 refineries around the world for an annual of £240,000 sterling. DRL has access to information collected by Moboil on refining, energy conservation, safety, efficiency monitoring etc. This relationship is vital to the company, because it provides the kind of head office corporate support that a refinery of DRL's size desperately needs in order to operate efficiently for a long time. As a result, there is a traditional trend in the company to follow all the recommendations of the technical advisor without much challenge.

THE HISTORY OF INFORMATION TECHNOLOGY AT DOCKSIDE REFINERY

INITIAL INVESTMENTS

The first attempt at introducing Information Technology was made in 1985. The parent company and official technical advisor, Moboil decided to provide DRL with one of its in-house developed applications. Simoil is a package that simulates the oil refining process according to Moboil's technology and know-how and was intended to be used by the Technologists to test various configurations of the plant equipment, and perform elementary scenario planning. Through the years Simoil has been enhanced. It is currently on version 9 and is one of Moboil's most successful software applications. Two company employees went through a basic training course on Simoil at Moboil's local headquarters.

Simoil had been developed on computer equipment supplied by one company, Digital. Dockside Refinery therefore made its first hardware investment in a microVAX, a minicomputer supplied by Digital. Two terminals were bought at the same time. The operating system for all Digital's computers was a proprietary one (VAX/VMS) designed by the company and used by few other computer vendors. Until 1989, the VAX was the only serious hardware equipment in the refinery. During this period, Moboil supplied the refinery with another package, a General Ledger application. Two more elementary applications were developed, one for Payroll, and the other for Personnel (more accurately to hold records of the staff leaves), both of which ran on the VAX.

Personal Computers were also being introduced at this time. Four PC-XTs were bought, and used for standard packages such as word processing and spreadsheet analysis using Lotus 123. As there was no Information Technology department all the support for the hardware and software used was provided externally, mainly by the vendors. By 1989, these Personal Computers were under heavy use. Some complex spreadsheets had been developed, especially in the Technological and Oil Scheduling units (a Burner Fault Diagnosis Expert System, laboratory information system for the technologist's laboratory), which shows the degree of sophistication and creativity of the refinery's employees. Most of these programs have proved successful and are still used today as basic working tools. At least one model developed at that time was written in a programming language, COBOL. This is one of the early programming languages primarily used for commercial applications development that predates the arrival of the high level business application package. The programme ran on a Personal Computer and was written for the oil scheduling section.

In 1988 John Connell was hired to take charge of Information Technology, together with the other responsibilities of the Administration Department. He is now the top management team member officially responsible for decision making and strategy in Information Technology. He is a very enthusiastic individual who keeps himself up-to-date with modern developments in Information Technology. A constant driver for change, he is always eager to introduce new software systems to the company, many times underestimating the difficulties and complexities these changes may bring to the end users. As a result, he often finds himself isolated from the user community of DRL, who tend to face his enthusiasm with mistrust.

PROPOSAL FOR THE FIRST MAJOR SYSTEM DEVELOPMENT (THE REFINERY INFORMATION SYSTEM)

By 1989 it had become apparent to the management that Information Technology was an underused resource with a great potential. The information needs of the company were constantly growing and some sort of computerisation was clearly needed. DRL asked for the help of the parent company. Moboil's first action was to recommend that it was best to ".. *keep it simple*" taking into account the size of the refinery and the nature of its business. In their view it was not worth while building in-house development skills or creating a separate Information Technology department.

The Information Systems section of Moboil undertook the first Information Technology study for DRL. It was obvious to everyone in the company that the first project should be developed for the Operations department. Hence this was a feasibility study for an "Operations Statistics Database" which subsequently became known as the Refinery Information System (RIS). The objectives of the study were to establish the magnitude of the system and to recommend a suitable system architecture. The benefits from the development of such a system were identified as being:

- an increase in the refinery product yield (produce a more profitable mix of products),
- a reduction in the refinery energy consumption
- an overall improvement in management effectiveness due to a faster overview of operations.

These benefits were estimated to give payback in 0.78 years, making a lot of happy accountants.

At that time, Moboil was heavily dependant on the VAX architecture, so they recommended the purchase of a second MicroVAX minicomputer for this application. Ingres, a sophisticated database package which could be used on VAX machines was recommended for the creation of the database and the development of the application. The report was submitted to the Managing Director, Peter White in December 1989.

Peter White has little background knowledge in Information Technology and is constantly frustrated by the fact that he has to rely on consultants advice in this area. In this case he consulted the only two managers with any great understanding of Information Technology and it's use, John Connell and the Refinery Information Manager, Ian McGregor. Ian McGregor is an ex-Shift Supervisor, who has immense experience of the operations side of the refinery. He is an Information Technology fan, largely self taught, who like John Connell reads constantly to keep himself up-to-date with modern developments. He was assigned to his present position at the beginning of the Refinery Information System project.

Despite widely different backgrounds, experience and personalities, both these men combined to argue against the proposed hardware platform. Their view was that the company should not "lock" itself to a single vendor's platform, especially one that was based on an ageing technology like VAX/VMS. Instead DRL should move to a more "open" environment where hardware equipment and software applications could come from many vendors, increasing the choice and bargaining power of the company. The UNIX operating system was proposed as the most promising platform for a multi-user environment. UNIX, unlike VAX/VMS, is freely available to everyone. Many vendors, both software and hardware, provide products that work with UNIX in some version. The proposed database package, Ingres, for example was available in a version that would work on UNIX.

Opposition came from both Digital and the top management team, who reacted unfavourably to the idea of disregarding Moboil's recommendations. "*How can we possibly know better than them?*" was their attitude. However Peter White exhibited great trust in his own advisors and led the board to reject the VMS/Ingres option and choose UNIX/Ingres.

The need for many people to be able to access this system simultaneously when installed meant that some form of network would be required. In 1989 the standard design for Ingres was a star formation in which every terminal was connected directly to the minicomputer running the database. However, John Connell and Ian

McGregor made a case for the new client-server structure. At that time this was still an emerging technology and not a proven solution as it is today. Client-server supports distributed computing. It is possible to locate the database on a server (which is just a powerful workstation) and then locate many different applications on other client machines (usually microcomputers). The architecture more clearly separates the two aspects of a major database system; the applications that may vary from individual to individual or over time and the data that is the core resource common to them all. John Connell and Ian McGregor persuaded the top management team of DRL to invest in a client-server network. The IS section of Moboil evaluated the hardware for the selection of a server. They recommended an NCR Tower 500 server machine, running the AT&T version of the UNIX operating system.

Since the company had no development expertise of its own, it was necessary to hire a software house to develop the system for them. Seven companies responded to the invitation to tender with widely differing prices. Only candidates with local associates were considered. Two emerged as serious possibilities, one from UK and the other from Maumi. The UK candidate had a good reputation and offered a very competitive price. However, they proposed to do the Analysis stage in Maumi and the Development stage in UK, blocking the chance for interaction with DRL during the most crucial phase of the development cycle. The other candidate was Maumi's largest software house. They were also the general representatives of Ingres and under that identity had already been in contact with DRL, over an initial study on network topologies for Ingres. They had the advantage of being in Maumi for the whole of the development cycle and after the implementation. In the end, the local candidate, InfoSys, was selected, basically because of DRL's fear that due to the complexity of the project and the company's high operational dependency on it, they would need continuous, immediate on-site support over a longer period, and InfoSys was the only one that could provide this support.

DESCRIPTION OF THE REFINERY INFORMATION SYSTEM

The Refinery Information System collects readings from the plant and produces hourly and daily reports on the efficiency/utilisation of the refinery. Part of the application is aimed to support the Laboratory (Technology department) in their systematic (24 hour) testing of the quality of the oil products. It is a fairly complex application that incorporates over 200 forms, 150 reports, some of which use up to 10 database tables each, with calculations involving thousands of iterations. One iteration could call for the retrieval of 10,000 records. The data inputs and outputs are shown in figure 2.

The System is a tool to support the work of the Operations Department, in particular the Shift Operators, who will be able to have real time supervision of the Refinery plant. It also supports the people in the Technological Department, mainly the staff of the Laboratory that need to perform constant analysis of the oil products. However, information which is already stored in the database could be obtained with little extra effort and is potentially very useful to both the other departments.

As an information system, it is a Strategic importance/mission critical system, not only because of its functions and the way they are linked to the Business Strategy of the company. It also acts as the backbone on which all future applications will rely, since it handles almost all the acquisition and storage of information in the Refinery Database.

Ian McGregor, the system's sponsor and one of its original designers comments:

" The Refinery Information System has a great future because it is designed to be able to connect to and exchange information with, all the control points of the refinery as soon as the pneumatic control instruments are upgraded to full electronic mode. Of course an immediate replacement of these instruments would mean a huge investment. However, it is gradually happening, and the information system will follow and connect, step by step. At the end we will have a fully automated, intelligent refinery plant which will be easy to monitor and simple to control."

THE DEVELOPMENT OF THE REFINERY INFORMATION SYSTEM (RIS) AND THE START OF THE PERSONNEL INFORMATION SYSTEM (PIS)

During the years 1990-92, DRL's Information Technology activities were focused on proceeding with the RIS project and on making everyone familiar with this new resource. The lengthy development time was largely due to the need to create the database. All information relating to the refinery had to be collected and coded. The construction of a corporate data model for a company the size of DRL is a huge task. The system grew up over this period to include almost all of the operating data of the refinery. With this project on the way and looking good, the decision for a new application, the Personnel Information System (PIS) was taken.

FIGURE 2
INPUTS AND OUTPUTS TO THE REFINERY INFORMATION SYSTEM

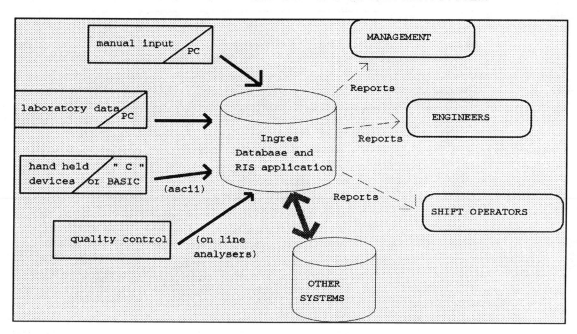

The new system will be used to track productivity and costing. Based on the working hours data that are input to the system by the employees themselves, the supervisors will be able to retrieve and calculate information on budgeting and costing of various tasks or projects, perform more effective Project Management, control overtime and plan Holidays and Sick leaves of the staff. Generally the introduction of the system addresses the areas of Personnel Records, Salaries and promotions, Training, Attendance and Leave records. The application is planned to replace a set of manual procedures together with the old Payroll application on the VAX, which is now out-dated and does not provide any of the required information. The PIS consists of two modules: a personnel system and a time costing system. It will have users from all the Departments of the Refinery, including Administration, Personnel, Accounts, Operations and Engineering, who will be able to create ad-hoc queries and reports, as well as extract information into spreadsheets for further analysis.

InfoSys developed both systems, using the same tools and many of the same people. Generally the two systems have many aspects in common. However, there are important differences between them, beyond their scope, size, or programming complexity. There were differences during the initiation, development, and implementation stages. These show how the experiences from the development of the RIS during the two years that passed before the start of the PIS project have "matured" the relationship between InfoSys and DRL.

With the first system, instead of arriving at a final agreement on the requirements of the client and the functional specifications of the application before the start of the development procedure, the programming started immediately. This is not what happened with the second system where the InfoSys manager explained that, " ..*no matter how difficult or painful it was, we arrived at a deal and we signed the specifications before any line of code was written*".

Another difference between the two projects, was the approach to written documentation. There was none for the System Analysis phase of the first system. The development started directly using the Ingres tools, after a basic session of database design. After the completion of the project, other tools will had to be used to carry out reverse engineering and produce the System Analysis documentation. For the second system, a formal methodology was followed resulting in much more complete documentation and a shorter development time.

The importance of having a project sponsor on the client's side was recognised and both projects had a sponsor. For the Refinery Information System it was Ian McGregor, the Refinery Information Manager and for the Personnel Information System it was John Connell, the Administration Manager. Ian McGregor was totally dedicated to the RIS, whereas John Connell had it on top of his other responsibilities. Ian McGregor's job was to act as a liaison between DRL and the developers. His duties, at the moment, refer specifically to that project. He has learnt Ingres well enough to write forms, and even debug the RIS forms to a certain degree. Being an extremely self-motivated person he has also ended up being *the* person responsible for Information Technology in the company. Apart from his RIS duties he deals everyday with troubleshooting, is the Network & Database administrator and takes care of the installation of every new software product that comes to the company. He has acquired a different approach on Information Technology to that of John Connell. He is less enthusiastic and more cautious when it comes to introducing new systems to the company. His attitude is the product of his experiences over the development period for the RIS, during which he says " *... I had the chance to confirm that it rarely happens the way they tell you it will at the presentation*".

HARDWARE DECISIONS

From 1989 onwards the company invested steadily in building an Information Technology infrastructure in the Refinery. The NCR Tower 500 machine was installed as server on the network which began to spread over the site. The major initial usage of the system was for those modules (fixed assets, general ledger and inventory) that were moved from the microVAX to the new UNIX machine, together with Ingres version 6.0 and the Ingres Development Tools. More Personal Computers were bought and connected to the network utilising the File Transfer Protocol (FTP) module mainly for file sharing on a common network drive. By mid 1993 more than 20 PC 386 machines using the MSDOS operating system had been acquired many of which were distributed to the administrative personnel. By this time 3 operating systems were being used at the refinery, VMS on the VAX, UNIX on the servers and MSDOS on the Personal Computers. Since the MicroVAX computer has never been connected to the network it is only the last 2 groups that can communicate.

Towards the end of 1992 and after two years of development and usage, it was realised that the NCR Tower was too slow for the RIS. The first modules delivered, were running at a very poor speed. It was then that an Information Technology consultancy firm, NET-Advice Consultants Ltd, was employed to undertake an analysis with the general objectives of "*...compiling a system specification based on the requirements of current and future DRL needs*".

NET-Advice's report submitted to the Managing Director in November 1992 supported the original decision to build a client-Server network. They assessed two options for upgrading the NCR Tower:

1. A Single processor machine to be used as Database Server (NCR 3447 or Digital 5900) @ US$ 45000
2. A Multi-processor machine with scalable upgradability (NCR 3450) @ US$ 84000. (This was the cost of the machine with one processor only)

The second server had the option of adding up to five more processor cards in order to upgrade its power. Multi-processing at the time was a general trend in the Information Technology industry for heavy duty databases, however, at least for the foreseeable future DRL had no plan to introduce multi-processor designed Operating Systems and software applications. The multi-processor machine (NCR3450) had about the same performance as the single processor (NCR3447), when run with one processor. NET-Advice's recommendation was to buy the multi-processor and trade-in the NCR Tower 500. The reason was its expandability capabilities, which gave the best price/performance options. DRL bought the multiprocessor at a price of US$84,000.

IMPLEMENTATION AND USE OF THE REFINERY INFORMATION SYSTEM

The Refinery Information System was planned to be implemented gradually as the separate modules were delivered. By mid-1992, the system went live in the Control Room, where the shift operators started acquiring data from the plant and storing them in the Database. The modules supporting the Chemical Laboratory at the Technological Dept were also delivered and put to use. There were some training sessions organised by staff from InfoSys, but the main part of the user training was carried out by Ian McGregor himself, who supported each group of users through the first weeks after the system's introduction. By today (1993), the system is being extensively used by the Operations and Technological departments. The quality of decisions has clearly improved, especially that of the control room operators who now can more easily monitor and control the plant.

However the system has not expanded to cross-company usage as fast as was planned. The central database has an enormous potential to cover all the possible information coming out of the plant. The designer/administrator of the database is not given the feedback and suggestions he wants from the refinery's employees, suggestions that would enable him to enhance the functionality of the system. One of the reasons for this drawback is the general culture of the company.

The refinery's departments operate autonomously, with as little interaction as possible and the general atmosphere does not favour transparency of information across the company or any co-operation between people from different departments. Politics is rather complex and extends from the line workers where operators compete with the technologists and engineers, right up to the top management team, where the non-engineer John Connell, is somewhat underestimated by the rest. Many of the middle managers in the departments consider the information they possess as a reflection of their power. Consequently, many people regard the RIS and the central database as the Operations' and not the Refinery's information system. Thus, they believe that making real use of this system and storing their valuable information in it, means transferring part of their power to the Operations Department and to its manager. In separate interviews, neither the head of the technology or the engineering department saw any potential for further applications in their departments.

RECENT DEVELOPMENTS; OFFICE AUTOMATION AND THE OIL SCHEDULING MODEL

A number of packages have been bought to support specific departmental functions. AutoCad, Microsoft Project, Maintenance MMS and Codex (a Moboil engineering codes specification program) for example are all installed on the workstations of the Engineering Department. Such types of applications can also be found at the workstations of the Technological Department. Their common characteristics are that they are all single user applications and apart from a few that run on the MicroVAX, the rest are MSDOS based. *Simoil* is running on the MicroVAX. However, the newly arrived latest version of Simoil is designed to run on the more powerful 486 PC. Hence, the MicroVAX is gradually retiring from use.

In Spring 1993, NET-Advice was asked to undertake another study, this time ".. *to review the whole network and produce an Office Automation Strategy with the main objective of increasing personnel productivity and effectively allocating computer resources*". The decision for this study was taken in an effort to find solutions to a number of problems DRL had with their Information Technology environment. These included the existence of various different programs of the same utility (3 different spreadsheets, 5 word processors...) which created various incompatibilities. However, the most important problem of all was memory management on the network. This was a problem for users on the network who needed to run <u>both</u> the office automation programs <u>and</u> the Ingres applications. They often had to reboot their Personal Computer workstations using a different configuration in order to run the desired application.

NET-Advice recommended the use of the new NCR 3450 machine as a file/application server as well as a database server and the adoption of a Graphical User Interface (Microsoft Windows). This would support all applications (market and developed) used by the refinery, offer a common user environment and undertake the memory management function.

This time however, unlike the previous occasion, the management of DRL decided to ignore NET-Advice's recommendations. Ian McGregor was seriously concerned about the memory problems on the network. These were primarily due to the memory resident programmes of Ingres which needed to be loaded before any application could be run. He knew that some of Ingres's modules could not work with Microsoft-Windows, so he was reluctant to accept that Windows could work. In contrast, John Connell was anxious to introduce a Graphical User Interface, being primarily concerned with the Office Automation of the company. The consultants focused on those issues too. The disagreement of the two internal experts managed to confuse Peter White, who received the impression that NET-Advice was trying to "sell" him a nice looking solution to a problem he did not have, ignoring the real problems of the company's Information Technology systems. By mid 1993 no further action had been taken on this issue.

Despite DRL's earlier decision, in 1989, to standardise on the UNIX operating system together with the Ingres database package, a decision was made in 1993 to develop a new application in COBOL to replace the old program used by the Oil Scheduling Unit. The project was assigned to a local software house, Compu-TECH. This angered Ian McGregor who declared that he " ...*found out about the details of this project after the contracts with the developer were signed.*" Elaborating on his views, he explained that the functions of this new application include the storing and manipulation of data that is already contained in the main Ingres database of the refinery. The new COBOL application will not be compatible and cannot make use of this already acquired and stored

298

information. The staff of the Oil Scheduling unit will have to use reports provided by the RIS in order to deduce and re-input data into the COBOL's information repository, resulting in the duplication of information and waste of time and effort. He also claims that the risk of errors has been increased due to the greater amount of human intervention. Following Moboil's earlier recommendation, Dockside Refinery has not created an Information Technology department or built any form of in-house development expertise. However, the company employs a lot of skilful people who, when they realise the potential of Information Technology, will teach themselves how to create programs and use various commercial applications. Information Technology expertise is primarily located in three groups; the people with standard spreadsheet and Personal Computer database skills (Lotus 123, dBase III+, etc.), the staff able to read, understand and write simple COBOL programs in the Oil account section, and the two men, John Connell and Ian McGregor.

CURRENT BUSINESS THREATS

Recent financial figures, published in the country's business press, show that the total cost of DRL production remains lower than CIF cost for the same product package, despite a declining trend. However, a predicted decrease of the freight rates due to other investments in finished product tankage, is expected to make importing products marginally cheaper than processing crude at DRL. Unless there is some sort of change, the refinery's prospects seem rather discouraging, giving food to various discussions concerning the fate of DRL, in the country's mass media. The various scenarios for the company fall into two main categories. According to them, Dockside Refinery Ltd can either continue to operate in the present form, as a petroleum refinery, or shut down its refining/production facilities and continue to operate as a central depot station for receiving and distributing the imported finished petroleum products to the rest of the island.

In order for the first option to work effectively, certain investments are necessary to bring the refinery up to date with the modern Safety & Environmental regulations and the new product specification requirements imposed by the United Nations Standards Committee. However, despite the government's commitment to undertake its share of the above investments, there is uncertainty as to whether the parent company and the other minor shareholders are willing to inject more capital into the company.

THE COMPANY'S BUSINESS STRATEGY

During the summer of 1993, Peter White circulated a memo in an effort to communicate to all employees the company's strategy. His aim is to avoid any change of the refinery's operations and to strengthen its negotiating position against any future threat. In the memo he identified the following four Criteria that must be met if DRL is to survive:

The cost of its products remains lower than the import cost
- Product specifications meet modern standards
- Environmental pollution remains within the limits stipulated by legislation
- Safety standards are maintained on behalf of both the workforce and the public at large

Elaborating on the first of the criteria, he outlined what he considered the most important aims for the company at this time:
- **The Maximisation of the plant on-stream time**. This is crucial since around 80% of the total operating costs are fixed.
- **The Maximisation of plant effectiveness**. It is important to reduce waste products such as RFG and maximise the production of those products like LPG which are the most expensive to import.
- **The Avoidance of waste** and improvement of working practices while maintaining good industrial relations. These aims can only be achieved by improving the performance of the plant.

THE ROLE OF INFORMATION TECHNOLOGY

DRL is in a difficult business position. Information Technology was not the cause of this situation but could be a crucial contributor to the refinery's survival. Before planning for the future, however it is important to identify where Information Technology has been poorly applied in the past and understand how this came about. Peter White needs advice on how to improve DLR's performance in using Information Technology. He needs proposals that will help the company to survive and to ensure it's longer term health.

ENDNOTES

[Teachnotes are available from the author].

REFERENCES

Bacon J (1990) Organisational Priciples of systems decentralisation JIT 5(2)

Brown A (Ed.) (1992) Creating A Business-based IT Strategy Chapman Hall

Brown A (1994) Getting value from an integrated information System to be published EJIS 1994

Earl M. (1989) Management Strategies for Information Technology Prentice Hall

Grindley (1992) Information systems issues facing senior managers: the culture gap JSIS 1(2) p57-62

Hodgkinson (1992) IT structures for the 1990s: organisation of IT functions in large companies J Information & Management 22

Kaplin R (1986) Must CIM be justified by faith alone? HBR March-April p87-95

Kovacevic & Majluf (1993) Six stages of IT strategic management Sloan management Review 34(4) p77-87

Legge K, Clegg C and Kemp N Ed (1991) Case Studies in Information Technology, People and Organisations NCCBlackwell

McKersie & Walton (1991) Organisational structure & IT. In The Corporation of the 1990s Information Technology and Organizational Transformation (Scott Morton M Ed.) Oxford University Press

Peters G (1990) Beyond strategy - benefits identification and management of specific IT investments JIT 5(4) p205-214

Remenyi DSJ, Money A and Twite A (1991) A guide to measuring and managing IT benefits NCC Blackwell

Scott Morton M Ed.(1991) The Corporation of the 1990s Information Technology and Organizational Transformation Oxford University Press

Venkatramen N (1991) IT-induced Business Reconfiguration. In The Corporation of the 1990s Information Technology and Organizational Transformation (Scott Morton M Ed.) Oxford University Press

Willcocks & Mason (1987) Computerising Work Paradigm

Windeatt & Knox (1992) Catalyst: a prgramme for change JIT

CHAPTER SEVEN

FRANCINE HAREL GIASSON
AN EDUCATOR, FIRST AND FOREMOST[1]

Francine Richer and Laurent Lapierre
Ecole des Hautes Etudes Commerciales de Montréal
MONTREAL, QUEBEC, CANADA

Abstract

This case describes the personal and professional development of Francine Harel Giasson, a brilliant teacher and a case method virtuosa. Her passion for her profession and her commitment to teaching have allowed her to develop exceptional relationships with her students. As a result, her classes often evolve into authentic happenings.

AN EDUCATOR, FIRST AND FOREMOST

With a wide generous smile lighting up her face, Francine Harel Giasson defines herself as follows: "First and foremost, I am an educator."

And a researcher.

And a non-conformist.

But she is also the little girl from Dorion Street who now travels comfortably in university circles and lives right across the street from the École des Hautes Études Commerciales.

She was a serious student who liked school--a top student.

She is a woman who grew up proud of her feminine heritage, in a Québec society in the midst of rapid change.

She is a woman who plays by the rules, but can make room for unconventional behaviour.

She is a woman who has known many firsts in her life and her career.

She is also a wife, mother, and grandmother.

Francine Harel Giasson is a professor at the École des Hautes Études Commerciales. She served as Director of Academic Studies at HEC from June 1, 1985 until May 1991, when she completed her second and last term.

I am totally at ease in this world of HEC where the profession includes teaching, research, contributing to internal operations, ensuring outside exposure for the school. My career here revolves around thought and action, and intellectual life itself includes practical applications as well as the critical analysis aspect. My daily routine gives me a chance to meet people from a variety of educational and philosophical backgrounds, of different ages and statuses. All of these aspects are important to me. I find them stimulating and I take a great deal of pleasure in them. Indeed, I tend to blend all these pleasures and enjoy them all indiscriminately.

THE LITTLE GIRL FROM DORION STREET

Francine Harel Giasson has teaching in her blood. Her grandmother taught school, as did her father and one of her aunts. Her mother also has a teaching certificate. In the Harel family, school was a valued treasure. For young Francine, it was a destination for special outings. As a youngster, she would go along with her father

---

[1]Translated from French by Helene Kaufman and André Cyr

or her aunt for certain activities. She knew that on those days, the rules could be bent slightly.

Her mother had high academic ambitions for her children. She made sure that they were accepted to the right convents and private preparatory colleges. When her oldest daughter was still in elementary school, she clipped a newspaper article for her about the first woman to win the Colin Award--a prize for the highest marks on the provincial matriculation exams--and another about the actuarial profession.

Another strong presence in the family was Georges Fleury, the parish priest and a close friend of Francine's father. On Saturday nights, the priest would babysit the Harel children. He was an eloquent speaker and with one or two of the children sitting on his lap, he would prepare his sermon for the next day. This is probably where Francine Harel developed her interest in communication.

At the Harel home, the class preparation book, the mark record book and the yellow report cards were familiar objects which the children were absolutely forbidden to make dirty. Francine Harel helped her father with correcting his students' assignments, often entering their marks in his record book or calculating totals and averages. She was her father's assistant. She was literally enveloped in a love of teaching. At a very young age, as the top student in her class, she was explaining work to others and helping them with homework over the phone. When she was in Grade 7, she even helped students who were having trouble in Grade 9. So, it was no surprise that she skipped Grade 2 and her first year of high school in the traditional classical humanities program of that time. Except for a brief flirtation with the idea of studying law, a temptation which she quickly rejected, Francine Harel Giasson has always known that she would end up teaching. She still knew this when she went back to school at the age of 30.

A TEACHER IN AN EVOLVING SOCIETY

THE FAST-TRACK

As she finished her classical humanities[1] program at the collège Marguerite-Bourgeoys de Montréal, Francine Harel chose to pursue a teaching career. She chose teaching because she loved it, but also because as the oldest child in a family of modest means she wanted to find a fast way to make a financial contribution to the family income. She promised herself that she would pursue more advanced studies at a later date.

Francine Harel registered in a program leading to a teaching degree at the *Institut pédagogique* (Teacher's College) affiliated with the *Université de Montréal*. With a Bachelor of Arts, it would take a year to earn a teaching certificate in this program. At the same time, with special permission, she began taking courses towards a science-mathematics teaching certificate, on Saturdays and during the summer. So, in short order she earned a Bachelor of Arts in 1959, a Bachelor of Education and an "A" level teaching certificate in 1960, and a special science-mathematics teaching certificate in 1961. She completed her teacher training at the age of 21, two years ahead of the usual length of time for such studies, and she had already been teaching a normal load for two years.

Her training was not the usual teacher training at the time. Generally, teachers went to teacher training school where they took four years to complete the "A" level certificate, allowing them to teach elementary or secondary school. The other option was to study for two years and earn a "B" level certificate needed to teach elementary school. The students in the fourth year of the "A" certificate program were in the same class as the students who had earned a Bachelor's degree who chose to go straight into teaching instead of first pursuing an undergraduate degree. The teachers' colleges, like the private preparatory colleges, were not co-ed.

In the last year of the teacher training program, the emphasis was on "methodology": methodology of language arts, mathematics, history. These "methodology" courses, now called "didactics," covered the ways and means of teaching, recipes, class preparation, and so forth. Basically, this was akin to the plumbing of teaching, and the courses held nothing new for the girl who had been "her father's assistant."

Nevertheless, she was interested in the philosophy of education as well as the texts of the great educators throughout the ages, and general psychology, child and adolescent psychology, and developmental psychology.

When she was a student teacher standing in front of elementary and high school classes, she was not in the least bit fazed. At the age of 19 she found it quite natural. Yet, now at 50, she is always nervous before she starts teaching a class.

Her experience of one-week student teaching sessions at the Sainte-Catherine girls' boarding school, where she had attended high school, was in fact just an extension of her summer job of play area monitor. She integrated imagination and play into her teaching.

A *BELLES LETTRES*[2] CLASS OF HER OWN - A FIRST!

When she was almost 20 and was studying for her Bachelor of Education, the principal of the collège Marguerite-Bourgeoys, Mother Saint-Sylvius, asked Francine Harel to teach at the college and to take over one of the three *Belles Lettres* classes. This was a first! The traditional girls' colleges were run by nuns and most of the teachers were nuns. Never before at the collège Marguerite-Bourgeoys had the responsibility for a class been entrusted to a layperson. The integration of lay teachers, especially in the traditional and prestigious institutions, had only just begun in the early 1960s.

Francine Harel Giasson has great admiration for the nuns who educated her. It was under their wise tutelage that she was able to accelerate her studies and thanks to their financial support that she attended the collège Marguerite-Bourgeoys. She has wonderful memories of her years at the collège, during which she developed a taste and appreciation for all those free cultural activities which she still enjoys so much. You will often find Francine Harel Giasson at concerts in the parks, the many outdoor festivals, noon-time concerts at Place Desjardins and Maison Alcan. And she is an avid devotee of the Québec City Summer Festival.

She is also aware of the respect she was shown by her teachers. She felt that she was recognized to be a gifted student, but was also regarded as a responsible person, with an instinct for teaching and respect for the values imparted by the institution.

So, at the age of 19 Francine Harel became a *Belles Lettres* teacher at collège Marguerite-Bourgeoys. She taught Latin, mathematics, and chemistry. She told herself that she should be capable of teaching what she had been taught and what she had understood when she was in *Belles Lettres* herself. Therefore, she prepared her classes from one week to the next or even from one class to the next. At that time, she made a more of a mark on her students in terms of human relations than in terms of the content of her teaching. She is also aware of this. She was young, tall, a talented layperson. In short, she was a new model for these students. Indeed she was also an emerging model for the nuns, who were around 45 years old, and were taking her trigonometry and differential calculus courses in the summer to prepare for their own Bachelor's degrees.

Francine Harel has the following to say about that first teaching experience:

Since that time, teaching has been the major thread of my professional life. My main passion is to awaken a taste for learning in others, to guide their learning, to help them discover the joy of having understood complex concepts and situations, to have established links or proposed new ideas, to see in their eyes the satisfaction of having exceeded their limits. No effort can be too much to reach these goals, neither in terms of content nor the form the instruction may take.

A WIFE, MOTHER AND GRANDMOTHER

At the end of 1961, Francine Harel became Francine Harel Giasson. As was customary at the time, she resigned from her full-time teaching position. However, she did continue to teach six hours of *Philo I* mathematics. She became pregnant almost immediately, and that led to another first: a layperson, teaching and pregnant, among the nuns.

The economic reality facing the young family pushed Francine Harel Giasson to earn more. In addition to her six teaching hours at the collège Marguerite-Bourgeoys, she took on a teaching load at the collège Saint-Denis in Montréal. This was a public lay college which accepted boys and girls who either had been expelled from other colleges or could not abide by their strict rules. This was Québec in 1962-63. The educational system, as traditional society in general, was on the eve of profound change.

Thus, the students attending this public college, located in a private home on Saint Denis Street, were considered "marginals or outsiders." Francine Harel Giasson taught *Versification* there. These youngsters had to be cajoled into learning and working. The teacher felt that her students were sharp, despite the high drop-out rate over the year.

That year Francine Harel Giasson met students who were very different from those at collège Marguerite-Bourgeoys and the Sainte-Catherine boarding school. They did not do well under some of the traditional structures of educational institutions. Though she is a highly disciplined woman, with a very distinguished style, Francine Harel Giasson considers herself to be a non-conformist as well. As a student, she did not like the chemistry labs where you had to perform experiments to find an answer which was written on the next page in the textbook anyway. With these so-called "marginal" students, Francine Harel Giasson was patient and counted on her fundamentally tolerant mentality, as well as on her appreciation of people with spunk and spirit. Indeed, Francine Harel Giasson is an individual with infinite respect for others and situations. She has faith in everything alive and lively. She admits that she tended to pay lipservice to the disciplined structures. While she did not breach the structures, she did give people, herself included, elbow room. Perhaps in these students she saw some of her own past, the little girl from Dorion Street who had unconsciously made concessions to the very formal system she had grown up in and was able to tolerate because of her special gift. Nevertheless, this system was no longer **the** answer nor was it the only path to acquiring knowledge, the only way to exist in this Québec society in the midst of the Quiet Revolution, the reorganization of its educational system and the marshalling of its hydroelectric resources.

In short, Francine Harel Giasson values different people.

She commuted between collège Marguerite-Bourgeoys and collège Saint-Denis throughout her first pregnancy. Moreover, since she and her husband were the only members of the Giasson family living in Montreal, she went each day for three months to visit her mother-in-law in the hospital at the Cancer Institute. In her words, "It was a whole winter, and what's more, our car was a real klunker!"

At that time, the expression "maternity leave" had not even been invented. Francine Harel Giasson taught her classes right up until she gave birth. Isabelle was born on April 29, 1963 and, much to the amusement of the doctors and nurses, the young mother continued correcting students' papers in her hospital bed. She was back in the classroom two weeks later.

She learned her lesson. It became clear that accumulating part-time teaching hours is hard work for little income. To save her strength and energy, Francine Harel Giasson sought a job as a full-time teacher, with a real salary and more steady working conditions. The Montreal Catholic School Commission was just opening a section of so-called "classical" studies for gifted students in a public high school. She taught French, religion, and primarily mathematics at the école Marie-Reine classique from 1963 to 1967. She was also the group leader in mathematics. She found this attempt at expanding access to classical studies very interesting. Indeed, for the first time the study conditions and the structure of the humanities courses became accessible to the general public. School hours were extended to 6 p.m. and there were classes on Saturday mornings, with Wednesday afternoons off. The girls in these classes were highly motivated students who, in many cases, would not have had the opportunity to enroll in a private preparatory school. They were top students attending a regional school. The atmosphere was excellent. These schools were run by nuns, but there were many lay teachers like Francine Harel Giasson. There was a high degree of *esprit de corps* among these teachers since they had been students together in the same private schools.

On December 4, 1964, Benoît was born and his mother continued her teaching career in the classical section of the new Marguerite-de-Lajemmerais high school on Sherbrooke Street in the east-end of Montréal. The science and general sections were located next door to the humanities section. The enriched, average, and below-average streams replaced all other divisions of students at the secondary level. With the creation of general and professional teaching colleges, generally known as Cégeps, the Quebec government abolished the last four years of these classical programs, i.e. *Belles Lettres, Rhétorique, Philo I and II*.

At the secondary level, Francine Harel Giasson taught mainly lecture courses. The students' assignments were exercises and math problems which the teacher corrected regularly and which formed the basis of new explanations or the starting point for new lessons the following day in class. Her students were highly motivated. In 1970, she was teaching a group of 9th grade students, in the below-average stream, but who had the ability to move up to the average stream through make-up classes. This experience appealed to Francine Harel Giasson because it was true teaching: "They needed more help than usual."

In 1970, Francine Harel Giasson left secondary education and the Montreal Catholic School Commission.

SHE HAD IT ALL, BUT...

Since she had earned her teaching certificate in 1961, Francine Harel Giasson had been considering going back to school one day.

In 1970, economic pressures weighed less heavily on her family and on her professional aspirations. Benoît was starting kindergarten. It was the right time to make her move. Logic dictated that she should go back to university to study mathematics, but something was holding her back.

Reconciling family life with professional interests, her union experience, and serving as chairman of the PTA had all given Francine Harel Giasson a firm grasp on real life. Her entire managerial baggage in 1970 consisted of her husband's business experience (Bertin Giasson was a graduate of the École des Hautes Études Commerciales - HEC), her own experiences as a student and a young mother trying to make ends meet each month, and the experience of purchasing their own home. At a meeting of the finance-investment circle, her husband happened to run into François Charette, a finance professor at HEC. As a result of their conversation, Francine Harel Giasson learned of the existence of a recently created MBA program at HEC and the possibility of being accepted into this program without any prior courses in business administration. According to François Charette, she had a good chance of being accepted. Without further deliberation, she decided to apply. She filled out the application form very carefully, highlighting her academic achievements and her experience, which was certainly relevant.

In accordance with the school commission regulations, she had to resign from her teaching position and request her pension even before she had a positive response from HEC, but she was confident that things would turn out all right.

The Assistant Dean, Denis Duquette, finally notified her: "You have been accepted."

Going back to school breathed fresh air into Francine Harel Giasson's career. She earned her MBA in 1972 and her Ph.D. in management in 1981. Her doctoral dissertation, directed by Professor Jean-Marie Toulouse, was entitled "Perception and Current Conditions of Promotion Factors Among Women Middle Managers in Large Frenchspeaking Québec Firms in the Private Sector.[3]

It was a pleasure to be a student again in a class, going from one course to the next! It was exhilarating and relaxing. It was also marvellous to be in a school of educators. She loved the lectures. As she put it herself, she was drinking from the well. In the second year of the MBA, Jacques Parizeau[4] was one of her professors. She discovered the case method and the artists of teaching using this method.

DISCOVERY OF THE CASE METHOD

When she first entered HEC, Francine Harel Giasson did not know anything about the case method, but she quickly realized that she liked it.

I had been working for ten years. I was not in management, but I did have a good instinct for it. This is what the case method lets us, as students, verify.

The case method suited her personal affinity, present in 1970 as it is now, for confronting ideas and practices.

She also believes, an educator's reflex, that this method can be used in other fields.

In the MBA program, the majority of courses are given according to the case method. Thus, as an MBA student, she was always in the process of preparing cases, and she realized that this type of course plays a major role in a student's organization of time. She understood the relativity of the concept of the "right answer" as a criterion of success in a course, as well as the special qualities of the "culture" of the MBA program.

Her fellow students, like herself, were enthusiastic and enjoyed learning and working on the cases in marketing, finance, and administration. These concerns far outweighed the quest for good marks. The goal was truly to acquire useful reflexes in the practice of management. She still believes that this type of program must seek to establish genuine group support and the personal commitment of the students in their learning process.

ON USING A CASE, BY FRANCINE HAREL GIASSON

Francine Harel Giasson first taught the case method at the Saint-Jean Military College where the new Bachelor of Administration program was established in 1972.

Another first: she was the first woman professor in a military college in Canada. This time, she was able to count on her past experience. She found that, "Being a civilian in a military college is a lot like being a lay person in a religious college." She taught administration, personnel management, and policy. She had her students work on cases in every class.

While she was teaching at the Saint-Jean Military College, she was also working at HEC with Pierre Laurin. In the framework of a research project on the integration of university graduates in small and medium-sized businesses, she wrote a case, prepared classes, and wrote an article. In addition she taught an undergraduate day course in management at HEC.

She was 32 years old.

As a student she had been trained according to the case method. So Francine Harel Giasson structured her first courses around her own class notes from the MBA and common sense.

I did bits and pieces selected from what had been taught to me at the HEC. I did a lot of imitation.

I did the best that I could. It seemed to me that I knew before I walked into the classroom, that for me, it was a good method. I also knew that it was a hard method for the teacher.

I had no theory on the cases. I had only practical knowledge and it was practical knowledge from a student's perspective, at that. When I was preparing my courses I would often refer to the teaching notes of my more senior colleagues such as Marcel Côté, Pierre Laurin, Paul Dell'Aniello, and Bertin Nadeau for background reading. What would come back to me in a flash of inspiration would be the techniques of people able to lead a discussion for an hour and a quarter on a given case.

Even now, when Francine Harel Giasson prepares a class according to the case method, she puts herself in her students' shoes and she thinks back to her former professors.

A TWO-STAGE PREPARATION

Francine Harel Giasson identifies two separate stages in the preparation of a course using the case method. The first stage involves an overall general preparation which addresses the objectives, the foundation, the content; the second stage is an immediate preparation focussing on the form, an extremely meticulous form.

General Preparation
The general preparation is actually the course outline.

As the years go by, I spend more and more time on developing this course outline and I think that it is a reflection of my student life. As a student, I liked having a good course outline which I could refer to throughout the semester; it would let me know what to prepare for the next class or if I could skip a class on a particular day. Thus, I constructed my course outline with this in mind. Once I have set this outline, I am the type of person who will not go back and change it.

The course outline must deal with the general objectives of the course. Once the topics and the underlying theme have been chosen, the course is then broken down into thirteen specific objectives corresponding to each weekly session.

Thus, using the general outline of the course, from one class to next, it is possible to locate this course in relation to the preceding ones and in relation to those which will follow it. The learning objectives are specified in terms of "the student will be capable of...": be capable of making a complete analysis of an issue, be capable of defining such and such a concept, be capable of solving problems at such and such a level of difficulty. These are the operational objectives; if possible, at the three levels of knowledge, technical know-how, and behavioral know-how.

In this course outline, the students finds all the work they will have to do, all the readings, the evaluation method, and the percentage breakdown of the final mark.

This document, concretely translating the effort of structured planning of the course which the professor is giving, constitutes a very valuable communication tool, on the one hand between the professor and the students, and on the other hand, between the professor and his/her colleagues in the same field or in other disciplines.

Experts in university teaching are unanimous in acknowledging the importance of a good course outline in terms of both guiding the student through the learning process and encouraging a valuable pedagogical reflection on the part of the professor who is preparing the next session.[5]

The first hour of the class is spent primarily presenting this course outline and discussing it. Francine Harel Giasson does not put the course outline into the printed set of course notes. She brings it with her and it is her first "gift" to the students.

The second hour, she presents and discusses the first case. She also brings it with her, since she has found that the students may have trouble obtaining the course notes before the first class.

Nothing should spoil the first class, especially something like not having essential papers. I feel that the first class has a major impact, the message that it gives: Here we are going to roll up our sleeves. We will gain enormous satisfaction from our work, but we will work hard.

Out of respect for my students, I rarely deviate from what is indicated in the course outline. If I make changes, it is for the following year.

Immediate Preparation

In the week preceding a class, and especially in the hours before a class, the teacher concentrates essentially on its form. I really don't leave the form to chance. In the case method, there is a lot of preparation of questions. I always have a series of questions.

In her eyes, the opening question is the most fundamental. For some of the subsequent concepts, there may be two or three alternative questions. All three are written down.

I will choose one or the other depending on what has already been raised in the conversation. Within each of the questions, I am capable of leaving enough room for all sorts of interpretations. But, my questions are always focussed.

Her course preparation does not include much written text. There are questions, but really very little text, maybe four pages, maximum, with large spaces left blank, for different scenarios!

I concentrate a great deal on what is happening in the class, rather than on the questions that I will ask afterwards. I am paying close attention to what is going on in the class. I am very attentive.

IN CLASS

A learning and communicating experience

What takes place in the class is basically a learning and communicating experience.

I have a dual objective when I teach with the case method. One of the goals deals with the actual topic at hand, but there is another goal: by speaking in class, the students are also learning the craft of management, they are developing communication skills. Regardless of the issue under discussion, for me the way that each student speaks about it is as much a learning experience as learning the content itself. The message is clear:

Each and every one of you has the best idea in the world. You have prepared the best report in the world. It is truly the way in which you will speak about this report to the people who count which will determine whether your idea takes off or gets buried in the cemetery of good ideas.

I really buy into this idea that managing, to a very great extent, is communicating.

Listening on two levels

Francine Harel Giasson finds that this is quite tiring, since this type of method requires you always to be listening on two levels: you cannot lose the train of the discussion, nor lose sight of the specific learning objectives targeted, but you also have to be stimulating.

She structures her immediate preparation of the course on the basis of these two levels of listening.

Aside from the questions, the immediate preparation is a search for variations, alternatives: the use of games, very few transparencies, an illustration, role playing/simulations, a little surprise. She takes a vote at the beginning of the class, for example, launches the discussion, sets half the class against the other. At the end of the discussion, she takes the vote again.

I want very much for my students to be thinking of things. To make sure of that, I rely on my instincts and I look out at the students' eyes which can tell me whether they are working or they are thinking about something else.

I am obsessed by a fear of being boring. This probably comes from the audience side of me, whether at the theatre, movies or ballet. I detest being bored; I don't mind if it makes me cry or it makes me laugh or it makes me shout. But I don't want to be bored. I don't want any flops. Yet, it doesn't have to be me who gives the show.

To complete her immediate preparation, to make her feel secure, Francine Harel Giasson puts everything together in a file folder including the various details and information on the case. For example, it may include the class notes of a professor who has already given the course, some additional calculations, notes typed in large print so they are easier to read from far away on looseleaf paper.

Whatever it takes

In class, Francine Harel Giasson will do whatever it takes:

Give me any story, fiction or non-fiction, from the business world or not, and I will try to do something with it which will be useful in management.

I have learned a great deal outside of the official corpus of the discipline and I want to share it with my students. Plays, novels, short stories are excellent teaching tools.

Indeed, she has already used Racine's *Britannicus* to illustrate the different sources and aspects of power. *Britannicus* is not a case; the students are well aware of it. They welcomed this perspective and understood the keen knowledge of the human being, the brilliant intuitions of this author. They appreciated this "trip" outside of business firms to visualize and understand power games.

Similarly, a sensitive short story by Madeleine Ferron, "*L'avancement*," from the collection *Le Chemin des dames* relates the feelings of a woman who has been appointed a credit union inspector and is about to make her first rounds. In a short story of just eight pages, these concepts of the identity of women who do so-called "men's jobs," the difficulty that men have to make room for them, this requirement that women have to succeed in this man's world are described with finesse. Such a tool allows the students to understand, to feel, to smile, and not only to argue.

Time is also part of this immediate preparation of the course. "I am a maniac when it comes to time." For each question, a time limit is set in advance, and this limit is respected. Whatever has not been learned this time, will be learned another day. We did what we could with that particular twenty minutes.

Francine Harel Giasson prepares to enter the class as if she were an actor walking on stage. She has intense moments of painful stage fright.

The last half-hour before a class, I am in a total panic, no question about it. Even if I have the feeling that everything will turn out fine, the last half-hour is extremely difficult. I want to take strength from my pain. I end up standing up, pacing about, a little like a bear in a cage. Just half a minute into the class, I can hardly remember the feeling. It's very much like giving birth.

FORMALIZATION OF LEARNING

In the case method, a major portion of the learning objectives is related to an awareness that there are divergent opinions, that the drastic solutions are not the best ones. The students know that there is a conceptual content underlying the discussion of a case. Some expect the professor to supply the "right answer." So, how can we formalize the learning content without making the students passive?

Regularly, at certain intervals in the semester, to help the students register what they are learning in the course through the case method, Francine Harel Giasson devotes an hour and fifteen minutes to summarizing the major elements of the information drawn from the readings which complement the cases to be prepared.

According to Francine Harel Giasson, it is preferable to keep these special reviews of the readings separate rather than integrating them into a case discussion. This would reduce the case to an exercise. The readings are not systematically excluded from a discussion of a case, but in the class discussion, the action contained in a case takes precedence over them. However, if the students are to take these readings and the information they contain seriously, they have to be paid some attention by the professor in a well-identified segment of the course.

She sometimes purposely "forgets" to make those end-of-course review lectures where the students are waiting for the professor to finally reveal the "right answers." Generally speaking, she does a review at the end of the course. She is very disciplined and she employs only the concepts and the vocabulary used by the group. She is very careful to add nothing of her own so she ends up giving the students a mirror of their work, thus making them responsible for their learning. However, she has already established the analytical grid on which she will list the students' contributions.

Another form of review, which is highly personal and indispensable for her, is that she forces herself to write down her own impressions of the class which has just ended. Basically, she is writing a self-critique as a professor. Being able to do this self-critique is "a badge of maturity." The following year, she rereads these notes and uses them to improve the course outline.

It is very worthwhile, but it takes an iron discipline. When I leave the class, the only thing I feel like doing is going home, stretching out in my lazy-boy, with a drink in my hand.

FRANCINE HAREL GIASSON, EDUCATOR

PASSION, A PRIORITY

In class, I give priority to action, to provocation, to passion, to individuals taking a stand.

Francine Harel Giasson demands several hours of preparation from her students. The students have to read the case and do other readings. These hours--and not minutes--of work are necessary to understand the case, to make the connections with the things they have learned or read in an article, to encourage intellectual considerations, to refer to live situations, to make calculations, to propose solutions.

During the course, the case always takes precedence. Within the course the readings have marginal or complementary value.

When the students see that it is true, that you are really building based on what takes place in the class and on what they bring to it, then they apply themselves to it.

THE INDIVIDUAL, A PRIORITY

When she gives an evening course, she does not assign team work before the class discussion; it would be too much to ask these adults to have to plan other meetings. For the full-time students, it's another story.

Francine Harel Giasson takes an interest in all of the aspects of interpersonal relations in class.

She gets to know her students very quickly; she feels that it is very important to identify them correctly and to address them by name. She uses nameplates and each student has an information card and a photo. In response to these students, who are sometimes surprised by this requirement, she says:

You have chosen a school where the people are not numbers, they are individuals. I will not agree to teach classes to anything except people.

For many years she used to learn the names of her students rapidly by playing with the information cards and photos with her own children. You guess and you get to keep the card. "But, the children are grown up now."

She remarks that in class the students make the professor's job easier by always sitting in the same spots.

On the technical level, she finds that the U-shape of most of the HEC classes favours group discussion, a certain dramatization and the professor's movements.

Francine Harel Giasson checks herself in the mirror before going into the class and prepares herself as if it were a job interview; this is out of pride as well as respect for her students. She conducts herself in a very official manner in the classroom. When she teaches large groups, she remains standing. She walks around the room. She moves closer to one individual or another to give him/her more attention. She moves away from one who speaks softly to encourage them to speak up. She stands behind a student who is speaking directly to her as the professor, so as to explicitly encourage him/her to address the other students. She likes to walk around to create a more relaxed atmosphere, because teaching is different than "presiding."

Time management, time itself, is always a point of mutual respect.

Like a train, I start on time and I finish on time, though I don't go so far as to stop in the middle of a sentence. I am extremely reserved with regard to what I believe I am showing them. Whatever I didn't show them today, I will show them another day and if it isn't me, it will be another professor, or it will be life.

MANAGING THE SILENCES

Silences in class are another one of her conquests of maturity.

At the beginning, I had a tendency to intervene right away. Now, if I have decided that the next sentence will come from the class, there is nothing that will budge me.

For me, silences are extremely important and easy to live with once you've tried them. This tool is important so as not to develop student passivity which I fear so much. If there is a silence and the professor speaks up, it's over. The student does not feel responsible for the next silence. He/She has just categorized that as something under the professor's responsibilities.

There are different sorts of silences. Aside from waiting silences, there are the silences of groups which are half-dead, where the discussions fall flat.

At those times, I rouse someone's passions, no matter whose. This is when I use my instincts.

The class may be divided in two, without taking into account individual opinions, roles are assigned. Irony, provocation rather than intellectual reference points, but especially passion! Francine Harel Giasson admits that when she does not succeed in triggering passion, she feels empty, ashamed and she wants to fade into the woodwork after a class.

ESTABLISHING COMPLICITY

While there are silences in the dynamics of a group, there are also individual silences, those of students who have not made up their minds to speak. Some of the most bashful students can be gently questioned, prodded. Others will need a more personal meeting. Francine Harel Giasson calls them to her office. Sometimes they can get used to the idea of communicating. During a face-to-face meeting, an agreement, a sort of complicity will be established between the student and the professor. This complicity may grow out of one or two sentences prepared in advance and inserted at an appropriate moment.

I establish little plots...two sentences to say during the next class, without worrying too much about whether they are said at the right moment. The person will say them just to break the ice, to get past the point of never having spoken. If it goes well, I reinforce it. If it was not very successful, I will arrange things so the student can save face. I am even prepared to let something false take place in the class at that precise moment.

She may arrange with the student that she is going to address him/her first and give him the time to read what he has written on a well-prepared sheet. She does not put pressure on these students who are trying to break the ice without having spoken to them in advance and without having set up a plan. Francine Harel Giasson is proud of the success rate she has had with her system of interpersonal contracts with students who have trouble getting up the nerve to speak in class for the first time.

On the other hand, there are those who speak too much, the ones who are too brilliant, the show-offs, or the specialists in the art of digression. Francine Harel Giasson pushes and provokes the show-offs. She even pushes them a lot. She enjoys going one-on-one with the big talkers.

When the big talkers have been speaking for too long, she will ask to hear three new voices within the next twenty minutes. At other times, she will push a student who has come up with a good idea, but has not developed it enough to go further. This is to bring out the *crème de la crème*. When there are digressions, she leaves it up to the group which will either integrate them into the discussion or will ignore them. If there is a confrontation, she will do some "decoding" in the group. If the situation becomes untenable, she brings the group back towards her challenge: the learning.

In a course with Francine Harel Giasson, there is a lot of laughter, both at her jokes and at those of her students:

My idol is Clémence Desrochers. If I didn't like to laugh, if it hadn't been a part of me, I would have made a concerted effort to insert laughter into my personal development program. There is so much complicity in humour.

In class, Francine Harel Giasson counts on her qualities as a communicator. She rarely relies on technical innovations; there are few videos or audio-visual presentations. She will use them on occasion, as a surprise. Her primary concern

is that each individual in the class is treated well and that the group learns that there are opportunities to learn all around us. I am not concerned with building the group. What concerns me most is that no one should leave without taking something to heart.

THAT PROFESSOR-STUDENT RELATIONSHIP

To do a good job teaching, especially in a university environment, you yourself have to be skilled at intellectual exercise, a craftsman of the development, structuring and dissemination of knowledge.

Professors have to feel good about themselves and be aware of the dynamics which develop between themselves and each of their students. The quality of the relationship which must be established between them seems to Francine Harel Giasson to be a determining factor in the process of growth which takes root in the professor as well as in the student.[6]

The activity of teaching is essentially a form of communication.

Each time a professor teaches, what he/she is saying to the students is that they exist and he/she exists. He is also telling them who they are for him and who he is. Clearly, teaching, being a form of communication, cannot be summed up as the simple transmission of knowledge. Teaching touches one of the most sensitive nerves of human beings, their respective identity.

Identity is the representation that an individual makes of himself, his personal answer to the question "who am I?"

For Francine Harel Giasson, this identify is not a monolithic nucleus. It is more like a kaleidoscope, with several constant facets, but which are activated according to the circumstances. Mother, professor, researcher, manager, wife, and so forth.

We are able to build this identity based on the regard of others for us and the impact of this regard. No matter who the professor is, her own visions, her own values relative to the identity of her students will be transmitted relatively explicitly in her teaching and the implicit message will be as strong as the official and explicit message.

Envisioning teaching as an art of communication has helped Francine Harel Giasson reflect upon her pedagogical practices, so as to improve them and to highlight difficulties which seemed to have very mysterious origins.

The greater the distance is between the identify of the teacher and that of the students, the more the teacher will have to have an open mind and heart if he/she wants to avoid the pitfall of contempt, on the one hand, and that of distrust, on the other hand.[7]

THE QUALITIES OF A CASE

If I like the case, I have the feeling that it will go well, and if I don't like the case, I feel that it won't go well. But, it's not always true.

Her favourite cases are those of decision-making, cases which raise questions such as: "What would you do in so and so's shoes?" "What is happening?" "What would you take into account?" "Let's change places now. What decision would you have made?" "What will happen next?"

Basically, she opts for the cases which allow the student to anticipate and to take a stand in a given situation, as in management. There are no answers to the questions which were raised to get the discussion underway. However, there is the awareness of pursuing very specific learning objectives.

WRITING A GOOD CASE

Francine Harel Giasson has written few cases. Under the direction of Pierre Laurin, she wrote "Gauthier & fils" (1973), "La pépinière Bernier" (1973), and "Steinberg - Beaucoup" (1976). She found the experience highly instructive. She co-authored the case "Jutrex inc." (1983) with Marie-Françoise Marchis-Mouren.

To write a good case, Francine Harel Giasson favours an approach in which there are interviews and an observation period. Yes, it is a good idea to spend several days on site particularly when the situation involves several people or makes reference to a decision of the firm rather than to individual dynamics. This observation period is important to get a feel for things, to take notes, to identify incidents. In the case of "Gauthier et fils," she felt the void around a man. "I have never forgotten that void."

She writes her cases as short stories which place us in the situation in a few pages. Once again, her main concern is to avoid boring her students. She instinctively chooses to narrate so that it is interesting.

Figures, yes figures.

I also like for there to be figures. I am always loathe to talk about management without some figures to back me up. I find that it is not credible. Yes indeed, I like figures.

Episodic cases also hold special interest for her because they integrate elements of time. She would design them differently, a little like the actual life of a board of directors. Before a board meeting, the members study their papers. At the board, new facts are presented by an internal manager or by a member of the board. You have to get the picture rapidly.

Francine Harel Giasson regrets that when she was a student she did not have enough opportunity to practice this skill of making links by taking these new facts into account. It has been through her experience as a manager and a member of boards of directors that she has realized its importance.

Other elements of information in the cases deal with customs or ways of doing things in firms. She considers this information very useful as an initiation to business, yet on condition that students be encouraged to develop or preserve an adequate critical spirit. It is good to know that things occur in such and such a way in firms, but that does not mean that these things cannot change and that there is no place for progress and innovation.

PROBLEMS ENCOUNTERED

The first problem that she admits encountering is one of teaching and excellence.

I believe that I am someone who works hard in terms of the simplicity of concepts, syntheses. Throughout life, I've been told: Oh Francine, with you it's so clear now!

In terms of teaching, clarity worries her. Is it in her nature to motivate students to make an effort? Indeed, learning by the case method requires students to work up a sweat.

I motivate people to be enthusiastic, but perhaps not to work. Since I need to work hard to arrive at simplicity, it seems to me that it should be the same for them. I do not hesitate to give a really low mark to a student who does not invest enough time and effort in the course. I have a biting sense of humour which drives me to confront this student with his mediocrity publicly. I try to do this as infrequently as possible, but sometimes I do it.

Teaching a case which she has written herself has already caused problems. She admits this difficulty and ascribes it to the fact that she was too sure of herself with regard to this case. On these occasions, some references are in the professor's head, but are not in the text. In fact, the professor and the students are not working on the same case. It shows and it is felt. However, this can be corrected and since then she pays particular attention to sticking to the text that the students have in front of them. If she brings in new official elements--which the students like very much--it is after the actual discussion has taken place and without invalidating the decisions made on the basis of the written text.

Another problem is giving the same class twice in one week. She does not succeed in drawing out the same quantity and the same quality of energy. If the first class has gone well, she relaxes and the second one does not go as well. If the first class has not gone well, she has to prove herself out of pride and it is the second class which will be better. Moreover, if she gives the same course the following year, she refers to her notes and incorporates whatever lessons she learned to make the process work better.

In the case method, it is important for the students to evaluate their learning by themselves because they will find it difficult to see their progress.

As a professor, however, I do not find it more difficult to measure the students' learning. For the students who leave the classroom with very few notes, they may have the impression that they have not learned very much.

I take the luxury of helping them to realize that they are learning something. Among other things, I show them that they have changed their minds during a class by taking a vote at the beginning of the class and again at the end, or I deal with the same case or another very similar one at the beginning and the end of the semester. I ask for a written text each time and I compare them to show the students that they have changed. After all, changing is a form of maturing.

EVALUATING STUDENTS IN THE CASE METHOD

Evaluation of students in a course given according to the case method must be based essentially on the case. I have a credo of ongoing or continuous evaluation. I despise exams that count for 100% of the final mark. I am never looking for the correct answer when I grade a case. I don't care what decision has been made, but I give marks for how the decision is justified, the list of elements which have been taken into consideration, and the correct anticipation of the consequences of that decision.

In fact, Francine Harel Giasson is not concerned when a bad decision seems to have been made. A bad decision cannot leave her indifferent! However, she will remain true to her original criteria even though she acknowledges that it takes some effort on her part.

Francine Harel Giasson is quite comfortable with her method of evaluation. Since there are several evaluations, no one fails unless they really deserve to. It is easy for her to pinpoint who has done satisfactory, above average, or outstanding work.

As part of this continuous evaluation, each week she asks her students to write a short page on the case and she takes the four highest marks from the semester. "So it's not like a guillotine." But the short page helps to get them thinking, it fosters class participation and decision-making. It helps her adjust her teaching to what the class has actually understood. One or two cases will be the basis of more detailed assignments and the exam will be a case.

At the mid-term, she gives the students the mark that she would have given them to date if it had been the time to evaluate their class participation. If there is a big gap between her mark and what they think they deserve, she asks them to write down the mark they would give themselves. If there is a big difference between the two marks, she reconsiders the matter.

WHAT ATTITUDE MAKES THE CASE METHOD WORK BEST?

When you teach the case method, confidence is the most important attitude. This confidence that one has in the interaction between the few reference points made by the professor and the wisdom, the strength of the group always produces something: "It always works!"

She finds the following comparison borrowed from Paul Dell'Aniello, a former colleague, very inspiring. He compares teaching the case method to conducting a jazz band. A jazz band has certain reference points, but there are always long improvisations. It is not like a classical orchestra which plays by following score.

I have my reference points, just about every twenty minutes. Within these twenty minutes, it is improvisation and the "happening." My job is to see to it that the "happening" part takes place.

MANAGING AND TEACHING MANAGEMENT

Francine Harel Giasson, was the Director of Academic Studies at the École des Hautes Études Commerciales from June 1985 to May 1991; as part of her related duties she has also served as Chairman of the Programs Council, member of the Pedagogical Council, member of the Administration Committee, member of the Committee of Vice-Rectors, Academic Affairs of the Conference of Rectors and Principals of Quebec Universities (CRÉPUQ), and member of the Commission des études of the Université de Montréal. The Registrar's Office, the Recruitment, Microfilm, and Institutional Research Offices, as well as the Office responsible for the Quality of Communication all reported to her. Thus, she was a manager at HEC.

From the very beginning, I wanted to cast my role under the banner of mutual aid among the members of the team, of collaboration with our other partners in the School, of respect for students, and assistance for entrepreneurship, whether it involved launching new programs, revising existing programs, creating an Office Responsible for the Quality of Communication or reversing a trend in the recruitment of Cegep students.

She has also taken on a management role as a member of the board of Loto-Québec since 1982, and a member of the board of John Labatt Ltd. since May 1987.

Yes, the teaching of management is a mental reference in her way of managing. Cases pop into her head spontaneously. Similarly, mental references drawn from her experience as a mother and from the role models in her life, her mother, her mother-in-law, and her grandmothers, also come to mind.

Her desire to have her managerial experiences nourish her teaching is evident. She takes notes. During the sabbatical year which separated the end of her mandate as Director of Academic Studies and her return to full-time teaching, she planned to work on integrating her management experience into her teaching.

In the final analysis, managing and teaching are the same profession. Both are largely arts of communication.

She is now working with Laurent Lapierre to develop a course focusing on the development of human resource management skills. Drawing on her recent six years of experience as head of a team of some 80 people, of her successful endeavours, as well as her less successful ones, she wants to contribute to developing a better mastery by her students of those arts which are effective in human resource management.

In her teaching, Francine Harel Giasson deals with organizational experiences and integrates many anecdotes drawn from family life. When she speaks about rivalry, what could be more concrete an example for her students than sibling rivalry, or rivalries between in-laws? Power is illustrated in children's street games. The one who brings the ball is hardly ever thrown out of the game, even if the kid is a pain.

When we speak to young students about the world of business, we are speaking about a world which they do not know.

It seems to me that it is reassuring for people to see that if you are able to get along in a game of ball in the street, you may also be able to get along in a management committee.

Just as she is with her children and her grandchildren, with whom she was and still is more of a play area monitor than a school teacher, this mother, who found homework-time to be one of the most joyful moments in her life, gets a thrill out of her work as a manager when she sees a light of enthusiasm go on in those she works

316

with.

She speaks fondly of the Registrar's Office:

I put too much into the Registrar's Office to let that part of my work go unmentioned. When I first started there, it was a major challenge and I feel that I contributed a great deal to carving a respectable place for that office and its staff in the life of the HEC and to having made it a dynamic, efficient and warm place to work.

I do not teach people to work in my teams, but when I am capable of stimulating people to strive for more, when I see people being able to do things this year that they couldn't do last year, I am overjoyed. That sort of thing makes me melt like butter.

I learned a great deal from them and my future teaching will benefit greatly from that experience.

THE WOMEN, MANAGEMENT AND ORGANIZATIONS GROUP

In 1981 Francine Harel Giasson co-founded the Women, Management and Organizations research group and was its leader for several years. Her research interests deal with the place of women in organizations, the reconciliation between career and family and organizational life. After all, that was the topic of her doctoral dissertation.

I have chosen the issue of women in management as my field of research. On the one hand, my thesis work taught me that there was so much to be done on this topic in Québec and, on the other hand, the increase in the number of women students enrolled in HEC led me to believe that it would be an area of growing interest for the School and for the future of our graduates. So I began with the simplest things: lists, portraits, and reviews of the literature. My thesis work also showed me that there are certain patterns that women have followed, at least for a given environment and era, and that traditional comparative methodologies, though able to highlight how women were similar to or different from men, were less effective at revealing their own dynamics. Thus, we needed to give women the chance to speak themselves; to do this we had to design original research instruments.

I studied women in management--which is a slightly marginal theme in relation to management *per se*--but through this process I learned a great deal about managers in general.

What the experience of women has done in particular is that it has forced people to make explicit many aspects of organizational life which usually remain implicit.

This is how my conferences on career, which were originally based upon the study of the experience of women, have progressively become recognized as contributions to the comprehension of the career in general and they have been requested by mixed audiences, and even by majority-male audiences. Likewise, questions designed to be part of questionnaires or interviews for women, apt to reveal how they have taken family matters into account, have proven to be possible improvements to the research tools applicable to men which, up until now, have generally ignored these aspects, though they are probably important in reality.

In 1991-92, she and Marie-Françoise Marchis-Mouren, her long-time research associate, completed a study on the vestiges of feminine culture in the actions of women managers.

I have always liked working as part of a team; I am sure that it was a way for me and my partners to do more and better than if we had been working alone. Marie-Françoise became my research assistant shortly after she earned her MBA. She has the gift of a rigorous mind and a great sense of organization. She also has an excellent background in languages and management. She is now a renowned consultant, a respected analyst, and a well-liked speaker.

CULTURAL DOMESTIC HERITAGE AND ORGANIZATIONS

The cultural domestic heritage passed on from mother to daughter is, in essence, the integration of the inner world and the outer world, from the rational to the affective, this ability to harmoniously and simultaneously accomplish tasks of different natures and levels.

Francine Harel Giasson chooses the example of the organization of a family Christmas Eve gathering to illustrate an integrated process.

The women plan the evening long in advance. They decide on the menu: meat pies, stew, turkey, fresh rolls. In the country, pieces of meat are set aside when the animals are slaughtered in the fall.

They have to extend all the invitations and make sure there is an appropriate present for each guest. Everything must be ready for the big day.

The day of the celebration, the women see to it that the atmosphere is congenial; they make sure that everyone is enjoying themselves and is happy. The potatoes have to be baked to perfection, and ready at the same time as the main dishes.

While the fact of being well-fed and sated corresponds to the material aspect, the fact of being happy and content falls into the affective aspect of the event. For a Christmas Eve gathering to be successful, everyone has to be full and content.

In addition, despite all the work required to make the celebration a success, no one should feel guilty or responsible for the mother's fatigue. Thus, at the time of the celebration, there should be "nothing left to do but the flowers and the fruit."

This state of non-division between the rational and affective dimensions of life is drawn more from the role of the mother than that of the father, according to Francine Harel Giasson, and women managers are likely to bring this into organizations. They do not, however, hold a monopoly on it.

I am afraid of the opposition that is found both in psychoanalysis and in other fields, between the inner world for women and the outer world for men.

I am not comfortable with the idea that women will humanize firms. What is the basis for thinking that women are more human?

As far as I'm concerned, there are two heritages, two different ways of participating in the human project and I am not able to say that one or the other is more human.

Organizational life in the industrialized world has certainly exerted a great deal of pressure in the direction of a break between reflection and action, between the rational and the affective. For all sorts of reasons, women have been visitors in this universe but "there is nothing there that has been forced by nature."

Francine Harel Giasson knows many men who are "feminine" in some respects and who are marvellous "mothers" at work.

I am far from being the most maternal person on the HEC management committee!

A keen knowledge of people, an excellent sense of organization, a certain of poise in the face of the unexpected are part of the so-called feminine heritage. She identified this same ability to do several things at the same time and on different levels, with an extraordinary sense of timing in her mother, her mother-in-law, and her grandmothers. The accomplishment of specific domestic chores in such a broader perspective of caring for and taking an interest in people, the quality of the atmosphere in which these people are growing, working and living every day requires special management skills, the mastery of that art of communicating, the ability to think of the routine in the big picture of real life.

All these women who have bequeathed this feminine cultural heritage were educators first.

She cannot understand why these disciplines have failed to draw on the wealth and wisdom of homemaking knowledge, in spite of the fact that it was not developed in the organizational world.

Here we get into the values of our society. There has never been a degree conferred for homemaking.

Yet, if we were to study the process of transmission of this knowledge from generation to generation, the discipline of education would learn a lot.

RECONCILING FAMILY AND CAREER

Francine Harel Giasson has researched how women reconcile family and career, especially among women chartered accountants,[8] but primarily she has done her own reconciliation. In the Harel family she was the intellectual. She was expected to do intellectual things, but few domestic tasks. When she finished her schooling, she was proud to contribute to her family's well-being.

She was lucky to have become a teacher two years after the Montreal Catholic School Commission had abolished the regulation requiring married women to resign. It should be borne in mind that the legal incapacity of married women in Québec had only been lifted in 1964. The effect of this legal incapacity was that a married woman could not be a party to a contract. If a married woman could not enter into a contract, then a woman who wanted to work was only allowed to practice the same profession as that of her husband. Francine Harel Giasson is very aware of the "firsts" in her career, but...

I always had to be more imaginative than demanding to get ahead in my career.

She also decided that her feminist involvement would focus on how society and situations would have to change so that women in general would have access to worthwhile careers or jobs. One should not have to be a heroine or have all the luck: money, exceptional talent, grandparents available to take care of the children, good babysitters, an open and intelligent husband. Society and companies have to support this reconciliation between family and career, rather than leaving it all to the couples themselves.

There have to be some new models on the rise.

Her own socialization was different: she had been recognized as talented, as a girl with bright prospects for the future. The socialization of her husband in a family where the father and mother ran the general store while taking care of the children facilitated her career. The general store and the Giasson home were not separate entities. Everyone took care of whatever had to be done without specific job descriptions assigned to each individual. This integration of the affective life into the working life allowed for the individuals to develop in harmony and for the family life to be more prosperous.

Nowadays, young couples are more independent, more or less out of choice. The support provided by the grandmothers is different. These grandmothers are not less tender and affectionate, but they are often working women themselves. Francine Harel Giasson describes herself as an "unworthy grandmother."

SELF-TRAINING IN THE CASE METHOD

Francine Harel Giasson received on-the-job training in the case method. Workshops or teacher training sessions which she has attended have never dealt with the case method, but rather on learning profiles, leading small groups, audiovisual, the use of the video. She enjoys these sessions which give her the opportunity to set aside a few days to think about teaching, outside of the city, in a country inn, outside of daily life.

Though she is an educator teaching education in a doctoral program in management, she is not a reader of pedagogical treatises. She prefers novels and plays.

I can't say that I have ever known of a bad method. I do know of bad uses of a method.

Moreover, she uses more than one teaching method. In 1982, she resumed lecturing for the new course in organizational behaviour in the second year of the Bachelor of Commerce. Later on, she gave the seminar "Femmes et gestion" (Women and Management) at the Masters and Ph.D. level in the form of a research seminar for a small group. In the pedagogy seminar in the Ph.D. program, she uses the lecture exposé and teaching exercises are delivered by the students and videotaped. As she sees it, the case method is one method among others. "Loyal, but not exclusive; that's the story of my life," she says with a certain smile.

The same objectives are not reached with each of the methods. The lecture course is good for creating impressions and transmitting information, but it is not as strong for developing skills. Conferences and talks transmit more impressions, preferences, and enthusiasm, but little in the way of information. And what could be better than a book or an article to provide information?

Francine Harel Giasson is allergic to the expression "active method" because it seems to imply that the other methods are passive:

All learning is active.

The so-called active methods refer only to an outward activity of the person, thus in the strictest sense of the activity of learning.

During a course taught using the case method, when one student is making a presentation, he/she is active; but does that mean that the other students are passive?

She would like to develop some role-playing, along the lines of the work done by the troupe in the Théâtre Parminou[9], with audience participation to change the scenario of a case or a role-playing session.

She has trouble getting into in-basket simulations, just as she used to have trouble with laboratory experiments. But she adores debates. The challenge of a debate is real; the object is to present your arguments better than your opponent presents his.

Francine Harel Giasson wants something to happen in class, not just for the sake of making some noise. Otherwise, it would be better to stay home and read a good book on management.

This something which happens in her classes, it is something to do with a contagious enthusiasm, passion, a passion for management and communication.

A student who is not thrilled with management should change majors.

She helps people to become better communicators. She passes on tricks and advocates a teaching method incorporating success in small steps. First, ask questions rather than taking a stand, participate in a round table discussion before giving a conference. Her advice to professors who want to learn to use the case method is to read cases, participate in discussions of cases, give such a course for the first time in a sheltered workshop, surrounded by colleagues and videotape the course. Simply watching this video will be highly instructive.

Francine Harel Giasson is a generous woman. She likes to help others and to inspire them.

"Go for it! You can do it!" How many times do I say those words in a week!

She is also a realistic woman.

I firmly believe that in a life, we do not do too much; no one does, in any case. The only reason that we, as professors, have to feel proud of what we do, is that many of us get together to train people.

The only thing that I find reassuring--otherwise I would die of fear--is that the students will have many professors. As a manager, I would never hire a student who had had only one teacher. It is our diversity that allows us professors to sleep at night.

ENDNOTES

1. Translators' note: The *Cours classique* (Classical Humanities) was taught in private catholic schools until the late 1960's. The curriculum was based on classical Greek, Latin and French humanities. The program was made up of eight academic years respectively called *Éléments latin, Syntaxe, Méthode, Versification latine, Belles-lettres, Rhétorique, Philo I* and *Philo II*. Graduates earned a Bachelor of Arts degree.

2. Translators' note: Approximately Grade 12.

3. Translators' note: Written under the original title: *Perception et actualisation des facteurs de promotion chez les femmes cadres des grandes entreprises québécoises franchophone du secteur privé.*

4. Translators' note: Jacques Parizeau is now leader of the opposition in the Quebec National Assembly.

5. HAREL GIASSON, Francine, "Un bon plan de cours", [A Good Course Outline] HEC, 1987, p. 1.

6. HAREL GIASSON, Francine. "The teacher-student relationship in the training of women on an international level," conference prepared for the workshop "Women, training, and management, CETAI-FGE, HEC, August 1987, p. 96 and p. 98.

7. *Ibid*. p. 103.

8. Translators' note: the Canadian equivalent of the Certifed Public Accountant in the United States.

9. Translators' note: The *Théâtre Parminou* is an experimental theater troupe which uses improvisations with audience participation to address specific issues, such as integrating handicapped workers in the organization. The troupe acts as consultants in different public or private organizations.

MONIQUE LANDRY'S SECRET?
PLAYING THE GAME AND A TALENT FOR ORGANIZATION[1]

Francine Richer and Francine Harel Giasson
Ecole des Hautes Etudes Commerciales de Montréal
MONTREAL, QUEBEC, CANADA

Abstract

This case presents the life and career of Monique Landry who was a member of the Canadian Parliament and a cabinet minister in Brian Mulroney's government. The case describes her personal development and highlights the nature of key political skills. It allows for an in-depth discussion on Monique Landry's own brand of leadership and on her vision of the leadership phenomenon.

Monique Landry agreed to see us at her Ste-Thérèse home while workers were completing a renovation project. Her short hair with highlights, blue eyes and clear complexion give her the healthy look of someone who enjoys the great outdoors.

"My husband has gone down south for the winter. I decided to stay here and have some work done in the house. It doesn't take the two of us, after all."

On October 24, 1993, Monique Landry was member of Parliament for Blainville-Deux-Montagnes, one of the largest ridings in Canada. In addition, she was also Minister Designate of Heritage Canada, Communications Minister, Secretary of State and Minister responsible for Francophone affairs. On the evening of October 25, 1993, she was about to become a private citizen once again: "In politics, when the wave comes, it comes."

That evening, Kim Campbell's Tories went down in a stunning defeat, retaining only two seats in Parliament. This was the harsh judgement of the Canadian people that put a final end to the Mulroney era. "I say this without bragging, I was ready for defeat. I remember Francis Fox.[1] He had been crushed by his 1984 defeat, but he acted like a gentleman. On Election Night, he came to see me to offer his congratulations. He also offered to brief me on the major projects in the riding. In an attempt to comfort him, I told him that it was perhaps better to be defeated than to end up sitting in the opposition, especially after having been a minister . At that point, he told me that when you are in politics, any seat in the Commons is better than nothing. I remembered that.

"I remembered Walter McLean's advice. He was Secretary of State when I was appointed as his parliamentary assistant. Walter was an Ontario MP, a Presbyterian minister who had been in parliament since 1978. His advice had been: "Monique, don't neglect your family and your friends, because politics will not be there for ever." I followed his advice, I looked after my family and my friends.

"I had accepted the idea that one day I would be defeated. In 1988, I won with one of the largest majorities in Canada. In 1993, when the campaign began I believed I would be reelected. I thought we would fight a good battle. Kim was popular. Everything was fine. When we started to slide, I realized that I might lose my seat, but for a long time, I thought I could hold on to it."

Three weeks before the vote, the polls confirmed that she had a chance to win. Everything is still possible right up until the end of a good campaign.

"We won in 1988 thanks to Free Trade, but then the blunders started piling up. I knew we were losing ground, I had accepted the idea that I might lose.

" I think it's important not to take it as a personal defeat; it's simply a change in the political climate, just as

---

[1]Translated fromFrench by André Cyr and Helene Kaufman

in Francis Fox's case in 1984.

"I haven't been affected, really not. In fact, I feel fine, really really fine. I've turned the page, I will keep on working for the Party, but active politics is over for me, for good. It was such a hectic experience that I have no intention of ever doing it again. I'm not bitter. I seem to be discovering a whole lot of things that I now have time to do, such as this renovation project, for instance."

Once the renovation is finished, Monique Landry intends to redecorate her house. One of her walls is covered with mementoes of her years in office and photographs of various heads of state, such as Gorbachev and Aquino.

"These are my rooms. Here, downstairs, I have about thirty boxes of archives and a box full of photographs that will have to be filed. I would like to make an album of my main trips, whenever I have time."

She does not miss her active life, she has plans. Her husband is retired, but she is not. Monique Bourbeau-Landry was born on December 25, 1937 in Verdun. She is now 56 years old and she feels the time has come to step back.

"In the month following the election, I closed all of my offices, said goodbye to my employees, got the paperwork done. I bought a car, sold my Ottawa condo and moved. You see the furniture in the den, it comes from the condo. I set up my office in the room next door. My husband and I went on vacation down south from November 20 to December 19. During the holidays, we entertained a lot, and I cooked more than I have in years.

"I loved that. I pulled out my Pol Martin cookbooks. I made the desserts that my children loved when they were little, I prepared lasagna for one, chicken pie for the other, brownies, etc. I cooked more than I ever did during the past ten years. I entertained my family and my friends. I even had time to read a few books."

Monique Landry received a number of offers, but she still has not accepted any of them. She would not be happy in a nine-to-five job, but she wants to keep on working, to take on new challenges.

"I've always had projects going my whole life, large ones and small ones, as well as an urgent need for action. I'm curious, and I'm an entrepreneur. The month down south with my husband was great, I needed to relax and take stock of my life. But I wouldn't live like that for six months. I'm 56 years old, it's not very young, but it's not very old either.

"I watched the Speech from the Throne and the Question Period on television without any regrets. I can't believe it! I hated the Question Period. It was such a free-for-all! I'm much too active for that kind of thing. I respect democracy, but I still believe that that Question Period is a waste of time in a busy day."

It used to take Monique Landry "the better part of an hour" to prepare for Question Period. In the Canadian parliamentary system, ministers do not receive written questions in advance as they do in the United Kingdom. In Canada, ministers must review all of their files in case there is a question on one of them.

"You have employees who are specifically assigned to this job. They read the papers from all across the country and prepare briefing notes that we read while eating a soup or a salad. You try to anticipate all the possible questions, then you go into the Commons, you sit and you wait for questions, while there is so much work waiting to be done!

"I'm not a good parliamentarian, I know people who thrive on parliamentary life. Not me. It's normal that the Government should be accountable, but we should have a more efficient system. If we used the written question system, all the ministers wouldn't be forced to be in the Commons."

When a minister has to be away, he or she must arrange for a substitute to be there. His files are given to another minister who stands in for him.

"Your files are in the hands of another minister or you take someone else's files. In the UK, Mrs. Thatcher only had to be in the Commons once or twice a week. Brian had to be there every day, unless he was out of the country. As for me, I'm an active person and I like to keep moving. I like to take a project and carry it through from start to finish. I'm not a good parliamentarian."

CHILDHOOD

Monique Bourbeau-Landry is the daughter of Antoinette Miquelon and Auguste Bourbeau, a surgeon. She is the youngest of four children, three girls and a boy.

"My mother became a widow when she was 39 years old. She had four children aged nine, seven, five and three. We lived in Abitibi at the time. I am a Bourbeau, the sister of André Bourbeau, who is also a minister, but in the Quebec provincial government. When my father died, my mother sold everything, and we moved to her hometown in the Eastern Townships. I don't really remember that part of my life.

"Mother was rather authoritarian. She raised us according to the standards of the day, which were certainly stricter than those of the current generation. It was fine with me.

"I was only three years old when my father died. The only memories I have of him are the stories that mother told me. My mother is still alive, she's 94 years old, and has been living in a nursing home for the past few years. She was very proud of her children, we were her whole life, her reason for living.

"She was very strict, and she kept us on a short leash. Father went to medical school at the *Université de Montréal* and studied surgery in Paris. They were married in 1929 and went on a honeymoon to Paris.

"My mother never had to earn a living. Although my father had left a small estate, my mother, with the help of her brothers, invested her capital soundly. She kept the family going on the income of two rental properties, and put all of us through university. We even spent a few summers in a lakeside cottage. We weren't rich, but we always lived well.

"I have good memories of my childhood, even though we didn't have a father. My mother was always there for us.

"I wasn't really spoiled because I was the youngest; I remember that my oldest sister, Louise, who was very conservative, always thought that my mother was too indulgent with me. When I went to school in Montreal, I started having boyfriends at a very young age, and my sister was worried; we were not really on good terms when I was about 13 or 14 years old."

Monique Landry considers that she had normal relationships with her brother and sisters, although there were some difficult moments, as is the case in all families and was later the case with her own four children. This did not keep them from being a close-knit family. When her brother André entered university, the family moved from Sherbrooke to Montreal.

"I was an easy child, a conscientious and diligent student. In Sherbrooke, I did well and skipped a year. I started getting involved in different activities such as the Girl Guides which I loved. I was very very enthusiastic.

"I've always been a total person; when I liked something, I would throw myself wholeheartedly into it.

"In Montreal, I went to boarding school at *Les filles de la sagesse* . I was in charge of recreational activities. I often represented the convent in inter-school activities.

"I liked discipline, even loved it. I was very happy to be a boarding student. This doesn't mean that the convent had any special influence on me. I was a good student. I liked to study. I'm a team player, which is why I like politics, but I only became active in party politics much later."

One summer, she worked as a counsellor in a camp for handicapped children in Joliette.

"This was something I had decided on my own, and I had been accepted. I still didn't know that I would go into physiotherapy."

Monique Landry became active in the Catholic Youth Movement, which was very popular at the time.

"I was a delegate; we went to regional meetings. I was also very active in sports."

Later on, at the *Université de Montréal*, she remained active in student government.

"I was a delegate for my faculty in the AGEUM.[2] I was in the first physiotherapy class at the *Université de Montréal*. You see, it's quite different from what I did later on!"

To give us an idea of her character Monique Landry explains how she was accepted at the *Université de Montréal* when she was 16 years old.

"I had completed Grade 12 in the science profile, but I'd never gone to junior college, and this is one of the reasons why Dr. Gustave Gingras was so reluctant to accept me in his program.

"This program wasn't offered at the *Université de Montréal* when I decided to go into physiotherapy. I had been accepted at McGill. During the summer, I read in the paper that Dr. Gingras wanted to open a school of physiotherapy, and that classes would begin the following December, so I asked for an interview and I went to see him. I was sixteen years old at the time. He told me: "I don't want sixteen year old girls in my program. I want ten or twelve students tops for the first year. I want mature girls who are in their twenties and who are already nurses or who have a good background, because I want them to become professors. That's what I'm looking for."

"I was so determined and persistent, and I insisted so much that he finally accepted me. I was the youngest member of the class, but I was very determined."

A VERY TRADITIONAL YOUNG LADY

By her own admission, Monique Bourbeau was a very traditional young lady, with occasional restrained bouts of rebellion.

"My mother raised us on her own. To give you an example, I wanted to study commerce when I went to university, but my mother was against it. In her opinion, commerce was for boys. In our family, the three girls studied medical disciplines. My father had been a doctor. My two sisters studied medical technology. My mother wanted me to become a nutritionist. I was a bit rebellious, but I finally gave in. Mother argued that girls didn't go into faculties like commerce. "You'll probably get married and be busy raising children," she told me.

"In 1984, when I was elected to Parliament, my brother had already been a member of the provincial legislature since 1981, in opposition. In 1985, after his reelection, he was appointed to the cabinet. When I became a minister in 1986, my mother, who was already quite ill, did not even believe that I was a member of Parliament. She said: "That's impossible, Monique is married and she has four children. She cannot be an MP." When people talked to her about me, she said they were wrong, it was her son, not her daughter, who was in politics. She never really realized. She would have been so proud."

Politics was not often discussed in the house, but Louise, the eldest of the family, was an active member of the Progressive Conservative party and worked for several candidates in the Montreal area. She also worked on fund-raising campaigns for the provincial Liberal party in which her brother was active. Michèle, her other sister, lived in Quebec City. She was less active in public life.

There is a great-grandfather on the Bourbeau side who was a Conservative MP in Ottawa and who defeated Sir Wilfred Laurier[3] in his own riding during a by-election. In the Miquelon family, on her mother's side, there is also a great-grandfather who was a Conservative member of the provincial legislature. Antoinette Miquelon had three brothers who were attorneys and were all active in politics. One of them was a member of the provincial legislature and minister in the Cabinets of Maurice Duplessis, Paul Sauvé and Antonio Barrette.

"My mother was not really into politics, but she was very proud of her brother Jacques, the minister. We were a close-knit family. Her brothers came to visit us. Of course, they talked politics. Over the years, I started following current events and I became interested in politics.

"Particularly during the Trudeau years, I really loathed Trudeau. I didn't like his arrogance, I still don't like him even now.

"As far as I'm concerned, politics really boils down to organization. It's one of my strong points. I like to be involved in organizations. I'm a good organizer. I think I do a good job on committees, but I would never have thought of going into active politics."

Monique Bourbeau studied at the *Université de Montréal* for three years. That is where she met her husband, Jean-Guy Landry, who was studying dentistry. She worked for two years at the Montreal Children's Hospital. She was the first francophone to be hired by that institution.

"I went on a student exchange in the last year of my program. I spent a whole summer in Toronto. I was not bilingual, so I went to Toronto to improve my English.

"I worked for two years, my husband graduated a year after me. We got married and we settled down in Ste-Thérèse, where Jean-Guy opened his dental practice. It was not easy to travel from Ste-Thérèse to Montreal. There was no highway in those days. It was suburbia, I would even call it living in the countryside. I went into private practice, I saw my patients at home, or they came to our house. I continued working even after our first children, the twins, were born.

"I was quite traditional when I got married, but my husband didn't object to the fact that I kept working in physiotherapy. "

The couple had four children, three boys and a girl. Monique Landry became involved in the local Ste-Thérèse community in the areas of education and extracurricular activities.

"I sat on the board of directors of the Parent-Teacher Association and of various recreational organizations. I was also what was called a *patroness* at the time."

At one point, the priests at Lionel Groulx College felt that the auditorium could be put to better use. They asked a group of women to set up an organization called the Ste-Thérèse *ciné-théâtre*. Monique Landry became its secretary-treasurer.

"We operated for several years. We hired companies like *Le Théâtre du Nouveau-Monde* and singers like Gilbert Bécaud. We set up a committee of honorary patrons, and we collected funds. I was very active in that organization."

A sports enthusiast, Monique Landry became a member of the Rosemère Golf Club. She was the club's champion for eight years, including seven years in a row.

"In fact, I taught the basics of golf to my children. The students, and particularly the twins, were soon better than their teacher."

She inevitably ended up in a high-level position in the various organizations in which she became active.

"I was active in the pastoral movement. I was even a lay delegate on an advisory committee set up by the St-Jerome bishop! These were difficult years for the Catholic Church. I still went to Church a great deal in those days and, after a rather difficult period of reflexion, I gave up on the whole thing, like many members of my generation."

Her husband, Jean-Guy, was a municipal councillor for 12 years. She took care of his organization. This was probably when she really became interested in politics.

"I had it all: a good husband, good children. I didn't work outside the home for several years, but I wanted to go back to work. Perhaps I should have gone back to school, but I didn't really have the courage to do it. My husband had some reservations about my going back to work.

"There was a year of painful evolution. My husband would argue: "what are you complaining about? You have everything that you need. You have lots to keep you busy, why would you go back to work? I don't want to get back home and find that dinner is not ready." Jean-Guy worked in the evenings, he was on a tight schedule; you see, that's the kind of evolution that I'm talking about."

Finally, in 1975, Monique Landry made up her mind and went back to work. She took a part-time job in advertising.

"I found a job immediately in the local papers. My husband was quite upset. I also did advertising jobs for Time magazine. After that I met people with whom I set up a wine company. I took courses on wine. That caused a major upheaval in our house."

When she became a partner in this venture, Monique Landry worked hard, travelled to Europe and often participated in evening wine-tasting sessions.

"My husband went through a few difficult years with his wife who was a bit too... I was aware of it. After that, he became a good partner.

"I was still a very traditional person with respect to my activities: you know domestic chores and all that... I had a cleaning lady who came in to help... but I also had four children. The twins, Jacques and Robert, were born in 1959; Michel was born in 63; and my daughter, Dominique, in 1967. I went back to work when my daughter entered kindergarten. I was lucky to be very healthy and energetic.

"When I think about that period, I wonder how I managed everything. On weekends, I bought groceries for the whole week. I cooked and I froze everything. When I came home from work, I would prepare everybody's dinner. I went to Europe on a regular basis for my wine business. When I was gone for two weeks, everyone would scream, but they had to get used to it. During those years, although I had been married for more than ten years, I really made my mark. My husband finally accepted all of these changes.

"I'm not a person who is happy to stay home. Even in the years when I was not working outside the home, I was always very active in community affairs, school committees, and even the provincial Liberals."

ACTIVE POLITICS

Monique Landry has been a very active member of the federal Conservative Party since the 1970's, when the provincial Liberals asked her to take over the presidency of the Groulx riding association which was then run by a management committee. She was not even a member of the Quebec Liberal party! She participated in the "No" campaign of the 1980 referendum and, at that time, met the senior officers of the provincial Liberals.[4]

"I had decided I wanted to be involved in the referendum campaign on the "No" side. I was the only Tory on the team, they called me the "blue baby"[5]... I worked from 8:00 AM until midnight throughout the whole campaign. After that, the Liberals asked me to take over the presidency of the Groulx riding association until they could reorganize it with local people.

"Even before that, as early as 1971, I had been asked to lend a hand to the Conservative party. I was very involved in politics, I hated Trudeau and, to get it out of my system, I decided to support the Conservatives. My political involvement started at that time. I organized fund-raising dinners and campaigns. I even went on a provincial tour with another person."

During the federal campaign of May 1979, when Joe Clark was elected Prime Minister, Monique Landry sat on the organizing committee in Quebec and worked fifteen hours a day for the party.

"I did the same job in 80 when Joe Clark was defeated. I bought the wine company after the referendum campaign. I stayed out of from politics from 1980 to 1984.

"In '84, I sold my shares in Cordevin International. There was a Canadian company interested in buying us, and I was ready to sell. My partner did not agree. So he had to buy me out according to the buy-and-sell agreement we had negotiated at the beginning of our partnership.

"In 1984, I called my friends at the Conservative party. We knew that there was an election coming up. I told them that I would be available if they needed me. They immediately asked me to start a membership drive throughout Quebec, and I went on tour."

Then a close colleague of Brian Mulroney asked her to be a candidate.

"I said no way, just as I had in '79! I never intended to go into active politics. I have a talent for organization, but I didn't see myself in the forefront, on the stage. At that point, they twisted my arm a bit. They told me I was afraid of Francis Fox, the incumbent MP, who was too big a candidate for me. They even offered me another riding, if I wanted.

"My children had been too young in 1979, but this was no longer a problem in 84. I had nothing to lose. We had a family dinner. The kids thought it was really funny. My husband agreed... after giving it due consideration. I agreed to run without really knowing what I was getting into...

"On the other hand, I am a winner! In politics as in golf, I play to win. And I'm a fighter! When I want to win, I put everything I've got into it. When I ran against Francis Fox, I had the same feeling as when I won my first golf championships. I said to myself: "I can do it."

"I set up my own organization, because there was absolutely nothing. The Conservative party simply didn't exist in Quebec. In my riding, there was a grand total of five registered Tories."

Her organization got off the ground in April 1984. The election was called in July, and the vote took place on September 4. Francis Fox lost, and Monique Landry became MP for Blainville-Deux-Montagnes, one of the largest ridings in Canada.

"I needed support, so I went out and got it. I had one of the largest ridings in the country. While I knew the eastern part pretty well: Ste-Thérèse, Rosemère, Bois-Brillant, Blainville and Ville de Lorraine, I was much less familiar with the western part: St-Eustache, Deux-Montagnes, Ste-Marthe-sur-le-Lac, St-Joseph and Pointe-Calumet. I made as many contacts as I could. I started calling on the people I knew. I held a press conference with the support of a few friends and Jean-Guy. I spent my days on the phone, with the phonebook by my side. I called lawyers, and I asked for the names of the presidents of Chambers of Commerce, local leaders, municipal councillors, and so on. I asked to meet them.

"People started coming on board. There were five, then ten, then twenty. You have to recruit those who are ready to support you and give you time."

While the organization needs a hard core, it also needs representatives from each municipality, from each sector. There must be representatives from the business community, the professions, and the social community in general. Monique Landry had very few contacts in the western part of her riding, but people were ready for change. "A bit like in the last election," she said.

"They were all very enthusiastic. I think I appealed to them and it wasn't hard to get their support. I even financed my campaign with a fund-raising party organized locally by those who had decided to support me. I took care of the organization. Normally, in an election campaign, you select an organizer who looks after the campaign. I organized my own campaign until the election was called. After that, things went very smoothly because I had set up a solid organization.

"I have to admit that everyone complained because I was much too involved in the organization. I found it difficult to stay away from the organization. I always wanted to fight clean campaigns. From the very beginning, I warned Francis Fox: "Be prepared, I have nothing against you personally, but I have a lot against your party."

The family went through a tough time during this period, but was very supportive. They worked hard. They left home, came back, had dinner, went door to door, and so on. They would often get together to assess the progress of the campaign. At first, her husband did not realize what he was in for when his wife won the election.

"I remember one evening we got back home and Jean-Guy told me, "Monique, I can't believe it, you're winning." I told him, "It's about time you realized. I've known for the past fifteen days that I was winning". I knew it, I felt it. Three weeks before the September 4 election, Francis Fox knew it also. Fox didn't live in the riding. The party had sent him to other ridings throughout the whole campaign. When he came back to his own riding, it was too late.

"On Election Night, it was euphoria! The next day, when we read it in the *La Presse*, we all began to realize it was for real."

All of a sudden, the house was empty. The twins had completed their education and had good professional careers, but they were still living at home. They bought a condo together. Michel was studying mechanical engineering at Sherbrooke University. Dominique, the youngest, and her father were, therefore, alone in the house. The mother MP moved to Ottawa and came back only on weekends, well most weekends.

"We had had an intense life as a couple and a family. Until then, we shared all of our leisure activities. We did sports, golf in the summer and tennis in winter. I played tennis at seven in the mornings with the boys. We played from 7:30 to 8:30 and I went to the office after that. We also had cultural activities, we went to the theater or the movies at least once a week. We played bridge with our friends. On Thursdays, we had dinner in town. All of a sudden, Jean-Guy was left alone without his wife at home.

"In a sense, it was my revenge, as I enjoyed telling him from time to time. My husband had been president of the Quebec Order of Dentists. At that time, I was the wife behind the president. I went to his conventions. All of a sudden, our roles were reversed. He didn't particularly like senior citizens' dinners or various other social functions, but he was there when I needed him. "Mister Monique Landry" as he was called from time to time. On Fridays and Saturdays, I often attended riding activities and, as External Affairs Minister, I was often out of the country.

"My daughter found that really tough. Dominique was seventeen years old when I was elected and she wrote letters that would tear my heart out. She told me that she missed her mother, and so on. On the other hand, it helped her develop a good relationship with her father.

"I am very much of a "phoner". When I left Ottawa, I called Jacques and Robert. I spoke to the kids every weekend and I tried to invite them for dinner every other Sunday. Actually, it was usually every third Sunday, but I always kept in touch with the kids. Always, always, always. It was very important for me."

The day after the election, everyone relaxed a bit and started getting ready for the big change ahead. Monique Landry was waiting to hear from the party and started packing up for Ottawa. During her first days in Ottawa, she had to find an apartment and move into her office. She also had to set up her riding office, close her campaign headquarters and hire her staff.

LEADERSHIP? WHAT MAKES SOMEONE A GOOD LEADER?

Monique Landry has just started thinking about what makes someone a good leader. During her political career, she worked with Joe Clark, Brian Mulroney and Kim Campbell.

"Brian was a magnificent leader. People said a lot of bad things about him, but he's a great leader. He had his troops in the palm of his hand. At the national caucus meeting, which was held every Wednesday morning in Ottawa, some MP's would get a bit jittery. Brian had a way of bringing people together! I was always impressed. I have unbounded admiration for Brian Mulroney's leadership. Leadership is simply something that you have. At the end of the national caucus, everyone was hyped up. He had a way to cheer us up. He was clever, he was extraordinarily skilled at rallying people.

"Personally, I'm a team player, I work well in a team, and I'm loyal. I defend my ideas, but I know that I can't always win. In fact, this is what happens in Cabinet. The chief must reconcile divergent opinions, particularly among regional representatives.

"I remember that in the General Motors affair, which was the major issue in my riding, I had Brian Mulroney's support at the national caucus. The issue had made headlines the day before. Some said that we have to support the plant, others argued that it wasn't the government's role. I got really scared. I knew that the plant would close if the government didn't support it, and 3 500 jobs would be lost. Brian told me not to worry. He never missed a caucus. Often, he didn't say a word, he just listened and took notes. He supported me. Nobody argued. His mind was just about made up".

"Brian is such a charming man. He would often phone on Sunday morning. At one point, there was a front-page article in the *Journal de Montréal*; there was a picture of my brother and me, back to back, the two ministers, brother and sister, with the Quebec and the Canadian flags. On page three, there was a long article on our family. At 9:30 on Sunday morning, the phone rang. It was the Prime Minister. I asked my husband, "What did I do wrong?""

"Brian told me he had just read the *Journal de Montréal* and that he didn't know my family history, he didn't know that my mother had brought us up on her own. He was sorry she was in the hospital. He was so nice."

According to Monique Landry, Brian Mulroney was very generous with all of his MP's. He would help all of them. He knew how to bring maverick MP's back into the fold. Brian Mulroney's major asset was his extraordinary network throughout the country. He knew who to ask to reach another person. But above all, he was very warm. Monique Landry is positive about this, "You would hear people talking about it. "Brian called, he asked about my wife, my son..." He really cared about his MP's.

"Kim did not do that. Kim had no network at all. I have high regard for Kim Campbell, but there's no comparison between her and Brian Mulroney. Leadership is probably an innate quality.

"I supported Kim from the very beginning. Brian's retirement was a very difficult moment. As soon as the leadership race was on, the major players were already known: Kim Campbell, Jean Charest, as well as Joe Clark, Michael Wilson, Perrin Beatty and Barbara McDougall. I was very close to Michael Wilson. I got along well with him and I liked him a lot. He called and asked me if I would support him and manage his leadership campaign in Quebec.

"I gave it some thought. In politics, the first order of business is to win the election. Who's the best person to win the election? What kind of person do we need to project a new image? I prepared my own set of criteria, and I really made an in-depth analysis before I came to a decision. Unfortunately, I told poor Michael that he was much too closely linked to all that made us unpopular: difficult budgets, tax hikes, cut-backs here and there, the GST, all of these things that people didn't like. I thought he couldn't win that election. It had nothing to do with Jean Chrétien, but rather with the fact that people were fed up. Michael could not represent renewal, he was too closely identified with the Mulroney era."

Monique Landry came to two possible alternatives: Kim Campbell and Jean Charest, both of whom were from a younger generation. Kim Campbell was 46, she was a bright woman who had had a brilliant career in Ottawa. Convinced and convincing, she had acquired a good reputation at the Department of Justice where Monique Landry thought she had done very well. She might be a bit distant, but she had leadership qualities, a good background and was sufficiently knowledgeable to be a leader.

"I love Jean Charest. He is the same age as my sons. In my opinion, that makes him too young. He still doesn't have enough experience to become a leader. Give him another ten years!

"I also thought that English Canada would like to have a Prime Minister who came from another province than Quebec. After Trudeau and Mulroney, it seemed like a good thing. We could win Quebec with Kim and Jean Charest as her second in command. A woman from the West, 46 years old, good background, a much longer career than Jean's... I finally decided to support Kim.

"I really liked her leadership race. She had really thought it over. I admit she was disappointing during the election campaign. Kim did not have... And that's the main difference between Brian and her... Kim did not have deep roots in the party. She had no natural allies. She did not have a good network in the party. You really need a national network. Brian is a pro at working the phones. Brian had his boys all over the country. He would give them a ring from time to time. Kim has a very different style, she does not communicate as well as Brian. She's not as considerate with people.

"Kim decided to keep to her role as party leader, not out of snobbery, but without considering the importance of human contacts, and of having the right people around her. During the election campaign, she received very poor advice and she made disastrous decisions.

"She wanted so much to break with the Mulroney era, that she turned her back on a lot of things. She thought that her reputation would be enough to win the election. It was a big mistake. We ended up in an election campaign without a program, although we thought we had one."

As many of her colleagues, Monique Landry felt that her party was sliding relentlessly towards defeat. The party proved incapable of turning the tide, and its leader continued to accumulate serious mistakes.

"Kim certainly has major skills, but leadership is simply something that you have or that you don't. Could she have developed it during the campaign? I don't think so. At that level, it would have taken a highly determined woman. Maybe Kim wasn't strong enough for that.

"In politics, you need a network. You'll never make it on your own."

That being said, Monique Landry would go so far as to say that her friend Brian was a bit macho. Apparently, he found it hard to trust women. On the other hand, he was very kind.

"I think that on the whole, Brian was satisfied with my work, and he liked me a great deal. I was a good minister. He often said so to his closest supporters in the party.

"Brian had a tendency to play father-knows-best with women, to make sure the "girls" stayed in line. You always felt that he was holding back a little. I admired him a great deal, but I'm positive about this."

How does one know that he or she is a leader? Applied to herself, the word "leader" still sounds surprising, raises questions, and brings back memories.

"I can see that in the riding, for instance, I always had people behind me who supported me and who remained loyal. Since 1984, there are of course people who left me, but I never made an enemy in politics. Even the dissidents left on good terms. We remained "good friends." They often came back during the next campaign.

"In 1988, I had organizers who were there in 1984. They had gone their own way in the meantime because they got involved in other activities. I called them and they said, "For you, I'll come back." I must have a way of bringing people together. I may not be really aware of it, but the fact remains that many people were loyal to me."

What is the secret behind that loyalty? Monique Landry ascribes it to her constant, long-term presence in the riding, and to the fact that she always remained true to herself.

"As a minister or an MP, I never changed personalities. I go to the grocery store or the drycleaner's. People are often surprised. I tell them, "You know, we have to eat too!" I drove my own car on weekends. I went shopping for my own clothes. Some people suggested that I should get a dresser, but I refused. It's too personal. I like to keep in touch, to see for myself what's going on. That's probably why people remained loyal.

"I've received letters and testimonials after my defeat, letters from very ordinary people in the riding, veterans, senior citizens' groups, whom I adored. I was very close to social groups, very very involved. That's probably why people were so disappointed when I was resoundingly defeated.

"I held organization meetings in the fall before the campaign. I had a committee of twenty people. No one was missing. We met for entire mornings on Saturdays in late August and early September. At times, I made personal phone calls, but most of the times I asked my secretary to call the meeting on Saturday from 9 AM to 10 AM. She called everyone and they would all be there. I also held several brainstorming sessions on Saturday mornings, to get the details of the situation on specific issues. People would tell me, "we'll do it for you." But at a certain point, they were no longer happy with Brian."

MINISTER... WHEN IT COMES RIGHT DOWN TO IT... IT'S A BOYS' GAME

To be a minister, and do your job, you have to play the game.

"And it's quite a game... If you're even moderately ambitious, you have to play by the boys' rules. It's a boys' club. By and large, the game remains a man's game even if things have changed somewhat since women have entered politics."

At the time of her first election, Monique Landry already had good contacts within the party, contacts close to Brian Mulroney.

"I'm a realistic woman. The sky isn't the limit. My two feet are planted firmly on the ground. I did not want to become a minister.

"I was appointed parliamentary secretary to the Secretary of State, and I was very happy that I was not appointed to the Cabinet at first. I know many people who failed miserably because they had no political experience when they became MP's and ministers all at once.

"When you arrive, you don't know the environment; you don't know the network; you don't know the civil service. Being parliamentary assistant gave me a chance to learn these things. I held that position at the Secretary of State for a year and then at International Trade until 1985.

The parliamentary assistant's job is to support the minister in his work. There is no job description. It evolves according to the quality of the relationship with the minister. The minister asks his parliamentary assistant to take care of the things that he does not have time to do.

"When I was External Affairs Minister, for instance, I did not have the time to travel as much as I should have. If a given mission appeared relatively less important to me, I would send my parliamentary secretary. The minister might also ask his secretary to deliver a speech. In the Commons, when the minister cannot be there, his parliamentary secretary stands in for him. It's a good training ground, because it allows the secretary to better understand the complexity of the civil service and to follow the evolution of various files."

When one becomes a minister, Cabinet alliances are very important. Some of them come naturally, others demand more work. It's easier to work with certain colleagues than with others.

"The best example is Joe Clark. Joe Clark was External Affairs Minister. Joe is an extraordinary guy. He has a wife, Maureen McTeer, who definitely helped him make the right choices. Joe is a guy who considers a female colleague on the same level as a male colleague. Not everyone is able to do that.

"You can tell the machos immediately, the men who regard you as a little girl. There was one of them who called me "*My little Monique! How is my little girl this morning?* "You know? I wanted to scream!

"Men-women relationships are not always easy because some men do not regard women as chums, friends, or colleagues. There is a boys' network and you feel a bit left out. You really have to be able to play the boys' game to be in politics. Otherwise, you go through hell and you become very aggressive. You must take some and leave some, so to speak. You can usually tell immediately if you can work with a given person, you don't need to see his or her life story. You have to cultivate your strongest allies. Natural alliances are a matter of character, and of education as well."

The situation is evolving, but not as fast as she would have thought.

"I had always thought that people from my generation would be more open, and that the younger generation, like my sons, would be even more open. This not necessarily the case. To a large extent, it's a matter of education, of mentalities. As far as I'm concerned, men are slowly getting used to the notion that women can be their equal. On the other hand, they cannot develop that concept if they don't have it.

"It's a tough environment. It's not easy. You have to be very strong, set your goals, and follow up on them with a great deal of determination. Projects simply don't move if you don't go ahead, and if you're not consistent, if you don't push constantly. The federal machine is so big! So heavy, so hard to move. Civil servants have so much power!

"If you want to get anywhere, you have to be clever and persistent, you have to play the give-and-take game. People will ask for favors, you grant them one and you let them know that, "now you owe me one." That's the way it goes."

A minister's life is very hectic, and there is really very little time to develop friendships. Days are busy from 7 AM until 9 PM. For politicians, Ottawa is not a leisure city. In addition, the power of ministers is far from obvious.

Apart from Question Period, Parliament sits from 11:00 AM till 6:00 PM. Bills follow one another. Ministers have their on-duty shifts in the Commons.

"I was on duty every Monday afternoon from four to six. I would bring a pile of documents to be signed, nothing to read, because it was so difficult to concentrate. The silly things that can be said in the Commons. Debates are so long! People can talk about 56 000 different things that are absolutely unrelated to the Speech from the Throne or the ongoing debate."

Monique Landry has held several different portfolios. She considers that the minister must apply the same talent from one Cabinet position to the next: the capacity to read and understand the reports that have been prepared by the virtually omnipotent civil servants!

"When I was minister responsible for CIDA[6], I had a 3 billion dollar budget. The minister sets the main goals, but the day-to-day management is in the hands of civil servants. There are so many things that you don't see. Civil servants have so much discretionary power. The minister does not see everything. Discretionary powers are delegated at different levels and civil servants protect each other. It's quite a scene."

The minister is accountable to the people. Civil servants are fully aware of that, and they protect each other. At times, decisions are made without the minister's explicit agreement. "Everybody gives you the run-around, and you can't put your finger on the problem," says Monique Landry. "The minister has a very, very hard life!"

"But your days are so full! You just wouldn't believe the agendas that we have! At first, I had a hard time to accept that I couldn't spent more time on my files. I wanted to know everything about my department.

"I think that one of my strengths was my ability to surround myself with very devoted and loyal people. I had magnificent teams. I had the same chief of staff for the last four years, Gilles Dery. We made a good team. We were on the same wave-length. You can't think about everything or see everything. Gilles Dery took care of employees and looked after the department. I had five or six people who worked with me, the chief of staff, the press secretary, the executive assistant... All of the documents which came from the civil servants went through them depending to their area of expertise. They made recommendations.

"You get home in the evening with briefcases full of documents. I rarely got back to my apartment before nine o'clock. Then, I usually worked until midnight or one o'clock in the morning every night. I would read the briefing notes that my staff had prepared. When I agreed, I simply signed. Otherwise I met with my staff on the next day and asked more questions. I didn't always agree with their recommendations, I saw just about everything, excepting routine stuff. That I delegated."

Her staff and her civil servants appreciated the fact that her work was important for her, that she showed so much enthusiasm.

"My staff did a magnificent job. People often talk about the bureaucracy, usually negatively, because it's too heavy, because it's inefficient. As a rule, people such as deputy ministers, assistant deputy ministers and department heads are excellent team members who work hard to promote their files and who are happy to see their minister take the matter to heart and ask questions. I had the reputation of knowing what was going on in my department."

Her experience at Cordevin International had not prepared her to deal with a large bureaucracy.

"As a vice-president, I spoke to all our partners, and we all knew what was going on. I had never been in a large corporation. The civil service is really an awesome machine. Control systems are incredible, supposedly because we are accountable to Parliament. The machine is heavy and cumbersome. Things move forward very slowly."

At the beginning of her political career, her goal was simply to do better than Trudeau's Liberals.

"I think you have to be realistic. You don't go to Ottawa thinking that you'll change everything. You realize how slow the government bureaucracy can be, but you have goals, you have things that you want to accomplish.

"At CIDA I had developed a new policy called *A Shared Future*. However, I was not successful in bringing in the administrative changes that would have improved CIDA's performance. That was my biggest disappointment in politics. I worked very hard, I hired SECOR, a consulting group. They studied the question for a whole year. I then developed a really good plan, but I wasn't able to get it passed. I was short one vote. Just one!

"In January, I knew that there was a Cabinet reshuffle coming. That study had just cost the government a million dollars. I knew it would be shelved if I didn't bring in my reform. I was right, it was never implemented. The minister who followed did not have the same priorities as I did."

As Secretary of State, and later on in June, under Kim Campbell, she decided to work on what was most likely to be done in a short time, because she knew the election was coming.

"I managed to get a 110 million dollars of new money for French-speaking communities outside Quebec, to allow them to manage their own schoolboards. This right is recognized in the constitution. For years, French-speaking communities outside Quebec had been claiming from their provincial governments the right to manage their own schoolboards. Provincial governments refused to grant them these powers as long as the federal government did not contribute any money. In fact, this amounted to a constitutional recognition on our part.

"When I announced the good news in Winnipeg, it was one of the most beautiful moments of my career. I never saw so much electricity in a room. People were so moved. I'm married to an Acadian. I am a bit familiar with the life of cultural minorities, but I never thought it would be so moving. These people had fought all their lives for the survival of their language. People were so happy that they were cheering and crying. I had to stop speaking because I was so moved.

"I had decided to work on that issue because I thought it was an injustice. I could not understand how provinces had put the ball in the federal government's court. I could not see what they had to lose. There are so many English-speaking colleges. I was convinced by these lobbying groups. Canada spends money on education in Third World countries and cannot even help its own minorities survive in their own language. That was really my pet project. I work very hard for three months, studying the financial impact of the issue and lobbying different people. I think I succeeded."

Another one of Monique Landry's accomplishments is the agreement on copyrights which allows for royalties on blank tapes, since they are used to copy original works.

"The department of External Affairs, among others, had always been opposed to these royalties because they were afraid the Americans would retaliate."

As a minister, Monique Landry sat in the Cabinet, as well as on various committees on economic development and trade, foreign policy and defence, legislation, and parliamentary planning.

"Depending on her portfolio, a minister reports to one of these commitees; it must support her project. First, you must make friends on the committee. Once the project has been approved, it moves to a higher level.

The Operations Committee is a small committee made up of five or six powerful ministers, including the Finance Minister. When you get to that level, you must have already secured the Finance Minister's support."

The life of a minister also includes beautiful memories and wonderful trips.

"My most wonderful trip was to China and Thailand with Madam Sauvé when she was Governor-General of Canada. The Governor-General never travels without a minister. Because she is not a member of the government, she cannot speak on its behalf.. My husband came with me. In this album, you see us before our appointment with the President of China, at the Three-Gorge Dam, the largest dam in the world, at the King of Thailand's ball, at receptions and banquets. In Shanghaï, I learned of the birth of my first grand-daughter. Madam Sauvé was as excited as I was.

"I visited about half of the countries in Africa. I was responsible for Francophone affairs, I was head of the delegation to Chaillot. There were difficult moments, but there were also good moments."

Monique Landry replaced Benoît Bouchard as political minister responsible for Quebec. Members of Parliament represent society in all of its diversity.

"As political minister for Quebec, you have to pamper your MP's. In a sense, you're like a mother or a father for them. You must always try to keep everything running smoothly, to meet these people, to look after their projects. Usually, MP's go directly to the minister in charge, but there are several English-speaking ministers who don't speak any French. Some MP's will complain that the minister does not pay attention to their files. Then, they come to see the political minister of Quebec, in this case me, to argue their case."

Monique Landry's role in regional structures and activities was very time consuming. As regional minister for Laval, she oversaw seven ridings, and, therefore, had to look after seven conservative MPs.

"I held regional caucuses regularly to advance regional issues. At times, it was painful to work with poorly disciplined people who really did not think like me! They were good MP's, but they didn't work the same way I did. I had a high opinion of them, however.

"In this respect, Brian was very demanding of his ministers, because it was important to him to keep his MP's happy. That was his strength, the essence of his leadership, he made sure that everyone was happy. These regional meetings were held regularly before the Quebec caucus which met every Tuesday from 6 to 8 PM."

These regional caucuses took up time that Monique Landry could have devoted to important issues, the aboriginal question, for instance, a complex issue without any apparent solution.

The two saddest moments in her career were Brian Mulroney's resignation and the defeat of the Meech Lake Accord.[7]

"On the night when Meech Lake failed, the Cabinet was in session in Ottawa. Newfoundland still had not decided. During the Cabinet session, television sets and phone lines were available. Brian went out once or twice. He made a few phone calls. At one point, he adjourned the meeting. We were watching television, we were waiting for news from Newfoundland.

"Brian came back. We all sat down, and he told us the Meech Lake Accord was dead. A sad moment. Everybody was disappointed, defeated, we all cried. It was unbelievable. This is one of the rare times when I revealed my emotions on television. Journalists often complained that I was too cold, not like Benoît Bouchard who often showed his feelings in public. Journalists like that kind of thing. Robert de Cotret was next to me. He put his hand on my shoulder. I was really crying, I was shattered. I was sad for all Quebecers.

"If the Meech Lake Accord had passed, the issue would have been settled once and for all, and we could have moved on to other things. We would have had to change the history of Canada. In that sense, what I experienced was really living history."

There were other difficult moments before that big disappointment, such as the resignation of Lucien Bouchard,[8] a personal friend of Brian Mulroney's.

"Brian is so loyal to his friends. Friendship is something sacred for him, and he was surrounded by friends. He thought they would be his best supporters."

Monique Landry regards herself as a realistic woman who is fully aware of her capabilities, her potential and her limitations. When she was approached to join the leadership campaign, she could not believe that people would even consider it.

"I know where to stop. When I entered politics, I did not have an exceptional background. To be Prime Minister, you must be a politician through and through. You must like all aspects of politics, and there are so many of them. To be Prime Minister you must be an excellent parliamentarian, a good speaker, you have to be so versatile."

In the final analysis, it was by keeping in touch with people that Monique Landry did not lose her head in this hectic life.

"I cannot really say that power was such a glorifying experience for me. OK, I have power, I'm the minister, I decide. Anyway, we didn't really have that much room to manoeuvre. It's not because you're a minister that you're going to change the whole world. No I don't miss that at all. I'm proud of the political experience that I acquired along the way.

"People were very kind. I never had a real negative experience. I was never badly treated, even by demonstrators; by journalists, yes, with their annoying questions.

"There were a few demonstrations in front of my office, for instance, high school students who were opposed to the Gulf War. I met with their representatives when I came back from Ottawa. I spent an hour with them and went to their school to meet with the students and explain the government's policies. I was very well received. I also had to deal with farmers and their tractors. I wasn't upset by these events.

"I always felt very comfortable defending the government's decisions. When you discuss an issue in Ottawa, the Gulf War, for instance, it's a team decision. Brian listened to us. He would ask a minister to explain the pros and cons of the question. A consensus would emerge. We all knew that Brian might change his mind against the majority. To do a good job as a team player, it's important to feel comfortable to discuss and to participate in the decision process. There was never a decision which I felt was going to become a matter of conscience."

On issues such as abortion, the death penalty, the vote is free in the Canadian Parliament. It is up to the Members' individual conscience. This is not the case on issues of government policy, in which the party takes precedence.

"At times, I would have liked to go further, or not as far, but in general, it was always defendable. I was always comfortable with the positions we adopted. I never tried to hide."

WOMEN IN POLITICS

How do women make out in politics? Is it more difficult for them?

"I am convinced that women who go into politics ask a lot more questions than men before they make their decisions. Men enter politics for 56 000 different reasons, such as power or prestige, without ever asking themselves if they have the necessary background. Before I made my decision in 1984, I thought about it for a long time; I discussed it with my husband, with a cousin who's a businessman in Montreal, and with a few friends. I asked myself if I had the right background, the training and the experience to be in politics. After a few months in Ottawa, I realized that there were many people who had never even asked themselves these questions! In a political landslide, anybody can get elected."

"I would say that women are much more conscientious about their job. I think the best MP's in Ottawa are probably women.

"I would say politics is tougher for women. You always have to be perfect. The social aspect is very time-consuming. You receive all kinds of important invitations for your department or for the government, a dinner in Montreal, another one in Toronto. A man has a few suits and a few shirts. A woman must always be impeccably dressed.

"On top of that, I am proud! Do you see that closet? It contains my minister's clothes, as I like to say, quite different from my personal clothes which are in my bedroom. I'm a very organized woman. Here are the blazers, there are the skirts, accessories, blouses and shoes. I was so well organized that it became a habit.

"I can do my own hair. I wash my hair and in half an hour I'm ready to go.

"I do my own shopping. I go into boutiques, and in a couple of hours I find the clothes I need. When I went on a trip, I needed a daytime wardrobe and evening clothes. When I was at External Affairs, I went to Africa three or four times a year. I virtually had a special wardrobe for Africa. You visit projects in difficult conditions. You need light clothes that are easy to wash in your hotel room at night and that dry quickly. In the evening, I would hang my clothes and pack my suitcases for the next day. I never bought cotton or silk clothes, only permanent press.

"I don't like people to touch my personal belongings, I take care of it myself.

"At the risk of being repetitive, I am a very down-to-earth person, and my two feet are planted firmly on the ground. I'm very pragmatic when it comes to using my time and I'm very efficient. I had absolutely horrendous agendas. At times, I took on too many things. I wanted to please everyone."

Monique Landry has a rather small circle of close friends. She has a best friend whom she has known ever since she was thirteen. They are very close to one another, and they talk to each other once a week even in the most hectic times.

"Her husband died of cancer. It was very painful. I was very close to her. I'm very selective in my friendships. I don't have time to see people whom I don't like.

"Jean-Guy is also quite loner. He became quite self-sufficient when I went to Ottawa. I often tease him about it, and he has a good sense of humor. In February 85, for his birthday after the election, I gave him a microwave oven and a cookbook, and I told him, "Here, have fun." He tried. He had never bought groceries in his life before 1984. Since then, he's developed a few recipes, his cooking skills are improving. He even made dinner when I preferred to eat at home on Friday evenings when I came back from Ottawa. He didn't have a large repertoire of meals, but..."

Pragmatic, dynamic and enthusiastic, Monique Landry will soon join her husband down south for a few weeks, until spring comes. Spring will bring new projects, large and small...

ENDNOTES

1.   Francis Fox was MP for Blainville-Deux-Montagnes and Minister in the Liberal government under Pierre Elliot Trudeau. In Canadian federal politics, two major parties have traditionally alternated in office: the Liberal Party of Canada and the Progressive Conservative Party of Canada (or Tories).

2.   Translator's note: *Association générale des étudiants de l'Université de Montréal* or University of Montreal Student Association.

3.   Sir Wilfred Laurier was the Liberal Prime Minister of Canada from 1896 to 1911.

4.   At the time of the Quebec Sovereignty referendum, the law required that all participants campaign under the "Yes" banner or the "No" banner, regardless of the political parties and the level of government (provincial or federal) to which they belonged. Hence, Quebec provincial Liberals, who were opposed to sovereignty, worked side by side with federal Conservatives in the "No" camp.

5.   Translators' note: Blue is the traditional color of the Progressive Conservative Party in Canada. The color of the Liberal Party, both provincial and federal, is red.

6.   CIDA: Canadian International Development Agency.

7.   Under the Trudeau government, the Canadian constitution had been repatriated from Great-Britain to Canada over Quebec's objections. The Meech Lake Accord was an attempt to give Quebec a satisfactory status and corresponding powers within the Canadian constitution.

8.   Lucien Bouchard was then a member of Brian Mulroney's Cabinet. After he resigned from the government, he founded the Bloc Québécois. Since October 1993, he has been Leader of the Official Opposition in Ottawa.

THE LAKE BERN INTERACTIVE CASE

Jack Ruhe
Saint Mary's College
NOTRE DAME, INDIANA, U.S.A.
Steven Nyers
DYCAST, Inc.
LAKE ZURICH, ILLINOIS, U.S.A.

Abstract

Lake Bern, a mid-sized aluminum die casting, machining, and assembly operations, was purchased by a Swiss Investment Group, Strauss, Inc. of Zurich, Switzerland in 1988 as a leveraged buyout from the founder. Strauss, Inc. intended to use the low dollar value relative to the Swiss franc to purchase a number of U.S. companies, maintain ownership for five to seven years, capitalize on high management fees, and then sell them at a significant capital gain and an expected rate of return of 30%.

Within months profitability began to slide and eventually major operating losses were incurred under two CEOs. They experienced major communication and morale problems with the large multi-cultural workforce from Central and Latin America that led to quality and operating loss problems. A third CEO was able to formulate and implement a successful turnaround strategy following concepts he learned in MBA school. The CEO will discuss the case and the most recent financial results of the Turnaround strategy.

INTRODUCTION

COMPANY BACKGROUND

The Lake Bern Company is a mid-size aluminum die casting, machining and assembly operation offering a variety of capabilities to the automotive, industrial machinery, computer, power tool, engine and appliance markets. The business was started by Glenn Robertson in 1961. Robertson, having had extensive education and experience in the industry, decided to capitalize on his technical expertise and work for himself as an entrepreneur. The company, under his direction, grew in sales volume to $20 million by 1988. The company had, over the years, developed a reputation for possessing the capabilities of producing extremely complex, low porosity, dependable products.

Keys to the company's success included early engineering efforts in porosity control so critical to the automotive market, coupled with the utilization of vacuum assist in the die cast production process. Porosity control is critical for parts utilized in high precision, functionally heavy duty applications; e.g.: combustion engine components. Porosity is basically the entrapment of air in a casting which tends to weaken its internal integrity. The vacuum assist is an air evacuation process and is applied to a die cavity before molten metal is introduced so as to eliminate air in the cavity as the metal is added.

The company's early entry into the sophisticated computer market provided the impetus for expansion into machining and assembly operations. Customer demands led to the development of an in depth, formal quality assurance system. Competition is heavy within a 100 mile radius of the plant's location. The customer base is situated primarily in the U.S.; however, some products are sold to Middle Eastern and European Countries.

RESOURCES

Facilities

Lake Bern performs all operations from one facility consisting of 70,000 square feet, of which approximately 5% is assigned as office space. Approximately 2/3 of the available space is occupied by the die casting operation, with the remaining 1/3 dedicated to machining and assembly operations. The building is 22 years old and requires some renovation.

Employees

There are two hundred total employees, all but fifteen of which are involved in the manufacturing process. The company has a non-union work environment. The work force is heavily weighted toward Hispanics (90%).

SALE OF COMPANY

In the summer of 1988, Glenn Robertson was approached by a Swiss Investment Group, Strauss, Inc. of Zurich, Switzerland regarding the possibility of purchasing the company. Strauss, Inc. was actively investing in holdings in the United States throughout the decade of the Eighties. During this period of low value of the U.S. dollar relative to most other currencies, foreign investment in the United States was at an all time high. Strauss, Inc.'s method of investment was to purchase companies, maintain ownership for from five to seven years, while capitalizing on handsome management fees (10% per annum of original capital infusion). During the holding period, expectations were to substantially grow the business, while retiring the secured debt; then selling the company, thereby enjoying a significant capital gain. The expected internal rate of return was in excess of 30%.

Strauss, Inc. was interested in the Lake Bern Company primarily because, even though die casting was a mature manufacturing industry, there was significant growth potential in purchased finished parts (casting, machining and assembly). The future appeared outstanding. In November, 1988, after extensive due diligence, a leverage buy out was consummated. The principal investors had purchased the company for $13.5 million, $5 million of which was capital investment, with the remaining $8.5 million funded by a British Bank, with all assets pledged as collateral to secure the loan.

NEW OWNERSHIP DILEMMA

Almost from the beginning of the takeover, the company's profitability began to slide, and eventually, major operating losses were being incurred (Reference: Financial Statements - Exhibits A & B attached which reflect the company's financial condition after three years under the new ownership). This occurred principally because the previous owner was not contracted with to operate the company for a period of time during transition, coupled with the fact that very little technical depth (beyond the previous owner) existed in the company.

By the fall of 1991, the company had gone through two presidents. The first of these was a graduate engineer hired by the previous owner who recommended him as the individual capable of leading the company into the future. After a year and a half, it became quite apparent that this individual had no managerial capabilities, and further, was the cause of serious problems with specific customers. The next president was hired through an Executive Recruiter, and appeared to have the necessary qualifications and background to run the company. After a year, it was apparent that this individual also was not a capable senior executive; that he had gained his experience in a larger organization with a substantial support staff in place. The Swiss investor group, at this point, was frustrated; nevertheless, it commenced a search for its third president. This time, however, there was a serious need to effect a turnaround for survival. A national executive recruiting firm had been engaged to scour the country for an individual with leadership skills, with exposure to the foundry and machining business, but equally important, with in depth experience in turnaround situations.

The executive search centered on T. S. (Steve) Egert. His experience as a C.E.O. in a casting environment, coupled with his experience in handling a reorganization for a foundry operation in South Wales, Indiana interested the executive recruiter. Egert was approached as to his interest in considering accepting the challenge of turning around another manufacturing firm. A meeting was arranged with the principal Swiss investors during which details of the company's history and its current economic plight were shared. After several meetings over a three month period, a comfort level of trust was developed; and an offer for employment was received by Egert.

Personal Background

Egert had joined his previous firm as the Chief Financial Officer, after having spent several years in accounting and finance positions in both the manufacturing and service business sectors. After 12 years in the financial area, Egert became Vice President of Administration for a period of four years; then served as President and Chief Executive Officer for six years during which period the company underwent its greatest challenge; that of having to effect a formal plan of reorganization under Chapter 11 of the United States Bankruptcy Law. After having successfully met this challenge, and further having gained an Executive M.B.A. at a local national university, Egert began to feel that his job was becoming void of significant fulfillment.

Personal Decision/Philosophy

Egert, after having been offered the presidency at the Lake Bern Company, was now faced with a choice that had many negatives and very few positives. Over the years, Christian principles became the center of Egert's business philosophy. His confidence in the efficacy of Christ's role in his life is illustrated by an extract from one of his speeches which dealt with the choice of this job offer:

As a Christian, I appealed to the Lord for guidance. I firmly believe that God has a plan for each and every one of us. I sought for a confirmation that this opportunity was the proper direction for me. Words from the Bible and other readings seemed to indicate that I should give up my comfortable situation and move on to greater challenges.

Despite these inclinations, Egert knew that the move to a neighboring state would be hard on his wife, Joan, a professional herself who held a position as Human Resource Manager in a local company in South Wales. Nevertheless, fortified with the aforementioned inspirational thoughts, he decided to accept the position. Egert and his wife further decided, temporarily, that they would have a commuter marriage, with Egert coming home only on weekends because his new company had many obstacles, with no assurances that they could be overcome, coupled with the fact that he valued his wife's need for a career opportunity.

PHASE I - STRATEGY FORMULATION

DATA GATHERING

Egert recognized that it was going to be essential to gain the cooperation and confidence of all members of the organization in order to successfully ascertain the root causes of the problem or problems within the company. Gaining cooperation would not be an easy matter. An attitude of distrust had developed between management and the hourly employees in the most recent years. As previously mentioned, 90% of the hourly employees were comprised of Hispanics from various parts of North, Central and South America. Unfortunately, very few of the managers spoke Spanish; consequently, communications posed a major problem in that translators were necessarily required, which left much to be desired. The Hispanic work force in most instances were limited to the more menial jobs despite specific competencies by some who had received higher education in their native countries. Others had received little or no training in order to qualify for the higher paying jobs which, of course, created a feeling of discrimination. Also other problems surfaced with regard to the salaried group in that over the years some favoritism toward the Caucasian or the American employee did exist in certain functional areas (e.g. engineering, and quality). Some managers enjoyed certain perks such as country clubs, fancy autos, etc.

Over time, management had allowed the production operation to get completely out of control, with excessive waste created because of poor quality. Internal scrap was regularly running in excess of 20% when the industry norm was 6-8%. Substantial overtime was necessary in an endeavor to service customers, yet late deliveries continued to escalate. The excessive internal scrap created the necessity for rework in an attempt to salvage production. In any event, inferior product was still reaching the customers, which of course caused complaints, a slowing of payments on account and customer discontent. Business was being lost to competitors because of the lack of performance. Competitors were brutal, taking every opportunity to criticize the company and encouraging its customers to shift their work to them.

Relations with suppliers had also deteriorated as rumors spread regarding the very real possibility of failure of Lake Bern. Many suppliers had either cut off supplies or put the company on a C.O.D. basis. Cash management was practically nonexistent, with severe cash shortage problems occurring on a regular basis.

Outside legal fees for questionable services were also draining on the profitability. Once inside the organization, it became readily apparent that the depth of the problems were far more broad than even Egert had imagined. Nevertheless, being committed to the challenge, it was time to move forward with the development of a plan.

THE TURNAROUND STRATEGY

At the commencement of the strategic formulation phase, Egert met with all senior and middle managers, and shared his philosophy and ideas as to how to collaboratively address the task of turning the company around. He indicated that without their total commitment, without the full and complete cooperation of all, success could not be achieved in this endeavor. This must have struck a harmonious cord, since all expressed a willingness to formulate change. They wanted the company to succeed; and were desperately looking for direction, however, he had some reservations on the competency of two managers.

Fortified with that knowledge, a series of brainstorming sessions was embarked upon examining internal and external influences, the end result of which was the development of a list of areas requiring change. Egert then proceeded to weave these ideas into a coherent turnaround strategy. This strategy, properly implemented and maintained, would provide the basis for reducing the negative trends of the company. The specific functional strategies formulated included:
- Personnel Realignment/Replacement
- Cash Control Involving Budget Development, Cost Reductions, Creditor Relations and Customer Collections
- Operating Plans
- Customer Relations to Increase Sales and Curb the Loss of Business
- Evaluation Systems to Monitor Effectiveness of Plans
- Capital Expenditures Requirements
- Structural Reorganization

PHASE II - THE IMPLEMENTATION AND EVALUATION

Egert remembered vividly from his MBA days that "The Strategic Management Process does not end when the company decides what strategy or strategies to pursue. There must be a translation of strategic thought into strategic action. This translation is much easier if managers and employees of the company understand the business, feel a part of the company, and through involvement in strategy formulation activities become committed to helping the organization succeed. Without understanding and commitment, strategy implementation efforts face major problems."

IMPLEMENTATION PROCESS

Personnel
- Reassignment/Replacement of Senior Management - There were five (5) Senior Managers on staff responsible for:
  - Sales
  - Operations
  - Engineering
  - Quality Assurance
  - Finance/Administration

After extensive, serious evaluation as to capabilities, attitudes and responsibility performance, it became apparent that three (3) of the five (5) managers would either have to be replaced or reassigned.
  - The Operations Manager was reassigned to Technical Sales; the Operations were split into two (2) divisions, die casting and machining/assembly, with responsibilities assigned to separate, existing middle management personnel.

- The Engineering Manager was terminated and replaced by an extremely competent individual with the necessary tools to scientifically resolve problems.
- The Quality Assurance Manager was terminated and replaced by an individual with state of the art technical capabilities.

Needless to say, Egert became a highly visible individual, having made these initial moves. It became apparent to all employees that things would be different; that there were no sacred cows as it were in the organization.

Next, having gained everyone's attention, Egert called a series of meetings with all employees, salaried and hourly, to explain that their management was in the process of developing a survival plan; that all employees would be required to share in the pain; that there would be equal sacrifices, beginning with the President of the company.

Cash Control

- Cost Reductions - because operating losses were running rampant, with negative cash flow strangling the company, immediate action regarding cost reductions were required.
  - All overtime requiring double time pay eliminated
  - Excess staff and hourly employees laid off
  - Salary and wage concessions - implemented 10% reduction across the board
  - Employee health care withholdings were doubled
  - Management perks eliminated or reduced (company cars, dues, etc.)
  - Eliminated/minimized ridiculous use of outside legal counsel
    Concessions are never readily accepted, consequently, problems were anticipated. Upon announcement of concessions to the employees, two situations developed:
  - Three (3) salaried employees (10%) terminated
  - Hourly employees contacted the Communications Union for possible representation.
    The salaried employee situation was not difficult to overcome. Replacements were simply hired. The hourly employee situation posed a much more significant problem. The company had two-hundred (200) hourly folks, 90% of whom were of Hispanic origin. The prospect of dealing with union representation was not exciting, particularly when the name of the game was to improve productivity.
    A major campaign was undertaken over a five (5) week period to ward off a union organization attempt. Significant research was conducted on the union. Posters were prepared and displayed in the plant. Egert, personally, conducted meetings twice each week explaining the company's position, the game plan, where the company is headed, why the company should remain non-union, shared horror stories about this particular union. When the vote was taken, the employees voted in favor of the company, thus affording management the opportunity to demonstrate what can be done. Obviously, all employees were disheartened by the 'take aways,' and yet there was enough believability in what was trying to be accomplished, that most agreed to support the endeavor.
- Budgetary Development - Thirteen departments were established with detailed expense projections prepared by individual department managers and reviewed by senior management. A monthly monitoring process was also established in order to compare actual vs. budgeted costs.
- Unsecured Creditors - A repayment plan for the unsecured creditors group was developed. Egert, personally, met with each major creditor and explained the company's dilemma. He shared the company's plans for the future and financial statements, then presented a liquidating balance sheet, which indicated that should the company be forced to liquidate, there would be no surplus funds for the unsecured creditors group. To illustrate the magnitude of the problem, the company owed $1.8 million to three hundred (300) vendors, obligations that were seriously delinquent. The proposal included:
  - Front end payment (5% or less of balance due)
  - Monthly payments of from six (6) to thirty-six (36) months
  - Opportunity to continue to supply product
    All but three (3) vendors agreed, with these three (3) filing suit. These situations were resolved by enhancing the front money and reducing the number of monthly payments. These were

successfully settled out of court.

- Secured Creditor - The next major issue to be addressed was the secured bank debt. The bank, after weeks of serious negotiations, agreed to forgive 55% of the debt in return for a 25% equity position in the company. Additionally, the company successfully negotiated for a two (2) year moratorium on principal debt reduction, along with the bank agreeing to waive interest during that time frame.
- Customer Collections - The last piece in the puzzle of cash control was to meet with all major customers to review the economics of the situation and provide assurance that the company would not be filing for protection under the U.S. Bankruptcy Law. However, it was emphasized that their help was required, that it was essential they comply with payment terms of net thirty (30) days.

Operations/Sales

The last major strategy to be implemented dealt with Operations. As previously mentioned specific personnel changes were made:

- Hiring of Vice President of Engineering
- Transfer of Operations Manager to Technical Sales
- Repositioning of Casting and Machining Managers
- Hiring of Quality Assurance Manager

As an aside, a very special man was hired to head up Engineering. During the interview process, it surfaced that he was also an individual with Christian beliefs. Egert firmly believed that the sharing of these beliefs was primary in this individual's decision to join the company. Shortly after he arrived, a commitment was made to spend a short period of time together each morning asking for guidance and counsel on conducting the affairs of the company. It is believed, that these moments, more than anything else, was the key to the successful turnaround of the company.

Several procedures were implemented during the first few weeks after personnel changes were in place:

- Machine Capability Studies
- Employee Training
- Converted from Three Shift/24 Hour Operation to Two Shift/20 Hour Operation

Within a matter of just a very few weeks, in-house scrap performance began to improve. Before the aforementioned changes, in-house scrap was running in excess of 20%. This number reduced to 16% after the first month, then to under 10% within three (3) months.

Because of the dramatic improvement in fallout for scrap, overtime was minimized; but more importantly, the past due order situation was reduced significantly, thereby allowing for the first positive signs with customers that perhaps a viable supplier did exist with the company. The positive change in quality improved delivery performance thereby re-establishing credibility with all major accounts. This stopped the flow of lost business and assisted in stabilizing the company.

Strategic Plan

During the time that strategies were being formulated and implemented, a Business Operating Plan was also developed including:

- Sales Game Plan - Target Markets
- Sales Forecast
- Operating Budgets
- Cash Flow
- Capital Expenditure Budget

Evaluation and Control

The plan was agreed to and approved by the management group and the investors, it then became the criteria for evaluating the effectiveness of the Strategic Plan.

CONCLUSION

During the ensuing months, the company returned to profitability, new sales have been awarded, credibility within the industry has been re-established. It is now being recommended as a qualified capable source to produce critical products.

The attitude and enthusiasm of the employees abound, energized by the positive changes that have been experienced over the past two years. The employees, without question, are the key to successful selling. A debt of gratitude is owed to each and every one of them.

The company is truly back from the depths of a difficult situation, though not completely home free as yet. The next fiscal year will prove just how far the company has come. This year should allow the company to experience a significant ramp up in sales, thus affording the opportunity to return to the level of prosperity enjoyed in the past. (An updated set of financial statements will be forthcoming).

This story is a real life experience, as well as a demonstration of what can be accomplished by people helping people, working together in a spirit of cooperation,

with a focus on a common goal.

LAKE BERN COMPANY
BALANCE SHEET
JANUARY 31, 1992

ASSETS

CURRENT ASSETS		
CASH		$ 352,200
ACCOUNTS RECEIVABLE-TRADE		1,514,500
ACCOUNTS RECEIVABLE-OTHER		2,500
INVENTORIES		705,900
PREPAID EXPENSES		299,700
TOTAL		2,874,800

PROPERTY AND EQUIPMENT		
AT NET HISTORICAL COST		5,317,500
CURRENT YEAR ADDITIONS		124,500
LESS: ACCUMULATED DEPRECIATION		(2,564,200)
TOTAL		2,877,800

INTANGIBLE ASSETS		
INTANGIBLE ASSETS		1,250,000
ASSET WRITE-UP TO FAIR MARKET VALUE		3,874,000
LESS: AMORTIZATION		(1,875,500)
TOTAL		3,248,500

OTHER ASSETS		
DEPOSITS		1,600
EMPLOYEE LOANS		5,300
TOTAL		6,900
TOTAL ASSETS		$9,008,000

LIABILITIES AND NET WORTH

CURRENT LIABILITIES		
NOTES PAYABLE-CURRENT PORTION NBD		85,900
ACCOUNTS PAYABLE		1,730,600
ACCRUED EXPENSES		1,012,100
ACCRUED MANAGEMENT FEES		698,400
ACCRUED INCOME TAXES		0
TOTAL		3,527,000

LONG TERM DEBT		
MORTGAGE NOTE NBD		58,000
NOTES PAYABLE BSC FAC A		4,916,000
NOTES PAYABLE BSC FAC B		2,234,300
NOTES PAYABLE BSC SUBORD. NOTE		1,000,000
TOTAL		8,208,300

OTHER LIABILITIES		
RESERVE FOR TOOL REPLACEMENT		447,100
TOTAL LIABILITIES		12,182,400

NEW WORTH		
CAPITAL STOCK		$5,105,200
RETAINED EARNINGS		(7,393,100)
CURRENT YEAR EARNINGS		(886,500)
TOTAL NET WORTH		($3,174,400)
TOTAL LIABILITIES & NET WORTH		$9,008,000

EXHIBIT B

LAKE BERN COMPANY STATEMENT OF OPERATION
FOUR MONTHS ENDED JANUARY 31, 1992

	ACTUAL	BUDGET	VARIANCE
SALES			
CASTING SALES	$2,800,000	$2,785,000	$15,000
IBM ASSEMBLIES	283,000	281,000	2,000
METAL	1,331,600	1,620,000	-288,400
FREIGHT	2,600	0	2,600
SALES RETURNS	-116,000	0	-116,400
SALES DISCOUNTS	-2,300	0	-2,300
NET TOOLING SALES	0	0	0
TOTAL	4,298,500	4,686,000	-387,500
COST OF SALES			
LABOR	1,626,700	1,250,840	-375,860
OVERHEAD	1,004,800	832,800	-172,000
METAL	1,226,800	1,495,200	268,400
OTHER MATERIAL	4,100	0	-4,100
IBM ASSEMBLIES	207,700	232,000	24,300
SUBCONTRACT PURCHASES	173,700	87,400	-86,300
LABOR/OVERHEAD INV. VARIATION	-125,100	0	125,100
TOTAL	4,118,700	3,898,240	-220,460
GROSS PROFIT	179,800	787,760	-607,960
	4.2%	16.9%	
GENERAL & ADMINISTRATIVE EXPENSE	235,900	221,500	-14,400
SELLING EXPENSE	191,900	216,500	24,600
TOTAL	427,800	438,000	10,200
OPERATING INCOME	-248,000	349,760	-597,760
	-5.8%	7.5%	
401K & BONUSES	0	22,900	22,900
INTEREST EXPENSE	245,600	267,100	21,500
OTHER (INCOME) EXPENSE	-8,000	-5,200	2,800
MANAGEMENT FEES	215,300	166,000	-49,300
DEPR FMV FIXED ASSETS W/U	36,100	185,400	149,300
AMORT INTANGIBLES	84,200	-84,200	
AMORT OF NON-COMPETE	65,400	0	-65,400
INCOME BEFORE TAX	-886,600	-286,000	-600,160

ETHICAL RESPONSIBILITY OF CORPORATIONS TOWARD THEIR EMPLOYEES AND RETIREES: A CASE STUDY

Abdel M. Agami
Old Dominion University
NORFOLK, VIRGINIA, U.S.A.

Abstract

This case was developed on the basis of library research. It is based on real persons and real events. Its purpose is to stimulate students' thoughts as to the ethical responsibility of corporations toward their employees and retirees, especially in the area of providing retirees with medical care and other post retirement benefits.

INTRODUCTION

March 2, 1993 was a nice day in Costa Mesa, California, where Kazimir "Casey" Patelski lives, but he was not enjoying the day at his residence. Instead he was in Washington, DC on this day, where winter was still going strong. As he was going over the notes he had prepared for his testimony before the Senate Subcommittee, he could not help but let his mind wander. At the age of 65, retired last year after twenty-eight eventful years of hard work as an engineer for McDonnell Douglas, his responsibilities included directing mission control for the Apollo moon launches. He was thinking that he should be in sunny California enjoying his retirement; instead Mr. Patelski was sitting in his wheelchair, disabled, with his legs paralyzed for eighteen months now as a result of a resurgence of the polio that he contracted as a college student almost fifty years ago. As if this was not bad enough, he was not feeling a bit good about the task ahead of him. He came to Washington, DC to testify against the same company to which he had given his youthful and productive years, the company that promised to take care of him when he got old or sick. But what else could he do after officials at McDonnell Douglas announced that they will not pay medical insurance premiums for him beyond 1996.

In his testimony before the Senate Subcommittee Mr. Patelski said that he feels betrayed and is "damn angry" that McDonnell Douglas Corp. has decided to scrap health benefits for retired workers. He accused the company of reneging on its promise to provide lifetime health coverage for himself and his wife. "I doubt that a person like me is going to be able to obtain health insurance...I simply do not know what the long-term outlook is on my medical condition but it does not take a rocket scientist--which I happen to be--to realize that I am going to have continuing medical costs...I'm upset and I'm damn angry they've gone back on their promise." In response to Mr. Patelski's emotional testimony, Barbara Anderson, a spokeswoman for McDonnell Douglas, said the company "tried to balance the needs of retirees against the needs of the corporation...We reserved the right to modify or amend or terminate the coverage (of retiree health plan) at any time" [Rosenblatt, 1993].

Marie Esposito, age 68, retired from Primerica Corp., a financial services concern previously known as American Can Co., after 19 years of service. She was an executive secretary and retired as a result of shutting down the department where she worked. She is single and lives alone, has high blood pressure and an ulcer. Presently her monthly medical cost runs to $177.67 a month which is covered by Primerica's policy of post retirement medical insurance. Primerica announced its intention to discontinue this policy. The company set December 23, 1992 as the deadline for seven thousand and eight hundred retirees to agree either to pay the full cost of continuing coverage, or go without it. The retirees learned of the deadline only three weeks before December 23, 1992. Marie Esposito said "They told us, either you take it by December 23 or you drop out and cannot be reinstated." She wonders, "Was it a scare tactic? If it is, they're doing a good job on me. I'm single.

I live alone. I have no one I can turn to." She said that it will cost her $144 a month to continue the coverage on her own. She presently gets a pension of $240 per month. She said, "I can't swing the $144 for medical coverage, which I desperately need" [Freudenheim, 1992].

Curtailment or elimination of retirees' post retirement benefits in McDonnell Douglas and Primerica are not two isolated cases. At least twenty-three large corporations have curtailed or eliminated their retirees' post retirement benefits, and in particular the health benefits they were providing thousands of retired employees. Dozens more have announced that they will not provide these benefits to future employees. Many companies are hiring more part-time staff to avoid the cost of fringe benefits. The reasons for this general trend by companies toward curtailment or elimination of retirees' post retirement benefits, in particular medical coverage, is the rapid increase in the cost of medical care in recent years, the requirement by the accounting profession for businesses to accrue the total cost of these benefits rather than expensing only the amount paid during the year, the lack of legal requirements to provide these benefits, and the absence of tax incentives for corporations to provide post retirement benefits for their retirees.

THE ESCALATING COST OF MEDICAL CARE

The cost of medical care is not only high; it is expected that it will go even higher as people live longer because the U.S. population is aging rapidly. The cost of medical care has increased 164 percent since 1980--nearly twice the rate of increase for homes, and four times as much as the increase in the price of cars. Premiums paid to insurance companies have increased to three or four times the rate of inflation. Some claim that insurance premiums nearly doubled from 1987 to 1991. Medical care presently eats up 12 percent of the U.S. Gross National Produce (GNP). The general price level increase is expected to continue at 3 to 7 percent while the medical trend rate (the total increase in the cost of providing medical care due to increases in cost per service, increased utilization of services, and advances in medicine and medical technology, and excluding the increases due to aging of the population) is expected to increase annually by 15 percent over the next 20 years. If these expectations materialize, we would be spending about 40 percent of our gross national product on medical care, as compared to the 12 percent we presently spend.

CHANGE IN ACCOUNTING FOR POST RETIREMENT BENEFITS

Before the Financial Accounting Standards Board (FASB), the primary entity responsible for establishing generally accepted accounting principles, issued Statement of Financial Accounting Standard (FAS) 106--Employers' Accounting for Post retirement Benefits Other Than Pensions--employers funded post retirement benefits on a pay-as-you-go (cash) basis and also deducted the amounts funded from income in the year they were paid. Post retirement benefits are all the benefits the employers provided retirees after retirement other than pension or retirement income. They usually include benefits such as health care, tuition assistance, legal services, etc. However, the medical care benefit is the most common and the most costly benefit.

The FASB was concerned about the lack of information in financial statements about the obligation of corporations to retirees for post retirement benefits. On February 19, 1981, the Board issued a discussion memorandum entitled "Employers' Accounting for Pensions and Other Post-employment Benefits" in which the Board raised the issue of how Post-employment benefits other than pensions should be accounted for. In 1982, the FASB published "Preliminary Views, Employers' Accounting for Pension and Other Post-employment Benefits," in which the Board tentatively concluded that the cost of Post-employment health care and life insurance provided to retirees should be accrued during the service lives of the employees expected to receive benefits. The FASB did not consider the pay-as-you-go basis to be acceptable. The Board reiterated those views in the 1983 Discussion Memorandum, "Employers' Accounting for Pension and Other Post-employment Benefits." In February, 1984, the FASB reached the conclusion to deal with the issue of accounting for Post-employment benefits separately from pension cost. In 1984, the Board issued FAS 81, "Disclosure of Post retirement Health Care and Life Insurance Benefits." FAS 81 required employers to disclose information related to the benefits provided and the employees covered, description of the employer's current accounting and funding policies for those benefits, and the cost of those benefits recognized for the period. In April, 1987, the Board issued Technical Bulletin No. 87-1, "Accounting for Change in Method of Accounting for Certain Post retirement Benefits," which allowed companies that change their method of accounting for post retirement benefits from cash basis to accrual basis to either account for the change prospectively or recognize the cumulative effect of the change in net income of the period of the change. On February 14, 1989, the FASB issued an Exposure Draft, "Employers' Accounting for Post retirement Benefits Other Than Pensions." Public hearings on the Exposure Draft were conducted in October and November of 1989. In December, 1990, the FASB issued Statement of Financial Accounting Standards No. 106, "Employers' Accounting for Post retirement Benefits Other Than Pensions." This statement significantly changed the current practice of accounting for post retirement benefits on a pay-as-you-go (cash) basis by requiring employers to accrue, during the years that the employee renders the necessary service. The Board believes that measurement of the obligation and accrual of the cost based on best estimates are superior to pretending that no obligation exists prior to the payment. In the Board's opinion, failure to recognize the obligation prior to its payment reduces the usefulness of financial statements.

IMPACT OF FAS 106 ON THE FINANCIAL STATEMENTS OF CORPORATIONS AND MANAGEMENT REACTION

To measure the impact of the 1989 FASB Exposure Draft, "Employers' Accounting for Post retirement Benefits Other Than Pensions" which proposed the accrual during the service period of employees, of the cost of post retirement benefits rather than the current practice of accounting for post retirement benefits on a pay-as-you-go basis, the Financial Executive Research Foundation sponsored a study to test the impact of the new proposal on 26 companies. This study showed that if the method of accounting for post retirement benefits proposed in the Exposure Draft was adopted by those corporations, their pre-tax income would decrease by 2%-20%. Furthermore, those companies' expense for post retirement benefits would increase to 2-6 times of what it is presently as a result of adopting the new proposal [Coopers & Lybrand, 1989].

In 1991 the Institute of Management Accountants (previously the National Association of Accountants) sponsored a research study to investigate the effect of FAS 106 on 10 small and medium-sized employers. The study found that the cost of post retirement benefits for those employers under the new accounting standard amounts to 2-7 times the cost under the pay-as-you-go basis for mature employers, employers having fewer than six active employees for every retiree. It amounts to 8-45 times the cost under the pay-as-you-go method for immature employers, employers having six or more active employees for every retiree [Coopers & Lybrand, 1991].

As the 1992 annual reports of corporations are becoming public, evidence of the impact of FAS 106 on the financial statements of corporations who adopted FAS 106 currently is becoming available. McDonnell Douglas has recorded a charge of $942 million as the cost of adopting FAS 106, and this after saving $676 million by deciding to eliminate the health benefit program for retirees by 1996 [Rosenblatt, 1993]. General Motors Corporation reported $20.8 billion as the cost of adopting FAS 106 in 1992, i.e., the future health care cost of its retirees. Ford Motor Co. reported $7.5 billion as the cost of future health care of its retirees in 1992. Sears Roebuck & Co. claims that the cost of future health care of its retirees is $1.87 billion [Shean, 1993].

Many companies used the impact of new accounting standards on their financial performance in 1992 to justify the curtailment or elimination of post retirement benefits, particularly medical care, as was pointed out earlier. However, several organizations have accused employers of using the new accounting standard as an excuse to reduce their costs and losses. For example, Cathy Ventrell-Monsees, a workers' right manager at the American Association of Retired Persons (AARP) said, "Companies have had several years' notice that they would have to comply with the accounting rule...To come out in this last quarter of 1992 and say, 'We are compelled to eliminate benefits because of FAS 106 accounting' is the weakest excuse for hurting people just to save money." Representative Ron Wyden, Democrat from Oregon and a member of the House Select Committee On Aging, asked the General Accounting Office to investigate the cancellation of retiree health benefits. He said, "My sense is that we're going to see more and more scheming to use FAS 106 and other accounting sleight of hand and dump seniors and get out from under paying health benefits" [Freudenheim, 1992].

COMPANIES DO NOT HAVE A LEGAL LIABILITY TO PROVIDE RETIREES WITH POST RETIREMENT BENEFITS

Presently there is no law that requires corporations to provide retirees post retirement benefits, medical or otherwise. The 1974 Employee Retirement Income Security Act (ERISA) does not give retirees the right to vested interminable post retirement or health benefits. However, most courts have looked first to the contract between the employer and its retirees and have considered the intent of the parties as reflected in the written provision of the plan document to establish the extent of the employer obligation and the rights of retirees. Other sources used by courts for clarification of the rights of retirees and the obligation of employers include collective bargaining agreements between employers and retirees, documents distributed to employees, discussion with employees prior to retirement, and pattern of conduct. Generally courts have looked to the plan document and have only consulted other documents when the plan document was not clear or was ambiguous. Courts have generally upheld curtailment or elimination of post retirement benefits only in cases where the plan document contained clear, explicit and unambiguous provisions that gave the employer these rights [Corporate Liabilities for Retiree Benefits, 1988].

The termination or reduction of post retirement benefits including health care benefits for active employees who are not yet retired but may become eligible for these benefits have not yet been tested in the courts. Only suits by retirees have been tried in courts to-date.

ABSENCE OF TAX INCENTIVE FOR CORPORATIONS TO PROVIDE POST RETIREMENT BENEFITS

Under current tax laws, health benefits are excludable from the retiree's income and deductible by employers as compensation expense. The deduction, except in limited cases, is available only in the tax year in which the cost of the benefit is incurred and is limited to the amount actually paid to retirees and/or paid as premiums to insurance companies. The tax laws generally do not allow deductions of amounts contributed in excess of the amounts paid. There are two exceptional cases to the general rule of deducting only cost paid. The first is when the post retirement benefits are incorporated with the pension plan as an ancillary benefit under Section 401(h) of the Internal Revenue Code. In this case pre-funding the cost of benefits would be tax deductible by employers and the benefits received by retirees would be excludable from their income. However, to qualify for this treatment the post retirement benefits must be "incidental" to the total benefits (no more than 25% of the entire contribution). The second exceptional case is to fund the post retirement benefit through the use of Section 501(c)(9) of the Internal Revenue Code known as Voluntary Employee Beneficiary Association (VEBA). Under this section the employer contributions are tax deductible to the employer and the VEBA's income generally will not be subject to taxes. However, the amount that is deductible is limited to contribution based on current medical cost; a projection for future medical care cost cannot be incorporated in the deductions [Bazzle, 1989].

A number of legislative efforts were made in Congress to encourage corporations to voluntarily provide for retirees' post retirement benefits as well as to sufficiently fund them. For example, in April, 1989, Representative Rod Chandler (Republican from Washington), Representative Ronnie Flippo (Democrat from Alabama), and Senator David Pryor (Democrat from Arkansas) introduced legislation that would allow employers to deduct pre-funding retiree post retirement benefits [Brostoff, 1989]. In June, 1989, the House Ways and Means Committee introduced a proposal that would permit companies to use excess assets from over-funded pension plans to fund post retirement benefits [Birnbaum, 1989]. This effort was successful and resulted in the 1990 Budget Reconciliation Act which became effective in 1991.

QUESTIONS

1. Should companies be legally obligated to provide their employees post retirement benefits (medical care, life insurance, etc.)? Are they morally or ethically obligated?
2. Should companies be allowed to renege their promises to provide post retirement benefits to their retirees?
3. Which is a more serious problem to society: companies turning their backs on promises they gave to their employees and retirees, or going out of business as a result of fulfilling the promises they gave employees?
4. Who, in your opinion, should provide for the cost of medical care? The government? corporations? individuals? Why?
5. Should the accounting profession have considered the possible impact of FAS 106, "Employers' Accounting for Post retirement Benefit Other Than Pension," on the behavior of executives and action of companies such as curtailing, changing or eliminating post retirement benefits before the Financial

Accounting Standards Board reached its decision as to how to account for post retirement benefits? In other words, should accounting standards be established on the basis of their merits and conceptual support only, or should economic and social consequences be taken into consideration in addition?

INSTRUCTOR'S NOTE

This case was developed on the basis of library research, mostly from cuttings the author made from daily newspapers such as The Wall Street Journal, The New York Times, and his local newspaper, The Virginian Pilot. It is based on real persons and real events. The author used, successfully, this case in his intermediate accounting course in Spring, 1993 in the topic "Pensions and Other Post retirement Benefits." This course is an undergraduate course, a required course for accounting students and an elective for other business major students. However, this case can be used in other courses such as a seminar in accounting theory, either under-graduate or graduate; also the case could be used in a finance course or a course in business ethics.

The objectives of this case are: to stimulate students' thoughts and discussion as to the legal vs. moral and ethical responsibility of corporations toward their employees and retirees, especially in the area of providing retirees with medical care; and to help students understand and appreciate the magnitude of the cost of medical care and how to provide for it. It also encourages students to understand and appreciate the process of establishing accounting standards, more specifically to get himself or herself involved in the debate over the issue of whether accounting standards should be based on conceptual justification only or should take into consideration economic and social consequences and other complexities of the "real-world."

REFERENCES

Bazzle, K., "Funding Post retirement Benefits." Management Accounting (April 1989), pp. 27-29.

Brinbaum, J., "Shift in Funding of Pension Plans Mulled in House." The Wall Street Journal (June 21, 1989), p. A2.

Brostoff, S., "Congress Gets Retiree Health Benefit Bill." National Underwriter--Life & Health/Financial Services Edition (April 24, 1989), pp. 2 and 5.

Coopers & Lybrand. Retiree Health Benefits: Field Test of the FASB Proposal. Morristown, NJ: Financial Executive Research Foundation, 1989.

Coopers & Lybrand. Retiree Health Benefits: How To Cope With the Accounting, Actuarial, and Management Issues. Montvale, NJ: Institute of Management Accountants, 1991.

Corporate Liabilities for Retiree Benefits. CPA Magazine (May 1988), pp, 6-8.

FASB. Discussion Memorandum: An Analysis of Issues Related to Employers' Accounting For Pensions and Other Post-employment Benefits. Stamford, CT: FASB, 1981.

FASB. Preliminary Views of the Financial Accounting Standards Board on Major Issues Related to Employers' Accounting For Pensions and Other Post-employment Benefits. Stamford, CT: FASB, 1982.

FASB. Discussion Memorandum: An Analysis of Additional Issues Related to Employers' Accounting For Pensions and Other Post-employment Benefits. Stamford, CT: FASB, 1983.

FASB. FASB Technical Bulletin 87-1: Accounting For a Change in Method of Accounting for Certain Post retirement Benefits. Stamford, CT: FASB, 1987.

FASB. Exposure Draft: Employers' Accounting For Post retirement Benefits Other Than Pensions. Stamford, CT: FASB, 1989.

350

FASB. <u>Statement of Financial Accounting Standards No. 106: Employers' Accounting For Post retirement Benefits Other Than Pensions</u>. Stamford, CT: FASB, 1990.

Freudenheim, Mit, "Firms Paring Retiree Benefits." <u>The Virginian Pilot</u> (December 25, 1992).

Rosenblatt, Robert A., "McDonnell Douglas Betrayed Its Retirees, Rocket Scientist Says." <u>The Virginian Pilot</u> (March 4, 1993).

Shean, Tom, "Accounting Rule Leaves a Trail of Red." <u>The Virginian Pilot</u> (February 14, 1993).

STRATEGIC BAR CODING DECISIONS: A MULTI-STAGE APPROACH

Sandra S. Lang
Greenville College
GREENVILLE, ILLINOIS, U.S.A.
Marvin Tucker
Southern Illinois University at Carbondale
CARBONDALE, ILLINOIS U.S.A.

Abstract

The business depicted in this case is a manufacturing plant, a cost center. To reduce costs and increase quality, the plant manager would like to expand their present bar coding system. Exactly what to include in this bar coding system is the crux of this case. Students will be expected to suggest items to introduce into the system and the order in which they should be added since the project is to be accomplished in stages. The students will have to look at the production process to determine what information will be beneficial for relevant feedback and efficient quality control.

ANDERS RUBBER COMPANY

Anders Rubber Company (ARC)[1] is a company that makes rubber roofing sheets for destinations throughout the world. The production plant is located in a community of just over 5,200 people and employs 180 workers. ARC is a division of Anders, Inc. and is a cost center. Tim Fields, Plant Manager, spoke regarding his operation. "We are a nonunion plant and use a participatory form of management. We have done this since hiring our first employee fifteen years ago because we feel it is the smart way to do business from both a moral and conscience standpoint. This past year there was a change in CEOs at Anders. The prior CEO's management style did not necessarily mesh with this plant's methods, but he liked the results we achieved and therefore used a hands off approach with us. What we are doing works. Including our employees in the decision-making process wasn't begun as a fad with us. Neither were we forced into it out of desperation as many companies have been. It was our choice. We are also fortunate in that we are able to pay at the top of the wage scale for the area and to provide an excellent benefits package. These things build loyalty.

"We expect and receive a good deal of input from the employees in regard to production and safety. We meet weekly with the employees and listen to their ideas. We have implemented many, ranging from some which are simple but effective, to more complex systems or equipment changes. The employees not only make suggestions, but work with us throughout the process to plan just how to make their ideas work; whereas, if similar concepts came from supervisors or support staff we would have kinks to work around to adapt them to our particular situations. The employees think through these little, often irritating obstacles before the idea takes on a tangible form. This approach makes the design phase of projects longer than the average, but allows for a shorter implementation and start-up phase, as well as a much more effective solution once the installation or change is completed.

"Since our employees are typically deployed in teams of four to seven, cross training is an important factor in keeping production running smoothly at Anders. There are no set breaks where everything stops for fifteen minutes. When a employee takes a break or has to be away from a station, his or her machine is not shut down. Instead another employee takes over."

352

PRODUCTION

ARC makes two thicknesses of roofing--.045 gauge and .060 gauge. They run three shifts continuously throughout the year with Saturdays worked when necessary.

Rubber roofing is produced in several steps, depicted in Exhibit 1. Raw materials (oil, carbon black, polymers and compounds) are first mixed via three computer-controlled formulas. The mixing is done in two stages. Samples are taken after the mixing process and tested at an onsight lab to insure that quality standards are met. These green sheets produced in this mixing stage then are calendared and rolled with a liner. At this stage, a computer continuously checks and adjusts thickness variances of 1/2 of one-thousandth of an inch or more. It is here also that the gauge is set. In the calendar process, the sheets are gauged to one-half the gauge desired, and two sheets are laminated together. This two-sheet lamination process virtually eliminates the possibility of imperfections in the sheet and gives strength to the finished rubber roofing product.

From the Calendar Area the rolls are taken to the Automated Sheet Building Machine (ASBM) in the Building, Curing and Postcuring Area. Here they are unrolled and placed together by machine with overlaps of a minimum of one inch. They also are dusted with mica dust, which prevents the material from sticking to itself when rolled. Any defective sheets discovered are rolled into what is called a pigg and routed back to be reworked. The rework rate at this level in the process is under 10%.

Next, the readied sheets, now approximately 50' by 300' in size, are rolled in Dartek wrap (not unlike a cellophane wrap in appearance). Both this wrap and the mica dust are important aides in the vulcanizing process during which gases are emitted. The mica dust and the wrap allow the gases to be vented out the ends of the rolls. The wrapped, rolled sheets are moved on sleds rather than by forklift as was the case before reaching the ASBM. The rolls are put into the vulcanizer in groups of five. After vulcanizing, during which the seams have been set and the sheets cured, the sheets are rerolled and allowed to cool.

The final step in the process involves unrolling the sheet, cutting it to ordered sizes, and rolling each finished sheet after visually inspecting for flaws. If defects are found in a cured sheet, spot repairs are made or the sheet is downsized to minimize the amount of cured rubber scrap. Normally, cured scrap has to be sent to a third party to be ground up, enabling it to be reused in the process. This procedure is both expensive and time-consuming. The amount of cured rubber scrap is less than 1%, which keeps this expenditure down. If a seam problem is detected, there is a press and seam table within the plant which enables ARC to fix them. Added Tim, "The repaired seam doesn't look the same as the original, but it is as strong or stronger and our customers know this."

Production and finished sizes of sheets are scheduled from the main offices. ARC employs a modified JIT system in that the amounts and gauge to be produced are determined by orders actually received. However, since there are peak periods of demand for the product (determined by weather for construction periods throughout the world), a limited amount of stockpiling needs to be maintained at all times. Inventory is monitored closely. Throughput time (from raw materials to shipping) is generally three and one-half days, but production can be accomplished in a minimum of twelve hours when necessary. The size of the order is, of course, a crucial determinant of throughput time. Custom orders take longer.

These finished rolls are moved by forklift to the warehouse attached to the plant, and they are then encased in bags the color of which indicates the size and gauge. This color coding facilitates locating the proper rolls for loading the trucks for shipping.

Tim Fields spoke of a problem ARC has been experiencing. "For three months now the rubber hasn't wanted to separate from the liner at the ASBM when it was unrolled. We had been working with only one formula, but now we use three. Formula changes are made for performance reasons or for cost control. The most recent formula changes were made strictly for cost control, as a substitution was made for cost considerations alone. We've decided that the problem we're having is due to this recent formula change, and corrective actions are being considered. I think that with a better bar coding system we would have been able to pinpoint the problem sooner."

BAR CODING

Recently, the decision was made to change computer consulting firms and update their computer system to increase work station capacity and capabilities. Tim Fields would like to incorporate a bar code label system that would integrate with the computer system to enable management to track a finished product back to the raw materials comprising it. A determination as to which factors to include in the code, if one were to be implemented in this area, is yet to be defined.

Primary objectives of expanding the present bar code system are to: enable ARC to build customer relations; trouble shoot problems that may show up at final inspection by pinpointing the machine on which that specific piece was calendared or assembled; locate which batch that sheet was a part of; and to identify the supplier of an inferior raw material.

There is a limited bar coding system in place as displayed in Exhibit 2. However, according to Dan Morrison, Production Manager, there are two major drawbacks to the present system: 1) the coding enables them to check back only as far as the calendar stage; and 2) the computer capabilities make a search regarding interrelated data both cumbersome and impractical.

An entire new system is not elicited; rather an adaptation of the present system to facilitate management decision-making and control for the cost center is sought via more proactive participation by all who are involved and/or use the system. Users could include the cost center management, accountants, lab technicians, production employees, and main office personnel.

Dan Morrison explained the present system of bar coding. "Production labels are generated at the calendar stage to identify the formula used, gauge, brand (ARC markets under two at present), time of production, shift and roll number for that shift (1, 2, 3, . . .). At the ASBM, that bar code is wanded into an ASBM data file. Defects are recorded to enable feedback to calendaring. Normally, this is the last place this coding is used. If a problem surfaces later, it can be checked inasmuch as the information would be in the computer.

"At ASBM, a pole ticket, or tag, identifying that sheet is introduced into the system. This ticket stays with the sheet (although it isn't actually attached as it does not physically go through the vulcanizer) through to the inspection station.

"At the inspection station, defects are identified as to the general area on the sheet on which they are located. The defects are given coordinates to be fed into the computer. This data is overlaid on a grid, not unlike a football field, so that possible defect patterns can be identified. This design has proven especially helpful in identifying recurring problems as this is usually an indication of a problem with a machine, and identifying the area on the machine where the problem is helps the employees trouble shoot and correct.

"A second bar code label is made at this final inspection point which is attached at the end of the cardboard core of each roll of rubber roofing that is produced. This information is also put in the computer for possible future use. The code contains the finished size of the roll (width & length), pole number (taken from the pole ticket), gauge, and brand. At this point, the pole tickets are sent to the accountant and kept temporarily as physical evidence of production in the event that there are any inventory questions." Dan paused and added, "To my knowledge a manual search of these tickets has never been necessary. The tickets are destroyed periodically."

"Each bar code label has two tear-off stubs, one of which is taken off as the roofing is warehoused where a scanner wands the information in. This input is used by the main offices where the information is compared to that generated at inspection to verify that the roll got from packaging to the warehouse. (A roll with a defect may have been pulled.) Any differences are reported to ARC and tracked down. Since a perpetual inventory is used, this procedure provides an inventory check.

"The second tear-off tag is removed as the roll is loaded onto a truck for delivery. These tags are held for a short time (not more than one week) to look to in the event of a delivery complaint, after which they are destroyed. Also, they can be used to trace lots for a possible recall if a defect is noted upon delivery. Presently, all of these checks are done manually if or when they become necessary."

Dan explained one of the issues regarding enhancing the bar coding system. "To institute a complete womb-to-tomb bar coding system would require a completely integrated computer program. Since ARC has made the decision to change consultants, now is the time to expand its bar code system if it is going to do so." He added, "We should update the work stations to go with a new bar coding system. The current bar code information is tied to the pertinent data within the system. However, the present response time is too slow, which discourages inquiries and the result is that we usually do the research manually." Dan paused before continuing. "With our present system, it can take over six hours to 'search' for a piece of requested data. Therefore, decisions frequently are made sans the use of the computer applying only the readily available information. The result is that decisions are made without complete data." He added, "Fortunately this approach has worked satisfactorily to date.

"Also, we have a lot of older data on tape, but we do not use it. It may not even be compatible with a new data structure and would then be useless. That may not be a major problem or loss though, as it is not used now. Our practice is to keep six months of information on the computer."

Dan continued, "New computer consultants were sought mainly because of our dissatisfaction with the service of the consultants we had. Sometimes after a call they would not come for weeks. Part of the problem may have been due to the fact that they were essentially a two-man operation. These new consultants (a larger firm) are currently familiarizing themselves with our present system and determining whether an alternative data base would speed up the process of linking files."

COMPUTER INFORMATION

Joseph Thompson, Plant Controller, spoke of ARC's expectations regarding the expansion of the present bar code system. "One of the main reasons we changed computer consultants was because we wanted someone who could take us to and through the next phases. We have a general idea of what we want and would like the new firm to work with us. They have two roles to play in our future--expanding the bar coding into other areas and updating our current programming code to make it more user-friendly. That way we could make some of our own changes. The present program is in Quick Basic. Information is on-line as it is input and immediately accessible by a user, which is important to our operation. We would, however, like to implement a data base that is more understandable to the layman.

"At present, the bar coding system is used only from the calendar to the warehouse. We want to expand the system in stages. We want to be able to reach back to the vendor (lot number, name, and the like) with each number or sheet number from the bar code, enabling us to call up additional pertinent information. Reaching forward we would like to include the carrier and destination in the system to have that information available for future reference.

"Billing could also be incorporated into the system. Presently, bills are done from the main office. The information for each order is put into the computer as it is produced and orders are done by exception. Back orders are taken out of the program, and those orders remaining in the system are assumed shipped and thus billed and faxed to the customer. If the information could be taken from the positive shipments by bar code, they would be more traceable--the ultimate.

"Keeping tract of measurements and defects is a monumental job. It is in our plans to add one terminal and upgrade one this year (1994). This should enable faster searches on the file server when a problem does arise. Since the current program is in modular form we can add building blocks to the system in the future.

"We want the bar coding system to be complete--back door to front door--enabling us to trace a product from source to shipping. At this point in time we are not considering how to cost custom work or to trace cost drivers for Activity-Based Costing (ABC). There is an ABC system in place, but the chief accountant who spearheaded its installation was transferred and therefore the system is not being utilized fully."

CONSIDERATIONS

ARC does not want to merely trouble shoot, but, more importantly, to be able to prevent problems before they occur. ARC has a good relationship with its employees and wants to maintain the high degree of loyalty they have developed. Can they generate certain records and still avoid the "Big Brother is Watching" impression? Some items Tim wishes to incorporate are bar code identifiers for each component so that a batch's ingredients can be traced. A problem here would be the oil and the carbon black, as new deliveries are added to prior shipments and stored in bulk until used. He would like to see formulas and batches identified for each finished roll.

According to Tim, the accounting information generated is a rear-view mirror approach. He would like to see the reports sooner and geared more to his needs. Could bar coding help here?

Also, direct labor is not the principal cost driver in this industry, although when asked, he sheepishly admitted that overhead is presently allocated on the basis of direct labor. Most problems that arise during production are machine- or ingredient-related. Perhaps bar coding could help identify the true cost driver(s) for future revamping of the overhead allocation process.

A last important consideration is the fact that each decision has to be justified to the head corporation offices. Therefore an overall picture has to be presented with each step outlined as to reason for its inclusion as well as the order chosen for its implementation.

FUTURE DECISIONS

The questions facing ARC are as follows:

1. What items should ARC incorporate into its revamped bar coding system and in what order of priority?
2. Discuss how ARC can use the information suggested in your answer to (1) above?
3. How can expanding the bar coding system aid customer relations?
4. Can this adapted bar coding system help reduce ARC's rework rates? Discuss.
5. Explain how identifying suppliers of inferior raw materials would improve rework rates?

TEACHING NOTES

Opinions from students are likely to be quite wide and diverse on the issues raised in this case. This diversity should be encouraged. The students will be faced with the restrictions and frustrations that they will encounter on the job. However, there are three possible main emphases that are likely to surface: tracking ingredients to vendors; production trouble-shooting; and accounting-related problems. Students may select one or a combination of these for a principal line of analysis. The specifics regarding how the bar coding system should be expanded will vary from student to student.

ENDNOTES

1.   The company depicted in this case has requested to remain anonymous. Therefore, all names used throughout are fictitious.

EXHIBIT 1
LAYOUT OF THE PLANT AND THE FLOW OF THE MATERIAL DURING PRODUCTION

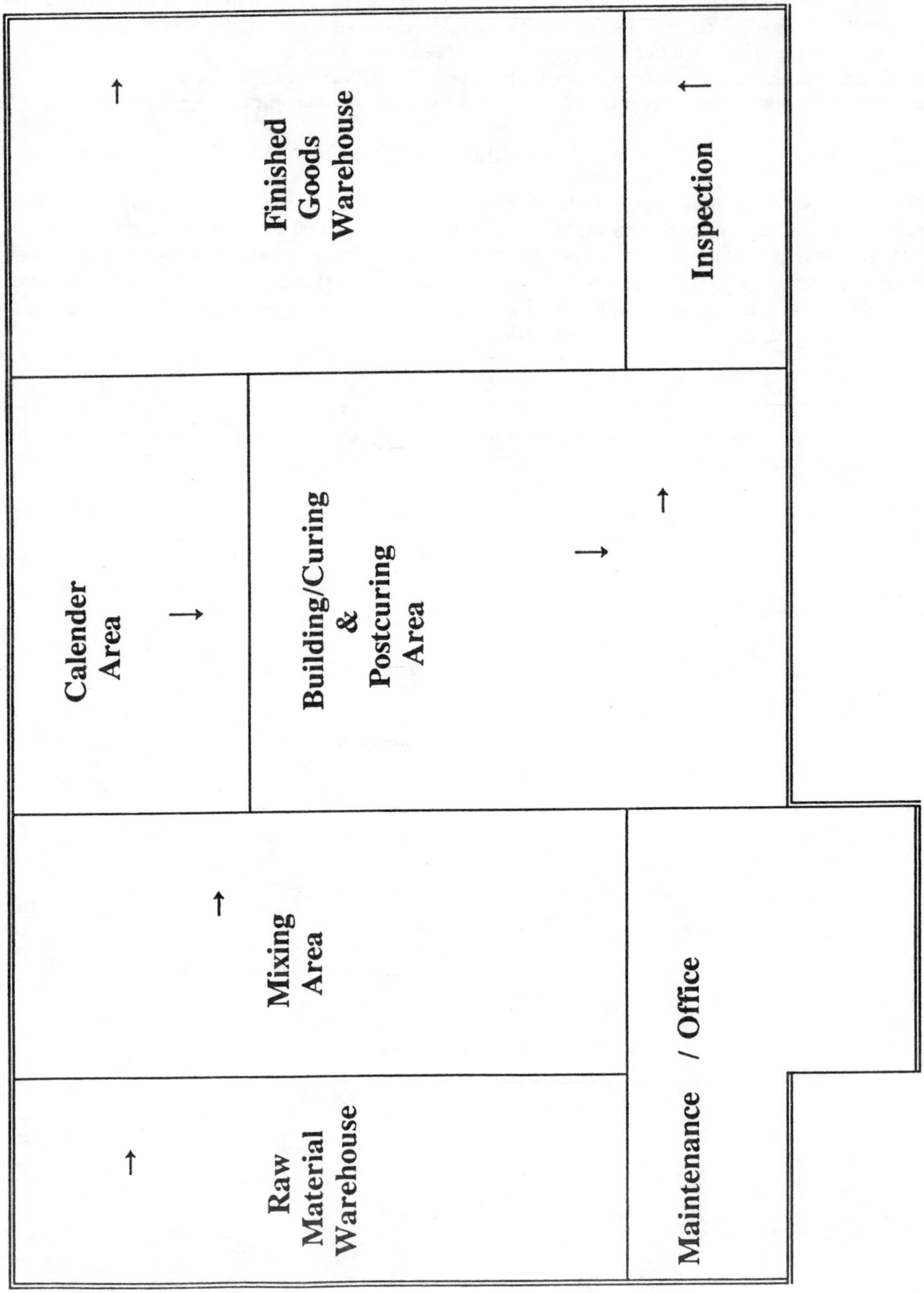

357

EXHIBIT 2
PRESENT BAR CODE LABEL COMPONENTS

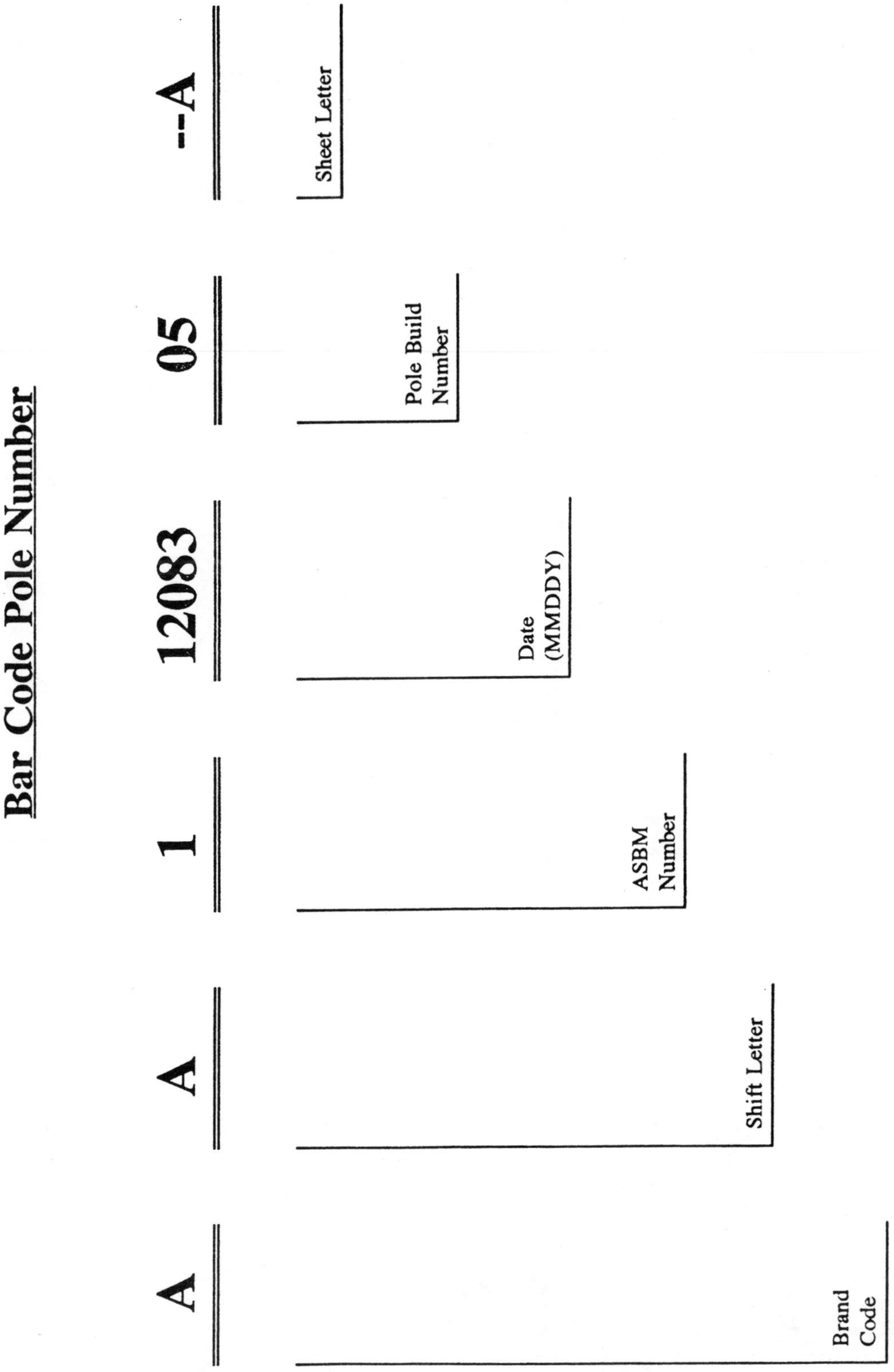

Bar Code Pole Number

A   A   1   12083   05   --A

Brand
Code

Shift Letter

ASBM
Number

Date
(MMDDY)

Pole Build
Number

Sheet Letter

QUANTITATIVE HISTORY OF WESTINGHOUSE:
ANALYSIS OF CORPORATE PROFITABILITY, 1951-1991

Richard H. Franke
Loyola College
BALTIMORE, MARYLAND, U.S.A.
Timothy W. Edlund
Morgan State University
BALTIMORE, MARYLAND, U.S.A.
John P. Milner
Westinghouse Electric Corporation
PASADENA, MARYLAND, U.S.A.
Sajjan M. George
Maryland National Guard
BALTIMORE, MARYLAND, U.S.A.
Thomas K. Hagigh
The Wine Merchant
BALTIMORE, MARYLAND, U.S.A.

Abstract

Westinghouse Electric Company, historically known as an engineer's company, has experienced repeated crises, resulting in major losses, followed by new Chief Executive Officers and major retrenchment. An examination of the economic history of the firm, together with an examination of variations in real profitability over 1951-1991 is explained by both external and internal influences. These have included disruptions by a major strike, default in delivering on uranium contracts, and adverse results from commercial real estate loans. Other factors are the economic and political environment, fuel price inflation, general inflation, corporate capital intensity, leadership, and the firm's culture. Historical interpretation suggests modifications in future strategy.

For a hundred and eight years, Westinghouse has been "an engineer's company," with great diversity in its use of technology and its fields of business [Rieser, 1958: 87; Westinghouse Electric Corporation, 1986; Novack, 1988]. Pioneering accomplishments have been in electricity, transportation equipment, radio, television, radar, analog computers, nuclear power generation, and a variety of electronic, power, space, defense, and environmental systems.

However, in the period since World War II, Westinghouse's sales and especially profits have lagged behind General Electric, the primary competitor in many of its businesses [Business Week, 1958; Rieser, 1958; Forbes, 1965; McDonald, 1967; Business Week, 1977; Economist, 1992]. Westinghouse diversification extended in the 1960s and early 1970s to supplying uranium fuel at guaranteed prices for nuclear power plants [Eagan, 1980; Financial World, 1980; Yokell and DeSalvo, 1985]; and, beginning in 1986, to supplying funds for commercial real estate and finance [Novack, 1988; Schroeder, 1991; 1993].

This quantitative historical analysis seeks to identify and disentangle possible causative factors to explain wide differences in corporate performance since 1950, over the four decades of modern business history. The previous two decades included economic depression, world war, and post-war recovery, which are likely to overshadow ordinary business phenomena. Thus, analysis since 1950 may be optimum for understanding of behavior and economic performance of modern business.

360

METHODS

Real performance. The data in Table 1 are obtained from Moody's Industrial Manuals, with income data over the past decade updated using Moody's Handbook of Common Stocks for Fall of 1993. But it seems clear that Westinghouse sales of almost $13 billion in 1991 were not really more than ten times the sales of one and a quarter billion dollars in 1951: Using the GNP and GDP deflators in Table B-3 of the Economic Report of the President for 1991 and 1993, it would require $5.46 in the currency of 1991 to equal the value of just one dollar in 1951. Thus, rather than a ten-fold rise over 1951-91, real sales of Westinghouse rose by only 89%. Similar differences are seen for after-tax income in comparing the first two columns of Tables 1 and 2.

The third columns in the tables are more problematic. Equity is a "book value" figure accumulated over the years since the beginning of corporate life, expressed in a variety of dollar values. With general inflation, rather than having stability or deflation, equity almost always is understated. In the case of a venerable corporation such as Westinghouse, correcting this understatement may result in a several-fold increase for real (constant-value) equity. The method here, described by Franke and Edlund [1992: 362-3], requires adding up the equity changes adjusted to real terms year by year (with an estimate made for the average vintage of capital in some early year). In this case, Westinghouse equity in 1951 (the average of end of year 1950 and 1951 figures) was estimated (based on rapid rate of increase in equity during years preceding) to be in 1946 dollars, and exactly calculated additions from 1951 to 1991 were made to this base in 1951.

The return on equity figures of Tables 1 and 2 express their income figures as percentages of equity year by year. Since in Table 1 the book value of equity is disproportionately understated, the resulting ratio--here labeled "ApparROE" for apparent return on equity--is overstated. The oranges-divided-by-oranges "RealROE" presented in Table 2 shows consistently smaller real figures for corporate profitability.

External factors. Economic growth rate of the national economy since the previous year often affects current spending decisions of various sorts. Since many Westinghouse products are heavy industrial equipment, business cycle effects on corporate economic performance are to be expected. "EcGrow" data presented in Table 3 were obtained by calculating the year-to-year growth rates of real GNP or GDP, taken from Table B-2 of the Economic Report of the President for 1991 and 1993.

Political party of the President of the United States, with a lag of a year or two for different policies to take effect, might be expected to have an impact on business performance [Hibbs, 1987: ch. 7]. For the United States economy from 1949 to 1984, Marcus and Mevorach [1988: Table 1] showed 73% higher real economic growth with Democratic than with Republican administrations, at little cost in terms of higher inflation (perhaps a Phillips' curve response to lower unemployment). Franke and New [1984] explain relative benefits of the Democratic political party largely through increased capital utilization that accompanies increased (if slightly more expensive) employment. In this case, the political party effect is lagged a year after the year of inauguration; for example, the latest shift from Democratic to Republican, early in 1981, is assumed to have economic effect during the year of 1982.

Currency inflation since the previous year might have negative influence, as it reduces real value and makes purchases more difficult. In businesses such as those in which price competition exists (as with General Electric), Westinghouse may be unable to raise their products' prices as much as their costs rise, reducing income and thus return on equity at times of higher inflation. Inflation is calculated as growth of GNP or DP deflator, from Table B-3 of the Economic Report of the President for 1991 and 1993.

Fuel inflation might affect adversely power plant customers of Westinghouse, as well as raising their own costs of operation and their costs of supplying fuel on contracts agreed to earlier. "FuelIn" is calculated as growth of the motor fuel price index in the Economic Report of the President for 1988, Table B-59, updated with later editions.

External/internal disruptions. There are three classes of major disruption to ordinary operation during the post-war period at Westinghouse: The Uranium price rise and default, with costs of reimbursement to customers; Westinghouse Credit Corporation 1986-91 involvement in commercial real estate loans and subsequent losses; and the strike against Westinghouse from October 1955 to March 1956.

In Table 3, "Uranium" expresses the percentage distribution of the costs of utility settlements with Westinghouse, calculated from data in Exhibit 1 of Yokell and DeSalvo [1985]. This factor can be expected to relate negatively to Westinghouse Real ROE.

"CommRE," or commercial real estate, is an index of commercial construction from Table B-50 of the Economic Report of the President for 1993, beginning in 1986 (when Westinghouse initiated aggressive lending operations). Prior to 1986 (prior to these operations), the nonvarying value for 1986 is extended back to 1951. Variation in this measure (of national real estate activity) can be expected to relate positively to Westinghouse performance (negatively when it decreases).

"Strike" is a dummy variable, with 1 during the years of the strike and 0 otherwise. It can be expected to relate negatively to corporate performance, as production and sales diminish.

Internal factors. As presented in Table 2, "CapInt" or capital intensity is the ratio of the primary elements of production, an index of the ratio of capital (equity) to labor (employees). As shown by Franke [1987b] for the financial industry, and indirectly by Buzzell and Gale [1987: ch. 7] and Franke and New [1984], increasing the capital:labor ratio can diminish capital utilization and capital productivity, although there may be benefit to labor productivity. While the factor can be expected to affect capital profitability (RealROE) adversely, Westinghouse appears aware of the need to utilize capital equipment at a relatively high level [cf. Business Week, 1963: 93], and with astute leadership adverse impact of rising CapInt may be minor.

Continuing in Table 3, corporate culture--largely determined by top corporate leadership--is measured by content analysis of the verbal reports to shareholders in Westinghouse annual reports (the second year's report following each of six chief officers' assumption of those responsibilities). The computer content analysis process is described by Franke and Edlund [1992].

Achievement motivation is an entrepreneurial, independent, innovative, and individualistic orientation, as described through observation and analysis by McClelland [1961]. However, as shown by Franke [1987a; 1992], at least for nations, entrepreneurial and individualistic cultures are less effective at economic growth than are those that are more collectivistic. Ach in the corporate culture of Westinghouse, as expressed by the imagery of its chief officer or his representatives, may be expected to benefit technological pioneering, but to affect net economic performance adversely.

Affiliation motivation has been shown by Skolnick [1966] to be an expression of concern over friendly interpersonal relationships, but also to suggest lack of social effectiveness. Work in firms by Kock [1965] and for nations by Franke [1974] suggests that Aff can be expected to affect performance adversely.

Power motivation is shown in several studies to benefit performance in organizations and nations [see Franke, 1974; McClelland and Burnham, 1976]. A combination of high power motivation and low affiliation motivation, termed interactive motivation ("Int"), has been shown to benefit firm and national economic performance [Franke, 1974; 1992; McClelland and Boyatzis, 1982], and can be expected to be beneficial at Westinghouse.

Analytical procedures. Following development of real corporate data and zero-order correlation of the Real ROE dependent variable with independent variables, multiple regression is performed stepwise, controlling for significance ($p < .10$, two-tailed), multi-collinearity (correlation of independent variables below .5, or tolerance > .75), and lack of significant serial correlation in time-series analysis. The procedure is similar to that described by Franke [1980] and Franke and Edlund [1992].

RESULTS

Correlations of Real ROE with independent variables in Table 4 utilize both the Pearson and the Spearman techniques, the latter to reduce outlier distortions. During thirteen of the years from 1951 to 1991, there were major disruptions that may have affected performance, with some very high and very low performance values. Since they mask ordinary effects, separate correlations for the remaining 28 years show these results.

For the 28 ordinary years, political party (Democratic = 1; Republican = 0) shows the positive effect on Westinghouse Real ROE that was expected. For inflation measures, there are Pearson effects, negative as expected but not verified by Spearman correlation. Only economic growth does not show significance, although results are positive as expected.

For the 41 years in total, the results of disruptions to ordinary operations are as expected, but not always significant. The uranium settlement costs are related negatively but insignificant to profitability. National commercial real estate building is related positively, with the 1990 and 1991 drop indicative of performance decline for the company. The long strike had a negative effect, although marginally significant only with the Spearman coefficient.

For internal factors in the 28 ordinary years, Table 4 indicates negative effects of greater capital intensity, of greater achievement motivation, and of greater affiliation motivation in corporate culture. On the other hand, power and interactive motivation are positively related to performance. With major disruptive factors removed,

362

differences in corporate culture appear to be important determinants of differences in Real ROE.

Table 5 shows interrelationships of independent variables. For example, uranium default costs are highly related to fuel inflation in general, so that entry of either may be viewed as expressing effects of the other in a regression equation.

Table 6 provides a regression model explaining 74% of the variance in Westinghouse profitability over 1951-91. With tolerance greater than .75 at each step of independent variable entry, there is little multi-collinearity. With a Durbin-Watson coefficient close to the neutral point of 2.00, Durbin and Watson (1951: table 5) show no significant serial correlation, indicating that the equation is well specified and that significance levels for the equation as a whole and for individual variables are as stated.

CONCLUSION

The disruptive influences of commercial real estate decline in 1990 and 1991 and the strike in 1955 and 1956 are in first and third positions in a regression model explaining year-to-year variation in Real ROE. A third factor that disrupted ordinary operation, costs from the uranium default, is associated with fuel inflation, which was the second variable to enter the model. This entry, rather than that of the Uranium variable, indicates that fuel inflation itself diminishes corporate performance, as the power industry which Westinghouse serves is affected.

Corporate culture, as measured by affiliation motivation expressed by corporate leadership in the report to shareholders, is a fourth but highly significant factor in Westinghouse profitability. Greater task focus, with an effective rather than a neurotic social orientation, is indicated by lower affiliation (or higher interactive) motivation. Variation in a second corporate factor, capital intensity (capital/labor ratio in real dollars of equity per employee), also explains variation in corporate profitability over the 41 year period.

Both of these factors, internal to Westinghouse, are consistent with literatures that describe performance benefits from low-affiliation corporate culture and from the higher capital utilization associated with higher employment relative to capital inputs. Westinghouse and other corporations may use motivational selection and training approaches to establish productive corporate cultures [cf. McClelland, 1985; Franke, 1992]. As noted explicitly by Westinghouse President Burnham two decades ago [Business Week, 1963: 93], investment decisions may be made contingent upon high, multiple-shift capital utilization.

The external factor of inflation, and in particular of fuel inflation, is uncontrollable. However, effects on profitability are felt over a period of up to a year or two following the inflationary period, allowing at least short term prediction of the need for belt tightening. With Westinghouse already exposed to energy prices through their major customers' susceptibilities, further corporate exposure to fuel price changes (as by fixing uranium fuel sales prices) should be avoided.

A second external/internal factor, labor peace, has a clear measure of importance in the regression model of Table 6: Five and a half percent of Real ROE was lost to the 1955-56 strike, after controlling for four other significant factors. Finally, as a basis for corporate strategy, it should be emphasized that Westinghouse is "an engineer's company," with experience and skills in the physical sciences, engineering, and high technology, as applied to manufacturing and customer needs. Diversification into other fields, such as commercial and real estate finance, seems to divert from the company's mission, real accomplishments, and aptitudes, and should be avoided.

Through a quantitative historical evaluation of a major American corporation over the post-war period, profitability variation is described and explained. Elements of this explanation can be used, at least as a starting point, to suggest useful steps in establishing corporate culture and directing corporate behavior.

REFERENCES

Business Week. 1958. How Westinghouse's three-man management works. May 17: 84-86, 88, 93.

Business Week. 1963. Breaking a pattern of woes. August 31: 90-93.

Business Week. 1977. The opposites: GE grows while Westinghouse shrinks. January 31: 60-64, 66.

Buzzell, R. D., and Gale, B. T. 1987. The PIMS principles: Linking strategy to performance. New York:

Free Press.

Durbin, J., and Watson, G. S. 1951. Testing for serial correlation in least squares regression, II. Biometrika, 38: 159-178.

Eagan, W. 1980. The Westinghouse uranium contracts: Commercial impracticability and related matters. American Business Law Journal, 18: 281-302.

Economist (London). 1992. Westinghouse: Felled by finance. February 1: 77-78.

Financial World. 1980. The uranium cloud passes. May 1: 40-41.

Forbes, 1965. Westinghouse Electric. June 1: 24-29.

Franke, R. H. 1974. An empirical appraisal of the achievement motivation model applied to nations. Unpublished doctoral dissertation, University of Rochester, Rochester, NY.

Franke, R. H. 1980. Worker productivity at Hawthorne. American Sociological Review, 45: 1006-1027.

Franke, R. H. 1987a. Achievement motivation and national economic performance. Proceedings of the Southern Management Association, 24: 31-33.

Franke, R. H. 1987b. Technological revolution and productivity decline: Computer introduction in the financial industry. Technological Forecasting and Social Change, 31: 143-154.

Franke, R. H. 1992. The relationship between cultural training and economic performance. In H. E. Glass and M. A. Hovde (Eds.), Handbook of business strategy: 1992/1993 Yearbook: 7-1 to 7-21. New York: Warren Gorham Lamont.

Franke, R. H., and Edlund, T. W. 1992. Development and application of a longitudinal procedure for quantitative case analysis. In H. E. Klein (Ed.), Forging new partnerships with cases, simulations, games and other interactive methods: 361-372. Needham, MA: WACRA--World Association for Case Method Research and Application.

Franke, R. H., and New, J. R. 1984. Presidential personality and national economic performance. Paper presented at the annual meeting of the American Association for the Advancement of Science, New York.

Hibbs, D. A., Jr. 1987. The American political economy: Macroeconomics and electoral politics. Cambridge, MA: Harvard University Press.

Kock, S. E. 1965. Foretagsledning och motivation. (Management and motivation.) Helsinki: Affarsekonomisk Forlagsforening.

Marcus, A. A., and Mevorach, B. 1988. Planning for the U.S. political cycle. Long Range Planning, 21 (4): 50-56.

McClelland, D. C. 1961. The achieving society. Princeton, NJ: Van Nostrand.

McClelland, D. C. 1985. Human motivation. Glenview, IL: Scott,Foresman.

McClelland, D. C., and Boyatzis, R. E. 1982. The leadership motive pattern and long term success in management. Journal of Applied Psychology, 67 (6): 737-743.

McClelland, D. C., and Burnham, D. H. 1976. Power is the great motivator. Harvard Business Review,

364

March-April: 159-166.

McDonald, J. 1967. Westinghouse invents a new Westinghouse. Fortune, 76 (October): 143-147, 176, 178.

Novack, J. 1988. What's a Westinghouse? Forbes, 141 (April 4): 34-36.

Rieser, C. 1958. The changes at Westinghouse. Fortune, 58 (August): 87-90, 142, 144, 146.

Schroeder, M. 1991. Has Westinghouse Credit become a debit? Business Week, April 8: 76-77.

Schroeder, M. 1993. The decline and fall of Westinghouse's Paul Lego. Business Week, March 8: 68-70.

Skolnick, A. 1966. Motivational imagery and behavior over twenty years. Journal of Consulting Psychology, 30: 463-478.

Westinghouse 1986. Centennial Review: 1886-1986.

Yokell, M. D., and DeSalvo, C. A. 1985. The uranium default: Westinghouse and the utilities. Public Utilities Fortnightly, 115 (February 7): 20-25.

TABLE 1
WESTINGHOUSE PERFORMANCE OVER TIME--IN THOUSANDS OF CURRENT DOLLARS (UNADJUSTED FOR CHANGES IN DOLLAR VALUE), AND IN PERCENTS

Year	Sales	Income	Equity	ApparROE
1951	1 240 800	64 600	578 500	11.17
1952	1 454 300	68 600	625 300	10.97
1953	1 582 000	74 300	670 300	11.08
1954	1 631 000	84 600	740 000	11.43
1955	1 441 000	42 800	779 550	5.49
1956	1 525 400	3 500	784 900	.45
1957	2 009 000	72 700	796 750	9.12
1958	1 895 700	74 700	845 800	8.83
1959	1 910 700	85 900	897 300	9.57
1960	1 955 700	79 100	944 200	8.38
1961	1 913 800	45 400	967 700	4.69
1962	1 954 500	57 100	971 050	5.88
1963	2 127 300	47 800	969 950	4.93
1964	2 271 200	76 700	976 500	7.85
1965	2 389 900	106 900	1 010 900	10.57
1966	2 581 400	119 700	1 065 750	11.23
1967	2 900 700	122 500	1 137 700	10.77
1968	3 296 100	135 000	1 225 250	11.02
1969	3 509 200	149 900	1 324 300	11.32
1970	4 313 400	127 000	1 428 100	8.89
1971	4 630 500	175 300	1 622 400	10.80
1972	5 086 600	198 700	1 844 900	10.77
1973	5 101 100	161 900	1 943 450	8.33
1974	5 798 500	28 100	1 929 550	1.46
1975	5 862 700	165 200	1 939 300	8.52
1976	6 220 900	223 200	2 053 700	10.87
1977	6 221 000	271 300	2 200 050	12.33
1978	6 779 800	311 300	2 350 400	13.24
1979	7 443 100	-73 900	2 336 500	-3.16
1980	8 514 300	402 900	2 389 950	16.86
1981	9 367 500	438 000	2 675 300	16.37
1982	8 745 400	449 300	2 997 850	14.99
1983	9 532 600	449 000	3 314 750	13.55
1984	10 264 500	535 900	3 630 300	14.76
1985	10 700 000	605 300	3 513 550	17.23
1986	10 731 000	670 800	2 859 500	23.46
1987	10 679 000	738 900	2 860 000	25.84
1988	12 500 000	823 000	3 508 500	23.46
1989	12 844 000	922 000	4 089 500	22.55
1990	12 915 000	268 000	4 140 500	6.47
1991	12 794 000	-1 086 000	3 825 500	-28.39
Mean:	5,420,345	202,853	1,872,323	10.10
SD:	3,899,904	316,541	1,091,542	8.56

Note: Equity is the "book value" or addition of all current values of contributed capital plus retained earnings.

TABLE 2
WESTINGHOUSE PERFORMANCE OVER TIME--IN THOUSANDS OF 1982 DOLLARS,
NUMBERS OF EMPLOYEES, THOUSANDS OF DOLLARS/EMPLOYEE, AND PERCENTS

Year	RealSal	RealInc	RealEq	Employ	CapInt	RealROE
1951	4,943,426	257,370	2,981,959	103,466	28.821	8.63
1952	5,703,137	269,020	3,166,939	110,618	28.630	8.49
1953	6,108,108	286,873	3,342,036	117,656	28.405	8.58
1954	6,201,521	321,673	3,609,086	119,936	30.092	8.91
1955	5,297,794	157,353	3,756,937	116,500	32.248	4.19
1956	5,428,470	12,456	3,776,286	120,454	31.351	.33
1957	6,903,780	249,828	3,817,719	126,811	30.106	6.54
1958	6,382,828	251,515	3,984,556	121,612	32.764	6.31
1959	6,285,197	282,566	4,155,937	113,694	36.554	6.80
1960	6,329,126	255,987	4,308,955	113,790	37.868	5.94
1961	6,133,974	145,513	4,384,639	112,118	39.107	3.32
1962	6,126,959	178,997	4,395,257	109,680	40.073	4.07
1963	6,565,741	147,531	4,391,836	112,568	39.015	3.36
1964	6,903,343	233,131	4,411,897	114,425	38.557	5.28
1965	7,070,710	316,272	4,515,046	114,410	39.464	7.00
1966	7,375,429	342,000	4,674,493	120,245	38.875	7.32
1967	8,079,944	341,226	4,877,455	128,699	37.898	7.00
1968	8,742,971	358,090	5,115,363	134,288	38.092	7.00
1969	8,817,085	376,633	5,370,976	138,993	38.642	7.01
1970	10,270,000	302,381	5,624,765	143,230	39.271	5.38
1971	10,429,054	394,820	6,074,534	152,500	39.833	6.50
1972	10,938,925	427,312	6,564,083	171,884	38.189	6.51
1973	10,305,253	327,071	6,769,395	188,934	35.829	4.83
1974	10,737,963	52,037	6,742,535	196,674	34.283	.77
1975	9,886,509	278,584	6,759,746	182,648	37.010	4.12
1976	9,858,796	353,724	6,946,674	163,496	42.488	5.09
1977	9,243,685	403,120	7,171,138	151,170	47.438	5.62
1978	9,390,305	431,163	7,386,693	141,585	52.171	5.84
1979	9,469,593	-94,020	7,368,258	143,515	51.341	-1.28
1980	9,935,006	470,128	7,433,322	145,384	51.129	6.32
1981	9,965,426	465,957	7,750,907	146,677	52.843	6.01
1982	8,745,400	449,300	8,083,433	146,546	55.160	5.56
1983	9,174,783	432,146	8,394,271	139,089	60.352	5.15
1984	9,530,641	497,586	8,692,523	129,888	66.923	5.72
1985	9,648,332	545,807	8,585,707	125,892	68.199	6.36
1986	9,421,422	588,938	8,003,812	124,397	64.341	7.36
1987	9,096,252	629,387	8,004,244	118,168	67.736	7.86
1988	10,305,029	678,483	8,547,604	116,059	73.649	7.94
1989	10,169,438	730,008	9,016,909	120,802	74.642	8.10
1990	9,821,293	203,802	9,056,475	118,868	76.189	2.25
1991	9,331,875	-792,123	8,821,925	114,719	76.900	-8.98
Mean:	8,222,426	306,333	5,690,133	132,490	45.670	5.34
SD:	1,897,178	244,069	2,060,758	22,577	14.752	3.21

Note: Real equity is the accumulation of all equity additions, as measured in constant 1982 dollar values.

TABLE 3
EXTERNAL AND INTERNAL FACTORS IN CORPORATE PERFORMANCE

| Year | External Factors | | | Ext./Int.Factors | | | | Internal Factors | | | |
| | Party | | | FuelIn | | CommRE | | | Corp. Culture | | |
	EcGrow		Inflat		Uranium		Strike	Ach	Aff	Pow	Int
1951	10.34	1	5.02	2.92	0.0	69.5	0	-2	-4	11	15
1952	3.90	1	1.59	2.57	0.0	69.5	0	-2	-4	11	15
1953	4.01	1	1.57	5.94	0.0	69.5	0	-2	-4	11	15
1954	-1.33	1	1.54	2.74	0.0	69.5	0	-2	-4	11	15
1955	5.56	0	3.42	1.33	0.0	69.5	1	-2	-4	11	15
1956	2.05	0	3.31	3.47	0.0	69.5	1	-2	-4	11	15
1957	1.67	0	3.56	4.05	0.0	69.5	0	-2	-4	11	15
1958	-.77	0	2.06	-1.33	0.0	69.5	0	-2	-4	11	15
1959	5.84	0	2.36	1.24	0.0	69.5	0	-2	-4	11	15
1960	2.22	0	1.64	2.89	0.0	69.5	0	2	1	3	2
1961	2.61	0	.97	-1.19	0.0	69.5	0	2	1	3	2
1962	5.31	0	2.24	.55	0.0	69.5	0	2	1	3	2
1963	4.11	1	1.57	-.22	0.0	69.5	0	2	1	3	2
1964	5.34	1	1.54	-.33	0.0	69.5	0	5	-1	2	3
1965	5.79	1	2.74	3.83	0.0	69.5	0	5	-1	2	3
1966	5.78	1	3.55	2.21	0.0	69.5	0	5	-1	2	3
1967	2.86	1	2.57	3.09	0.0	69.5	0	5	-1	2	3
1968	4.15	1	5.01	1.40	0.0	69.5	0	5	-1	2	3
1969	2.44	1	5.57	3.25	0.0	69.5	0	5	-1	2	3
1970	-.29	1	5.53	.86	0.0	69.5	0	5	-1	2	3
1971	2.84	1	5.71	.66	0.0	69.5	0	5	-1	2	3
1972	4.98	0	4.73	1.22	0.0	69.5	0	5	-1	2	3
1973	5.20	0	6.45	9.76	0.0	69.5	0	5	-1	2	3
1974	-.54	0	9.09	35.39	0.0	69.5	0	5	-1	2	3
1975	-1.26	0	9.81	6.82	0.0	69.5	0	5	-1	2	3
1976	4.89	0	6.41	4.16	0.0	69.5	0	5	-3	2	5
1977	4.67	0	6.66	5.79	5.5	69.5	0	5	-3	2	5
1978	5.29	0	7.28	4.30	18.4	69.5	0	5	-3	2	5
1979	2.48	1	8.86	35.30	44.3	69.5	0	5	-3	2	5
1980	-.17	1	9.03	38.97	24.4	69.5	0	5	-3	2	5
1981	1.94	1	9.68	11.32	7.4	69.5	0	5	-3	2	5
1982	-2.55	1	6.38	-5.23	0.0	69.5	0	5	-3	2	5
1983	3.57	0	3.90	-3.34	0.0	69.5	0	5	-3	2	5
1984	6.78	0	3.66	-1.51	0.0	69.5	0	7	-2	1	3
1985	3.35	0	2.97	.84	0.0	69.5	0	7	-2	1	3
1986	2.74	0	2.71	-21.86	0.0	69.5	0	7	-2	1	3
1987	3.43	0	3.07	4.04	0.0	68.9	0	7	-2	1	3
1988	4.46	0	3.32	.69	0.0	71.5	0	10	-1	3	4
1989	2.51	0	4.12	9.61	0.0	73.9	0	10	-1	3	4
1990	.93	0	4.12	14.34	0.0	72.5	0	10	-1	3	4
1991	-1.27	0	4.26	-1.77	0.0	54.8	0	2	-5	7	12
Mean:	3.01	.44	4.48	4.83	2.38	69.4	.05	3.5	-2.1	4.3	6.4
SD:	2.83	.50	2.90	10.28	8.18	2.5	.22	3.6	1.6	3.9	5.1

Note: A further internal factor, capital intensity, is in Table 2.

TABLE 4
CORRELATIONS WITH WESTINGHOUSE REAL PROFITABILITY, REALROE

	1951-91 (41 years)		28 Ordinary Years, excluding: major strike (1955-56); extraordinary uranium costs (1977-81); commercial real estate activity (1986-91)	
	Pearson r	Spearman rho	Pearson r	Spearman rho
Independent Variables				
Year	-.26	-.19	-.44*	-.48**
External Factors				
EcGrow	.34*	.21	.26	.17
Party	.24	.32*	.47*	.54**
Inflat	-.23	-.26	-.38*	-.20
FuelIn	-.24	.01	-.43*	.22
External/Internal Disruptions to Ordinary Operation				
Uranium	-.24	-.15	--	--
CommRE	.68**	.13	--	--
Strike	-.22	-.28(*)	--	--
Internal Factors				
CapInt	-.24	-.18	-.22	-.42*
Corporate Culture				
Ach	.01	.04	-.42*	-.31(*)
Aff	.09	-.14	-.57**	-.53**
Pow	.03	.05	.54**	.31(*)
Int	-.00	.17	.58**	.55**

Note: (*)p < .10, *p < .05, and **p < .01, all two-tailed (without testing for serial correlation: see Table 6).

TABLE 5
INTERCORRELATIONS OF INDEPENDENT VARIABLES

(Pearson r: n = 41 years in upper right, 28 years in lower left)

	External Factors				Ext./Int.Factors			Internal Factors			
	EcGrow	Party	Inflat	FuelIn	Uranium	CommRE	Strike	CapInt	Ach	Aff	Pow
1951-91 (41 years)											
Year	-.14	-.42**	.23	.06	.21	-.11	-.28	.91**	.86**	.15	-.71**
External Factors											
EcGrow		-.03	-.33*	-.23	-.08	.21	.05	-.13	-.12	.03	.10
Party	.01		.06	.18	.21	.05	-.18	-.32*	-.18	-.07	.08
Inflat	-.36*	-.08		.57**	.51*	-.01	-.09	.10	.37*	-.08	-.41**
FuelIn	-.24	-.07	.54**		.64**	.13	-.04	-.05	.13	-.02	-.12
External/Internal Disruptions to Ordinary Operation											
Uranium	--	--	--	--		.02	-.07	.12	.12	-.17	-.18
CommRE	--	--	--	--	--		.01	-.13	.22	.32*	-.13
Strike	--	--	--	--	--	--		-.22	-.35*	-.27	.39*
Internal Factors											
CapInt	.03	-.28	.07	-.32	--	--	--		.72**	.04	-.47**
Corporate Culture											
Ach	-.10	-.15	.49**	.08	--	--	--	.65**		.51**	-.88**
Aff	-.05	-.14	.06	.09	--	--	--	.12	.56**		-.66**
Pow	.11	.18	-.41*	-.06	--	--	--	-.58**	-.96**	-.74**	

28 Ordinary Years, excluding disruptions

Note: *p < .05 and **p < .01, two-tailed (without testing for serial correlation: See Table 6).

TABLE 6
REGRESSION MODEL: WESTINGHOUSE PROFITABILITY OVER 1951-1991

% Real ROE = - 64.235

+ 1.029 * CommRE   t = 8.51 (p < .00005)
- 0.115 * Fuelln   t = -4.34 (p = .0001)
- 5.499 * Strike   t = -4.05 (p = .0003)
- 0.562 * Aff   t = -2.93 (p = .0059)
- 0.047 * CapInt   t = -2.41 (p = .0213)

Equation F = 19.96 (p < .00005)
Variance Explanation = 74.04%
Variance Explanation, adjusted, = 70.33%
Durbin-Watson Coefficient = 1.81 (no significant serial correlation).

THE TEACHING NOTE:
LET'S AGREE TO DISAGREE

James Clinton
University of Northern Colorado
GREELEY, COLORADO, U.S.A.
James Camerius
Northern Michigan University
MARQUETTE, MICHIGAN, U.S.A.

Abstract

The teaching note is many things to many casewriters and case teachers. Differences exist as to what should be included in the teaching note and even the process by which the teaching note is developed. This paper discusses the rationale for the teaching note and contrary views with respect to: objectives, methods of analysis, classroom-tested cases, qualitative vs. quantitative emphasis, the epilogue, and teaching methods. Differing opinions concerning teaching note development, content, and use, are a good sign that the casewriting discipline is healthy and likely to continue to adapt to a changing environment.

INTRODUCTION

Although the teaching note bestows the mantle of respectabiity upon the written case, its author, and those organizations that sponsor casewriting as a legitimate exercise in scholarship, not all casewriters agree upon the contents of the teaching note. The discussion that follows attempts to highlight some of those issues that continually swirl around the subject of the teaching note.

RATIONALE FOR THE TEACHING NOTE

The teaching note generally is acknowledged by those who use cases in the classroom to be an inseparable adjunct to the case. Consequently, although a case without a teaching note does not make the instructor's task impossible, the absence of the teaching note does place an unnecessary burden upon the instructor who is unfamiliar with the background and research that went into development of the case.

Analytical talent is not equally distributed in this world and not all case instructors, regardless of experience and academic achievement, can quickly and authoritatively digest a case whole, expostulate at length about crucial case elements and relationships, develop alternative strategies, and cite pertinent theories reflected in the case content.

The case instructor's security blanket, the teaching note, however, moderates instructor anxiety and sharpens his or her intellect before engaging students in classroom dialogue about case nuances and complexities. The teaching note facilitates case discussion and, most reassuring of all, is always available for professional consultation.

ESTABLISHING CASE OBJECTIVES

ALTERNATIVE TEACHING NOTE PROCESSES

Some case authors believe that the casewriter's primary task is to first write a relevant case in an interesting manner. Only then should the teaching note be prepared. The opposite tack is to write the teaching note and then the case, ensuring that case teaching objectives are achieved. Either approach can accomplish the same end, and the sequence is neither transparent nor significant to the case teacher.

BROADLY-DEFINED OBJECTIVES

Case objectives establish case parameters and focus. In some cases, the objectives may be exhaustive in detail and leave no aspect of the case unexplored. This litany of objectives may or may not be overly ambitious, depending upon case content. Conceivably, the teaching note may grossly exceed the written case, both in complexity and sophistication, creating unwarranted expectations within the case teacher concerning the nature of the case. Conversely, the objectives, even though they be many and feasible, may offer little, if any, challenge, actually belying case content that is both interesting and significant. Clearly, those case teachers who rely heavily upon author-identified objectives as a determinant of case selection, will discover that neither of these two alternative scenarios presents a valid basis for instructor choice.

NARROWLY-DEFINED OBJECTIVES

The conservative, less ambitious casewriter may develop only a single issue in a very limited way, anticipating that other cases will be used in a progressive, building block approach to achieve a cumulative learning experience for the student. The casewriter, in the view of the authors of this paper, should not be penalized or hectored for setting limited objectives. The casewriter may wish simply to provide a vehicle for classroom discussion that clarifies textbook theories and concepts, leaving advancement of the boundaries of current knowledge on the subject to more ambitious case researchers. This incremental approach may disappoint the case teacher, however, who formulates a vision for the case's content and potential beyond that conceived by the casewriter. Such an instructor longs for a significant expansion of the case analysis and collateral reading references that facilitate a more robust case discussion and learning experiences for both instructor and students.

MATCHING OBJECTIVES WITH CASE CONTENT

The appropriateness and feasibility of case objectives are of continuing concern to casewriting stakeholders, such as the World Association for Case Method Research and Case Method Application (WACRA), the Society for Case Research (SCR) and the North American Case Research Association (NACRA). The SCR, for example, specifies that the analysis provided in the teaching note should be based on material contained in the case and be consistent with case data [Cabell, 1990]. The caution, in this case, is the need for teaching note objectives that accurately complement the case, specifying no more than what is attainable, given the particular case data.

MULTIPLE STAKEHOLDERS EVALUATE OBJECTIVES

Interpretation of whether or not case objectives are feasible and associated with a valid analytical exercise may not be a simple matter that is objectively determined. Adequacy of case objectives may simply be a function of who makes that determination. Consider that the casewriter and his or her teaching note is beholden to a variety of stakeholders who may have different agendas. First, are peer reviewers of organizations such as WACRA, the SCR, or NACRA, or the reviewers and editors of publications associated with these organizations. Second, is the instructor who will utilize the teaching note as a teaching aid.

PRIORITIZING STAKEHOLDERS

A potential third stakeholder is the casebook author in search of an addition to a soon-to-be-published case text. Fourth, the casewriter must satisfy his or her personal criteria as to the intent of the case and the analytical scope and depth of the teaching note. Fifth, the casewriter's employer typically is anxious that its members engage in scholarly activity that results in published materials such as cases accompanied by teaching notes. There may be other stakeholders as well. It would be a rare case that satisfied all of these stakeholders. What is the casewriter to do? There is no generic approach; the decision is unique to the casewriter who must decide for him or herself which stakeholder or set of stakeholders is paramount.

THE ROLE OF THE REVIEWER

One obstacle that many casewriters encounter is the situation in which their concept of what the case is all about and what it should accomplish differs from that of a reviewer who determines whether or not the case should be published in a scholarly journal. There are many reasons for such conflict. Only a few will be cited here. A reviewer, for example, may be preoccupied with a particular analytical device or academic theory and attempt to condition acceptance of a case upon inclusion of such analysis or discussion that fits case content into such theory. The parallels perceived by this reviewer may or may not apply, but can create havoc within a casewriter who fails to see such application – but who, for whatever reason, is anxious that the case be accepted for publication.

A peer reviewer might consider the case objectives either overly ambitious or unnecessarily restrained, inappropriately dampening the case's potential. Since the casewriter must accede to the strong admonitions of his or her peer reviewers, typically members of the major casewriting organizations identified above, the casewriter learns that the scope of objectives and the process by which they are identified often is a collaborative undertaking -- which may or may not be all that bad.

THE COMPLETE TEACHING NOTE

ASSESSING ADEQUACY OF CASE CONTENT

The casewriter can't anticipate all possible questions and issues and, even if he or she did, space limitations suggest otherwise. As a minimum, the teaching note should enable the case teacher to understand the key issues, particularly if the case is complex. The teaching note ratchets up a notch in quality if it also cites linkages between case content and the appropriate discipline, theories, and concepts. A note that further discusses how the case is related to contemporary issues in applicable environments facilitates expanded classroom discussion.

Just as casewriters alone do not determine the adequacy of case teaching objectives, neither are they the final arbiters of the completeness of the teaching note. Some case reviewers, for example, demonstrate an insatiable craving for inclusion of just a little more information in the teaching note to unconditionally ensure that the instructor using the case will be adequately prepared to teach the case. A more reasonable approach is to limit the focus of the case and provide an analysis in the teaching note that addresses no more than key issues and problems and obvious, significant concepts that apply.

SIGNIFICANCE OF TEACHING NOTE VS. CASE NARRATIVE

The former approach may lead to teaching note excesses that ensure that the note far exceeds the length of the case which, at present, tends to be the exception. If this possibly interminable approach were taken, then the major academic focus would be on the note and not the case narrative, symptomatic of goal displacement [Wheelen and Hunger, 1992] wherein the focus is on method and means as outlined in the note, versus the end purpose of creating a student-learning document, as revealed in the case narrative. Since cases are the means by which students hone their problem-solving skills and concurrently discover the uniqueness and commonality of organizational issues and problems within varied environments, preoccupation with the teaching note would seem an inappropriate bias.

CASE ANALYSIS

Ideally, the casewriter's analysis should include: assumptions, where appropriate; why particular data were chosen as support; and an interpretation of such data. When the casewriter's logical argument is clearly presented, the case instructor can then determine to what extent he or she agrees with the casewriter.

DEFINITIVE VS. TENTATIVE APPROACH TO ANALYSIS

The casewriter who presents the content of the teaching note as the definitive analysis and instructional approach may not only diminish the creative instincts of the case teacher but also antagonize those who tend to use the teaching note as a guide rather than an absolute. A teaching note presented as a tentative document, however, and one susceptible to amendment, is likely to encourage case teachers to reflect upon, interpret, and perhaps modify the teaching note rationale submitted by the casewriter, thus expanding case teacher learning. Tentative in this instance should not be confused with a casewriter who is uncertain or unsure. Rather, the emphasis here is on openness and a humility that accepts differences and the value of the contributions of others.

The tentative casewriter is likely to be receptive to the candid comments of reviewers and willing to adapt the nature of the case to accommodate differing views, not because of a compulsion to do so, but because such views enlarge his or her own concept of the case's potential. This casewriting philosophy may be anathema to those case reviewers and case teachers who favor a deliberate approach that sets out definitively where the casewriter stands with respect to the issues and applicable concepts, and advocates a preferred course of action, stated in no uncertain terms and accompanied by a strongly-advocated rationale.

The case teacher, who is assumed to have a mind of his or her own, is free to accept or reject this analytical assertiveness. Which approach is better? Again, case teachers are a mixed lot and either technique will find either favor or disfavor, depending upon the reader's biases and predispositions.

THE QUESTION-ANSWER FORMAT

Analysis of the case may take various forms. One approach is to pose questions addressing the critical case issues and present the casewriter's analysis in the response that follows. This framework complements the usual dialogue between instructor and students and serves to prompt the case teacher in conducting class discussions. The case teacher may find the content of the casewriter's answer to a question a useful and adequate analysis, and go on from there. On the downside, however, the questions may be trite or incompletely answered, and questions of a more substantial nature not included. Nevertheless, the question-answer combination can serve as a helpful starting point that leaves the case teacher room to exercise his own initiative and creativity.

THE NARRATIVE ANALYTICAL FORMAT

A second analytical approach is to develop a narrative analysis using one or more analytical tools or models. The casewriter, for example, may use the problem-solving technique that examines alternatives and costs and benefits associated with those alternatives, and arrive at recommendations that include a documented rationale. The author might also employ a Strengths, Weaknesses, Opportunities, Threats (SWOT) analysis; specialized financial techniques that, for example, estimate a company's likelihood of survival; statistical formulas associated with the marketing and production functions; or a sensitivity analysis that utilized computer software such as LOTUS 1-2-3.

THE ECLECTIC APPROACH

A third approach would include both questions and answers and one or more analytical methods, presenting the case teacher with a smorgasbord of analytical choices. The case teacher is free to limit his or her discussion to one approach or the other or embellish the classroom experience with various analytical perspectives. When case data provide the opportunity to apply a specialized analytical technique, the casewriter would be remiss if he or she were to omit that particular technique from the teaching note. Otherwise, there doesn't seem to be any special reason why one approach should be preferred to the other, so long as the quality and content of the note address the critical case issues and the case objectives outlined in the teaching note are met.

Just as in the cases themselves, teaching thrives on diversity, rather than lockstep conformity. The case can be made for each of these analytical approaches. Preference is instructor-dependent, based upon which approach is compatible with the instructor's comfort level and his or her preferred approach for class discussion. No matter which analytical approach is adopted by the casewriter, one element that is a constant is the essential inclusion of the casewriter's logical thought processes, either reflected in or inferred from the analysis.

FURTHER ISSUES

Imbedded within the previous discussion are multiple issues that concern the casewriter, the case teacher, and those who evaluate the case product. These issues include: 1) the inclusion of material in the teaching note that does not appear in the case narrative, 2) the value of student input in the evaluation of a case, 3) a quantitative vs. a qualitative emphasis in the case analysis, 4) the contribution of the epilogue to the teaching note, 5) approaches to teaching the case, and 6) the extent to which casewriter creativity is enhanced or diminished by standardized casewriting criteria. The merits of opposing views are advanced.

INCLUSION OF MATERIAL IN THE NOTE NOT IN THE CASE

One regional casewriters' group cautions casewriters not to include material in the note that is not available to students, so as to preserve student self-esteem and avoid the situation of the all-knowing case teacher [Southwest, 1993]. On the other hand, some casewriters believe that inclusion of such material provides the case teacher with the option of using such material to enrich classroom discussions -- not to encourage instructor arrogance. Perhaps the issue is one of how the case teacher should utilize such material and not whether it should be included at all.

CLASSROOM-TESTED CASES

Those who publish cases -- both editors and casebook authors -- typically wish to know whether the case has been classroom-tested. The presumption is that if the case has been classroom-tested, inadequacies and inaccuracies have been weeded out through heightened exposure and extended discussion. A "shakedown cruise" enables the instructor to identify and clarify ambiguities and produce a more user-friendly product.

Students as Expert Reviewers

Students, however, may not make the best critics. It seems surprising, moreover, that experienced editors and casewriters appear to believe that student case analysts can offer critiques that are more perceptive than those developed by either peer reviewers or editors. Although student perspectives may illuminate their personal concerns, the quality of their insights can vary, depending upon the incentive they have to critique their instructor and his or her responsivenenss to such criticism.

The Issue of Dependency

Students who are in a dependent relationship with the instructor tend to avoid offering candid comments where there is the risk that the instructor may take offense. Peer reviewers have no such restraining influence, and their comments generally are uninhibited and undaunted by the casewriter's views, increasing the likelihood of an undiluted critique. On the positive side of classroom-tested cases, however, is the self-discovery available to the casewriter who, just through the process of exposure of the case, may very well detect anomalies or opportunities to amend and improve the case or the teaching note, or both.

QUANTITATIVE VS. QUALITATIVE CONTENT

Some case teachers complain that far too often, the teaching note tends to emphasize a qualitative analysis and slight the more appropriate quantitative perspective. This may simply be the bias of those who are more comfortable with objective data and computer-assisted games that tend to arrive at a resolution of complex environmental factors, in contrast to a qualitative approach that tends to be flexible, sometimes ambiguous, and uncomfortable for those anxious to identify the "correct" answer. On the other hand, the absence of a quantitative analysis that clearly would have demonstrated the value of such a technique as a decision-making tool reflects adversely on those who participated in the development of the case, namely, casewriter, peer reviewers, and editor. All parties concerned should be alert to those instances where such quantitative analysis brings another dimension to the case analysis.

Customary Calculations

Most peer reviewers and both the SCR and NACRA suggest that the teaching note include calculations that students normally would be tasked to do, as well as those which enable interpretation of the data somewhat beyond the level that the average student would undertake. There appears to be common agreement that where financial statements appear in the case, ratios should be calculated. In some instances, time value of money calculations would assist in the evaluation of alternative strategies. Case teachers could also benefit from calculations that reflected alternative circumstances and performance, for both the internal and external environments – to the extent that relevant data were contained in the case or could be derived from case data.

VALUE OF AN EPILOGUE

Both the SCR [Society for Case Research, 1993] and NACRA [North American, 1993] reference the epilogue in teaching note discussions and seem to infer that where the outcome of a situation is known, an epilogue is desirable. Students typically are anxious to know what happened in a particular situation, so that they can compare their recommendation against the course of action taken by the case principals. The inference is that what happened subsequently was the one best solution to the situation and that anyone who had chosen that solution obviously was blessed with a superior intellect. Of course there is always the possibility that the situation was overtaken by events beyond the control of management and that an epilogue merely relates what action the organization actually took, regardless of whether it was a considered action, a decision taken on the spur of the moment, or one forced upon them by others.

Risks in Relying Upon Reality

The epilogue contained in the teaching note is information not available to students and to that extent it does give the instructor the edge. Those who oppose such instructor one-upsmanship, to be consistent, should oppose the inclusion of an epilogue. So long as an epilogue is included, there is the danger that the instructor will tend to favor that particular action and endow that action as the "school solution." An unresolved issue, i.e., the absence of an epilogue, places greater pressure upon both student and instructor to develop logical arguments to support their positions. Irresolution tends to emphasize the thinking processes rather than whether or not one came up with the "right" answer.

TEACHING CHOICES

The case teacher typically questions how he or she can make the best use of the teaching note. The instructor may choose to use the note simply as a resource supplement, to be accessed for additional information beyond that available in the case. He or she may even carve out an idiosyncratic approach consistent with his or her comfort level and previously successful experiences. Such behavior is typical of the seasoned case teacher, who may use the teaching note only as an afterthought, having selected the case primarily for the relevance and usefulness of the case narrative itself. This individual consults the teaching note only to compare his or her personal views on case content and instruction and then proceeds to present the case in accordance with his or her professional opinions, free to disregard the quality of the analysis that went into development of the teaching note.

The Moderately-Experienced Instructor

Case instructors with intermediate levels of experience may use the teaching note as a departure point for the classroom discussion and appreciate the insights offered by the instructor concerning case content and suggested methods for developing the case material.

The Novice Instructor

The novice instructor, on the other hand, may use the teaching note as a crutch to lean on, bolstering his or her own opinions on how the case situation should or should not be resolved. The novice is likely to rely heavily upon the suggestions contained in the teaching note, including teaching approaches that may differ significantly from his or her preferred teaching style.

The Appeal of Diversity

In view of instructor differences, there is small likelihood that a teaching note will satisfy all those who use it, for whatever purpose. Moreover, there is no compelling reason why the case teacher should follow the casewriter's chosen path. Consequently, teaching notes that contain multiple suggestions on case teaching approaches will benefit a larger number of users, stimulate case teaching creativity, and perhaps promote broader casewriter perspectives.

CREATIVITY VS. STANDARDIZATION

A major issue raised in this discussion is the degree of flexibility or rigidity that is appropriate for the teaching note and whether or not all teaching notes should be evaluated in terms of a common denominator. To the extent that the three premiere casewriting organizations -- WACRA, NACRA, and the SCR -- specify in detail case content, creative casewriting that lies outside existing well-defined boundaries may be inhibited. Just as instructors are expected to encourage creativity and originality among their students, these three casewriting organizations might consider extending similar latitude to their membership.

CONCLUSIONS

This discussion has offered insights in areas of special interest to casewriters, and was intended to generate further, extended discussion concerning the nature and purpose of the teaching note so that those who either develop or utilize this instructional resource will collaborate in developing an improved product that will benefit as many stakeholders as possible.

The differences cited should not be interpreted as symptoms of confusion and disarray, but rather the result of healthy disagreement and the prevalence of creativity and individuality in casewriting and case teaching, supporting the authors' belief that the casewriting discipline is healthy and thriving. Just as companies must constantly reinvent themselves to adapt to a changing environment, the lack of agreement and constant state of ferment which seems to be the norm in casewriting bodes well for the utility and relevance of cases.

RECOMMENDATION

Differences among casewriters should be encouraged, not discouraged. The premier casewriting organizations -- WACRA, NACRA, and the SCR -- should cherish the differences of their members and resolve that there is no ideal way to write a case, thus continuing to spawn dynamic, creative casewriting that is attuned to our changing environments.

REFERENCES

Cabell, David W.E., Cabell's Directory of Publishing Opportunities in Business and Economics, 5th ed. (Beaumont TX: Cabell Publishing Co., 1990), pp. 126-130.

"Call for Cases, Papers, and Proposals," Southwest Case Research Association (SCRA), 1993, p.3.

"Evaluation Criteria for Business Cases," handout, Society for Case Research (SCR), 1993, p.4.

North American Case Research Association (NACRA), handout, 1993.

Wheelen, Thomas L. and Hunger, J. David, Strategic Management and Business Policy, 4th ed. (Reading MA: Addison-Wesley Publishing Co., 1992), pp. 317-318.

CHAPTER EIGHT

.

ENCASING THE CASE METHOD

Bedford A. Fubara, Jide S. Olutimayin, Alph. Tlhomole
University of Botswana
GABORONE, BOTSWANA

Abstract

The case method approach in teaching is new in Africa and especially so in Botswana for two reasons. First is the fact that no case method book has been developed based on the Botswana business environment. Second, case method books developed in other African environments do not bring the here-and-now-experience necessary for Botswana students. The Southern African political experience is different from the rest of Africa and Botswana is probably the only politically stable environment in Africa that will encourage business activities in the foreseeable future. The region has been peaceful for more than 20 years now.

This paper is meant to describe our approach in employing the case method in teaching business policy at the University of Botswana. It also describes the encasing experience of students writing cases. These may be used in future in conjunction with existing foreign cases. Part of our ambition is to de-mystify the case writing skill as something attainable in any environment.

We find that our students' (based on the students' reports) understanding of business policy has increased through the use of the case method approach as compared to the traditional teaching method. We can also report that students have shrugged off their shyness to speak in class and have become completely immersed in the quest to solve the problems posed by cases presented to them. Besides, they have reported that the process of writing their own case has driven home the class lecture on the environment of business and the need to position a business competitively.

INTRODUCTION

A case is a body of information describing a business situation. It is basically a reporter's account of the elements of thought and the interpersonal relations among managers/employees that have characterized a particular action environment. Comprehensive cases are to be analysed rather than solved. The analyses may be presented or developed orally in classroom discussions or in written reports. In either form, the analysis must start with a focus on the central issues or problems that represent an accurate sizing up to the situation. An argumentative thesis that explains in further detail the important action elements on the case can be developed. The argument must be supported by the factual interpretive evidence from the case itself and not from vague generalizations and opinions. A final step in analysis is usually to suggest actions or decisions that appropriately follow in the action situation analyzed [Fubara, 1985].

METHODOLOGY

In this study, a class of 65 final year students who have been taught during their four-year study period at the University of Botswana with the traditional method were given four weeks lectures on business policy/strategic management concepts. Thereafter they were taught how to analyse management cases and were required to analyze one case per week [and present the case to the class]. [The case were] chosen from the 35 cases in the Higgins and Vincze [1993] book.

The class was divided into five groups of 13 students each. Each group elected a group leader and on the date of presentation, five of the students in each group were appointed by their group members to form a panel to present their case. The remaining members of the group joined the other members of the class on the class floor to listen to the case and to raise questions on various functional and strategic issues or to support and sometime to justify the points made by the panelists.

The 65 final year Bachelor's degree programme students in the School of Accounting and Management Studies major in different disciplines: accounting, management, accounting and statistics, accounting and public administration or accounting and economics. Those who successfully complete the course work are expected to graduate in July, 1994.

During the presentation by each group, questions were asked by students from various backgrounds. Questions came from management, accounting, and economics majors and from those with related interests. Arguments tended to be tilted toward assessing the performance of the organization in questions related to profitability. Some majors in management tended to ask questions relating to personnel management or strategic management; some were concerned with liquidity and other financial ratio. Students showed much concern over situations where some organizations wanted to borrow in order to realize some visions, but had a high debt equity ratio, or situations where the philosophy of the company was to make some senior staff to "own stores in the stores" as in the case of Wall-Mart Stores Inc. [Higgins and Vincze 1993].

FINDINGS AND DISCUSSIONS

The intriguing issue about the case method is that, on one hand, each group that presented its case worked hard enough to avoid embarrassment from their class mates who were listening to their renditions. On the other hand, some students studied the case to be presented so well that they were poised to point out the errors of the presenting team probably in retaliation for the way questions were thrown at them during their own presentation. On the day of presentation each of the 65 students received a copy of the analysis of the case from the presenting group a few minutes before the presentation. It was often observed that some members of the class were always anxious to make speedy reviews of the paper in order to pick holes in the presentation and with various definitions, as they raised queries on the financial performance of such companies. The instructors made fundamental remarks on issues of principles when they thought that the students were missing the point of the discussion.

The system created conflict or criticism as a venue for learning. In attempting to pick holes in their colleagues' presentations, students carried out in depth analysis of the case before class sessions and proffered answers to issues that were not obvious from the case material. For instance, there was an argument as to whether a firm was incorporated since it was not indicated in the case. One student was quick to discover from the financial records that the company had issued common stock which convinced everybody that the firm was an incorporated body. Classes were held thrice a week. Although students had two tutorials a week, they were encouraged them to use those tutorial periods for preparing their cases or for working out answers to take-home quizzes issued in class.

Some conceptual questions were given as home work materials fortnightly to be answered in groups and for onward transmission to the instructors for grading. Each student who took part in preparing a case was required to attach his/her own individual analysis to the group summary as a way of ensuring that no student 'hid behind others' in the group assignment. To enforce this, a student was penalized for not attaching his individual case analysis to the group work. This method was adopted because some group leaders were not strong enough to persuade some of their mates to surrender their home work as attachment, as some of the students thought it would expose their lack of understanding of the case, especially when discussions would show their 'deviations from the central gravity.'

To encase this teaching design in learning, the instructors designed a questionnaire for the students to collect data/information on the business operations in Botswana, particularly in Gaborone, where students could have access to business organizations easily. Each student was required to visit a company of his choice and to hold interviews through the structured questionnaire, where possible. The objective was to empower the student to write-up his own case for proper documentation. No cases had been written before about companies operating in Botswana. I n some situations, students were requested to leave the questionnaire behind for functional managers to complete, because the data requested required expertise in marketing, production, finance, accounting and personnel. To enrich their case write-ups, students were encouraged to speak with the Chief Executive Officer of the company. The faculty believed that the organization would be operating from conceptual lens and because it was assumed that he would have information written (or unwritten) about the company from its beginning stages.

To assess this encasing-the-case-method, a questionnaire was administered to the students to find out their reactions to the case-method approach in learning the subject of business policy and strategic management. The result show that a majority of the students (90%) stated that they understood the concept of business policy better than they had when only the traditional lecture method was employed. Some of the students admitted that certain issues taught with the traditional lecture method became more meaningful when they started analysing the group cases. Other students also reported that some conceptual issues became more meaningful when they went about collecting the information for encasing the concept of business policy. And from the data collected from the firms, some students were able to see the need for an integrating business policy course. More surprising to the students were the attitudes of the companies which in some instances refused to give out information about themselves even in areas such as the Chief Executive Officer's (CEO's) assessment of the company's market share.

A majority of the students reported that the case method created more opportunity than the lecture method for students participation. All (100%) reported that case method encourages group participation, rapport among students and encourages understanding of team actions.

Students were required to react to the assignment to collect data for writing up their own cases. All (100%) agreed that the assignment created an opportunity for them to learn how to collect information. Furthermore, the course motivated them to learn techniques they could employ when trying to meet important people.

In response to "In your own words, state what you have gained so far in being involved in case analysis in your group and in class" the following samples can be seen as indicative of the total picture.

a) I have now seen the need to express my opinion and the need to listen to other people's opinion.
b) I can now reconcile from this case method what I have been taught in other different courses
c) I gained in group discussions because in general, the individual group members participated quite well.
d) It has helped me to analyse a case in a better and in a more organized fashion. It has improved my own way of thinking and the approach I now make towards a case is more strategic and broad.
e) This is the first time that I am writing up my own case and it has been a worthwhile experience. I have never been involved in a subject like this before. The case analysis in groups and in class has been an enriching exercise. I have been exposed to a variety of situations and knowledge and have enjoyed the 'brainstorming' in my group. I have also enjoyed being a group leader.
f) Case analysis improves how you think, how you approach a problem and how to interpret the information you have in front of you. Since it deals with real cases, it helps us to better understand real world problems. On the whole case analysis has helped me to channel my way of thinking. It broadens the mind.
g) In my own group I came to realize that the business world is full of problems and to solve such problems, you have to be patient and get ideas from other members which may aid you in solving the problems. Each case needs to be read thoroughly in order to get its meaning. Again in the group, other members may not be willing to work. Therefore to encourage team spirit you have to encourage them to work hard for the ultimate results.
h) Improved public speaking (confidence); ability to analyse cases in the business environment was improved
i) Enhanced my ability to analyse cases; appreciation of the importance of active group participation in case analysis; a better view of the overall business environment.
j) Working in a group has taught me to be patient when working with other people because each member of the group wants his/her point to be taken as being right. Arguments at times help because I experienced that I ended up understanding some of the things through arguments during group discussions. I have not started writing up my case yet, but to get information for the case, I sweated. I had to run around and actually begged for information from companies. I realized that in Gaborone, companies are not willing to help when it comes to giving information about their business.

From the comments extracted from a few students, it can be easily observed that the case method as it was set up did expose students to the business world.

384

CONCLUSIONS

Our conclusion is that the case-method of teaching management courses is useful, and more useful when it dovetails traditional teaching method encased with the students writing up their own cases to experience the here-and-now situation in real business activities. A major finding in this study is the fact that students who had opportunity to do vacation jobs with any of the firms in Botswana, found it less difficult to break-through the company's resistance in releasing information, especially where firms (most of them with foreign component) were afraid of business espionage.

LESSONS FOR CASE METHOD TEACHERS

Part of our ambition in designing the business policy course this way is to be able to document some of the happenings in the business environment of Botswana. More importantly it is our desire to de-mystify the foreign text-book cases we used and to promote the understanding that businesses do not work in a vacuum but in a real environment.

REFERENCES

Fubara, B. A.(1985); Business Management Principles and Strategies (University Press Ltd), p.203.

Higgins, J.M. and Vincze, J. W. (1993); Strategic Management, (The Dryden Press, New York).

THE RELEVANCE OF THE CASE STUDY SYSTEM AND OTHER TEACHING TOOLS IN AN AFRICAN SETTING: AN EXPERIENCE AT FOUR AFRICAN UNIVERSITIES

Jide S. Olutimayin
University Of Botswana
GABORONE, BOTSWANA

Abstract

The inadequacy of indigenous teaching and learning materials has been recognised as a constraint in development efforts in Africa (Centre for Management Development, 1985). In order to increase the supply of indigenous teaching aids for education and training, some organisations in Nigeria have conducted Case Study and Case Writing Workshops. Arising from my participation in one of the workshops is the urge to try some of the techniques discussed on different grades of studentship in four Universities situated in two sub-regions of the African continent. These techniques have produced very encouraging results, thus increasing the arsenal of teaching materials in Africa.

INTRODUCTION

Teaching is an art [Lambo, 1993]; this statement is a challenge to an earlier thought that had been suggested, and indeed impressed, that teaching was a science [Fubara, 1985]. Both positions have their merits; in some people/teachers, effective teaching is in-born and is as natural to them as getting out of bed in the morning; in others, the effectiveness has to be worked for, and is, therefore, hard-earned. To the "naturally-born" teachers, teaching with/through case studies may seem uncalled for as they believe they can, and do get through to the students adequately without employing the Case Study System; they would rather supplement their (theoretical) teaching with "simple examples" which they do not consider as case studies.

Perhaps these differing thoughts might not have emerged if there had been more evidence in Africa of the effectiveness of the Case Study Method as a teaching tool. This work is therefore an attempt to evaluate the system as a tool in a teaching and learning situation and to see the extent to which other teaching techniques can increase learning in an African setting. Some of these tools are simulation, videos, industrial visits and attachments, and simple in-the-firm researches.

The exercises were expected to improve the critical thinking and analytical skills of the working managers and the MBA students who were also working managers. In addition, it was expected that these techniques would help the students to improve their scores in classroom tests, particularly the undergraduates.

METHODOLOGY

The line between the Case Study System on one hand, and some other tools on the other, may not be clear. All of them have the same objective; the bottom-line is getting through to the students in the most effective way (this objective of effectiveness will be discussed in this paper). These teaching tools were applied in different situations to complement conceptual teaching.

The Video Session Method was applied on working managers because the other three methods stood better chances of being applied in undergraduate studies. And since the level of studentship is the same as in Case

386

Study Method, the results can be compared. The teaching techniques were:
- **Simple Research and Report Writing on Specific Cases** at the University of Ibadan, Nigeria (West Africa) (1985-89).
- **Video Sessions** at Peace & Peasant in Lagos, Nigeria (West Africa) (1987-92).
- **Industrial Visits and Attachments** at Ogun State University, Ago-Iwoye, Nigeria (West Africa) (1989-92).
- **Simulation Exercises** at the University of Swaziland, Kwaluseni (Southern Africa) (1992-93).
- **(Pure) Case Studies** for MBA students at the University of Botswana, Gaborone (Southern Africa) (1993 to date).

Each technique was chosen as adjudged to suit a particular learning situation.

SIMPLE RESEARCH AND REPORT WRITING

This technique was applied to Computer Science students in their third and fourth (final) years of study. Groups of students were made, in turn, to carry out simple research(es) in different areas as a way of amplifying what they have learnt in the classroom to confirm or deny their understanding of the topic. At different intervals, each group was asked to do two things:
(i) reteach' the particular subject to the class, while the other students were asked to rate how much the teaching had contributed to their further understanding of the subject;
(ii) each group was asked to write a short report on the work they carried out.

This provided the teacher an unbiased and indeed a fairly reliable way of assessing the students' understanding of the subject.

VIDEO SESSIONS

Peace & Peasant is a firm of consultants engaged in running Management courses, Computer application courses, Information Technology courses, etc for their clients. Students were drawn mostly from the management cadre (top, senior and intermediate). Initially, courses were run only in classroom versions, but latter ones were `spiced' with video recordings, at times in parallel with the teaching, and at other times, after the formal classroom teachings. At the start, the ratio of classroom teaching to videos was about 2:1, but was decreased to 1:1, and later to about 2:3, based on the encouraging results. Students were asked to explain the subjects to the class,
(i) after the formal teaching, and
(ii) after the supplementary videos.

INDUSTRIAL ATTACHMENTS

The Department of Mathematical Sciences offered courses in various combinations of Mathematics, Computer Science, Accounting, Economics and Statistics. Although the students were registered for different degrees, the bulk of their learning had a common base. To those who initiated and developed the programmes, this common-base concept would give them a balanced chance to assess and graduate the students as broad-knowledged ambassadors of the department. On the author's assumption as the Coordinator of these courses, the practice was introduced whereby students were made to go on industrial attachments for nine months (one academic year) during which they were exposed to real-life applications of what they had learnt in three years in the classrooms. They were also to produce technical reports on their experiences on the work they did during the nine months.

SIMULATION EXERCISES

The second and third year students of the Department of Computer Science and Physics seemed to have difficulties in understanding some of the concepts taught in the class. We therefore thought of trying out the idea of making them simulate the application(s) of these topics; this may be likened to the very popular, old and successful idea of Do-It-Yourself. Tests were administered after topics had been covered in the class, and other tests after the simulation exercises.

(FORMAL) CASE STUDIES

The Case Studies Method was tried on postgraduate working managers. The <u>Masters in Business Administration</u> programme drew students from various disciplines. The case study system was applied in the area of Information Systems; students were asked to analyse cases as Take-Home-Assignments and also in the class. The Take-Home-Assignments were reviewed in the class after grading. This practice was increased from a twice-a-term exercise to a fortnightly affair. The <u>table below</u> is a composite of the characteristics of the various tools.

TABLE 1
CHEMISTRY OF THE STUDY

Learning Material	Region of Study	Level of Studentship	Area of Concentration of Students	No. of Students
Simple Research	W. Africa	Undergraduate	Computer Science	67
Video Sessions	W. Africa	Managers	Industrial Business Management	Average of 24 per course
Industrial Attachments	W. Africa	Undergraduates	Applied Sciences and Social Sciences	76
Simulation Exercises	S. Africa	Undergraduates	Applied and Pure Sciences	93
Formal Case Studies	S/Africa	Post-graduates Working Managers (MBA)	Business and General Management	11

FINDINGS AND OBSERVATIONS

As can be observed from Table 1, the study covered (geographically) different areas of two sub-regions. The emerging results can therefore be taken as reasonable and true representations of the reality in the continent. Secondly, the background of the students ranged from sociology, through pure sciences, to applied sciences. The study can therefore be said to have taken care of all spheres of human operations and orientations. In addition, the Table reveals varying numbers of
students per learning tool, ranging from (as low as) 11 to (as high as) 93. This suggests that the size of a learning group is not a factor for the success or otherwise of a learning material. However, this assertion might be more authoritative if the group sizes were reversed or rearranged for the learning tools.

SIMPLE RESEARCH AND REPORT WRITING

The Simple Research tool ended on positive notes:
- the students understood the basic principles governing research activities as well as its demands, and the ability to mount one;
- it provided knowledge of data gathering and collation as well as processing same;
- it enabled the students to compare theoretical/classroom knowledge with practical realities of the outside world;
- when the students were asked to 'reteach' their respective subjects on which they did their research it was

observed that their abilities showed marked improvement compared with earlier efforts before the research. This can be adjusted as an <u>oral</u> success.
- their written reports on their research also reflected a high degree of understanding of the subjects they had worked on.

TABLE 2
REACTIONS OF STUDENTS TO VIDEO SESSION METHOD

Responses	No. of students that gave the response	No. of students as a percentage of total students
Tool allows more relaxed atmosphere	24	100%
Tool allows us to learn by seeing, hearing and thinking	23	96%
Tool allows us to make meaningful contributions in the class	24	100%
Tool provides a meaningful relationship between the subject and our jobs	22	92%
Tool enables better understanding of the overall subject	24	100%

TABLE 3
A MEASURE OF EFFECTIVENESS IN A GROUP OF 24 WORKING MANAGERS
USING THE VIDEO METHOD

Claims by students	No. that said yes before the Video	% age of total Students	After the video	% age of total students
Able to explain the subject to the rest of the class	14	58%	23	96%
Able to query some aspects of the subject	20	83%	24	100%
Able to relate subject effectively to personal work	16	67%	22	92%
Scores over 50% in Tests	18	75%	24	100%

VIDEO SESSIONS

As we indicated, the ratio of classroom teaching to video sessions was reduced from 2:1 to an even ratio of 1:1, a reflection of the impact the video sessions seemed to have made on the students. The result showed marked improvement. However, to confirm or deny this observation as a true factor of this seeming success, the ratio was further reduced to a 2:3 relationship. The results were now even more encouraging than in the 1:1 situation suggesting that improvements resulted more from video sessions than from classroom teachings. In their comments, the students related their success to the fact that video sessions provided more relaxed atmospheres than classroom situations, and that the video pictures must have been very carefully selected such that they were very pertinent to the subjects they were supposed to cover.

When asked to indicate what they had gained from the application of this tool, the students gave encouraging responses, some of which are shown in Table 2. Some of their claims, when asked to relate this tool specifically to their academic performance, are also shown in Table 3. These Tables reveal evidence of perceived effectiveness of the tool.

INDUSTRIAL ATTACHMENTS

Assessments of these industrial programmes were two fold:
(a) through the reports the students produced: these were assessed in terms of originality, grasp/knowledge of the subject, ability to express oneself effectively, ability to communicate ideas and knowledge clearly, etc.
(b) Collating the performances of these students in past years (i.e. Years 2 and 3), and comparing them with their performances in Years 5.

The assessments revealed considerable improvements in their technical reports over their term papers produced in Years 2 and 3, i.e. before the students went on the industrial attachments. In addition, more than 95 percent of the students (in 3 consecutive years) raised their performances in Year 5 of their study (i.e. after the industrial attachment programme), compared with their performances in Years 2 and 3 of their study. We had reasonable convictions to believe that the teaching and learning material was a major contributing factor to these improved performances. An evidence of this belief is shown in the Table below:

TABLE 4
COMPARISON OF STUDENTS' PERFORMANCES
BEFORE AND AFTER INDUSTRIAL ATTACHMENTS

Period Collated Performances	1989 - 90 Session	1990 - 91 Session	1991 - 92 Session
Average Scores of Class Before Industrial Attachment	54%	58.5%	57.8%
Average Scores of Class After Industrial Attachment	61.4%	65%	66.8%

SIMULATION EXERCISES

The result here was very similar to the industrial attachment situation because the programme resulted in better performances in class tests after the simulation exercises. In another dimension, the students did not only score higher after each simulation exercise, their scores were progressively higher. Our table of evidence was identical to earlier tables, and is therefore omitted.

FORMAL CASE STUDIES

The most striking feature of this tool was that the students always scored higher in case studies than in tests administered in conceptual subjects. It was also observed that their scores in theoretical tests began to improve as more cases were introduced and treated. Perhaps these positive situations are reflections of the fact that the students on the programme were working managers and were therefore more interested in problem-solving programmes than theoretical ones. In any case, the notable fact is that the tool has proved very effective indeed in a teaching and learning situation. It was also discovered that the students were happier that they learned, more than with the marks they obtained.

Because this group of students were working managers, we compared their responses with those of other working managers in video session methods. This comparison is shown in Table 5.

TABLE 5
COMPARISON BETWEEN STUDENT'S REACTIONS
TO THE CASE STUDY METHOD AND THE VIDEO SESSION METHOD

Case Study Method		Video Method	
No. of students with positive responses	As % age of total no.	No. of students with positive responses	As % age of total no.
11	100	24	100
11	100	23	96
11	100	24	100
11	100	22	92
11	100	24	100

*The small differences might be due to the difference in group size or could be due to the effectiveness of the tools. All the same, they are very comparable.

CONCLUSION AND RECOMMENDATIONS

As stated in the Introduction, the line between a formal case study on the one hand, and the individual tools on the other hand, may not be very clear because they all produce the same results - getting through to the students in an effective way. Perhaps, a more detailed study which reverses the application of these techniques might reveal which tool is more suitable for what learning situation, what group size, what location, and what benefits. At that point, the effectiveness of each learning tool may then be more accurately assessed, focusing on students' keen participation in the class - how much they contribute to discussions. Other areas of assessment would include how much the students enjoy the teaching, how much the sessions stimulate them to come up with examples that further enhance their understanding of the topic, and more importantly, the extent to which the tools increase their performances in tests, assignments and examinations after the application of these techniques.

Perhaps such a study would also answer the following questions:- Has it oriented their learning toward producing results? How much time does teaching the subject take using the tools, when compared with direct teaching delivery? In other words, has it increased or decreased the number of hours for getting through the subject and getting through to the students? How much notes (or workload) are the students subjected to by these techniques?

However, for now, we are happy to report that, on the whole, the individual tools have proved to be very relevant and effective in teaching and learning situations. This paper is therefore stressing the need for developing countries - in particular African countries - to employ more of these teaching methods and pursue their developments more vigorously. For instance, hitherto only the Case Study Method had been recognised as an effective tool in a teaching and learning situation, and some efforts are being made to produce local case materials [Fubara, Olutimayin, Tlhomole, 1994]. But now that this study has shown that the Video Session Method can produce similar results with the Case Study Method in similar situations, there is need for African institutions to reinforce their efforts in this direction to produce their own local videos that are relevant and pertinent to their local situations.

In this regard, this paper therefore further calls for linkage ventures between the advance nations of the West and institutions in the developing world. It is making a special appeal for African countries. Such linkages could be with the recipient institutions directly, or they could be channelled through some organisations, or through their various governments, in that order.

REFERENCES

Centre for Management Development (CMD) (1985); <u>Management Case Book</u>; Management Village, Lagos, Nigeria (Foreword Note).

Fubara, B.A. (1985); "The Gulf Fisheries Company Ltd", in <u>Management Case Book</u>; (Centre for Management Development, Lagos, Nigeria) (Pp.181 - 186).

Fubara, B.A., Olutimayin, J. Tlhomole A. (1994); "Encasing The Case Method". Paper for the 11th International Conference on Case Method Research and Application; Montreal, Quebec, Canada (June 19 - 22 - 22, 1994).

Lambo, E. (March, 1993); <u>Better Health in Africa</u>; (The World Bank Africa Technical Department, Human Resources Division) (Technical Working Paper No. 7).

392

TEACHING CASE WRITING AND CASE METHOD TEACHING IN A DIFFERENT CULTURAL ENVIRONMENT: A CHALLENGING EXPERIENCE[1]

Danielle Desbiens
University of Quebec at Montreal (UQAM)
MONTREAL, QUEBEC, CANADA

Abstract

Teaching case writing and teaching by the case method in a different cultural environment is a challenging experience. The teacher is forced to consider the philosophy of education and is confronted with sociological phenomena. This paper presents a classroom experience which occurred in January and May 1991 at the Universidad Autonoma de Guerrero in Mexico. The objectives, the context and the course plan components are described. More specifically, the author discusses insights and knowledge gained from this experience.

INTRODUCTION

The author's intention in this paper is to describe various issues associated with the use of cases in a non-American environment. Teaching how to write cases and how to teach with cases in a different cultural environment is a challenging experience. The teacher is forced to consider the philosophy of education and is confronted with sociological phenomena such as social status of university professors and leadership processes. In these circumstances the educational objectives, the communications mode, the teacher's role, implicit and explicit values of teaching, are important factors, as much as the actual learning content.

DESCRIPTION OF THE TEACHING EXPERIENCE

This article is based on two workshops given in a program sponsored by the Canadian International Development Agency (CIDA) to support the training of teachers at the Acapulco School of Tourism, which is affiliated with the State University of Guerrero (UAG). The program's objective was to develop the UAG's autonomy in offering the Master's program in tourism management in Acapulco. The students who attended the workshops had finished their doctoral studies. Some students were professionals in the field of management, others were teachers. During their studies, all of the students had taught at the undergraduate or at the master's program level. In fact, in exchange for receiving a scholarship, students were required to assume teaching duties.

Given the future teaching role of the students, the Canadian coordinator of the program decided to end the training with a workshop on the case method [teaching]. Knowing that there are very few Mexican cases, I accepted the challenge, giving myself the specific objective of breaking the vicious circle of "no cases - no use of the case method - no motivation to develop cases."

A first workshop was developed with a view to giving participants the opportunity to learn the writing process. The specificity of this objective came from the fact that our goal was to have Mexican cases written by Mexicans and for Mexicans. The second workshop on teaching with cases was necessary in order to build on the initial investment, due to the students' reactions in the first workshop. While they [the students] appeared to be motivated, they lacked confidence and information on how to use the cases they had written.

Educational objectives and course plans were prepared for both workshops. They were developed from the author's own experience with Leenders and Erskine and from various workshops given to colleagues. The

394

educational objectives and course plans are presented here, not because it is suggested that they be used as a model, but rather to enable the reader to understand what was learned.

EDUCATIONAL OBJECTIVES, COURSE PLAN AND EVALUATION

FIRST WORKSHOP: HOW TO WRITE CASES

Over a period of two weeks, the five-day workshop included the following:
1. Presentation of the method, discussion of its advantages and disadvantages, strengths and limits;
2. Presentation of the research steps and writing process;
3. Identification of the objectives and preparation of the first interview;
4. Writing of the first paragraph, structuring of the information;
5. Identification of the missing information and preparation of the second interview;
6. Final version and teaching plan.

In order to maintain their [students'] motivation and to delimit the learning process, the students were asked to write a case to be used in a course in which they were actually involved. The main objective was to give the participants the opportunity to go through the process of researching and writing a case. The final product was not to be complex, but rather a simple case adapted to *their* [emphasis added] students' needs in the field in which they were teaching.

Evaluation was a program requirement. A first assignment was due on the third day. The students had to write a draft of the first paragraph, develop the structure of the case as well as a teaching plan. Another assignment involving presentation of the case and [preparing] teaching notes was to be submitted at the end of the workshop.

SECOND WORKSHOP: TEACHING WITH CASES

The second workshop, which was intended to be a follow-up to the first course, was based on the same formula of a five-day workshop given over a two-week period. The ideas, notions and models developed in Bédard, Dell'Aniello and Desbiens [1991] were used in structuring this workshop. The steps were: determination of educational objectives, case selection, course planning, choosing leadership style, development of teaching aids, case analysis. Group process and feedback were the main pedagogical tools. A major portion of the time was planned for practice in class with the students' own cases. No formal evaluation was made. In addition to the work in class, the students professors were invited to write down what being a teacher or teaching means to them.

INSIGHT AND KNOWLEDGE GAINED

HOW TO WRITE CASES

On the first day, it was obvious that the students had not experienced the case method. For unknown reasons, perhaps because of a lack of relevant material or a lack of time, the case method had not been used in their training. Those few students, who had experienced the method in other programs, remembered it only as a small group discussion with no particular learning content. None of the students had ever used cases in their teaching. A few students were preoccupied with their research paper and were interested in cases as a qualitative research method.

A discussion on the method's advantages, strengths and limits had been designed to help the students to determine why they would use the method in their teaching. This discussion appeared to have remained on a theoretical level. The students had not made the connection between theory of the case method and its use in class.

While preparing the course, I had thought that the students had experienced the method, Therefore, I had planned to put the emphasis on the process of writing cases and had not expected giving a demonstration of the method. To my surprise, I was asked repeatedly to explain how cases should be used in the classroom. Due to their lack of experience, the students did not have a clear idea of how they themselves could use the method.

The case writing process and its various research activities generated reactions. The majority of the students thought that they had only to tell an interesting story. In a way, carrying out the research activities was a matter of trust for them: they followed the process step by step. I had to be very concrete in my teaching. My experience of teaching a course on interviewing helped me to give them tips and a list of do's and don'ts which were very much appreciated.

At each step along the way, there were problems, but not necessarily the ones I expected. The students' difficulties were particularly evident when the time came to define and choose the educational objectives to be attained in their course using the case method. They did not appear to be familiar with the use of educational objectives, which is the starting point of the case writing process. As expected, writing the introductory paragraph and structuring the information were difficult steps [for them to understand] to understand, and because of the students' lack of experience with educational objectives, the preparation of teaching notes also posed a problem.

Nevertheless, with a lot of support, the students wrote their first paragraph and established the basis for their teaching notes. At mid-session evaluation, each student was met individually and all the difficulties were discussed. This step appeared to be a turning point in their learning. The students had problems at all levels. I was able to fill the gaps. Without these individual meetings, I would not otherwise have been able to clarify misconceptions experienced at various stages of the process. Since then I have decided to use this type of individual supervision in all of my workshops in the future, especially when teaching in a different country.

As for the case writing style, a few students were looking for recipes. I did not want to suggest or recommend a specific model but wanted them to be confident about their own style of interviewing and writing. As doctoral students they had enough experience to have developed their own writing style. Through an analysis of translated material, a list of do's and don'ts was created.

During the two-week period over which the workshop was given, the students' motivation seemed to be very strong. All of the students participated actively, although as a teacher, I had the impression that they were answering very much in the sense of what they thought was expected. Even though everyone had written a case by the end of the course, I questioned whether they really understood the process - the objective of the workshop.

HOW TO TEACH WITH CASES

The second workshop took place four months later. During the first workshop, each student had prepared a teaching plan to be used in his or her course. But few of the students had experimented teaching with their case in the classroom. One had written a second case (he was the lone exception). For the majority, their fear had been stronger than their motivation. In the discussions, they gave excuses such as "they did not know how to do it;" "they did not want to take the risk." There were some negative evaluations from the few who had tried: "My students did not like it;" "It is not teaching;" "It is impossible in my field to use cases;" "My group is too large." Once I overcame my surprise - they [the workshop participants] had appeared so enthusiastic in January - I decided to work from these difficulties. In the process I and became more convinced of the importance of having the students experiment during the workshop. So, I allowed more time for the students to practice teaching and to give feedback in class and insisted that the majority of them participate. In a way, they were learning on three levels: as participants (practice teaching session), as observers (integrating the concepts) and as students (experiencing the method).

The practice teaching session in class gave the students the opportunity to realize that they were better than they thought. They did not have a clear notion of group processes. However, due to their teaching experience, they had a good idea of how to go about facilitating a session. Although at first, they had a tendency to imitate. Later they gradually became more personal in their teaching.

In relation to the learning process, the students were not accustomed to expressing their feelings, nor [were they able] to openly analyze a teaching process. In a sense, they were not used to giving feedback to colleagues. They had known each other for years, but not in their professional field. They gradually became involved. After two or three experiences, there was more interaction in the group. The students were better able to give each other useful feedback, their argumentation was more relevant and their feelings were expressed more clearly.

A demonstration, planned early in the course, was very helpful. This gave all of the students a common reference point. They could compare. However, the students' feedback allowed me to assess their level of understanding. They were applying the concepts more easily then during the first workshop and [they were] making the connection to educational objectives.

The process of working on one or many possible solutions or decisions was not understood very well. When playing the professor's role, the students had a tendency to control the process in a more or less "question and answer" formula, looking for the best and sole solution or decision. Could this be an indication of Mexicans' preferred leadership style? A discussion on the students' philosophy of teaching was revealing on this subject. For a Mexican (at least for this group of Southern Mexicans), teaching is basically knowledge communication. The feeling of authority related to the image of "the person who knows" seems to be a fundamental value. Having the students participate in the class, taking the students' experience into consideration, pushing the students to find solutions on their own, not providing their own [the teacher's] interpretation, were all anxiety producing factors for the majority of the student-professors in this workshop.

CONCLUSION

When a person teaches how to write or to use cases in a different cultural environment, he or she must be aware of the fact that every step may be influenced by cultural considerations: the planning, the way one teaches, the content. Everything that is done, is culturally loaded, even the use of the method itself. "The medium is the message."

At first, I was concerned with culture, mostly in relation to the case as an instrument. From my point of view, the cultural considerations were respected because the authors were completely autonomous as to the content of the cases. I was prepared to respect their way of writing, of structuring the information, etc. The students were Mexicans writing for Mexicans. I was responsible only for teaching them the process. This experience gave me the opportunity to see how much the use of the case method questions basic values in teaching: we have to know why we teach business administration to know what we are looking for in the case method; the interaction between students and professors and the roles played by each party are culturally oriented; the non-directive approach and the degree of participation that the students are allowed are socially determined. In some cultures where the autocratic style of teaching is predominant, the use of the method may be more problematic. We can thus question its universal applicability.

Most of all, the case user has to change his attitude or the image he has of his students. He is no longer the master and the students his disciples. In the case of these Acapulquenians, they had: 1. to take into consideration that many of the undergraduate students already knew how to do business because entrepreneurship is well developed among young people in Acapulco, and 2. to refrain from giving their own solution to the case.

The fact that educational objectives in the field of administration may be very different from one community to the next, has to be taken into consideration. In promoting the case method, we are promoting an approach which aims to develop individual judgment, fast reactions and rationality in decision-making. It is a mode of interaction with the "authority" and with colleagues. With the case method, the student is no longer silent in front of his professor, he can express his disagreement with colleagues' opinions and he will probably do the same in his workplace. Can this method be adapted to every country?

The case method is very demanding for the teacher who uses it without concern for the cultural context. It requires sufficient ego-strength and confidence to allow uncertainly and argument. If, in addition, the pedagogical method does not correspond with habitual modes of interaction in business, its use can be destabilizing in many ways. One may ask whether the method is appropriate in every country and what might be the impact of its use.

KNOWLEDGE GAINED AND SUGGESTIONS

1. The premise about the popularity of the method [in Mexico] is false. The use of the case method is not systematic or generalized in the teaching of business administration. Students with scholarship in administration, even at the doctorate level, may never have been exposed to the method.

    When teaching a course on or about cases in a different cultural environment it is imperative that a demonstration be given. Do not assume that every student in business administration knows what a case is. As well, not all students will have the same experience of the method. The demonstration gives the group a common experience which serves as a reference point for all of the students. Students must first understand how one teaches with cases before learning how to write cases.

2.   Try not to introduce a positive bias for the method. Rather, discuss educational goals in teaching business administration.

     In terms of the teaching process, it is important to check not only the participants' knowledge of the method, but their motivation to use it, before giving any information on the method itself. Even though it may appear logical to structure the course by first presenting the method and then having the students react to it. Native students may just be polite to the guest lecturer.

3.   Considering the importance of pre-established educational objectives as a means of facilitating the first case writing experience, it is important to teach what an educational objective is and to discuss the problems involved in teaching skills, particularly decision-making [skills].

4.   It is important to take the time to make future users realize how much they already know and to put the emphasis on their own writing experience. Students who experience case writing for the first time may lack confidence in their skills.

5.   Learning by doing is a good method, and when we teach how to write cases, it is often at the end of the process that the students realize what they have learned. It is appropriate to have the participants go through the entire process. Students are not always aware of the selective perception process or their own personal biases. They tend to write their own analysis in order to show that they know what it is about. The use of teaching notes is very useful to counterbalance this tendency.

6.   In terms of pedagogical training, the practice teaching session is the most valuable way of getting students involved. It is important to push them to give feedback.

ENDNOTES

1.   Presented at the 1992 WACRA Congress, in Limerick, Ireland.

THE CASE PROGRAM OF THE "ECOLE NATIONALE D'ADMINISTRATION PUBLIQUE" (ENAP)

Michel Paquin
Ecole nationale d'administration publique
MONTREAL, QUEBEC, CANADA

Abstract

The paper describes the experience of the "Ecole nationale d'administration publique" which started in 1990 a case program whose objective is to promote the use of (teaching) cases in the School's programs. The paper consists of two parts. The first part describes what has been done in the field of training the instructors. The second part of the paper discusses what has been achieved in the field of writing cases.

INTRODUCTION

In 1990, the "Ecole nationale d'administration publique" (ENAP), the School of Public Administration of the University of Quebec, decided to start a case program with the objective to promote the use of (teaching) cases in the School's programs. Few teachers of public administration have had the opportunity to become familiar with the case method, and those who are interested in using cases do not find a sufficient number of good cases in French. The case program is designed to cover the training costs of the instructors interested in using the case method and the costs related to writing cases. The purpose of this paper is to first present what has been done in the field of training and to describe what has been achieved in the field of writing cases.

TRAINING THE INSTRUCTORS

Many instructors considering the case method think that a case must be used to apply previously delivered theory to specific problems. The teacher presents the theory and the tools necessary to solve a problem and then the problem the students have to work on. Such way of using cases does not allow to take full advantage of the case method which aims to simulate the decision process in a real context where both the ways of solving a problem and the solutions are debatable. To simulate managerial reality in the classroom, the class must look for its own solution, not that of the instructor. Thus, when an institution promotes the case method, training is important to have the instructors using the case method effectively.

At ENAP, the training of the instructors was planned as a two-step process. First, the instructors had to participate in a demonstration session so that they could see as a participant in case discussion what the case method is in the classroom. Second, the instructors interested in using the case method were offered a two-day training workshop to develop their skills.

The best way to have a group of people understand the case method is to have those people involved in the analysis of a case and the discussion of it in the classroom. Thus, a demonstration session was proposed to any instructor interested to know what the case method is. The instructors who registered for the session received, a few days in advance, a case that had to be discussed in the classroom. The participants were instructed to analyze the case individually before the session so that they would be ready to participate actively in the discussion. The case, used in one course of the Master of Public Administration Program, was written by one of the School's professors and it illustrates quite well the possibilities offered by the case method in some courses. The case discussion in the classroom started right after the presentation of the session's program. The session was led by a university professor with a lot of experience in using the case method in the classroom and

400

in training for teaching with cases.

The case discussion, which lasted about ninety minutes, was followed by a discussion on the participants' learning. First, the discussion focused on what had been learned in analysing and discussing the case, which is a good way to highlight the kind of learning the case method promotes, and after on what had been learned while observing how the instructor was proceeding, which is a good way to highlight the instructor's role and how he should behave. The rest of the session dealt with the basic characteristics of the case method, the different ways of using the case method (whether or not to give instructions to the participants, whether or not to suggest readings, individual analysis, small group discussion, ways of discussing in the classroom), the organization of the period of time dedicated to the case discussion, the instructor's behavior in the classroom, and the evaluation of the students.

Following the demonstration session, some professors concluded that the case method was not for them but others were really interested to try it. However, those interested felt that they had to acquire some skills, particularly in conducting case discussion in the classroom. This aspect is the most critical one, for the fear of losing control of the situation in the classroom is being considered the main problem by those who plan to use the case method. Thus, to reinforce the interest in the case method, we had to pass to another step which is training for teaching with cases.

We considered two options regarding training for teaching with cases. First, we considered a training workshop for our staff only. That option was rejected because training for teaching with cases requires a minimum number of participants to simulate what goes on in the classroom and we were unable to reach that number. Then, we considered another option, to have our teaching staff follow one of the training workshops offered regularly by some institutions, for example Harvard University or the University of Western Ontario. In the meantime, the Canadian Centre for Management Development (which is the Canadian Government's training agency for senior management) invited our teaching staff to participate to its annual workshop on training for teaching with cases. This training workshop is offered in French. We accepted this invitation and since 1991 some members of our teaching staff participate to the CCMD's annual training workshop.

At CCMD, the case method is used throughout the two-day workshop. The participants receive a series of cases and some texts on the case method and the role of the instructor. The first day, the instructor teaches four cases, one of them being a case dealing with a management problem. This case illustrates the use of cases for training in management. The three other cases describe problems met in the classroom while using the case method. They deal with some basic abilities the instructor has to master. The discussion of the cases is completed with two lectures, one on teaching with cases and one on the instructor's role. In the evening, the participants have to prepare, in small groups, a teaching plan for a case that will be discussed in the classroom the day after, each group being given a different case. Each participant must also analyze individually all the cases that will be discussed the day after.

The second day, some of the participants have the opportunity to conduct a classwide discussion of a case. For each case to be discussed, one member of the group in charge of the case acts as an instructor and facilitates the classwide examination of the case's problems and issues, the decision-maker's options, and recommendations. The participant acting as an instructor must follow as closely as possible the teaching plan prepared by his or her group. The group members do not participate in the discussion but they act as observers of the person acting as an instructor. They have to check how well the instructor follows the teaching plan and how well his/her behavior is adequate while conducting the discussion. After the classwide case discussion, the participants are asked to make some comments on the teaching plan followed and the instructor's behavior. At the end, the instructor in charge of the workshop makes some comments and concludes the discussion.

The workshop on teaching with cases gives the participants an opportunity to get some skills but these skills will be fully developed only after a lot of experience. For the instructors who have some doubts about their way of conducting a case discussion, we suggest two things. First, ask permission of a colleague who has the reputation of being a first-class instructor to watch him in action. Second, ask him to watch you in action and make some comments.

WRITING CASES AND TEACHING NOTES

Those in the field of public administration considering teaching with cases written in French face the problem of case supply. There are many good cases but the field is so large that, in many areas, it is difficult to find cases suiting the instructor's objectives well. Therefore, ENAP supports its staff willing to write cases and teaching notes or willing to have cases written under their responsibility.

In Canada, there are three suppliers of cases in public administration: the Institute of Public Administration of Canada (IPAC), the Canadian Center for Management Development (CCMD), and the "Ecole des Hautes Etudes Commerciales de Montreal" (HEC).

IPAC case program is a clearinghouse for cases and instructor's notes written by professors or practitioners in the field of public administration. It has published a large number of good cases which can be used in a variety of Public Administration, Public Policy and Canadian Politics courses. Unfortunately, IPAC's cases rarely address managerial problems at the operational level (for example, problems related to human resources management or work design) and only a small proportion of IPAC's cases are available in French.

CCMD uses in its training programs cases written by its own staff or, upon its request, by practitioners or authors. CCMD's cases deal with problems met in the federal public administration and are sold through IPAC. CCMD's cases are available in both English and French.

The "Ecole des Hautes Etudes Commerciales de Montreal", the School of Business Administration of the University of Montreal, has a case program ("Centrale de cas") which publishes and sells cases written mainly by or under the authority of the School's staff. HEC publishes its cases in French only. Most HEC's cases are in the field of business administration, but some cases describe problems met in public organizations, for example in hospitals, social services agencies, educational organizations, and municipalities.

ENAP's teaching staff using cases may buy some from the sources just mentioned, but they can also decide to write their own cases or have someone doing it under their authority. Most of the time, the instructors prefer to hire an assistant or a case author and ask for the case program's financial assistance. The choice between a case writer or an assistant depends on many factors. A case writer is a professional author who is more experienced and more autonomous than an assistant who is usually a student in our Master of Public Administration Program. But a case of an average length (about ten pages) written by a professional writer may cost 5,000 canadian dollars while the same case written by an assistant costs less than 2,000 canadian dollars.

Whoever writes the case, the instructor has to play an important role. First, he has to decide for what purpose the case is prepared and what are the learning objectives, in particular the basic skills and the kind of decision-making capacity the case wants to develop. One of the difficulties often met by case writers is precisely the lack of clear objectives given by the instructor. Clear orientations are important because they define what information to look for and how to write the case.

Second, the instructor has to find a situation fitting his or her objectives. For that, many sources can be used. The instructor may look at his or her experience as a consultant. Colleagues may be aware of interesting experiences. Students with a practical experience are also good informants. Finally, public sources like academic or professional journals and newspapers may also be very useful. In general, it is better to consider many possibilities, some more interesting than others. To choose the best situation, we apply criteria like the degree of adequacy to the objectives, the degree of interest for the students (which depends on identification with the organization and the situation under study), the probability to get clearance for publication, and finally practical aspects like traveling costs.

It is up to the instructor, not the author, to get the authorization from an organization to undertake field research for a case, and it sometimes happens that the research must be abandoned because the situation is not what we thought, or because the organization under study does not cooperate well or refuses to give clearance for publication. Therefore, when we do research for a case we must expect a possibility of failure.

The instructor is also responsible for the case validation. First, the case must be validated by people in the organization under study. Those people will underline the missing facts and will validate the description of the situation. A case may also be reviewed by colleagues who are also case writers. They will underline problems with the presentation of the facts, the style of writing, etc.. Students may also be used to check if a case has the necessary information, if it is clear, etc. But the final test for a case is in the classroom. It sometimes happen that a case fails to meet this test. For various reasons, the students don't like the case.

The instructor who writes a case or has a case written under his or her direction usually also writes a teaching guide. The teaching guide gives the instructors some guidelines about the way to use the case in the classroom. Most clearinghouses publish cases under the condition that a teaching guide also be written. At ENAP, writing a teaching guide is not mandatory but we strongly recommend it when a case is used by more than one instructor.

Instructors or assistants who undertake writing a case often look for some guidance. There are some writing workshops where participants work under the guidance of experimented case writers. We recommend to the instructors planning to write cases, or even planning to have cases written by an assistant, to participate to a writing workshop. To be able to give useful guidance to an assistant, it is important to have some experience in writing cases.

At ENAP, we have not yet organized writing workshops, but to provide some guidance to case writers we published a note on case writing. In addition, we published for the instructor's guidance a note on writing a teaching guide. The note on case writing has sections on the definition of a case, the method of case research (sources, workplan, data collection), the case writing process (outline, style of writing , disguise), the case validation and testing, and complementary documents. The note on writing a teaching guide gives a definition of a teaching guide and present the sections found in such a document: case summary, learning objectives, case analysis, how to use the case in the classroom, instructions to the participants, and what happened in practice. The case writers and the instructors find that the notes on case writing and on writing a teaching guide are very useful.

CONCLUSION

Four years after its debut, the ENAP case program's achievements are significant. Four years ago, the case method was used in only three or four courses. Now, the case method is widely used in a variety of courses at the graduate level: Public Management, Organization Design, Organizational Behavior, Management of Change, Culture and Power in Organizational Analysis, Public Policy Analysis, Program Evaluation, Human Resources Management, Strategic Management, and the Preparation Seminar for Internship. The case method is also used in training seminars for Senior Management. During this period of time, about thirty cases were written or are in process of being completed. Some cases are bought from IPAC, CCMD and HEC but ENAP's cases now count for a significant proportion of the cases used at the School.

In conclusion, let's mention some key factors of success that may apply to any institution pursuing the objective of promoting the use of the case method. First, senior management must be involved. At ENAP, the case program was an objective of the 1990-94 Development Plan supported very strongly by the Director General. Second, budget must be available for training, for case writing (according to the circumstances, this aspect is more or less important because it depends on the availability of good cases in the market), and for technical assistance and publishing. Third, we must be patient and not expect spectacular achievements right at the beginning. After all, we have to convince people to change strong habits and to invest much effort in training, in changing their way of teaching and, in some instances, in writing cases.

USING THE CASE METHOD WITH AN INTERNATIONAL ACADEMIC AUDIENCE

Patricia S. Tulin
University of Hartford
WEST HARTFORD, CONNECTICUT, U.S.A.

Abstract

As the case method of study continues to gain acceptance as an important pedagogical tool for business education throughout the world, business faculty may be asked to train faculty from countries other than their own on its use. This paper discusses the experience I had at the 1993 Krakow Faculty Development Workshop, introducing the case method, including case writing, to 31 faculty participants from various Polish institutions.

INTRODUCTION

The case method of study has been integrated into many, if not most, of the American business schools largely because of its enormous value in teaching skills such as issue analysis, problem-solving and outcome assessment. As Business schools seek to export their methods to other countries, part of that process may involve teaching other faculty the value of the case method. This past July, I had the opportunity to do just that as part of the 1993 Krakow Faculty Development Workshop, held in Bukowina Tartzanska, Poland.

Introducing the case method to an international audience comprised of academics provided certain unique challenges. It was important to appreciate the sophistication of the audience, understand differences in their attitudes and training, and adapt the format to accommodate such barriers as language proficiency.

THE 1993 KRAKOW FACULTY DEVELOPMENT WORKSHOP

The 1993 Krakow Faculty Development Workshop was the result of an agreement between a Consortium of American Universities and The Jagiellonian University in Krakow, Poland.[1] The agreement has as one of its goals the development of quality Polish faculty resources committed to business management education. The Workshop consisted of 31 Polish participants, representing faculty from a variety of Polish institutions.[2] In addition to academics, practitioners attending the Workshop included a Social Service Administrator for the city of Krakow, an administrator in the Bureau of Promotion and Offers (the "economic development" office) for the city of Krakow, and a representative from the non-profit Business and Progress Foundation.

The participants were divided into functional teams according to their areas of interest: Finance, Management, Marketing, Entrepreneurship and Public Administration. Each team consisted of five members, except Public Administration which had six. Each of these teams was lead by a Consortium faculty member, assisted by an appointed Polish team leader who was expected to take an active role in conducting the Workshop. Professor Kathleen Sloan[3] and I acted as Consortium Co-leaders of the Public Administration team.

In addition to the division into functional teams, the Workshop was further divided into morning and afternoon sessions each day. The morning sessions were comprised of all 31 participants, while the afternoon sessions were used to break off into individual teams for in-depth substantive discussions of the discipline and to prepare for the team's presentation before the whole group on assigned mornings. Each team was responsible for conducting two of the morning sessions, so the participants would be exposed to each of the five disciplines at least twice during the ten-day Workshop, and would witness a wide variety of pedagogical techniques. In addition to the case method, other techniques included use of technological tools such as videos and computers, simulations, brain-storming and cross-functional discussion groups.

INTRODUCING THE CASE METHOD TO THE PUBLIC ADMINISTRATION TEAM

Prior to arriving in Poland, we had been told that much of the pedagogy in Poland's universities remains formal lecturing, with students listening to the lecture and reiterating what they "learned" back to the professor in the form of a comprehensive examination. We believed it was very important to introduce more active, participatory learning to the participants - primarily using the case method which encourages the use of role playing, simulation and scenario development to facilitate analysis and discussion.

In addition to this inherent preference for passive learning, another obstacle we encountered was the participants' understanding of what constitutes the "case method". Although all of the academics on the Public Administration team said that they had used the case method to varying degrees in their classes, their idea of the method appeared to be for the professor to present a problem and the student to give the "correct" answer. This approach is certainly an improvement over the more passive, lecturing model which is commonly used in Poland, but it is not the case method as used in the United States, where the emphasis is on issue-spotting and identifying a range of solutions.

We introduced the team to the case method during the first afternoon session, using the Harvard Business School case "Ordering Floppy Disks in Poland".[4] In one page the case describes the steps involved for an advisor to Poland's undersecretary of state for European integration and foreign assistance to order floppy disks for a computer. It concludes that it takes four people and five steps to get the disks. This case generated a very lively and interesting discussion. Issues such as "good" versus "bad" bureaucracy, participatory government, management science and time/motion studies, the role of the legal system in instituting changes, and more were considered. We demonstrated how to use the case for active learning through role-playing, calling on various members of the group to take on the role of the bureaucrat, the person ordering the disks, and so forth. We pursued the fact that in the United States this same thing might happen, and stressed the use of cases to develop theoretical constructs. We also stressed the need to bring the theoretical discussion back to the facts of the case in order to fully appreciate the complexity and reality of problem-solving and change management.

Interestingly, we noticed a difference between the academics' and practitioners' attitudes when we finished demonstrating our approach. The practitioners were very enthusiastic, while the academics remained slightly skeptical of its utility in the classroom. This probably reflected the academics' formal training and the fact that their students, unlike American graduate students, have had little or no practical experience.

On the fourth day, the Public Administration team made its first presentation to the entire Workshop in the morning session. Professor Sloan and I used the first half of the session to briefly present the topic of business/government interaction and to demonstrate how to use the case method. Prior to the session we had provided copies of the Harvard Business School case "United Technologies and the Closing of American Bosch"[5] to all participants and asked them to prepare it for discussion. We chose this case because it illustrates the public/private nexus. The case involves the handling of the closing of a 76-year-old plant in Springfield, MA and the corresponding loss of 900 manufacturing jobs. The "cast of characters" is familiar: management arguing that conditions beyond its control required the closing in order to maintain profitability and insure the continued economic health of the corporation and thereby provide jobs; labor charging a "clear pattern of mismanagement and disinvestment"; the Springfield Mayor charging lack of good faith on the part of United Technologies for its failure to accept the city's assistance which was offered in return for leaving the plant open; and then-Governor Dukakis expressing surprise and disappointment based on the fact that UTC had given numerous assurances that the plant was not going to be closed. The legal requirements of the Massachusetts plant closing law were also questioned, since they contained no mandatory restrictions on plant closing procedures but only voluntary actions. This raises the issue of whether UTC complied not with the letter of the law (they did) but with the spirit of the law.

The case was well-received by the Workshop participants. In opening the discussion we had an advantage because we were co-teaching. We began the discussion by one of us acting as facilitator and the other playing the role of Springfield's mayor. This allowed us to demonstrate role-playing before actually turning to the participants for their contributions. We had used this technique in the afternoon session with the "Floppy Disk" case and found that it was tremendously useful in encouraging the participants to become active. Although it was very clear that the participants were extremely bright and well-educated in their discipline, it was also clear that they were somewhat entrenched in the passive lecture method. Additionally, there were various levels of

405

English ability. In order to be chosen as a participant, one of the requirements English proficiency. However, some of the participants were not as comfortable with English as others. It was therefore difficult during the early days of the conference to determine whether the person you called on to play a particular role was hesitant because they did not understand, were not prepared, or simply could not express themselves very well in English.

After we completed our demonstration of the case method, we turned the rest of the morning session over to the Polish team leader, Professor Wieslaw Kisiel, who discussed local government in Poland and used the "Ordering Floppy Disks" case to lead a discussion. We were pleased that Professor Kisiel, who apparently had never used the case method in this manner, proved to be a "quick study" and lead the discussion with skill and style. Much of the excitement and interest which we had witnessed in our previous use of the case with the Public Administration team was duplicated in the larger setting of the Workshop.

USING CASE WRITING TO ENHANCE THE CASE METHOD

Based on the excitement we witnessed on the part of the Public Administration team when they were introduced to the case method and the fact that we were working with a highly intelligent, advanced group, we decided that it would be useful for them to write a case and present it to the Workshop.[6] We had brought with us a series of articles concerning the Pratt & Whitney threats of plant closings in Connecticut, which formed the basis for their case-writing exercise. In addition to this material, we provided the group with samples of additional Harvard Business School cases plus an assortment of cases which our Public Administration graduate students had written. At subsequent sessions with the group we provided additional material about Pratt & Whitney and further instructions concerning case writing. We particularly wanted them to be thinking about how the case could be integrated into their teaching, since this is the most useful and enriching purpose for writing cases.

On July 14 the Public Administration team presented its case, "Pratt & Whitney and Threatened Plant Closings" to the Workshop. On their own initiative and with minimum guidance from us, the team had developed a format for discussing the case which involved the entire team and encouraged active learning on the part of all Workshop participants through the use of role-playing. Each of the teams within the Workshop were assigned a role (Entrepreneurship was State Government, Finance was Local Government, Marketing was Pratt & Whitney, and Management was the Trade Union) and were asked to prioritize various decisions which needed to be made concerning the case (pertaining to employment, wages, benefits package, taxes and regional development). The teams were given time to meet and discuss the issues in order to agree on the priorities. When the participants reconvened, each team was given the opportunity to defend its position and the teams negotiated in order to reach a compromise. This negotiation process led to the identification of many issues which inform the discussion about business/government relations, such as the trade off between jobs and revenue, the impact of lower employment on tax revenues and government's ability to provide services, the role of government as a purchaser of goods (in this case, jet engines) with the corresponding significance of changed geo-political realities leading to loss of income for business, and the appropriate amount of "incentives" such as tax abatements which might be offered to encourage businesses to remain in the state.

To close the discussion, one team member, Professor Marek Fila, succinctly summarized many key points from the case: the conflict of interests; the "war" over money and the trade off between current exigencies and the needs of future generations; the importance of gathering all pertinent information before making decisions; the bias contained in the materials used for the case; and, most important from our perspective, the similarities between the situation outlined in the Connecticut case and the realities of Poland in its efforts to adjust to a market economy. Participants were quick to realize that the changing political climate in Connecticut and the United States, especially regarding the decrease in spending on military contracts which directly impacted Pratt & Whitney, played an enormous role in the plant closing case. They were also interested in learning how, if at all, Pratt & Whitney and the state of Connecticut had responded to these changes. At the close of the session, we concluded that the participants understood the connection between the case method and the problem-solving skills needed to successfully understand and address public administration issues.

CONCLUSION

In using the case method with an international audience of academics, it is important to keep in mind several points. First and foremost, we found it was essential to respect the talent and intelligence of the participants at the Workshop. These were our academic peers, so it was important to stress the use of cases as an additional pedagogical tool, which can enhance, rather than replace, their teaching methods. The participants had reached a measure of success based on formal lecturing and were not about to unilaterally discard the formal lecture in favor of the case method; there is no need to do so.

Second, language can be a significant barrier with an international audience. We found that we had to alter our initial plan to conduct the entire Workshop in English because doing so had the effect of dampening discussion on the part of many participants who were not fluent in conversational English. Since facilitating discussion is one of the primary reasons for using the case method, it was counterproductive to insist on English when that acted as a barrier to discussion. We therefore allowed the entire final session, where our team presenting its case to the whole Workshop, to be conducted in Polish. Although this made it more difficult for us to monitor, since we required an interpreter, it greatly enhanced the learning environment for the participants.

Third, we found it was very useful to understand some of the substantive issues which concern the international audience. Before attending the Workshop, Professor Sloan and I did some reading on issues such as local government and privatization in Poland. This allowed us to pick cases which we believed would address areas of interest for our audience. We were also fortunate to find the "Floppy Disk" case which immediately caught their attention since it was set in Poland.

Finally, from the beginning of the Workshop it was made clear to us by our team members that they were not interested in hearing only about the achievements of American business and how Poland could benefit. The participants were certainly intelligent enough to understand that there is something to be learned through trial and error; they wanted cases that dealt with not only the successes of business/government relations in the United States, but also the failures. The plant closing cases were particularly resonant for this audience, as Poland struggles with the dislocations of instituting a market economy after 45 years of communist rule.

I suppose it should be mentioned that none of these points differs very much from how you should treat any audience - international or domestic - respect their intelligence and create an atmosphere for learning which is both comfortable and stimulating.

ENDNOTES

1. The Consortium consists of The University of Hartford, The University of Massachusetts, Boston College and Columbia University. Other American faculty at the 1993 Workshop represented The University of Massachusetts and Boston College. This was the second such Workshop, the first was conducted in July, 1992.

2. The institutions represented included: The Jagiellonian University, including the School of Self-Government, Institute of Psychology, School of Public Health and Institute of Economics; The Academy of Economics; The Warsaw School of Economics; and the Krakow Academy of Agriculture.

3. Associate Professor of Public Administration, Chair, Department of Public Administration, Barney School of Business and Public Administration, University of Hartford.

4. Harvard Business School Case No. C16-92-1139.0 (1992).

5. Harvard Business School Case No. 9-386-174 Rev. 5/86 (1986).

6. In the Public Administration program at the Barney School, we often require students to write cases. As students gain experience in the analysis of case studies, it is useful to take it a step further and require them to write their own cases; the skills that they have learned in studying cases are thereby put to use. An added benefit to our program in recent years is that we have accumulated many excellent cases written by our students.

INTERACTIVE PROGRAMMING ENVIRONMENT
THE NIDE PROJECT

Anne-Marie Hugues
Muriel Walas
CERAM, Département Informatique
SOPHIA ANTIPOLIS FRANCE

Abstract

The CERAM group offers graduate and postgraduate programs in Management, Finance and Computer Science. The case study, we describe here, is used in the MS program in Software Engineering. It is a somewhat peculiar project in terms of its interdisciplinarity. It finds its place within the same discipline: Software Engineering. The reader will discover how the different software components interact strongly within a project just as the various services do within an enterprise.

SOFTWARE ENGINEERING

Programming has long been considered an abstract field for a "happy few." This way of thinking gave rise to the famous software crisis [Bro 75], [Boe 81], and demonstrated that introducing methodology while constructing software products had become a necessity. The vocable Software Engineering appeared for the first time in 1968 at a NATO meeting that took place in Germany. The first conference on Software Engineering was held in 1973 and IEEE Transactions on Software Engineering began in 1975. The terms began to be widely used in the early Eighties. We notice that it contains the word Engineering as in Civil Engineering or Mechanical Engineering. This analogy is justified: the completion of major projects as a dam or a space shuttle could not be carried out without a minimal methodology defined by Civil Engineering or Mechanical Engineering. All alike, Software Engineering emerged as an organizing force to define a set of **methods, techniques and tools** that guarantee the feasibility, quality and reliability of a software product.

As we can see, Software Engineering is a fairly recent discipline, some even say it is an art. Because of its young age, we find in software production some odd attitudes that would look odd in some older disciplines. For instance, we would be amazed to see a mechanic engineer make his own screws or wheels, or a bricklayer his own bricks. Until a fairly recent period, a software engineer could not believe his work could be reused by anybody in another context. Much time has been wasted rewriting programs which had already been written and tested, just because the software business was such an abstract activity that it seemed easier to redo than reuse... This attitude now belongs to the past, or at least we may presume so. We commonly speak of the reusability of programs and we see it as a quality criterion that will imply better productivity and reliability. It can be achieved by using an object oriented approach and is made possible by the use of objects libraries that software engineers can get from their enterprise, buy or get gratis from a network. This example leads us to detail the methods, techniques and tools which make Software Engineering.

METHODS

Software engineering has long been assimilated to a sole set of methods. Just because it was what was actually needed at a time where the anarchy prevailing in the field of software production required some kind of rationalisation. Just as a firm is organised as a set of units to produce a service or a product, likewise software production implies the definition of tasks each requiring a specific knowledge.

When we start out to build a house, we assume we have a proper design. We build it and test it to see for example if it is waterproof. A manager who runs an enterprise must have an objective and a strategy to reach it. It seems natural to do the same while constructing software products. Software engineering has to deal with a simple problem solving paradigm:

WHAT
      HOW
          DO IT
              TEST
                 USE

The software process can be described through a development life cycle implementing that paradigm. Various model of life cycle now exist [Blu 92] [Som 91]. All stress the necessity of sharing projects into well defined tasks. Boehm [Boe 81] first described the waterfall model, so called because it emphasizes the flow of the decomposition activities: each task must be completed, documented and endorsed before moving to the next one. Phases are organized in a logical fashion: steps that cannot proceed until a higher decision is made await that decision: i.e. the validation phase cannot start until the product is done. Each phase includes some review process by the whole team involved in the project (customers, technicians, experts, bankers...). Product acceptance is required to be able to use the output of a phase as input to another one. This organization is the result of rigorous statistics [Boe 81] proving that the later an error is found the more expensive it is to repair it. We could further our comparison with Civil Engineering saying that it is cheaper to move a wall on a plan then it is in real life. The process is iterative, i.e. if the product of one phase is not satisfactory, the whole phase starts again until acceptance. One of the management goals is, of course to limit the number of iterations.

Although the maintenance phase does not explicitly appear in the life cycle development, a lot of research is now being done on methods, tools and techniques to improve that phase. They tend to give more reliability, reusability and extensibility to the products. No wonder when one knows that about 60% of the budget of software engineering is concerned with maintenance, versus only 40% for the development of new projects [Lis 80].

The V life cycle (Figure 1)

The waterfall model has been then refined into the V model which we develop now. Whereas in the waterfall model, the output of one phase is used as input to only the following phase, in the V model, they are shown as going to both the next decomposition phase and the matching composition phase. So the preparation of the last tasks is anticipated (e.g. the preparation of the tests is made at the time we deal with the requirements since it is the moment we exactly know what the product is supposed to do). This anticipation induces the acceleration of the integration process and of the validation phase. Let us see each phase in details.

System requirements: this phase produces a set of goals and objectives that represents a response to a need. The hardware / software constraints are described. The major decisions during that phase are connected with feasibility. We then define how hardware and software will be integrated.

Software requirements analysis: the actual software development life cycle starts here. We express precisely the WHAT of the problem solving paradigm, which must fit the system requirements needs. This phase produces the first deliverable in the computer system engineering process: the system specification. It includes a functional description of each system function, the allocation of each element of the system; the constraints (quality criteria, time or space constraints, urge to use a particular software...) expressed in the previous phase are described more precisely, the cost and the schedule are determined. The man-machine interface is well defined here and the first version of a user's manual must be provided. The V life cycle model recommends to produce during that phase a validation plan, that is a way to prove that the software product fulfills the system specification (needs and constraints), this plan is a set of tests the product will pass successfully when it is done. It is most important that the customer (requester) and the software developer should agree completely on the result of that phase since all these documents are the basis of the contract they are signing.

High level design: from now on, the customer won't be much aware of what is going on. Whereas he was somehow a leader during the system requirements , he cannot master the HOW of the problem solving paradigm, i.e. which are the components of the system. Though it is most relevant for the customer to understand the importance of that HOW phase. Most of the quality criteria he(she) will appreciate during the maintenance phase will rely on the high level design. To further the analogy with mechanical engineering, we agree that a car driver does not have to understand how his (her) engine works, provided he can drive the car (through the user interface) and knows where he wants to go (the objectives of the system requirements). But what happens if the engine breaks down? He (she) will have to pay more or less and wait for a longer or shorter period depending on the design of its engine and the accessibility of its different parts. The methods used in high level design aim at only one goal: build modular software products [Mey 88] so that it facilitates their development, readability, extensibility and testing. This phase produces the description of each module and an integration plan which will be followed during the integration phase to obtain the final product. The integration tests are also defined during that phase.

Detailed design and coding: these are the highly technical phases, they must have been carefully prepared by the previous ones. We enter the fabrication process, it must be done in respect with the quality rules described in the quality manual on which the customer and the developer have agreed and that may fulfill some commercial standards.

FIGURE 1
SOFTWARE DEVELOPMENT V LIFE CYCLE MODEL

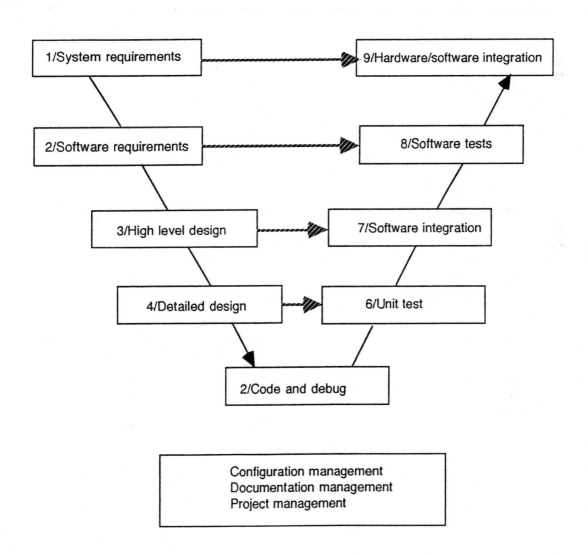

410

Methods used during each phase

The implementation of each phase relies on a few specific methods which won't be described here, we just give some reference for further reading.
- Specification methods (SADT [SAD 89], SART [WaMe 85]),
- high level design methods ([You 79], [War 75], [Jac 75], [Boo 91], [Rum 91], [ShM 88] [Tar 89],
- coding methods (which are actually programming techniques and will be discussed later on),
- validation methods [Mye 79].

These methods will be implemented through the use of what is commonly known as CASE tools.

TOOLS

The tool is useless if the method is not mastered. If you try to saw a tree in your backyard with a powerful chain-saw but without any predefined method, the tree will in all likelihood crush your house down...The reverse is true, if you ask a wood cutter to fell your tree with a diminutive saw, even if he has a thorough knowledge of the method, the job will take him ages... It will be even worse if he handles a hammer instead of a saw.

The problems raised by software engineering tools are the same as those described in the example. On the one hand, we see that the software engineer must be familiar with the methods before he applies them, and on the other hand to allow him (or her) to apply the methods he (she) must be provided with the adequate tools.

There are a good many Computer Aided Software Engineering tools which can be used in various contexts. They provide the necessary instruments to software construction and cover the whole development life cycle.

They can be federated in some kind of structure (Softbench of HP, Concerto of SEMA Group, Enterprise II of Thomson) or used in a tool kit manner. Here are some of them:
- Specification tools are the oldest and by the way the most widespread on mainframe and on micro computers (Teamwork, Graphtalk, STP, Foundation, Excelerator...). Most of the time they provide graphical editors and some of them can generate code in a high level language.
- Programming environments can be as simple as an operating system (OS) or a complete language oriented environment including a syntax editor, a debugger, a pretty printer, a compiler or an interpretor, cross reference display (Object center for C++, ADA environments...). The tool NIDE under consideration in section 3 belongs to this category.
- Tests generators (Mercury Interactive, ASA) and static analyzers (Logiscope, Battleware of Mac Cabe Inc...) enable the user to calculate metrics on the code giving information on its quality [Mcc 76].
- Configuration managers enable the reconstruction of multi-users, multi-machine versions of the same product [Tic 85] and are most valueable during both development and maintenance phases.
- Specific tools: Database management systems (Oracle, Sybase, Informix, Ingres...) [Kor 92], man machine interface prototyping (Aida, Architect, NSDK...) performance or charge simulators (QNAP SIMULOG), Local Area Networks (Ethernet, Novell), Wide Area Networks (Transpac, Bitnet, Internet), expert systems (SMECI of ILOG), real time operating systems (OS9).

Some other tools are used in Software development but are of general interest:
- Word processing software (Word, Word perfect, Framemaker, Interleaf...) is used to produce the associated documentation. Project management technology (Project of Microsoft...) helps managers to track and plan a project by use of PERT and Gantt diagrams. Groupware tools (e-mail, news, teleconference tools...) [Kar 94] also play an important part in the everyday life of a computer specialist and of any professional, since more and more time is devoted to that type of activity.

TECHNIQUES

Programming techniques are those which first come to mind. To the beginner, this term means writing computer programs. This technology has evolved dramatically over the last 35 years [Set 89]. If we agree that the first modern language is FORTRAN (1958), we easily measure the gap with today's languages (C++, Ada...). While the first generation of programmers wrote programs for computers to calculate, we are now facing problems of developing full information systems; whose parts may already have been developed and must yet be maintained.

Modern languages provide the programmer with some high level instructions enabling him (her) to express simply the problem to be solved. Moreover, they offer means of giving an ultimate description of a given algorithm and apply it on different types of data (genericity). They provide ways of implementing encapsulation of data and treatments, i.e. defining libraries that can be reused in different contexts [Boo 91]. To put it simply, we can say that nowadays programs are written to be read by human beings and not only to be executed by machines, and so for obvious quality and productivity reasons since we all know that staff costs are far ahead of hardware costs.

Networking plays an important part in Software Engineering. After the mainframe based organization of the seventies, after the emergence of micro-computers in the eighties, we are now heading toward an open system organization relying on telecommunication technologies and distributed computing. This progress has been made possible thanks to advances in computer theory and specially in the field of inter process communication and task parallelism [Mil 80].

THEORY

It is difficult in such a fledgling discipline that borrows from various fields, to distinguish technique and theory, all the more so as it is true that today's theory is the technique of tomorrow.

The level of nowadays programming languages (C++ [Str 86], Ada [Als 93], Eiffel [Mey88], ML [Mil 88]...) has been reached thanks to the efforts made in computer theory [Gri 81], language theory [Hop 69] and algorithms [Knu73]. Actually if it is now clear that readability is one of the major qualities required from a program, we must understand that it has been made possible only because more readable programs can efficiently be translated on the hardware. Research made in the sixties [Hop 69] [Aho 86] regarding syntax analysis have led to generic tools like LEX [Les 75] commonly used over the last decade.

The programmer's dream would be to give mathematical evidence that his program implements its specifications. Unfortunately, this property is generally undecidable. Nowadays research on programs semantics tend to obtain in this field results that can be compared to those obtained in the domain of syntax analysis. Directions are numerous for the research now carried out: formal specifications and automatic code generation [Jon 86], formal specification of the language semantics and automatic generation of translators [Kah 87], description of the behavior of a reactive system and automatic generation of the program command system [Ber 87].

THE CERAM M.Sc. in SOFTWARE ENGINEERING

THE FRENCH MASTERES SPECIALISES

French *Mastères Spécialisés* aim at training specialists with a solid theoretical background and a genuine industrial approach. These postgraduate programs cover one year and are designed for students who have recently graduated (with a french bac +5 degree or an equivalent foreign title) or professionals in continuing education with the same level of studies. This label is certified by the french Conférence des Grandes Ecoles.

PHILOSOPHY

The CERAM MS in Software Engineering with its 10 years' experience, and more than 300 graduates in activity is both the oldest and among the best of the french MS. It is aimed at training aims to produce developers of software applications, software tools designers, software development managers who will not only be able to find a job right after their training but still be efficient after 10 or 20 years because their knowledge of concepts will enable them to keep up with the technological progress.

Indeed we do witness at dramatic changes in the computer business. After the "roaring" seventies when anyone could become a computer specialist after a mere training in a specific computer language, there are now more and more unemployed in this branch and the market demand provides fewer opportunities more narrowly defined. The days are over for programming technicians; foremen are now required covering many different disciplines and viewing the future as well for the development of products as for their maintenance and the necessary investments in terms of staff, software and hardware.

If we notice that progress of fundamental computer science research are available in the commercialized products after a period of 5 or 10 years, if we bear in mind that it may take 10 years for the cost of some heavy investments in computer science to write themselves off; we wont be amazed to see such a discrepancy between the glamorous vision of computer science in research labs and the industrial world as it is with its constraints and compromises. The postgraduate program we propose, borrows from these two worlds and enriches itself from their relationship.

THE MS in SOFTWARE ENGINEERING PROGRAM

With so many different technologies, the mastering of concepts and methods will guarantee lasting knowledge. The program covers most of the disciplines of Software Engineering as well from the theoretical point of view as for the practical one. It is organized around different trends and is completed with an internship and projects.

Program execution environments
- UNIX environment development
- Man machine Interface (X-window / Motif)
- Artificial Intelligence
- Relational and object oriented data bases
- Networks (LAN, WAN)

Quality software insurance
- Software process (V life cycle, ISO 9000)
- Specification methods (SART, Entity Relationship Model)
- Object oriented design (OOA/OOD, OMT, HOOD...)
- CASE Tools (Teamwork)
- Validation techniques (reviews walkthrough)

Programming techniques
- Structured programming with C
- Object oriented programming with C++
- Functional programming with ML
- Logical programming with Prolog
- Parallel programming (Ada and Esterel)

Theory
- Finite Automata
- Grammars and compilers (LEX, YACC, CENTAUR)
- Logic and semantics
- Agorithms

THE NIDE PROJECT

Programming environments are among the most useful tools in software engineering. They are most useful during the coding phase and enable the programmer to write programs using a syntax-directed editor, a debugger, a pretty-printer and some graphical tools. The case study we demonstrate here is the major project of the MS in Software Engineering. It takes place after 3 months of basic training when students know object oriented programming and software development process. They must complete an interactive development environment for the NOGO language (Nogo Interactive Development Environment) which is a subset of the ADA language. The project covers a 3 months period and follows the V life cycle. To start with, the students are given the requirements and must hand back a fully tested and documented product.

REQUIREMENTS

As we often find it in industry, a prototype (CIDE) describes the software functionalities on a dummy language Calc. The language NOGO itself is described through its grammar and semantic rules. The list of constraints the product must fulfill is also given.

Prototype CIDE (Calc Interactive Development Environment)

The prototype is a programming environment for a desk calculator language. The language Calc has no control structure and no type definition or procedure calls.

FIGURE 2
DIFFERENT VIEWS OF THE SAME PROGRAM

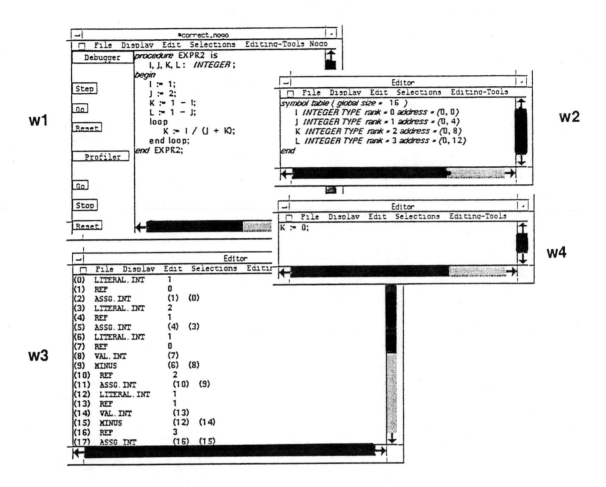

Among the functionalities of the prototype, we will underline the possibility of visualizing different views of the program in different windows using the given graphical interface as we see it in Figure 2:

• source code written in NOGO by the programmer (f1: upper left window),
• symbol table, list of the symbols used in the program which is calculated by the prototype (f2:upper right window),
• binary code (f3: lower left window),
• memory state during program execution, displaying program variables values (f4: lower right).

The interesting part of the prototype CIDE , that has to reproduced in the NIDE project, is that any user interaction on a window causes some kind of interaction on any other window with the interrelated components.

Example: we enlighten (using the mouse) a variable in the source code, it will be colored in blue in this window (f1), but as well in the window displaying the symbol table (f2), in that displaying in the binary code (f3), and its value in memory as well (f4).

These information are most valueable for the programmer since they may help to the debugging or the transformation of the program for instance to run it on a parallel machine.

FIGURE 3
SYNTAX DIRECTED EDITOR

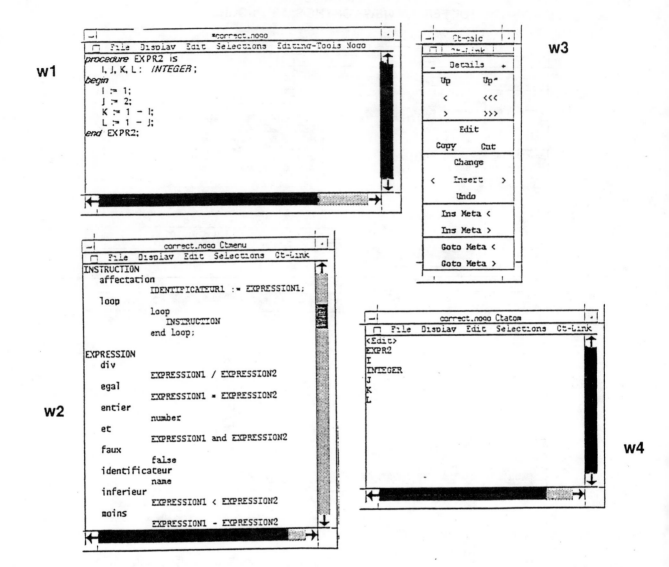

w1
w2
w3
w4

As shown in Figure 3, the prototype provides a syntax directed editor:

- source code written by the programmer, (f1: upper left window),
- Ct-calc menu providing insertion, deletion, modification of program constructors (f3: upper right window),
- Ct-menu menu provides the user with the different possible syntax elements at this point, that is done using a meta-language (f2: lower left window),
- Ct-atom menu provides the list of the different lexical elements of the language (f4: lower right window).

So the different syntax constructors are displayed in a window (f2), the different lexical elements in another one (f4). A menu (f3) enables the programmer to take some elements of the window (f2) or (f4) to build his own program (f1). This tool makes the programmer task easier, since he can avoid syntactic mistakes. The tool can also be used as a tutorial for the apprenticeship of a new language.

This prototype CIDE has been made by the CERAM professors using the CENTAUR interactive generator of programming environment [Jac 90]. This tool considerably reduces the time spent to build a programming environment for a new language. It is build above LEX and YACC and provides various meta-languages to define the syntax, the semantic, the pretty print . It works on an abstract syntax tree that represents the program.

NOGO language definition

The NOGO language definition is described with a BNF grammar and a list of semantic rules [Dio 87]. NOGO is an ADA subset with types and procedures declaration. The parallel aspect of ADA has been removed as well as the pointers, genericity and overloading which would have been too difficult to compile.

Constraints

The product must be developed under Unix, using CENTAUR [Jac90] and the text editor emacs in respect with the project development plan given at the beginning of the project.

Deliverables

At the end of the project, students must hand back a programming environment with the same functionalities as the prototype CIDE but for the NOGO language and the associated documentation (maintenance manual, reference manual, user's manual, installation manual) [Ami 94].

PLURIDISCIPLINARY

We have seen that software engineering is an interdisciplinary discipline. To teach it we had to find a project at the cross-roads between orthogonal and complementary disciplines. To go back to the classification we previously gave regarding software engineering, we look now at the pluridisciplinarity [multi-] of the project as long as techniques, methods and tools are concerned.

Methodological acquisitions

One of the objective of the *Mastère* is to give the student an industrial approach in software development. This project faces the students with actual industrial development conditions, the need of respecting a development plan, and taking into account the different constraints and insure the delivery of product and documentation. The student finds here the same context as in his (her) future job or internship.

As in an industrial context each phase is validated and a documentation is produced. The organization of the project (staff, planning, hardware, software) is the responsibility of the students who obviously must justify themselves with their professors. In this context the professors act as a manager, the part of the customer being played by an industrial partner. It enables the student to understand the customer-developer relationship. The project is developed in respect with the V life cycle model. The specification method which is used is SADT, together with an object oriented approach.

Technical acquisitions

The development of the NIDE project needs the use of different programming languages: ADA (whose NOGO is a subset), LISP (used to communicate with CENTAUR), PROLOG (through an experience of logical programming with TYPOL, a internal language of CENTAUR allowing the expression of the semantics in a natural way [Kah 87]), intermediate language OIL (Optimizable intermediate language between high level language and assembly language). The project being developed in a Unix environment, the students must use their knowledge in C. This project focuses on structured programming and object oriented techniques.

One of the most important problems in the 1990s is the definition and programming of man machine interfaces. The NIDE project provides the students with the opportunity of designing a graphical interface and let them think of its ergonomy. The implementation relies on Motif tools used through CENTAUR resources.

Another interesting point of the project is that it lets the different views of a program to communicate. This is made possible by using the software bus of CENTAUR, Shop talk [Cle 90]. Through its programmation the students get familiar with programming in a distributed environment.

Theoretical acquisitions
The compiler course is fundamental in a Software Engineeringcoursess. It is essential for us to understand how a high level structure is translated into machine code. Moreover, many software products leads to the translation of one language into another one, (command language, manipulation language...) The NIDE project gives a chance to see all the phases of the compiling of a language from the grammar definition to code generation and the execution. It uses modern tools of compiler generation (LEX, YACC, CENTAUR).

The students acquire the skill while imitating the prototype style which is a good way of learning specially in the computer field. This imitation is made possible only because the students have attended theoretical courses: graph theory, semantic and logic, meta language use.

CONCLUSION

The NIDE project will be further published as an annex of a book dealing with compiling techniques whose readers will be able to access NIDE via NFS. A further development could be to widen the scope of our project and find more interdisciplinarity in it. It would be most interesting to build a full development environment and include it in a CASE Tool taking into account the specification and design phases. We also plan to develop a configuration manager next year whose implementation will need the use of a data base that could be done by the students of the Master in data base of CERAM. We could even think of commercializing the product and in that case the marketing could be done by the students of the CERAM business school !!!

ACKNOWLEDGEMENTS

This project owes a lot to the CROAP team of INRIA Sophia Antipolis who provided us with the CENTAUR environment and their time and specially Gilles Kahn and Laurence Rideau. We also want to thank Bernard Dion, former Director of CERAM, and professor at the MS in SE , for the time he spent on the prototype. And obviously this project could not have been done without the generations of students who have helped to build it and improve it .

REFERENCES

Ada Reference Manual, Alsys, 1993

Compilers: Principles, Techniques and Tools, (Addison Wesley , 1986)

V. Amidi Nouri & Al, NIDE Manuel d'utilisation, dossier de specifications fonctionnellles, dossier de conception globale, (CERAM Sophia Antipolis France, 1994)

G.Berry, Esterel V3 Programming Examples: programming a digital watch in Esterel, Rapport technique, (Ecole Nationale Superieure des Mines de Paris ,Sophia Antipolis, France, 1987)

B.I. Blum , Software Engineering, a Holistic View, (Oxford University Press, 1992)

B.W. Boehm Software Engineering Economics, (Prentice Hall, 1981)

G. Booch, Object Oriented Design with Applications, (Benjamin Cumings 1991)

F.P. Brooks, The mythical man month, (Addison Wesley, 1975)

D. Clement, V. Prunet, "Proposal for a Message Handler based on Object Encapsulation" , (SEMA Group, Sophia Antipolis, 1992)

D. Gries, The science of Programming, (Springer Verlag, 1981)
J.E. Hopcroft, J.D Ullman, Formal Languages and their Relation to Automata, (Addison Wesley, 1969)

I. Jacob, CENTAUR, Manuels d'utilisation, The Mantle, The Crust, SEMA, Paris, France

M.A. Jackson, System Development, (Prentice Hall, 1982)

C.B. Jones, Systematic Software Development using VDM, (Prentice Hall, 1986)

G.Kahn, Natural Semantics , Rapport de recherche No 601, INRIA, Sophia Antipolis, France

A. Karsenty, "Le collecticiel: de l'interaction homme-machine à l'interaction homme-homme", TSI Vol 13 n0 1/1994, AFCET , France

H.F. Korth & A. Silberschatz, Database System Concepts, (Mac Graw hill, 1992)

M.E. Lesk, "LEX- a lexical analyser generator" Computing Science Technical Report 39, ATT Bell Laboratories, Murray Hill, NJ, 1975

B. Lientz & E.G Swanson, Software Maintenance Management, (Addison Wesley, 1980)

J. Mc Cabe "A complexity Measure", IEEE Trans , SE-2:308-320, 1976

B. Meyer, Object Oriented Software Construction, (Prentice Hall, 1988)

M. Miloni, A.M. Hugues, Interpreteur OIL Manuel de Reference , CERICS, 1990

R. Milner, "A Calculus of Communicating Systems", Lecture Notes in Computer Science 92, (Springer Verlag, New York, 1992)

R. Milner & Al, The Definition of Standard ML, ECS-LFCS-88-62, Laboratory for Foundations of Computer Science, University of Edimbourgh

G.J. Myers, The Art of Software Testing, (J. Wiley, 1979)

J. Rumbaugh & Al, Object oriented Modeling and design, (Prentice Hall, 1991)

Sommerville, Software Engineering, (Addison Wesley, 1991)

S. Shlaer , S.J Mellor, Object oriented Systems Analysis, (Yourdon Press, 1988)

IGL Technology, SADT un langage pour communiquer, (Eyrollles , Paris, 1989)

R. Sethi, Programming Languages, (Addison Wesley,1989)

H. Tardieu, A. Rochfeld, La méthode Merise principes et outils, (Editions d'organisation, Paris, 1989)

W.F. Tichy, "RCS- A system for Version Control", Software Practise & Experience, 15:637-654, 1985

J.D. Warnier, Logical Construction of Programs, (Van Nostrand, New York, 1975)

M.Walas, Description du projet NIDE, CERAM 1993, Sophia Antipolis, France

P.T Ward, S.J Mellor, Structured Development for Real Time Systems, (Yourdon Press 85-86)

E.Yourdon, L.L. Constantine, Structured Design, (Prentice Hall, 1979)

AN EXPERIMENTAL USE OF A SEQUENTIAL CASE IN POSTGRADUATE MANAGEMENT TRAINING

Adam Koch and Andrew Rodger
Swinburne University of Technology
MELBOURNE, AUSTRALIA

Abstract

This paper presents the experience since 1991 of using a certain category of a case, on an experimental basis, in one of the subjects taught in a postgraduate course at an Australian university. To enable proper evaluation of this experience, background information on the course and the students, as well as some suitable concepts and analytical tools are presented. At the same time, some cross-cultural aspects of management education are signalled.

INTRODUCTION

A case is a valuable '*connecting link which draws together the experience of the executive on the job, the executives (and potential executives) in management development programs, and the researcher in his efforts to understand the process of management. The written cases are catalysts to speed the process of learning from experience*' [Towl, 1969]. Most major case studies are meant to simulate some salient characteristics of the business environment, such as time pressure and limited amount of information, and help improve students' ability to identify key issues and construct practical solutions to the problems defined by them.

The current opening up of the Australian economy and its deregulation requires a more effective use of resources; in seeking optimal allocation of their resources and skills, many companies show an increased propensity to apply them outside the traditional confines of their market. Current major restructurisation of the Australian economy is seen as a necessary condition for the economy to resolve its external and internal debt problems. In line with the transformation of the business environment, the need for a comprehensive analysis of implications of such transformation on the framework and conduct of strategic analysis, was becoming more and more evident. In acknowledging this a recommendation was made in late 1990 to either find or write up a suitable case study for the benefit of Marketing Management 2 (MM2) unit taught at the postgraduate level at an Australian university.

The postgraduate business administration training program offered by that university increased since 1990 its emphasis on enhancing students' familiarity and skills required in successfully dealing with the demands of the contemporary international business environment. In particular, the decision was taken around that time for the course curriculum to assist the students in embracing the basic tenets of global competition and corresponding strategies that have seen an increasing prevalence in a number of industries worldwide. A case depicting a complex transformation of a domestically oriented company into one following the global concept was found to be most appropriate. Due to the acute shortage of case studies presenting such process in a broad perspective, a case on a hypothetical company (Blue Star Ltd) was written, in which subject convener's relevant business experience and the knowledge of authentic facts proved to be helpful.

The Blue Star's motive has been chosen to demonstrate how existing skills and resources may be successfully transferred to other product and/or geographic markets by companies that seek new sustainable competitive advantages. As Porter [1980] indicates, '*the entry into an industry ... of an established firm is often a major driving force for industry structural change... [such a firm has] skills and resources [...] different from those of existing firms. Also, firms in other markets may be able to perceive opportunities [...] better than existing firms because they have no ties to historical strategies and may be in a position to be more aware of technological changes occurring outside the industry that can be applied to competing in it.'*

The Blue Star sequential case not only deals with the issues of international business strategy, in themselves a formidable challenge to many students with no prior exposure to international business, but it also comes in a learning format far removed from those best known to the students in question. This paper attempts to present some problems in selecting and running this particular case and, to explain their origin. In doing so, we hope it may contribute to a better understanding of the guidelines one should go by in choosing the best case for a particular learning situation. We shall start from outlining the analytical framework that was used to decide about case difficulty. [The Blue Star case is available from the authors on request].

HOW DIFFICULT A CASE NEEDS TO BE

The degree of difficulty of a case is an issue of paramount importance, yet one that not always is given sufficient attention. In their study, Leenders and Erskine distinguish three degrees of case difficulty and describe them by asking the questions typical for every individual degree:

- *'Here is a problem, here is a solution. Do you think the solution fits the problem? Are there some alternatives that might be considered?'* (first degree)
- *'Here is a problem. Give me a reasonable solution.'* (second degree)
- *'Here is a situation. What are the problems? What are the solutions'* (third degree).

In a more analytical approach, one could compare cases by looking at three aspects of their difficulty [Leenders and Erskine 1978, 127], namely:

- a conceptual dimension
- *an analytical dimension*
- *a presentation material dimension,*

with a number of *difficulty ranges* available for each aspect/dimension. To assist in qualifying cases properly, the relevant ranges for every dimension would need to be defined operationally. A proposal of a case dimension summary by Leenders and Erskine (see Table 1) describes the kind of information to be provided in each case category, explains the meaning of the case dimensions and of the difficulty ranges in that context and also specifies the most pertinent specific learning objectives. We found this framework very useful in selecting a case whose level of difficulty would most closely match the requirements of a particular learning situation. Educational and professional background of the students, their relevant experience and career objectives, familarity with the case method as well as the learning objectives of the course constitute major feedbacks in this selection process.

CHOOSING AN APPROPRIATE FORM OF A CASE

Apart from a decision regarding the level of difficulty, the teacher also needs to determine the form of the case that would suit best the needs of his students at a certain stage. What are the options ?

Generally, we have two categories of cases: **comprehensive** (that incorporate all functional areas of a company) and **specialised**. Sometimes a third category of **minicase** is regarded as worth separate mention, as it is often a dominant form in the introductory stages of business education and does not require a similar depth of analysis. Most cases provide the students with essentially all data they are to work with, whereas *'in most organisational and marketing situations it is the creation or acquisition of the data that is the crucial problem'* [Cohen and Miaoulis 1978].

In selecting a case that would be appropriate for a certain learning situation, a number of factors needs to be considered. We shall refer to some of them in more detail here. **Determining the case study objectives** defines problem area(s) on which the analysis will focus and thus helps reduce the search effort considerably. A list enumerating a number of possible **areas of analysis** is shown in Table 2.

A relevant, general framework that might be used in developing a more accomplished method of selecting a most appropriate type of case and its degree of difficulty is presented below (Figure 1). Several simple verbal rating scales of the kind shown below would allow for each of the significant factors to be considered in the selection.

TABLE 1
CASE DIMENSIONS - SUMMARY

AXIS	CASE DIMENSIONS	RANGE	INFORMATION GIVEN IN CASE	EXPLANATION OF CASE DIMENSION AND RANGE	OBJECTIVE OF CASE
X	ANALYTICAL DIMENSION	1	— Decision situation, issue or problem; — Alternatives considered; — Decision made	This is what the company did. What do you think of it?	Develop ability to appraise decisions and actions.
		2	— Decision situation, issue or problem	This is the decision facing the company. What should they do?	Develop ability to analyze and identify alternatives, select appropriate alternative and present action program.
		3	— Decision(s) or issue(s) not clearly presented; — Background information supplied	Here is some information about a company. Do you think they have problems and if they need to make some decisions or set some policies? If so, which and why and how and when?	Develop ability to identify issues and alternatives and present appropriate action program.
Y	CONCEPTUAL DIMENSION	1	— Concept straight forward, "simple"	Almost everyone involved will readily grasp it with minimum additional explanation, e.g. chain of command, ratio analysis, batch or continuous flow processes, "push or pull" promotion.	In all cases of this dimension the objective is to give the reader practise in identifying, understanding and using the concept(s) involved.
		2	— Concept of medium difficulty; — Simple combination of concepts	Needs further clarification through class discussion or instructor. May also be a combination of several simple concepts, e.g. R.O.I., E.O.Q., funds flow, pro forma statements, authority vs. responsibility.	In all cases of this dimension the objective is to give the reader practise in identifying, understanding and using the concept(s) involved.
		3	— Concept difficult; — Cross functional situation or policy situation; — Complex combination of concepts	Needs extensive clarification. High likelihood that a number of readers may never fully understand. Could be a combination of several concepts, e.g. cost of capital, pricing, industrial dynamics, motivation.	In all cases of this dimension the objective is to give the reader practise in identifying, understanding and using the concept(s) involved.
Z	MATERIAL PRESENTATION DIMENSION	1	— Small amount of information; — Clearly presented	Amount of information required for analysis relatively small. Minimum amount of extraneous information. Relatively short case.	To work with the information so that there is minimum distraction from educational objectives under X and Y. Useful for introductory courses and cases addressing X2, X3 and Y2, Y3 situations.
		2	— Average amount of information; — Clearly presented	Some extraneous information given. Length of case about normal.	To approximate more closely real life situations and to give the reader some exercise at sorting information.
		3	— Large amount of information and/or not clearly presented or; — Crucial information missing	Considerable extraneous information. Long case or tough case because of missing information.	To force the reader to do his own sorting of material or to specify what additional information is required before a decision may be made.

Source: Leenders and Erskine, 1978

TABLE 2
CASE AREAS

Branding	Positioning
Business to business	Price
Consumer behaviour	Product
Direct marketing	Product definition
Distribution	Product development
Environment	Promotion
International	Retailing
Market research	Segmentation
Market planning	Services
New product	Strategies
Not-for-profit	

FIGURE 1
CRITERIA FOR SELECTING A CASE

A. **First-hand experience in solving business problems**
None   Very substantial

B. **Business education**
None   MBA+

C. **Career objectives**
No job changes   Change of industry & of job

D. **Gaps in individual skills**
No gaps in crucial skills   Lack of crucial skills

E. **Stage of the course**
Introductory   Final

F. **Depth of experience in using the case method**
None done   Extensive experience

G. **Instruction style**
Autocratic   Participative

H. **Depth of contact hours**
Minimal   Sufficient to all students

I. **Diversity of students professional backgrounds (in the classroom and in individual teams)**
Several diverse backgrounds   The same background

J. **Level of students' motivation**
Only minimal effort to be expected   Ready to fully stretch themselves

It would appear that **the degree of difficulty of cases to be selected should in general grow as we move to the right end of every scale** below.[1] Naturally, each of the dimensions or aspects of difficulty would require a separate consideration.

At a more advanced level, attempts are usually made by those responsible for selecting appropriate cases to provide a variety of case categories that would be capable of helping the participants in the acquisition or adequate enhancement of their analytical, problem definition and resolution skills. Many leading management education institutions spare no efforts in simulating in their courses circumstances that very closely resemble the relevant work environment. One way of approximating it would be by using so-called **sequential cases**. By releasing information on a certain business situation in stages, and having several separate discussions, one is likely to encourage students to do more research on their own, use other teams'/colleagues' opinions and ideas as inputs and modify their view of the situation as well as recommendations.

Obviously, the social context (eg attitudes to competition, strength of the desire to excel and the status of formal learning) and the educational philosophy play an important role in both determining the appropriate degree of difficulty and, in choosing a suitable form of a case. Considerable divergences in practice and expectations exists between various countries and different universities/teaching institutions. Postgraduate management training courses such as the Australian Program of Training for Eurasia conducted since 1991 by a consortium, of which Swinburne University of Technology is a part, furnish plentiful observations in this respect.

THE PROFILE AND OBJECTIVES OF THE COURSE

The course had its first intake in 1975. It was designed as an alternative to MBA for students who were unable or unwilling to commit themselves to the greater demands of the latter in terms of its duration, cost and the requirement at that time for at least one year of the MBA to be completed on a full-time basis.

COURSE STRUCTURE

Nine compulsory subjects formed the core of a the postgraduate course:
* 2 units in accounting and finance,
* 2 units in marketing,
* 2 units in organisation behaviour,
* 1 unit in economics,
* 1 unit in quantitative methods, and
* one capstone unit (Business Policy).

These were completed over two years (4 or 5 semesters) of part-time study. Whilst content has changed over time, the course structure has remained largely unaltered. An important contributing factor in its early and continuing success was the delivery mechanism. Nearly all formal tuition took time on a Monday morning, between 8.00 am and 12.30 pm, leaving the evenings and weekends to individual study and team work. This of course required time release from employment, and therefore the approval of the employer and often negotiations with the student's work colleagues. The result was that the conflicting demands facing the students were managed 'up front,' significantly reducing the normally high dropout rate for part-timers.

The backgrounds of most of the staff that taught in this course include periods of experience in business, consulting and industry. The course had therefore a distinct and strong applied profile.

STUDENTS

90% of the students on this course were university graduates across all academic disciplines; they hold management or supervisory positions in private enterprise or public institutions. The balance were very senior and entrepreneurial managers with outstanding work records, who had not completed an academic program at the university level and did not hold any university degrees. The average age of the students was mid 30's ranging from late 20's to late 40's.

Whereas, at its inception in the mid 1970's the course attracted students employed in comparatively large organisations, today a greater balance of participants is seen, from small to medium sized firms. There had also been a notable increase in the number of applicants coming from engineering and non-business backgrounds, such as the welfare sector, the performing arts and medicine.

The implication of this trend is that most professions now recognise the need to supplement and complement their respective academic discipline training with a competence in management skills and enhanced entrepreneurial capabilities.

Due to the variety of educational profiles, professional experiences, and career prospects, an accurate diagnosis of the students needs would have demanded a case-by-case approach, an option never seriously contemplated under the existing structure of the course. The decision not to offer a semi-flexible curriculum

424

(of a kind similar to one presented in the Appendix B) that could have accommodated the aforementioned diversity had had a paramount influence on the teaching philosophy and methodology in this course and had created some problems that could have been best studied by examining the feedback provided by the trainees during and after their Blue Star case experience. Indeed, some of them indicated that they were disappointed with a fixed curriculum in international marketing, that disregards the true variety of students interests and belies the complexity of the discipline.

INTERNATIONAL COMPONENT OF THE COURSE

The MM2 unit was a hybrid, composed of two independent subunits, Marketing Research and International Marketing, each taught by a different academic. The decision to combine and compress these two reflected the belief of the course convener that the basic framework of the course and its curriculum should not be modified,[2] the total number of classroom hours for the entire course should remain the same and the changes may only occur within the units taught.[3]

As there had been no tradition of a separate unit in International Marketing or any other international discipline in this course, chances of introducing a separate thirteen weeks unit in International Marketing or International Business at the expense of an existing unit looked rather slim at the time. It was believed that subunit convener's professional experience in international business from Europe would reinforce the practical slant of the course, add to the variety of perspectives represented by the staff and offer sufficient benefit to the students despite the briefness of the unit.

THE BLUE STAR CASE BACKGROUND

In 1990, an emphasis in the international segment of MM2 was put on demonstrating the specificity of international marketing, discussion of basic types of international strategies and, on teaching students some elementary skills needed in international trade. Due to vast discrepancies in relevant experience between the students, this approach could not satisfy many: it was old hat for some students, not much relevant or too difficult for some others.

The then Head of Marketing suggested building the subunit around a case study which was hoped to stimulate students to undertake a more active and more intense study of the relevant body of knowledge, and result in a very effective teamwork. The case to be offered was supposed to discuss the transformation of a company from one that followed the domestic strategy in business and then, through regio- and polycentric stages, has eventually assumed a global approach to formulating business strategy. After some futile search for a comprehensive case, or a series of cases on the same company, that would match the order, the convener decided that it may be both quicker, and more convenient, to write one.

In doing so, he leaned on his work experience, offering students an expert knowledge of the industry in question. In an attempt to test students abilities to carry out a substantial research, he deliberately restricted the amount of background information to be released to them. As the Marketing Research segment immediately preceded International Marketing, some desirable integration of both parts of the unit was likely to occur, in itself a worthwhile outcome.

To simulate the management environment and relevant strategic planning processes, a decision was taken to use an uncommon form of a sequential case. It was hoped that students will be thereby encouraged to revise their views and recommendations as they are provided with new bits of information and advised of new strategic directions considered or undertaken by the hypothetical company. Even though a sequential case of study requires substantial amount of work, the potential of so-called syndicates that form autonomous work groups with essentially stable membership and prepare major team assignments in most subjects throughout the course, was thought to be adequate for the task that included reassessing the Blue Star capabilities in a broader market context, evaluating various business development alternatives and market entry options, and recommending strategic directions.

CASE CONTENT

The hypothetical situation demonstrated in the case draws on the convener's experience. The case was developed to demonstrate some particular issues related to the simultaneous task of a very substantial business profile change and globalisation, undertaken under volatile conditions in the external environment and draws on the concept of **capabilities based competition**, that focuses on the non-specific skills and resources of a company (ie those that can be implemented in various product markets). When compared with more 'traditional' cases, it requires a considerable relaxation of the geographic and product market focus. The Blue Star case challenges the 'static' framework of SWOT analysis[4] and instead proposes a 'dynamic' one, in comparing the relative strengths and weaknesses between the companies that come from different product markets and/or geographic areas, which is a much more complex and difficult proposition.

LEARNING OBJECTIVES

A qualitative observational evaluation of students needs conducted by the convener in 1990 showed that a number of skill gaps or deficient skills needed to be addressed:[5]
- carrying out the 'dynamic' type of SWOT analysis,
- defining crucial capabilities (ie those believed to be most important in the market in question) and evaluating their strength relative to the competition,
- combining capabilities in order to create a new business entity that would possess a sustainable competitive advantage (SCA), or a number of SCAs, in a new market environment,
- defining the information requirements of the requisite analysis and finding some crucial information missing from the case,
- defining the feasible market entry modes and evaluating their relative attractiveness, including the assessment of accompanying risk(s),
- analysing general market opportunities in areas outside the product expertise of students
- proposing alternative ways of enhancing existing capabilities through a range of, mostly, organisational measures,
- understanding the influence of the information provided piecemeal by the instructor and the implicit assumptions by the students on the strategic recommendations made by them at every stage,[6]
- appropriately utilising the insights and differing points of view of other syndicate members in conducting the analysis and preparing the team report.[7]

To ensure an appropriate focus in their Blue Star analysis, students were then briefed on the associated learning objectives during the introductory session[8]

LESSONS LEARNT

The experience of four semesters during which the case was used (semester 2, 1991 - semester 1, 1993) had shown a considerable degree of uneasiness with some students through their entire Blue Star project[9], a reaction that we believe might be largely attributed to a high level of its difficulty[10] and the experience based expectations of Australian graduate students.

Often, their first reaction to the case was one of bewilderment; with all their work experience, most of them felt they should be given a detailed description of all steps to be taken in the analysis, together with a list of possible decision options. In trying to get their instructor to substitute this case with a more orthodox one, some of them would protest during the introductory sessions that they had never done such a case before. Their teacher's retort: 'That is exactly why you might need to do a case like this now' could not have modified these sentiments decisively. With some students this disposition was amplified by their tendency to minimise their study effort and aim at just 'getting the piece of paper,' as some of them have indicated during interviews conducted by Newton [1993].

It would appear that some of them might have regarded a case study in its more traditional format (ie fully released at the outset of the analysis instead of being sequential, posing moderate analytical and conceptual problems and requiring only minimal extraneous research) as a goal *per se* rather than a means of acquiring some practically meaningful analytical skills.[11]

TABLE 3
THE BLUE STAR CASE LEARNING OBJECTIVES

1. To show the relativity of strengths & weaknesses of a company not only with respect to various geographic area/markets/sets of actual competitors but also with regard to various industrial activities/functions and other product markets (potential competitors).
2. To show how some of the company strengths/specific skills may be successfully employed in new areas, thus establishing for it a new, sustainable international competitive advantage.
3. To demonstrate the meaning of an adequate marketing research and intelligence effort and an appropriate management and planning style for the success of a company turning international/global in the challenging and volatile world market conditions of the nineties.
4. To analyse a variety of geographic and entry mode alternatives that a company may contemplate today and to demonstrate that some of them are feasible, when an appropriate strategy is adopted and suitably implemented.
5. To show the need to regularly analyse market opportunities outside the normal product market confines of the company and suggest some practical ways of doing this.
6. To demonstrate how a long-term competitive position can be established by a company going through a sequence of moves and business ventures that provide the company with additional business experience, skills, contacts, cash and other resources needed to establish a suitable form of presence in some strategically important regions/product markets by the end of the transformation process.
7. To enable the students to carry out a self-analysis of their decision-making approach in resolving some complex business problems by looking at:
   - the impact of informational inputs on their recommended strategies,
   - the sufficiency and robustness of support provided by themselves, and
   - the consequences of the need to revise their strategic recommendations.
8. To compare and discuss student's personal recommendations with other syndicate members.

OTHER OBSERVATIONS

1. During the briefing session very few students were willing and able to ask questions pertaining to the techniques to be used in this case analysis; the percentage of those that subsequently sought some relevant advice during the convener consulting hours was around 10%.
2. Students were in general poorly prepared for class discussions, diffident and unwilling to contribute; the teacher's part in it was therefore often dominating which was neither intentional nor desirable. Some students thought that the instructor confused them deliberately by withholding important information they were supposed to find themselves.[12]
3. Many students mentioned the foreign background of their teacher in international marketing and, quite openly, the cultural insensitivity on the part of some students as possible causes of some interpersonal difficulties that negatively affected participation in class discussions; some of them were prepared to admit that their preconceptions and perhaps their prejudging this learning experience were indeed responsible for the major part of the problem.[13] According to Newton, some interviewees described their international business study as a parallel experience in 'inter-cultural dynamics' and suggested that 'you really need the right framework to learn from another culture [...] the framework involves patience, courtesy and interest in others.'
4. Very rarely did the students attempt to review the evolution of their focus in the strategic analysis of the international business opportunities for Blue Star, and their recommendations following the release of subsequent case stages.
5. External sources meant to fill in the informational gaps in the case were not always used critically enough: their selection of sources was at times indiscriminate and/or the information obtained was not duly processed so as to become useful in making robust recommendations.
6. Many students might have remained hostages to an educational approach in which analytical tools such a SWOT analysis are used in one, unmodified form that is applied to a vast variety of situations; they rarely come to uncover these methods' underlying assumptions, which renders these students vulnerable to some

misconceived usage of them.

7. Even though the case does not seem to be very difficult conceptually, still the relative unfamiliarity with international marketing issues[14] might have reduced some students' self-confidence and caused some passivity, inadequate preparation and timidity in class as well as little originality in their contributions.

8. Students interviewed by Newton [1993] reported that they found the contents of the International Marketing segment '*demanding but ultimately rewarding*,' some of them, though, were '*initially concerned about coming to terms with the unit and felt ambivalent about its merits*.'

9. Even though students' feedback regarding the International Marketing segment rarely contained comments as drastic as those referred to Cohen and Miaoulis [1978], yet their supposition: [...] *students value faculty members that make them comfortable: who give answers and direction, appear to be decisive, sure of themselves, knowledgeable about the ways of the corporate world, articulate, cool under fire, and who are able to handle large groups and difficult classroom situations*' would hold true for the leaning experience presented here, together with their interesting finding about the commonality of scapegoating as a form of group defence against a teacher considered too powerful by his students.

EVALUATION OF LEARNING BENEFITS

Over four semesters Blue Star seems to have achieved a fairly moderate degree of success. As no formal evaluation of its effectiveness could have taken place we need necessarily to found our conclusions on some written comments by students made available to:

- Newton (1993), while conducting his research in which he attempts to evaluate some aspects of the effectiveness of the course as a whole, and to
- the subject's convener in the form of written comments of the teams in their reports.

While this approach obviously lacks the rigour of a proper scientific examination, by referring to our prior diagnosis of deficient skills, we may attempt to roughly assess the relative impact of this learning experience on the level of relevant skills with the course students. It appears that with exception of two of those skills ("*combining capabilities in order to create a new business entity that would possess a sustainable competitive advantage (SCA), or a number of SCAs, in a new market environment*" and "*appropriately utilising the insights and differing points of view of other syndicate members in conducting the analysis and preparing the team report*") in relation to which no improvement in students skills could have been ascertained, in all other instances some moderate degree of skill enhancement with some if not most students/teams could have been noticed.

A particularly satisfying result appears to have been achieved in the case of "*analysing general market opportunities in the area outside product expertise of students*," where external contacts of the students have proven to be very effective in providing the needed extra information on the product markets embraced by the analysis. Even in the latter case, the discrepancy between the best and worst teams was very considerable, though. Due to the lack of practical experience in international business, most of the students were rather vague in: "*defining the information requirements of the requisite analysis and finding some crucial information missing from the case*" and "*defining the feasible market entry modes and evaluating their relative attractiveness, including the assessment of accompanying risk(s)*"; those with some relevant experience fared much better.

The degree to which each of the express objectives of this case study seems to have been achieved, is demonstrated in Figure 4 above.

CONCLUSIONS

This learning experience would have brought more benefits to the students had:

- their professional (but not necessarily educational) backgrounds been less diversified;
- they been better prepared to cope with intercultural problems when studying International Marketing [Newton 1993];
- their time budget would have been less strained (instead of being a segment of MM2, International Marketing should have been taught as a separate unit or indeed a string of electives to enable tailoring the focus to the needs of every distinctive group of students);
- there had been an adequate level of course integration and appropriate ways of encouraging and accommodating changes to the curriculum and individual syllabi in operation;
- a more focussed approach had been adopted (less learning objectives and topics to be prepared but more

in-depth examination);

TABLE 4
EFFECTIVENESS OF THE BLUE STAR CASE AS A LEARNING EXPERIENCE

1. To show the relativity of strengths & weaknesses of a company not only with respect to various geographic area/markets/sets of actual competitors but also with regard to various industrial activities/functions and other product markets (potential competitors): minimal improvement in demonstrated competence, with very few teams only.
2. To show how some of the company strengths/specific skills may be successfully employed in new areas, thus establishing for it a new, sustainable international competitive advantage: **good overall understanding by the majority of students who conducted appropriate external research**.
3. To demonstrate the meaning of an adequate marketing research and intelligence effort and an appropriate management and planning style for the success of a company turning international/global in the challenging and volatile world market conditions of the nineties: **two or three teams only have demonstrated sufficient grasp of practical implications** (had students spent more time comparing factual basis, assumptions, conclusions and recommendations of other teams, their benefit would have probably been much more substantial).
4. To analyse a variety of geographic and entry mode alternatives that a company may contemplate today and to demonstrate that some of them are feasible, when an appropriate strategy is adopted and suitably implemented: **a substantial improvement with most of the students, although many lacked analytical competence and , often, commitment to eg compare implications of particular entry mode alternatives properly**.
5. To show the need to regularly analyse market opportunities outside the regular product market confines of the company and suggest some practical ways of doing this: **general comprehension and support demonstrated, few practical insights however shared with the class**.
6. To demonstrate how a long-term competitive position can be established by a company going through a sequence of moves and business ventures that provide the company with an additional business experience, skills, contacts, cash and other resources needed to establish a suitable form of presence in some strategically important regions/product markets by the end of the transformation process: **most of the students were able to embrace the logic of at least some of the moves by Blue Star; only few attempted to grasp the entire idea behind Blue Star transformation.**
7. To enable the students to carry out a self-analysis of their decision-making approach in resolving some complex business problems by looking at:
    *   the impact of informational inputs on their recommended strategies,
    *   the sufficiency and robustness of support provided by themselves, and
    *   the consequences of the need to revise their strategic recommendations:
    only those equipped with inquiring minds performed satisfactorily in this respect; there had been no evidence of such analysis having been comprehensively conducted by any individual, neither in writing nor orally.
8. To compare and discuss student's personal recommendations with other syndicate members: **students in general were rather reluctant to expose their recommendations to their peers' critique (both outside and inside the classroom) and apparently not consider this relevant in preparing their report; some exchanges of views did take place in few groups, of which the convener was made aware.**

*   the students would have possessed higher order of skills in *divergent thinking*[15] and be at the same time less inclined to follow the Freudian *pleasure principle*;[16]
*   more time would have been spent on discussing some issues pertaining to the category of markets and market entry modes in question (either in preceding units or during extra workshops);
*   the co-convener responsible for the 'international' segment would have spent more time with his students prior to, and during the teaching period, trying to establish their weaknesses and fears and build mutual trust

and confidence in students;

- more adequate assessment techniques had been adopted that would have minimised the risk of students from the same team delegating the various assignments to one or more of their number rather than participating in a truly group analysis and solution generation.

It would appear that about half of the students failed to fully appreciate the need to resist premature closure on the problems signalled in the Blue Star case and the significance of taking on problems answers to which were neither clear nor certain (compare with findings by Cohen and Miaoulis [1978]. Most of these students seem to have remained in doubt as to whether this learning experience was what they actually needed at that stage of their study. In attempting to push students in their sequential case study as far as he would like to, the instructor realised that indeed full success requires a great deal of art, and perhaps, some luck as well.

On the strength of this particular evidence, resorting to the collusion to '*cling to a relationship based upon the security of knowledge and spurious certainty, rather than to allow the reality of uncertainty to intrude too far into the classroom*' [Jaques 1991] would have probably turned out on this occasion a safer option even if not necessarily more effective one.

ENDNOTES

1. The only notable exception from the general rule formulated above would probably be only necessary when accounting for the degree of students diversity, where a case-by-case approach would seem better suited.

2. The idea of a semi-flexible curriculum that could have addressed the need to accommodate the diversity of educational and professional backgrounds of the students as well as their career prospects has not been considered, due to its fundamentally different philosophical provenience.

3. Some students reported [Newton 1993] certain degree of confusion with regard to the rationale of the decision to combine two distinct segments into one unit.

4. The 'static' framework of the SWOT analysis is defined here as one in which only the relative strengths and weaknesses of the actual current competitors are assessed only, while the 'dynamic' one involves a much wider spectrum of possible entrants into the market in question, as a result of various changes in business environment characteristics, including the relative attractiveness of investment that may be affected by the ease of market entry and exit.

5. Obviously, the above gaps don't apply uniformly to all students; all of them were however common and important enough to guide one in selecting an appropriate case format and contents.

6. The sequential style of the case, with information being released in stages, all of them very concise, particularly lends itself to the demonstration of the above.

7. This list must not to be analysed in isolation from the structure of the course curriculum and the course objectives; some of the skills believed to be either lacking or deficient were necessary in the subsequent subjects, some of them seem to be an indispensable component of the professional competence in the nineties.

8. The above draft of Learning Objectives differs from one that was used initially in that it specifies some of them in a more detailed manner.

9. An unforeseen curriculum change that was introduced in the second half of 1993 has effectively prevented the International Marketing convener from carrying out an appropriate survey that could furnish relevant quantitative information; still the authors believe that the qualitative part of their study is far more significant.

430

10.   In our opinion, it would rank in the Range 3 on the **analytical dimension**, the Range 2+ on the **conceptual dimension** and the Range 3 on the **material presentation dimension.**

11.   No wonder, some of them would repudiate any less typical form of case. In their feedback, some other would attribute their positive grades to a lucky chance, which probably reflects their belief that a case with *'decisions and issues not clearly presented'* (Range 3 of analytical dimension) can not offer an adequate learning benefit.

12.   Similar observations were reported, for instance, by Cohen and Miaoulis [1978].

13.   A comprehensive internal study by Newton [1993] documents these phenomena.

14.   The percentage rates of students with some kind of prior exposure to international marketing usually varied between 5 and 15; students were supposed to study an international marketing textbook while taking the Marketing Management 2 unit.

15.   Divergent thinking is defined by Jaques as one that *'tends toward the novel and speculative, toward revising the known and explaining the undetermined'* [Jaques 1991].

16.   It essentially says that whenever some conflict arises between the demands of reality-testing and the demands of the more primitive values within us which seek for magical solutions, the latter will prevail.

REFERENCES

Charan, R., "Classroom Techniques in Teaching by The Case Method," Academy of Management Review, (July 1976), pp.116-123.

Cohen, A.R. and G.Miaoulis, "MBA Student Anxiety and Overreactions: Learning from Linking The Required OB and Marketing Courses," Exchange: The Organisation Behaviour Teaching Journal (1978, Vol.3 No 2), pp.11-19

Dooley, A.R. and W.Skinner, "Casing Casemethod Methods," Academy of Management Review (April 1977), pp.277-289.

Jaques, E., "Creativity and Work" (International Universities Press Inc., Madison Connecticut, 1991).
Koch, A., "

Blue Star Ltd: Changing a Business Orientation,"1991 (an unpublished case used in the course discussed in the paper)
Leenders, M.R. and J.A.Erskine, Case Research: The Case Writing Process (The University of Western Ontario, School of Business Administration: London, Canada, 1978)

Newton, J., "Learning from The Experience in Management Education," Melbourne, 1993 (an unpublished report).

Towl, A.R.; To Study Administration by Cases (Harvard University, Graduate School of Business Administration: Boston, 1969).

CHAPTER NINE

SIMULATIONS FOR PLANNING:
ONE TOOL FOR RE-ENGINEERING EDUCATION

Ronald R. Tidd
Syracuse University
SYRACUSE, NEW YORK, U.S.A.

Abstract

This paper discusses how commonly used software is combined with a flexible conceptual structure to produce computerized planning simulations. Prototypes are being tested in an advanced tax course for undergraduate accounting majors, although the simulations' technical and theoretical foundations generalize to many courses involving microeconomic decisions. The simulations provide a feasible, effective, and efficient means of integrating computers into the curriculum, in a manner that helps students develop the cognitive skills that are necessary for professional success.

INTRODUCTION

Many stakeholders support re-engineering the educational process, including the education of aspiring and practicing accountants [Arthur Andersen & Co., 1992 and Jensen 1992]. Like all business professionals, accountants require a different set of skills and knowledge to succeed in the information age that is supplanting the industrial age. Notably, they must have a foundation on which to build a program of life-long learning [Accounting Education Change Commission, 1990], and it is not apparent that our centuries-old pedagogy contributes to the construction of that foundation.

It is apparent that computer technology is one appropriate tool with which to build [Bonwell and Eison 1991, Kinard 1991, Purcell 1993, and Williams et al 1988]. The extant literature indicates that computers can enhance the teaching and learning functions by providing, for example,

- multidimensional feedback and guidance (audio, textual, and graphical) on a timely basis, and
- "housekeeping" for repetitive tasks (e.g., calculations) that otherwise divert constrained cognitive resources away from conceptual issues.

Properly designed computer assisted learning tools also support learning that transcends time and space. In an educational process that is reengineered with computer technology, accounting students become their own educators; professors become mentors and facilitators.

This paper examines computer simulations as one fruitful application of computer technology that provides numerous benefits. The simulations are 1) designed to help undergraduate accounting students in their second tax course integrate concepts from a variety of sources, and 2) developed with spreadsheet and word processing software that is commonly used by educators. Furthermore, the simulations' analytical structure generalizes to virtually any tax in any jurisdiction: economically rational taxpayers seek to maximize the net present value of after-tax wealth, given a statutorily-specified tax policy that comprises a tax rate schedule and a tax base. All tax planning involves strategically shifting components of the tax base to take advantage of differential tax rates. Thus, the methodology, like the technology, transcends time and space. The methodology also generalizes to many decision environments that rely on economically rational decision makers.

In the sections that follow, this paper develops a foundation for integrating computer technology into the curriculum by reviewing the role of and the costs and benefits of computers and simulations in the academic process. Then, the design and implementation of prototypes based on this foundation are discussed, with an emphasis on the ability to creatively employ commonly used software (spreadsheet and word processing) to prepare effective learning tools without expert programming skills. The outcome is a system that is feasible, effective, and efficient for a broad segment of business education.

FOUNDATIONS FOR COMPUTER SIMULATIONS

In the reengineered educational process of the information age, educators must be mentors and facilitators; students will be active participants in mediated learning systems that are delimited by creative applications of information technology, not by classrooms and class schedules. The demands of these redefined roles motivates this project's integration of personal computers and simulations into a tool for re-engineering.

DEFINING THE ROLE OF COMPUTERS

Computers have broad application to the academic process, as the following taxonomy suggests [Jensen and Sandlin 1992]:
- computer aided teaching, which involves an active interface between students and instructors in a classroom or via a network;
- computer aided instruction, which entails self-study with computerized applications; and
- computer managed instruction, which maintains course and performance records, provides test databases, etc.

While these are not mutually exclusive classifications, the taxonomy provides a useful and commonly used structure. This research focuses on computer aided instruction (CAI), which encompasses drill lessons, tutorials, and interactive dialog software. As discussed in a following section, CAI also includes computerized simulations, although that is not a traditional application and the literature is not extensive.

EXAMINING THE COSTS AND BENEFITS OF INTEGRATION

Irrespective of how they employ computers, educators must examine the costs and benefits before integrating them into their classrooms. The costs of integration can be material. The acquisition costs of hardware and software represent the largest resource expenditure [Frand and Britt 1992], although costs continue to decrease and there are significant discounts for academic purchasers. The incessant evolution of software and hardware exacerbates the problem, making it difficult for educators to stay abreast of the technology that graduates will encounter.

There are also costs associated with the design and implementation of course material. In an early generation of courseware (circa 1975) for example, one study reported that approximately 8,000 hours of programming time were required to develop material for an elementary accounting course [Helmi 1986]. This in not acceptable in an environment of constrained academic resources. It is also dangerous, as the existing faculty incentive systems do not support the necessary exploration of new methdologies [Frand and Britt 1992]. Explorers are at risk with respect to promotion and tenure decisions.

Those who do not feel constrained by the incentive system must still be sensitive to the costs that students incur. Out of control technological creativity impedes the learning process by first distracting, then alienating and boring students. Students can also be overwhelmed by the instructor's overzealous expectations for the assimilation of topical material and computer technology [Tidd 1993]. This can be problematic when students are required to jump between platforms (e.g., DOS to Apple to mainframes) during the course of their academic careers. It can also impede mastery of course material, as students focus on learning how to compute rather than computing to learn.

These costs are countered by numerous benefits:
1. personalizing study by removing constraints of instructor availability and class schedules [Bonwell and Eison 1991]
2. shifting laborious calculations and housekeeping work to the computer and outside of the classroom [Crookall 1988 and Williams et al 1988]
3. reducing the amount of time necessary to learn material [Bonwell and Eison 1991]
4. providing hands on experience with important technology [Williams et al 1988]
5. attracting the attention of a visually-oriented (MTV) generation of students.
6. leveraging resources by using media that is easily edited, stored, transported, and reused [Jensen and Sandlin 1992]

Most relevant to the re-engineering process, computers force students to become actively engaged in their education, while pushing educators into the background [Crookall 1988].

Item 2 warrants additional commentary. Novice decision makers lack the cognitive skills that expert decision makers use to solve unstructured problems encountered in the business world. The development of those skills is hindered by training problems that are too demanding with respect to content or solution requirements: a novice's limited cognitive resources are spread between problem states, solution goals, and ill-defined ideas about which solution path to take [Sweller 1988]. Properly designed computerized problems help develop cognitive skills by providing organizing structures and feedback that relieve the strain on cognitive resources [Kachelmeier et al 1992].

DETERMINING THE ROLE OF SIMULATIONS

The traditional business simulation presents a competitive game in which participants manipulate firm-specific price and production parameters as they vie for market share. Simulations can be more broadly defined [Thomas & Hooper 1991]:

> A computer based instructional simulation is a computer program containing a manipulatable model of a real or theoretical system. The program enables the student to change the model from a given state to a specified goal state by directing it through a number of intermediate states. Thus, the program accepts commands from the user, alters the state of the model, and when appropriate displays the new state.

Thus, simulations can include constrained decision-theoretic ("what if") models that accounting and finance professionals frequently use in micro-level planning.

Research suggests that computerized simulations are most effective when used to consolidate isolated concepts and principles into functional units (*integrating* programs) [Thomas & Hooper 1991 and Williams et al 1988]. They also provide exposure to a variety of situations tailored to meet the learning objectives. That includes risky situations where practicing professionals could lose life, wealth, or reputation, if it were not a computerized exercise [Jensen 1992]. Finally, simulations can help students mature intellectually [Arthur Andersen 1992]: the organizing structures, linkage between choices and outcomes, and the consolidation of isolated concepts contribute to the development of abstract reasoning.

APPLICATION OF COMPUTER SIMULATIONS

The computer simulations in this project are responsive to the theoretical foundations. They help students realize the general course objective of providing them with the skills, knowledge, and professional orientation that will help them engage in life-long learning. Concomitantly, the simulations do not place undue demands on educational resources, including instructor time.

DESIGN METHODOLOGY

The simulation design contributes to the learning objective by directing students' cognitive resources and energies away from solution processes and towards solution and topic concepts. In part, this is accomplished by including features that organize and expedite the solution process, including the mind-numbing calculations that permeate accounting education. These housekeeping and navigational features remain constant between different simulations, so as to minimize the technological learning curve. These features are discussed in the following section.

The design also relies on a conceptual characterization that is consistent with the course objective and generalizable across tax regimes and taxpayer types: every tax system comprises a tax rate and a tax base that are imposed by the public sector. Private sector taxpayers want to maximize the net present value of after-tax wealth, subject to the tax system. A taxpayer pursues this objective by tax planning that strategically shifts components of the tax base (**TABLE 1**) to take advantage of differential tax rates. Several different simulations have been designed within this conceptual framework. Each simulation allows students to practice with a different shifting concept or a different area of tax law.

TABLE 1
COMPONENTS OF TAX BASE

Tax Base Components	Examples of Strategic Shifting
Taxpayers	Transfer income-producing property to taxpayer with lower marginal tax rate.
Accounting Periods	Incur and expense research and development costs in period with higher marginal tax rate
Accounting Methods	Elect accelerated depreciation methods for periods with higher marginal tax rate.
Taxable Amounts (inclusions, exclusions, and deductions)	Invest in assets that generate capital gains or pay exempt income

SOFTWARE TECHNOLOGY

Educators are empowered by the evolution of software. Features previously accessible to skilled programmers, now are accessible to skilled (but not expert) users of common spreadsheet and word processing applications. The simulations in this project comprise elements produced in both types of software.

Spreadsheet software [2] provides the engine for the simulations and several enhancements that facilitate computing to learn rather than learning to compute. First, instructor-prepared pro forma worksheets provide an analytical structure for each problem (**APPENDIX A, FIGURE 1**). This approach allows students to focus on solution concepts rather than solution processes. It also ensures a structure that emphasizes the targeted concepts and introduces them to appropriate workpaper design. Second, user-friendly dialog boxes expedite data entry into the worksheet (**APPENDIX A, FIGURE 2**). These boxes provide a familiar type of interface, guide students through the solution, and counter deficient keyboard skills.

[3] Third, the completed worksheet (**APPENDIX B, FIGURE 1**), summary tables (**APPENDIX B, FIGURE 2**), and graphs (**APPENDIX B, FIGURE 3**) present multi-dimensional feedback on the consequences of each choice. For example, students can see the composition of the total tax burden and how tax burdens and after-tax wealth are distributed between cooperating taxpayers.

The most complicated part of the system is the series of buttons that help students navigate the simulation. Each button is assigned to a macro function (*macro*) that facilitates completion of the simulation in one of three ways (**TABLE 2**). The preparation of effective macros is simplified and automated by recorders that are included in modern applications. When activated, recorders translate the preparer's keystroke and mouse actions into the code that becomes the macro. While many educators will find it useful to understand the programming code in the resultant macro, it is not critical for success.

TABLE 2
NAVIGATION BUTTONS

Purpose of Button	Examples in Appendices
Activates the next stage of the solution process	"ALT #1" button, Appendix I, Figure A, which opens dialog box, Figure B
Provides feedback on completed stages	"Type of Tax" button, Appendix I, Figure A, which displays graph, Appendix II, Figure C
Presents help with a concept or consideration.	"Help" button, Appendix III, Figure A, which activates a Help Index (Figure B) from which to select a Help Topic (Figure C)

The custom help files illustrated in **APPENDIX C**, **FIGURE 2** and **FIGURE 3**, are compatible with the help files in applications based on the Windows operating system. Thus, they are a familiar feature of the current computing environment, that provide educators with the ability to present timely and useful guidance with pop-up definitions and hypertext (jump) topics. There is specialized software that simultaneously simplifies development and produces printed documentation. However, custom help files can be prepared with word processing software [4] (as these were) and minimal special skills [Boyce 1992], including the ability to use conversion software that is free from Microsoft Corporation. [5]

FUTURE EXTENSIONS

This paper discusses the output of the initial stage of a research agenda. A survey instrument will be administered at the end of the current semester (Spring 1994) to assess student response to the prototypes. Student and instructor impressions will then be used to refine the simulations for future use and study.

Subsequent stages will involve rigorous assessment of the effectiveness of the simulations as a learning tool. An experiment will use a between-subjects design, in which students enrolled in the course will be randomly assigned to one of two groups. Two experimental learning tasks (defined by two different conceptually and computationally demanding tax topics) will be devised. Each group will be a treatment group for one task and a control group for the other task. Both groups will be presented with the same problems for each task. The treatment group will use simulations, while the control group will solve the problems. To measure learning under the different formats, a test over the subject matter will be administered to each group immediately after completion of the learning task. Demographic data will be collected and used with the performance measure in a co-variance analysis.

Alumni who were educated with the methodology will be surveyed approximately one year after graduation. The survey instrument will reflect a bifurcated interest with respect to the simulations. The primary interest is whether the methodology contributed to the expert problem solving skills that they used during the first year of employment. The secondary interest is whether the simulations helped with computer skills and work habits/techniques.

ENDNOTES

1. The topics include the allocation of tax brackets between related corporations, the timing of gratuitous transfers, owner-officer compensation, and distributions by complex trusts.

2. Excel for Windows version 5.0.

3. This is a critical feature for the assessment stage of the research agenda when the efficacy and efficiency of the methodology is evaluated.

4. Word for Windows version 6.0.

5. Microsoft Excel Custom Help File Conversion Utility, from Microsoft Product Support Services.

REFERENCES

Accounting Education Change Commission. Objectives of Education for Accountants (Position Statement No. One). (Torrance, CA: Author., 1990).

Arthur Andersen & Co. (1992). Critical Thinking, Interactive Learning, and Technology: Reaching for Excellence in Business Education, Thomas J. Frecka, ed. (Chicago: Author, 1992).

Bonwell, C. C. and J. A. Eison. Active Learning: Creating Excitement in the Classroom, ASHE-ERIC Higher

438

Education Reports , no. 1 (The Georgre Washington University School of Education and Human Development, 1991).

Frand, J. L., and J. A. Britt. Where are Business Schools in the Process of Computerization? Ninth Annual UCLA Survey of Business School Computer Usage (The John E. Anderson Graduate School of Management at UCLA, 1992).

Helmi, M. A. "Integrating the Microcompuer Into Accounting Education- Approaches and Pitfalls," Issues in Accounting Education, (Spring 1986), pp. 102-111.

Jensen. R. E. "The Paradign Shift in Technology and Learning: Teaching Will Never Be the Same." Unpublished manuscript, Trinity University, Department of Business Administration, San Antonio, 1992.

Jensen, R. E., and P. Sandlin. "Why Do It? Advantages and Dangers of New Waves of Computer-Aided Teaching/Instruction." Unpublished manuscript, Trinity University, Department of Business Administration, San Antonio, 1992.

Kachelmeier, S. J., J. D. Jones, and J. A. Keller, "Evaluating the Effectiveness of a Computer-Intensive Learning Aid for Teaching Pension Accounting," Issues in Accounting Education (Fall 1992), pp. 164-178.

Purcell, J. D. "Designing New Learning Environments," Technical Horizons in Education Journal, (Autodesk, 1993), pp. 2-3.

Sweller, J., "Cognitive Load During Problem Solving: Effects on Learning, "Cognitive Science (April-June 1988), pp. 257-285.

Thomas, R. and E. Hooper, "Simulations: An Opportunity We Are Missing," Journal of Research on Computing in Education, (Summer 1991), pp. 497-513.

Tidd, R. R. "Integrating Computer Technology into the Tax Curriculum: Stage One," in Proceedings of The 21st Annual Conference of the International Business Schools Computing Association (Denver, July 25, 1993), pp. 485 - 491.

Williams, J. R., H. C. Herring III, J. H. Scheiner, and M. G. Tiller, Framework for the Development of Accounting Education Research, Accounting Education Series, Vol. 9 (American Accounting Association, 1988)

Appendix A

Pro Forma Workpapers

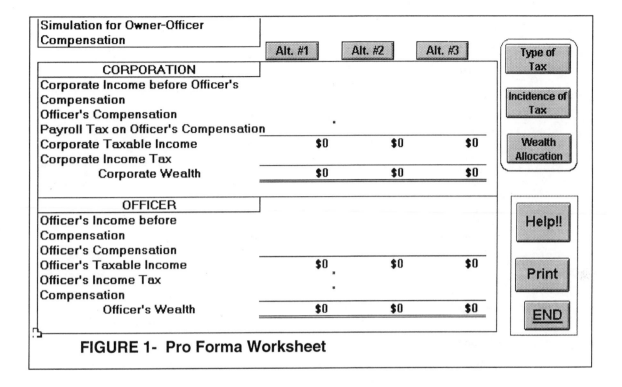

FIGURE 1- Pro Forma Worksheet

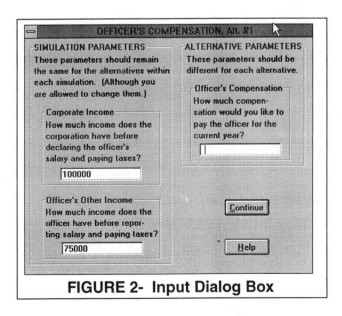

FIGURE 2- Input Dialog Box

Appendix B

Feedback and Output

CORPORATION			
Corporate Income before Officer's Compensation	$100,000	$100,000	$100,000
Officer's Compensation	($75,000)	($60,000)	($45,000)
Payroll Tax on Officer's Compensation	($4,400)	($4,400)	($3,600)
Corporate Taxable Income	$20,600	$35,600	$51,400
Corporate Income Tax	($3,090)	($5,340)	($7,850)
Corporate Wealth	$17,510	$30,260	$43,550
OFFICER			
Officer's Income before Compensation	$75,000	$75,000	$75,000
Officer's Compensation	$75,000	$60,000	$45,000
Officer's Taxable Income	$150,000	$135,000	$120,000
Officer's Income Tax	($39,930)	($35,280)	($30,630)
Payroll Tax on Officer's Compensation	($4,400)	($4,400)	($3,600)
Officer's Wealth	$105,670	$95,320	$85,770

FIGURE 1- Completed Pro Forma Worksheet

TYPE OF TAX	#1	#2	#3
INCOME TAX	$43,020	$40,620	$38,480
PAYROLL TAX	$8,800	$8,800	$7,200
	$51,820	$49,420	$45,680
INCIDENCE OF TAX	#1	#2	#3
CORPORATE TAXES	$7,490	$9,740	$11,450
INDIVIDUAL TAXES	$44,330	$39,680	$34,230
	$51,820	$49,420	$45,680
WEALTH ALLOCATION	#1	#2	#3
GOVERNMENT	$51,820	$49,420	$45,680
CORPORATE	$17,510	$30,260	$43,550
INDIVIDUAL	$105,670	$95,320	$85,770
	$123,180	$125,580	$129,320

FIGURE 2- Summary Table

Appendix B

Feedback and Output

(continued)

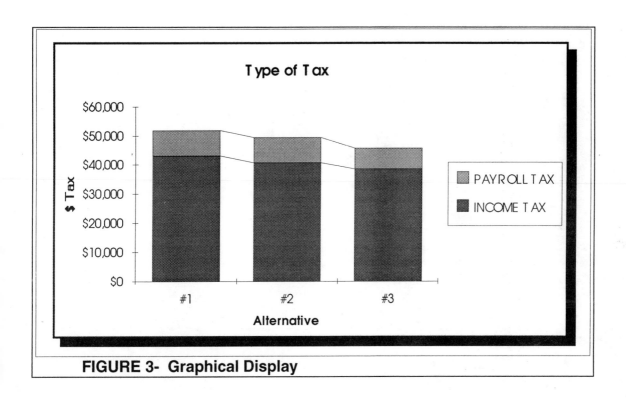

FIGURE 3- Graphical Display

Appendix C

Navigation and Help

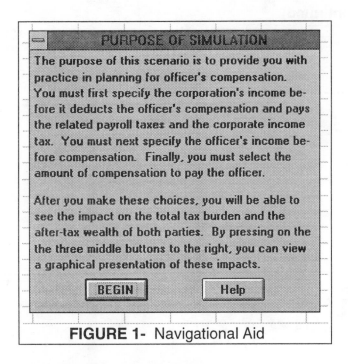

FIGURE 1- Navigational Aid

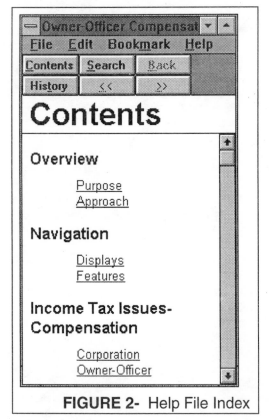

FIGURE 2- Help File Index

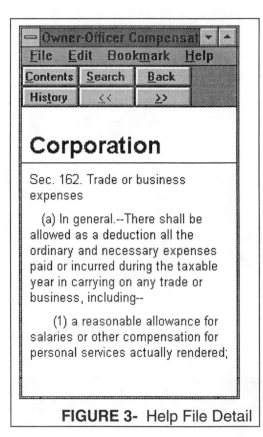

FIGURE 3- Help File Detail

THE PRODUCTION OF CASE STUDIES ON THE MANAGEMENT OF COOPERATIVES: THE EXPERIENCE OF THE ÉCOLE DES HÉC IN MONTREAL

Marie-Claire Malo
École des Hautes Études Commerciales, Montreal
MONTREAL, QUEBEC, CANADA

Abstract

The École des HÉC has the indisputable merit of being the Francophone institution with the longest tradition of teaching in the management of cooperatives, while also being the most important producer of case studies in this field.

In order to gain a better understanding of this comparative advantage and to acquaint others with it, we have analyzed the production of case studies on cooperatives at this management school. Our goal was to highlight the characteristics of case study production in this institution, and, in particular, to expose the prime conditions of success which have prevailed there. Each corpus of case studies has both a starting point: the need for pedagogical material, and an end point: its use in class. The research and writing up of cases take place in between these two points.

In terms of teaching itself, following an unsuccessful attempt to introduce courses on the management of cooperatives as a permanent part of the bachelor's program in business administration (a three-year undergraduate program of day classes), "cooperativology" finally found its niche in the certificate program (evening classes). The course "Gestion et organisation des coopératives" has been offered at the HÉC since 1979. With the support of research assistants working at the *Centre de gestion des coopératives*, founded in 1975, a first series of cases studies was realized for the purposes of this new course. From the beginning, the Centre has always constituted a source of support for the research and writing up of case studies dealing with the distinctive features of the management of cooperative associations. The production of cases was stimulated on the one hand by a number of conferences (for example, "Stratégie et organisation de l'entreprise coopérative", "Les coopératives de travail pour le maintien et la création d'emplois", etc.), and on the other hand by research projects (for example, "Pratiques de sélection des membres dans les coopératives d'habitation"). A thematic analysis in the series "Coopératism", published by the former *Centrale des cas*, reveals the existence of case studies in all cooperative sectors. Although each cooperative organization can be said to be the "combination of an association of individuals and of a business reciprocally linked by a double relation of activities and membership" [Vienney, 1980], there are also different types of cooperatives which have their own corresponding "cooperativized functions", including stock management in the case of suppliers' cooperatives, human resources management in employee cooperatives, and marketing in client cooperatives [Malo, 1979 and 1983]. Cases which examine the practices specific to cooperatives generally address the "cooperativized" function and the function of relations with members, both of which are common to all associative bodies and which forcibly interface with one another [Malo, 1991].

With the exception of the sector of cooperatives of financial institutions, the offer of cases generally exceeds the demand for cases. In order to understand this apparent imbalance, it is important to recall that the student population has shifted from the "new" to the "old" type of cooperatives; meaning from those emerging out of new social movements (ex.: democracy of users and workers) toward those linked to the movement of economic nationalism [B. Lévesque, 1991]. In the class "Gestion et organisation des coopératives", employees of the Desjardins credit unions now form the dominant group. To adjust the offer to this new demand, we are seeing

444

a refocusing of the production of case studies on savings and credit unions, thanks to the initiative of the professor who teaches this course and to the director of the *Centre de gestion des coopératives*. The experience of the École des HÉC thus reveals a dynamism characterized by innovation, by the contribution to a new field of knowledge, and by the capacity to adapt to the evolution of demand in the milieu.

This overview of the situation brings to light one of the first conditions of success for the production of case studies on the management of cooperatives: the relationship between the writing of cases and specialized research linked to the field itself of cooperative organizations. The experience of the HÉC is also characterized by a second condition of success: that of institutional support in the process of generating cases, but not only in terms of financing the salaries of research assistants or of reducing professors' teaching loads to allow them time to write up cases. Indeed, until quite recently, services related to the case study method at the HÉC's *Centrale de cas et de documents pédagogiques* had the precious advantage of being organized according to the "one-stop service" model. However, recent budget cuts have put an end to the existence of this central unit, and the various services have been, or will be, redistributed among other internal or peripheral units in the school, in order to continue the implementation of a policy of institutional support. For example, linguistic revision may come under the responsibility of the direction of the quality of communication, while the diffusion of cases has been conferred on the *Coop HÉC*, which is the largest cooperative in the teaching milieu in Quebec and which has offered an order service for specialized books on administration for several years.

Thus, three institutional aspects cohabit in the process of the lasting development of case studies in the management of cooperatives: a specialized research centre which maintains relations with a milieu having specific practices; the backing of support services at the different stages of the process; and a study program which offers the ideal site for the diffusion of case studies; that site being the class of students who either work or intend to work in the field where the practices exposed in the cases are encountered. It goes without saying that the institutional approach privileged here to derive the conditions of success of the production of case studies in the management of cooperatives in no way detracts from the individual and personalized approach, according to which other elements also contribute to the success of the process. These additional elements include the quality of the relationship of the professor-researcher with practitioners, with support service employees and with students [Malo and Poulin, 1993]. Certainly, transferring the experience of the HÉC requires that one take into account both the institutional and the interpersonal aspects of the case study development process. It also requires that one draw on Quebec's especially rich expertise in cooperation, [Lévesque and Malo, 1991], and, in particular, on the École des HÉC's specialization in the management of cooperatives [Malo, 1988].

REFERENCES

Lévesque, B., Les coopératives au Québec : deux projets pour une société distincte) Collection des Cahiers de la Chaire de coopération Buy-Bernier de l'Université du Québec à Montréal, 1991).

Lévesque, B. and M.-C. Malo, "Quel avenir pour la recherche universitaire sur les coopératives?", Revue des études coopératives, mutualistes et associatives (n° 39, 3rd semester, 1991), pp. 87-99.

Malo, M.-C., "Managing the Co-operative Association", pp. 71-82 in Bold and Hammond, Empowerment Through Co-operatives (Canadian Association for Studies on Co-operatives, 1991).

Malo, M.-C., "Le point sur la recherche en gestion des coopératives à HÉC", pp. 23-41 in Gibbs, La recherche sur les coopératives (Collection des Cahiers de l'Association canadienne française pour l'avancement des sciences, 1988).

Malo, M.-C., La fonction de relations avec les membres : champ d'activités et structuration (Collection des Cahiers du Centre de gestion des coopératives de l'École des HÉC de Montréal, 1983).

Malo, M.-C., Une typologie des coopératives : associations et entreprises (Collection des Cahiers du Centre de gestion des coopératives de l'École des HÉC de Montréal, 1979).

Malo, M.-C. and A. Poulin, L'écriture d'un cas de caisse populaire (forthcoming, Proceedings of the CIRIEC-

Canada, 1993).

Vienney, C., <u>Socio-économie des organisations coopératives</u> (Édition de la Coopérative d'information et d'édition mutualiste de Paris, 1980).

COMPUTER VISUALIZATION IN TEACHING MATHEMATICS: A CASE OF LEARNING BY DOING

Yuanqian Chen
Central Connecticut State University
NEW BRITAIN, CONNECTICUT, U.S.A.

Abstract

Computer graphics plays an important role in improving students' logic and deductive skills. Computer software "Tarski's World" is one of first software which aim at helping students with their logic and reasoning abilities. It provides an environment where students could visualize abstract logic concepts. Moreover, students may learn logic rules and theorems by creating their own environments and by playing games with computers. We will analyze this software, especially its features of connecting logic laws and their meanings by visualization and its interactive features that encourage learning by doing.

INTRODUCTION

Mathematicians have long been aware of the value of visual tools both for teaching and as heuristics for mathematical discovery. Recent progress in computer graphics has generated a renaissance of interest in visual representation and visual thinking in mathematics. The development of many excellent computer software, such as Maple, Mathematica, and Derive, enables mathematicians to help students learn mathematics concepts through computers and graphing calculators. Visual thinking and development of visual tools through computer graphics could make major contribution to mathematics education.

So far, most of the use of computers as visualization tools in teaching mathematics falls in the areas of calculus, linear algebra, and differential equations, where graphing is essential in developing concept. One of the most successful use of computer visualization in teaching mathematics is calculus. Mathematical educators working with "calculus reform" have been tremendously successful in introducing computers and graphical calculators in teaching calculus. The Harvard Calculus Consortium, which has been one of the leading groups in the calculus reform, has proposed the "rule of three" in teaching calculus: every topic should be presented geometrically, numerically, and algebraically. They continually encourage students to think about geometrical and numerical meaning of what they are doing. As they put it "it is not our intention to undermine the purely algebraic aspect of calculus, but rather to reinforce it by giving meaning to the symbols" [3]. Computer software and graphing calculator provide excellent tools in implementation of geometrical presentation of mathematics concept. The impressive graphing ability of computer software in two dimensional plane and three dimensional space has made visualization of concept much easier and brought tremendous change in the way many mathematics subjects were taught.

The success of using computers in teaching calculus can be attributed partly to the nature of calculus itself: many ideas of calculus were developed by graphs and numerical tables, and mathematicians have been using graphs to teach calculus since the subject was born. Graphs and other visualization methods have been integral parts in teaching calculus, and the development of computer software makes graphing easier and more flexible. However, unlike calculus, many areas of mathematics deal with reasoning techniques where formal rules and symbols are very important, and graphing is not an integral part in developing such mathematics concepts, and hence visualization does not come naturally and easily as it does in calculus where visualization in a two dimensional plane and a three dimensional space plays an important part in understanding the concepts. This brings up a question: what can computer software do to help students learn abstract concepts and deductive skills?

One of such areas is logic which deals with theory of deduction and reasoning. In logic, students learn why some reasoning is correct and other reasoning is faulty, and become skilled at telling one from the other. The deductive theory is implemented by the language of first-order logic which is precise and rigorous. Logic is offered at different levels of mathematics, from introduction of logic in high school mathematics to symbolic logic at the graduate level. As a foundation of many branches of mathematic, logic is used whenever a rational inquiry is needed. The development of logic concepts is based on formal rules.

Logic is regarded by many students as hard and abstract. When students study logic, they often leave a first course in logic having learned what seem like a bunch of useless formal rules. They may have little understanding about why those rules, rather than some others are used. And they are unable to take any of what they have learned and use it in other fields of rational inquiry. Indeed, many come away convinced that logic is both arbitrary and irrelevant. The real problem, as Barwise and Etchemendy put it, is a failure on the part of logicians to find a simple way to explain the relationship between meanings and laws of logic [4]. In particular, we do not succeed in conveying how the meanings of sentences govern different methods of inference, and which are valid and which are not. It is this problem that mathematicians try to solve with computer visualization such as Tarski's World, and its approaches are innovative and inspiring.

This paper examines the roles visualization plays in teaching formal language and reasoning skills. We will examine the case of using computer program Tarski's World and study the roles played by computer graphics in teaching logic skills: description of subjects and their relations, constructions of counter examples and active learning process of playing games with computers.

BACKGROUND

Tarski's World is motivated by what the creators see as a failure of existing text books on logic to show that the study of a formal language provides the means by which we can understand the relationship between meaning and logic. The creators of Tarski's World have two main aims, to introduce a formal language of first-order logic and then to use it to teach the notion of logical consequence.

In logic, one needs to learn a new language, the language of first order logic. Like Latin, this language is not spoken, but unlike Latin, it is used every day by mathematicians, philosophers, computer scientists, linguists, and practitioners of artificial intelligence. The mastery of the language of first order logic is essential in studying logic. The language has emerged over the past hundred years. In the late 19th century, Gottlob Frege, Giuseppe Peano, and Charles Sanders Peirce independently came up with the most important elements of the language, known as the quantifiers. Since then, there has been a process of standardization and simplification, resulting in the language in its present form. It is used in mathematics and other areas where absolute clarity, rigor, and lack of ambiguity are essential. The very idea of artificial language that is precise, yet rich enough to program computers, was inspired by the language of first order logic.

There are two ways to learn a second language. One is to learn how to translate sentences of one's native language. The other way is to learn by use language directly. In teaching logic, the first way has always been the prevailing method of instruction. There are serious problems with this approach. Some of the problems stem from the simplicity, precision, and elegance of the language of first order logic. This results in a distracting mismatch between the student's native language and the language of the first of logic. It forces students trying to learn logic to be sensitive to subtleties of their native language that normally go unnoticed. While this is useful, it often interferes with the learning of the language of first order logic. Students mistake complexities of their native tongue for complexities of the new language they are learning.

The computer program Tarski's World adopts the second method for learning first order language. Students will be given many tasks involving the language, tasks that will help them understand the meanings of sentences in the language. Only then will students be asked to translate between English and first order language. Correct translation involves finding a sentence in the target language whose meaning approximates, as closely as possible, the meaning of the sentence being translated. To do this well, a translator must be fluent in both languages. Tarski's World provides a simple environment in which the language of first order logic can be used in many of the ways that we use our native language. In this environment (it is called a "world" in Tarski's World), students will learn how to put the language to more sophisticated uses. This environment is also used to demonstrate the meaning of logic laws.

THE PROGRAM

The program itself supports an interpreted first-order language for a logic which is first order with equality. It has three main components, a "World module", a "Sentences module", and a "Keyboard module", each of which occupies one of three windows that appear on the screen when the program is run.

The World module displays a picture of a world, a Tarski's world, that displays certain objects: cubes, tetrahedra, and dodecahedra and certain relationships among them like being Large, Larger, LeftOf, or BackOf. This world provides, in a very direct and easy to understand way, an interpretation for the sentences which appear in the Sentences module. The Sentences module displays a list of sentences that can be checked for well-formedness, sentencehood, and truth in the interpretation as given by the currently displayed world. The Keyboard module provides an alternative way to enter a sentence, and many people find it easier to use than the physical keyboard.

Tarski's World displays an impressive flexibility of use. In addition to checking sentences against world, new worlds may be constructed so as to conform with a given set of sentences. A wide range of interaction is possible, and the program is used to illustrate each new structure in the language. The program can be made to play the HenkinHintikka game, a game for checking the truth value of a sentence interactively. The program can also be used very effectively to demonstrate the invalidity of arguments by building worlds that refute them.

The language of first order logic is built of atomic sentences which correspond to the most simple sentences of English, sentences consisting of some names connected by a predicate. The first order language used in Tarski's World takes the letters a through f plus n1, n2,... as its names. For predicates, Tarski's World use Tet, Cube, Dodec, Small, Medium, Large, =, Smaller, Larger, LeftOf, RightOf, BackOf, FrontOf, and Between. Some examples of atomic sentences in this language are Cube(b), Larger(c,f), and Between(b,c,d). The software can be used in the following areas:

(1) Check sentence against world

Students may open a World in the Tarski's World, and a Sentence World , and evaluate the truth value of each sentence in the given world. After their evaluation, Tarski's World can verify their answers. Students may also describe a World by sentences in first order logic, and then verify if their sentences correctly describe the World.   The following are examples of World and Sentence.

FIGURE 1
WITTGENSTEIN'S WORLD

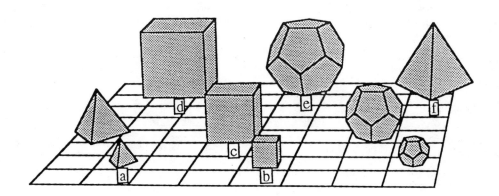

FIGURE 2
BERSTEIN'S SENTENCE

1. $\forall x \; Cube(x) \to Small(x)$

_____

2. $\exists a \; Cube(a)$

_____

3. $\exists v \; Cube(v) \wedge Medium(v) \wedge Larger(v, c)$

_____

4. $\exists u \; (Small(u) \wedge Cube(u)$

_____

5. $\forall w \; (Tet(w) \to \exists z \; Dodec(z) \wedge Larger(w, z))$

_____

6. $\forall x \; \forall y \; \forall z \; LeftOf(x, y) \wedge LeftOf(y, z) \to LeftOf(x, z)$

_____

7. $\forall x \; \forall y \; (Larger(a, b) \to Cube(a) \wedge Dodec(b))$

_____

8. $\forall x \; \forall y \; Cube(x) \wedge Cube(y) \to LeftOf(x, y)$

_____

9. $\forall x \; (Cube(x) \to \exists x \; Between(x, x, y))$

(2) Truth table is supplemented by games

The three basic connectives in logic are conjunction($\wedge$), disjunction($\vee$), and negation($\neg$). The traditional way to teach these connectives is to use truth tables. The Tarski's World provides another way to teach connectives: playing games with computers. It is an active process of learning, and in particular, it enables students to find out why their initial claim is wrong if they lose to computer. The following table summarizes game rules for conjunction, disfunction, and negation.

GAME RULES FOR $\wedge$, $\vee$, AND $\neg$

Form	Your Commitment	Player to Move	Goal
PvQ	TRUE	you	Choose one o P,Q
	FALSE	Tarski's World	that is true
		you	
PvQ	TRUE	Tarski's World	Choose one of P,Q
	FALSE		that is true
$\neg$P	either	---	Replace P by $\neg$P and switch commitment

When a student stakes out a claim about a world with a complex sentence, he is committed not only to the truth of that sentence, but also to the claims about its component sentences. For example, if a student is committed to the truth of P∧Q (read "P and Q") then he is also committed both to the truth of P and to the truth of Q. Similarly, if he is committed to the truth of negation ¬P(read "not P"), then he is committed to the falsity of P. This allows us to play a game that reduces complex commitments to more basic commitments. The Later claims are much easier to evaluate. To play the game, one needs to enter a guess about the truth value of the current sentence in the current world. This guess is one's initial commitment. The game is of most value when this commitment is wrong, even though one won't be able to win in this case.

For example, if you commit to the truth of P∧Q then you have implicitly committed yourself to the truth of each of P and Q. Thus Tarski's World gets to choose either one of these simpler sentences and hold you to the truth of it. If one of them is false, it will choose that one. If both are true, or both are false, it will choose at random. If you commit to the falsity of P∧Q, then you are claiming that at least one of P or Q is false. Tarski's World will ask you to choose one of the two and thereby explicitly commit yourself to its being false. If you lose a game, you could always back off step by step, and find out where it goes wrong.

(3) Translation

An important skill that students need to acquire is that of translating from English to the language of first order logic. After students are familiar with logic and know how to express themselves in logic, the translation is lot of fun. In Tarski's World, students are first asked to describe a world, before they are asked to translate English sentence to first order language, and vice visa. For example, one may open boole's world (figure 3) and describe some features of this world. If a student incorrectly describes the world by sentence: Between(e,d,a), then it does not take long for him to see that mistake. For he is able to visualize that such relation does not exist in the world.

With this preparation, the translation between English and first order language becomes much more natural and easier, for it is clear to students that both language are used to describe world. Logic teachers sometime have trouble explaining to students why their translation is not correct, for students fail to see the connection between logic sentences and the reality described by these sentences. With World, students may actually see why their translation does or does not reflect the structure of the world. If they fail to see this, they could always play game with Tarski's World and find out.

FIGURE 3
BOOLE'S WORLD

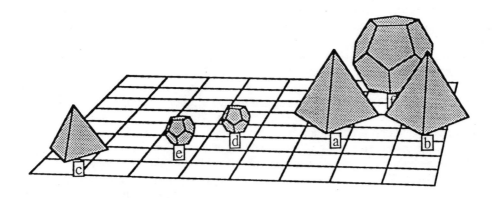

<u>(4) Construction of counter examples</u>

Since students can create their own "world" any way they desire, Tarski's World can be used to construct counter examples. A counter example to a statement is an example in which the condition of the statement holds, but the conclusion fails. By seeing a counter example or constructing a counter example, students could have a better understanding of certain logic rules.

CONCLUSIONS

I used Tarski's World when I taught discrete mathematics to computer science majors. Discrete mathematics covers propositional and predicate logic, however, the formal proof technique and the first order set theory are not covered. As computer science majors, students feel very comfortable and natural to use computer software in their study. The class performance and students responses is very encouraging. The major improvement is that students are able to relate logic laws to its meanings. They feel comfortable and natural to disprove a statement by constructing a counter example. They are also able to appreciate the precision of first order language, without trying to match it with their native language. Compared with other available software for teaching mathematics, many of Tarski's World's approaches to visualization of mathematics concepts are original.

1. The most innovative approach in the Tarski's World for teaching logic is the creation of "World." First of all, the world is essential in connecting logic laws to its meanings. To make abstract logic rules and theorems understandable to students, it is necessary to have an environment where students could visualize how the language of first order logic describes the environment and how the logic rules governs the environment. The "World" in Tarski's World provides such an environment.

   Being fluent in the language of first order logic is essential for one to learn logic, and the way Tarski's World used to teach the language of first order logic is to ask students to use the language, to play with the language before they translate between English and first order language. The "World" is essential in helping students learn language, it actually allows students to play between language and world, just like everyone learns his mother tongue.

   Secondly, it makes counter example construction much easier. In mathematics, to show a statement is false, one needs to find a counter example, i.e. to find a case in which the assumption of the statement is true, but the conclusion does not hold. Students always find it harder to disprove a statement than to prove a statement. Part of the reason is that they have a given assumption in hand when starting to prove a statement, and they feel that they have nothing to start with when trying to disprove a statement. Sometimes, constructing a counter example to disprove a statement may take much more work than to prove, and some creative and elegant counter examples are very famous in the history of mathematics. In Tarski's World, students can create their own world, and finding a counter example can be something that they can "play with." By creating their own world in which a certain logic statement is not true, they understand why the rule does not work, for it fails in a certain world. It is encouraging to see students trying to refute a statement by counter example after they have learned how to use "Tarski's World."

   Thirdly, an important feature of Tarski's World is its dynamic character. The reasoning often takes the form of successively adding or modifying a diagram. This makes it a very convenient form to use in one-on-one discussions at a blackboard or in front of a class. Its game function also provides an interactive learning process, for it can be used as an alternative to the more traditional approach that uses truth tables, making the problem much more fun than the drudge of endless truth tables.

2. Tarski's World does an excellent job balancing variety and flexibility. As a software designed to help students develop skills of language of first order logic, it is easy and fun to use. students are able to play with it right away without any special training. Interaction is almost wholly mouse driven. The world created by Tarski's World is simple enough for students to work with and yet flexible enough to accommodate many complicated logic rules. There only three shapes - cube, dodecahedra, and tetrahedra; three sizes - small, medium, and large; and simple relations - back of, in front of, right of, left of, larger than, smaller than, and in between. It displays an impressive flexibility of use with a high-quality user interface. Tarski's' World has many pre-created worlds, and students may also create as many worlds as they desire.

453

3. Tarski's World is most effectively used together with the text book, the Language of first order logic. The book is packed with interesting exercises and problems which make imaginative use of the program. Equally, the program provides essential support to students as they work through these problems. The supplement book "Tarski's World 3.0" includes hundreds of exercises in construction formulas and proofs.

4. Tarski's World is meant to develop language and reasoning skills, and it offers little help in the construction of formal proof. The formal proof technique is one of the most difficult techniques to learn. All the proofs used by mathematicians are informal, and a formal proof of a simple statement may appear to be very long and confusing. Another software, "Hyperproof" extends Tarski's World in formalizing the proof methods. To be fair, it is not the purpose of Tarski's World to develop formal proof skills, and if the function of formal proof is added to the Tarski's World, then it will compromise the users-friendliness of the Tarski's World.

The originality and innovation of Tarski's World make it an ideal choice for a first course in logic, particularly for those students who lack a formal mathematical background.

REFERENCES

Andrews, P., An Introduction to mathematical Logic and Type Theory, 1986

Goldson, D. and Reeves R., "Using Programs to Teach Logic to Computer Scientists," Notices of the American Mathematical Society, February 1993, vol. 40, No. 2

Hughes-Hallett, D. and Gleason, A. M., Calculus, John Wiley & Sons, Inc, New York, 1993

Barwise, J. and Etchemendy, J., The language of first-ordered logic, Center for the Study of Language and Information, Sanford, 1992

Barwise, J. and Etchemendy, J., Tarski's World 3.0, Center for the Study of Language and Information-Lecture Notes, 1991

Zimmermann, W. and Cunningham, S., Editors, Visualization in teaching and leaning mathematics, Mathematical Association of America, 1991

EVALUATION OF THE PROCEDURAL STEPS IN THE DEVELOPMENT AND PRODUCTION OF AN INTERACTIVE CASE STUDY

J. G. Gallagher, D. P. Stevenson & R. S. Scott
Napier University
EDINBURGH, SCOTLAND

Abstract

Drawing on the experiences of producing an interactive case on an industrial company the following observations were made. In today's screen dominated world there is increasing pressure to produce case studies in formats other than paper. The application of multimedia techniques utilising sound, vision, animation and hypertext may well be the basis of case presentation for the future. This format allows increased student centered learning and overcomes some of the perceived problems associated with case study usage. Development of the interactive case required that the case study writer call on additional expertise and harness them to produce a multi-skilled teaching and learning platform. The result of this was that writing the case took on a greater future orientation than was normal in a `paper' based case.

CASE GENESIS

The development of the multimedia, interactive case study was a direct result of the production of a `paper' based case study on Kwik-Fit Holdings Plc. the market leader in automotive replacement parts in the U.K. and European markets. Use of this case in class situations produced good results and feedback from the student body. But, it was felt that there was more to offer in the case than could be developed by the traditional `paper' based format. Consequently, examination and evaluation of this potential was undertaken by `doing', by producing an interactive case study.

There can be little doubt that in the future more and more teaching and learning will occur through the application of multimedia techniques. Currently, case studies are presented to students in either `paper' based format or in a `paper' and `video' enhanced format. In either format content is more important than packaging. Consequently, merely repackaging the case study in multimedia format will not, of itself, produce a good case study.

Simply put, good case studies have to be `sexy': they have to attract and hold the interest of the participant. They often contain a catalyst of change sometimes in the form of a critical event or complex situation or dominant personality which redirects and refocuses the organisational growth and development. The students are expected to analyze the situation and bring to bear the theory they have absorbed to develop feasible solutions to the situations confronted in the case. The development of computer based, interactive case studies allows a method of presentation which enhances this process. It should not though, be viewed as a total replacement for traditional `paper' based case studies and their concomitant class discussion. Rather it is seen as a tool which augments good teaching practice. Good case study development and preparation still remains within the domain of the good case writer.

It would be fair to say that computers should be used to do what cannot be done either on the printed page or with blackboard and chalk. There is no substitute for the symbiotic development of ideas and solutions generated by students in a lecturer led, class based, case discussion. There is no definitive solution to any given case study. There are though, a number of routes to a number of possible solutions. The interactive case has the advantage that it can present to the student what the company actually did and the rationale that lay behind its decisions whilst still allowing the student to explore other options.

Development of interactive case studies based on the marriage of multimedia technologies and `live' industrial situations and laid down to CDIs and/or CD ROMs formats will enhance the teaching and learning process. The interactive case study will do this by offering more than simply a better presentational appeal, it will allow a better quality of learning experience for the student. Key personnel in the case study companies speaking, answering and justifying for themselves are used to directly explain why certain decisions were taken or the rationale behind those decisions. Drawing directly on this personnel base a more realistic and digestible picture can be drawn of the situations the company faces. The objective here is to incorporate, in the system, solutions to a number of key questions which students are likely to raise. Consequently, by accessing a menu of pre-digitised answers the students should, therefore, through their interrogative skills, be able to form an appropriate line of questioning and solution generation possibilities to carry them through the case.

By introducing the dimensions of sound, speech, video images (still and moving) animation and hypertext to case material. Students will, therefore, gain a more realistic and colourful appraisal of the main participants (management and staff) and the environments and problems they face.

A further aspect of the interactive case is that at pre-determined points theory menu prompts will enable the students to access theoretical foundations. This is achieved by the introduction of a lecturer `figure' on the `disc' to discuss and direct the student to the relevant theory bases required to augment and illuminate their solution generation. Effectively, relevant theory is laid down to be accessed when and if the student needs and augmented by lecturer interpretation of the application of such theory to the case material.

One of the prime objectives of the development of the interactive case study was to try to overcome some of the perceived flaws of case study learning. For example, not all students are naturally participative in class discussion, nor do they learn at the same rates, nor do they have the same educational bases and disciplines to start from. Consequently, the development of the interactive case study was aimed at promoting the incremental development of student centered, problem solving, teaching and learning materials. It was hoped these would help increase the effectiveness of learning by enabling the students to organise their own work to overcome the difficulties associated with complex unstructured problems.

Therefore, for the students the important feature of the interactive case study is the capacity to control their own pace and direction of learning. At present, students are confronted by the strictures of a predetermined syllabus or teaching programme. A programme, moreover, which may already be under `political' pressure to be shortened. Nevertheless, whatever the programme, it is usually followed religiously with subject areas and theory being taught sequentially week by week. Depending on the structure of the material laid down on the `disc' the students will be capable of choosing those areas on which they wish to concentrate. Consequently, students will be learning in a less stressful environment where they control the pace and direction of learning. The interactive case can be viewed, therefore, as a vehicle which allows students to review theory and its practical applications in a broader and less hostile environment.

Interactive cases are the tools not of tomorrow but of to-day. From their usage accrue some specific benefits not the least of which are increases in staff productivity and efficiency. These will accrue from student centered learning based on the ability to network the `disc' thereby reducing staff/student contact. In addition it will provide a vehicle to support student centered learning on distance/open learning courses.

DEVELOPMENT OF MULTIMEDIA CASE

Four basic skills are necessary in developing the multimedia case:
1. Case writing skill
2. Software application skill
3. Photographic/Video skill
4. Graphic skill

If it is to be seen as more than just a gimmick, the combination of these four areas is critical for the development of the interactive case. Consequently, the case writer will have to develop new skills which will allow him/her to combine other disciplines with that of the core case writing skill.

Initially, the process of developing the base material and structure for the interactive case lies squarely on the shoulders of the case writer. This means that he has to, if not learn then certainly develop his skills base. To a great extent he has to foresee how the interactive case will unfold and how the parts will relate to each other. Essentially, the case and the teaching notes are being combined into the one script. A script with parallel, though interlinking story lines.

A fundamental skill of case writing is that of interviewing. It is the bread and butter skill of case writing but one which undergoes subtle changes when the addition of videoing is added. Often the interviewee will feel uncomfortable about being videoed with the result that part of the interviewers task was to calm taut nerves and develop a process of active stress reduction.

Normally, a case study is written after the secondary data has been generated and the parameters set and subsequently reinforced or amended following interview with the key participants in the company. Generation of interactive material at the outset has to be more predetermined. It is essential that at the interview stage more threads are followed to generate the necessary data for use in all aspects of the interactive case development. Teaching notes are therefore, seen not as a passive result of the development of the case but as an integral part of the complete teaching vehicle. Their development has therefore, to run in parallel with that of the case itself as they will be merged with underlying theory in far greater depth than that normally experienced with traditional paper based cases.

One result of this was that the format of the interview had to be based on a more structured dialogue with the result that time spent with the interviewee increased dramatically. Partly, this was due to the need to obtain the correct visual quote and partly to the need to obtain on screen the underlying significance and relevance of such a quote. Unfortunately, as with any interview situation the result is that in reality only three or four minutes of footage may be used. Nevertheless, the need to obtain quality material is a driving force in case development which cannot be denied.

One further aspect of interactive case development is the amount of co-operation and trust that must be built with the case study company. Access to personnel at all levels of the company as well as access to operational data demands much from the company. It is essential, therefore, to build a working relationship which will endure throughout the period of production of the interactive case and long afterwards. This is necessary if the shelf life of the case is to be longer than that normally associated with `paper' based cases. Where a case study may have a four year life expectancy the interactive case can expect more. Effectively, new editions will prove relatively easy to develop as the majority of the material laid down to disc will be unaffected in the short run by all but the most violent changes.

DEVELOPMENT AND APPLICATION OF ADDITIONAL SKILLS

In developing the multimedia case study the software skills used are not those of the conventional programmer, i.e. they do not involve writing a screed of code in a current fashionable language (C, Visual Basic etc). With the interdisciplinary nature of multimedia the software skills required are, to an extent, more complex.

The basic skills used in production of the interactive case are those of the applications developer: someone who can use and modify existing, commercially available, software. The onus therefore is not on producing new, bespoke, software but to tailor existing software to the needs of the case study. This is not to say that conventional programming skills are of no use. Much commercial software includes a dedicated 'scripting language', which can be used to customise the software.

As mentioned earlier, the case study must be written with a view to it being transferred into a multimedia format from the beginning. Merely transferring an existing case study from paper onto disk will more than likely produce a paper based case study on the computer rather than an interactive learning tool. This distinction is important as multimedia is an umbrella term for a collection of communication tools and the strength of multimedia is as an effective means of communicating information, in whatever form is most appropriate.

In this respect the case study will form the script from which the interactive version will be produced. At this stage techniques such as story-boarding can be used to produce an idea of what screens will look like and of how information will be presented, e.g. video, text, animation sound etc. Design and ergonomic issues must be addressed. The interface between the computer and the user (student or staff) is of vital importance. The quality of the interface will determine the useability and ultimately the success of the application. Even when the content is first rate, if the means of accessing it are below par then the success of the application will be jeopardised.

From the storyboard a prototype of the application can then be built. This provides the dual function of ensuring that the design is technically feasible and works as envisaged.

The selection of the software and hardware to be used is of importance when the distribution of the application is considered. Is the application to be written for PC, Apple, CD-I, or a combination. Each platform is inherently different, although each can produce similar results and each offers its own advantages/disadvantages.

The multimedia case study includes the dimensions of sound and video, which come with their own problems.

Sound is probably the easiest to overcome as sound-cards are relatively cheap to purchase and could feasibly be shipped with the case study, in PC format. Apple Mac's come with a sound capability anyway and CD-I uses the television as the viewing medium which again has a sound capability. However in the case of the PC, the sound files can also be directed to the internal speaker of the PC.

Capturing, storing and playing back video from a digital source is more difficult. Cards and software exist for PC and MAC which can achieve this, but at a price: both in terms of money and quality. Although digital video technology at the moment is 'good enough' it is still not the same quality as 'pure video'. There are basically two solutions. The first requires hardware playback of video, which is not as costly to develop, but requires a relatively expensive card to be purchased by the user. The second requires a software only playback of the video, which is costly to the developer, but does not require any additional hardware on the part of the user.

The amount of storage space (i.e. memory) needed for the application is going to increase dramatically with the inclusion of both video and sound as the files used for each tend to be very large. Especially video where, typically, one minutes full motion video use approx 11 Megabytes (equivalent to 8 HD floppy disks). Even with file compression technology such as fractals (again a high investment cost) it is obvious that a distribution platform with a high storage capacity must be found. CD-ROM is the obvious choice as they are cheap to produce and CD-ROM players for both MAC and PC are also cheap to purchase. One CD-ROM disk can hold 650MB (approx 464 HD floppy disks) of information.

These considerations must be made at an early stage as they are vital to the distribution strategy for the multimedia case study. Obviously it will be more beneficial to students if it can be run on machines which they have access to. This infers that a high development cost strategy would be best as this will enable the case study to be run on virtually standard machines.

One consequence of this dependence on combining disparate skill areas is that costs are measured in hundreds of man hours rather than units of man hours. Total production costs of interactive case studies are by definition very high.

MEDIA CENTER/FACULTY COLLABORATION: PRACTICAL GUIDELINES FOR PRODUCING VIDEOTAPES FOR CASE-STUDY APPLICATION

Jean-Henry Mathurin
Robert DeMichiell
Fairfield University
FAIRFIELD, CONNECTICUT, U.S.A.

Abstract

In the last two decades, the rate of change has increased on a worldwide basis. This acceleration requires that educational programs incorporate methods and techniques more responsive to global and competitive markets. Students must be more productive, work on teams, hone presentation skills, and think critically and actively in order to enter future executive careers. Several scenarios are discussed to demonstrate the use of videotaping as an effective technique in courses focusing on the design and application of technology. Special liaisons between media staff and faculty are necessary for making the classroom come alive. Guidelines for developing and implementing case-studies with a video tape component are provided to assist faculty in using this medium effectively.

VIDEOS AND CASE STUDIES: PREPARE AT THE ONSET

"Industry On Parade" was a popular television show in the early 1950s. Each week, this 15-minute program demonstrated how such household items as the electric light bulb were manufactured, tested, and packaged. It was fascinating to observe the step-by-step process that went into the production of these everyday items. Video production is also a step-by-step process, where success depends on carefully following a procedure through pre-production, production and post-production stages. Though the scope of this article does not permit a detailed treatment of this process, information will be discussed to provide an overview, a general awareness of the process and a realization that video production does not simply happen haphazardly or spontaneously. This is especially true when considering integrating video into case studies. Rather than an add-on, video design has to be incorporated with case-study methodology from the outset. In such an amalgamation, the three key words are: preparation, preparation and preparation.

MEDIA CENTER RESOURCE SUPPORT

Fairfield University's Media Center maintains a full in-house audiovisual production facility and a staff of media professionals who assist faculty to incorporate instructional media into their curricula. Media coordinators at Fairfield work closely with faculty to provide a wide range of media services, including the production of instructional video programs. Video production has taken on a greater degree of importance recently with the installation of a campus closed-circuit television distribution system. With the system's distribution originating in the Media Center, video programming can now be telecast across campus to classrooms, presentation facilities, and student residences. Besides Public Broadcasting Service programs and a variety of special programs down-linked by satellite, this campus TV system carries commercial and University-produced instructional video programming. Increasingly, faculty are accessing this resource, incorporating telecast materials into their courses, and exploring the potential of producing original instructional video programs.

CLASSROOM/STUDIO TAPING

Original video programs can be as simple as recording an event with a VHS camcorder for the archives, for library reference or for student/instructor self-evaluation. Introduction to Systems Design Process, an information systems course, is a good example of such programming. This School of Business course examines techniques for selecting, installing and operating computer systems and their peripheral devices and relies heavily on case-study methods. Essential to the course is an interactive teaching methodology. However, detailed note taking, in the attempt to document the extensive materials covered in each class session, is detrimental to the smooth flow of the student/instructor dialogue. Instead of solely listening to what is being said and participating in that dialogue, students split their attention between that and taking notes [Christensen, 1991].

Video presents a viable solution. Using a single-camera, VHS remote unit, classroom sessions are videotaped throughout the semester. Each session's tape and copies are deposited in the University library's reference section the very next day. Confident that any marginalia taken during class can be supplemented in detail by viewing a video transcript, students can focus primarily on the concepts being developed in class and participate in the on-going student/instructor dialogue.

During the past decade, the authors have video taped twenty-five sessions from varying information systems courses. These tapings included capture of formal student presentations with multiple cameras, case-study environments and business activity, student interviews of business executives, and communication among and within student teams as they conduct project work.

In addition to classroom sessions, pivotal team presentations are videotaped in studio. When formal responses to a document requesting proposals from competitive student teams are required, confidentiality of negotiation is an issue [DeMichiell, 1988]. By taping in a studio, only those teams involved with the presentation are present. Once confidentiality is no longer an issue, previously competitive teams can then view and critique tapes of each other's presentation. Using multiple cameras, these presentations are shot contiguous, "black-to-black"--a relatively simple taping where the program begins with a fade from black to an opening shot, progresses through the beginning, middle and end of the program, and closes with a fade to black. From the Media Center's perspective, such requests have the advantage of providing maximum benefit to the requesting instructor and to his/her students, while requiring minimum production logistics or resources.

MAJOR PROJECTS

At the other end of the original video programs spectrum, production can involve a highly orchestrated series of shots or sequences where considerable time and effort are expended to show and say the right thing in the right way. Unlike the simple, straight-forward VHS classroom or black-to-black studio taping, such programs can involve remote location sites, scripting, and post-production editing and are more manpower and resource intense. Requests for such programs are justifiably categorized as major projects and their needs and feasibility of production are carefully evaluated before committing University resources.

The video program "Czechoslovakia in Transition" is a prime example of this high-end programming. During the summer of 1990, WACRA selected Prague, Czechoslovakia, as the site for its symposium, **Czechoslovakia in Transition, Developing Strategic Initiatives with Case-Study Methodologies.** One of the goals of the symposium was to document case-study data of a developing nation, highlighting problem-solving exercises, as well as interactive group discussions and creative-thinking sessions. Video was selected as the medium of choice because of its unique ability to allow an environment to be experienced on a more experiential level than allowed by the more traditional print medium. Instead of reading about a group's interaction, video allows that interaction to be seen, to be heard, to be experienced [Klein and DeMichiell, 1991].

A faculty member of the School of Business and a member of WACRA's Symposium Planning Committee approached the Media Center for production and personnel support. Though the request involved an outside agency, the Media Center makes every attempt to support faculty in their professional-related activities, especially when the final product has classroom application. "Czechoslovakia in Transition" met this initial prerequisite but production could not be considered until Media Center staff researched the existence of commercial, pare-produced programs with similar content.

Using "Video Directory Plus," a **Variety Magazine** CD database, 80,000 video titles were scanned within minutes. No existing program was found that covered the proposed content and purpose of "Czechoslovakia in Transition." A more traditional search of print references also confirmed the uniqueness of the proposed program and its candidacy for its possible production. Time and effort expended in such research is always time well spent, especially in today's economic climate.

Preliminary Funding Issues

Once the Media Center gives a "go ahead" for production, the client usually asks, "How much will it cost?" Unfortunately, this question is premature. There's no magic ratio between dollars spent and the length of a program. Among other considerations, cost is a function of the size and caliber of the production crew, the number of remote location sites or studio days required, the use or not of professional narration, the amount and type of music selected, the degree of post-production special effects, client expectations and the "glitz factor"--the addition of costly, cosmetic bells and whistles which result in a prettier though not necessarily more communicative program.

Production format also impacts on cost. Fairfield can produce a master tape in both VHS (Video Home System) and U-Matic (3/4-inch cassette) formats and has in-house post-production editing facilities for both. Considering any other production format can significantly increase the price of doing business. For example, in tape stock alone, upgrading from U-Matic to a 1" broadcast format results in a jump from $25.00 to $100.00 per hour for tape. It also requires renting format-specific recording equipment and post-production editing facilities and, in general, significantly complicates production logistics.

Costs are also a matter of time, production quality and program content. A high-quality, content-involved program with a short turnaround time will be more costly than one with a more generous production schedule, less complicated content, or lower production quality expectations. Bottom line? Asking for a dollar amount at this stage of production is like asking a building contractor how much a house will cost without specifying its size, design or location. The message, rather than cost, should be the first major concern.

Designing Videos With a Message

Deciding on the message to be communicated is the single most important decision in creating a successful video program [Worth, 1991]. A formula for success is a single, focused, well-articulated message, in the proverbial 25 words or less, targeted to a well-defined audience. Even so, it is often difficult to avoid the temptation--usually because of budgetary concerns--to diverge from this formula, cramming several, and often conflicting messages into a single program. Success also depends on knowing the target audience's background. An audience's homogeneity, age, sex, occupation, economic status, ethnic background and familiarity with content material all impact on how receptive that audience will be to a program's message. To be successful, know your message and know your audience.

These and other issues, such as how a program will be treated artistically, technically, and content-wise, are all summarized in a document called a treatment. Usually only one to two pages long, a treatment also identifies what an audience is expected to do or know after viewing a program. Are they to retain detailed information, undergo a change in attitude, demonstrate emotion, or acquire new skills? A treatment is not etched in stone. It's a working document that serves as a reference when evaluating possible new changes in direction or emphasis. A treatment also serves as the basis for the development of a program's cost proposal, budget, production schedule and the all-important shooting script.

Writing the Script

Writing for video is an art form of its own. Video relies on a subtle combination of the spoken word and visual symbols, or icons, to communicate. Unless one has had experience writing for such genre, there's a tendency to include tangential and intrusive bits of information--exceptions, buts, ifs, and on the other hands--creating needless communication barriers. It is highly recommended that a professional script writer be hired to write a script for any major video project. Not only does this save time, it allows the faculty member to focus on his/her area of expertise--writing the case study. Also, experience has demonstrated time and time again that a professional writer can always visualize and express the content better than even the content expert. After an initial fact-finding session, a professional script writer will submit a rough draft ready for review, followed by a second draft and a final or approval draft. Usually, a script is submitted in a two-column format. In one column, the script writer will indicate anything that will be said (narration) during the program and identify who's speaking. Music and special sound effects are also identified in this column. In the second column, the writer will describe proposed graphics, alongside their appropriate narrative component in the other column. It's important to ensure that the writer has clearly conveyed the main message outlined in the video treatment and that this main message is continually reinforced through the development of the script. In addition, ideas must flow smoothly from one idea to another. Simplicity and brevity are the keys to a successful script. A word of caution: Though constructive input is always desired and of value, final approval for any component of a video program, especially the script, should rest with the faculty member for whom the program is being developed.

Remote/Studio Production Insights

As mentioned earlier, video production does not simply just happen. Anticipation of needs and identification of client expectations are also important ingredients for success. Though a request may come in simply as, "I need a VHS setup," it is routinely followed up by Media Center support staff. Two questions that prove invaluable are, "How do you plan to use the setup?" and "How do you plan to use the recorded tape?" What may have been perceived by the requesting instructor as a simple, straight-forward request may prove to be otherwise upon answering these questions. The Media Center once received a request to videotape a presentation in one of the University's larger halls. The request was for a simple VHS camcorder to be located at the back of the hall. Upon inquiring how the instructor planned to use this tape, he responded that he would like to submit it to Public Broadcasting Service (PBS) for airing. For a multitude of reasons, his expectation was not realistic and demonstrated a lack of understanding of basic production requirements.

The same can happen when planning remote location or studio shoots. Not only do a client's expectations have to be clearly identified, the means by which those expectations can be executed have to be clearly understood. The process of staffing such shoots is a good example. A remote crew consists of a director, at least one camera person, one video/audio engineer, possibly a make-up artist, and at least one production assistant or grip. In a studio, additional personnel could include a technical director, a Teleprompter operator, floor manager, font/graphic operator and two more camera operators. For the most part, these people are free-lance agents charging by the day which can vary from eight to ten hours, with significant overtime penalties for each additional hour over the limit. Their fees vary from $100 a day for a grip to $300 a day for a director. In addition, these free-lance agents expect full or partial payment even if a shoot is canceled by an act of God (i.e., inclement weather or a power failure). If a production requires a lighting director, he/she will have to survey or visit the remote site prior to the taping date to evaluate lighting and AC power requirements. Such a survey day is considered a full working day and full payment is expected [Zettl, 1992]. Similarly, for a studio shoot the set design and lighting are done the day before. Be prepared to pay at least a half-day rate for studio facilities and personnel for set design and lighting. Other out-of-pocket expenses can include travel, food, and hotel accommodations. Clearly, a good understanding of these considerations not only impact production scheduling and logistics, but also a production's budget.

Audio is an often overlooked component in video production. As mentioned earlier, video relies not only on visual symbols or icons to communicate, but also the spoken word. Though a picture is often said to be worth a thousand words, the question always remains, which thousand? While teaching an audiovisual production course, this point was illustrated by using a political cartoon featured in a national newspaper. After deleting the words in each character's balloons, copies of the cartoon were distributed to the students. They were then asked to interpret what they perceived to be the intended message of the cartoon's illustrator. This particular cartoon had what appeared to be a men's athletic locker room as its background. In the foreground was a burly stereotype of a weightlifter holding a small labeled jar. A coach, with a clipboard in hand, was facing the weightlifter. Only two of the 20 students correctly interpreted the general subject being addressed by the cartoon, because they had been closely following the issue of abuse of steroids by athletes. In the unaltered cartoon, the weightlifter is saying, "Gee coach, I'm getting worried about these steroids you've been giving me." The coach replies, "Don't be ridiculous, Jennifer!" The visual icons of the cartoon, by themselves, could not communicate the intended message. It required the combination of words in conjunction with the icons. Similarly, successful communication of a video's message must rely on its accompanying audio component, as well as on its visualization. No matter what level of video production is being considered, good, clean audio is essential to successful communication.

Post-Production Parameters Impact on Production

It is also important to recognize that production and post-production are closely intertwined and difficult to separate. Approaching production without a good understanding of post-production requirements, courts disaster. This is true not only for the media professional, but also increasingly true at Fairfield for faculty who wish to produce their own programs using VHS format. A good example is a lack or poor understanding of the editing process. Time and time again, a faculty member will use his/her camcorder with the anticipation of editing the visuals into a program, only to learn later that these visuals are not usable. The most common error is not allowing sufficient time in the record mode before and after recording a desired visual sequence. A camcorder not only records visual and audio components on tape, but also records a special technical or control track. It is this control track that allows the playback and recording machines of an editing system to work together and ensures that an edit takes place exactly where it has been programmed to occur. Turning a camcorder's power off "breaks" the control track. In itself, this is not bad. However, it's important to realize that post-production editing systems require five seconds both before and after a programmed edit. Therefore, out in the field, it is always advisable to make sure that you are in the record mode at least five seconds before and after capturing that visual sequence of choice, with no break in control track in between. Instead of being too quick on the trigger, when in doubt or framing a shot, use the PAUSE button instead of the ON/OFF switch. Control track is not broken in the PAUSE mode.

Poorly executed camera techniques can also cause post-production headaches. One of the greatest misuses is the PAN shot. In a PAN shot the camera moves from point A to point B by rotating the camera left-right or right-left. When justified and well executed, it is an extremely effective shot. When used for its own sake and poorly executed, it's gut wrenching, especially when executed without a tripod. In most situations, a simple shot sequence is more than sufficient. One recommended sequence opens with a ten second, static wide shot of the scene to be taped, followed by a zoom-in to a close-up shot of the point of interest in that scene. After waiting ten seconds, zoom-out to the original wide shot. Editing-wise, this sequence eliminates post-production hindsight woes--"Why didn't I take that extra shot?" It goes without saying that the use of a good tripod is always recommended. Also, make those zoom-in and outs fairly fast. A slow zoom is seldom used.

"Czechoslovakia in Transition" posed an additional post-production challenge--- electronic compatibility or standards. Presently, three video standards dominate the world's markets--NTSC (National Television System Committee), PAL (Phase Laternate Line), and SECAM (Sequentiel Couleur a Memoire). NTSC differs from PAL and SECAM in the number of lines of resolution produced and the type of electrical power used. NTSC video has 526 lines of resolution and operates on 60 cycle-per-second AC or alternating current, while PAL and SECAM produce 626 lines of resolution and operate on 50 cycles-per-second ACcurrent. PAL and SECAM standards differ from each other in the way they encode color. The important point, however, is that production equipment designed for one standard, and tapes produced on that standard, are not compatible with the other two. Czechoslovakia uses SECAM and 50 cycles-per-second electrical current; the United States uses NTSC and 60 cycles-per-second current [DeLuca, 1991].

Initially, consideration was given to producing "Czechoslovakia in Transition" in a 3/4-inch format because of quality considerations. However, the University's NTSC-compatible equipment would not operate in Czechoslovakia and renting SECAM-compatible equipment proved prohibitive budget-wise. Fortunately, an option presented itself. After several calls to manufacturers, it was determined that most NTSC, VHS camcorders sold in the United States operate on either 50 cycles-per-second or 60 cycles-per- second AC current. Though this meant down scaling from a 3/4-inch production format to VHS, electronic compatibility was no longer a concern. The moral: always keep in mind post-production concerns when planning production.

GUIDELINES FOR FACULTY/MEDIA STAFF COLLABORATIONS

Guidelines for assisting faculty to incorporate effective videotaping techniques in the development of case studies are:

a. Contact a media professional. Whether requesting a simple VHS classroom remote or a major project, your college's or university's media professional will assist you to assess needs and production feasibility and establish realistic production expectations;

b. Research existing commercial titles before committing department or institutional resources;

c. Develop a program proposal or treatment if production is warranted. Such a treatment should address the following: What is the target audience? What is the main message of the program? How will the program contribute to the better understanding of one or more aspects of the case scenario? What content will be covered by the program? How will this content be treated artistically and visually? What will be the production/distribution format? And, when will the program be used?

d. Submit a formal written proposal for approval. This process varies from institution to institution. Be sure

464

that all appropriate approvals have been granted before continuing with the project;

e. Develop a shooting script;

f. Identify out-of-pocket expenses. Before drafting a production budget it is essential to not only anticipate obvious out-of-pocket expenses, but "hidden" expenses as well;

g. Draft a production budget upon approval of proposal. Educational media production facilities charge for services rendered on either an in-house rate or an outside rate. Typically, projects requested by faculty and targeted for campus consumption are charged the lesser, in-house rate. Some facilities will contribute production facilities, equipment and even manpower as in-kind services;

h. Appropriate sufficient funds upon approval of the budget. In most instances, it is the responsibility of the requesting faculty to appropriate sufficient funds to cover expenses outlined in the production budget. Many production facilities will not issue work order numbers or initiate production on unfunded projects;

i. Establish a production schedule. Adhering to these agreed upon production deadlines is a critical element in keeping project costs within budget;

j. Establish an approval chain. The saying that a camel was a horse created by a committee should be a strong enough recommendation to keeping the approval chain short;

k. Consider post-production considerations when approaching production;

l. Determine level of participation in the actual production. At some schools, the media center assumes the role of producer. Faculty are encouraged to participate in the production process to what ever level and degree they are willing. Faculty credits may include: creative producer, content consultant, or script development; and,

m. Establish ownership of the property. In many universities, projects produced with university resources are the sole property of the University--all rights reserved.

CONCLUDING COMMENTS

Video programming is a step-by-step process where each step impacts on the other. The most important first step in this process is to seek assistance from a media professional. He/she will be able to help you determine production requirements, as well as plan and organize a production strategy that will conserve your time, effort and resources.

From a case-study perspective, the most important step is to incorporate video design into case-study methodology from the onset. Don't add video to a scenario in hindsight. Also, the final video product directly relates to the case-study environment, learning objectives and overall atmosphere of faculty/student fact exploration. It is important to remember that video design has a direct bearing on what and how students approach their problem-solving experience.

Bringing a video program to life out of all the words and sounds and pictures that you have selected is one of the most satisfying experiences that you can imagine. It's a unique creation--your creation, one made possible by effective media center/faculty liaisons.

REFERENCES

Christensen, R., Education for Judgement (Harvard Business School Press, 1991), pp. 15-30.

DeMichiell, R., "Computer Contract Negotiations: Videotaping Student Driven Confidential Cases," in An International Forum, Hans Klein, ed., WACRA, 1988.

DeLuca, Stuart M., Instructional Video, (Focal Press, 1991), pp. 42-47.

Klein, H. and DeMichiell, R., "Capturing Case Study Data With Videotapes: Experience in Czechoslovakia," in Managing Change, Hans E. Klein, Ed., WACRA 1990.

Worth, R., Creating Corporate Audio-Visual Presentations (Quorum Books, 1991), pp. 76-84.

Zettl, Herbert, Television Production Handbook, Fifth Edition, (Wadsworth, Inc., 1992), pp. 573-581.

LEARNING AND MANAGING
LOCAL INDUSTRIAL NET WORKS
USING CASE METHODOLOGY

Jean-Luc Fleureau
E.N.S.I.E.T.A.
BREST, FRANCE

Abstract

Learning the implementation of a local industrial network, then managing it in an optimal way, implies an important number of constraints on resources including financial resources. To maximize scarce resources we have developed a simulation tool representing a flexible production workshop. Its originality lies in the fact that it ties computer simulation to real production machines. Students program industrial robots in order to optimise the movement of parts from working area to working area..

INTRODUCTION

The "Ecole Nationale Supérieure des Ingénieurs des Etudes et Techniques d'Armement" (E.N.S.I.E.T.A.) located at Brest (France), is a multi-disciplinary college which trains generalist engineers mastering cutting-edge technologies. Issuing engineering diplomas since 1934 it constitutes, together with the E.N.S.A.E.,[1] the E.N.S.T.A[2]. and the E.N.S.I.C.A,[3] the pool of engineering colleges depending on the D.G.A[4]. Created to assure the initial formation of military engineers, its role expanded to include the formation of civil service personnel. The training offers many perspectives in the sectors of electronics, mechanics, pyrothechnology and shipbuilding.

The E.N.S.I.E.T.A. is composed of six laboratories of study and research which offer college course work:

- Laboratory of mechanics,
- Laboratory of fluid simulation,
- Laboratory of materials,
- Laboratory of electronics,
- Laboratory of signal and image processing,
- Laboratory of automation.

The automation laboratory admits also students from other schools in BREST (U.B.O.,[5] E.N.I.B.,[6] I.I.I.[7]). This arrangement permits the sharing of research results with teachers and practitioners. The following disciplines are being taught at the lab: automation, electronic of power, electro-technology, automation manufacturing and automation.

It is in the context of teaching industrial automation where we have used case methodology. This study represents the implemention of a local industrial network between interconnected programmable robots. The case methodology is indispensable if we want to correctly understand the goal of such a network and to implement a solution. The subject posed to the students is the management of a flexible workshop. Besides the didactic aspect, the originality of the project lies in the fact that the simulation on computers and the use of real production machines are linked. Indeed, the parts conveyor belts, unwieldy and expensive, are simulated on a computer controlled by an industrial programmable robot. The existing machine tools are used without any operator. With a sense of humour, we can say that this *complex* study is composed of a *real part* and an *imaginary part*. The remainder of the paper will attempt to describe these two parts and their utilisations.

SIMULATION OF THE OPERATIVE PART

The automation laboratory has twelve equipments bays composed of industrials programmable robots connected to computers (FIGURE 1). Computers, equipped with graphics screen, are used to simulate numerous operative parts of industrial automatisms. Furthermore, connecting an operator desk increased the realism of the process control.

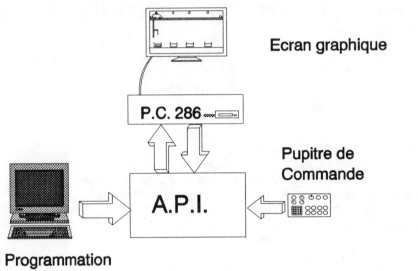

Ecran graphique

Pupitre de Commande

Console de Programmation
en langage GRAFCET

Figure 1
(liaison API et ordinateur)

As of today, the laboratory has realised four simulations: automatic laundry, concrete factory, treatment of surfaces and flexible workshop. This powerful tool allows on one hand, to modify quickly the subject of the proposed practical work, and on the other hand to use 100% of the capabilities of the programmable robot (boolean, analogic, numeric, network, etc...). Each object of the simulation is created with the help of D.A.O[8]. software, and then saved in a file. The last part of the job requires the animation of the different objects generated by the robot and to report back to the robot the state of the different sensors of the operative part.

UTILISATION OF THE MACHINES

In addition to the computer simulations, we use real machine tools with numerical commands, capable to manufacture parts made of steel and aluminum. These machines are connected and guided by the industrial programmable robots (which may send via a specific network the appropriate codes to the machine). According to these orders, the machine executes the specified job. Of course, in the context of a flexible workshop, the machine loads its parts and its tools in automatically.

DESCRIPTION OF THE FLEXIBLE WORKSHOP

The objective of the proposed student project is to simulate the functioning of a flexible workshop. One of the main advantages of our approach is to be able to adjust the reaction of the workshop to each change in demand.

It is possible for a part at the entrance to the system, to determine totally automatically its manufacturing scale and consequently its routing. The flexible workshops, therefore, are particularly suited to manufacturing management techniques such as the Kanban method. However, this implies a more delicate implementation and management than for a linear workshop; one must, for example, deal with and solve eventual conflicts.

Global working of the workshop

The workshop is composed of 4 work stations(FIGURE 2), normally equipped with robots or machine tools with numerical commands. The specific tasks for each work station are the following:

work station 0 (B0): Handling robot,
work station 1 (B1): Numerical controlled tower,
work station 2 (B2): Numerical controlled grinding machine,
work station 3 (B3): 3D control machine.

Each work station, managed by a group of students, is served by a continuous rotating conveyor, which is simulated by an area. This conveyor is in linked with the central conveyor, managed and simulated by another area. This central conveyor distributes pallets used to transport the parts to the different machines. The workshop is started with a specific parametrable configuration for each working area; it corresponds to a workshop halted in a special state at the end of a day, and re-started in the same state the next morning.

Principle of parts manufacturing

The manufacturing is driven by labels affixed to each pallet. This label defines the order of the operations to be executed on each part, for example *turning, reaming and finally control*. After the programmable robot '0' has read such a label, students have to move the part to the different work stations, managing the external internal loops. When many parts are being transferred, each loop has operate smoothly to be avoid *conveyor saturation*.

Notion of quality

To simulate reality, the possibility of spoilage has been included in the simulation process: at the beginning of the simulation, the percentage of spoilage may be indicated for each work station. Then randomly and according to this percentage, a certain number of parts are rejected without further work being performed.

Technologic application

Technically, the programmable robots (TSX 47 et TSX 67)[Télémécanique,1987] of the external loops are respectively connected to machine tools or robots. When the simulation indicates to the robot that a part is on a machine, students have to send to it the appropriate orders to do the required work. As soon as the task is finished, machines and robots send back to the controllers a code specifying the result of the operation: *terminated or on error*.

Programming language

The programming language used is the GRAFCET [Bouteille,1992]. It authorises a graphical specification of sequential automatisms program controllers. The data is exchanged between the different robots in two ways: either in a broadcast mode or in a point to point mode. The first one is used to broadcast common data to all the controllers connected on the network, for example, the level of saturation of the workshop or the state of the manufacturing in progress. The second mode is used to indicate to two adjacent loops the type of part in transfer or the result of a previous output (notion of scrap).

INTEREST OF THE CASE METHODOLOGY

The interest of the case methodology in this instance is trivial. Indeed, during the implementation of a local network in an industrial field, numerous problems appear. From this report, the first question that a teacher may ask is: "how can we reproduce such problems, so that students can recognize them and learn to deal with them." This concern prompted us to implement this project with the tools described earlier.

After a general introduction to local industrial networks, our students begin to work on the "pseudo-real" case. This project involves groups of maximum ten students. The time allowed per student to solve the problem is 30 hours. Nevertheless, to obtain a proper functioning of the workshop, a minimum of 45 hours is necessary. These additional hours represent efforts outside the regular course. This allows to gauge their interest and their ability to plan their time commitments. The students' first contact with the project requires reading and understanding the entire project. Then they have to dispatch the different tasks, according to their respective

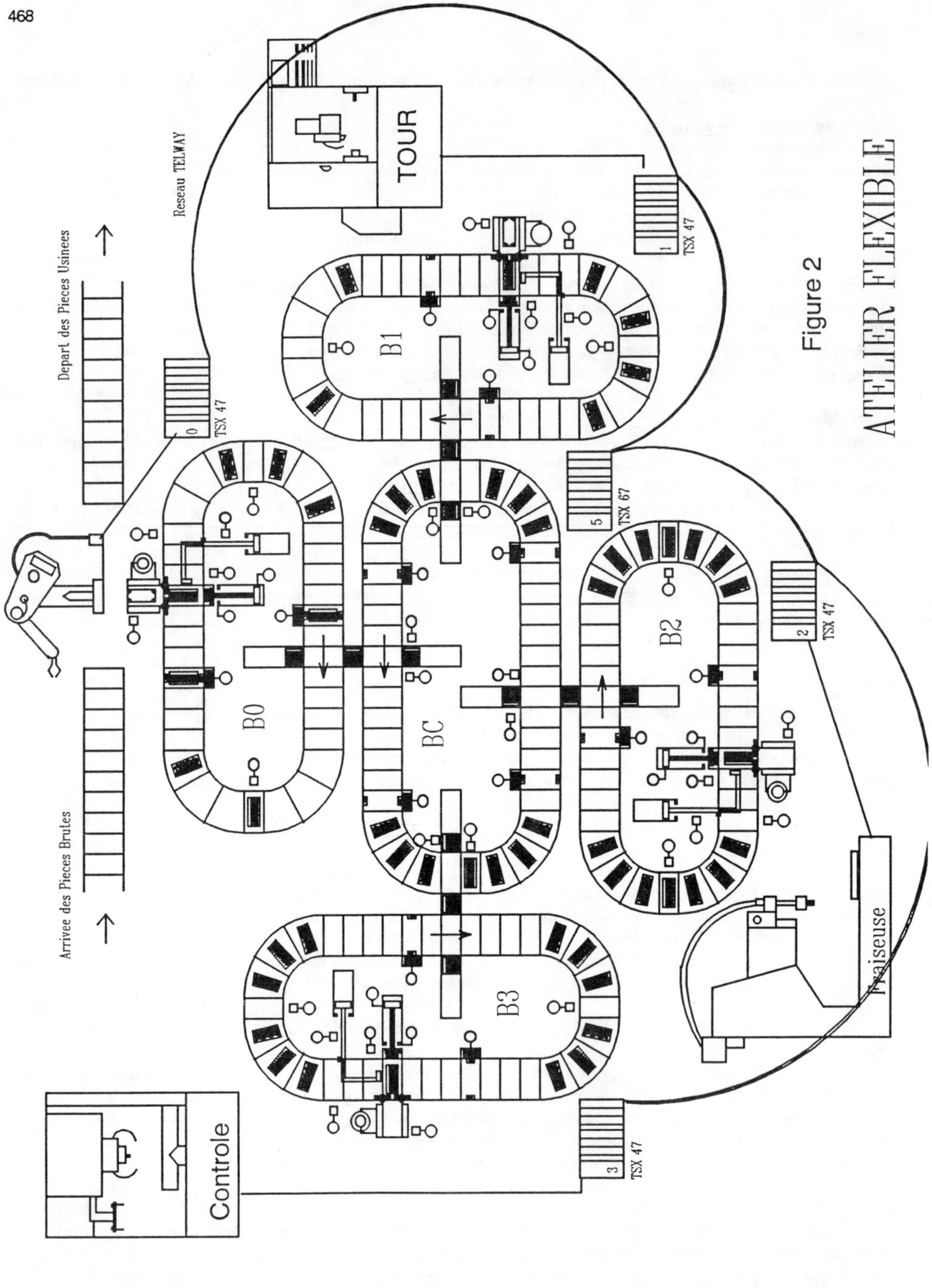

468

ATELIER FLEXIBLE

Figure 2

Reseau TELWAY

Depart des Pieces Usinees

Arrivee des Pieces Brutes

TOUR

B1

B0

BC

B2

B3

Controle

Fraiseuse

TSX 47   1
TSX 47   0
TSX 67   5
TSX 47   2
TSX 47   3

relationships to the five work stations (four external conveyors and a central conveyors; two students per place). They then analyse the problem and program the controllers(robots) with the help of the tools learned during cours lessons (GRAFCET, communication between controllers, etc...). Of course, they [the student] have to organise and attend regularly meetings to discuss the progress of each group, the problems they have encountered, etc... If communication between the different groups of students is working, communication between the different machines will not encounter any difficulties and the flexible workshop will then work properly.

CONCLUSION

This first experience of the implementation of a local industrial network is intellectually very satisfying for the students. They do not feel to be involved in routine class assignments, with "pre-defined" questions and answers, but rather that they are doing the work of an engineer.

Finally, the human aspects of such a project has to be underlined. Indeed, at the beginning of the work, we insist on the fact, that a network is first a way of communicating. Therefore, to work effectively with many individuals (10 in our case), we have to learn to communicate and to agree with each other on a common strategy of driving the workshop and managing the production. In most instances the result depend on the homogeneity of the group. However, working together effectively is an experience which cannot not be taught scientifically.

ENDNOTES

1.   Ecole Nationale Supérieure d'Aéronautique.

2.   Ecole Nationale Supérieure des Techniques Avancées.

3.   Ecole Nationale Supérieure d'Ingénieurs des Constructions aéronautiques.

4.   Direction Générale de l'armement.

5.   Université de Bretagne Occidentale.

6.   Ecole Nationale d'Ingénieurs de Brest.

7.   Institut d'Informatique Industrielle.

8.   Dessin Assisté par Ordinateur.

REFERENCES

Bouteille,N.,"Le GRAFCET", Cépadues édition,Paris,1992,144 p.

Télémécanique,"TSX 47: manuel de programmation", documentation technique,1987,200 p.

LEARNING LOGISTICAL SYSTEM DYNAMICS USING CONTINUOUS SIMULATION RELATIONSHIPS BETWEEN THE PRINCIPAL DOCTRINES AND LEARNING TECHNIQUES

Daniel Thiel
Tours Graduate School of Management
TOURS, FRANCE

Abstract

We have tackled the problem of teaching business logistics. Our vision and knowledge of the industrial world and particularly its logistics are obviously not the same as that of our graduate and post-graduate students without professional experience. Therefore, our teaching difficulty consists in adopting the means of transferring knowledge to this specific public.

We chose the system dynamics approach using continuous simulation. We placed this type of training in relation to different traditional teaching doctrines and methods. We also compared our teaching method to different traditional learning methods like interactive, interrogative, intuitive and active methods.

COMPLEXITY OF LOGISTICAL SYSTEMS

We retain the definition given by the Council of Logistics Management : «*Logistics is the process of planning, implementing and controlling the efficient, cost-effective flow and storage of raw materials, in-process inventory, finished goods and related information from point of consumption for the purpose of conforming to consumer requirements.*» [Bowersox, 1978] According to this description, we studied the logistics of production and distribution systems. Our current knowledge of logistical systems is often empirical. We identified two essential types of working :

- the first one, which we call «procedural», is based on a formal reasoning and on deterministic bases,
- the second one, called «expert», is based on usual job rules acquired by an «organizational training».

In reality, many decisions easy to make,[1] are essential to the real time control of the industrial activity. In the short term, we observed companies, with objective of improving their ability to respond, quickly overcome simple problems or even, simplified problems by reduction of complexity level. Meanwhile, globally, really complex problems are not solved. For instance, in some companies, how can we explain (and try to improve) a too high level of inventories, apparently necessary to guarantee a satisfactory customer service? The responsibilities of such an anomaly are varied and can be attributed just as easily to the production tool, little flexible and unreliable, as to the bad quality of information and order transmission. For this reason, we direct our teaching programs towards essential mechanisms for appropriate implementation to overcome such dysfunctions.

TYPES OF KNOWLEDGE TO BE ACQUIRED

Generally, the different types of knowledge to be acquired in the field of logistics area can include many aspects : static, kinematic and dynamic. Within the scope of industrial systems description (see Figure 1), we have noted the inappropriate static description of logistical flows. These operating systems like production, transportation or handling tools, are only physical supports which are uninteresting for a first understanding of the complex dynamics of flows. For that reason, we prefer to orient our teaching programs towards the knowledge of materials and information movement instead of towards substructures and installations which are of course necessary to carry out the operations.

FIGURE 1
DIFFERENT VISIONS OF LOGISTIC EDUCATION

	Aspects	Educational objectives
LOGISTICS ≠	STATIC ASPECT	Structural knowledge of operating systems
LOGISTICS =	KINEMATIC ASPECT	Structural knowledge of driving systems
	DYNAMIC ASPECT	Knowledge of the flow dynamics

That is why we retain the system dynamics approach as a way of investigating complex logistic systems. We offer a kinematic description of industrial systems which is characterized by information and driving systems and by an operating system described in two dimensions : uncertainty and complexity. The behaviour dynamics is observed by model simulations with different scenarios.

THE PROBLEMS OF LEARNING

Industrial systems described in term of feedback structures, are in general too complex to be treated by mathematics and their dynamic behaviours can only be represented by non-linear models. An efficient, objective and relevant method should consist in observing in real time, on the shop-floor, the decisions taken in the systems and in analyzing the consequences. J-C. Moisdon [1984] also said that, «we can only analyze a working organization when it is set in motion, just as a force field unveils its structure when we can observe the movements of the objects which are immersed in it.» But the delay of this approach is too long and explains the ordinary use of computer simulation. One of the major problems of simulation model building is its validation. In this way, it is advised a priori to draw from existing theories for building a model which can be completed or adjusted by a ground observation (according to B. Walliser [1977] who considers that it is a circular process which can start at any phase). This behaviour investigation method currently presents deficiency because no laws exist to describe particular problems frequently present in industries, for instance : reducing production cycles in case of decreasing productivity, reorganizing production and increasing capacity upon demand, etc. Only general theories like system theory or some decision theories can help us model industrial complex systems.

LEARNING LOGISTICS USING SYSTEM DYNAMICS THEORY

First, we describe the cognitive process of learning based on system dynamics principles. Then, we position this type of teaching in relation to certain educational doctrines and methods.

THE COGNITIVE PROCESS

In the industrial field, we often note that many management consultants who advise personnel polyvalency, production flexibility, cycles reduction, total quality control, industrial investments, etc... reach today the limit of

FIGURE 2
DIFFERENT WAYS Of REPRESENTING KNOWLEDGE

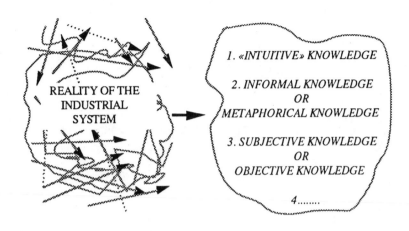

FIGURE 3
A METHOD TO FORMALIZE KNOWLEDGE

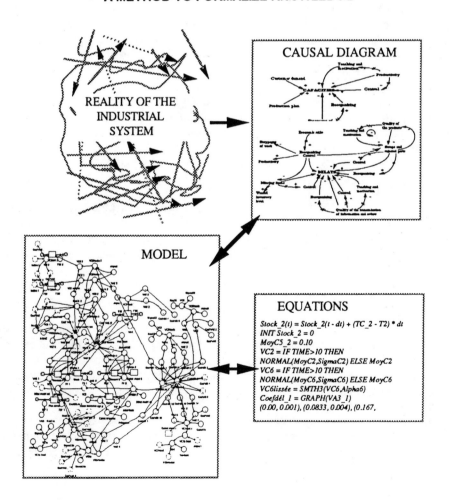

their efficiency. Many successive and partial political choices do not lead to the expected results. These consultants often base themselves on their past experiences, which lead unfortunately to failure. Even if R.J. Trotter et J. Mc Connel [1980] noticed that «the previous experience had an important place in problems solving and that people often look for solutions which have had some success in the past», P. Senge describes the limit of this learning by experience. According to him, there are some cases where the observation of the consequences of each of our actions are not visible. «When the effects of an action become irrelevant to our visual field, it is not possible anymore to learn by experience.» [Senge 1990]

How should we prepare future managers for these complex systems? Teaching using system dynamics is an original method which stimulates intelligence through the conceptual phase completed by practical simulation experimentations. Furthermore, Alain [1959] said that «the mind becomes active only as it comes in contact with experience.» According to Dewey, the intelligence method, as it shows itself in several steps of experimental process, implies that we keep track of ideas, activities and observed consequences. «Reflection must be capable of reviewing and globalizing. Reflecting is to consider in retrospect what has been done in order to free the various significations which become for the intelligence some sort of capital placed in reserve for future experiences. Here is the core of the intellectual organization and the discipline of the mind.» [Dewey 1968] The objective of teaching by modelling as we advise, is in accordance with E. De Bono's [1976] quote that says that «*the teaching of thinking is not the teaching of logic but the teaching of perception.*»

How can we represent our industrial system knowledge? We observe in the following figures the different ways of representing knowledge of complex systems. A first approach (fig. 2) develops very qualitative aspects more or less objective and more or less formalized. The second one (fig. 3) presents the classical way according to Jay W. Forrester theory [1969 and 1984].

We shall not compare these two modes of knowledge representations because they are complementary. The first phase that we advise, consists in discovering the reality by immersion in the company and try to extract objectively relations between different variables through a systemic vision. This is what we call a «systemic audit» which allows us to apprehend the complex reality. The second phase enriched by the first one, consists in translating these subjective, informal or intuitive[2] knowledge in a model which is progressively built from the causal relations (non-linear in most cases). As specified by A. Bensoussan [1982], «the first objective of modelling is positivist, it allows the developing of knowledge models. The second aspect, which is normative, aims at helping the practitioner to «objectivize» the pictures that he perceives as subjective ...»

We advise the system dynamics approach to apprehend logistics, starting from elementary knowledge conceptualization and progressive building of models. «Thinking in terms of systems» according to P. Senge's demonstration [1990], implies having the ability to understand what are the key relationships which influence behaviours present in complex systems when it is necessary, and what is the managers' capacity when they have to «consider these sets».

Referring to our Figures 2 and 3, Figure 2 corresponds to a knowledge representation mode that we call «expert» and Figure 3, a procedural mode corresponding to the logical model building phase.

EDUCATIONAL DOCTRINES AND SYSTEM DYNAMICS TEACHING

We have chosen to present three doctrines, the first one is coming from science schools and the two others, from new schools. They were the most interesting to develop here and to compare with different aspects of our teaching.

SPENCER'S DOCTRINE

According to Spencer [1885], «our mind works inevitably from the concrete to the abstract» (in Alain's view [1959], «all our conceptions must bear the double mark of the human order and the preliminary abstraction ... Progress of the mind goes from the abstract to the concrete.») We do not enter into an epistemological controversy but we try to position our educational method in relation to these two assertions. In the modelling phase, we construct an abstract model from the concrete reality, but our own epistemological reference is abstract and inspire our concrete way of formalizing.

The construction of causal diagram develops «the power to observe with precision and to think independently» [Spencer 1885]. Moreover, Spencer specifies that in the studying of sciences, «relationships presented to the mind are causal relationships; and when they are taught accordingly, the student does understand them as such.» He also emphasizes that the student must find by himself as often as possible the teacher, saying as little as possible. We think that teaching based on system dynamics, contributes to a spontaneous development of intellectual activities and motivation.

DEWEY'S DOCTRINE

After a critical study of the English empiricism, Dewey [1947] agrees with Rousseau and recommends the student to think as well as to handle («*Learning by doing*», was Rousseau's [1762] and Froebel's [1861] expression). In system dynamics, the simulation results analysis requires us to look back at the model structure and so, to alternate with handling and thinking.

We don't always agree with some of Dewey's assertions which consist in defining, «the relationship, within the experiment, between past works and future events», because the past can be a source of judgment errors faced with complex problems.

DECROLY'S DOCTRINE

According to Decroly [1929], in educational practice, many processes are in contradiction with the classical theory of the induction and the deduction reasoning. In his opinion, the basic and visible event is that mental work at any stage, is or can be dominated, established, or anyway influenced by different tendencies of the subject. «In order to name this particular aspect of our mental activity, we offer «globalization» which is convenient to describe the perception stage.» At the initial phase of reality perception, we try hard to develop a systemic vision which could correspond to this cognitive function of globalization.

TRADITIONAL LEARNING METHODS AND SYSTEM DYNAMICS TEACHING

Method, technique and process are sometimes difficult to distinguish, because the same expressions can cover very different realities. As education developed, Cousinet [1949] thought that the word method has changed meaning because most methods were, naturally, empirical. «They were worth what empiricism itself is worth, which is the result of badly conducted experiments ... Consumer, in this particular instance the student, was on the receiving side.»

THE DIDACTIC METHODS

The traditional «didactical» methods are not against a system dynamics education. But we advise avoiding all preliminary acquisition of static methods given by predefined theories. It is necessary that the student using models, discover different control mechanisms in companies, instead of learning the E.O.Q. (economic order quantity) for instance.

THE INTERACTIVE METHODS

The methods called interactive, because they use simulation games, have the major disadvantage of substituting the playing aspect for the real interest of the student. Alain [1969] said : «Easy attention is no attention at all», and Rousseau's [1762] opinion was that : «Among so many remarkable methods to shorten the study of sciences, we would dearly need one of us to provide for a method to study them all with pain.» Using management games even very limited ones, conceived by the students themselves, is the solution that we advocate in our approach to logistics using system dynamics.

THE INTERROGATIVE METHODS

According to a UNESCO book [1981], titled *The Educator and the Systemic Approach*, it is interesting to ask some easy questions which directly speed up the thinking system. The interrogative methods, in particular the Socratic method, consider that knowledge must be conjured up in our minds which are in a latent state. These particular thought processes are present in our progressive modelling phases, which include the coupled cybernetic mechanisms of complex logistical systems.

THE INTUITIVE METHODS

The intuitive methods provide direct knowledge by observation, without intermediate intellectual operation. According to Piaget [1970], «intuition stays phenomenistical because it imitates reality's outlines without correcting them, and egocentric because it is constantly centred according to the moment's action : therefore, it lacks the balance between the assimilating of things to the thinking schemes, and the accommodating of the latter to reality.» That is the reason why this method is not appropriate for studying the flow dynamics of companies. Nevertheless, we agree with Comenius [Leif, 1959] who claimed that «not only do we look in order to know, but also to understand by going down to causes.» This is the phase of constructing the causal diagram. Spencer's [1885] opinion is that this type of teaching, is only the rational organization of empirical knowledge by application of observation methods and induction rules.

THE ACTIVE METHODS

According to Piaget [1970], the active methods consider that the actual experience must be deep and elaborated by a lively thinking which will improve it. Dewey [1947] offers that «a sharp mind must obtain qualities which will later strengthen its reasoning by :
1) the regular use of reflection, interest, attention, caution
2) the power to set up relationships between close and distant, present, past, and future objects
3) differentiating quickly the essential from the accessory
4) the need for testing, which is the highest level of intellectuality.»
In Mialaret's [1983] opinion «action and thinking are connected.» In taking action, we furthered the development and the exercise of thinking; firm and solid thinking manages better the action and gives it more effectiveness. The active methods' basic objective is to produce this reaction of the personality and to strengthen the mental activity by real and original exercise. The teaching based on system dynamics contributes to develop this double relationship between reflection (through the modelling phase) and action (through the simulations).

COUSINET'S METHOD

The art of research is the most important part of what Cousinet's [1949] method developed. In his opinion, it is much more important to see what the students are really doing, than to try searching for what they know, because doing is much more interesting and more in accordance with their nature. System dynamics as a teaching tool for a new subject, is appropriate for this knowledge transfer by action.

LEARNING BY SIMULATION GAMES

«Exceeding the training objective and approaching experimentation,» was A. Kaufmann's [1976] opinion about games. According to E. de Bono [1976], «Games have an internal logic and a good player quickly learn his internal logic because it is repeated so often. Life, unfortunately, has not such internal logic ...» Cousinet [1949] thought that many games played by pleasure, do not further one's knowledge because these two notions, pleasure and progress, are both amphibologic. Nevertheless, it is possible not to be particularly interested in things which can give us pleasure, but during an activity with some interest we can find forms which do not offer any pleasure but for which we are conscious of for our own objective.

J. W. Forrester [1969] said about games that «there are some close similarities between the business game and the full dynamic model. A few decisions are made by the human participants as the game progresses. In both there is a mathematical model, usually there is a computer, both concentrate on the business system, and both aspire to enhance understanding of the broader business scope. Here the similarities end.»

Games conceived by system dynamics models and which allow an analysis of the causes, are more efficient to understand complex phenomena (see Machuca 1992 and 1993 for example].

SUMMARY

According to D. Freedman [1993], «managers believe that they understand what relations between cause and effect inside their organizations are, whereas in fact links between action and its result are more complex than could be imagined.» P. Senge call this the «dilemma of the deep assimilation.» «To succeed in a linear approach gives satisfaction; to succeed in a non-linear, holistic, heuristic approach brings pleasure in discovering our own significance» [L.V. Williams 1986]. B. Richmond [1986] considers that evolutionary fusing of three threads : educational process, thinking paradigm and learning tools, can successfully create a permanent change in the way people learn.

EXAMPLE OF A LOGISTICS TEACHING PROGRAM

MODELS OF INDUSTRIAL SYSTEMS

The industrial systems are generally described by technical, economical, and social aspects.[3] Indeed, the driving decisions emerge from an industrial organization constituted by people and technologies.[4] In relation to the problematics of industrial logistics which consists in assuming a permanent activity control, the descriptive model based on complexity and uncertainty[5] of its environment seems to be the most suitable.

LEARNING MODELLING

We developed a teaching approach based on progressive system modelling.[6] First, we ask our students either to conceived limited models to understand different mechanisms in materials management for example (according to the types of models presented by J. Lyneis [1988] in «*Corporate Planning and Policy Design: A System Dynamics Approach*»). Then, they work on more complex generic[7] models and observe «in vitro» counter-intuitive behaviours. In this second phase, the educational objective of simulations consists in improving the understanding of complex behaviours and in guiding the driving of these systems. The system dynamics is activated by fluctuations of the most sensitive variables. Our approach also consists in trying to bring together the multiple cinematic structures identified by students with the dynamics of some industrial behaviours, independently of the physical activities of different companies. Therefore, it is not an analysis of a particular logistical system, but a research of relationships between different industrial structures and typical primitive behaviours. The numeric results only have a relative comparison value between different elaborated models.

This active method [according to Piaget, 1970] allows us to apply the simulation results to the companies and gives us the possibility to modify industrial system driving. It also allows us to improve the performances of the essential regulation loops in uncertainty.

CONCLUSION

This teaching implies a global vision of industrial management. It is composed of a basic theoretical system analysis and modelling applications. Systemic audits of industrial units contribute to the global perception of these complex feedback systems. Therefore, we just emphasize the necessary effort to a logistic management learning by systemic modelling teaching. This approach brings a larger and multi-disciplinary vision of industrial systems and vision of its dynamics to management.

ENDNOTES

1. Programming decisions according to H.A. Simon [1960].

2. H.A. Simon asserts that intuition is a recognition phenomenon [1969].

3. J. Woodward was particularly interested in sociology as an explicative tool of organizational phenomena [1971].

4. According to P. Baranger, it seems necessary to establish a relation between complexity and technology [1992].

5. Typology proposed by J.P. Kieffer and Y. Gousty [1986 and 1988].

6.   This educational process and the combining tools were used in a second cycle teaching progam (industrial logistics course) and two postgraduate programs (in production management and logistic business courses. In the last one, the concerned public have generalist engineering or management backgrounds with solid bases in statistics and mathematics [see Thiel 1992 and 1993a].

7.   These models are described in Thiel [1993b and 1992c]. 8. These indicators were picked in our previous survey [see Thiel 1993b]. 9. According to J.W. Forrester [1969]: «a high precision of results is secondary to improving knowledge.»

REFERENCES

Alain, *Propos sur l'Éducation*, Presses Universitaires de France, Paris, 1959.

Baranger, P., «Gestion de la production; un état de la littérature récente», XIèmes journées nationales des IAE, Annales du management, 1992, p. 73-86.

Bensoussan, A. «La recherche en gestion», Colloque FNEGE, Nancy, 1982, p. 5-29.

De Bono, E., *Teaching Thinking*, Penguin Books, 1976.

Bowersox, D.J., *Logistical Management*, Macmillan Publishing Co., Inc., 1978.

Cousinet, R., *Une méthode de travail libre par groupes*, Les Éditions du Cerf, Paris, 1949.

Decroly, O., *La fonction de globalisation et l'enseignement*, Maurice Lamertin, Bruxelles, 1929.

Dewey, J., *Expérience et éducation*, Librairie Armand Colin, Paris, 1968 from the original title *Experience and Education*, Edition Kappe Delat Pi. Heidelberg College, Ohio, 1947.

Forrester, J. W., *Industrial Dynamics*, MIT Press, Cambridge, Massachusetts, 1969, p. 344-361.

Forrester, J. W., *Principes des systèmes*, Presses Universitaires de Lyon, 1984.

Freedman, D., «A science, management,» Harvard-l'Expansion, Spring 1993, p. 6-13.

Froebel, F., *L'éducation de l'homme*, L. Hachette et Cie, Paris et Ferdinand Claass, Bruxelles, 1861.

Gousty, Y. et J.P. Kieffer., «Une nouvelle typologie pour les systèmes industriels de production», Revue française de gestion, juin-juillet-août 1988, p. 104-112.

Kaufmann, A., R. Faure et A. Le Garff., *Les jeux d'entreprises*, Collection Que sais-je?, Presses Universitaires de France, Paris, 1976, p. 71.

Kieffer, J.P., *Les systèmes de production, leur conception et leur exploitation*, Thèse d'État, Université Aix-Marseille III, 1986, p. 40-48.

Leif, J. and G. Rustin, *Pédagogie générale par l'étude des doctrines pédagogiques*, Librairie Delagrave, Paris, 1959.

Lyneis, J.M., *Corporate Planning and Policy Design : A System Dynamics Approach*, Pugh-Roberts Associates, 3, Cambridge, 1988.

Machuca, J.A.D., «The Need for a New Generation of Business Games for Management Education,» System Dynamics Review, n° 22-1, 1992.

Machuca, J.A.D., M.A.D. Machuca, A. Ruiz et J.C. Ruiz., «Systems Thinking Learning for Management Education and Transparent Box Business Games. What Are Our Ideas and How Are We Going About It in Sevilla?,» Second European Congress of Systems Science, Praha, Czech Republic, 1993.

Mialaret, G., *Introduction à la pédagogie*, Presses universitaires de France, 6, Paris, 1983, p. 124-134.

Moisdon, J-C., «Recherche en gestion et intervention», <u>Revue française de gestion</u>, sept-oct 1984, p. 61-73.

Piaget, J., *Introduction à l'épistémologie génétique*, from the original title *Genetic Epistemology*, Columbia University Press, New York, 1970.

Richmond, B., «System Thinking : Critical Thinking Skills for the 1990s and Beyond,» <u>System Dynamics Review</u>, 9-1993, p.113-133.

Rousseau, J-J., *L'Émile*, livre 3 : 198, 1762.

Senge, P., *The Fifth Discipline : The Art and Practice of the Learning Organization*, Doubleday, New York, 1990.

Simon, H.A., *The New Science of Management Decisions*, Evanston, Harper and Row Publishers, New York, 1960.

Simon, H.A., *The Sciences of the Artificial*, MIT Press, Cambridge, 1969, p. 91.

Spencer, H., *De l'éducation intellectuelle, morale et physique*, Félix Alcan Éditeur, 1885, p. 48-64.

Thiel, D., «Formation systémique à la modélisation des systèmes de production» in Actes du premier Colloque européen *Productique et Formation*, PRO FORMAT-92, Marseille, 1992, p. 191-195.

Thiel, D., «Enseignement systémique et complémentarité des modèles stochastique et continu de systèmes de production» in Actes du Congrès AFCET 1993 Systémique et Cognition, colloque *Communication, information et esprit d'entreprise*», Afcet, Paris, 1993a, p. 51-59.

Thiel, D., *Management industriel, une approche par la simulation*, Economica, Paris, 1993b.

Thiel, D., «Modèles génériques de comportement des systèmes de production», <u>Revue internationale de systémique</u>, Afcet, Dunod, 7 (2), 1993c, p. 117-142.

Trotter, R.J. and J. Mc Connel., *Psychologie, science de l'homme*, Les Éditions HRW Ltée, Montréal, 1980, p. 185-221, from the original title *Psychology, The Human Science*, Holt, Rinehart and Wintson, 1978.

UNESCO, *L'éducateur et l'approche systémique*, Manuel pour améliorer la pratique de l'éducation, Organisation des Nations Unies pour l'éducation, la science et la culture, Paris, 1981.

Walliser, B., *Systèmes et modèles, Introduction critique à l'analyse des systèmes*, Éditions du Seuil, Paris, 1977.

Williams, L. V., *Deux cerveaux pour apprendre*, Les Éditions Organisation, Paris, 1986, from the original title *Teaching for the Two-Sided Mind*, Prentice Hall.

Woodward, J., *The Structure of Organisations*, Pugh, 1971, p. 56-71; and excerpts from *Management and Technology*, H M S O , 1958, p. 4-21.

CHAPTER TEN

POLITICAL ALIGNMENTS AND INTERNATIONAL ACCOUNTING STANDARDS: THE CASE OF TAIWAN

Karen Cascini
Sacred Heart University
FAIRFIELD, CONNECTICUT U.S.A.
William Thomas Stevens
St. John's University
NEW YORK, NEW YORK U.S.A.

Abstract

Culture and environment are powerful forces. Accounting principles may be viewed as an economic measurement manifestation of their influence. Countries adopt accounting principles in accordance with the needs of their environment, their culture, and their perceptions of their role in the world or their desired political alliances. In this paper, the authors present some preliminary evidence suggesting that a nation's political and economic policies can be analyzed, in large part, by studying its accounting standards. Using the Republic of China (Taiwan), a country far removed from the western world both culturally and environmentally, as an example, it is shown that their adoption of a particular set of accounting standards indicates an alignment, economically and politically, with the United States of America.

INTRODUCTION

The problem of communicating financial information across national boundaries has long been recognized. Further, when the information is prepared under different legal systems, varying tax statutes, divergent social, political and demographic environments, dissimilar languages, ethnic and national cultures, and separate accounting rules, the problem of interpreting widely different data is compounded exponentially [Schroeder, et al., 1991: 723].

The complexity of the problem can be appreciated from the following report on a typical international joint venture [Most, 1991]:

The Japanese Saison Group and Scandinavian Airlines System (SAS) own 60% and 40% respectively of Inter-Continental Hotels Corporation, with subsidiaries in 46 countries . . . One [can imagine] the accounting Babel that this combination represents. Saison is a Tokyo-based, family controlled, conglomerate of 120 mostly unlisted companies. SAS is a Stockholm-based airline controlled by Scandinavian governments [Denmark, Norway, and Sweden]. Inter-Continental was founded by Pan American World Airways, and presumably endowed with a U.S.- type accounting system managed by U. S.-trained accountants. Its $1 billion of debt is owed in a number of countries, and besides being accountable to parents speaking very different accounting languages, Inter-Continental must also present financial statements to many lenders who speak yet others.

Enthoven [1976: 1] had earlier characterized and summarized the problem of interpreting and reporting activities for international enterprise by commenting, ". . . harmonious economic and social development . . . is probably the most pressing problem facing our current civilization, and neglecting or evading this problem could well lead to disastrous economic, social, and political consequences.

PURPOSE OF THE PAPER

In this paper we: (1) briefly trace the International Accounting Standards Harmonization Movement. (2) show that national cultural issues and accounting principles are inextricably linked and are not only environmentally related but are also political in nature; (3) demonstrate that national cultures tend to be controlled by attitudes of dominance on the part of some nations; and (4) using as preliminary evidence the case of the Republic of China (Taiwan, but hereafter ROC), a nation about as culturally distant from the United States as it is possible to be, we suggest that non-dominant countries tend to adopt accounting principles based on political alliances or economic alignments. Further, if the accounting principles they adopt are unaligned to a dominant power, the nation has visions of its eventual world-wide influence or dominance. We show that the ROC through its 21 basic recently adopted accounting standards [Soong, 1992] is aligned politically and economically to the United States.

The Republic of China was selected as the basis for the preliminary thesis that a nation's accounting standards represent its politics and economic policies because it has become a large-scale international manufacturer and exporter.

THE INTERNATIONAL ACCOUNTING STANDARDS
HARMONIZATION MOVEMENT

Each nation has its own accounting rules which tend to mirror certain elements of that nation. A country's economic, legal, and political systems : stage of technological development or sophistication ; culture and tradition ; and various other socioeconomic factors all influence the development of accounting standards. Today businesses are international in scope and they have economic activity that crosses national boundaries. They seek investment capital in foreign markets, and they conduct their operations through facilities in foreign countries. Given the growth of international business activity, and especially international investment, comparability of accounting standards has a high priority. Although there was little disagreement that greater harmonization of accounting principles would facilitate international investment, there was no agreement on which general approach should be followed to achieve this harmonization.

The concept of establishing international standards of accounting germinated around the turn of the century when, in 1904, the First International Congress of Accountants was held in St. Louis. This idea reached maturity as a result of the Tenth International Congress, with the formation of the International Accounting Standards Committee (IASC) in 1973 by the leading professional accounting bodies in nine nations : Australia, Canada, France, Germany, Japan, Mexico, the Netherlands, the United Kingdom and Ireland, and the United States. IASC presupposed that a set of uniform international accounting standards or principles (hereafter referred to as generally accepted accounting principles of GAAP) could be established, thus making accounting and financial reporting global. IASC possessed no sanctions and had no real authority to impose its findings on the nations more or less committed to participation in IASC's primary mission of identifying the appropriate and relevant standards [Hepworth, 1977; IASC, 1983]. The committee soon discovered two major barriers blocked its progress : (1) the strong hold culture -- ethnic, national, and professional — had on an individual nation's accounting principles; and (2) the general unwillingness of some nations, in particular the United States, as represented by the newly created FASB, to modify its accounting principles to conform with global views, maintaining an attitude that, more or less, the world had to adopt American principles. This view persists although FASB continues to provide assurance in a general, if rather vague way, of its commitment to harmonized accounting standards [Beresford 1989].

HARMONIZATION RATHER THAN UNIFORMITY

Uniformity in accounting standards quickly yielded to "harmonization." Harmonization was perceived as a practical compromise that would lead to "the reconciliation of different accounting and financial reporting systems by fitting them into common broad classifications, so that form becomes more standard while content retains significant differences," the initial step in a movement towards achieving the desired end product of uniformity, "the elimination of all alternatives in accounting for economic transactions, other events, and circumstances." [Cairns, 1989].

The search for harmonized principles continues but, till now, has been unproductive insofar as satisfying urgent needs are concerned. To illustrate, disagreement by member nations over the mandated uniform accounting standards to be used after the 1992 creation of the European Economic Community (EC), led the EC to abandon, at least temporarily, its requirement for uniform EC accounting standards. The cultural forces in individual member nations were too powerful to be renounced no matter how common the economic needs of the union. The EC recanted its mandate and each member nation was basically allowed to retain its own standards.

At present, IASC is proposing three GAAP classes: (1) 12 standards for which agreement was relatively easily secured; (2) 10 standards for which some nations have demanded local modifications; and (3) three standards which have defied general agreement and acceptance [Purvis, et al., 1991]. Other possibilities for standards are, at the moment, ignored and no agreement has been formally reached. The situation remains in limbo since "Different regions of the world are subject to different values, social mores, political implications, religious beliefs and economic constraints." [Bernard, 1991: 102]. Frequent and periodic public expressions of assurance that a full set of agreed-upon international standards are "just around the corner" [Cowan, 1991], but somehow the long-promised standards never seem to materialize.

IS INTERNATIONAL HARMONIZATION OF ACCOUNTING PRINCIPLES ATTAINABLE?

A number of researchers do not see cultural commitments as the impediment to harmonization [i.e., Most, 1991], asserting that these cultures have changed in the past and are constantly undergoing change. Early and post-World War II Japan and the creation of the EC are cited as examples. It is concluded that harmonization is "a worthy objective" that, generally, has the conceptual support of the world-wide accounting profession. "Harmonization" is seen as "the elimination of all alternatives in accounting for economic transactions, other events, and circumstances," a movement that is primarily cost driven. Using the Inter-Continental example cited supra, the current multitude of national "accounting standard-setting" processes and their resultant standards is seen as uneconomic and, coupled with auditing difficulties, dramatically increases "cost of capital and corporate operating expenses."

Accordingly, the argument runs, that the search of harmonization should be focused on a set of universal accounting truths or a conceptual framework that is acceptable to world-wide financial markets, derived from a scientific approach based on economic uniformities resting on "internationally understood logic and conceptual coherence" of the basic accounting measurement issues of recognition, classification, and disclosure [i.e., Anthony, 1987; Most, 1991].

While this view may be conceptually commendable, we conclude that international harmonization of accounting standards is unlikely to ever come to pass because of two overwhelming cultural constraints, constraints far more powerful than ethnicity or environment: (1) the professional culture of governance over accounting standards, a seemingly localized, narrowly focused matter that, cumulatively, becomes global; and (2) the national culture of supremacy present in some nations—a desire to be the dominant player in international affairs, a self-perceived mission or role of global leadership.

THE CONSTRAINT OF PROFESSIONAL GOVERNANCE

The long-standing, overwhelming desire of professions to govern and, thus, control the practice of the profession is well known. Practitioners of Medicine, Law, Engineering, and Religion, among others, constantly strive to maintain and, if possible, expand the boundaries of their authority over their profession. It is no different with accountants.

THE ECONOMICS OF GOVERNANCE

Despite some relatively impotent constraints, the accounting profession has succeeded in preserving both functional and operational governance, especially in the United States. This is also the case throughout much of the world; even where accounting rules are rooted in specific legislation, that legislation has largely been spearheaded by the profession. So strong is the profession's preoccupation with governance, that "Lord" (then Sir Henry) Benson has, with firm and tireless steadfastness, exhorted the accounting profession world-wide to resist any proposed accounting standards, no matter how appropriate they might be, if they are not first and directly promulgated by the accounting profession [Benson 1981].

The accounting profession's great concern over governance is as much basically economic as it is publicly altruistic. Accounting simplification is the profession's economic enemy. Large international accounting firms have massive infrastructures that must be supported by fees if they are to survive. Simplification will reduce rather than expand revenues. Harmonization, as noted *supra,* has been largely accepted by the world-wide accounting profession as a cost reduction program, but it is highly debatable either that any cost reductions that might result will flow through to the public or that harmonization will be accepted if it results in fee-reducing simplifications. Based on the historical track record of the profession, it is doubtful that harmonization will come to pass if it involves shifting governance to some other body. Indeed, there is a movement, unjustified from an educational viewpoint, to require "professional" accountants, that is, certified public accountants, to have not less than 150 credit-hours of formal education *almost without regard to the content of the additional educational credit requirements.* This is a natural consequence of a profession. Its members must, somehow, be set apart from others, by licensing, by education, by examination, by experience, by restriction of functions, or by whatever other means will set the practitioners apart from their fellows. One needs only to review the history of the jurisdictional strikes that plagued the United States after World War II to see the economic significance of governance.

The risks of professional governance have long been recognized—governance of the military profession in the United States has always been vested not in the profession but in the laity. In countries where this is not the prevailing situation or is a weak case, the abuses of the military are well known.

We contend the accountants will be unlikely to surrender their local governance authority. This suggests that attaining of agreement on the common ground of international accounting and a global governance removed from their authority is highly unlikely. It is simply not in their best economic interests to do so. But a more serious deterrent to harmonized international accounting standards lies in the national culture of *supremacy.*

THE NATIONAL CULTURE OF SUPREMACY

Supremacy, the national drive to international dominance impacts dramatically on international accounting harmonization. The influence of culture on society, business, economics, and accounting is well known. Examples are Marx [1986], who dealt with powerful influences of culture on a socially global basis, Schein [1988], who concentrated his studies on organizations, Scott [1931] focused on accounting, Miranti [1991] was concerned with the accounting profession, while the Spindlers [1990] viewed America as a cultural entity; but these examples need not be repeated here. Our concern is the drive for world domination exercised by once powerful, currently powerful, or emerging powerful nations. Cases of nations seeking international domination are well known, such as Hitler's German Third Reich, Japan's Asian Co-Prosperity movement, and the 70-plus-year Soviet Union's push to extend communism to the world, among others. However, we will generally focus only on the culture of supremacy, the bent for dominance that drives the domestic as well as international actions of the United States of America, in recent years, arguably the most powerful and influential nation in the world.

THE AMERICAN CULTURE OF SUPREMACY

When the British colonies that would become the United States of America were a small and seemingly impotent revolutionary force seeking and succeeding in overcoming what was, at the time, the most powerful nation in the world, Great Britain, a hardy and adventuresome national character was being forged. Hardened by the rigors of the frontier and a history of having never lost a war (until, perhaps, Viet Nam), the United States became the most powerful nation in the worlds [Spindler, G. and L, 1990]. Often viewed as the saviour of the world after intervening in World Wars I and II, rebuilding the world through mechanisms like the Marshall Plan and, already filled with a sense of power, the United States became the center of world finance, banker to the world, the major world-wide economic force as both merchant and creditor. Through a sort of welfare mindset, America distributed its largess to those nations of the world who would, more or less, acquiesce to the American viewpoint on politics, economics, and morality or, at least, offer them lip service. With the United Nations action in Korea, the United States became widely viewed as the world's policeman. The United States began to seek to dominate the world, to be benevolent, benign, but supreme.

ACCOUNTING AND NATIONAL SUPREMACY

In the case of accounting the United States has also demonstrated an unrelenting commitment to the culture of national supremacy. As we have seen, FASB has "paid lip-service to the objective of harmonization" but ,in practice, the board has been largely unyielding insofar as accepting modifications of American GAAP unless the changes arise from FASB itself or, possibly, the American Securities and Exchange Commission (SEC) where the true authority for establishing accounting standards technically lies. Harmonization, in the FASB frame of reference, is desirable only if it reflects FASB rules, an attitude representing not only the sentiment of national supremacy but also likely reflects the view of the American accounting profession given its commitment to governance. Indeed, FASB's chairman has indicated that harmonization was not likely to come about in the near future [Beresford, 1989]. This attitude of the American right to dominance in financial matters persists even though, as we have seen, 80 or so nations indicated, in late 1991, that they were on the verge of adopting an IASC-developed "internationally accepted set of accounting rules," which has yet to come to fruition.

OTHER NATIONAL SUPREMACY CULTURES

While the United States seems, at the moment, to possess the most powerful cultural bent towards supremacy, it is not limited to the United States. To illustrate, Japan has, at least twice, changed its public cultural profile from the days of military dominance, but there is considerable evidence that Japan has, in fact, not abandoned its view of Japanese supremacy, but merely shifted its accomplishment mode from war to economics [Cunningham 1992]. The United Kingdom continues to hanker after Victorian days when the sun never set on the British empire and, as the father in *Mary Poppins* proclaimed, "The British pound is the envy of the world." The EC's plan for a single European currency seems stalled at this writing by British unwillingness to abandon the pound. And, among others, the question of what the effect of the reunification of Germany will have on their latent culture, national pride, or bent to dominance remains to be answered.

THE EMERGENCE OF NEW
NATIONAL SUPREMACY CULTURES

It must be recognized that while national supremacy leanings do not easily die, they are also not constant. Russia and its political brand of extreme socialism is currently on the wane as a major power but communism is far from dead and a new national exponent of the philosophy may arise and claim a place in the international arena as a major player in global affairs. New national powers emerge from time to time, just as the United States came into existence as a major global force over time and as a consequence of events. Japan, at the moment, is clearly becoming a major global economic force. Other nations are likely to gain world wide power in one form or another over time.

ACCOUNTING STANDARDS AND THE DEVELOPMENT
OF NATIONAL SUPREMACY

It is the general message of this paper that an examination of a nation's accounting standards may provide some of the first indications of the embryonic stages of becoming a global power. One needs only to examine the accounting standards adopted by a nation to deduce its political leanings. A country choosing to adopt the American set of accounting principles (subject to some local ethnic cultural differences) may be evidence that nation has chosen to align itself economically and probably politically with the United States. If the communist concepts of accounting are adopted, the alignment is to socialism in one form or another. If the nation follows the general rules of Japan, this provides evidence of an alignment with that emerging power.

But if a nation's accounting principles do not follow any established political or economic alignments, this would seem to provide some evidence to the effect that nation views itself as an emerging global economic and potentially politically dominant force or, alternatively, has chosen to remain fully independent and nonaligned.

The ROC has, in recent years, adopted a set of 21 accounting standards. Prior to adopting the new set of standards, their accounting principles were largely a hodge-podge mixture of diverse standards lacking cohesiveness. How does the ROC currently view itself? An examination of their 21 accounting standards may provide some indication of its future view of itself.

ANALYSIS OF THE REPUBLIC OF CHINA'S ACCOUNTING STANDARDS

Even though the ROC has a unique culture, it appears that the United States' influence has been important in establishing the ROC's accounting tradition. The ROC's accounting standards tends to be relatively conservative and secretive compared to the Anglo-Saxon countries. A study of the ROC's accounting standards reveals that, primarily, the accounting principles used in the ROC are similar to those followed in the United States. There are, however, certain significant differences as well as some relatively minor ones [Evans, et al, 1994].

FIXED ASSETS AND INFLATION

The principal differences between ROC and American accounting principles lie in the area of fixed asset evaluation and impairment. While the United States, through its standard-setting body FASB, does not require the reevaluation of fixed assets and is silent on the matter of asset impairments. The ROC allows reevaluation of fixed assets, wasting resource assets, and/or intangible assets provided ROC price levels rise by 25 percent or more [Soong, 1992: 52].

This provision is understandable when one considers the ROC environment. In the past, the ROC has been subject to fluctuating currency values and inflation, a cultural and environmental situation of considerable economic significance not present to the same degree in the United States. Indeed, inflation in the United States had been regarded as relatively minor, so much so that an official attempt (through FASB 33) to insinuate inflation into the financial statements was abandoned as essentially meaningless.

FIXED ASSET DISPOSITIONS AND
DEFERRED INCOME TAXES

Gains on the sale of fixed assets are not taken to income in the ROC but, instead, are credited directly to equity [Soong, 1992: 65]. This seems rational for the ROC since an inflation factor of 25 percent or more mandates asset reevaluation. To include dispositions of such inflated assets in the income statement would distort the concept of operating income (for the same reason, the American all inclusive, segmented approach to income determination is not employed in the ROC) and, moreover, would subject the firm to taxes on what is essentially unrealized income.

Adhering to a similar rationale, the ROC does not actually require deferrals of income taxes, making the recognition of deferrals optional [Orsini, et. al., 1993, ¶38.2]. Deferred taxes are officially an accounting requirement, but the implementation rules have not been finalized. This is possibly due to the difficulties experienced in the United States with this issue, especially with respect to deferred tax assets. Since it has been shown that the current American deferred tax rules provide a vehicle for income smoothing [Casabona and Stevens, 1993], and the wide swings in inflation and price level changes common to the ROC, management's perceived need for some mechanism for dampening these effects and, thus, smoothing income seems desirability. The optional approach to tax deferrals seems to satisfy this desire. In any event, in a nation with a volatile economy and current rates subject to dramatic gyrations in value from time to time, deferred taxes becomes difficult to express in terms that are meaningful for future, often uncertain events.

MINOR DIFFERENCES

A number of other minor differences also exist between ROC and American accounting principles. These seem to be largely environmentally or culturally based. Some pertain to lease constraints [Soong, 1992: 39]. Others deal with the matter of pension accounting [Soong, 1992: 16] which is currently being reevaluated. Consolidation rules, insofar as the treatment of goodwill is concerned, also differ [Soong, 1992: 54-56]. And there are several relatively minor differences concerning disclosures [Soong, 1992: 56]. These differences can each be traced to significant variances in culture or environment and are not generally germane to our paper.

SUMMARY AND CONCLUSION

Our basic contention in this paper is essentially preliminary. Much more in-depth study is needed to finalize the conclusion that non-dominant countries establish their accounting principles as much on political grounds as on their cultural and specific environmental considerations.   Using the ROC as a detailed example indicates that there are a number of factors that influence the level and sophistication of financial reporting practices in a particular country.   The United States has been economically, politically, and militarily supportive of the ROC and is one of the major, if not the major market for ROC Products.

Other countries seem to exhibit similar tendencies. Egypt, for example, now heavily dependent upon American foreign aid, has largely adopted American accounting principles. Eastern bloc countries once dependent on the Soviet Union largely adopted Russian accounting treatment rules. With the break-up of the union, some of these countries are studying the reformation of their accounting standards. While the transition is not yet complete, it will be interesting to see if the new principles follow those of their principle supporters or customers. We suspect they will. But this conclusion must await finalization of the changes and their analyses.

The culture of a nation coupled with the environment in which it exists, and the global political and economic forces of its world, are powerful factors. A nation's accounting standards, we believe, tend to be tangible manifestations of those factors.

REFERENCES

Anthony, R. N.   "We Don't Have the Accounting Concepts We Need." *Harvard Business Review*. January-February, 1987: 175-83.

Benson, Sir H. "Establishing Standards Through a Voluntary Professional Process Across National Boundaries." in *The International World of Accounting Challenges and Opportunities,* John C. Burton, Ed. (Reston, Virginia: The Council of Arthur Young Professors, 1981: 27-48.

Beresford, D. R. "Internationalization of Accounting Standards: An Update on the Role of the FASB." Unpublished paper presented at the *Annual Meeting of the American Accounting Association.* Honolulu, Hawaii, August 1989.

Bernard, M. C. *Opening the Middle East Through Accounting.* Unpublished Master's Thesis, St. John's University, Jamaica, New York, 1991.

Cairns, D.   "IASC's Blueprint for the Future." *Accountancy.* December 1989: 80-83.

Casabona, P. A., and W. T. Stevens. "Income Tax Accounting: a Proposal for Caribbean and Latin American Countries." *Proceedings of the 8th International Congress of the North American Economics and Finance Association, 1993:* 45-56.

Cowan, A. L. "International Accounting Rules Advance." *New York Times.* December 2, 1991: D1, D5.

Cunningham, L. "Japanese Lead the Way in Economic War." *Fourth Estate.* Spring, 1992: 1.

Enthoven, A. J. H. "Social and Political Impact of Multinationals on Third World Countries (and Its Accounting Implications)." Paper presented at *60th Annual Meeting of the American Accounting Association.* August 1976.

Hepworth, J. A. "International Accounting Standards." *Chartered Accountant in Australia,* August 1977: 74-97.

Greenhouse, L. "Justices Hear Case on Right of U. S. to Kidnap Foreigners." *New York Times.* April 2, 1992: D22.

[IASC] International Accounting Standards Committee (IASC). 1983. *Objectives and Procedures.*

490

MacNeill/Lehrer News Hour,   Public Broadcasting Service, June 2, 1993.

Marx, K.   *Capital: A Critique of Political Economy,* 3rd Ed., trans. S. Moore and E. Aveling. New York: Popular Library, 1986.

Miranti, P. J., Jr. 1991. *Accountancy Comes of Age: The Development of an American Profession, 1886-1940.* Chapel Hill, North Carolina: University of North Carolina Press.

Most, K. S. (citing a 1991 *Wall Street Journal* report).   "Towards the International Harmonization of Accounting." Unpublished ms., *Association of Chartered Accountants in the United States.* 11 pp. (courtesy of author).

Mueller, G., H. Gernon, and G. Meek. *Accounting: An International Perspective,* 2nd Ed. Homewood, Illinois: 1991.

Orsini, L. L., J, P. McAllister, and R. N. Parikh. *World Accounting.* New York: Matthew Bender, 1993.

Purvis, S. E. C., H. Gernon, and M. A. Diamond. "The ISAC and Its Comparability Project: Perquisites for Success." *Accounting Horizons.* June 1991: 25-44.

Schein, E. H. *The Culture of Organizations.* Reading, Massachusetts: Addison-Wesley, 1988.

Schroeder, R. G., M. Clark, and L. D. McCullers. *Accounting Theory, 4th Ed.* New York: John Wiley and Sons, 1991.

Scott, DR.   *The Cultural Significance of Accounts.* New York: Henry Holt, 1931.

Soong, T. N. *The Accounting Profession in Taiwan, Republic of China.* New York: American Institute of Certified Public Accountants, 1992.

Spindler, G. and L. *The American Cultural Dialogue and its Transmission.* New York: The Falmer Press, 1990.

Tyler, S. "U. S. Strategy Plan Calls for Insuring No Rivals Develop." *New York Times.* March 8, 1992: A1, A14.

THE INTERNATIONALIZATION OF COLLEGES
THE CASE-STUDY OF COLLÈGE DE BOIS-DE-BOULOGNE

Bernard Lachance
Collège de Bois-de-Boulogne
MONTRÉAL (QUÉBEC) CANADA

Abstract

In this text, the Director-General of Collège de Bois-de-Boulogne will outline the approach used by the college to internationalize its activities, the results obtained by the adoption of the College's Administrative Council of a *Declaration of Intention Regarding Internationalization* and the difficulties encountered in putting such a policy into action.

INTRODUCTION

At the beginning of 1990, aware of the challenges posed to Quebec by the free movement of goods and people between countries, Collège de Bois-de-Boulogne decided to commit itself to internationalization. Even as early as 1990, the economic forecasters were predicting, not only that we must increase the number of college graduates, but that 50% of these same graduates would have to participate in international activity by the year 2000, either through dealing with foreign partners or customers or through direct overseas involvement. The new Director-General of the college was given a mandate to involve the college more closely with the community and with the outside world. The challenge was all-embracing because it was, and still is, necessary to prepare our students to become citizens of the world. Up to that time, without being excessively inward-looking, the college had limited its participation to the Greater Montreal area and to the network of Quebec community colleges. We had therefore to embark on a new and important direction which involved not only the setting-up of new services but above all a change of cultural attitudes in our very organization.

THE SITUATION AT THE BEGINNING

Collège de Bois-de-Boulogne is one of 47 academic and technical community colleges in Quebec, providing either a compulsory 2-year programme for university-bound students or a 3-year technical programme complete in itself. The college receives about 3000 full-time students every year, together with 10 000 part-time students, many of them following custom-made programmes requested by 150 client companies. 70% of our students will go on to university. In 1990, the college was already on its way to internationalization since 24% of our students were new Quebecers, coming from some forty different ethnic communities. The 3-year technical programmes offered by the college are all in the service sector and thus form part of the training of professionals who will be working in a significantly multi-cultural mosaic.

We had to take into account other factors, particularly the difficulty of financing activities not specifically mentioned in the student curriculum and the failure, at that time, of colleges to acknowledge the international dimension in their educational mission as they then perceived it. We must also note that colleges are bound by both financial and pedagogical constraints which leave them little room to maneuver. Colleges are institutionalized bureaucracies. The college, while maintaining the high standards required of its students and focussing carefully on the needs of its clientèle, has always organized itself on the principle of respecting the sense of responsibility of its faculty and staff. This is in turn made it necessary that each member of our college community accept and assimilate all the changes implicit in our new venture. We therefore had to adopt a strategy which promoted individual participation.

THE STRATEGY WE CHOSE

The Director-General immediately assigned the responsibility for overseeing the implementation of the internationalization policy to one senior member of the management team. He was relieved of all other duties and devoted his time entirely to coordinating such an implementation. A former Secretary-General of the college, he and the Director-General then worked out the strategy necessary to establish an institutional programme of internationalization.

The first step was to identify those members of the college community who had come from overseas or who had overseas experience. It was thought that these people would already be particularly receptive to the new approach. Of our 250 members of faculty and staff, 80 were so identified. Meetings were arranged with a number of them and eight were invited to sit on a committee to advise the college administration on what further steps should be taken. Four were teachers and four were involved with adult or daytime education in a non-teaching capacity. The Director-General and the International Development advisors were *ex officio* members of the committee. The second step, and no doubt the most important, was to produce a *Declaration of Intention Regarding Internationalization* which defined the direction the college would take.

The Declaration explained why such a policy was essential, defined its goals, described the services which would be introduced and finally outlined the steps necessary to realize the objectives of internationalization.

The Declaration had to be brief, clear and acceptable as a consensus. It was deliberated over by a number of bodies within the college before being officially adopted by the Administrative Council on June 12, 1990. The principal elements of the Declaration :

1. The college has three aims :
   a) to prepare the students for life in a changing world and to equip them to work in a competitive global market;
   b) to enrich the knowledge and experience of all the members of our college community, to improve the quality and the relevance of our teaching and related activities and to raise our social and international consciousness;
   c) to improve the position of the college in a competitive market.
2. The college envisages three categories of activity to achieve its goals :
   a) the introduction of internationalization as a component of existing programmes, new programmes, exchanges, study-periods abroad, and other new initiatives;
   b) the welcome of foreign students into existing and new programmes, together with active recruitment of such students through activities like exchange schemes and sending our own people for study-periods abroad;
   c) educational services overseas.
3. The college will participate if the following conditions have been met :
   a) the training of personnel;
   b) the development of international awareness and a consensus on content;
   c) the welcome of foreign students here for a practicum and the sensitization of personnel and students going overseas;
   d) partnership in the carrying-out of projects;
   e) the self-financing of these activities.

So that this Declaration would have its full impact on all college activity, it had to become part of the thinking of every sector of the college. To this end, we carefully avoided setting up a new body. Rather, we planned to involve as many participants as possible. We used the following strategies :

- At the purely educational level, we introduced four new courses, each in a different discipline, into the list of complementary courses and into the list of choices offered specifically to students of Human Sciences and Administration. The four courses were International Economics, Anthropology - the study of different world cultures, Geography - the map of the world and International Politics.
- With the cooperation of the Quebec Association of Forwarding Agents, the college introduced a new major in International Commerce.
- With the same end in view, our Adult Education Service, in cooperation with the Federal Development Bank, introduced a practical business programme for those small and medium-sized businesses interested in exporting their product.
- The college increased its attention to its Modern Language School and developed new initiatives, including

language immersion sessions. A sixth modern (Asiatic) language was added to our range of linguistic offerings.

- Four different teams participated in overseas projects : in Niger, Cambodia, Equatorial Africa and Martinique. Twenty of our personnel were involved. Other, less intensive projects were undertaken in a number of other countries.
- Study-periods abroad and student exchanges were arranged in three different departments within our Technical and Vocational sector.
- Our personnel participated in twenty visits abroad and we received almost as many visitors at the college.
- Our Department of Student Services sponsored groups of students who undertook to sensitize the student body by organizing competitions with international themes and intercultural activities. One group concerned itself particularly with promoting intercultural awareness on our campus.

These first steps were undertaken in the years following the adoption of the *Declaration of Intention*. For the most part they were outlined in the programme of proposed activities published annually by the college. On average, a hundred people were involved from all the departments and services committed to the internationalization of our college.

Less than a year later, the college adopted a second *Declaration of Intention*, focussing particularly on intercultural education and the integration of new Quebecers into the life of our college community. The declaration sought intercultural rather than multi-cultural education. We aimed for one integrated culture rather than a profusion of parallel cultures so that we might enrich our shared knowledge with mutual understanding. The publication of this new Declaration was followed by a number of new initiatives, including : the publication of a guide against racism called *Living in Harmony*, professional development courses in interculturalism for personnel and faculty, courses in French for those who find difficulty with the language, a special programme, "Transition-Québec", to help newcomers integrate into our educational system and our job market, and many others. This second Declaration was complementary to the first. It was adopted separately and was the basis of a whole different series of initiatives, coordinated by a new appointee who nevertheless worked in close collaboration with the supervisor of our international cooperation programme.

After one more year we had established our presence in five different countries. Groups of our students, small in number for the moment, have a total immersion experience once a year in South America in planned environments. Four business groups have already made their first overseas commercial venture. Our first graduates in International Commerce have already entered the job market. The college has established a sizable network of partnerships across Canada and the world.

Every year, usually in February, the Administrative Council of the college receives a status report on the implementation of the Declaration. The results are interesting. Nearly half of the constituent departments and services of the college have been involved in one or another of the international activities. More than 100 of our personnel have been involved, some for the first time. More and more of our students have been sensitized to internationalization in various ways. There is much still to be done, especially when we look at what has been achieved by similar institutions in other countries. We still have to find more ways to get our students into immersion experiences overseas, the only real way, I believe, for them to truly understand and be comfortable with cultures other than their own.

DIFFICULTIES ENCOUNTERED AND AN ANALYSIS OF STRATEGIES

Some of the difficulties we met were foreseeable. Finance remains a major obstacle. It was only by acting as an executive agent for the Canadian Agency for International Development in certain projects that we were able to find, in part, the salaries of the two administrators who oversee our programme of internationalization. The annual cost of the college's international cooperation programme is in the order of $500 000. Our teaching costs are met by the provincial budget but our real problem lies in funding student activities, particularly immersion experiences abroad. We knew it would be a difficulty and we have not yet found a solution. Perhaps the problem is not entirely ours to solve. A second problem is in the recruiting of foreign students. We have had to delay this innovation because of a lack of available places. The urgency of the problem has, however, diminished since we are receiving many new students from immigrant families of various ethnic origins. More spaces would also become available if the college were to be enlarged. We have already made a submission to the Quebec Minister of Education to this effect.

As regards a collective support within the college of our project to internationalize, we have made great strides, especially in those areas where a large number of our personnel have learned from personal experience the advantages of living internationally. However, some of our people still have a problem distinguishing between the exoticism and the educative value of our innovations. Others are hostile to any change that will disturb their daily routine. Still others believe that the financing of our international projects is done at the expense of other college activities. Nevertheless, we have brought a majority to assimilate the new outlook and to seek the new goals.

There is one last difficulty, perhaps inherent in any action of this kind. It is not always easy to share collectively any experience and knowledge individually acquired. It is not always easy for one group to share with the whole community the enrichment it has enjoyed.

The strategy we chose, to establish an advisory committee which would meet regularly to examine developments, to make any necessary adjustments, and to interact at an informal level with the community as a whole on an individual basis, seems to have proved a good one. The creation of this committee and our Declaration of Intention are the two cornerstones of our whole collective movement to internationalization. It is only the beginning. There are many battles still to be won.

AN ANALYSIS OF CORPORATE GOVERNANCE PRACTICES: THE CASES OF GERMANY, JAPAN, AND THE UNITED STATES

Curtis C. Verschoor and Kevin S. Woltjen
DePaul University
CHICAGO, ILLINOIS, U.S.A.

Abstract

Corporate governance practices in publicly held companies have come under greatly increased public scrutiny in recent years. Causes include a substantial increase in the size and strength of financial institutions and particularly a greater public awareness of the importance of institutional investors to capital markets. A comparison of authority sharing governance practices in several countries having large well-developed capital markets raises questions for international investors and is the basis of recommendations for future actions.

INTRODUCTION

The increased importance of institutional investment entities, especially pension and other retirement funds, has been due to several factors. First, the past ten years have witnessed extraordinary returns from both debt and equity investments. Returns to investors from shares listed on the New York Stock Exchange averaged 16.2 percent annually between 1982-1992, while foreign equity markets averaged over 14 percent. The Salomon Brothers Bond Index averaged 11.7 percent over the same years. Only partly resulting from inflation, these returns have led to dramatic increases in the total value of institutionally managed investment funds.

Another consideration in the United States is that American society as a whole is taking greater personal responsibility for funding its own retirement. Thus, workers are investing more in retirement and pension funds, such as 401k's and profit-sharing plans. Longer life expectancy and improved retirement life styles have also resulted in increases in the amounts devoted to retirement and other institutional funds.

These causes have resulted in a dramatic growth of institutional investment vehicles and a heightened market presence for institutional investors and money managers. These factors have enabled them to obtain a significant ownership position in all of even the largest public companies. Managers of these assets are beginning to take more active roles in influencing the corporations in which they represent shareholders. Changes have also resulted from the widely perceived need to protect the value of their investment positions from unnecessary market risk and the competition to increase their rate of return. This is a specific requirement necessary to fulfill an investment manager's fiduciary duty. These actions force the issue of shared authority to the forefront [Paefgen, 1992].

Systems under which shareholders can own enough shares of voting common stock in a corporation to command the attention of management are a form of shared authority. A great variety of management styles and corporate governance arrangements are available to smaller, more entrepreneurial corporations. Thus, this paper is limited to discussion of authority sharing corporate governance practices in only publicly held corporations.

AUTHORITY SHARING IN VARIOUS COUNTRIES

Although widely practiced in other countries, the concept of authority sharing was new to the United States until the recent emergence of institutional investors. American banks are presently barred by law from acquiring large portions of businesses in spite of the fact they are widely considered very capable investment managers.

Such statutes include the McFadden Act[1], the Glass-Steagall Act[2], and the Bank Holding Company Act[3].

On the other hand, many European and Asian nations, including Germany and Japan, have corporate governance practices which focus on financial intermediaries like banks who share control over corporate direction with internal management. Thus, these countries provide practical illustrations for countries such as the U.K. and the U.S. to review in determining the value of these conventions.

The presence of these practices abroad is also relevant because as today's capital markets become increasingly internationalized, the search for first-class investments is not limited by national borders. Foreign capital markets are eager to manage American assets. Similarly, the New York Stock Exchange (NYSE) as well as stock exchanges in other financial centers, competes to attract listings of the largest international corporations. Financial systems designed to monitor and provide market liquidity for such corporations are generally considered very congruent, most notably in the German and Japanese markets. However, since different regulations and disciplines do exist in various market places, international investors need to know these differences before risking their capital.

This paper will examine the German and Japanese employment of corporate governance practices of shared authority. It will examine differences in the regulations and disciplines in these financial markets, two of the world's largest. The discussion will also evaluate what shared authority practices may be appropriate in other countries, such as the U.S. or the U.K. This will be accomplished through a comparison of the costs and benefits shared authority practices provide.

CORPORATE GOVERNANCE PRACTICES IN GERMANY

German banks influence the actions of German publicly held corporations to a much greater degree than their American counterparts. German national banks can enter corporate boardrooms because they, like Japanese firms and increasingly like American institutional funds, hold concentrated voting blocks. These large positions arise from a combination of "direct ownership of stock, control over investment companies, and, most importantly, authority to vote stock that the bank's brokerage customers own but deposit with the bank." [Roe, 1993] This combination of the functions of banking, operation of mutual funds, and acting as a broker is patently illegal in the United States.

Control over large voting blocks and hence the proxy system, translates into board representation, and these representatives have the power to make managerial changes. Thus, German banks can influence management, or share corporate authority with internal management. Corporate governance in Germany vests authority in two boards of directors, a management board and a supervisory board. Interestingly, many believe the management board is the board with the most power, since it essentially manages daily decisions. The real power of the supervisory board is its oversight functions and its position of electing the members of the management board.

HISTORY OF CORPORATE GOVERNANCE IN GERMANY

The vast power of German banks developed in the late 19th century when Bismarck built German industry by "creating great banks as engines of development." [Roe, 1993] The statist political government allowed a central bank to provide liquidity for the German banks' long-term investments. The banks naturally wanted some governance influence over the investments made with funds they lent and thus banks became immersed in corporate affairs. However, when the newly unified German state subsequently taxed transfers of securities, as with most tax laws, a loophole emerged. Stockholders could avoid paying the tax by selling ownership but not physically transferring the securities. As stockholders preferred to deposit stock for safekeeping with bigger banks which could better match customers' sales and purchases, banks gained control over the proxy system. Thus, their role in corporate governance expanded exponentially.

Control of investors' proxies and the unlimited ability to directly invest in Germany corporations allow German banks to together elect virtually all of the stockholding side of the supervisory board. Because a bank representative is normally elected chairman, he becomes the "tie-breaker" when the worker half of the supervisory board unites to oppose the stockholding side on an issue. Despite the relative deliberateness with which banks have obtained their power, there has been intense political pressure to set up some controls on bank power over corporate affairs.

The first check on bank power came after the German Revolution of 1918. The Parliament sought to calm revolutionary forces by designing a system that gave workers a formal voice in corporate affairs--co-determination. [Buschgen, 1979] The system has since been dramatically enlarged, with its current format set in 1976 after labor strikes in the 1970's intensified and commanded attention. Under this system, employees in big corporations elect one half of the supervisory board, and the shareholders-banks elect the other half. Besides appeasing the strong German populist constituency by having banks share power with employees, co-determination also makes this system appealing from a democratic standpoint because there are checks and balances on authority.

German politics brought labor and capital together in the corporate boardroom while American politics have fragmented these groups. The presence of employees reduces the power banks can wield in boardrooms. It thus "makes powerful intermediaries more politically palatable in Germany than they have been in America." [Roe, 1993] While American reservations may be dissipating now that banks are not the sole powerful intermediaries, German banks are presently under intense political pressure from forces not unlike those in the United States that historically disabled financial intermediaries. [Dornberg, 1990]

CURRENT DEVELOPMENTS IN GERMAN CORPORATE GOVERNANCE

German corporate executives have recently expressed their desire to get bankers out of supervisory boards, even if the doors are closed and private. However, managerial negative attitudes toward banker power are ambivalent. Managers praise the value of a banker ownership capability to thwart a hostile takeover although they condemn any banker interference in internal corporate affairs.

Even members of the German Bundestag wish to "limit the percentage of equity a bank could maintain in a nonbank enterprise and cut the number of supervisory board positions a banking executive could hold." [Dornberg, 1990] German financial institutions are now concerned that American-style legal restrictions may be imposed. In the United States, powerful interest groups combined with anti-bank emotions have produced laws restricting the scope of corporate activities banks can pursue.

To reduce similar protests in Germany, German banks, including Deutsche Bank (Germany's largest bank) have attempted to lower their public profile by announcing that in the future, they will be using their stock ownership position less aggressively. As a signal of these intentions, Deutsche Bank has announced it will sell a 3 percent stake in Daimler-Benz to US investors. Although this will reduce its shareholdings to 25 percent, the bank will likely retain its position of supervisory board chairman. Daimler is Germany's largest private-sector corporation and is ranked 16th in the world. It has also begun the process of becoming listed on the New York Stock Exchange. This action is viewed as a signal that German companies are willing to become more open and responsive members of the global corporate community.

SUMMARY OF GERMAN CORPORATE GOVERNANCE

In summary, Germany's corporate governance structure uses shared authority quite well. It formally and directly obligates internal management to respond to both large shareholder (bank) and employee interests. This reduces managerial agency costs and improves decision making by bringing more considerations and information into the process.

CORPORATE GOVERNANCE IN JAPAN

In some respects, Japan's structure of corporate governance is similar to that of Germany. Both systems are largely owned and controlled by huge financial intermediaries. Japanese financial institutions, however, differ from their German counterparts because in Japan they derive their power from cross-ownership, not proxy control. Japan's corporate governance structure includes shared authority because these large cross-ownership blocks share authority with corporate management.

At the heart of this cross-ownership is the keiretsu, an intricate group of intermediaries and firms that own some of each others' stock, at times amounting to half or more of the others' stock. Existing for the last 25 years, the typical keiretsu consists of four or five other investors, including banks and insurers. They typically each own about 5 percent blocks of stock in an industrial firm to create a strong four or five-holder stockholder coalition with only 20-25 percent of the outstanding stock. This authority sharing through cross-ownership is the result of cultural ideology and political maneuvering, not only by the Japanese people, but also by the United States occupation forces after World War II.

HISTORY OF JAPANESE CORPORATE GOVERNANCE

The political environment after World War II compelled the Allied Powers to essentially rewrite Japanese law based in large part upon American legal principles. The Supreme Commander, Allied Powers (SCAP) in the person of Douglas MacArthur, was entrusted with establishing this new society. SCAP initially sought to fragment firm ownership by breaking up zaibatsus, the predecessors of keiretsus. The plan prohibited Japanese banks from owning more than 5 percent of another firm's stock, a law similar to the later enacted American Bank Holding Company Act [Cox, 1993].

When communism in China and war in Korea emerged, however, SCAP partially abandoned the full fragmentation goal and sought primarily to build a stable economic ally. To build up the ally, SCAP allowed banks to develop close relations with industry, but did not allow intra-industry ties to emerge. This fostered the movement of stock from individuals to banks and insurers, and a drastic cross-ownership of finance and industry resulted, giving Japanese financial institutions their entrance to corporate authority. There are other factors contributing to the rise of Japanese banks to power. However, SCAP's altered political policy cleared the path for such actions.

Japanese culture stimulated this post-World War II cross-ownership of corporations which today is the foundation of authority sharing in Japan. Three centuries of isolation, ending in 1850s, resulted in Japan's stress on the Confucian ideal of the `primacy of the group' which grew out of the principles of filial piety and compromise, and subordinated the individual to the community. This group ethos is seen by "the tendency to frame disputes in terms of social rights and to resolve them by informal means," [Gibbons, 1990] or compromise, and not by litigation.

Many in the United States advocate adaptation of the Japanese non-litigious dispute resolution models, similar to mediation or arbitration. They are less expensive, less time-consuming, and result in higher compliance rates. However, there are major drawbacks to a system which tries to have all disputes settled out of court. The major problem with a system that does not use formal litigation is the lack of precedent, and the avoidance of public resolution on some issues desperately needing it. [Goldberg, et al., 1992] For its own good, Japan needs to litigate alleged securities violations to create this precedent and structure because "although the Tokyo Stock Exchange is the largest securities exchange in the world in terms of market capitalization, there is wide distrust, both inside and outside of Japan, of its securities markets." [Cox, 1993]

PREVAILING REGULATORY SYSTEM IN JAPAN

Japan's current regulatory system is commonly known as one of administrative guidance, and "reflects the pervasive Japanese philosophy that close ties between the regulated and the regulator is one of the greatest virtues of the Japanese financial system." [Cox, 1993] The relatively small number of powerful groups, keiretsus, have thrived because they have immense financial power. They are also able to control the compromise-based system managed by the friends they have developed in the Ministry of Finance, the government agency regulating large public corporations, using administrative guidance. The practice of moving from an elite policy-making ministry position to a position in the industry they previously regulated is known as "descending from heaven." The United States calls this practice a revolving door, and has raised questions about the direct movement of individuals from governmental regulatory positions to a private business with which they formerly had relationships.

The power held by the five largest financial institutions and industrial firms in their keiretsus, is far greater than the power held by the largest 25 investors of the largest American firms. The five largest holders of Toyota, Nisson, Matsushita, and Mitsubishi control roughly 20 percent of the total voting stock. On the other hand, the largest 25 investors in General Motors, IBM, and Exxon vote less than 20 percent of the total.

Although Japan technically has some means for stockholders to influence a firm's management, little influence is actually exerted by outsiders. First, representatives of financial intermediaries interact with the managers of corporations in monthly keiretsu Presidents' Council meetings, which are similar to supervisory board meetings in Germany. However, since financial services firms and industry are so closely related, this supposed check on authority actually gives the powerful groups carte blanche in corporate affairs. Japanese companies must each have an annual shareholder meeting. However, since almost all are scheduled for the very same day of the year, real outsider influence is again nearly impossible.

On the surface, it would appear that Japan was beginning to adopt corporate governance conventions practiced in other countries. These include the implementation of changes in the Japanese Commercial Code in October 1993 (which only relates to smaller private businesses), and a trend of emerging individualism which may in time force the legal culture to reformulate the substance of corporate laws affecting large corporations. Other than the omnipresent governmental ministries, there is little effective outside influence over corporations in Japan today. As an outsider, the foreign investor is well advised to beware.

SUMMARY OF JAPANESE GOVERNANCE

Therefore, although Japan's system of cross-ownership requires Japan's corporations to `share' their management authority with powerful intermediaries (i.e., keiretsus), because its cross-ownership is so encompassing, the concept of authority sharing is erased as the keiretsus control all authority. The close cooperation between industry, finance, and the governmental ministries facilitates management making decisions without any external interference.

CORPORATE GOVERNANCE IN THE UNITED STATES

As noted earlier, the size of institutional funds (particularly both private and public pension systems as well as mutual funds) has increased dramatically in recent years. As institutional funds have grown in size, they have also acquired corporate power in the form of voting rights. In the past, institutional investors tended to vote retention of the management slate of directors. More recently, however, American institutional funds have been seeking a greater say in the boardrooms of companies in which they have significant investments to fulfill fiduciary requirements and thus satisfy their investor beneficiaries.

Rather than just selling the shares of corporations they found out of favor, two groups of interested parties have arisen. The first group uses the concept of "relationship investing" by actively targeting corporations whose performance has been sub-standard. Through direct consultation and proxy influence for election of directors dedicated to make changes in management, they report having achieved significantly higher investment returns than otherwise would have occurred. The other group uses less direct methods by persuading corporations to change policies through spotlighting adverse publicity on them.

BENEFITS OF AUTHORITY SHARING

To determine the propriety of authority sharing in the United States, it is necessary to examine both the virtues and concerns it raises. A significant benefit is an increase in managerial accountability. Authority sharing may be most relevant when crises hit, because this is when shareholder representatives meet with directors and management to work up solutions. Senior management presumably tries to avoid these crises and the threat of displacement which directors can employ. Similarly, authority sharing personifies the various stakeholders having an interest in a company's affairs. This may increase managerial motivation by awakening them to the real and sincere shared interests involved. Authority sharing activities may also impose peer pressure upon the managers.

A third benefit of authority sharing is its facilitation of monitoring by multiple intermediaries. Institutional investors can ensure each constituency involved with the corporation that senior management keeps the corporation's, rather than its own, best long term interests always at heart. Another benefit is a tendency toward improved decision making as more parties inherently bring more information, wisdom, and experience to the process. A structure which contains shared authority also encourages power sharing, not domination, and fosters better understanding at the authority level. These virtues lead to the underlying benefit to all -- improved decisions that considered the interests of all stakeholders.

DISADVANTAGES OF AUTHORITY SHARING

Simultaneously, authority sharing can also be a severe drain on a corporation if the authority rests in too few hands, or hands which represent the same interests. For example, Japan's system of shared authority does not really fan out authority to more constituencies than management because of the cross-ownership keiretsu phenomenon. In Japan, all those with authority have similar interests, and therefore few shareholder perspectives are considered in the decision-making process for strategic decisions. Thus, authority is controlled by only one group in Japan, the keiretsu. Having the corporate authority dominated by a few groups leads to conflicts of interests which can lead to mutual managerial self-protection. For example, in Japan those in control seek to insulate their fellow keiretsu friends from problems.

American culture has also shaped our system of corporate governance and strong government regulation. The strength of the entrepreneurial spirit and emphasis on individual rights may add costs and result in uneconomic confrontation between government and business.

DEVELOPMENT OF U.S. GOVERNANCE PRACTICES

Dramatically, the United States commitment to securities regulation began in response to the effects of the Great Depression. In the early 1930's, the Senate Banking and Currency Committee found a catalogue of offenses believed to be at the heart of the stock market overheating in the heady 1920's. These findings highlighted the abuses by corporations that preceded the market's crash and emphasized the regulatory laxity that existed under the state laws governing the monitoring of corporate activity. It is interesting that these factors closely parallel those found in Japan today. The revelations of abuse and experiences of manipulative practices resulted in strong federal corporate and security laws and a culture of zealous regulation that continues to the present.

A system with built-in checks and balances should be inherently more stable over a longer period. This concept of rigorously enforced regulation is the basis for the system employed in the United States. The SEC acts as an eternal watchdog, employing "chain link fences" to ensure honesty and fair dealing through strict disclosure requirements containing real teeth.

COMPARISON OF GOVERNANCE PRACTICES

A prominent difference between German, Japanese, and American corporate systems is the degree to which owner-shareholders influence the actions of corporate managers. In Japan and Germany, corporate officers of the large firms have made decisions considering the influence of the votes of large blocks of stock. There are several advantages to authority sharing, but a fundamental benefit is that agents of institutions with large blocks of stock interact regularly with management. This constant interaction reduces the inherent conflict of interest between managers and owners, known as agency costs. This shared authority reduces potential abuses by management, such as insider trading or conflict of interest transactions.

The role of institutional funds in corporate America is dramatically expanding and evolving. Some such investors have sought to combine their voting power to exert more influence over management. Other institutional funds have sought less bullying tactics considering the business of ganging up as dysfunctional. Though the means may differ, the ends are the same - to foster truly independent corporate boards. Independent boards are the best avenue to reduce conflicts between management and shareholders (agency costs) and maximize corporate long-term profitability. This new function being undertaken by American institutional funds is invaluable. It provides American corporations with the main advantage of foreign systems-- investor interaction with management. This American form of shared authority will increase the efficiency and profitability of corporate America, making this concept one of significant importance.

RECOMMENDATIONS

In summary, therefore, the optimum structure of corporate governance in public corporations may be one that reduces agency costs while also maximizing the activities designed to benefit the interests of all constituent stakeholders involved. This can be achieved through increasing the opportunities for effective interaction of intermediaries between shareholders and management. A new proxy rule issued by the SEC will facilitate such interaction.

Because of the differences in corporate governance practices in various countries, investors in securities of foreign corporations should understand the culture within which authority sharing is practiced in the corporation's home country. They should also carefully investigate the amount of information given to and control allowed by shareholders before making significant investments in such securities.

ENDNOTES

1.   The McFadden Act restricts the extent to which national banks can establish and operate branches in more than one state.

2.   The Glass-Steagall Act limits the type of securities businesses American banks can engage in.

3.   The Bank Holding Company Act of 1956 requires American banks to remain passive investors by prohibiting bank affiliates from controlling more than 5% of a corporation's stock.

REFERENCES

Buschgen, H.E., "The Universal Banking System in the Federal Republic of Germany, Journal of Corporate Law and Securities Regulation(January 1979), pp. 1-32

Cox, J.D., "Regulatory Competition in Securities Markets: An Approach for Reconciling Japanese and United States Disclosure Philosophies," Hastings International and Comparative Law Review(Winter, 1993), pp. 149-164

Dornberg, J., "The Spreading Might of Deutsche Bank," New York Times, September 23, 1990, pp. D 28

Gibbons, D.J., "Law and the Group Ethos in Japan," International Legal Perspectives(Fall, 1990), pp. 98-110

Goldberg, Sanders, Sachs, Dispute Resolution, 2nd ed., (Little, Brown & Co., 1992)

Paefgen, T.C., "Institutional Investors Ante Portas: A Comparative Analysis of an Emergent Force in Corporate America and Germany," published by American Bar Association, Section on International Law and Practice, Summer, 1992, pp. 327-376

Roe, M.J., "Some Differences in Corporate Structure in Germany, Japan, and the United States," Yale Law Journal(June, 1993), pp. 1927-1998

WINNERS IN SCIENCE AND TECHNOLOGY
A CASE FOR THE DEVELOPING COUNTRIES
OF SOUTHERN AFRICA

Willem H J De Beer
Technikon Pretoria
PRETORIA, TRANSVAAL, SOUTH AFRICA

Abstract

Science and Technology are the creators of wealth. The European Economic Community stated that 40-80% of the economic growth of developed countries can directly be attributed to the implementation of new science and technology. Science and technology constitutes a major impetus to the economic growth of any nation, irrespective of the level of its national development. A country like Singapore's vision is that science and technology is the key to economic growth. Since 1980 they have invested in science and technology as part of a program to generate economic growth. Since then the standard of living has improved manifold in Singapore. According to the World Bank Atlas of 1990 the countries that are serious about the development of science and technology are showing excellent economic progress. The percentage change in the gross national product per capita from 1980 to 1989 was +8,8% for Korea, +5,7% for Singapore and -0,8% for South Africa.

What will be the characteristics of a developing country to be a winner in science and technology. The following are suggested and will be discussed. They are:
1. An appreciable percentage of the GDP must be invest-ed in the development of science and technology.
2. Between 65-80% of the money spent on the research and development of science and technology must be provided by the private sector.
3. Government and private industry must collaborate in the formation of a National Science and Technology Board with the vision to develop the country into a centre of excellence in selected fields of science and technology so as to enhance the country's inter-national competitiveness in the industrial and service sectors.
4. The principles of the management of science and technology must be understood and applied.
5. To be a winner in science and technology the country must develop its human resources.
6. Winning nations have industries with flat structures, which eliminate rigidity in the system and allow responsible workers to be entrepreneurial.
7. Winning nations appreciate the value of long term academic research, but they also actively promote short-term and medium-term research developments, directed toward economic upgrading.
8. Winning nations apply science and technology to conserve the environment.
9. Winning nations regard their skilled labour force as an asset and not as a cost.

ACTIONS TO BE TAKEN BY A DEVELOPING COUNTRY IN
SOUTHERN AFRICA TO BECOME A WINNER IN SCIENCE AND TECHNOLOGY

1. An appreciable percentage of the gross domestic product (GDP) must be invested in the development of science and technology. The developed nations of the world typically spend approximately 3% of their GDP on research and development. South Africa spends about 1% and the figure remains fairly

static. In the countries of the Pacific rim the percentages are increasing and they plan to invest even more in the development of science and technology. The situation is illustrated in Table 1.

TABLE 1
INVESTMENT IN SCIENCE AND TECHNOLOGY
AS PERCENTAGE OF THE GROSS DOMESTIC PRODUCT

Country	Investment in science and technology (% of GDP)
Singapore	0,2 (1978) 0,9 (1990) 2,0 (1995)
South Africa	0,96 (1985) 0,88 (1989) 0,86 (1990) 1,04 (1991)
South Korea	0,50 (1950) 2,0 (1990) 4,5 (2000)
Canada	2,7 (1981) 2,8 (1987)

2. Between 65% to 80% of the money spent on research and development of science and technology must be provided by the private sector. Not how much is spent is the only important factor, but also who spends the money. In the developed nations between 65% to 80% of the spending is by the private sector. In the developing countries as low as only 20% of the spending is by the private sector. It is a well-known fact that in general the private sector is a better creator of wealth than the government. In table 2 (Clarke, 1991) the situation is illustrated.

TABLE 2
RELATIVE CONTRIBUTIONS TO RESEARCH AND DEVELOPMENT
IN SCIENCE AND TECHNOLOGY

Country		Government (%)	Private Sector (%)
Japan	- 1984	20	80
UK	- 1981	26	74
USA	- 1984	29	71
West Germany	- 1983	40	60
France	- 1984	46	54
South Korea	- 1982	41	59
South Africa	- 1985	72	28
Central African Republic	- 1984	74	26
Brazil	- 1982	77	23
India	- 1982	86	14

3. Government and private industry must collaborate to form a National Science and Technology Board. The vision of this board must be to develop the country into a centre of excellence in selected fields of science and technology to enhance the country's international competitiveness in the industrial and service sectors. The focus is on mastering science and technology in niche areas that will contribute

to economic growth. B G Lee Hsien Loong [1992] the Deputy Prime Minister of Singapore said that they started by embarking on an industrialization program to generate economic growth. For industrialization to succeed the key was to be competitive inter-nationally. Singapore became a Newly Industrializing Economy (NIE) and since then their standard of living has improved manifold. To stay competitive they plan to move beyond manufacturing and operating machines efficiently into more sophisticated activities with greater design and innovative content. Singapore's vision is that science and technology is the key to economic growth. Winning nations have a national science and technology plan with targets and key recommendations clearly spelt out. Development of science and technology must be results-driven, producing results eventually relevant to the country's economic competitiveness.

4. Winning nations in the science and technology apply the principles of the management of science and technology. The National Research Council (1987) stated that the management of science and technology links technology, science and management disciplines to plan, develop and implement technological capabilities to shape and accomplish the strategic and operational objectives of an organization. It concerns the process of managing technological development, implementation and diffusion in industrial or government organizations. Hequet [1991] stated that the management of science and technology is a motley array of financial analysis, technology, manufacturing, strategic planning, comparative technologies, etc. It is the mastery of the mundane. The Asians seem to be masters of the management of science and technology. Although the British, Americans and Germans are the pioneers of technological advancement, the Asians master its mass production. Winning nations understand that the value of science and technology does not lie in the pursuit of science and technology for its own sake, but in the benefits a country derives from the implementation of the products of science and technology in the creation of wealth. The management of science and technology translates customer's needs into technological and product-design specifics. Table 3 compares the economic parameters of developed and developing countries.

TABLE 3
ECONOMIC PARAMETERS OF SELECTED DEVELOPED
AND DEVELOPING COUNTRIES

Country	GNP Millions US dollars (1991)	% real growth 1980 - 1991	GNP per capital US dollars (1991)	% real growth 1980 - 1991
Australia	287 765	2,8	16 590	1,2
Botswana	3 335	9,3	2 590	5,8
Canada	568 765	3,1	21 260	2,1
France	1 167 749	2,3	20 600	1,8
West Germany	1 516 785	2,3	23 650	2,2
Hungary	28 244	0,5	2 690	0,7
Japan	3 337 191	4,3	26 920	3,7
South Korea	274 464	10,0	6 340	8,8
Lesotho	1 053	2,7	580	0,0
Malawi	1 996	3,5	230	0,1
Mauritius	2 623	7,2	2 420	6,1
Mozambique	1 163	-1,1	70	-3,6
Namibia	2 051	1,6	1 120	-1,5
Singapore	29 249	7,1	12 890	4,9
South Africa	90 953	3,3	2 560	0,9
Swaziland	874	6,8	1 000	3,1
USA	5 686 038	3,1	22 560	2,1
Zaire	8 123	1,6	220	-1,6
Zambia	3 394	0,7	420	-2,9
Zimbabwe	6 220	3,6	620	0,2

Source: The World Bank Atlas, The World Bank, Washington, DC, 1992

Table 4 compares the growth of production of selected develop-ed and developing countries.

TABLE 4
GROWTH OF PRODUCTION OF SELECTED DEVELOPED
AND DEVELOPING COUNTRIES

Country	Average annual growth rate (%)									
	GDP		Agriculture		Industry		Manufacturing		Services	
	70-80	80-91	70-80	80-91	70-80	80-91	70-80	80-91	70-80	80-91
Australia	3,0	+3,1		2,6		+3,6		2,1		+3,7
Botswana	14,5	9,8	8,3	3,0	17,6	10,7	22,9	7,5	14,5	10,3
Canada	4,6	3,1	1,2	1,6	3,2	3,0	3,5	3,1	6,6	3,3
France	3,2	2,3		1,9		0,9		0,6		2,9
West Germany	2,6	2,3	1,1	1,8	1,7	0,9	2,0	1,4	3,5	2,6
Hungary	5,2	0,6	2,8	0,9	6,3	-1,6			5,2	2,4
Japan	4,3	4,2	-0,2	1,2	4,0	4,9	4,7	5,6	4,9	3,7
South Korea	9,6	9,6	2,7	2,1	15,2	12,1	17,0	12,4	8,8	9,3
Lesotho	8,6	5,5	0,2	1,8	27,8	8,2	18,0	12,8	13,6	5,3
Malawi	5,8	3,1	4,4	2,4	6,3	3,3		3,9	7,0	3,7
Mauritius	6,8	6,7	-3,3	3,2	10,4	10,1	7,1	11,2	10,9	5,8
Mozambique		-0,1		1,6		-3,6				-1,7
Namibia		1,0		0,3		-2,0		1,7		3,1
Singapore	8,3	6,6	1,4	-6,6	8,6	5,8	9,7	7,0	8,3	7,3
South Africa	3,0	1,3	3,2	2,6	2,3	0,0	4,7	-0,1	3,8	2,5
Swaziland										
USA	2,8	2,6	0,6		2,1		3,0		3,3	
Zaire										
Zambia	1,4	0,8	2,1	3,3	1,5	0,9	2,4	3,7	1,2	0,0
Zimbabwe	1,6	3,1	0,6	2,2	1,1	2,1	2,8	3,1	2,4	4,0

Source: World Development Report, Oxford University Press, New York, 1993

From table 4 it is fairly obvious that the countries of the Pacific rim, where the components of the management of science and technology are practised, are very prosperous. Very interesting is Botswana and Mauritius where the high growth can be attributed to improved education. In Table 5 the structure of production of selected developing and developed countries is illustrated.

TABLE 5
STRUCTURE OF PRODUCTION OF SELECTED DEVELOPING
AND DEVELOPED COUNTRIES

Country	GDP millions of US dollar		Distribution of GDP (%)							
			Agriculture		Industry		Manufacture		Services	
	1970	1991	70	91	70	91	70	91	70	91
Australia	39 330	299 800	6	3	39	31	24	15	55	65
Botswana	84	3 644	33	5	28	54	6	4	39	41
Canada	73 847	510 835	4		36		23		59	
France	184 508	1 199 286		3		29		21		68
West Germany	5 543	1 574 316	2	2	49	39	38	23	47	59
Hungary	203 736	30 795	18	10	45	34		29	37	55
Japan	8 887	3 362 282	6	3	47	42	36	25	47	56
South Korea	67	282 970	26	8	29	45	21	28	45	47
Lesotho	271	578	35	14	9	38	4	13	56	48
Malawi	184	1 986	44	35	17	20		13	39	45
Mauritius		2 253	16	11	22	33	14	23	62	56
Mozambique		1 219		64		15				21
Namibia		1 961		10		28		4		62
Singapore	1 896	39 964	2	0	30	38	20	29	68	62
South Africa	16 293	91 167	8	5	40	44	24	25	52	51
Swaziland										
USA	1 011 563	5 610 800	3		35		25		63	
Zaire										
Zambia	1 789	3 831	11	16	55	47	10	36	35	37
Zimbabwe	1 415	5 543	15	20	36	32	21	26	49	49

Source: Word Development Report, Oxford University Press, New York, 1993

It is interesting that in the developed countries industry and services are the main contributors to the GDP. In the developing countries agriculture is still a main contributor to the GDP, although many of them have large natural resources that they develop ineffectively because of a lack of technology. Typical examples are Angola (diamonds, petroleum), Malawi (limestone), Mozambique (coal), Namibia (copper, tin, uranium, diamonds) etc. These countries will have to manage their science and technology to create wealth.

5. Winning nations in the science and technology develop their human resources. Lee Loong (1992) said: "Our key assets will continue to be an open economy and an educated and skilled workforce. Science and technology is the key to economic growth while the strength of a nation depends on the talents and skills of the people." Educational institutions like schools, technical colleges, technikons and universities must not train in a vacuum, but their training should be customer-driven. This implies a healthy interaction with their most important customers, the relevant industries. The management of science and technology must be an integral part of the existing science and technology subjects. A winning nation has a program for the development of its human resources in the science and technology with its priorities driven by the relevant industry and the needs of the economy. In the training there must be a delicate balance between the scientific and technological contents and wealth-creating principles like creativity, innovation, entrepreneurship, financial implications of production, etc. Winning nations train people to have adequate knowledge of science and technology and who are enthusiastic to be successful in production, marketing, the international market and in the creation of wealth.

The World Competitiveness Report (1992) revealed that South Africa's education system is falling apart in some respects and is woefully deficient in others. The report emphasises that educated, skilled manpower is a country's most productive and vital asset. Without it, there can be no sustainable growth. Comparative studies show that Japan's high school level is about three times the standard of the West, while the West is about twice as strong at top university level - but this is not the advantage it appears to be. These Asian economies are very strong on sciences and mathematics. The education system is geared to meet the demands of a modern, technological economy. One should not equate education with university degrees only, where it is really about educating the huge middle stratum of secondary school children.

These Asian economies laid the foundations for their current success 20 years ago. It can take only two years to reverse an economic deficit, but 20 years to reverse a technology deficit and 20 years to reverse a skills and training deficit.

6. Winning nations have institutions with flat structures which eliminate rigidity in the system and allow responsible workers to be entrepreneurial - to make decisions about taking calculated risks. Managers in these winning organizations do not lead by rules and regulations but by their example by having a productive output of their own. Lewis W Lehrer [1990], the Chairman of 3M, said they believe in a process of divide and grow, because too large a division spends too much time on established products and markets. The corporate structure of 3M is designed to encourage innovators to take an idea and run with it. They recommend that the hierarchical pyramid should be flattened. Decision-making should be pushed downwards or outwards to where the organization interacts with the environment.

7. Winning nations appreciate the value of long-term academic research, but they also actively promote short-term and medium-term research developments directed towards economic upgrading. Lee Loong [1992] said that the products of research in science and technology should be implemented to create wealth in the short- and medium-term and the wealth created can be used to finance fundamental long-term research at universities.

8. Winning nations apply the management of science and technology to conserve the environment. This is very important especially with the ongoing population explosion and even primary school children must be taught the close relation between science and technology and the conservation of the environment which includes the available natural resources. Many problems are exacerbated by the growth of economic activity. Industrial and energy-related pollution (local and global), deforestation caused by commercial logging, and overuse of water are the result of economic expansion that fails to take account of the value of the environment. The challenge is to build the recognition of environmental scarcity into decision-making. With or without development rapid population growth may make it more difficult to address many environmental problems. In table 6 the population growth rate, energy use per capita (in kilogram oil equivalent), water use per capita (in cubic metre) and annual average percentage change in forest coverage are illustrated for selected developed and developing countries.

TABLE 6
ENVIRONMENTAL PARAMETERS FOR SELECTED DEVELOPED
AND DEVELOPING COUNTRIES

Country	Population growth rate (% p.a) 1980 - 1991	Energy use (oil equi- valent) GDP output (US dollar) per kg 1990	Water use per capita (cubic metre) 1970 - 87	Forest coverage: Annual average change (%) 1980 - 89
Australia	1,5	3,4	1 306	0,0
Botswana	3,3	5,9	98	-0,1
Canada	1,0	2,1	1 752	0,6
France	0,5	5,5	728	0,1
West Germany	0,1	5,4	668	0,1
Hungary	-0,2	1,0	502	0,5
Japan	0,5	6,7	923	-0,1
South Korea	1,1	3,0	298	-0,1
Lesotho	2,7	0,0	34	-
Malawi	3,4	5,3	22	-2,6
Mauritius	1,0	6,0	415	-0,2
Mozambique	2,6	1,1	53	-0,8
Namibia	3,2	0,0	79	-0,2
Singapore	2,1	2,1	84	0,0
South Africa	2,4	1,2	404	0,6
Swaziland	3,5	3,5	-	0,7
USA	0,9	2,8	2 162	-0,1
Zaire	3,2	2,9	22	-0,2
Zambia	3,7	1,0	86	-0,2
Zimbabwe	3,4	-	129	-0,4

Source: The world bank atlas, The world bank, Washington, DC, 1992

From these figures it is fairly obvious that for some countries the red lights are flickering and they should apply the management of science and technology to use their resources more effectively.

9. Winning nations regard their skilled labour force as an asset and not as a cost. Maital [1992] quoted Robert Barro from Harvard that it is human capital (skills, dexterity and judgment) and not physical capital (factories, buildings, machines, natural resources, etc) that holds the key to persistent high growth in per capita income. The key to growth lies in the fact that people, unlike machines, can learn and what can be learned can be taught. As a result, investments that increase people's skills and productivity yield not diminishing, but constant and even increasing returns. Poor countries can catch up with rich countries if they have high human capital per person rates. The old theory that the standard of living only rises when you have either natural resources or plentiful capital seems to be wrong and the new theory says that a poor country can become better off by growing its own human capital - that is, creating a well-trained labour force. A poor country can acquire technology from a rich one. It can also borrow capital, but it can't acquire or borrow a superior workforce. It has to build gradually its own pool of skilled labourers who are able to use capital and technology to generate profits. If a nation has smart workers, then investors and their capital and technology will beat a path to its door.

Handy [1989] also said that the principal asset in an organization is its skilled people. If one tries to keep the people and the cost of wages as low as possible, one will get low quality people who are not very motivated or creative and the organization will not survive in the modern highly competitive world economy. Talented peoples have to be managed as talent-ed individuals in the knowledge that the key peoples are the key assets and that those assets could walk out of the door and leave an organization with just the office furniture and a few bare rooms.

CONCLUSIONS

1. The developing countries of Southern Africa spend too little of their GDP on the development of science and technology. In order to create wealth in a meaningful way they will have to increase their present investment of about 1% of the GDP to at least 2% of the GDP.
2. The private sector must invest more in the development of science and technology. The governments of the developing countries of Southern Africa must give enough incentives to private industry so that they invest at least 65% of the money spent on the development of science and technology.
3. There must be very close collaboration between Government and the private sector in constituting a national

body that will ensure that the country's natural resources are developed with optimal effectiveness. The ultimate goal must be to be a successful player in the global market.

4. The standard of education in science and technology must be raised. Training must also include the management of science and technology in order to ensure that the knowledge of science and technology is used for the creation of wealth and not only for the sake of science for science and technology for technology.

5. The developing countries will have to get rid of the bureaucratic structures and replace it with flat structures that are more flexible and promote creativity, innovation and entrepreneurship.

6. The developing countries will have to prioritize their long term, medium term and short term development in order to achieve economic upgrading.

7. The developing countries must realize that human capital and not physical capital holds the key to high economic growth. They can become better off by growing their own human capital, by creating a well-trained labour force. A developing country with smart workers can be sure that investors with their capital and technology will beat a path to its door.

SUMMARY

The message to the developing countries is simple and inescapable: success is built on producing goods and services quicker, cheaper and better than anyone else.

REFERENCES

Clarke, J B: "The intra-regional transfer of technology". Africa Insight, Vol 21; No 1, 1991.

Handy, C: The age of unreason (Business Books, London, 1989).

Hequet, M: "Management of technology." Training, vol 23(4) 1991.

Lee Hsien Loong, B G: "Singapore: Technology for economic growth." Scientific American, January 1992.

Lehrer L W quoted in Adair J: The Challenge of Innovation (Talbot Adair, 1990).

Maital S: "How poor nations can catch up" (Across The Board, June 1992.

National Research Council: Management of Technology: The hidden competitive advantage National Academy Press, Washington, DC, 1987.

World Competitiveness Report, IMD, Lausanne, 1992.

SOURCES

The World Bank Atlas, The World Bank, Washington, DC, 1992

World Development Report, Oxford University Press, New York, 1993.

STRATEGIC RECYCLING AGENDAS: A LOOK
AT HIGHER EDUCATION IN ALABAMA

Michael C. Budden and Tom F. Griffin, III
Auburn University at Montgomery
MONTGOMERY, ALABAMA, U.S.A.
Connie L. Budden
Auburn University
AUBURN, ALABAMA, U.S.A.

Abstract

A survey of state universities in Alabama indicates that all are involved in some form of formal recycling. Since 1990, the State of Alabama has mandated recycling programs at all state institutions. As was determined from the survey, most private colleges and universities in the state are engaged in some administratively sanctioned, formal recycling efforts. The primary materials recycled appear to be paper and aluminum products.

INTRODUCTION

The call to recycle materials where possible and thus conserve natural resources has been at the forefront of many ecologically-oriented groups' agendas since the first Earth Day was held in 1970. Significant recycling in recent years have centered primarily on efforts to recycle aluminum cans, newspapers, and in some areas, plastics. The success of these efforts vary geographically but are successful as evidenced by the fact that over 70% of aluminum cans are recycled in the U.S. annually.

State and local governments have noted that with the increased costs and potential pollution associated with landfill operations, incineration and other historical disposal methods, recycling may impact positively the waste disposal and natural resource utilization problems simultaneously. In response to the need to reduce solid waste materials several universities began recycling programs. For instance, Georgetown University initiated a recycling effort that included sending old books to Czechoslovakia, appliances and clothing to charitable groups, and a book swap for students. Georgetown's effort which recycled 463 tons of newspapers, paper, glass and aluminum in less than one year, was modeled after similar efforts at the University of Michigan and at Dartmouth College (The Washington Post, May 23, 1991). Hartwick College in Oneonta, New York and the State University of New York (SUNY) at Oneonta both instituted recycling efforts in response to higher landfill costs (New York Times, June 4, 1989). In still other states, private initiatives have helped over 1,000 schools begin recycling efforts which have reduced solid waste and in many cases made monies for the schools involved (BioCycle, October 1992).

In many areas, governmental units have begun mandating recycling within their jurisdictions and by their governmental units. Indeed, forty-eight states have enacted mandatory recycling legislation (Ching and Gogan, 1992). These various laws typically mandate the recycling of certain materials (eg. paper, plastic, aluminum, etc.) by either consumers, government agencies or both. Alabama for example, has implemented a law (Act No. 90-564) which requires that state universities and other state agencies take steps to recycle. Alabama law mandates that state agencies and public school systems initiate and manage recycling efforts within their areas of responsibility. State supported universities and colleges are considered state agencies under the aegis of the act. To ascertain compliance with the law to date and to get a preliminary assessment of its impact, a poll of universities in Alabama was conducted. The poll was conducted in the spring/summer of 1993. The phone survey sought information on recycling efforts from the Vice President/Vice Chancellor for Business Affairs on the various campuses. In several instances, at the recommendation of the individual initially contacted, the call was diverted to a more-appropriate individual on campus (eg. Director of Plant Operations, Recycling Coordinators, etc.) who were directly concerned with the effort or who were otherwise more knowledgeable of recycling efforts.

Though the law specifically mandates that state agencies and public school systems (including state universities (private schools are exempt from the act) must develop recycling efforts, the survey was not limited to state universities. In an attempt to see what privately-funded institutions were doing relative to recycling, several of the private institutions in the state were surveyed as well. Table 1 lists the colleges and universities in Alabama that were surveyed and indicates which materials are involved in each campus's recycling efforts, an assessment by each respondent indicating their perceptions of the effectiveness of the program and the disposition of any earnings.

FINDINGS

It can be seen in the table that a total of 21 universities were surveyed. Of these, fifteen are state supported institutions and six are private. The types of materials being recycled included paper, aluminum, yard waste, and glass. As one might expect, paper and aluminum were found to make up the bulk of materials being recycled. Only two institutions reported recycling glass and yard waste, two reported recycling oil, while three reported the recycling of cardboard. It should be noted that many respondents indicated that additional recycling initiatives were planned for the future. As for the disposition of the monies earned from recycling, the greatest use of the funds involved depositing the funds back into the university's general fund. However, a few schools plowed the money into scholarship programs, and still others used the funds to support activities ranging from club and organizational support, to housekeeping and even refreshments for the custodial staff. Six universities reported making no monies from the effort (or as stated in some cases - donating the materials to recycling centers). One university reported using some of its recycling earnings in its research efforts. Two others reported that the funds were reinvested in the recycling effort itself; for instance buying containers to hold the materials.

Generally respondents indicated that the universities in the state had been engaged in formal recycling efforts for three years or less. Four of the 21 indicated that they had been recycling for more than three years. It is apparent from the short longevity of these programs, that recycling efforts on campuses in Alabama are relatively new. Only one school, a private school, indicated that it had not yet begun a formal recycling program but was in the process of discussing such an effort.

Finally, respondents were asked their assessment of the effectiveness of their programs to reduce the amount of materials that historically would have been disposed of in landfills or through incineration. The great majority of respondents indicated that they felt their school's efforts were effective or very effective. Three respondents reported they felt their schools' efforts had been somewhat effective. A positive finding was that no respondent perceived that their school's efforts had been ineffective in reducing solid waste materials.

CAVEATS AND THE FUTURE

The findings of the phone survey reported above indicates that all state institutions in Alabama are engaged in some form of materials recycling. The effectiveness of such efforts appears to be well-received by those responding to the survey. The major caveat that may concern readers is whether or not the individual responding for any particular campus may have been the most knowledgeable individual on campus to respond. However, all respondents indicated knowledge of recycling efforts on their campuses and the findings are presented here. Future efforts by the authors will include developing cases based on the recycling efforts of some of the universities reported on in this study. An effort to monitor ongoing recycling efforts will be initiated in order to track noticeable trends in the recycling of university waste products.

SUMMARY

A phone survey of state universities in Alabama reveals compliance with the state's mandated recycling efforts. A review of private institutions in Alabama indicates that the great majority also engage in recycling efforts. Funds earned from recycling generally are deposited to the general funds of the universities.

Scholarships, research support, student activities, and the recycling program itself are often the beneficiaries of such efforts. Recycling efforts to date are viewed as meeting expectations of those involved and seen as effective in reducing the amount of wastes that would otherwise be disposed of in landfills or through incineration.

It is apparent that Alabama's universities are largely in a learning mode when it comes to recycling their wastes. As experience mounts, it is expected that improvements in recycling efforts will continue and many benefits will accrue to the State of Alabama and to its environment.

REFERENCES

BioCycle (1992). "Businesses Promote School Recycling," October, pp. 60-61.

Ching, Raymond and Robert Gogan, "Campus Recycling: Everyone Plays a Part," New Directions for Higher Education, Spring, No. 77, pp. 113-125.

The New York Times (1989). "Recycling Efforts Help Environment and Save Money," June 4, pp. 47-48.

The Washington Post (1991). "Georgetown Recycling Students' Throwaways," May 23.

University	Policy	Years	Paper	Alum	Glass	Other	Disposition of Earnings	Evaluation[e]
U. of Alabama	Yes	1-3	X	X			Donation	E
U. of Alabama - Birmingham	Yes	3+	X	X		Cardboard	Containers, Advertising, Scholarships	VE
U. of Alabama - Huntsville	Yes	1-3	X			Cardboard	Grants, Research	VE
U. of South Alabama	Yes	1-3	X	X			G. Fund	E
U. of Montevallo	Yes	1-3	X	X		Oil, Metal Yard waste	Donation	SE
Livingston State University	Yes	<1	X	X			Donation	SE
Auburn University at Montgomery	Yes	3+	X	X			Department Keeps	E
Auburn U.	Yes	<1	X				No Monies	VE
U. of North Alabama	Yes[a]	3+		X			Biology Scholarship	E
Troy State U.	Yes	1-3	X	X			G. Fund	SE
Troy - Dothan	Yes	1-3	X	X			G. Fund	SE
Troy - Montgomery	Yes	1-3	X				G. Fund	E
Alabama State	Yes	1-3	X				G. Fund	E
Alabama A&M	Yes	1-3	X	X			G. Fund	E
Jacksonville State	Yes	1-3	X	X			Donation	VE
Tuskegee[d]	Yes[b]	1-3	X				Discount on purchase	E
Samford[d]	Yes	<1		X		Cardboard	Recycling Program	E
Huntingdon[d]	Yes	1-3	X	X	X		Clubs, cleaning	E
Spring Hill[d]	Yes	<1[c]	X	X			No monies	SE
Faulkner[d]	No[f]							
Birmingham Southern[d]	Yes	3+	X	X	X	Plastic, Oil and Yard Waste	Refreshment for custodians	E

[a]Only one department, campus wide soon
[b]Currently applies to computer operations only
[c]Earlier program proved ineffective and was scrapped.
[d]Private schools
[e]SE - Somewhat effective; E - Effective; VE - Very effective
[f]Currently discussing organizing a recycling program

THE ENVIRONMENTAL VISION
OF THE WALT DISNEY COMPANY:
THE GREENING OF THE MOUSE

John F. Quinn
University of Dayton
Joseph A. Petrick
Wright State University
DAYTON, OHIO, U.S.A.

Abstract

The authors have researched the Environmental Policies of the Walt Disney Company, especially the park in Florida. After a short background on the company, particularly some early mistakes in development, the challenges for and progress in sustainable development, are discussed. Thus, water resource management, solid and hazardous waste disposal, new energy sources, transportation, environmental themes in films and television and environmental education of employees and the community are reviewed in terms of the new environmental vision of sustainable development.

INTRODUCTION

Walt Disney is a name known throughout the world as a symbol of "The Finest In Family Entertainment" [Walt Disney World, 1987]. This legacy has been developed through more than fifty years of bold, pioneering achievements. A blend of creative genius, imagination, and dedicated work has created a monolithic empire from just one man and his mouse. The Walt Disney Company of today has gone beyond being an entertainment giant and seems, at least on the surface, to be dedicated to innovations to create a more cohesive environment for all living organisms - a strong figure of leadership, by example, of the new environmentalism.

BACKGROUND

The late Walt Disney opened the gates at Disneyland in Anaheim, California in 1955. After only a few years of operation, Walt became disillusioned at what was taking place outside the gates surrounding his magical kingdom. Traffic was becoming a snarled mess and overdevelopment was rampant as everyone tried to capitalize on the Disney presence. The outside world was spoiling the illusion of what Walt Disney had in mind when Disneyland was created.

In 1965, Walt Disney launched his company into "the most significant decade of growth in its history" [Disney, 1993]. After purchasing 27,443 acres of pine forest and wetlands in Central Florida, Disney announced, "There is enough land here to hold all the ideas and plans we can possibly imagine." In his master plan for the 27,000 plus acres of property, he incorporated the ideas and dreams of a lifetime. As an ardent conservationist, Walt Disney, immediately set aside 7,500 acres as a nature preserve [Walt Disney World, 1987].

Phase I of the plan called for a "Vacation Kingdom" - a giant entertainment complex complete with hotels, camping facilities, shopping, entertainment, a theme park and a myriad of land and water recreational activities. Disney's greatest dream for the Florida project was EPCOT - Experimental Prototype Community of Tomorrow. The vision of EPCOT was a community of the future designed as an example for the world as it existed in 1965. He said "EPCOT will take its cue from the new emerging creative centers of American industry. It will always be introducing, testing and demonstrating new materials and systems - a showcase to the world for the ingenuity and imagination of American free enterprise" [Disney, 1993].

Unfortunately, Walt Disney died shortly after the ground breaking in 1966, before he would be able to see his dream realized. However, he did leave behind his brother, Roy, who dedicated the property. Roy Disney was determined that all 27,443 acres would be a testing ground to seek solutions to the challenges faced by communities--challenges such as conservationism, land use planning, water management, energy systems, communication, transportation and education.

Since 1966 The Walt Disney Company, which now owns a total of 29,000 acres (almost 43 square miles), has utilized less than a tenth of the total property including conservation lands. During this time Disney acknowledges that it truly has gone through a learning process and has admittedly made mistakes in many areas. It is a company unencumbered by existing paradigms with a strong belief in the quality of the vision of its founder.

LEARNING FROM MISTAKES

The Disney Company made mistakes but learned from them. The original budget to build the Magic Kingdom - the first theme park - was 13 million dollars. By the time the park actually opened it had cost overruns in excess of nineteen times the original amount. The economics were just a small part of the learning experience.

Most people have heard that there is an underground city under the Magic Kingdom, an area for Disney employees, "cast members" to make preparations before going "on stage" to service or entertain the "guests." What most people do not know is that "underground" is actually the first floor. The intricate labyrinth was built first, then earth taken from the building of a 200 acre man-made lake was used to fill in around the structure so that the Magic Kingdom could be built on the "second floor." What the engineers at Disney failed to realize was that by doing this they were actually changing the natural water table, a part of the Everglades ecosystem, the surrounding community, the Kissimmee River, and the Everglades. Today, there are pumps continuously pumping water away from the structure to keep the Kingdom from collapse.

This was the first indication to the Disney engineers that the ground in Central Florida was a giant sponge and that everything they would do in the future would effect the natural ecosystem. Even today Disney is learning more about the land they have developed. While building Pleasure Island, which opened in 1989 but was scheduled to open in 1987, the concrete used to create the island sunk seven times before they determined how to build a stable structure [Tuchman, 1989]. Needless to say they do not plan to build anymore islands.

Rather than focusing on their failures, it is equally important to see what the developers at Disney have done well. Environmentalism and development do not always have bipolar effects. "Walt Disney World...is one of the finest mixed-use developments that has ever been created in terms of its relevance to contemporary and future issues and the needs of society. It is a Master Planning effort unmatched in scale, which will have great impact for the development industry as an influential research tool and project model [Disney, 1993].

THE CHALLENGES OF LAND DEVELOPMENTS

As the Disney team designed the Master Plan, it became evident that the EPCOT goals of demonstrating new methods and using new materials would be extremely difficult to achieve within the existing boundaries of current building codes and zoning ordinances. The two counties, Orange and Osceola, in which the Disney property is located, had different standards and regulations. For EPCOT to proceed, a unified form of government was essential. One governing body was needed to provide basic public services to the property, as well as, provide the legislative and regulatory atmosphere necessary for private enterprise to build a "Community of Tomorrow." By working through existing legislation, representatives from Orange and Osceola counties and the Disney Company proposed to the Florida legislature a multi-purpose district operating under one governing body. In 1967 the Reedy Creek Improvement District was created as the governing body for the Walt Disney World Resort Community.

The district has the jurisdiction over the property owned by Walt Disney Company. Functioning like a county, it provides essential public services to the property such as fire protection, flood control, waste collection and environmental protection. The district receives all its income from taxes and fees imposed within its boundaries. A board of five supervisors conducts business in the district. Daily administration of the district is delegated to the general manager whose responsibility is similar to a city manager.

From the beginning, the district has placed significant emphasis on land use planning [Disney, 1993]. In 1974 the Board of Supervisors adopted two major documents - The Comprehensive General Plan and The Land Use Regulations. These documents established the ground work for future land use decisions and included in-depth studies in areas of drainage, topography, soil and vegetation. The formation of the Reedy Creek Improvement District has laid the foundation for the Reedy Creek Improvement District Comprehensive Plan. The Comprehensive Plan's document is evaluated every five years and currently reflects planning for the Walt Disney World property through the year 2000 [Disney, 1993].

In addition to the Reedy Creek District, Disney also established permanent management of all conservation areas. Under permanent management, a team of scientists provides insight into a diverse ecosystem of plants and animals. Nearly all species of wild birds and animals that reside in central Florida have room to survive and reproduce. More conservation areas will be set aside as additional development continues.

When EPCOT Center was under construction, Disney developers discovered that a rare species of woodpecker lived on the planned site for an EPCOT parking lot. Instead of destroying the birds' habitat, the decision was made to move the parking lot. The vice president of planning and engineering stated: "The commitment to keep such wildlife is still with the company today." As part of the education process, Disney has created a program entitled, Protecting the Natural Environment in Large Projects, as part of the American Society for Civil Engineers [Disney, 1993].

Recently, Walt Disney World was granted a twenty year permit to complete the planned building on the property. Part of the plan impacts 535 acres of wetlands. To mitigate the loss of the wetlands, Disney has purchased 8,550 acres of pristine wetlands on the Walker Ranch in Osceola County. The county has the largest concentration of bald eagles in the United States. The federal government only requires an equal swap for wetlands' development. The Disney swap for wetlands was endorsed by thirty environmental groups. Disney believes that it would be more beneficial to the environment to practice "mitigation banking" -- preserving and adding to large tracts of environmentally-sensitive land rather than the spot mitigation process that currently takes place [Stoker, 1991].

WATER RESOURCE MANAGEMENT

The first construction project carried out by the Reedy Creek Improvement District was a water control system consisting of canals, levees, and water control structures. The system was designed to control rather than eliminate surface water levels on the property. The canals were designed and constructed to curve as streams do naturally. Properly mulched and seeded with grass, man-made canals appear to guests as rivers complete with the expected flora and fauna [Florida, 1992].

Unlike dams and locks constructed by civil engineers and the Army Corps of Engineers, the water control structure of choice is a non-powered, double-ballasted water control gate designed by Emile Gate [Disney, 1993]. The control gates are balanced to float open when the water reaches peak levels and close when the peak resides. The gates require no power or human monitoring. Water is routed through the canals to 7,500 acres of wetlands. During periods of extreme rainfall, the wetlands serve as a holding basin and prevent flooding in the developed areas. "This wetland area is designed to protect and manage the land's natural beauty and wildlife and is permanently established as a conservation area for environmental research" [Stoker, 1991].

Wastewater management is another obvious environmental concern. During the planning stages of the Disney development, this had to be addressed early on of it was to appropriately serve the community and the environment. Central Florida rests on the Florida aquifer. Degradation and destruction of the aquifer would have a devastating impact on all of Florida, resulting in sinkholes, salt water intrusion, loss of drinking water and ultimate destruction of the environment. Disney's scientists responded to the challenge of recycling water that would supplement the natural replenishment of the aquifer [Disney, 1993].

The primary wastewater treatment plant is similar to the ones found in many communities. The water which is cycled through the treatment facility contains nutrients that promote growth of algae and other plants when released directly into surface waters. Although this water meets current Florida standards for discharge, Disney is currently experimenting with advanced treatments to release a higher quality waste effluent [Disney, 1993].

Disney has come under considerable criticism over its use of pesticides and herbicides in its efforts to create the picture perfect image for their developments. As a response to environmentalist outrage, the Disney name and the cartoon character, Goofy, were pulled from promotion of the product Greensweep [Daniels, 1988]. Now Disney is discontinuing the use of pesticides and herbicides and is involved in research where the "good bugs are killing the bad bugs."

A waste water spray irrigation system implemented in 1971 is now responsible for most property irrigation systems though it has taken many years to implement on such a large scale. The technologies added to the irrigation system in 1977, Wetland/Overland Flow and Percolation Pond/Overland Flow Systems, make this possible. Today over 10 million gallons per day are reclaimed [Disney, 1993]. These technologies will also enable future wastewater recycling for more than irrigation purposes.

Beginning in 1979 Disney began a research project combining Disney scientists, industry, government and academe together to research and experiment in liquid and solid waste management. The project was designed to test the purifying properties of the floating hyacinth plant and to research an alternative energy source. The research project resulted in two key findings: 1) the water hyacinth system required less than 50% of the energy needed to run a comparably sized, conventional secondary treatment system, and 2) the hyacinth is capable of treating primary water to secondary standards by filtering suspended solids and absorbing nitrogen and phosphorus through its root system [Disney, 1993]. The Gas Research Institute, the U.S. Department of Energy and the State of Florida are continuing the experiment in bio-mass energy production, using aquatic plants and municipal solid waste [garbage] for anaerobic digestion to produce methane gas [Gwinn, 1990].

In addition to this research, NASA is continuing research on the water hyacinth since it considers the plant feasible for space stations where it could be used in wastewater treatment and for the production of methane gas to generate electricity from fuel cells [Disney, 1993]. It may also hold a practical application for small municipalities and housing developments in tropical and subtropical climates [Stoker, 1991].

Walt Disney World is continuing its research through several different avenues: hydrology studies on the quantity and quality of surface waters, daily monitoring of air, water, land, agriculture, forestry, and animal inventories within the development areas, as well as, the conservation areas. In an effort to maintain the ecological balance within the Walt Disney World property, the Reedy Creek Improvement District "walks" each site to be developed in order to determine and protect the presence of rare and/or endangered species and also checks sites for land erosion in order to determine test methods to protect erosion [Walt Disney Company, 1992].

Several years ago, Disney attractions formed its own conservation committees to examine how water was used in the parks and how it could be better managed. Programs implemented by these committees included the utilization of low-volume sprinkler and drop irrigation systems, soil moisture sensing devices, toilet fixtures and rest-room faucets with infrared sensors, water efficient shower heads, ultra-low flush toilets, drought-tolerant landscaping and other water conservation measures. As a result of these efforts water consumption was reduced by over 40% [Sinclair, 1992]. Additionally, many of the water attractions in the theme parks now have "closed loop' water features by which water systems recirculate continuously. New water is added to these attractions only as a result of evaporation loss. Building design also plays a major role in water resource management. EPCOT's Spaceship Earth is the world's largest geodesic sphere. An innovative rainwater collection system keeps water from cascading off the structure by capturing it at midpoint and channeling it inside the sphere to pipes emptying into the Disney water control system.

DEALING WITH SOLID AND HAZARDOUS WASTE

Disney cast members and guests generate large quantities of solid waste annually. In efforts to curtail the generation of solid waste in its own products, Disney has created several "in-house" projects to eliminate waste by cutting down on its purchases of multi-wrapped packages. The effects of this project are subtle to the average consumer in the resort areas. However, the project has reduced paper waste by 400,000 pounds per year [Walt Disney Company, 1992]. Guests in Disney resorts are asked to participate in the Disney recycling programs which are explained in detail in every guest room.

Disney recently opened its own recycling facility on its property. This $4 million facility recycles guest waste and Disney employee waste from office and home. The facility is recycling office paper, newspaper, aluminum, tires, oil, glass, and plastics. In the last few years the recycling program has collected over 4,400 tons of cardboard, 46 tons of aluminum cans, 2,020 tons of mixed paper, 3 tons of plastic bottles, and 2,350 tons of lumber. This program has dramatically reduced a significant percentage of the resort's waste destined for landfills and the company believes the recycling program will double in size in the next year. Additionally, new recycling programs are being added, such as the polystyrene program.

In 1992 Walt Disney World added a new process to the Materials Recovery Facility. On a very large scale, Walt Disney World has created a state of the art composting system to handle its sewage sludge. The treatment facility processes the sludge into minimal toxic waste and the majority of the by-product is being used as a soil amendment by the Horticulture Department, and is also made available to employees for their own personal yard use.

CREATING AND DEVELOPING NEW ENERGY SOURCES

Disney uses co-generation systems to simultaneously generate electrical energy and low-grade heat from the same fuel source. This Central Energy Plant can produce approximately 50% of the annual electrical requirements for over 65% of the Walt Disney World Resort [Disney, 1993]. Utility systems are monitored throughout the resort through the use of computers within the Energy Plant. Many problems are programmed to be detected and automatically corrected without any human intervention. The Dynamic Economic Energy Dispatch System takes into account the methods of energy production available to the operators at the Energy Plant and suggests alternatives for operating the plant in the most cost-effective manner. This is an ideal utilization of computers considering the high cost of the energy sources.

Another innovative application of technology is the energy management system at EPCOT Center for the Universe of Energy exhibit - 80,000 photovoltaic cells on the roof of the pavilion convert sunlight into electricity. The 70,000 watts of electric current generated are used to power amusement-ride vehicles operated in the attraction [Disney, 1993]. Solar energy is being heavily researched and implemented throughout Disney developments.

In 1977 Walt Disney World Company was selected to participate in a federally funded solar energy demonstration project sponsored by the Department of Energy. A prototype office building was designed to be heated, air-conditioned, and supplied hot water through the use of solar energy. The results of the project led to more practical and cost-effective uses of solar energy for the general consumer and provided data to the technical community for future applications [Disney, 1993].

In response to the South Coast Air Quality Management District's Regulation XV, the EPA's National Clean Air Act and the Walt Disney Company's desire to contribute to improving traffic congestion and air quality, Disney introduced a new program called the "Frequent Freeway Flyer." This program rewards those employees who make an effort to car-pool, vanpool, use public transport, bicycle, or walk to work. Employees accumulate points for each day they participate in the program. For every 21 points, the employee receives a $10 gift certificate redeemable at The Disney Store. The program is flexible and allows employees to control how quickly the points accumulate. Interestingly, when this program was introduced it overrode the long term policy requiring employees to provide their own methods of dependable transportation to and from work.

TRANSPORTATION OF THE FUTURE - TODAY

Perhaps the authors' most vivid memories of the televised opening of Walt Disney World were of the monorail transporting guests throughout the park. Seeing that technology of tomorrow being utilized in the late 1960's (and combined with the Space Program) made the world of the animated Jetson family believable. Disney's transportation systems are designed to move guests and cast members efficiently throughout the property and provide additional guest entertainment. They also do something more important. They cut down on the emissions and congestion that would occur if guests and cast members were to use their own form of transportation. Disney transportation systems make public transportation fun and palatable for the community. The Monorail System is the primary transportation link between the main parking lot, EPCOT, the Magic Kingdom, and the resort hotels. The first monorail system dates back to the original monorail at Disneyland which began operation in 1959 [Disney, 1993].

Although Disney designed the Monorail System primarily as an attraction, it quickly became the primary transportation system operating and averages 50,000 miles per year with less than a one hour downtime period per year [Disney, 1993]. The monorail is a non-polluting, cost effective methods of transportation and is one of the few privately funded transportation systems in the country. So why isn't it more widely used? It is extremely expensive to build and the tracks operate best in moderate climates where there is little expansion and contraction of the cement girders. In fact it is so expensive (approximately $5,000 per foot) that Disney has yet to link its most current attraction the MGM Studios.

Vehicles throughout the property have been converted to operate on clean burning alternative fuels. In Disneyland over 80 service and attraction vehicles now run on compressed natural gas. This includes the water attractions such as the Jungle Ride and the 20,000 League submarines [Walt Disney Company, 1992]. Research continues at the Walt Disney World facility to constantly improve the use of clean burning and low emission fuels.

The Medway People Mover is another attraction/transportation system utilized within the Disney World resort. The Medway offered a revolutionary form of transportation through a unique propulsion system using a linear induction motor, which has no moving parts, include a nearly unlimited life expectancy, almost silent operation, low energy consumption, no pollution, no effect from inclement weather, and low maintenance [Disney, 1993].

In the summer of 1981 the Medway People Mover has its first public application at the Houston Intercontinental Airport. The Disney-developed transportation system has met the requirements of the Urban Mass Transportation Administration and is approved for "downtown people moving transportation." Because transportation systems are a critical component of the Disney resort, the system used in the theme parks must also be "part of the attraction." The Inductive Power Transfer System and Automatic Vehicle Guidance System are "firsts" in new methods of transportation. Inductive power coupling transfers electric power from a source in the roadbed to vehicles by electromagnetic induction across an air gap. Power is transferred without contact when the ride vehicles are stopped within the attractions. Because this system if non-contraction, it eliminates the wear and tear associated with direct contact power collection. The safety factor is high in such a system. Electrical conductors are not exposed to accidental contact and the system can be walked upon without hazard [Disney, 1993].

The most recent development in transportation has even far more reaching consequences. The Automated Vehicle Guidance System has sensor units mounted under the cars which detect signals from a guide wire and issue commands to the independent steering units on the front axles to keep the cars centered over the wire. Applications of this system may well go beyond the theme park transportation and may be a preliminary step towards a dynamic highway or road system where cars could be directed along highways by wires in the roadbed [Disney, 1993].

Be it bus, tram, watercraft, horse, bicycle, golf cart, or new forms of mass transit, the total Disney transportation network provides full-service mobility for guests away from their own personal vehicles. The overall effect of the transportation system is low pollution for high density areas, cost effectiveness management and reliability for everyone - a useful model for the country. Satisfying the need for independence but with a mind for the environment is a form of sustainable development in the transportation field [Transportation, 1991].

ENVIRONMENTAL THEMES IN FILMS AND TELEVISION

The Walt Disney Studio has established a relationship and has been working with the Environmental Media Association in an effort to include environmental messages in film and television programming [Disney, 1993]. Additional efforts are underway to develop network specials based on environmental themes. The internal Environmental Policy Department reviews all film and television scripts with the intent of including environmental themes when it is appropriate. With the same thoughts in mind the Environmental Policy Department reviews the themes at the resort attractions to evaluate additional environmental messages and assure accuracy for the existing attractions.

Within the past two years, Disney Studios has released two major films with environmental themes and a new film is scheduled to be released in 1994. All profits from Fern Gully, a major animated motion picture about the last rain forest and intended to educate children (and their parents) about the immediate need to start rain forest preservation, have been donated to the preservation of the world's remaining rain forests.

DISNEY'S ENVIRONMENTAL POSTURE WITHIN THE COMMUNITY

Disney is an entertainment, hospitality and consumer products organization that believes it has an obligation based upon public image to provide environmental leadership to heighten the awareness of environmental issues for all of its employees. The Corporate Environmental Policy Statement is given to each new employee during the orientation process and the policy is constantly being reviewed, updated and reiterated to employees so that it reflects recent innovations that are occurring internally within the organization. Externally the public sees a smiling mouse but is that the same image local governments and vendors see? For all their posturing and concern for the environment, Disney has recently sent a very mixed message to those public officials and residents of Anaheim and Long Beach, California - possibly jeopardizing their environmental image.

Disney makes no secret of the fact it is very unhappy about the community that surrounds the Disneyland park. Overdevelopment, lack of proper community services, crime, prostitution and a concentration of smog led Disney to search elsewhere in its plans to expand and create WESCOT (the west coast version of EPCOT). Disney looked to the nearby neighboring community of Long Beach for its expansion plans. Long Beach officials were willing to provide Disney with the tax abatements and other city infrastructure commitments that Disney demanded. But Disney dropped its environmental eye when it announced its plans for WESCOT--"our humanity, our history, our planet, our universe"--development which included Disney Sea. The "Sea" would require dredging and fill work of 200 acres of currently recreational port area. Disney even went so far as to propose a bill that would amend the current coastal policy to permit the construction. The bill died in committee as the cry from environmentalists was heard and Disney backed off.

Anaheim has conceded to give Disney the community and roadway improvements it has demanded and WESCOT will now be built in Anaheim. But what if Long Beach officials had given Disney what it wanted? Would all the environmental posturing have been severely tarnished if not destroyed over the wishes to expand and create more profits? How could Disney state publicly it was creating a land of vision, while it was acting to destroy a portion of the environment? This is a clear indication that Disney was willing to put itself before the needs of society [Zachavias, 1992].

A NEW VISION OF ENVIRONMENTAL RESPONSIBILITY

Disney has a great opportunity to make a significant environmental impact on society. Disney's challenge is to preserve the values and ethics that they have instilled in their employees and to reach out further into the community at large and sprinkle their Pixie dust.

"Imagineering" means if you can imagine it, it can be done at Disney. Disney has set the standards and presents strong leadership for society - provided that Imagineering maintains its integrity. Disney has played a powerful role that has enhanced the viability of a truly environmentally responsible society.

Disney has a new project for Imagineering. This new project reaches out to the community and carries Walt's dream to the next level. Celebration will be the name of the city that Disney will be building in Osceola County beginning in 1994. Celebration will be more than just an experimental community of tomorrow; it will be THE community of tomorrow. The community of the future is planned for 20,000 residents and 15,000 employees on 4,000 current acres of Disney property. Once complete and occupied, Disney plans to deed the community back to Oseola County to run and operate. Celebration will incorporate everything Disney has learned from EPCOT and puts their new vision of community sustainable development into practice.

CONCLUSION

The Walt Disney Company has built a strong environmental tradition from its founder's vision. Preserving that vision requires ongoing commitment to sustainable development as the most effective and responsible foundation for future growth. Disney has the ability to educate organizations and a great majority of the populous about what it means to be environmental stakeholders. Disney has proven that the tradeoffs for environmentalism can be consistent with development. The ultimate reward is an earth that can be tolerant of human life which has to change from "conqueror of the land community, to plain member and citizen of it." It implies intelligent respect for both environmental protection and economic development [Armstrong, 1993; Schmidheiny, 1992]. An innovative, pioneering spirit with vision and values, best describes the people who make up the Walt Disney Company - borne from one man's vision and committed to carrying forth his dream.

REFERENCES

Daniels, Stevie O., "Danger in Disneyland?," Organic Gardening, 35 (5), July 1988, 24-28.

Disney Enterprises, Innovation In Action, Walt Disney World Seminar Productions, 1993.

"Florida, Disney Swap: A Ranch for Wetlands," Florida Trend, January, 1992, 11-12.

522

Grimm, Matthew, "Disney's New Character: The Green Executive," <u>Marketing Week</u>, 31 (7), April 16, 1990, 22-29.

Leopold, Aldo, "The Land Ethic," in <u>Environmental Ethics</u> ed. by Susan J. Armstrong (Prentice-hall, 1993), 67-79.

Pfeffer, Jeffrey, <u>Competitive Advantage Through People</u>: <u>Unleashing the Power of the Workforce</u>, (Harvard Business School Press, 1994).

Schmidheiny, Stephan, <u>Changing Course</u> (MIT Press, 1992).

Sinclair, Lani, "Corporate Environmentalism Makes Good "Cents," <u>Safety and Health</u>, 146 (56) July, 1992, 77-85.

Stoker, Melissa, "Disney Develops with the Environment in Mind," <u>Orlando Business Journal</u>, October 25, 1991, 3-4.

Transportation Editor, "Maritime Industry and Disney Butt Heads," <u>Transportation Report</u>, 24 (6), December, 1991, 34-38.

Tuchman, Janice, "Building a Bigger Disney World," <u>ENR</u>, 15 (6), May 18, 1989, 4.

Walt Disney Company, <u>Significant Environmental Activities</u>, 1992.

Walt Disney World, <u>Walt Disney World Productions</u>, 1987.

Zacharias, Beth, "Disney's Planned City to Spur Tourism, Growth in Osceola," <u>Orlando Business Journal</u>, 88 (23), May 3, 1991, 22.

UP THE LEARNING CURVE:
A STRATEGIC ANALYSIS OF THE IMPACT OF ARBITRATION CASES ON COMPLAINTS INVOLVING SEXUAL HARASSMENT

Connie L. Budden
Auburn University
AUBURN, ALABAMA, U.S.A.

Abstract

The court system is burdened by the number of such complaints and the time involved in hearing them. The resolution of sexual harassment complaints through arbitration is becoming increasingly popular in that it saves time and money. Arbitrators are taking their lead from major court decisions when deliberating cases. Issues involving just cause, disparate treatment, and the credibility of witnesses are major concerns in deciding arbitration cases relating to sexual harassment.

INTRODUCTION

In recent years sexual harassment has become a very important legal issue. Freada Klein Associates estimate that the problem is costing large corporations about $6.7 million per year. The consulting firm indicates that 90% of the Fortune 500 companies have received sexual harassment complaints. Over one-third of the companies report being sued at least once over this issue and over one-fourth report being sued more than once [Fisher, 1993]. Clearly, sexual harassment qualifies as an area of management concern deserving attention.

Since it is a common perception that a basic responsibility of trade unions and management is the provision of a safe and healthy work environment for employees, sexual harassment, whose presence can be viewed as an undesirable and unhealthy work place factor, becomes an important issue in organizational development. Another basic responsibility for those in positions of authority in organizations is to ensure an equality of opportunity in the work environment which can only be accomplished if the issue of sexual harassment is adequately addressed [Kremer and Marks, 1992]. Management, in focusing on achieving the goals of a healthy work environment and equality of opportunity for all employees, should provide clear policies to identify and discourage sexual harassment and provide a clear recourse for employee action to prevent court cases [Morgan, 1993].

BACKGROUND

The large number of women entering the work-place in the 1970's coupled with a realization that women may have been subjected to work environments which were unnecessarily repressive due to sexual connotations/situations/expectations brought about the first sexual harassment cases to enter the courts [Twomey, 1989]. Recent studies of working women indicate that as many as 50% to 80% may have been the victims of sexual harassment [Meredith, 1992]. The high costs associated with litigation and the time involved in problem resolution due to the backlogs in many courts, have caused many grievants to turn to other methods of resolution including arbitration. Arbitration has the advantages of lessening the adversarial problems of litigation and developing a meaningful solution much quicker than a typical civil suit. In arbitration, the grievance may be brought by an alleged victim of the harassment or an employee who was disciplined for an alleged act of sexual harassment [Meredith, 1992].

The first cases involving sexual harassment saw courts reject arguments that sexual harassment was a violation of Title VII of the Civil Rights Act and as such was an insufficient basis for legal action [Crow and Koen, 1992]. The Equal Employment Opportunity Commission (EEOC) in the 1980's redefined sexual harassment as "unwelcome sexual advances, requests for sexual favors, and verbal or physical conduct of a sexual nature" when "submission to such conduct is made either explicitly a term or condition of an individual's employment and when submission to or rejection of such conduct by an individual is used as the basis for employment decisions," or when "such conduct has the purpose or effect of unreasonably interfering with an individual's work performance or creating an intimidating, hostile, or offensive working environment" [Crow and Koen, 1992]. This new, legal definition of sexual harassment is now recognized as a landmark move as it essentially discerned two types of sexual harassment. The first type, the quid pro quo arrangement of exchanging sexual favors for advancement or money had always held a specter of impropriety and was easily recognized. However, the second type involving the creation and or maintenance of an intimidating, hostile or offensive work environment added a new dimension to the concept of sexual discrimination.

The quid pro quo type of sexual harassment involves the expectation of sexual favors from an employee as a requirement or condition of employment, or the forfeiting of an economic benefit if the individual was already employed. A plaintiff in a quid pro quo case would establish a violation of Title VII of the Civil Rights Act [Crow & Koen, 1992; Twomey, 1989; Robinson, Allen, McClure, Duhon, 1993].

Sexual harassment involving a hostile environment exists in a work environment where an employee feels the work environment itself is sexually intimidating and offensive. The work performance of an employee can be negatively effected by the existence of a sexually hostile environment. This hostile environment basis for a complaint of sexual harassment is the most controversial aspect of sexual harassment and is difficult to prove [Crow and Koen, 1992]. The plaintiff in such a case may prove discrimination on the basis of a violation of Title VII [Twomey, 1989; Robinson, Allen, McClure & Duhon, 1993].

Sexual harassment complaints can be brought by men or women although most cases to this date involve women. In a recent sexual harassment case involving a male plaintiff, a Los Angeles Superior Court awarded Sabino Gutierrez $1.017 million in damages from California Acrylic Industries and Maria Martinez, its chief financial officer. The Gutierrez case is considered significant not just for the amount of the damages awarded but due to the fact that it involved a male employee who ostensibly was required to perform sexual favors for his female supervisor. Until the Gutierrez case, many people erroneously believed only women could be victims of sexual harassment in the work place.

In sexual harassment cases the plaintiff bears the burden of proof. In other words, the jury should rule in favor of the defendant if both sides present questionable testimony [Kadetsky, 1993]. In the Gutierrez case, several jury members felt both sides presented doubtful evidence but the jury surprised legal scholars when it ruled in favor of the plaintiff despite the conflicting testimony. Sexual discrimination experts and numerous lawyers proffer the belief that juries and members of our society in general, have a tendency to believe the testimony of a man before that of a woman. Perhaps that belief, if it exists, impacted the findings in the Gutierrez case.

ARBITRATION

Sexual harassment cases where a collective bargaining agreement exists can be brought to arbitration in two ways. First, the victim of the sexual harassment brings a grievance which alleges the harassment is in violation of a non-discrimination provision of the contract. The most common occurrences though have been situations where an employer disciplines an employee for sexual harassment and the employee brings the case to challenge the discipline on the basis of "just cause". The latter cases present a perplexing problem for unions in that they may find themselves in situations where they are called upon to represent the interests of both the accuser and the alleged harasser.

Arbitrators face a number of problems in dealing with sexual harassment cases. The first problem in arbitration cases involving sexual harassment is the burden of proof required. If the sexual harassment case is brought under a violation of contract provision, the burden of proof falls on the union. The union will then face the difficulty of dealing with the conflict of interest issue arising from its desire to represent the interests of all its members.

Court standards may cause confusion when they are being applied in arbitration cases. Adding to the difficulty is the fact that the problem for arbitrators in disciplinary cases is the application of "just cause" standards to specific situations involving sexual harassment. The employer in such cases may have to prove the sexual harassment took place in the work place knowing well that his statements and information presented may lead to possible civil suits arising from the occurrence. The last problem faced in arbitration cases involving sexual harassment is the fact that few arbitrators are currently recommending training and counseling for employees and victims involved in such cases [Meredith, 1992].

SUPREME COURT CASES

The U.S. Supreme Court has set several de facto standards for deciding sexual harassment cases. In Meritor Savings Bank v. Michelle Vinson, the Court dealt with the issue of a hostile environment and found that sexual harassment is a form of discrimination and a violation of Title VII of the Civil Rights Act. The case set the standard of sexual harassment as being severe enough to alter the conditions of employment and the creation of a hostile work environment. The case set forth the standard that discrimination existed if the sexual advances involved were unwelcome and not whether Vinson's participation in sexual intercourse with her supervisor was voluntary. The findings in the Meritor case concluded that employers may not be automatically held responsible legally for the sexual misconduct of their managers. However, the fact that an employer hadn't received notice of the harassment does not relieve the employer of liability in a case. The justices in the case found that the mere existence of a grievance policy doesn't protect the employer in complaints of sexual harassment involving violations of Title VII of the Civil Rights Act.

The most recent U.S. Supreme Court case involving sexual harassment, Teresa Harris V. Forklift Systems, Inc. dealt with the issue of the determination of a reasonable person standard of a hostile environment. Harris filed suit after quitting her job with a Nashville-based truck-leasing company because of the crude conduct of the firm's president. Harris alleged she was regularly insulted on the basis of her gender and targeted for sexual innuendos by the president of the company in the presence of other employees. Although Harris was unable to prove she was psychologically damaged by the behavior, the Supreme Court reversed the lower court findings and remanded the case for further proceedings. The action reaffirmed the standards set forth in the Meritor Case which stated that discriminatory behavior may exists if it is severe enough to create a "discriminatorily hostile or abusive working environment". The standard requires that only a "reasonable person" find the environment to be hostile or abusive for discrimination to exists. In determining whether the environment is hostile, all relevant factors should be examined.

In reviewing the Court's findings, the relevant factors to be considered in determining the existence of an abusive environment include the "frequency of the discriminatory conduct; its severity; whether it is physically threatening or humiliating, or a mere offensive utterance; and whether it unreasonably interferes with an employee's work performance." Another factor to consider is whether the employee actually found the work environment abusive which makes the "psychological well-being" of the employee an important consideration. All of these factors must be considered when determining whether a hostile work environment exists.

ARBITRATION CASES

As in civil cases, there are basically two types of sexual harassment cases for which arbitration have been and will continue to be used to bring about problem resolution. The first type involves a situation where an employee brings a complaint in response to discipline received for the alleged sexual harassment of another employee. The second type of situation arises from cases where an activity or environment (sexual harassment) is alleged to be in violation of a non-discriminatory provision of an employment contract. In arbitrating cases involving sexual harassment, arbitrators traditionally look to three major concerns. The three concerns involve whether or not just cause existed and whether the disciplinary action was appropriate, whether there was disparate treatment in the handling of disciplinary actions, and the credibility of those involved.

JUST CAUSE

The first issue addressed in arbitration cases is whether are not "just cause" exists for the discipline administered, and whether the disciplinary action was an appropriate remedy for an employee accused of sexual harassment. There are several standards used by arbitrators in determining "just cause". Some arbitrators use the reasonable doubt standard in the more serious sexual harassment cases with involve moral turpitude. Other arbitrators have used lesser quantums of proof such as clear and convincing evidence and a preponderance of the evidence.

In the Western Lake Superior District and Minnesota Arrowhead District Local 96, AFSCME.PERB Case, Arbitrator John W. Boyer Jr. used the clear preponderance of evidence measure to determine "just cause" as opposed to the "physical contact/favors/ touching" concept proposed by the union. The grievants were both suspended from their job for the sexual harassment of a female co-worker. The arbitrator in this case ruled the grievants behavior created a hostile work environment for the sexually harassed employee and denied the grievance of the union.

In the Memphis Light Gas and Water Division and International Brotherhood of Electrical Workers, Local 1288 Case, Arbitrator John F. Caraway found that "just cause" existed for the indefinite suspension given an account investigator for the sexual harassment of customers. The company did reinstate the grievant to a non-customer relations position which the arbitrator also upheld as reasonable.

Arbitrator William P. Daniel found that the employer in the Flushing Community School and International Union of Operating Engineers, Local 547 provided clear and convincing evidence of the charges against the grievant. Another issue looked at in this case was whether the discharge of the grievant was the appropriate remedy for the situation. Mr. Daniel considered whether the grievant was salvageable and whether rehabilitation would be possible. The arbitrator felt that certain mitigating circumstances made it possible to reinstate the grievant to his former position under certain conditions. The conditions included professional counseling at the employee's own expense over a period of sixty days and a continuing assessment of the employee's fitness over the period of his future employment. The arbitrator found "just cause" in this case but felt dismissal from employment was to severe a remedy and ordered reinstatement of the grievant pursuant to the conditions he specified.

In the King Soopers Inc. and United Food and Commercial Workers Local 7 Case, Arbitrator Marshall A. Snider looked at the issue of "just cause" and appropriate remedy. He used the standard of proof as being convincing and substantial since a termination of employment was involved. The grievant was terminated from employment for the sexual harassment of three female employees. The arbitrator found that the rules were not enforced consistently among employees and order the grievant reinstated with a twenty work-day suspension and back pay for any time past twenty days for which the grievant was not allowed to work.

Arbitrator Hartwell D. Hooper used the "clear and convincing" standard in determining "just cause" in the Duke University Case and Individual Grievant case. Mr. Hooper found that the grievant should be given a disciplinary suspension with counseling instead of termination. The grievant may be placed in a non-supervisory position if the University so desired.

In the Central Michigan University and American Federation of State, County, and Municipal Employees, Local 1568 Case, the arbitrator found "just cause" in the suspension and dismissal of a custodian for the sexual harassment of two female students. The arbitrator used the clear and convincing standard of proof in determining "just cause" in this case.

In most of the cases above, the standard of proof used is the "clear and convincing" standard of proof. Although this standard is less severe than the standard used in most criminal cases, most arbitrators use it.

DISPARATE TREATMENT

The next issue which was addressed in the 1990's arbitration cases is disparate treatment in determining the correct discipline in cases. In the Fry's Food Stores of Arizona and United Food & Commercial Workers case the Union claimed the grievant was singled out for more severe treatment than other workers had received for similar activities. Purportedly, in three previous cases, employees involved in instances of sexual harassment were given three-day suspensions and demotions rather than discharge. Arbitrator Raymond L. Hogler, ruled the instances of sexual harassment where the firm reportedly was easier on other employees were either sketchy or insubstantial and denied the grievance in this case.

In the case of General Dynamics Fort Worth Division and International Association of Machinists and Aerospace Workers, Local 776 the issue concerns disparate treatment in the discipline of the grievant and a supervisor who sexually harassed her. The grievant was discharged after sending a vulgar letter to the wife of a supervisor who had sexually harassed the grievant over a period of time. The supervisor was disciplined for the sexual harassment but the grievant was not notified and the sexual harassment continued after the disciplining. The company was found to have treated the grievant and supervisor differently in regard to penalties even though the conduct of both was comparable. The arbitrator ordered the grievant reinstated within 15 working days of the award and time lost is to be considered disciplinary suspension without pay.

The arbitrator in the case of City of Havre, Montana found that although the company policy stated a written reprimand was the correct discipline for abusive language first offense, the federal law allows the disciplining of employees who create a hostile environment.

The case of King Soopers also involved a consideration of disparate treatment. The arbitrator found that the grievant's discharge was shown to be a form of disparate treatment compared to past treatment of other employees under similar circumstances. The arbitrator in this case found that the suspension should be converted to a twenty-day disciplinary suspension.

CREDIBILITY

The next issue considered in the arbitration of sexual harassment cases is the credibility of the witnesses. Arbitrator Jerry A. Fullmer found "just cause" in the discharge of a newspaper distribution manager in the sexual harassment of a married gas station clerk. The arbitrator looked at the credibility of the gas station clerk in determining this case. He considered the following: 1.)that since the complaining witness came forth voluntarily and any rational person would dread going through the process the statement would be true. 2). The union and grievant claimed that the clerk was bringing charges because of a bad marriage and her boss wanted her to get revenge against the grievant over an argument. The arbitrator found this was not a reason to assume false testimony. 3.) The grievant at no time gave any indication he understood the importance of refraining from sexual harassment of other employees and customers. 4.) The arbitrator felt the clerks demeanor and appearance were appropriate for a witness. The Grievant seemed more mechanical and stoic. 5.) The clerk delayed in bringing the charge from June 1991 to March 1992 did not impugn her credibility because of her lack of access to the company policy. The arbitrator considered all of the above factors in determining the clerk was a creditable witness. The grievance was denied since the clerk was found the most creditable witness.

CONCLUSION

Recent Supreme Court cases have shown that a hostile work environment need not cause psychological damage to an employee to be a violation of Title VII of the Civil Rights Act. Important factors to be considered by arbitrators are discussed for arbitrators to consider in determining whether an environment is hostile and what a reasonable person standard entails. The important issues which arbitrators have faced in the 1990's are discussed and outlined. It is recommended that in the future, arbitrators consider including training and counseling recommendations in their decisions involving sexual harassment cases. Arbitrators may need to recommend counseling for the victims of sexual harassment. Another course of action in these cases may be the removal of the sexual harasser from the same department as the victim to prevent further problems [Meredith, 1992].

Organizations and employers also need to address the issue of sexual harassment by setting forth formal policies to discourage sexual harassment behavior on the part of employees. The policies should be clear and state the consequences of the behavior. The policy should set forth a clear set of recourse which victims of sexual harassment can follow to correct the situation. The EEOC definition of sexual harassment should be used in such policies with clear examples of what constitutes sexual harassment. These policy statements should be distributed to all employees and periodically reinforced [Culverhouse and Buford, 1991].

The policy should specifically define non-sexual harassment and define when that behavior becomes sexual harassment. The company should also provide a training program which clearly defines sexual harassment and addresses the various relevant issues. The training program should provide clear examples of harassing behaviors and clear examples of non-harassing behaviors [Shull, 1993]. The most effective training methods include lecturing, case studies, conferences, role-playing, and behavior-modeling [Culverhouse and Buford]. A combination of these methods may prove more successful than the sole reliance of any one method. It is important that the trainers receive adequate training and have an in-depth knowledge of the legal issues involved.

If organizations and managers would use concrete policies and training programs to prevent sexual harassment the number of court cases and arbitration cases involving sexual harassment would drop significantly. The work place would be more conducive to efficient work efforts and a more equitable work

528

environment would follow.

REFERENCES

Costello, Edward J. Jr., "The Mediation Alternative in Sex Harassment Cases," Arbitration Journal, March 1992, p. 16-23.

Crow, Stephen M. and Clifford M. Koen, "Sexual Harassment: New Challenge for Labor Arbitrators?," Arbitration Journal, June 1992, p. 6-18.

Culverhouse, Renee and James A. Buford, Jr., Sexual Harassment: Information For Employers and Managers, CRD-51, Alabama Cooperative Extension Service, Auburn University, Alabama, 1991.

Fisher, Anne B., "Sexual Harassment What To Do," Fortune, August 23, 1993, p. 84-88.

Kadetsky, Elizabeth, "Million-Dollar Man," Working Women, Oct. 1993, p. 47-79.

Kremer, John and Jenny Marks, "Sexual Harassment: The Response of Management and Trade Unions," Journal of Occupational and Organizational Psychology, 1992, p. 5-15.

Lavan, Helen, "Arbitration Of Sexual Harassment Disputes: Case Characteristics And Case Outcome In Public Versus Private Sector Cases," Journal of Collective Negotiations, 1993 Vol 22, p. 45-53.

Meredith, Susan R., "Using Fact Finders to Probe Workplace Claims of Sexual Harassment, Arbitration Journal, December 1992, p. 61-65.

Morgan, Lynn H., "Investigating Sexual Harassment," Security Management, September 1993, p. 156-157.

Robinson, Robert K., Billie M. Allen, Geralyn McClure Franklin and David L. Duhon, "Sexual Harassment in the Workplace: A Review of the Legal Rights and Responsibilities of All Parties," Public Personnel Management, Spring 1993, p. 123-136.

Shull, Glen R., "Stretching The Boundaries of Sexual Harassment," Training, September 1993, p. 74.

Twomey, David P., Labor and Employment Law Text and Cases, 8th edition 1989, p. 382-393.

LEGAL CITATIONS

Central Michigan University and American Federation of State, County & Municipal Employees, Local 1568, 99 LA 135 (Patrick A. McDonald, 1992).

City of Havre, Montana and American Federation Of State, County & Municipal Employees, Local 336, 100 LA 867 (Thomas F. Levak, 1992).

City of St. Paul and American Federation of State, County & Municipal Employees, District Council 14, Local 1842, 100 LA 105, (William J. Berquist, 1992).

County of Oakland and Oakland County Employees Union, 94 LA 451 (William P. Daniel, 1990).

Duke University and Individual Grievant, 100 LA 317 (Hartwell D. Hooper, 1993).

Flushing Community Schools and International Union of Operating Engineers, 100 LA 445 (William P. Daniel, 1992).

General Dynamics and International Association Of Machinists and Aerospace Workers, 100 LA 181 (Roy Francis, 1992).

King Soopers and United Food and Commercial Workers, Local 7, 100 LA 901 (John F. Sass, 1993).

Memphis Light, Gas and Water Division and International Brotherhood of Electrical Workers, Local 1288, 100 LA 291 (John F. Caraway, 1993).

Meritor Savings Bank and Mechelle Vinson, 477 US 57, 1986, p. 2399-2411.

Paragon Cable Manhattan and International Brotherhood of Electrical Workers, Local 3, 100 LA 905 (Florence Dreizen, 1993).

Plain Dealer Publishing and Newspaper & Magazine Drivers' Union, Local 473, 99 LA 969 (Jerry A. Fullmer, 1992).

Teresa Harris and Forklift Systems, Inc., 1993, WL 453611.

Summit County Board of Mental Retardation and Developmental Disabilities and Weaver Education Association, 100 LA 4 (Jonathan Dworkin, 1992).

Western Lake Superior Sanitary District and Minnesota Arrowhead District Local 96, 94 LA 289 (John W. Boyer Jr. 1990).

APPENDICES

WACRA
WORLD ASSOCIATION FOR
CASE METHOD
RESEARCH & APPLICATION

History

Founded in 1984, the World Association for Case Method Research & Case Method Application (WACRA) evolved from contacts of professors, researchers, policy-makers, professionals and business executives into a worldwide organization. These individuals shared the common interest of studying and applying the Case Method in research, teaching, planning, training and development. Professionals and academicians from fifty countries have participated in ten international conferences on Case Method Research & Application: Lausanne, Switzerland (1980), London, UK (1984, 1985, 1987), Waltham (Boston), USA (1988, 1989), Enschede, Netherlands (1990), Berlin, Germany (1991), Limerick, Ireland (1992), and Bratislava, Slovakia - Vienna, Austria (1993). WACRA is a Non-Profit Corporation, contributions and donations to WACRA are tax deductible under the U.S. Internal Revenue Code, Section 509(a)(2).

The Case Method

The Case Method can be defined in a broad sense by contrasting it with the lecture method. Instead of textbooks, the Case Method uses partial, historical descriptions of specific situations enabling students to discover and develop their own unique framework for problem-solving. The Case Method achieves this goal efficiently and effectively. Data and information are presented in narrative form to encourage student involvement by solving problems actively, by identifying sources of information necessary for problem-solving, by engaging in critical thinking and through group work. (The group work contributes to the development of individuals able and willing to work collegially, etc.). Although "cases" have been used in one form or another by both law and medicine for a long time, the Case Method in the teaching of management and other disciplines is relatively new. The Harvard Business School is well known for its innovative role in this regard. The method has applications far beyond the managerial, business orientation so familiar to many. New applications for the Case Method in disciplines other than management and business are being explored and research is being conducted on this basis. The Case Method is increasingly applied in higher education and educational administration, the instruction (and operation) of the social sciences, the arts, engineering, agriculture, strategic policy planning, and personnel development in different parts of the world. Several volumes of international case method research papers and presentations attest to WACRA's success in providing an important forum in "managing change in multi-cultural setting" and in promoting cross cultural dialogue and development in Higher Education and Training.

Objectives

The objectives of WACRA are to explain, research and advance the use of the case method in teaching, planning and training at all levels; to promote and encourage research using the case method, with special emphasis placed on studying the teaching effectiveness in varied teaching-learning systems; to coordinate development of interactive pedagogical methods involving the case method, simulations and games; to augment the available body of research and teaching materials; to foster interdisciplinary applications and to encourage cooperation with the public sector, the business community and other case method oriented professional specialties on a worldwide basis.

Functions

WACRA's main function at the present time is to coordinate research, to facilitate the organization of forums, public discussions, workshops, training sessions, lectures and conferences and develop a worldwide network. WACRA organizes annual conferences at various locations around the world to provide opportunities and encourage the exchange of ideas, the presentation of planned, on-going and completed research, and the sharing of applications, simulations and games. Papers and manuscripts accepted (peer review) and presented at the annual conferences are published. The WACRA NEWSLETTER informs members about ongoing research projects, employment (exchange) opportunities, new publications and releases, curriculum development and other developments in interactive pedagogy. WACRA supports and cooperates with national Case Method Organizations, with Case Clearing Houses worldwide and shares information with professional associations, agencies and corporations.

Advantages of Membership

Membership in **WACRA** carries the following advantages: you receive the WACRA NEWSLETTER; you are entitled to substantial discounts on WACRA publications; you receive preferential rates at all meetings organized by WACRA; you can receive training and assistance in case writing and teaching; once you are a member, payment of full registration fee for any meeting includes membership in WACRA for the following calendar year; you receive notices for all meetings and calls for papers; you have the opportunity for networking, consulting and to associate with other professionals working with cases, simulations and games on a truly international scale; you can become a leader in your profession and in the organization.

Membership

Membership in WACRA is open to all individuals and organizations in all countries who wish to advance the objectives of the association and advance professional standards in the field. The various classes of membership and annual dues which provide for the continuing support of WACRA, are as follows:

Regular Member US $38: Any individual (teacher, researcher, government official or representative, business executive, attorney, consultant) who wishes to assist actively in attaining the goals of WACRA.

Organization Member US $150: A special class of Membership through which other existing associations or organizations can lend their support in meeting the goals of WACRA. Associations and organizations eligible for this class of membership include foundations, educational, civic, community, governmental units, professional, business, and industrial groups.

Sustaining Member US $300: A special class of membership available to any individual or organization wishing to offer more substantial financial support to WACRA.

Associate Member US $30: Advanced students.

CALL FOR PAPERS
CASE METHOD

RESEARCH AND APPLICATION (INCLUDING CASE WRITING)

TWELFTH INTERNATIONAL CONFERENCE

Leysin, Vaud, SWITZERLAND

June 18 - 21, 1995

"THE ART OF INTERACTIVE TEACHING AND LEARNING"

With Cases, Simulations, Games, Videos and Other Interactive Methods

The case method can play an important role in solving problems and in teaching problem-solving, as well as in initiating and managing change. Thus this conference provides opportunities for participants to learn more about teaching using the case method and related instructional approaches in a variety of educational settings. Participants will have ample opportunity to meet colleagues from around the world with whom they can forge research partnerships. WACRA conferences are interdisciplinary multinational forums for scholars in the disciplines and professional fields (such as business, education, engineering, law, medicine, public policy, social work) and practitioners in business and industry, education and government.

Papers are solicited that analyze theory and practice using cases, simulations, videos and related instructional methods for problem solving, managing change and innovation. Priority will be given to papers that are interdisciplinary, international, and/or comparative. Papers reporting the application of cases in university and professional training programs in diverse settings and papers on the evaluation of the case method and its related forms for teaching and learning are encouraged. Contributions investigating the impact of the case study method on the (student) learning process are also solicited. Proposals for case writing & development and actual cases placed in diverse settings are invited, e.g. joint-cross-cultural cases. While a main focus of the WACRA conferences is on using cases for teaching and problem-solving, scholarly papers that report research using the case method are welcome. WACRA is particularly interested in scholarly papers that enhance the understanding and collaboration between and among international partners. The most innovative presentation and the outstanding paper are recognized.

Proposals (for presentation) and papers (presentation and consideration for publication), submitted in English or French, will be evaluated through a blind peer review process on the basis of (a) contribution to the understanding of the case method; (b) the appropriateness of the topic for a multinational, interdisciplinary audience; (c) the technical adequacy of the inquiry; and (d) originality. Proposals should include (three copies) of (1) Cover page,[1] (2) Proposal summary (not exceeding two double-spaced pages). The summary should state clearly the objectives, the framework, and the nature of the proposal and be responsive to the criteria used for review. The name of the author(s) should not appear on the summary. (3) Two stamped (or Post Office Int.Answer Coupon) self-addressed envelopes (which will be used to acknowledge receipt of the proposal and results of the review). All proposals and papers are due on or before January 16, 1995. Selected papers will be published.

[1]For the first author the following should be included: paper title, author's name, position, institution, address, tel., fax, bitnet. Information on additional authors should be provided on a separate page identifying the paper.

Au plaisir de se retrouver à Leysin pour une expérience stimulante et enrichissante.

W A C R A
WORLD ASSOCIATION FOR CASE METHOD RESEARCH & APPLICATION

23 Mackintosh Ave NEEDHAM (BOSTON) MA 02192-1218 U.S.A.
Tel. +617-444-8982 Fax: +617-444-1548 Internet: hklein@bentley.edu

Please post or share this invitation with colleagues!

Return to WACRA today!

INNOVATIVE TEACHING - WACRA '95 Conference Pre-Registration
LEYSIN (Canton de Vaud), SWITZERLAND - June 18 - 21, 1995

Last Name _____ First Name _____ Title_____ Institution/Company _____

Street _____ City, State, Zip Code, Country _____

Tel. ( ) _____ Fax: ( ) _____ E-mail address _____

	Theory	Application	Evaluation	Descriptors
I plan to: participate in the 1995 conference	_____	_____	_____	_____ _____
present a paper*	_____	_____	_____	_____ _____
conduct a workshop*	_____	_____	_____	_____ _____
conduct a simulation/game*	_____	_____	_____	_____ _____
make a demonstration*	_____	_____	_____	_____ _____
organize a round-table*	_____	_____	_____	_____ _____
organize a panel*	_____	_____	_____	_____ _____

*Please indicate the best category fit of your proposal and provide <u>descriptors</u> of the main topic of the paper, e.g., (1) marketing, (2) pedagogy (3) video (4) simulation (5) game.

I will be interested in accommodations as follows: Hotel yes/no. International airports are Geneva and Zurich. There are excellent and frequent train connections from both airports to Leysin (via Lausanne and Aigle), about 75 minutes from Geneva.

Please mail:	Additional information as it becomes available:	yes/no	Inf. on **WICS** - **WACRA** Interactive Case Sessions:	yes/no
	Manuscript preparation guidelines:	yes/no	Inf. on **WILS** - **WACRA** Interactive Learning Sessions:	yes/no
	Call for proposals:	yes/no	List of publications:	yes/no
	Recent **WACRA** NEWSletter:	yes/no	Membership information:	yes/no
I would like to:	Join the **WACRA** Bulletin Board:	yes/no		
	Chair/moderate a session:	yes/no	Assist in conference preparations and manuscript review:	yes/no

I will be accompanied by _____

Please invite the following colleagues: _____

WACRA
World Association for Case Method Research & Application
23 Mackintosh Ave
NEEDHAM (BOSTON) MA 02192 U.S.A.
Tel. +617-444-8982; Fax +617-444-1548; Internet: hklein@bentley.edu

Non-Profit
Organization
US Postage
Paid
Permit #59889
WALTHAM, MA

To:

109406

DEMANDE D'ARTICLES

WACRA '95 - Douzième Conférence Internationale sur la Méthode des Cas
(Recherche, Application et Écriture)

LA PÉDAGOGIE INNOVATRICE

LEYSIN (Canton de Vaud), SUISSE du 18 au 21 juin 1995

La méthode des cas peut jouer un rôle important lorsqu'il faut résoudre des problèmes et enseigner à résoudre des problèmes tout comme lorsqu'il faut entreprendre et gérer le changement. Par conséquent ce congrès offre aux participants la possibilité d'apprendre plus sur l'enseignement par la méthode des cas et les méthodes d'enseignement qui s'y rattachent dans des situations éducatives variées. Les participants auront l'occasion de rencontrer des confrères d'un peu partout dans le monde avec lesquels ils pourront développer des partenariats de recherche. Les congrès de WACRA sont des <u>forums interdisciplinaires et multinationaux</u> pour les universitaires dans les disciplines traditionnelles et les domaines professionnels (y compris la gestion, l'éducation, l'ingénierie, le droit, la médecine et les politiques publiques) tout comme les praticiens dans les domaines des affaires, de l'industrie, de l'éducation et du gouvernement.

Nous sollicitons des articles qui analysent la <u>théorie</u> et la pratique en se servant de cas, de simulations, de vidéos et de méthodes d'enseignement s'y rattachant pour résoudre des problèmes et gérer le changement et l'innovation. La priorité sera donnée aux articles interdisciplinaires, internationaux et/ou comparatifs. Nous encourageons les articles qui décrivent l'<u>utilisation</u> de cas à l'université et dans des programmes de formation professionnelle, dans diverses situations, ainsi que les articles qui traitent de l'<u>évaluation</u> de la méthode des cas et de ses différentes formes utilisées dans un contexte d'enseignement et d'apprentissage. Nous aimerions recevoir des articles qui documentent l'impact de la méthode des cas sur le processus d'apprentissage de l'étudiant ainsi que des articles qui traitent de l'écriture de cas et de son développement. Nous acceptons aussi des cas réels décrivant diverses situations comme, par exemple, des cas interculturels. Même si lors des congrès nous mettons l'accent sur la méthode des cas comme une méthode pour résoudre les problèmes, nous acceptons bien volontiers des articles académiques qui décrivent la méthode des cas comme une méthode de recherche. L'Association s'intéresse particulièrement aux articles académiques qui améliorent notre compréhension de la collaboration qui existe entre et parmi les partenaires internationaux. En fonction du thème de cette année et pour continuer sur la lancée de Montréal, nous voudrions lancer une invitation particulière à ceux qui parmi nos collègues souhaiteraient animer un cas. Nous prévoyons de souligner la présentation la plus innovatrice et l'article le plus remarquable.

Les projets d'articles (pour présentation seulement) et les articles (pour présentation **et** publication possible), <u>soumis en anglais ou en français</u>, seront évalués par des confrères de façon anonyme sur la base de (a) leur rapport à la compréhension de la méthode des cas; (b) la pertinence du sujet pour une audience multinationale et interdisciplinaire; (c) la valeur technique de de la recherche; et (d) l'originalité. Les projets doivent comprendre (trois copies) de : (1) la page couverture,[1] (2) un résumé du projet (au moins deux pages à double interligne). Le résumé doit clairement indiquer les objectifs, la structure et la nature du projet et répondre aux critères d'évaluation utilisés. Le nom du (ou des auteurs) <u>ne doit pas</u> apparaître dans le résumé. (3) Deux enveloppes pré-affranchies (ou contenant deux coupons postaux internationaux) avec vos nom et adresse (que nous utiliserons pour accuser réception du projet et pour vous informer des résultats de l'évaluation). **<u>Tous les projets et tous les articles doivent nous parvenir au plus tard le 16 janvier 1995</u>**. Les articles acceptés seront publiés.

N.B. La conférence a lieu en anglais et en français et les organisateurs sont tout à fait disposés à faire une session en espagnol ou en allemand si le besoin se faisait sentir.

[1] Le titre de l'article, le nom de l'auteur(s), son poste, son institution, son addresse, téléphone, fax, internet.

WACRA - World Association for Case Method Research & Application
23 Mackintosh Ave NEEDHAM (BOSTON) MA 02192 U.S.A.
Tel. +617-444-8982; Fax +617-444-1548; Internet: hklein@bentley.edu

Au plaisir de se retrouver à Leysin pour une expérience stimulante et enrichissante.

Merci d'afficher ou de partager cette invitation avec vos confrères!

SOLICITUD DE ARTÍCULOS

WACRA '95 - 12. Congreso International sobre el Método de los Casos
(Investigación, Aplicación y Redacción)

LA PEDAGOGÍA INNOVADORA

LEYSIN (Canton de Vaud), SUIZA del 18 al 21 junio de 1995

El método de los casos puede desempeñar un importante papel cuando se trata de resolver problemas y enseñar a resolverlos; es importante también cuando de trata de emprender y administrar cambios. Por lo tanto, este congreso ofrece a los diferentes participantes la posibilidad de aprender aún más sobre la pedagogía de este método y otros métodos de enseñanza relacionados con él, en diferentes situaciones educativas. Los participantes tendrán la oportunidad de conocer a sus diferentes colegas de todos los rincones del mundo, con quienes podrán desarrollar grupos de investigación y de enseñanza. Los congresos de la WACRA son foros interdisciplinarios y multinacionales para todos los académicos y practicantes de las asignaturas tradicionales y de los sectores profesionales (que incluyen la administración de empresas, la educación, la ingeniería, el derecho, la medicina) y los profesionales dedicados a los negocios y a la industria, a la educación y a las ciencias políticas.

Se solicitan artículos que analicen tanto la teoría como la práctica, mediante el uso de casos, simulaciones, videos y otros métodos de instrucción relacionados con la solución de problemas, la administración del cambio y la innovación. Se dará prioridad a los artículos interdisciplinarios, internacionales y/o comparativos. También se favorecerán los artículos que discutan y situen la aplicación de casos en universidades y en programas de entrenamiento profesional en diferentes contextos, al igual que artículos que evaluen el método de los casos. Se aceptarán artículos que traten del impacto de este método sobre el desarrollo del aprendizaje del estudiante y artículos que involucren la redacción y el desarrollo de casos actuales en diferentes situaciones (por ejemplo casos interculturales). Aun si el enfoque de los congresos de la WACRA es el método de los casos y el uso de este método como un instrumento de enseñanza y de ayuda a la solución de problemas, consideramos artículos de académicos que situen el uso de este método en el campo de la investigación. La WACRA está particularmente interesada en artículos académicos que aumenten nuestro conocimiento de la colaboración y desarrollo entre los miembros de organismos internacionales. Considerando el tema que se ofrece este año y para continuar con el experimento que se hizo en Bratislava, quisiéramos invitarle a participar a talleres de resolución de casos. Se tiene previsto señalar la presentación más innovadora y al artículo más relevante.

Un grupo de colegas evaluará, de manera anónima, los diferentes proyectos, artículos y casos presentados, en inglés o en francés, basándose principalmente en los siguientes aspectos: A) su contribución a la comprensión del método; B) la pertinencia del tema presentado para una audiencia internacional e interdisciplinaria; C) el valor técnico de la investigación; y D) la originalidad. Todos los proyectos deberán incluir (con 3 copias): 1) la portada[1]; 2) un resumen del proyecto, dos páginas, doble espacio. El resumen debe indicar con claridad los objetivos, la estructura, la naturaleza del proyecto y corresponder a los criterios de evaluación mencionados. El nombre del autor o autores no debe figurar en el resumen. 3) Dos sobres franqueables o acompañados con dos sellos de correo internacionales, con su respectivo nombre y dirección. Estos dos sobres serán utilizados para acusar recibo del proyecto y para informarle del resultado de la evaluación del proyecto presentado. **Todos los proyectos y artículos deberán ser recibidos antes del 16 de enero de 1995**. Los artículos seleccionados serán publicados.

[1] El primer autor debe incluir : el título del artículo, su nombre, su puesto, su institución, su dirección, teléfono, fax, bitnet. Las informaciones que se refieren a los otros autores vendrán en una hoja separada identificada con el título del artículo.

WACRA - World Association for Case Method Research & Application
23 Mackintosh Ave NEEDHAM (BOSTON) MA 02192 U.S.A.
Tel. +617-444-8982; Fax +617-444-1548; Internet: hklein@bentley.edu

Au plaisir de se retrouver à Leysin pour une expérience stimulante et enrichissante.
Le Agradecemos Anunciar o Compartir esta Invitación con sus Colegas!

Twelfth International Conference on Case Method Research and Application
June 18 - 21, 1995
Leysin (Vaud), Switzerland
Host Institution: IMD, Lausanne

Directions for Preparation of Your Manuscript or Abstract

Prepare your manuscript according to the following guidelines and send a CAMERA READY hard copy and on diskette a "Wordperfect" or ASCII text file prepared on IBM PC or compatible (DOS environment) or a text file by electronic mail (Bitnet). If you cannot send the diskette, include your check in the amount of $75 (payable to WACRA, drawn on an US bank or international money order).

1. Print your manuscript on 8-1/2 x 11" paper, SINGLE SPACED.
2. MAXIMUM length is 12 pages (NO EXCEPTIONS).
3. Print on ONE side of the paper.
4. Margins should be ONE INCH on **ALL FOUR SIDES OF THE PAPER.**
5. Use 10 pt standard type (NOT some fancy script type).
6. Print on a LASER JET or LETTER QUALITY printer, NOT on a dot matrix printer.
7. Make sure that the printed copy you send is of dark enough quality so that it is easily read.
8. List all ENDNOTES at the end of the paper (but before references).
9. List all REFERENCES (alphabetized) at the end of the paper. See back for sample. When referencing an item, use the following style: [Chow, 1983].
10. All paragraphs should be indented as shown on the back. Set your Wordperfect Tabs at 0.3" intervals relative to the left margin. DO NOT SKIP LINES BETWEEN PARAGRAPHS.
11. The first page should contain: Beginning on the **seventh** line from the top (1) the title, centered, ALL CAPITALIZED; drop two lines (2) the author's name (first name and lastname, without titles), centered; on the next line (3) the author's affiliation (name of institution centered; on the following line (4) the city, state and country, ALL CAPITALIZED; drop 2 lines (5) the word "Abstract;" drop one line, an abstract of the paper (100 words MAXIMUM, INDENTED .6 inches FROM THE LEFT AND RIGHT MARGINS); and (6) the beginning of the paper after having dropped one line at the end of the abstract. Use "tabs" to indent at the beginning of each paragraph.
12. Tables and Figures should be numbered (1, 2, etc.), SINGLE SPACED, and PLACED IN THE TEXT. A one inch margin on all 4 sides must remain free. **All Tables and Figures (Drawings) must be camera ready**.
13. There can be up to THREE levels of HEADINGS. The FIRST level is CENTERED, ALL CAPITALIZED and bold; the SECOND level is FLUSH WITH THE LEFT MARGIN, ALL CAPITALIZED and bold; and the THIRD level is FLUSH WITH THE LEFT MARGIN (lower case characters) underlined.
14. To enable us to consider your contribution for publication, we need to receive your completed manuscript **on or before March 25, 1995** at:

WACRA
WORLD ASSOCIATION FOR
CASE METHOD RESEARCH & APPLICATION
23 Mackintosh Avenue
NEEDHAM (BOSTON) MA 02192-1218 U.S.A.
Tel. +617-444-8982 FAX: +617-444-1548 Internet: hklein@bentley.edu

SAMPLE PAGE - TITLE OF THE PAPER

Hans Klein
Bentley College
WALTHAM, MASSACHUSETTS, U.S.A.

Abstract

This is a sample page containing a sample abstract, short sample body, and references. Front and back of this instruction sheet are printed in **Geneva Regular 10 pt and Geneva 14 pt (IBM PC)** fonts, except for the paper title: **Tiempo bold 14 pt**. Notice how this abstract is indented .25 INCHES from both the left and right margins. All headings (except third-level headings as below) including **TABLE 1, FIGURE 1, APPENDIX A** should be in upper case characters and bolded.

INTRODUCTION - FIRST-LEVEL HEADING

Above is an example of a first-level heading. Below is an example of a second-level heading. At the end of a sentence, after the period, insert **two** blank spaces. Use the "full" justification feature.

SECOND-LEVEL HEADING

Above is an example of a second-level section heading. The heading is flush left, in upper case characters and bold. Below is an example of a third-level heading. The third-level heading is (underlined) in lower case characters, except for the first word, nouns, etc.

Third-Level Heading

The third-level heading is flush to the left, in lower case characters and <u>underlined</u>. Included in this sentence is an example of a reference [Chow, 1983] appearing in **[square brackets]**. Avoid footnotes to the extent possible and use endnotes[1] instead.

ENDNOTES

1. This is an example of an endnote. All endnotes should be generated using the appropriate Wordperfect feature. The endnotes should be placed at the end of the paper, before references. Immediately following the automatic note number insert an "indent."

REFERENCES

Chow, C., "The Effects of Job Standard Tightness and Compensation Scheme on Performance: An Exploration of Linkages," <u>Accounting Review</u> (October 1983), pp. 667-685.

Previts, G. and B. Merino, <u>A History of Accounting in America</u> (John Wiley, 1979).

1000220674

WILKES UNIVERSITY LIBRARY